Western Mediterranean Prophecy

by

Harold Lee, Marjorie Reeves,
Giulio Silano

The apocalyptic writings of Joachim of Fiore were of fundamental importance in forming the world-view and shaping the historical consciousness of the later Middle Ages. The essential method employed by the Calabrian abbot consisted in the establishment of concordances between figures of the Old and New Testaments and those of later times in order to define the traits of important personages and events yet to come. This novel exegesis was developed within the context of a complex periodization of history which correlated historical currents with the Trinitarian nature of God and looked forward to an age of the Holy Spirit.

This original and apocalyptic view of history proved particularly attractive to the Mendicants and their supporters, whether these were fully orthodox or less so. They considered Joachim to be a prophet, ensured a wide audience for his works, and reshaped the abbot's prophecies into tracts that could speak more directly to their times and concerns. The *Breuiloquium*, an anonymous work composed in Catalonia, issued from the circles of Beguines and Third Order Franciscans who were such a large part of the religious scene of that time and place. The work presents in a summary fashion a Joachimite vision of the world and of society and attests to millenarian expectations in the tradition of the re-elaboration of Joachimite thought fashioned by such eminent Spiritual thinkers as Olivi and Arnold of Vilanova.

The Introduction to the critical edition of the *Breuiloquium* addresses the question of continuity and new departures in Joachimite thought in the fourteenth century. Particular attention is paid to writers in the tradition such as Arnold of Vilanova who were especially influential in Catalonian Spiritual circles. The potential and social context of the work is discussed both to assist in its intelligibility and to examine the concerns which led the anonymous author to the composition of the work. The Introduction and the edition of the *Breuiloquium* together form an interesting instrument for an approach to apocalyptic and prophetic literature of the fourteenth century, especially as it took shape in Catalonia.

STUDIES AND TEXTS 88

WESTERN MEDITERRANEAN PROPHECY

The School of Joachim of Fiore and the
Fourteenth-Century *Breviloquium*

BY

HAROLD LEE, MARJORIE REEVES,
GIULIO SILANO

PONTIFICAL INSTITUTE OF MEDIAEVAL STUDIES

Acknowledgement

This book has been published with the help of a grant from the Canadian Federation for the Humanities, using funds provided by the Social Sciences and Humanities Research Council of Canada.

Canadian Cataloguing in Publication Data

Lee, Harold, 1933-
    Western Mediterranean prophecy

(Studies and texts, ISSN 0082-5328 ; 88)
Bibliography: p.
Includes index.
ISBN 0-88844-088-X

1. Summula seu breviloquium super concordia Novi et Veteris Testam.   2. Joachim, of Fiore, ca. 1132-1202. Liber de concordia Novi ac Veteris Testamenti. 3. Bible — Prophecies.   4. Apocalyptic literature.   I. Reeves, Marjorie. II. Silano, Giulio, 1955-   .   III. Pontifical Institute of Mediaeval Studies. IV. Title.   V. Title: Summula seu breviloquium super concordia Novi et Veteris Testam.   VI. Series: Studies and texts (Pontifical Institute of Mediaeval Studies) ; 88.

BS647.2.L43 1988   220.1′5   C88-094357-2

Printed by Universa, Wetteren, Belgium

Distributed outside North America by
E. J. Brill, Leiden, The Netherlands
(Brill ISBN 90 04 08929 2)

Contents

THE SCHOOL OF JOACHIM OF FIORE

SUMMULA SEU BREVILOQUIUM SUPER CONCORDIA NOVI ET VETERIS TESTAMENTI

Preface

The idea of this edition was first conceived when one of the authors, examining the manuscript of the *Breviloquium* in the British Library, discovered that it was no mere summary of the Abbot Joachim's *Liber Concordie*, but a fourteenth-century re-statement of Joachimism which was of great interest. From the beginning, Dr. Morton Bloomfield, of Harvard University, encouraged the project and, at a later stage, Dr. J.N. Hillgarth, of the Pontifical Institute of Mediaeval Studies, gave valuable advice on the presentation of the edition and furthered its publication.

The editors of the text also wish to acknowledge their debt to Sr. Aurelio Gómez, Director of the Provincial Library, Tarragona, and to staff of the Chapter Library, Valencia; the National Library, Madrid; the Vatican Apostolic Library; the Department of Manuscripts, the British Library. They also wish to thank Dr. Hillgarth for his kind willingness to re-examine for them the Madrid manuscript.

It remains to be specified that the division of labour among the authors was the following: Harold Lee and Marjorie Reeves produced the study of the School of Joachim of Fiore; Dr. Lee was responsible for the Introduction to the text of the *Breviloquium* and for the table of dates; Harold Lee and Giulio Silano edited the text of the *Breviloquium*.

Harold Lee
Marjorie Reeves
Giulio Silano.

Abbreviations

For full references, see the Bibliography.

Journals and Institutions:

AF	*Archivum Franciscanum*
AFH	*Archivum Franciscanum Historicum*
AIA	*Archivo Ibero-Americano*
AK	*Archiv für Kulturgeschichte*
ALKG	*Archiv für Litteratur and Kirchengeschichte des Mittelalters*
AST	*Analecta Sacra Tarraconensia*
BISI	*Bullettino dell'Istituto Storico Italiano e Archivio Muratoriano*
DTC	*Dictionnaire de Théologie Catholique*
HJ	*Historisches Jahrbuch*
JWCI	*Journal of the Warburg and Courtauld Institutes*
MARS	*Mediaeval and Renaissance Studies*
PIMS	*Pontifical Institute of Mediaeval Studies*
PL	*Patrologia Latina*
REF	*Revista de Estudios Franciscanos*
RTAM	*Recherches de Théologie ancienne et médiévale*
SF	*Studii Francescani*
ZKG	*Zeitschrift für Kirchengeschichte*

Primary Sources:

Alia informatio	Arnold of Vilanova, *Alia informatio beguinorum*, and Perarnau, Josep, *L'"Alia Informatio Beguinorum" d'Arnau de Vilanova*
Allocutio	Arnold of Vilanova, *Allocutio super significatione nominis tetragrammaton*
Allocutio christiani	Arnold of Vilanova, *Allocutio christiani de iis quae conveniunt homini secundum propriam dignitatem creaturae rationalis*
apparatus	Eiximenis, Francesco, *Apparatus de triplici status mundi*
Arbor	Ubertino da Casale, *Arbor Vitae Crucifixae*
Aus den Tagen	Finke, Heinrich, *Aus den Tagen Bonifaz VIII*
Brev. and *Breviloquium*	*Summula seu breviloquium super concordia Novi et Veteris Testamenti*

Com. Cyrilli	Roquetaillade, Jean de, *Commentum super prophetiam Cyrilli*
De oneribus	Pseudo-Joachim, *De Oneribus Prophetarum*
De statibus	*De statibus ecclesiae secundum expositionem Apocalypsim*
De tempore	Arnold of Vilanova, *De tempore adventu antichristi*
Direct. Inquis.	Eymerich, Nicholas, *Directorium Inquisitorum*
"Dous Nous escrits"	Battlori, Miguel, "Dous nous escrits espirituals d'Arnau de Vilanova"
ESA	Arnold of Vilanova, *Expositio super apocalypsi Arnaldi de Vilanova*
Eulogium	Carreras y Artau, Joaquín, "La polémica gerundense sobre el antichristo entre Arnau de Vilanova y los Dominicos"
"Evangelium aeternum"	Denifle, Heinrich, "Das Evangelium aeternum und die Commission zu Anagni"
Expos.	Joachim of Fiore, *Expositio in Apocalypsim*
Exposició	Infant Peter, *Exposició de la visió damunt dita*
Informació espiritual	Arnold of Vilanova, *Informació espiritual al Rei Frederic de Sicilia*
Introductio	Arnold of Vilanova, *Introductio in librum Ioachim De semine scripturarum*
Lib. Conc.	Joachim of Fiore, *Liber Concordie Novi ac Veteris Testamenti*
Lib. contra Lombardum	Pseudo-Joachim, *Joachimi Abbatis Liber contra Lombardum*
Lib. Fig.	Joachim of Fiore, *Liber Figurarum*
Lib. Ostensor	Roquetaillade, Jean de, *Liber Ostensor*
Lib. Sec. Ev.	Roquetaillade, Jean de, *Liber Secretorum Eventorum*
Lib. Sentent.	Limborch, Philippus van, *Historia Inquisitionis, cui subjungitur Liber Sententiarum Inquisitionis Tholosanae, 1307-1323*
MEFRM	*Mélanges de l'École Française de Rome*
Obres Catalanes	Battlori, Miguel and Carreras y Artau, Joaquin, *Arnau de Vilanova: Obres Catalanes*
Passio Sanct. Apost.	Lipsius, Richard, and Bonnet, Max, eds., *Passio Sanctorum Apostolorum*
Postilla	Olivi, Petrus Johannis, *Postilla super apocalypsim*
Practica Inquis.	Gui, Bernard, *Practica Inquisitionis*
Psalt.	Joachim of Fiore, *Psalterium Decem Chordarum*
Quat. Evang.	Joachim of Fiore, *Tractatus super Quatuor Evangelia*
Raonament	Arnold of Vilanova, *Raonament d'Avinyó*
Responsio	Arnold of Vilanova, *Responsio ad cavillationes adversarii veritatis* (old title); *Tractatus quidem in quo respondetur obiectionibus que fiebant contra tractatum Arnaldi de adventu antichristi* (new title)

Septem Sigillis	Joachim of Fiore, *De Septem Sigillis*
Sibyl Erithrea	*Vaticinium Sibillae Erithreae*
Super Esaiam	Pseudo-Joachim, *Super Esaiam Prophetam*
Super Evang. Mat.	Olivi, Petrus Johannis, *Postilla super Evangelium Matthei*
Super Hier.	Pseudo-Joachim, *Super Hieremiam Prophetam*
Vita St. Benedicti	Joachim of Fiore, *De Vita Sancti Benedicti et de Officio Divino secundum eius Doctrinam*

Secondary Sources:

"Collections"	Reeves, Marjorie and Beatrice Hirsch-Reich, "The *Figurae* of Joachim of Fiore: Genuine and Spurious Collections"
Die Spiritualen	Ehrle, Franz, "Die Spiritualen, ihn Verhältnis zum Franziscanerorden und zu den Fraticellen"
Escritos condenados	Canovas, Elena and Piñero, Felix, *Escritos condenados por la Inquisición*
Franciscan Order	Moorman, John, *A History of the Franciscan Order*
Historia	Menendez y Pelayo, Marcelino, *Historia de los Heterodoxos Espanoles*
HL	Bignami-Odier, Jeanne, "Jean de Roquetaillade (de Rupescissa), Théologien, Polémiste, Alchimiste"
Influence	Reeves, Marjorie, *The Influence of Prophecy in the Later Middle Ages*
Lectura	Manselli, Raoul, *La "Lectura super Apocalypsim" di Pietro di Giovanni Olivi*
"Profecies Catalanes"	Boligas i Balaguer, Pere, "Profecies Catalanes dels segles XIV i XV. Assaig bibliografic"
R	Bignami-Odier, Jeanne, *Études sur Jean de Roquetaillade*
Relaciones	Carreras y Artau, Joaquin, *Relaciones de Arnau de Vilanova con los Reyes de la casa de Aragon*
"Scrutamini Scripturas"	Lee, Harold, "Scrutamini Scripturas: Joachimist Themes and *Figurae* in the Early Religious Writing of Arnold of Vilanova"
Visionarios	Pou y Marti, José Maria, *Visionarios, Beguinos y Fraticelos Catalanes*

Introduction

It is curious that among a number of critical editions and studies of works attributed to Joachim, both genuine and spurious, made during the last hundred years, the *Breviloquium* has been almost completely overlooked. It was mentioned by Denifle and it appears in Russo's *Bibliografia* among Joachim's genuine works, but otherwise it has been virtually passed over.[1] The reasons for its neglect are probably twofold: first, it was taken to be a summary of the *Liber Concordie* and as such was regarded as of no great significance; secondly, the manuscripts were few and of these two were in Spain.[2] One in the British Library would have been easily accessible, but, in general, scholars interested in Joachimism have not examined the resources of English libraries closely. A copy recently discovered in Rome by Professor Bloomfield appears to have been unrecognised before, and Professor Lerner has even more recently found excerpts from the *Breviloquium* in French prophetic anthologies at Tours and Rouen, and a Catalan excerpt at Carpentras.[3] The work is, in fact, most interesting. It is not a digest or summary of the *Liber Concordie* but a highly individual synthesis made by a mid-fourteenth-century Joachite — almost surely in Catalonia — who certainly used the *Liber Concordie* extensively but also incorporated material from other works of Joachim, from the pseudo-Joachimist prophecies and from the works of previous Joachites, especially the *Postilla super Apocalypsim* of Petrus Johannis Olivi. From these materials he constructed a revised system of Joachimism as a veritable "tract for the times." For us, the interest of the *Breviloquium* lies chiefly in the light it throws on Joachimism in Spain, especially Catalonia; in its uniqueness as a late Joachimist work; in the skill and originality with which the unknown author shaped his prophetic material into a new system.

[1] Heinrich Denifle, "Das Evangelium aeternum und die Commission zu Anagni," *Archiv für Litteratur und Kirchengeschichte*, 1 (1885): 92; Francesco Russo, *Bibliografia Gioachimita* (Florence, 1944), p. 20 (where it is placed among the *opere autentiche* of Joachim). See also Emil Donckel, "Studien über die Prophezeiung des Telesphorus," *Archivum Franciscanum Historicum*, 26 (1933): 52; Leone Tondelli, *Il Libro delle Figure dell' Abate Gioacchino da Fiore*, 2nd ed. (Turin, 1953), 1: 117-118; Morton Bloomfield, "Joachim of Fiore," *Traditio*, 13 (1957): 251, n. 4.

[2] For the complete list of MSS, see the Introduction to the Text, infra, pp. 152-159.

[3] Vatican City, Biblioteca Apostolica Vaticana, Vat. Lat. MS 11581; Tours, Bibliothèque Municipale, MS 520, fols. 52v-57v; Rouen, Bibliothèque Municipale, MS O.20 T 1 (cat. Nr. 1355), fols. 98r-99r; Carpentras, Bibliothèque Inguimbertine, MS 336, fols. 76v-116v.

The School of Joachim of Fiore

by

Harold Lee and Marjorie Reeves

1

The Joachimist Literature

Of Joachim's chief works, the author of the *Breviloquium* obviously knew the *Liber Concordie* best and found its whole method of concords congenial to his way of thinking. Joachim had used a double pattern of concords, sometimes seeing the two great Dispensations of history as rolling in parallel streams to the First and Second Advents respectively, sometimes applying his Trinitarian philosophy of history to construct sequences of concords in threes, thus pointing forward to the third age (*status*) of the Holy Spirit.[1] The author of the *Breviloquium* was deeply imbued with the concept of the three *status* and thus, as we shall see, tended to go even further than Joachim in working out patterns of threes. In the *Liber Concordie* much thought is expended on calculating the Last Things through the concords of the generations.[2] Although Joachim was too wise to predict exact dates, he nevertheless initiated an approach to the problem which became immensely popular. His own calculations suggested the period 1200 to 1260 as the crucial one,[3] but when this was past ingenious ways were found of pushing the date on to 1290, to 1335 and so on.[4] The author of the *Breviloquium* inherited not only the fascination of predicting dates but also Joachim's particular method of forming the final programme through studying the pattern of all the generations in history. Of Joachim's other two main works, he knew the *Expositio in Apocalypsim* but used it directly less often. For

---

[1] On Joachim's number-patterns, see Marjorie Reeves, "The *Liber Figurarum* of Joachim of Fiore," *Mediaeval and Renaissance Studies*, 2 (1950): 71-79; idem, *The Influence of Prophecy in the Later Middle Ages* (Oxford, 1969), pp. 17-20, 25-26; Marjorie Reeves and Beatrice Hirsch-Reich, *The Figurae of Joachim of Fiore* (Oxford, 1972), pp. 1-19.

[2] See especially Joachim of Fiore, *Liber Concordie Novi ac Veteris Testamenti* (Venice, 1519), fols. 11r-19r.

[3] Ibid., fols. 11r, 41v, 56v; idem, *Expositio in Apocalypsim* (Venice, 1527), fol. 9v; idem, *Tractatus super Quatuor Evangelia*, ed. Ernesto Buonaiuti (Rome, 1930), p. 35; Joachim of Fiore, *Lib. Fig.*, pl. 4.

[4] Infra, p. 113.

Joachites perhaps the most important element in the *Expositio* was the treatment of the manifestations of Antichrist. Joachim insisted that Antichrist was multiple and found this embodiment of evil in the Dragon with seven heads, as also in the two Beasts of *Apocalypse* 13 and other figures.[5] He saw the sequence of Dragon's heads in political terms, with the seventh and worst still to come. The combination of the two Beasts suggested to him a distinction between a religious and a political manifestation of Antichrist: the Beast from the land was to be a false religious leader or a pseudo-pope, while the Beast from the sea represented the onslaught of the infidel.[6] We must also note that the Roman (i.e. German) Imperium came under Joachim's severe judgement: it had provided a head of the Dragon and in its last phase was to be identified with Babylon.[7] We shall find all these ideas developed by Joachites and used by the author of the *Breviloquium*. He also made extensive use of Joachim's other basic number-pattern, that of sevens — especially the double sevens of seals and openings — but drew this from Joachim's small tract, *De Septem Sigillis*,[8] and from the schematisation of Olivi[9] rather than from the *Expositio*, where the "sevens" are so prominent. There is no indication that our author knew any other of Joachim's minor works, with one notable exception: the fact that he embellished his work with pictures suggests the influence of Joachim's *Liber Figurarum*[10] — although, as we shall see, the general style is very different — and his production of Tables of Concords at the end of the *Breviloquium* proves conclusively that he had at least part of the *Liber Figurarum* in front of him.[11]

The author of the *Breviloquium*, however, had not only Joachim's works, but a whole tradition of Joachimist literature on which to draw, including both writings falsely ascribed to Joachim and the books and tracts of some leading Joachites in the late thirteenth and the first half of the fourteenth centuries. The history of the pseudo-Joachimist works as a separate *genre* of prophetic literature has never yet been written. A full study would show how prophetic expectation was shaped and re-shaped by political and religious circumstance, mounted to a series of climaxes and was reborn after each collapse of hope. It is significant that only one of the pseudo-Joachimist

---

[5] *Expos.*, fols. 10r-11r, 132v-133r, 156r-v, 162r-165v, 166v-168v; *Lib. Fig.*, pl. 14.

[6] *Expos.*, fols. 162r, 166v.

[7] Ibid., fols. 173v-174r, 190r-192r, 196v, 134r-v; *Lib. Fig.*, pls. 16, 17.

[8] Joachim of Fiore, *De Septem Sigillis*, eds. Marjorie Reeves and Beatrice Hirsch-Reich, "The Seven Seals in the Writings of Joachim of Fiore," *Recherches de Théologie ancienne et médiévale*, 21 (1954): 211-247 (text: 239-247).

[9] Infra, p. 120.

[10] Infra, pp. 132-137.

[11] Infra, pp. 114-115.

works was theological in character — an attempt to re-state Joachim's exposition of the Trinity as against Peter Lombard.[12] This lies outside the main stream of Joachimist interest, which was focused on the application of Joachim's interpretations of history to contemporary events. Joachim's system of ages, states and times (*etates, status* and *tempora*)[13] provided a periodisation of history which gave prophecy its necessary framework. When, in addition, Joachim crowded the final divisions of history with portentous figures and events — the agencies of Antichrist, the spiritual men (*viri spirituales*) sent to guide the true Church through the Wilderness and across Jordan into the Promised Land, the fall of Babylon, the death of Antichrist and the advent of the future spiritual leaders of the third *status* — all the materials for high prophetic drama were present. In varying ways and with varieties of local colour the authors of the pseudo-Joachimist works adapted the framework and the *dramatis personae* of Joachim to their own contemporary needs.

The earliest of these works was really only a compilation from Joachim's figures to which an *Epistola subsequentium figurarum* was added.[14] Such visual representations (*figurae*) could proclaim prophecy to the eyes of impatient seekers much more directly than a treatise, and this early thirteenth-century anthology had a number of successors which must have been carriers of Joachimist ideas. In some of these, it is true, the figures are so garbled as to obscure the message, but such symbols as the Dragon with seven heads proclaimed their prophetic meaning openly. The tradition of using *figurae* persisted in various forms, as we shall see, down to the *Breviloquium.*

The first substantial work of pseudo-Joachimism, the *Super Hieremiam,*[15] raises questions of date, authorship and provenance to which we do not yet have clear answers.[16] It certainly emanated from south Italy, however, and

---

[12] *Joachimi Abbatis Liber contra Lombardum*, ed. Carmelo Ottaviano (Rome, 1934). This was written soon after 1234.

[13] Joachim's Latin terminology for ages, states and times is used throughout this study.

[14] For MSS of this and other figure collections, see Marjorie Reeves and Beatrice Hirsch-Reich, "The *Figurae* of Joachim of Fiore: Genuine and Spurious Collections," MARS, 3 (1954): 170-199; *Lib. Fig.*, p. 34.

[15] *Super Hieremiam* (Venice, 1516).

[16] On these and other problems, see Karl Friderich, "Kritische Untersuchung der dem Abt Joachim v. Floris Zugeschreibenen Commentate zu Esayas u. Jeremias," *Zeitschrift für Wissenschaftliche Theologie* (Jena, 1858), pp. 349-363, 449-514; Bernhard Töpfer, *Das Kommende Reich des Friedens* (Berlin, 1964), pp. 108-115; Marjorie Reeves, *Influence*, pp. 56, 151-153, 156-157; idem, "The Abbot Joachim's Disciples and the Cistercian Order," *Sophia*, 19 (1951): 362-367; E. Randolph Daniel, "A Re-examination of the Origins of Franciscan Joachitism," *Speculum*, 43 (1968): 671-676; Fiorella Simoni, "Il 'Super Hieremiam' e il Gioachimismo Francescano," BISI, 82 (1970): 13-46. S. Wessley is shortly to

was probably written in the early 1240s. The chief point of debate is whether the author should be sought among early Franciscans in south Italy or in a Florensian-Cistercian group of Joachim's immediate disciples. If certain prophetic statements which point directly to the two great mendicant orders are put on one side as possibly additional glosses, the internal evidence strongly suggests the second alternative. This view has however been challenged. Either way, our concern here is with the various elements which constituted the ingredients of such prophetic works.

In the first place, there is a confused political situation with emotions running high in the struggle between the papacy and the Hohenstaufen. Here fuel to feed anti-Hohenstaufen fires could be found in Joachim's pronouncements on the political role and fate of the German *Imperium*. Thus the author of the *Super Hieremiam* uses the device of a spurious dedication to the emperor Henry VI, and through the supposed words of Joachim menacing prophecies are spoken against "your posterity" (*tuus posterus*).[17] Secondly, Joachim's disciples are concerned to defend his reputation for orthodoxy by veiled hints at the machinations of enemies and his unjust condemnation by the supreme pontiff. They see this persecution as extended to his disciples, the future spiritual men, who will be forced to flee from the persecution of the false pope, who is to be the future Herod.[18] Thirdly, a sense of mission is running high. Whether the expected agents were the two Mendicant Orders or other *viri spirituales* still to be expected, or both, the main burden of the *Super Hieremiam* was to proclaim the great prophetic role of these men in the near future.[19] Fourthly, the juxtaposition of the greatest tribulation of all time — in which the Ark of the Church will be almost submerged — and the highest triumph of the third *status* fills the work with a dramatic sense of expectation.[20] These are themes which repeatedly stimulated the authors of the pseudo-Joachimist writings. The method used in this work is that of a running commentary on the text of the Book of *Jeremiah* in which certain identifications are made. Thus the kings from the north are German rulers and Henry VI is both serpent (*coluber*) and snake (*vipera*).[21] Egypt stands for France,[22] while Israel and Judah are the Greek and Latin Churches respec-

---

publish an article which supports the argument for a Florensian/Cistercian authorship rather than Franciscan. See also R. Moynihan, "The Development of the 'Pseudo-Joachim' Commentary 'Super Hieremiam'," MEFRM 98 (1986), 109-142.

[17] *Super Hier.*, fols. 14r, 45v-46v, 53r, 58r-v, 59v, 62r.

[18] Ibid., fols. 23r-v, 43v-44v, 59r.

[19] Ibid., Preface, fols. 1v-2r, 12v-13v, 18v, 20r-v, 23v, 24r-v, 25v-26r, 27v, 28r-v, 32r, 33v, 38r, 41r, 45r, 48r, 49r, 54r, 57r-58v.

[20] Ibid., fols. 2r, 3v-4r, 18v, 23r, 24r, 38r, 46v, 47v, 53r, 57v-58v.

[21] Ibid., fols. 3v, 4r, 14r, 45v, 46r, 59v.

[22] Ibid., fols. 7v-8r, 9r, 17r, 43v, 60r-v.

tively.[23] King Sedechias is equated with Herod and, together with Caiaphas and Pontius Pilate, these signify Pope Innocent III in league with the Pharisees, who are the Cistercians, against the true religious.[24] No general Joachimist framework is given and the whole adds up to the use of a commentary on the Old Testament prophecy as a vehicle for certain specific contemporary prophecies.

The sense of calamity and triumph, realised or impending, continued to invest the history of south Italy with high significance throughout the 1250s. Thus the Regnum was probably the seedbed which produced a crop of short pseudo-Joachimist prophecies during the final stages of the Papal struggle with the Hohenstaufen. The first of these, the *Vaticinium Sibillae Erithreae*, now dated to 1249,[25] shows a predilection for oracles invested with the mystery of eastern origin. This purports to be a gloss by Joachim on a sibylline oracle which is couched in the enigmatic language common to the so-called prophecies of the sibyls already circulating in the twelfth century. The text announces a succession of rulers, of whom the latest are identified in the gloss as the last Norman kings of Sicily, the emperors Henry VI and Frederick II and the Hohenstaufen brood. The series ends with the prophecy that "there will be no ruler beyond the seed of the eagle."[26] This is an anti-Hohenstaufen addition to the original sibylline text. The other clear point made in the text is the prophecy of the two new expected religious orders.[27] Thus the main themes are the fate of Imperial politics and the precursors of the new age.

Closely associated with this work in language and attitude towards the Hohenstaufen is the *De Oneribus Prophetarum*,[28] written in the same decade. This again purports to be addressed to the emperor Henry VI and, as in the *Super Hieremiam*, directs many dire prophetic warnings towards Henry's descendants (*tuus posterus*).[29] Part of it takes the form of specific prophecies

---

[23] Ibid., fols. 4r, 10r-v.

[24] Ibid., fols. 3v, 12v-13r, 23r-v, 43v, 44v, 47r, 48v, 52v-53r, 55v, 58r, 59r.

[25] *Vaticinium Sibillae Erithreae*, ed. Oswald Holder-Egger, *Neues Archiv der Gesellschaft für ältere deutsche Geschichtskunde*, 15 (1889): 155-173 (longer version); 30 (1904-1905): 328-335 (shorter version). All references are to vol. 15. Paul Alexander has pushed the date of the Joachimist version back from 1252-1254 to 1249. See his "The Diffusion of Byzantine Apocalypses in the Medieval West and the Beginning of Joachimism," *Prophecy and Millenarianism*, ed. Ann Williams (London, 1980), pp. 76-79.

[26] *Sibyl Erithrea*, p. 170.

[27] Ibid., p. 165.

[28] *De Oneribus Prophetarum*, ed. Oswald Holder-Egger, *Neues Archiv*, 33 (1907): 139-187. A somewhat different version is to be found in London, British Library, Royal and Kings, MS F. xvi, fols. 38-44.

[29] *De Oneribus*, pp. 139, 141, 144, 152, 153, 160-161, 164, 166-168, 181, 183; fols. 41r, 41v.

modelled on the 'Burdens' of Isaiah. Thus the Burden of Egypt is directed against France;[30] the Burden of Judah concerns Italy;[31] the Burden of Jerusalem is applied to the western Church[32] and the Burden of Tyre to the Kingdom of Sicily.[33] The Burden in Arabia deals with Britain and here the author makes an interesting allusion to the martyrdom of Becket which probably accounts for the dissemination of this work in England.[34] Babylon or Chaldaea is, of course, the German empire.[35] Some of these Burdens are treated twice over, but interrupting these are other sections of material in which some attempt is made to give a Joachimist framework. Here we have several more universal patterns: seven embodiments of evil set over against seven great leaders given by God; seven seals in the Old Testament and seven openings in the New; seven double persecutions; the three *status*; the seven heads of the Dragon.[36] But the emphasis is not on the exposition of Joachim's system so much as on the reiteration of certain themes in the interpretation of events, political and religious. First, once again, the Hohenstaufen are pursued with great venom, partly through the oracles of the Erithrean Sibyl and Merlin, partly through Biblical symbols. The serpent (*coluber*), the rapacious wolf (*lupus rapax*), the bear (*ursus*), the panther (*pardus*), the eagle (*aquila*), the lioness (*leena*) and the lion (*leo*), the serpent (*vipera*) which springs from the royal beasts, the flying serpent (*regulus volans*) are all pressed into service.[37] Henry's son will be the hammer of the Church (*malleus ecclesie*), the mist-enshrouded mountain (*mons caliginestus*) to fall in ruin, the evil precursor of Antichrist to match John the Baptist, precursor of Christ. He will unite Saracens and heretics against the Church and be the Pharoah or Herod to vex it.[38] Above all, he is the representative of the Dragon which persecutes the Woman.[39] And behind Frederick II there lurks a further apparition, a third Frederick, only hinted at in enigmatic phrases.

The second preoccupation is with the tempest which assails the world, described in Part 2 of the work as a "tempest throughout the world," which in the approaching sixth opening is to take its course through successive regions.[40] Naked Peter must gird on his coat and plunge into the waves; the

---

[30] Ibid., pp. 140-141, 174-177.
[31] Ibid., p. 142.
[32] Ibid., pp. 143-145.
[33] Ibid., pp. 146, 183-184.
[34] Ibid., p. 148. See Reeves, *Influence*, pp. 82-84, for Joachimist prophecies in England.
[35] *De Oneribus*, pp. 151-153, 172-173.
[36] Ibid., pp. 154-171.
[37] Ibid., pp. 150, 157-158, 184.
[38] Ibid., pp. 149, 156, 160-170, 172.
[39] Ibid., pp. 157-159.
[40] Ibid., p. 171.

Ark of the true Church will be nearly submerged but will finally be lifted on top of them.[41] Thirdly, the two new orders point the way towards the third *status*. Noah sends out the raven and the dove; the two explorers enter Canaan; the two future witnesses of the *Apocalypse* announce the end of the tribulation.[42] Taking a text from *Isaiah* 21.7, the author declares that the "chariot of the two horses" prefigures the two future orders.[43] The opening of the sixth seal — which is to occur "after the year 1200" — must see the two new orders leading the faithful across Jordan, that is, out of the power of the Hohenstaufen, as once Moses and Aaron led the Israelites out of Pharoah's clutches, and Paul and Barnabas released the young Church from Herod's Judaism.[44] Thus, although the *De Oneribus* is so preoccupied with detailed political prognostication, the work still has a clear sense of direction towards the third *status*, already initiated in 1200: "The third *status* will shine forth in the year 1200" as pre-figured by Pope Celestine. For there is no doubt that in the sixtieth year (1260) the Church will be released from labour and given peace.[45]

In a number of passages of the *De Oneribus* the opinion of Fr. Raynier is cited.[46] This links the work with a group of smaller pieces which must have been produced about the same time and probably also in south Italy.[47] An *Expositio super Sibillis et Merlino* is addressed to the emperor Henry VI, as also a small tract *De tribus statibus*. Three short prophecies belong to the same group: 1. a commentary on the number of the Beast of Apocalypse 13.18, beginning *Quia semper in stipendariis propriis*; 2. a prophecy concerning Sicily, beginning *Cum ad me ruine miseriam*; 3. a prophetic interpretation of the plagues of Egypt, attributed to Frater Raynier and beginning *Decem plagas quibus affligetur Egyptiis*. The *Expositio* is written in the same vein as the works we have just considered: attention is focused on the history of Sicily and the direful role of the Hohenstaufen down to the expected Third Frederick. These themes are discussed, supposedly by the Abbot Joachim and Frater Raynier, in terms of the enigmatic oracles attributed to Merlin and the Sibyls. The little tract on the three *status*, consisting partly of selections from the *Super Hieremiam*, is more concerned with the Joachimist framework of history, but is still strongly coloured by the

[41] Ibid., pp. 140-141, 151, 171-172, 178-179.
[42] Ibid., pp. 156, 160, 164; fol. 39v.
[43] Ibid., p. 177.
[44] Ibid., p. 154.
[45] Ibid., pp. 156, 170.
[46] Ibid., pp. 173, 182; fols. 39v, 41v.
[47] For MSS of all the works mentioned in this paragraph, see Reeves, *Influence*, pp. 520-521, 528-529.

same political outlook and contains the same menacing pronouncements against *"tuus posterus."* Of the three short pieces, the first is a political interpretation of the number of the Beast, the second is a similar prophecy on Sicily and the third takes the ten plagues of Egypt in the Old Dispensation as types of the seven plagues to come in the New Dispensation. Two interesting points in this whole group of works are the creation of fictional dialogue on prophecy between Joachim and Raynier, and the continuing obsession with the Hohenstaufen who still menace the future.

Written a decade later, the *Super Esaiam* has lost the immediate reference to the year 1260.[48] But close similarities in phraseology suggest that it emanated from the same group as the *Super Hieremiam* and the *De Oneribus*, while its dedication to Fr. Raynier links it with the tracts we have just discussed. It is a complex work. The first part consists of a commentary on chapters 1-10 of *Isaiah*, with marginal notes to the commentary. On fol. 9v a fresh heading — *Pars I de oneribus sexti temporis* — introduces a section on the Burdens of Isaiah. As far as chapter 13 on the Burden of Babylon, the commentary is in the same style as that of the *De Oneribus*, but then occurs what is best described as a geographical section in which, starting with Italy, the different regions, with their respective dioceses, are represented in diagrams accompanied by marginal notes.[49] After this the work returns to straightforward commentary from chapter 13 onwards, ending with a brief section on the prophecies of Habakkuk and Zachariah. Finally, there follows *Pars II de septem temporibus ecclesie* (fol. 49v), which seems to be a separate little Joachimist tract.

We find in this work the same motives in using Biblical prophecy as in the previous ones. There is, in the first place, the desire to identify the Old Testament peoples with those of contemporary Europe and to apply the denunciations of ancient prophets to them. For this purpose the Burdens of *Isaiah* were particularly appropriate. "The Burden of Babylon," writes the author, "according to concord signifies the Romans, just as Chaldea signifies the Germans; the Burden of the Philistines signifies the Lombards and other Italians; ... the Burden of the Desert of the Sea signifies the Africans and other infidels ... The Burden in Arabia signifies the Spaniards and Marchians."[50] These and other similar political interpretations run right through the work. The long chapter expounding the Burden of Tyre (*Isaiah* 23) in terms of the Kingdom of Sicily affords a particularly good example of this method, enumerating, amongst other things, five "plagues" of Sicily later

---

[48] *Super Esaiam Prophetam* (Venice, 1517).

[49] *Super Esaiam*, fols. 11r-27v.

[50] Ibid., fols. 9v-10v.

alluded to in the *Breviloquium*.[51] In the geographical section the note on the diocese of Cosenza (Calabria) as Galilee, the refuge for those who believed in the prophecies, is of special interest.[52] As once the Holy Family fled to Egypt and then found refuge in Galilee, so will the faithful remnant retreat to Calabria. The evil genius of the Hohenstaufen still broods over the scene. Thus, in the interpretation of *Isaiah* 30.6, Henry VI is identified as the "lioness," Frederick II as the "lion"; the "vipers" are to be Frederick's successors, and "the flying serpent" signifies the "elevation" of the son of perdition.[53] The figures of the eagle, serpent, and dragon's head are also applied to the Hohenstaufen.[54] But there are also more truly Joachimist intentions in this work. It affirms the immovable position of the Roman Church as the true Church. As the one true Ark, it must reel in the tempest but cannot sink. It is Jerusalem, Mount Syon, or Mount Carmel.[55] The role of an apocalyptic papacy is emphasized, and the theme of the two new orders of spiritual men is again announced through all the wealth of the Biblical symbols assumed to point towards them.[56] The author has grasped the true Joachimist expectation, not only because he believes himself to be at the beginning of the third *status*, but also through the concept of the spiritual understanding or intelligence (*spiritualis intellectus*) proceeding from the two testaments.[57] He believes that the Church will shortly be led across Jordan into its sabbath after conflict.[58]

All these points arise in the course of the commentary on *Isaiah*. In the second part of the work[59] we meet a different type of pseudo-Joachimist work one closer in intention to the *Breviloquium*, although much briefer. This is a tract expounding various Joachimist patterns, starting with that of the seven seals and openings and the seven *tempora* of the Church. It includes Joachim's distinctive pattern of the unequal division of Tribes and Churches into five-plus-seven from which he drew a promise of the third *status* and also his "number play" with the species of understanding (*intellectus*) equated with the seven spiritual gifts and three cardinal virtues.[60] But, in general, as

---

[51] Ibid., fols. 38v-41r. See infra, p. 172.

[52] Ibid., fol. 14r.

[53] Ibid., fol. 42v.

[54] Ibid., fols. 10v, 13v, 15r, 29r-v, 35r, 37r-38r, 39v-40v, 46v-47v, 49v, 59r.

[55] Ibid., fols. 2v, 5r-v, 7r, 9v, 11r, 20v, 28v, 33r, 43v, 58v.

[56] Ibid., fols. 2r, 6v-7r, 8v, 11v, 30r, 37r, 38v, 41r, 46r, 48r.

[57] Ibid., fols. 27r, 30v, 45v, 50r-v, 58v. The figure collection (*Praemissiones*) preceding the *Super Esaiam*, states the "procession" of the *spiritualis intellectus* explicitly.

[58] Ibid., fols. 3r, 27v, 31v, 33v, 46v, 48v, 59v.

[59] Ibid., fols. 48v-59v.

[60] Ibid., fols. 50v-51r; *Lib. Conc.*, fols. 31v, 39r, 57r; *Expos.*, fols. 16v, 28r, 48r; *Psalterium Decem Chordarum* (Venice, 1527), fol. 262r.

an exposition of Joachim's system, it is not nearly as impressive as the *Breviloquium.*

The *Super Esaiam* is nearly always preceded by a small figure-collection which, following the sixteenth-century editors of the work, we call the *Praemissiones.* These figures have been studied elsewhere[61] and the conclusion drawn that, though based upon what must have been authentic *figurae,* they are a mid-thirteenth-century production designed to present some of Joachim's main concepts in a form to catch the eye. They include the dragon with seven heads, intertwined circles, the wheels of Ezekiel, two trees and other images used by Joachim. When placed so as to precede immediately the prologue to the *Super Esaiam,* certain connections of ideas between them suggest that the figure-collection was designed to accompany the work. There are eight extant manuscripts containing the *Praemissiones*[62] and, together with several other separate collections of *figurae,*[63] they demonstrate the continuing circulation of Joachimist ideas in the thirteenth and fourteenth centuries by *figurae* as well as texts. The writer of the *Breviloquium* stood in this tradition.

One other mid-thirteenth-century production should be mentioned, since it was used as a yard-stick for Joachimism by the fourteenth-century inquisitors in Catalonia. This is the famous *Eternal Evangel* which appeared in Paris in 1254. We now know that this was not a new book but a compilation from Joachim' three main works, together with an introduction and glosses by a Franciscan, Gerard of Borgo San Donnino.[64] It was condemned and destroyed in 1255 and, so far as we know, no complete copies have survived. Our knowledge of its contents derives chiefly from the Protocol of the Commission of Anagni appointed by Alexander IV to examine it. Here full and careful quotations show the relationship between the more extreme interpretations of Gerard's introduction and the genuine tenets of Joachim. But in their furious attack upon the work, the Paris Masters of the university, led by William of St. Amour, drew up a list of thirty-one articles which give an extreme view of the dangerous doctrines contained in the *Eternal Evangel.* Few texts of the Protocol are known but the Paris articles were copied by

---

[61] Reeves, Hirsch-Reich, "Collections," MARS, 3 (1954): 183-194.

[62] Reeves, *Influence,* pp. 521-522.

[63] Reeves, Hirsch-Reich, "Collections," MARS, 3 (1954): 174-182.

[64] The fundamental research on this subject was done by Heinrich Denifle, who edited the Protocol of Anagni. See his "Das Evangelium aeternum und die Commission zu Anagni," ALKG, 1 (1885): 49-142. Bernhard Töpfer, in "Eine Handschrift des Evangelium aeternum des Gerardino von Borgo San Donnino," *Zeitschrift für Geschichtswissenschaft,* 7 (1960): 156-163, believes that MS A. 121 in the Dresden Sachsische Landesbibliothek contains part of Gerard's compilation.

various writers, including Eymerich in his *Directorium Inquisitionis*. Clearly, it was the Paris articles that inquisitors referred to when they cited passages from the *Eternal Evangel*.[65]

Standing by itself is the *Oraculum Cyrilli*, dated to the decade 1280-1290.[66] This does not share the common outlook and language which makes it clear that the whole group of writings from the *Super Hieremiam* to the *Super Esaiam* belong together. It is, for one thing, no longer involved in the struggle against the Hohenstaufen. This *Oraculum* has no obvious political viewpoint and affords no real clues as to its provenance. It exemplifies, however, the Joachimist predilection for eastern oracles as alternatives to Biblical prophecy, since it purports to be an oracle which Cyril the Carmelite received in a vision and sent to Joachim to gloss. Besides the text and gloss there are two letters supposed to have been exchanged between Cyril and Joachim, and a later, fourteenth-century prologue and commentary by a Fr. Gilbertus Anglicus. The letters stress the need for the gift of spiritual illumination to interpret such deep enigmas and one purpose of the work may have been to enhance Joachim's reputation for the exposition of prophecy.

There seem to be few consecutive lines of thought in either text or gloss and both are couched in the enigmatic language associated with the sibylline oracles. The text begins with some astronomical prognostications for the years 1254-1282 with political implications[67] and there is certainly a strand of political prophecy in its texture: the Roman Empire appears both as "Dragon" and "Great Eagle," while Sicily still occupies an important position.[68] But the main concern of this work seems to be the condition and the future of the Roman Church. There is no doubt that this is the true church — twice the gloss alludes to the double power, temporal as well as spiritual, wielded by it[69] — yet the sins of its false clergy are denounced under such judgements as: *Ve corone superbie brutorum*,[70] while the cardinals in particular are attacked as "possessed": "they are ventriloquists, consecrated by a malign spirit and concealed in the bellies of divines. Such are the cardinals of the Roman Church and other prelates."[71] Judgement will fall on the Church in the form of a great schism, typified in the story of Rehoboam and

---

[65] Infra, p. 62 and n. 5.

[66] *Oraculum Cyrilli*, ed. Paulus Piur in Karl Burdach, *Vom Mittelalter zur Reformation*, 2, Pt. 4 (Berlin, 1912), Appendix, pp. 220-327. For MSS and editions, see Reeves, *Influence*, pp. 522-533.

[67] *Oraculum Cyrilli*, pp. 251-258.

[68] Ibid., pp. 270-273, 308-309.

[69] Ibid., pp. 264, 278.

[70] Ibid., pp. 262-267.

[71] Ibid., p. 266.

Jeroboam, between the true people and a pseudo-pope.[72] The outcome of this is never explicitly forecast, but two passages embody the expectation of a final saintly pope under the figures of a miraculous bear (*ursus mirabilis*) and an unspoiled flower (*flos indifluus*).[73] The bear is to be a Roman pontiff properly elected who, before his election, will despise precious vestments as does the bear, called "miraculous" because he is discovered to be in "vile and despicable wool" among beasts. The "unspoiled flower" is also to be a future pontiff of sweet-smelling life, whose "newness (*novitas*)" will manifest itself in many ways, but especially "in changing and renewing the offices and dignities of the Roman Church." Whilst the idea had been slowly evolving from Joachim's prophecies, these are two of the earliest explicit references in Joachimist prophecy to the Angelic Pope upon whom so much later expectation was focused.[74] The *Oraculum Cyrilli*, in fact, initiates a new phase of Joachimist thought. In the earlier works the agents of renewal had been the two new orders designed to bring in the third *status*. Here the two new orders play no part, nor is the doctrine of the three *status* mentioned, but an arresting programme for the Church begins to take shape: schism on a great scale, to be followed by the triumph of a new and powerful leader of the "Spiritual Church." These hints in the *Oraculum Cyrilli* were to be taken up with great eagerness by fourteenth-century Joachites. First, the concept of the Angelic Pope emerges and then, in the work of Jean de Roquetaillade[75] and Telesphorus of Cosenza,[76] the whole programme of the Schism and the series of Angelic Popes is fully worked out.

The last group of pseudo-Joachimist prophecies follows the new line of emphasis on the necessity of spiritual revolution in the Papacy. These are the famous prophecies of the Popes, as contained in the earliest fifteen *Vaticinia de Summis Pontificibus* and the *Liber de Flore*, with the commentary on it

---

[72] Ibid., pp. 289-290, 298-300, 303.

[73] "Donec ursus mirabilis": hic ursus Romanus pontifex est. Etenim prout ursulus lictu seu lambitu parentum affigiatur, ita Romanus pontifex et quilibet verus prelatus ore seu lingua electorum preficitur; vel potest dici, quod talis pontifex, antequam eligatur, vestes despiciet preciosas velut ursus, qui est lana repertus vili et despicabili inter feras, propter quod mirabilis appellatur ... (*Oraculum Cyrilli*, p. 292). "Flos indifluus": ... Ex hoc intelligo futurum pontificem odorifere vite, aut fame futurum ac novitates magnas facturum. Flos quidem habet odorem in tactu et novitatem in ortu. Hec autem novitas, quam committet, poterit contingere multipliciter et maxime in officiis et dignitatibus Romane Ecclesie commutandis et renovandis. (Ibid., p. 295).

[74] On the Angelic Pope, see Reeves, *Influence*, pp. 401-415; Bernard McGinn, "Angel Pope and Papal Antichrist," *Church History*, 47 (1978): 155-173; idem, *Visions of the End* (New York, 1979), pp. 186-195, 328-330.

[75] Infra, pp. 78-80.

[76] On Telesphorus of Cosenza, see Reeves, *Influence*, pp. 325-330, 423-424.

and the *Liber Horoscopus*.[77] All were probably composed between 1303 and 1305 by the group of Spiritual Franciscans associated with Angelo Clareno. We are now in a different world from that of the mid-thirteenth-century Joachites and the demands made on prophecy are new. This little group of religious enthusiasts believed that in maintaining the Rule and Testament of St. Francis unadulterated they were defending the spiritual treasure of the future age. Their hope depended upon a spiritual revolution in the leadership of the Church. What they asked of prophecy, therefore, was the delineation of a series of Angelic Popes, placed in sharp juxtaposition to the worldly pontiffs under whom they had suffered, and to be expected shortly. Under cover of Joachim's name they could "prophesy" on the recent occupants of St. Peter's chair tellingly enough and then move over to real prophecy most convincingly. Thus the *Vaticinia* contained fifteen portraits of popes, with pictures and text based once more on an eastern model, the Byzantine Oracles of Leo the Wise, in which the unreformed succession from Nicholas III to Benedict XI is contrasted sharply with the following prophetic series.[78] Their model provided them with the device for effecting the transition: at the crucial moment the voice of God directs the electors to seek a new pope among the rocks of the most westerly of the seven hills. They find a hermit among the rocks and elect him as pope.[79]

The illustrations to the *Vaticinia* were no longer the diagrammatic *figurae* of thirteenth-century Joachimism, but actual pictures of popes, portrayed with various enigmatic symbols. They were immensely popular in the following two centuries, inspiring many artists to try their hand at rendering them in different styles and providing, perhaps, the model for the artist of the *Breviloquium*. The *Liber de Flore* had no illustrations but ventured further in its detailed prophetic programmes for the four Angelic Popes envisaged in it. The whole group of writings embodied a revolutionary attitude towards the Church in that the transition to the new age was to be sudden and brought about by the direct intervention of God in the election of these spiritual

---

[77] The pioneer study of this group of writings was made by Herbert Grundmann, "Die Papstprophetien des Mittelalters," *Archiv für Kulturgeschichte*, 19 (1929): 77-159; idem, "Die Liber de Flore," *Historisches Jahrbuch*, 49 (1929): 33-91. Grundmann produced strong arguments for ascribing them to Clareno's group at this date, but the evidence is not quite secure and the possibility of a slightly earlier date has been raised. See Marjorie Reeves, *Popular Belief and Practice*, ed. George Cuming and Derek Baker (Cambridge, 1972), pp. 107-134; idem, *Joachim of Fiore and the Prophetic Future* (London, 1976), p. 75; Emil Donckel, "Prophezeiung," AFH, 26 (1933): 29-104.

[78] Reeves, *Popular Belief and Practice*, pp. 107-134.

[79] In an unpublished paper Professor David Clark of Hope College has made an interesting study of the "cave" motif in relation to thirteenth-century spirituality and prophecy. This motif clearly continues into the fourteenth century.

popes. Yet the device of the papal succession preserved the continuity and authority of the church of Peter.

In this brief account we have attempted to survey the literary tradition of Joachimist works as inherited by fourteenth-century Joachites. This included the use of Joachim's chief number patterns of twos, threes and sevens, the appropriation of all the Biblical symbols used by him to herald the two new orders of spiritual men, and his expectation that after the greatest tribulation of all time the Church would shortly cross Jordan into the Promised Land of the third *status*. Through his system of concords between the Old and New Dispensations Joachim had pointed the way towards the use of Biblical prophecy in reading the signs of God's judgement upon the contemporary political scene and in identifying the manifestations of Antichrist. The mid-thirteenth-century Joachites, with their strong anti-Hohenstaufen bias, plunged deeply into political prophecy based on the Old Testament prophetic writings. Here, of course, they went much further than Joachim. Although their specific prognostications went quickly out of date, the continued circulation of these works shows the attraction of this type of prophecy. A clear shift of emphasis was made, however, in the latest pseudo-Joachimist writings. The politics of the mid-thirteenth century were shaken off and attention was focused on the judgement to fall on the false church, the violence of schism between the true and false churches, the secret refuge of the true Church, and the emergence, through revolution, of the triumphant sequence of Angelic Popes. These were some of the ingredients used by the Joachites of the fourteenth century.

2

Petrus Johannis Olivi

There were no further attempts to bring Joachimism up-to-date by means of prophetic writings under the Abbot's name. Instead, there appeared certain original and passionate missionaries who, seeking to read the signs of their own age, assimilated many of the Joachimist categories. At the turn of the thirteenth/fourteenth centuries Petrus Johannis Olivi and Arnold of Vilanova were thinking and writing in prophetic terms which exercised great influence throughout the fourteenth century over Spiritual Franciscans, Beguins, and others, especially in the south of France and Catalonia.

Petrus Johannis Olivi was born at Sérignan about 1248, and joined the Franciscan Order at Béziers at the age of twelve.[1] His intellectual abilities were soon recognized, and he was sent to Paris, where he studied under St. Bonaventura and took a bachelor's degree. He returned to his native province, became a lector to the friars, and sometime thereafter began to offend certain of his colleagues with the fervour of his preaching, which was probably in the tradition of Hugh of Digne (ob. 1257), who has been generally recognized as the initiator of the Spiritual movement within the Franciscan order. A treatise Olivi had composed on the Blessed Virgin was burned by order of the Minister General, and soon afterwards Olivi and his disciples were accused of teaching Joachimist doctrines, for which some of his followers were imprisoned. In 1282, after the Chapter General of Strasbourg, the Minister General turned Olivi's works over to a committee of Paris theologians, who condemned thirty-four of his propositions.

Olivi refuted the charges made against him in his *Responsio*, and triumphed over his opponents at the Chapter General of Milan in 1285. After

---

[1] This brief account of Olivi's life is based on John Moorman, *A History of the Franciscan Order* (Oxford, 1968), pp. 189-190, 193-194, 197. See also Franz Ehrle, "P.J. Olivi, sein Leben und seine Schriften," ALKG, 3 (1887): 409-452; Decima Douie, *The Nature and Effect of the Heresy of the Fraticelli* (Manchester, 1932), pp. 81-119; Malcolm Lambert, *Franciscan Poverty* (London, 1961).

another confrontation at the Chapter General in Montpellier in 1287, the charges against him were dropped. Shortly afterwards he was appointed lector to the friars at Florence, where he probably met Ubertino da Casale, and two years later he became lector at Montpellier.

At the Chapter General of Paris in 1292, Olivi carefully avoided criticism of Nicholas III's *Exiit qui seminat,* but managed to retain a strict interpretation of the *usus pauper.* He returned to his teaching in Montpellier, "attracting many," as Moorman has written, "by the depth of his learning, the purity of his life, and the modesty of his character."[2] After several years he moved to Narbonne, where he died in March 1298.

As a theologian and philosopher Olivi is still somewhat of an enigma. He wrote prolifically: more than sixty treatises are now firmly attributed to him.[3] He wrote commentaries on a number of books of the Bible, he lectured on the Sentences and produced *Quaestiones* on many philosophical and theological subjects, he made decisive contributions to the controversy on Poverty and the *usus pauper,* and replied to his critics in various responses. His reputation as an original scholar and thinker has steadily increased in recent years. The difficulties in appraising his contribution to medieval learning arise, first, from the fact that many of his works are still unedited, secondly, because his very individuality makes him difficult to "place" in relation to medieval schools of thought, and thirdly, because the argument on the extent of his Joachimism has tended to get him out of focus. As a disciple of Bonaventure, Olivi has often been labelled Augustinian, but others see him as intermediate between Bonaventure and Duns Scotus, and pointing towards the breakdown of the old "schools."[4] Perhaps the clue to all his thinking lies in his concern with salvation history and the mission of the Franciscan Order within it. Thus his thought on a whole range of philosophical and theological topics could be said to be directed, not towards achieving or maintaining a coherent synthesis of all knowledge, but to furthering understanding of God's purpose in history. His attitude to Aristotle illustrates this point: David Burr has shown that, as a scholastic philosopher, he was prepared to acknowledge and use the Philosopher at certain levels, but that the extreme cult of Aristotelianism came over to him as a deeply dangerous "sign of the times,"

[2] Moorman, *Franciscan Order,* p. 197.

[3] Dionysius Pacetti, *Petrus Ioannis Olivi, O.F.M., Quaestiones Quatuor de Domina, Bibliotheca Francescana Ascetica Medii Aevi,* 8 (1954): 15*-29*, gives a list of 64 works. See also Servus Gieben, "Bibliographia Oliviana (1885-1967)," *Collectanea Francescana,* 38 (1968): 167-195.

[4] See David Flood's masterly survey of changing assessments of Olivi's place in medieval thought in *Peter Olivi's Rule Commentary* (Wiesbaden, 1972), pp. 1-23.

and in this sense he saw Aristotle as a fore-runner of Antichrist.[5] The
originality and variety of his positions is exemplified by the fact that at various
times his views on marriage, grace, baptism, the divine essence, the nature
of the soul and the nature of "quantity" all came under attack,[6] as well as the
central issue of the *usus pauper* and — after his death — his apocalypticism.
Nevertheless, Olivi's character and his criticisms of both the Church and his
own order attracted growing numbers of disciples. We shall see later how his
followers, the Beguins, revered his works and circulated them even under
pain of death. In 1299 his books were burned by order of the Chapter
General of Lyon, but this did little to stem the growing influence of this
extraordinary man.

Although its importance should not be exaggerated, Olivi's apocalypticism
should be seen nevertheless not as a late aberration in his career, but rather
as a consequence of his overriding concern with God's work in history.
Within the context of this study, Olivi's expectations concerning the final
stages of history and the extent of Joachim's influence at this point in our
survey are central themes. In his study of Olivi's commentary on the
Apocalypse, Manselli concluded that Olivi owed only a superficial debt to
Joachim. Because Olivi deliberately disavowed Joachim's Trinitarian doctrine
Manselli argued that his conception of history was cut loose from Joachim's
Trinitarian reading of it, so that, though he mentioned the three *status*, he
avoided "appropriating" the separate Persons of the Trinity to each *status*.[7]
Moreover, Manselli found almost no evidence of that study of concords
between the Old and New Testaments which is a fundamental attribute of the
Joachimist view of history. Manselli concluded that "the Joachimism of Olivi
shows itself in this last work to be of quite moderate proportions," and
cautioned against "exaggerated opinions" of such influence.[8]

In our view, this judgement is not correct. Although Olivi's emphasis is
at times different from that of Joachim, his apocalyptic theory, as embodied
in his *Postilla in Apocalypsim*, is fundamentally and overtly Joachimist. It was
Joachim's pattern of double sevens on which he fastened most strongly, but

[5] David Burr, *The Persecution of Peter Olivi*, Transactions of the American Philosophical
Society, ns. 66, pt. 5 (Philadelphia, 1976): 25-30; idem, "The Apocalyptic Elements in Olivi's
Critique of Aristotle," *Church History*, 40 (1971): 15-29.

[6] Burr, *Persecution of Olivi*, pp. 44-61.

[7] Raoul Manselli, *La "Lectura super Apocalypsim" di Pietro di Giovanni Olivi* (Rome,
1955), p. 165; idem, "La Terza Età, 'Babylon' e l'Anticristo Mistico (a proposito di Pietro
di Giovanni Olivi)," BISI, 82 (1970): 47-79; Edith Pásztor, "Giovanni XXII e il Gioachimismo
di Pietro di Giovanni Olivi," BISI, 82 (1970): 81-111; idem, "Le polemiche sulla 'Lectura
super Apocalypsim' di Pietro di Giovanni Olivi fino alla sua condanna," BISI, 70 (1958):
365-424.

[8] Manselli, *Lectura*, p. 190.

the *Postilla* demonstrates that Olivi also derived his structure of history from the pattern of threes. Olivi states of the *Postilla* that "the most important intention of this book is to describe the seven ages (*septem tempora seu status*) of the Church and especially the sixth and seventh."[9] The fact that he uses *tempus* and *status* interchangeably for the seven periods of the Church which match the seven periods of the Old Testament need not bother us, for he goes on to distinguish Joachim's threefold division as that of the "general" *status*, specifically relating the seven *status* or ages of the Church to the second and third of the three "general" *status*.[10] He believes the Church to be standing in the sixth age,[11] and merges the sixth and seventh ages into the *tertius status generalis*, a conception which he explicitly attributes to Joachim.[12]

The concept of three *status* as fundamental to Olivi's view of redemptive history may be seen most explicitly in a passage from the *Postilla* which in turn includes a quotation taken verbatim from Joachim's *Expositio*. "As in the first *status* of temporal history," Olivi quotes from Joachim,

> it was the study of the Fathers to expound the great works of God undertaken from the beginning of the world, and in the second *status* from Christ until the third *status* it was the task of His children to seek the wisdom of mystical things and hidden mysteries in the temporal generations, so in the third [*status*] it remains for us to sing the psalms and rejoice in God, praising His great works and his multiform wisdom.[13]

Continuing in his own words (but still following Joachim's train of thought in the *Expositio*), Olivi describes the first age as that of God the Father, "terrible and fear-inspiring"; the second that of the Son, "teacher and

---

[9] Petrus Johannis Olivi, *Postilla super Apocalypsim*, Rome, Biblioteca Angelica, MS 382, fol. 105r.

[10] Ibid., fol. 105r.

[11] Ibid., fol. 1r.

[12] Ibid., fol. 52r.

[13] Ibid., fol. 31v; the italicised words in the passage below are those taken from Joachim's *Expos.*, fols. 84r-85v, and are those translated in the text:

Significatur etiam per hoc proprium donum et singularis proprietas tertii status mundi ... VIo statu ecclesie inchoandi et spiritui sancto per quandam antonomasiam appropriati. Sicut enim *in primo statu seculi ante Christum studium fuit patribus enarrare magna opera Domini incohata ab origine mundi, in secundo vero statu a Christo usque ad tertium statum cura fuit filiis quaerere sapientiam misticarum rerum et mysteria occulta in generationibus seculorum. Sic in tertio nil restat nisi ut psallamus et iubilemus Deo laudantes eius opera magna et eius multiformem sapientiam* et bonitatem in suis operibus et scripturarum sermonibus clare manifestatam. Sicut enim in primo tempore exhibuit se Deus pater ut *terribilem* et metuendum, unde tunc claruit eius *timor*, sic in secundo exhibuit se Deus filius ut magistrum et revelatorem et ut verbum expressimum sapientiae sui patris. Ergo in tertio tempore spiritus sanctus exhibebit se ut flammam et fornacem divini amoris ...

revealer"; the third that of the Holy Spirit, "flame and furnace of divine love."[14]

Olivi drew most of his interpretations of Old Testament and Church history from Joachim's *Liber Concordie*. He did not reproduce the entire system of concords, but tells us that it can be found in Joachim's works. The forty-first and forty-second generations are crucial, and in pin-pointing these Olivi tells us he followed Book V of Joachim's *Liber Concordie*.[15] These were the generations in which the translation of the Church from the sixth to the seventh *tempus* or *status* would be enacted. Olivi divided the seven ages of the Church as follows: first, the age of the Apostles from Christ until the emperor Nero; second, that of the martyrs from Nero to St. Silvester; third, that of the doctors from Silvester to St. Anthony; fourth, that of the anchorites from Anthony to Charlemagne; fifth, that of the regulars from Charlemagne to St. Francis. The sixth age is that of the evangelical men from St. Francis to the death of Antichrist; this is further sub-divided into six parts. The seventh and final age will last from Antichrist until the end of the world.[16] This, of course, represents an adaptation of Joachim's time-scale but the pattern is basically the same and Olivi adopted Joachim's concords of the double sevens, paralleling seven wars against the Church with seven wars of the Old Testament. Again following Joachim, he matched the seven perse-cutions of the Church to the seven heads of the Dragon and, finally, like Joachim, he saw the seven *tempora* of the Church corresponding to the seven general *etates* of the world's history: 1. Adam to Noah; 2. Noah to Abraham; 3. Abraham to Moses; 4. Moses to David; 5. David to Christ; 6. Christ to Antichrist; 7. Antichrist to the end of the world. To these patterns of sevens he added two of his own, establishing concords between the seven *status* of the Church and the seven days of creation, on the one hand, and the seven sacraments on the other.[17]

Obviously to Olivi an important element in these patterns of concords was that of the divinely-commissioned series of orders. The first five, corres-ponding to the five *status* of the Church, follow Joachim's sequence, but in place of Joachim's uncertainty about the sixth order we now have the evangelical men under St. Francis.[18] For the seventh *status* there is no special order. Olivi further supports his belief in the unique role of the evangelical

---

[14] *Postilla*, fol. 31v.

[15] Ibid., fol. 83v.

[16] Ibid., fols. 12v-13r, 2r-v.

[17] Ibid., fol. 12v for the seven days of Creation and seven *status* of the Church, fol. 12r for the seven sacraments.

[18] Ibid., fols. 53r-53v, 55v, 84r.

men by a pattern of threes which he takes directly from Joachim: as the synagogue was propagated by twelve patriarchs and the Church of the Gentiles by twelve apostles, so the final Church will be propagated by twelve evangelical men.[19] Once again he pushes this claim further by identifying this last twelve with St. Francis and his companions. There is no doubt that Olivi expected a flowering of history between the triumph of Antichrist and the consummation of time (*consummatio seculi*), and that St. Francis held in his mind a unique position as the initiator of this final epoch. In one line of thought particularly he combined a Christocentric view of history with a threefold pattern which exalted the epoch of St. Francis into a special category: this was the concept of the three Advents of Christ: first in the flesh, second in the spirit of evangelical reform when there would appear a "new age or new church," third in the final judgement.[20] The conformity of St. Francis was specifically placed within this eschatological framework of history: as in the sixth age (*aetate*), the Judaic religion having been rejected, the new Man Christ came with the new law and life and cross, so in the Sixth *status*, the carnal church having been rejected, the law and life and cross of Christ will be renewed (*renovabitur*). This process had already been initiated by the appearance of St. Francis, who bore the Stigmata of Christ, and is a figure for His life and Passion (*et Christo totus concrucifixus et configuratus*).[21]

Perhaps Olivi's revision of Joachimism is best illustrated in the following passage, where we see his interpretation of recent events within the framework of the crucial generations:

> For in the sixth year of the forty-first generation, the third *status* was initiated, running as yet concurrently with the second, and it also contains the opening of the sixth seal, running as yet concurrently with the fifth. For St. Francis, the angel of the opening of the sixth seal, was in that sixth year converted, which is the sixth year of the thirteenth century ... From that time all persecution of the evangelical *status* relates to the persecution of Antichrist. And by this reasoning, in the following forty-third generation there began the persecution in which the Paris doctors condemned evangelical poverty. In that same generation Frederick II and his accomplices persecuted the Church, for which reason he was deposed from the empire by Innocent IV at the Council of Lyons. ... Then Manfred, Frederick's son, usurped the kingdom of Sicily which was held by the Church, and was deposed and killed by Charles. Shortly afterwards, Conradin, the son of Conrad who was the son of Frederick suffered the same fate. Also, in the forty-third generation, Peter of Aragon invaded

[19] Ibid., fol. 56v; see *Lib. Conc.*, fols. 21r-22r.
[20] *Postilla*, fols. 7v-8r.
[21] Ibid., fol. 13r.

Sicily, and afterwards there followed great discord between kings and king-doms.[22]

Here Olivi follows the mid-thirteenth-century Joachites in his apocalyptic interpretation of political realities, seen, of course, from the perspective of a generation later. But the tumults of kings must be placed against the background of the secret beginnings of the third *status* and the persecution of the evangelical men who bear its treasure.

In the struggle of the great transition period Olivi saw the forces of evil as concentrated in the Carnal Church (*Ecclesia Carnalis*) and the manifesta-tions of Antichrist. The *Ecclesia Carnalis* is openly identified with the Whore of Babylon.[23] Just as the Synagogue, proceeding against Christ through Annas and Caiaphas, cast Him forth, so now the new synagogue, which is "the congregation of Satan," in rejecting evangelical poverty, has cast out Christ in the persons of his apostles, those who practise true poverty.[24] These false Christians are the *Ecclesia Carnalis* which attacks the principles of Christ and of St. Francis; as they have rejected, so they will be rejected.[25] Nowhere, however, does Olivi identify the Roman Church as such with Babylon. Indeed, he adopts exactly Joachim's position. The "merchants" (*mercatores*) and "businessmen" (*negotiatores*) of New Babylon are interpre-ted as various types of carnal ecclesiastics. Here again Olivi draws on Joachim's *Expositio* extensively, but Babylon and the Roman Church are never mentioned in the same breath.[26]

In the third division of the sixth *status*, the mystic Antichrist, precursor to the great Antichrist, is to appear. The mystic Antichrist, identified with the wild boar from the wood (*aper de silva*) of *Psalm* 79.14, and with Caiaphas

---

[22] Nam in sexto anno XLI[i] generationis initiatus est fundamentaliter tertius status concur-rendo tamen adhuc cum secundo initiata et est apertio sexti sigilli concurrendo tamen usque adhuc cum quinta. Franciscus enim tanquam angelus apertionis sexti sigilli est illo sexto anno conversus que est et sextus annus XIII centenarii ... ex tunc autem omnis persecutio sui evangelici status spectat ad persecutiones Antichristi. et secundum hoc in sequenti XLII a generatione cepit Parisius persecutio quorundam magistrorum condempnantium evangelicam mendicitatem. In ipsa ... fuit Federicus secundus cum suis complicibus persequens ecclesiam, propter quod et in ipsa ab imperio depositus fuit in Concilio generali per Innocentium IIII facto Lugdunii. ... Tuncquam Manfredus Federici filius usurpatorie regnum Sicilie contra ecclesiam tenens est per Karolum devictus et occisus. Et paulo post Corradus filius Corradi filii Federici. Et in XLIIa generatione Petrus rex Aragonum invasit Sicilie regnum. Et ex tunc secuta sunt multa discordia inter reges et regna. (Ibid., fols. 83v-84r).

[23] See the commentary on *Cecidit, cecidit, Babylon* (fol. 95r), where Olivi states that the *ecclesia carnalis imo vocatur Babylon hic et in XVII° et XVIII°, et tam ibi quam capitulo XVIII° vocatur meretrix magna.*

[24] Ibid., fol. 27r.

[25] Ibid., fol. 53v.

[26] Ibid., fols. 107r-108v; see *Expos.*, fols. 200r-202r.

and Herod,[27] is apparently to be a false pope, and may reign concurrently with the great Antichrist. Olivi is not entirely clear concerning the respective roles of the two Antichrists and the false pope; sometimes all three are distinguished, and sometimes the false pope seems to be identified with one of the two Antichrists. This ambiguity will be reflected in later Olivianist documents we shall consider: most of his disciples took the mystic Antichrist to be a false pope, but some apparently were not convinced of this, as, for example, Bernard de na Jacma.[28] In his study, Manselli concludes that Olivi displays a tendency to make the mystic Antichrist an antipope, and his view seems justified.[29]

The section in which Olivi discusses this matter in some detail begins with the passage in *Apocalypse* 13, *and they adored the dragon who gave power to the beast.* Of this beast Olivi comments that to adore the error and the following of this beast is to adore the dragon who is the author of that error and his following, or sect. According to Joachim, Olivi states, to adore the dragon is to adore that king in whom the devil in his evil power particularly resides.[30]

A second beast is then to arise — *and I saw another beast* — from among the nation of the faithful, and will place himself in league with the first beast.[31] This second beast will rise, as Daniel had prophesied, not in its own strength, but in the strength of the first. When it does rise, then will occur the temptation of the mystic Antichrist and his followers, who will cause men to adore cupidity and carnality or worldly glory.[32] This mystic Antichrist will give false signs, chief among them to be the following:

> First, that whoever contradicts his ecclesiastical authority shall be seen to be inobedient, contumacious, and in schismatic rebellion. Secondly, that whoever contradicts his teachers and doctors and the general opinion of the multitude will be seen to be stupid, insane, and heretical.[33]

---

[27] *Postilla*, fol. 68v.

[28] Philippus van Limborch, *Historia Inquisitionis, cui subjungitur Liber Sententiarum Inquisitionis Tholosanae, 1307-1313* (Amsterdam, 1692), pp. 307-309.

[29] Manselli, *Lectura*, pp. 224-225.

[30] *Postilla*, fol. 90v.

[31] Ibid., fol. 90v.

[32] Cum autem apostatrix bestia de terra religiosorum ascendet in altum cum duobus cornibus pseudo religiosorum et pseudo prophetarum falso similibus veris cornibus Agni, tunc erit validissima temptatio mistici antichristi. Surgent enim tunc pseudo christi et pseudo prophete qui facient ab hominibus adorari cupiditatem et carnalitatem seu terrenam gloriam bestie saecularis. (*Postilla*, fol. 92v).

[33] Primo scilicet sue ecclesiastice auctoritatis cui contradicere videbitur inobedientia et contumacia et rebellio scismatica. Secundo omnium magistrorum et doctorum suorum et que totius multitudinis seu communis opinionis omnium cui contradicere videbitur stultum et insanum et quae hereticum. (*Postilla*, fol. 92v).

Offenders will be handed over to the secular arm for punishment. This passage is one of those reproduced at length from the *Postilla* in the *Breviloquium.*[34]

From the evidence in Joachim's works and from accounts of the life of St. Francis and his associates, Olivi concludes that Frederick II is the "head wounded unto death" of *Apocalypse* 13.3, and that in the time of the mystic Antichrist, Frederick is to be revived in someone from his seed (*reviviscat in aliquo de semine eius*).[35] In order to obtain the kingdom of France, this descendant of Frederick will employ the false pope, who will attack the evangelical position, and place those of his own persuasion in the episcopate.[36]

This false pope is presumably to be identified with the mystic Antichrist, who has been brought to power by the seed of Frederick II. The beast who is adored is identified by Olivi as Antichrist, and the image of the beast, which is also adored, is identified by him as the false pope.[37] In the context of this passage, the false pope also appears to be the mystic Antichrist.

During the time of tribulation caused by the mystic and the great Antichrists, the temptations for the elect will be great. The learned doctors will take the side of Antichrist, and there will arise a locust-like swarm of religious disciples and detractors who will stir up enmity against those not favouring them and against all spiritual things, publicly attacking the life and spirit of Christ in the evangelical men, and solemnly condemning them.[38]

It may be seen here that Olivi is much more interested in the mystic than in the great Antichrist. Professor Brian Tierney[39] has suggested that, in putting forward his theory of papal infallibility, Olivi was expecting a pseudo-pope who would attack evangelical poverty and seek to overthrow what he regarded as Nicholas III's confirmation of Franciscan poverty in *Exiit qui seminat.* Intellectually, spiritually, and institutionally the true church is approaching its final conflict with the carnal church and the coming crisis is focused on the figure of the mystic Antichrist or pseudo-pope to be expected.

---

[34] See infra, p. 230.

[35] *Postilla,* fol. 93r.

[36] Ibid., fol. 93r.

[37] *siquis adoraverit bestiam* idest, antichristum, et eius bestialem sectam *et ymaginem eius,* scilicet in eius honorem factam vel per bestiam intelligitur rex tunc monarcha et per ymaginem pseudo papa quem ... faciet adorari ut deum seu potius ut ydolum. (*Postilla,* fol. 95r).

[38] De fumo autem predicti casus et apertiones exierint locuste idest religiosi illorum sequaces ac leves et volatiles ... et detractores que et contra omnes eis non faventes ... concitantur quasi equi currentes in bellum et que contra omnia multum spiritualia ... quoniam publice Christi vitam et spiritum in viris spiritualibus accerrime impugnabunt et solempniter condempnabunt. (*Postilla,* fol. 67v).

[39] Brian Tierney, *Origins of Papal Infallibility, 1150-1350* (Leyden, 1972), pp. 71-130.

It was this emphasis which gave Olivi's work special significance when John XXII began his suppression of the evangelicals.

Like Arnold of Vilanova, Olivi believed that he was living in the crucial times mentioned by Daniel — 1290 to 1335. In 1335 Antichrist would die, and the reign of grace and peace would begin. At the conclusion of the destructive work of the two Antichrists, ten kings would rise to destroy the carnal church. The evangelical men would return from their exile to regain their inheritance, and would convert the whole of Israel to the true faith. Enoch and Elijah would return to earth, which would at last be bathed in the great illumination, the *superhabunda lumina sapientiae Dei.*[40]

Olivi's work constituted the first major revision of Joachim's system. It put greater emphasis on the seven *status* of the Church, and provided a new pattern for the crucial sixth age, developing the concept of a mystic Antichrist as the precursor of the great Antichrist. Above all, it placed St. Francis and his followers within the Joachimist framework, endowing their role with the cosmic significance of a redemptive work which could be seen in concord with that of Christ himself. We shall find the *Breviloquium* drawing on the whole tradition of Joachimism, as developed in the thirteenth and fourteenth centuries, but more especially incorporating large portions of Olivi's revised version of that tradition.

[40] *Postilla,* fol. 32r.

3

Arnold of Vilanova

Arnold of Vilanova[1] occupied a position which provided for him throughout his career a base from which to pursue his apocalyptic speculations and evangelical preaching.[2] He was a confidant of four kings: Peter II of Aragon and his three sons, Alfonso II, James II, and Frederick III of Sicily. He played various roles for the royal family, as physician, alchemist, spiritual father, diplomat, and political adviser.[3] His position vis-à-vis the powerful house of Aragon and his reputation as a physician also provided another important connection as physician to popes Boniface VIII, Benedict XI, and Clement V. Consequently, his evangelical zeal was sometimes encouraged, and sometimes tolerated, to a greater extent than that of such contemporaries as Olivi.

[1] The bibliography of Arnold of Vilanova is assuming formidable proportions; consequently, we have cited only references directly related to this study of the Joachimist themes in his work. For a valuable annotated bibliography of Arnoldian scholarship, see Elena Cánovas and Felix Piñero, *Arnaldo de Vilanova: Escritos Condenados por la Inquisición*, Editora Nacional (Madrid, 1976), pp. 47-52. See also Miguel Batllori, "Orientaciones bibliográficas para el estudio de Arnau de Vilanova," *Pensamiento*, 10 (1954): 311-323, with a bibliography on spiritual movements during Arnold's time, and Josep Perarnau, "Bibliográfia teológica catalana," *Analecta sacra Tarraconensia*, 45 (1972): 121-235; idem, "Troballa de tractats espirituals perduts d'Arnau de Vilanova," *Revista catalán de teológia*, 1 (1976). Perarnau's *L'"alia Informatio Beguinorum" d'Arnau de Vilanova* (Barcelona, 1978) is especially important for its presentation of newly-discovered documents relating to the early history of Arnoldian Beguinism, and for an edition of Arnold's *Alia Informatio Beguinorum*. We shall refer in detail to this work in later chapters. In *Dos Tratados "espirituales" de Arnau de Vilanova en traducción castellana medieval* (Rome, 1975-1976), Perarnau has presented evidence for the spread of Arnold's work in Beguin communities throughout Castille and northwestern Spain in the late fourteenth and early fifteenth centuries. At the time of this writing, Perarnau was preparing an edition of Arnold's *De Helemosina et Sacrificio*.

[2] For biographical data on Arnold, see especially Juan Paniagua, "Vida de Arnaldo de Vilanova," *Archivo Iberoamericano de Historia, de la Medicina y de Antropologiá Médica*, 3 (1951): 3-83; idem, *Estudias y Notas sobre Arnaldo de Vilanova* (Barcelona, 1963); Canovas and Piñero, *Escritos Condenados*, pp. 15-44; Joaquin Carreras y Artau, *Relaciones de Arnau de Vilanova con los Reyes de la Casa de Aragón* (Barcelona, 1955); Miguel Batllori and Joaquin Carreras y Artau, eds., *Arnau de Vilanova: Obres Catalanes* (Barcelona, 1947), 1: 11-35.

[3] Carreras y Artau, *Relaciones*, p. 18.

Arnold was born sometime in the 1230s, probably in Valencia, learned Arabic in his youth, studied Latin, humanities and theology in the schools of the Dominicans, and by 1260 was a student of medicine at Montpellier. During this period, he received his clerical tonsure, became a master of medicine, and married Agnes Blasi, the daughter of a Montpellier merchant. There is some doubtful evidence that he may have studied at Naples during the next decade. In 1276, however, he was in Valencia, where in that year his only child, Maria, was born. In that year also, James I died, and his kingdom was divided between Peter II, who took Aragon, and James II, who began his rule over Majorca, Roussillon, the Cerdagne and Montpellier. By 1281, Arnold had become physician to Peter and had begun studies in Hebrew literature under Fr. Ramon Martí of the Friars Preacher. In 1282, Peter II became king of Sicily as a result of the Sicilian Vespers, and his wife Constance took the Infants James and Frederick to Sicily to rule for the house of Aragon. In 1285, Arnold attended Peter II in his last illness, was a witness of the king's second will and then in 1286 returned to Valencia. During this period Arnold had also been translating into Latin various Arabic medical works.

The period of his life which first directly concerns this study encompasses the years 1288 to 1298, during which Arnold wrote three important early religious treatises. During this period he also served Alfonso II and James II of Aragon, and Frederick III of Sicily, began a professorship in the school of medicine at Montpellier in 1289 (the same year in which Olivi joined the *studium generale* of that city), began his involvement with the Spiritual and Beguin causes, and took up his role as spiritual adviser to the royal family.

The major work of this period is the *De tempore adventus Antichristi*,[4] the first written evidence of his immersion in the Joachimist prophetic tradition, and of central importance to his entire religious and prophetic career. Batllori's discovery of a hitherto lost work of Arnold, the *Responsio ad cavilationes adversarii veritatis*,[5] has provided strong evidence for an early

---

[4] For the MS of *De tempore*, see Vatican City, Biblioteca Apostolica Vaticana, Vat. Lat. 3824, fols. 50v-78r. Parts of this work have been edited by Heinrich Finke, in *Aus den Tagen Bonifaz VIII* (Munster, 1902), pp. CXXIX-CLIX.

[5] Miguel Batllori, "Dos nous escrits espirituals d'Arnau de Vilanova," *Analecta Sacra Tarraconensia*, 28 (1955): 45-70. Batllori summarizes and reproduces portions of the *Tractatus quidem in quo respondetur obiectionibus que fiebant contra tractatum Arnaldi de adventu Antichristi* from Rome, Biblioteca Carmelitana, MS III, Var. I, fols. 46v-90r. The tract was know earlier in an inventory of Arnold's library as the *Responsio ad cavilationes adversarii veritatis*, the title used in this study. In the tract, Arnold describes the vision which produced the *De tempore*, and says that he kept the work secret for seven years. Perarnau, *Alia Informatio*, p. 177, believes the tract was written by a disciple.

date for *De tempore* (1288-1290 rather than, as formerly suggested, 1297-1298), and consequently a new sequence for Arnold's earliest religious works. Now earliest instead of latest in this sequence is the *De tempore* of 1288-1290, followed by the *Introductio in Librum Ioachim de Semine Scripturarum*,[6] followed by the *Allocutio Super Significatione Nominis Tetragrammaton*,[7] both of which were certainly written in 1292. This new order implies that Arnold's studies in Hebrew did not necessarily precede but probably coincided with his first exposure to the work of Joachim. Joachimism is the predominant and continuing influence on Arnold during this early period; Hebrew and cabbalistic influences are subordinate and, even in the *Allocutio*, less pervasive than had been thought.[8]

In the *De tempore*,[9] Arnold announces the coming of Antichrist in the late fourteenth century, and outlines a Joachimist sequence of events in the Last Times based upon a system of concord. He defends the propriety of attempting to make such calculations by invoking St. John's injunction to study the Scriptures (*scrutamini scripturas*), and by attacking the orthodox interpretation of St. Augustine's strictures on speculation concerning the end of history. In the version available to us, presumably the third, the tract has these two clearly defined objectives: it offers a prediction of the advent of the Last Times, and is at the same time a manifesto proclaiming the propriety and necessity of making calculations concerning the end of history. The version which survives is undoubtedly an enlarged version of both the original draft and the draft of 1297, and its second part is weighted especially towards the second objective.

The main subject of the first part of the tract (fols. 50r-68r) is Arnold's interpretation of the numbers 1,290 and 1,335, and other matters described by Daniel, which are held to mark the beginning of the sequence of events starting with the appearance of Antichrist and culminating in the Second

---

[6] *Introductio*, ed. Raoul Manselli, in *La Religiosità d'Arnaldo di Vilanova* (Rome, 1951), pp. 43-59. See also Beatrice Hirsch-Reich, "Alexanders von Roes Stellung zu den Prophetien," *Mitteilungen des Instituts für Österreichische Geschichtsforschung*, 67 (1959): 306. For *De Semine Scripturarum* — not part of Joachim's canon — see Vatican City, Biblioteca Apostolica Vaticana, Vat. Lat. MS 3819, fols. 1-18r-v.

[7] Edited by Joaquin Carreras y Artau, in *Sefarad*, 7 (1947): 75-105.

[8] Harold Lee, "Scrutamini Scripturas: Joachimist Themes and *Figurae* in the Early Religious Writing of Arnold of Vilanova," *Journal of the Warburg and Courtauld Institutes*, 37 (1974): 33-56. Prof. Carreras y Artau takes a different view, and argues for a more pervasive influence in the early work. See Joaquín Carreras y Artau, "Arnau de Vilanova y las culturas orientales," in *Homenaje a Millàs-Vallicrosa* (Barcelona, 1954), 1: 309-321; idem, "Arnaldo de Vilanova, Apologista Antijudaico," *Sefarad*, 7 (1947): 49-61.

[9] The following analysis of the *De tempore* is derived from Lee, "Scrutamini Scripturas," pp. 34, 35-42.

Coming and the consummation of history. Although there is at least one later addition here, the bulk of this section must surely have constituted the core of the vision of 1288-1290. According to Arnold, the fourteenth *centenarium* is to be the time of crisis, punctuated by three signs of the coming Last Judgement: the appearance of Antichrist, various astronomical phenomena, and, finally, the appearance in the heavens of the Son of Man (fol. 59r). The Last Judgement is apparently not to occur until the fifteenth *centenarium*. On earth, Antichrist is to be responsible for the corruption of the Church, and a period of great trial for all mankind, including physical cataclysm. All these trials are to cease during the final part of the Last Times, however, when a period of great tranquillity is to occur. Jerusalem will be returned to Christian rule, and the entire world will be converted to Christianity. There will be one flock and one pastor and the world will bask in the radiance of the Holy Spirit.

Arnold's approach to the problem of interpreting Daniel is fundamentally that of the fulfilment of patterns of history based on concord. Arnold argues that the traditional interpretation of the destruction of the yoke of sacrifice (*iuge sacrificium*) as having taken place during the destruction of Babylon by Nebuchadnezzar is insufficient in itself as the event which is to prefigure the end of the world. He does not deny its significance as an Old Testament figure, but argues that Daniel's prophecy is really intended to foreshadow the destruction of Jerusalem by Titus and Vespasian in New Testament times. This event in turn is the true figure or concord for the events of the Last Times, and is the sequence of events which is to be fulfilled in the fourteenth and fifteenth *centenaria*. From the destruction of the sacrifice,

> it follows therefore that the siege and overthrow of Jerusalem and the captivity of its people after the time of Christ was accomplished by Titus and Vespasian, and from that time that land and the profaned Jerusalem were frequently occupied and trodden underfoot by the Gentiles, and so it will continue to be until those times are fulfilled after which the plenitude of nations shall enter the Church of God and the conversion of the reprobates to the Catholic faith shall occur in the following century.[10]

The destruction of Jerusalem has a numerological significance which is also based on concord:

---

[10] Constat autem quod obsessio Ierusalem et eversio et captivitatio populi post tempus Christi fuit per Titum et Vespasianum peracta et ex tunc fuit illa terrena et sacrilega Ierusalem a gentilibus possessa et calcata frequenter, et etiam erit donec impleantur tempora post quam plenitudo gentium ingredietur ecclesiam Dei et conversionem reproborum ad fidem catholicam quod erit in sequenti centenario (*De tempore*, fol. 59v).

It follows also that Jerusalem was overthrown and its people captured by Titus and Vespasian in the forty-second year after the Passion and Ascension of the Lord because from the Passion until the Ascension there were precisely forty-two days.[11]

Arnold's concern with the concords of forty-two is consistent with Joachim's expectation of a third age, and indeed is explicable only in this context. In the *Liber Concordie*,[12] Joachim saw forty-two as the key number in the divisions of the three *status*: as it marked the end of the Old Testament, so the approaching forty-second generation of Joachim's time was to bring the third and final *status*. Olivi used this same reckoning in the *Postilla super Apocalypsim* of 1299 (discussed supra) to calculate the time scheme for Antichrist and the third *status*, naming dates consistent with Arnold's calculation. The third *status* is to begin in the sixth year of the forty-first generation with the appearance of Antichrist, and, as both Olivi and Arnold state, will find its consummation in the seventh *tempus* of the Church.[13] These concords are also found in the *Breviloquium*, fol. 44v.

Arnold's obsession with Antichrist meant that the emphasis placed by Joachim on the third *status* itself, the Age of the Spirit between Antichrist and the *consummatio seculi*, was given little prominence in the *De tempore*.[14] The years 1290 to 1335, which would encompass the great tribulation of the time of Antichrist, were his main concern. However, God's kingdom would be established before the end of his age, and the *renovatio*, so essential a feature of Joachimism, is explicitly forecast by Arnold. Quoting the oracle of Daniel (*Blessed is he who expects and survives until the year 1335*), Arnold describes the Joachimist expectation of tranquillity and spiritual leadership mentioned in our earlier summary of his views:

> Therefore truly he is said to be blessed who reaches that time, as the sacred doctors expound, because he will come to the time of universal tranquillity and peace in the Church, in which the truth shall be recognized throughout the entire world, and Christ shall be adored, and "there shall be one shepherd and

[11] Constat autem quod Ierusalem fuit eversa et populus captivatus per Titum et Vespasianum XLII° anno post passionem vel ascensionem Domini quoniam a passione usque ad ascensionem non fuerunt nisi XLII dies (*De tempore*, fol. 61v-62r).

[12] Joachim writes: Ostensis in testamento veteri et ex parte in novo locis precipuis concordiarum modo sub numero generationum querendi sunt termini generationum: ut sciat lector loca concordie per regulam numeri invenire: hac in re exerceat qui vult intelligentiam suam: incipiens unumcumque voluerit et ubicumque completum cernit esse numerum 42arum generationum. (*Lib. Conc.*, fol. 13r).

[13] Olivi, *Postilla*, fol. 84v.

[14] Arnold devotes further attention to this period in the *Introductio* and the *Expositio super Apocalypsim* (infra, pp. 35, 40-42), but not nearly as much as does Joachim.

one sheepfold (*erit unus pastor et unum ovile*)." This is that time of the opening of the seventh seal, of which it is said in Apocalypse 7, "and when the seventh seal was opened, there was silence in heaven," that is, peace and tranquillity in the Church, "as it were for half an hour." [15]

Having dealt with the predictions for the coming of Antichrist, Arnold then turned to the question of the propriety and necessity of predicting the Last Times, establishing a position he would be called upon to defend again and again. The crux of the argument lay in St. Augustine's treatment of the subject, for his pronouncements constituted the main case against apocalypticism: "The enemies of prophecy," Arnold claims, "assert that Augustine, in the eighteenth book of *The City of God*, says that it is not expedient for the faithful that they should know the time of the persecution of Antichrist." [16] Augustine had referred to the text in *Acts* 1.7 where, in reply to the disciples' question, "Lord, will you restore the kingdom of Israel in this time" Christ had answered, "It is not for you to know the times which the Father has put in His own power (*Non est vestrum nosse tempora vel momenta quae Pater posuit in sua potestate*)." Augustine commented that "in vain, then, do we attempt to compute definitely the years that remain to this world, when we may hear from the mouth of Truth that it is not for us to know this." [17] Those who try to calculate the end of the world use merely human conjectures, he continues,

> and bring forward nothing certain from the authority of the canonical Scriptures. But on this subject He puts aside the figures of the calculators and orders silence, saying, "It is not for you to know the times which the Father has put in His own power." [18]

Arnold argued that the theologians in Paris had simply misinterpreted Augustine's view, and offered an alternative exposition of the Augustinian position. He first points out that Christ's reply was not concerned with the advent of Antichrist, but with the "consummation of the age, and the final conversion of the Jews to Christ." Since Augustine must be absolved from charges of irrationality or ignorance, Arnold continues, we must conclude

---

[15] Finke, *Aus den Tagen*, p. CXXXIII: Ideo vero beatus dicitur, qui pertinget illud tempus, ut exponunt sacri doctores, quia veniet ad tempus universalis tranquillitatis et pacis ecclesie, in quo per universum orbem cognoscetur veritas et adorabitur Christus et "erit unus pastor et unum ovile." [*John* 10.16] Hoc est tempus apertoris septimi sigilli, de quo dicitur apo. VII°: "Et cum aperuisset sigillum septimum, factum est silentium in celo," id est pax et tranquillitas in ecclesia "quasi dimidia hora."

[16] Ibid., p. CXLI.

[17] St. Augustine, *De Civitate Dei*, 18.53 (PL 41: 616-617).

[18] Ibid.

that he himself was also referring, not to the time of Antichrist, but rather to the end of the age, when he stated that it was in vain "to compute definitely the years that remain to this world." [19] Secondly, Augustine's assertion that such a calculation is not possible by human effort means only human endeavour unaided by God, and does not preclude a combined effort, as it were. Indeed, since the divinely-inspired Scriptures constitute such a mixture of human and divine, and offer certain calculations, we may assume that they are legitimate targets for interpretation, and not placed out of bounds by Augustine's strictures concerning "the presumption of human curiosity." [20] Finally, although he does not discuss it here, the argument is certainly related to the point made elsewhere by both Joachim and Arnold that he who meditates on the Scriptures can receive divine assistance in their interpretation.

Indeed, the need to study the Scriptures is underscored again and again in the tract. To forbid the study of any part of the Scriptures is itself to disregard divine warnings:

> For since God says through John, "Study the Scriptures," and, the above exposition, as it is Catholic, pertains to the examination of Holy Scripture ... it follows that whoever forbids the study of Catholic matters to the faithful, puts himself in direct opposition to divine admonition and to the Holy Spirit. [21]

Christ himself, Arnold notes, quoted Daniel on the coming of Antichrist. Hence, it must follow that the divine inspiration contained in the Scriptures is intended to be understood by men, and has been given to them for their proper direction. [22]

The prophetic message which Arnold thus buttressed with such passionate argument was one which he believed every pastor should be transmitting to his flock: "Watch (*Vigilate*), and walk cautiously, since perhaps the final persecution of the rapacious wolf and the consummation of the present age are only too close." [23]

The *De tempore* certainly seems to have been seized upon by Joachites as a supporting text, for we shall find the author of the *Breviloquium* using

---

[19] Finke, *Aus den Tagen*, p. CXLII.

[20] Ibid., p. CXLIII.

[21] Nam cum Dominus inquit per Jo[annem]: "Scrutamini Scripturas," et predicta expositio, cum sit catholica, pertinet ad scrutinium divine scripture ... constat, quod, qui eam interdicit fidelibus et abduct a studio catholicorum, directe contrariatur divine monitioni et sancto Spiritui se opponit. (Ibid., p. CXLVI).

[22] Ibid., p. CXLV.

[23] Vigilate, ut caute ambuletis, quoniam forte iam nimis appropinquat ultima persecutio lupi rapacis et consummatio seculi presentis. (Ibid., p. CXLVI).

Arnold's approach to the crucial text in *Acts* as a direct defence of Joachimist concords: Man cannot know his end by his own calculations, but he may do so by the aid of divine revelation and through the concords of the Scriptures.[24] Moreover, Arnold's emphasis on the knowledge of the Last Things being made known only to the elect is echoed in the prologue to the *Breviloquium*, and his *vigilate* motif is combined with his call to heed the Scriptures in the opening lines of the prefatory poem.[25]

One more aspect of the *De tempore* demands comment: the tract does not mention Joachim, except to allude to the *De Semine Scripturarum*, the work erroneously ascribed to the Abbot. Arnold also draws twice on the pseudo-Joachimist tract, *Vaticinium Sibyllae Erithreae*,[26] but he believes it to be an ancient oracle. His main authorities are Daniel, Augustine, and Jerome. Why does he make no mention of Joachim's writings? The omission can hardly have arisen because Arnold was not yet familiar with these writings; by the time of its public presentation, Arnold knew at least three of Joachim's major works. The reason for this omission would appear to be that he was deliberately avoiding controversial sources in order to strengthen his argument among the orthodox. At the conclusion of his discussion of the crucial passage in Daniel, Arnold insists that "it is clear that by means of the revelation given to Daniel, the time of Antichrist can be revealed by exact computation. Nor does any one of the sacred commentaries deny this."[27] Christ Himself sets his imprimatur on this view, Arnold argues, Jerome and Augustine support it, and Augustine's approval of the Sibyl authenticates that source. Thus it seems that Arnold was determined to do battle with the Paris doctors on their own ground — the Biblical and Patristic tradition.

In the second work of this period, the *Introductio in Librum Ioachim de Semine Scripturarum* (1292),[28] Arnold moves from Antichrist and the beginning of the Last Times to calculations concerning the Second Coming and the end of history in the fifteenth *centenarium*, basing his calculations on passages in Daniel, on Augustinian numerology and the numerology of the alphabet expounded in *De Semine Scripturarum*. He also uses Augustine's explication of the fulfilment of historical events — *misterium*, or *figura* — to

---

[24] Infra, p. 94.

[25] Infra, p. 168. See the opening of the *Prologus* of the *Breviloquium* for a similar, but more restrained and condensed statement of this position. As we shall see, these themes persist in Arnold's later work as well.

[26] The *De Semine Scripturarum* is not by Joachim and is unrelated to the Joachimist tradition; see Reeves, *Influence*, p. 58. For the allusions to the *Vaticinium Sibyllae*, see Finke, *Aus den Tagen*, pp. CXXXII, CXLVII.

[27] See Lee, "Scrutamini Scripturas," pp. 42-48; *De tempore*, p. CXXXVIII.

[28] See Lee, "Scrutamini Scripturas," pp. 48-53.

construct his own technique of figural exegesis, which consists of a threefold analysis of *ordo*, *potestas*, and *figura*. The work is consummated in symbolic images which combine the Platonic universe with Joachimist prophecy, bringing to fruition Arnold's remarks in the *De tempore* concerning the interpretation of natural phenomena, as well as his remarks on the nature of cognition.

In the course of his argument in the *Introductio*, Arnold devotes himself to an extensive discussion of the millennium and its divisions as a figure of perfection, following Augustine, and begins to use his own interests in Pythagorean mathematics, the Platonic universe, and Joachim's numerology. Since the number 6 in mathematics is the first number which can be broken down into a perfect unity of parts, the sixth millennium must contain the *consummatio*. Arnold alludes here specifically to Joachim's writing on the number 6 in the *Liber Concordie*, and adduces Joachim's notion that the six days of creation are figures for the six *millenaria*. He also follows Joachim on the significance of 7 and 8, 7 related to judgement and 8 to eternal glory. At the conclusion of this section he refers the reader to the three major works of Joachim as corroboration of the *De Semine*.[29]

Having expounded *ordo* and *potestas* and their fulfilment in the *Introductio*, Arnold concentrates on the *figurae* of the letters of the Tetragrammaton in the *Allocutio super Significatione Nominis Tetragrammaton* (1292)[30] and here borrows from Hebrew exegesis. The technique he uses and describes in the *Introductio* is now applied to the letters of the Hebrew and Latin Tetragrammata, which are figures for the Trinity. Throughout this work as well, the themes of the study of Scripture, the revelation proceeding from that study, and the apocalyptic expectation predominate. The *Allocutio* ends as the *De tempore* began, with a prediction for spiritual crisis in the fourteenth century, and an outline for the sequence of events in the Last Times.

Arnold's central topic here is the Trinity, of course, and although his argument is too complex to follow in detail in this survey, its Joachimist underpinning may at least be demonstrated. Arnold was extremely interested in Joachim's commentary on the letters Alpha and Omega in their aspect as shapes of a triangle and a circle, and follows Joachim in seeing Alpha and Omega as signifying the unity of three-in-one of the Trinity: *ego sum trinus et uniformis*. However, he diverges from Joachim by giving equal emphasis

---

[29] De misteriis autem horum numerorum et aliorum qui infra millenarium continentur, quantum iam revelatum est, sufficienter tractavit his [a]uctor in quattuor operibus suis scilicet hoc presente et *Psalterio decacordo* et in *Expositione apocalypsis* et, pre hiis omnibus, *Concordia duorum testamentorum* (*Introductio*, p. 57).

[30] Lee, "Scrutamini Scripturas," pp. 48-56.

to the aspect of *principium et finis* in *Apocalypse* 1.8, and, after some tortuous exegesis, concludes that in Alpha, a distinction of the parts is visible, but in Omega there is no visible distinction. If these parts of the exegesis are uniquely Arnoldian, the general intent is similar to that of Joachim: the Tetragrammaton manifests the Trinity, and also prefigures the shape of history, which is nearing its climax.

In the matter of Arnold's debt to cabbalistic exegesis, one of the present writers has argued that although Arnold was influenced by cabbalistic sources, his use of the Jewish technique was more limited than Carreras y Artau has suggested.[31] Cabbalistic exegesis helped Arnold to formulate his technique of *figura in scripto*, but this *figura* is part of a threefold technique which is thoroughly Joachimist in intent and practice. In their broadest dimension, both the *Allocutio* and the *Introductio* may be viewed as attempts to develop an exegetical technique to buttress the pronouncements of *De tempore*, and to bring his wide-ranging studies within the bounds of the Joachimist expectation.

A fourth work of this period, the *Dialogus de elementis catholicae fidei* (1297), has a special interest for this study. This work, written for the sons of James II, is also occupied with numerology, and is deliberately constructed in 14 parts,[32] for the following reason:

> Why are fourteen articles of faith put forward? Because just as on the one hand there are fourteen joints [of the body] distinguished by the senses, so in the one Catholic faith fourteen principal articles of belief are laid down.[33]

The author of the *Breviloquium* divides his work into 14 *distinctiones*, exerting considerable ingenuity in the effort. It seems likely that he was following Arnold's exhortation.

As Piñero has noted,[34] this first decade of Arnold's religious writing did not contain the attacks on the clergy which characterized the writings which appear in the succeeding years, beginning in the period 1299 to 1303. In 1299, Arnold journeyed to Paris on behalf of the king of Aragon, James II, to negotiate a border difficulty with the French king, and took the opportunity to make the first public presentation of the *De tempore* before the masters of the Sorbonne. His views were met with vehement rejection at the university, and at the end of a day of debate on December 18th, Arnold was

---

[31] See supra, note 8.

[32] Cánovas and Piñero, *Escritos Condenados*, p. 21.

[33] Ibid., p. 21.

[34] Ibid., p. 22. The divisions of the years after 1299 are our own, as well as the specific references to Joachimism. Biographical references are based on Paniagua, Cánovas and Piñero, and Carreras y Artau.

arrested and spent the night in jail as an enemy of the faith. He languished there only for a day, when one of James' officials secured his release. However, the incident marked the beginning of a protracted "formal offensive"[35] against the theologians of the Sorbonne, carried on in tandem with a general campaign against the clergy, and indeed any laymen, princes or popes who had the temerity to defend the religious establishment from Arnold's charges of error and corruption. In the Joachimist context, the incident may be seen as a spectacular beginning to Arnold's mission as a *praedicator spiritualis*, warning of the present evils now visited upon the flock of Christ, and soon to get worse before they got better.

In 1300, Arnold returned to Barcelona to be rewarded by James ii for his services, travelled to Montpellier and Rome, wrote and preached against the Paris doctors, enlisted his patient Boniface viii's somewhat reluctant support in 1301, and in 1302 began a controversy with the Dominicans in the diocese of Gerona. Among his writings of this period are *De cymbalis Ecclesiae* (1301),[36] in which he presents himself as a prophet sent for the reform of the Church and suggests 1368 as the date for the appearance of Antichrist; *Philosophia catholica et divina tradens artem annichilandi versutias* (1302), in which he emphasizes the glory of poverty and its practice by that small band of its clerical adherents who are such a contrast to the worldly and therefore false church; the *Eulogium* (1302), the opening shot in his other offensive against the Dominicans in Gerona; and finally the *Apologia de versutiis et perversitatibus pseudotheologorum et religiosorum* (1302). The last two of these works will serve as evidence of both the outburst of evangelical preaching and the continuity of their Joachimist context for this period.

The primary theme of the *Eulogium*, also known as *La Polémica gerundense*,[37] is the contrast between the true and the false apostles, those who follow the true evangelical teaching of Christ and strive to imitate His own life, and those who fall prey to the snares of the devil. Of particular interest to this study is the revival of his argument in *De tempore* over the use of the Scriptures. He reminds the ecclesiastics of Gerona that they are still misreading St. Augustine and the Scriptures, especially the Pauline Epistles. St. Augustine, he insists, "who correctly understands all things," says in the

[35] Ibid. For an account of the episode of 1299, see Franz Pelster, "Die Quaestio Heinrichs von Harclay über die Zweite Ankunft Christi und die Erwartung des baldigen Weltends zu Anfang des xiv Jahrhunderts," *Archivio Italiano per la Storia della Pietà*, 1 (1951): 25-82.

[36] Cánovas and Piñero, *Escritos Condenados*, pp. 24-25.

[37] Joaquin Carreras y Artau, "La Polémica gerundense sobre el Antichristo entre Arnau de Vilanova y los Dominicos," *Annales del Instituto de Estudios Gerundenses*, 5 (1950): 33-58.

De trinitate that the "times which the Father placed in His power" shall be revealed in His great power to the elect in the times He has appointed.[38]

The *Apologia de versutiis et perversitatibus*[39] is noteworthy for its echoes of the new Joachimist synthesis developing in the early fourteenth century, shaped by Arnold in his unique fashion. The force of the argument in this tract is an attack on clergy and the cloistered as repositories for the seven deadly sins, and consequently as agents of Antichrist. Those who are humble and patient are truly of Christ; those who are not "are followers of the great Antichrist."[40] This reference to a *maximus Antichristus*, to which Arnold refers elsewhere as well, reflects the emerging concept in Joachimist circles of a great Antichrist who is to appear after one or more lesser of his kind, named by Olivi as a mystic Antichrist. The ecclesiastical followers of the great Antichrist, Arnold continues, desire to mingle with the worldly and the powerful, displaying a foolish appetite for worldly glory, moving away from their intended state to engage in giving worldly advice and promoting worldly business (*ad expeditionem negotiorum*),[41] until their thoughts are turned entirely away from the spiritual life. The picture painted by Arnold is precisely that sketched by the "father" in the *Breviloquium* to his little band of followers.[42]

The seventh sin described in the *Apologia*, the "consummation of all iniquity,"[43] takes precedence over the traditional *luxuria*. Arnold says that Christ named the Pharisees as an example of this seventh sin of the clergy, for the Pharisees (and the lawyers) knew Christ to be the Messiah, but condemned Him anyway. The reference is to those who now condemn the true Church in the person of the prophets of poverty and the Last Times, and leads Arnold to identify the number 7 with Judgement and the end of Time, as, following Joachim, he did in the *Introductio*. Again, it is the proper study of Scripture which is essential in order to prepare ourselves for the end. Commenting on 1 *Cor.* 10.11, which deals in part with the tribulations of the elect, Arnold writes:

> The malice of their adversaries clearly shows how necessity impels the faithful to arm themselves diligently in the Last Times with the truth of the sacred volumes.[44]

---

[38] Ibid., p. 41.
[39] Finke, *Aus den Tagen*, pp. CLXIII-CLXXII.
[40] Ibid., p. CLXVI.
[41] Ibid., p. CLXVII.
[42] *Brev.*, p. 175.
[43] Finke, p. CLXX.
[44] Ibid., p. CLXXI.

The following years, 1303-1306, saw continuing confrontations and continuing preaching, the beginning of a new phase in his relationships with James and Frederick, and, in 1306, another excursion into biblical exegesis. Arnold's activities at the *Curia* resulted in two incidents connected with his evangelical career in the year after Boniface VIII was succeeded by Benedict XI. In 1304, at Perugia and with Arnold in attendance, Benedict died suddenly of dysentery. Arnold had written to Bernard Délicieux about the state of the pope's health, and inadvertently caused suspicion to fall on Délicieux of complicity in the pope's death, as rumours of poisoning spread. Later, during the long conclave to elect a new pope, Arnold presented a protest over the retention of his writings, and was again arrested, to be freed once again through the intervention of James II. Eventually, Clement V was elected.

During this period Arnold had kept up his exhortations to the popes and the *Curia*, even going to the length of writing a letter to Benedict in which he claimed that Boniface's death had been caused by his failure to pay heed to Arnold's suggestions for reform, and urged Benedict to remedy this situation. After his release from prison in Perugia, Arnold travelled to Sicily in 1304, there to be received by Frederick II as "Plato resurrected."[45] In 1305, he went to the court of James II, where he read to assembled notables his *Confessió de Barcelona*, a polemic against the increasing number of clergy who disagreed with his views. By now Arnold was thoroughly disillusioned with the ecclesiastical hierarchy, and beginning more and more to place his hopes for *renovatio* in James and Frederick.

James and Frederick shared a sincere religiosity, a fervent loyalty to the Church, and strong brotherly affection. They diverged in temperament, however: James was a prudent, self-controlled and astute politician; Frederick was, as Carreras y Artau has described him, a "man of the heart,"[46] open-hearted and passionate, dedicated and consistent in his ideals. Arnold especially favoured Frederick. While James came to distrust Arnold and the apocalyptic role cast for him by his physician, Frederick consistently espoused Arnold's causes.

When in Sicily in 1304-1305, Arnold wrote for Frederick the *Allocutio Christiani*,[47] a document which marked a new dimension in his evangelical career in which he sought to realize his spiritual reforms through the framework of the state. The work has much of the political manifesto about it, is religious but not apocalyptic, and sets forth the general principles on

---

[45] Cánovas y Piñero, p. 32.

[46] Carreras y Artau, *Relaciones*, p. 43.

[47] *Allocutio Christiani de hiis quae conveniunt homini secundum propriam dignitatem creaturae rationalis*, Vatican City, Biblioteca Apostolica Vaticana, Vat. Lat. MS 3824, fols. 217-226r-v; Finke, *Aus den Tagen*, pp. CXCVII-CCI.

which all individual and collective reform must be based.[48] His central topic
is justice, and in his discussion of the just ruler he merges the civil and the
ecclesiastical. Carreras y Artau sees Arnold in this aspect

> as one of the purest representatives of the medieval theocratic conception of the
> State, which, far from separating the area of civil or terrestrial society from the
> divine or ecclesiastical, tends to conflate them, simply merging the political
> functions into the religious duties of the monarch.[49]

Before this new initiative bore fruit, however, Arnold returned to earlier
preoccupations in two works written in 1306, the first of which was the
Responsio ad cavillationes adversarii veritatis.[50] In this work, he enumerated
all the objections raised against the *De tempore*, among them charges that he
misinterpreted Augustine, indulged in false numerology, and committed a
variety of other offences both intellectual and spiritual. In the conclusion of
this tract, his Joachimist studies once again reveal themselves in the course
of a denunciation of his detractors. They are, he claims, plunging the Church
into darkness, and are clothed in the spirit of the dragon of the *Apocalypse*.
Continuing in this Olivianist fashion, he claims that as the primitive Church
was attacked by the ministers of fraud and oppression, so is the same thing
happening now: the true writings of the elect are attacked as false. His
examples are the condemnation by the Fourth Lateran Council of the view
of the Trinity set forth by Joachim and the attacks on the writings of Olivi.[51]

The purely exegetical work of this year is the *Expositio super Apocalypsi*.[52]
Although it concentrates on Arnold's desire for and warning of an imminent
renovation, the framework of this work is based on the seven ages and three
status of Joachim, the expectation of the Angelic Pope, and other themes of
the early fourteenth-century synthesis. These Joachimist themes are apparent
in the passages of Arnold's work which deal with the fourth, sixth and
seventh angels of the Apocalypse, and the sixth and seventh seals.

Joachim himself is enshrined by Arnold in the fifth *tempus*, along with
St. Hildegard, St. Cyrillus of the Carmelite Order, and "Horoscopus."[53]

---

[48] Carreras y Artau, *Relaciones*, pp. 44-45.

[49] Ibid., p. 45. Piñero (*Escritos Condenados*, p. 32), emphasizes the spiritual themes in
the work.

[50] See supra, note 5.

[51] Batllori, "Dos nous escrits," AST, 28 (1955): 56-67. On Joachim Arnold makes the
enigmatic statement: *qui fuit in omnibus predictis ab apostolis citra clarior, doctior Ecclesie
[?a] Christi.*

[52] Joaquin Carreras y Artau, ed., *Expositio super Apocalypsi Arnaldi de Vilanova* (Barcelona, 1971).

[53] ESA, p. 105. Horoscopus is probably an astrological appendix to the *Liber de Flore*. See
Reeves, *Influence*, p. 402.

These and other unnamed personages have given to the elect "certainty concerning the course of the final times of the Church" in the sixth and seventh ages. Of the opening of the sixth seal, Arnold notes that three principal events are to take place: the ruin of the Church, the perplexity of the elect, and the reformation of the Church by the elect. His gloss on this passage follows the general Joachimist interpretation:

> *A great earthquake* [*magnus motus terrae*] *occurred*, that is, a great subversion of the Church because of its great breaking away from the truth of Christ ... *Blackness descended* [*factus est niger*], that is, the darkness of impurity ... *As a sack-cloth* [*saccus cilicinus*], which signifies indiscriminate cupidity ... and *the stars* [*stellae*], the prelates of the Church, *fell to earth*, that is, from the rites of the spiritual life.[54]

Commenting on the four angels (*Post haec vidi quattuor angelos*), Arnold assigns topical identifications with the kings of Sicily, France, England, and Aragon, describes the offences of Frederick II against the Church in the thirteenth century, and the mournful condition of the Church itself in that age. However, the same period saw the appearance of St. Francis and St. Dominic and the beginning of true evangelical preaching, which is to be consummated near the end of the sixth *tempus*. Arnold announces the advent of the Angelic Pope who is to initiate the final renovation of evangelical truth, then follows Olivi's *Postilla* in describing the evangelical order: they will all be one in their zeal to promote this truth, and will all have the stigmata which were vouchsafed to St. Francis.[55] As in Joachim's *Expositio*, Enoch and Elijah are the types for the final triumph of the spiritual preachers, and we may speculate that Arnold saw himself and Olivi as consummators of those roles.

---

[54] ESA, pp. 106-107. The author of the *Breviloquium* glosses the same phrases as follows: *motus magnus factus est*, quia in toto orbe, maxime in romano imperio, fiendus est per guerras scilicet intestinas inter reges et principes et comunitates tocius populi christiani, tam in terra quam in mari, et multorum regum infidelium contra romanum inperium et ecclesiam insurgencium ... *Et sol*, seu summus pontifex, qui solus est in dignitate sua, *factus est niger*, seu obscurus quasi cuntis credentibus, radiis utriusque potencie obfuscatis, nam in tantorum errorum et persequucionum caligine erunt omnibus in derisum, sicut *sacus sicilicinus*, de pillis porcorum propter uilem et corruptam uitam cunctorum ecclesiasticorum in omni statu ... *Et stelle*, seu cardinales et prelati alii cum tota media gerarchia ecclesie, *ceciderunt super terram*, primo de celesti statu diuini cultus, secundo de sedibus seu locis suis uelint nolint, ut cursores leves. (*Brev.*, p. 219).

[55] Et omnes erunt uniformes in zelo promovendi hanc veritatem, et omnes habebunt signum Dei vivi praedictum. Stigmata namque quibus beatus Franciscus fuit a Deo corporaliter insignitus, licet per reductionem alicuius consequentiae possint dici signa Dei vivi ... (ESA, p. 111).

In the passage beginning *Et sextus angelus,*[56] Arnold describes a three-fold sequence for the sixth *tempus* which consists of the subversion of doctrine, a reformation by a true pontiff or Angelic Pope, and the appearance of Antichrist. The second stage, the reformation, is described in the commentary on *Et vidi alium angelum*, and marks the beginning of the third *status*. The Angelic Pope is to be overthrown by Antichrist, who in turn will be overthrown at the consummation of the sixth *tempus*.

The Seventh Angel[57] will bring the seventh and last *tempus* and the end of the third *status*, during which the faithful will be liberated from the tribulations of temporal persecution, and they will only have the Last Judgement to fear.[58] Arnold refers to only two events in this last sequence, the exaltation of the faithful in the temporal victory of Christ over his adversaries and the act of thanksgiving as much for that victory as for the Last Judgement.[59] As in the *De tempore*, his primary interest continues to lie in the events of the fourteenth century and the reformation he was himself trying to shape.[60]

In the last years of his life, from 1307 to 1311, Arnold continued to propagandize for the evangelical reformation to diverse audiences, continued to minister to Clement v, and involved himself even more closely in the affairs of James and Frederick. His recognition as a person of spirituality and influence may be seen in the request of the Aragonese Templars for Arnold to arbitrate for them in the dispute over that order which now arose, in his reception of a deputation of monks from Mount Athos worried over depredations against their monastery, and in his successful intercession for Ubertino da Casale and his group, who wished to present a petition to the pope in 1309.

Arnold acted as mediator for Frederick in the situation caused by the accession of Robert as king of Naples, Sicily and Jerusalem, and carried letters for both James and Frederick to the pope in the matter of a Crusade planned against the Moors. In a joint venture, the Castilians were to attack Algeciras and the Aragonese were to engage the enemy at Almería. Arnold encouraged the brothers James and Frederick to unite in a combined reformation of the church and a Crusade to rescue Spain and ultimately the Holy Land from the infidels. The manner in which he expounded this scheme

---

[56] ESA, pp. 135-136.
[57] Ibid., p. 151.
[58] Ibid., pp. 151-152.
[59] Ibid., p. 152.
[60] For further discussion of Arnold's seventh age in the ESA and its relation to the *Brev.*, see infra, pp. 98-100.

to the pope, reconstructed in the *Raonament d'Avinyó* in 1309, offended James and caused a break between them, but Frederick remained loyal to the end. In September of 1311, Arnold died near Genoa on a voyage from Naples to Avignon, presumably intending to render medical services to the pope.

Four works of this final period reflect the prophetic context of Arnold's own last times. With respect to his obsession with ecclesiastical reform, the *Llicó de Narbona* of 1308[61] continues the call to evangelical poverty among clerics and lay people. Its major theme is poverty, which is to be chosen and loved in this temporal state.[62] It was the path chosen by Christ, who showed the way by choosing a poor mother, birth in a stable, and who delivered manifold injunctions against the accumulation of riches.[63] Arnold attacks clergy, regulars, and even lay people who parade riches in defiance of Christ;[64] like Herod, who killed children in the flesh, the laity kill their children spiritually in giving them worldly values.[65] He repeats his earlier theme that wordliness detracts from the study of Scripture and the pursuit of justice.[66]

During these last years, Arnold saw two roles for James and Frederick which he believed were being played out in the Joachimist context. The first was revealed in the *Interpretatio in somniis Jacobi et Frederici*, written in 1308. Frederick seemed especially promising for a spiritual mission; he had dreamed as a child that his mother appeared before him veiled, and said "My son, I give you my benediction in order that you may apply yourself to serve truth absolutely."[67] After a second dream in which she appeared unveiled and carrying a gem of great beauty in her right hand, she told Frederick to summon Arnold for an interpretation.[68] The unveiled face was grace vouchsafed to Frederick, Arnold replied, the gem was "the ornament of evangelical virtue," to be worn publicly as much in regal dignity as in the mind.[69] Arnold then instructed Frederick on his role as an agent of God, discoursed on the public dispensation of justice by the just ruler, and noted that poverty should take precedence over wealth.

---

[61] See *Obres Catalanes*, pp. 141-166.
[62] Ibid., p. 143.
[63] Ibid., pp. 143, 144.
[64] Ibid., pp. 158-159.
[65] Ibid., p. 159.
[66] Ibid., pp. 161-162.
[67] Menendez y Pelayo, *Historia de los Heterodoxos Espanoles* (Santander, 1948), 7: 233.
[68] Carreras y Artau, *Relaciones*, p. 54; Menendez y Pelayo, *Historia*, p. 237.
[69] Carreras y Artau, *Relaciones*, p. 54; Menendez y Pelayo, *Historia*, p. 241.

To this spiritual mission was added the historical and prophetic mission of the Crusade. In 1309 James, accompanied by Arnold, was in Almería, ready to begin the campaign against the infidel. He dispatched Arnold to Clement v with a petition asking for a benediction for their forthcoming efforts. Arnold reconstructed his message to the pope in the *Raonament d'Avinyó* (1309),[70] in which he created his own context for the expedition in the spiritual and historical terms of Joachimism, endowing the Crusade with a three-fold mission. The first aspect of the Crusade was that James and Frederick had been inspired by God to promote the truth of Christianity "in all places," between Catholics and schismatics as well as among the pagans, and by means of the two swords of spiritual and temporal power (combined, as he had noted in the *Allocutio Christiani*, written for Frederick). The two kings would penetrate as far as the Holy Sepulchre and overthrow the entire Mohammedan religion. The second and third aspects of this mission emphasized the writing and teaching which they would spread throughout the world, to bring both errant Christians and pagans into the true faith. "Already," Arnold says of Frederick, that ruler

> has begun to found and maintain evangelical schools for men and for women, in which both rich and poor are being instructed in the evangelical life, which is the true Christianity. Some will be trained to preach, others instructed in various languages, so that they may be able to demonstrate the truth of the Gospel to everyone, whether pagans or schismatics.[71]

What Arnold expected to be initiated through the agency of the kings and their Crusade is that sequence of events he had described in the *De tempore*, when Jerusalem would be returned to Christian rule and the entire world converted to Christianity, ushering in a period of great tranquillity.[72] The only difference is that in the *De tempore*, the sequence has a derivative flavour; in the *Raonament*, the prediction has the immediacy of a scenario which Arnold believed was unfolding before his very eyes.

A further ingredient of the *De tempore* and the *Expositio super Apocalypsi* appeared in the *Informació espiritual al Rei Frederic de Sicilia*[73] of 1310. Although the siege of Almería had been broken off, Arnold was still hopeful for the teaching mission of Frederick and for his role as legislator. Frederick would be an initiator of that final sequence which would bring the appearance of the Angelic Pope, "who through the agency of that king will purify all

---

[70] *Obres Catalanes*, pp. 167-221.
[71] Ibid., pp. 220-221.
[72] Ibid., pp. 218-221.
[73] Ibid., pp. 224-243. See also *Relaciones*, p. 47.

Christendom, and will return it everywhere to the original truth, which is that of Jesus Christ and His Apostles." [74]

Arnold would not live to find a candidate for this spiritual pontiff, but he at least had the consolation of seeing the statutes suggested in the *Informació espiritual* put into law. In October of 1310, in the *Constituciones* promulgated at Messina, Frederick incorporated a number of Arnold's instructions concerning converted Saracens and Jews, and various matters of ecclesiastical rights into the royal document. [75] Frederick himself continued to live according to Arnold's teaching, and it was reported that the king's wife sold her jewels.

Frederick also followed Arnold in the matter of the Spiritual Franciscans. Arnold had received a public promise from him that he would protect adherents of evangelical poverty who sought refuge in his dominions, and in this matter Frederick remained scrupulously true to Arnold's memory. [76] In 1312 the group of Spirituals who had collected in Tuscany fled to Sicily, appealing in a letter to Frederick for the protection which they expected — and received. [77] In 1313 Clement V issued a bull against them, while the Minister-General of the Franciscan Order wrote to the King of Aragon in November 1313 asking him to prevail on his brother Frederick to expel the Spirituals from his kingdom and see that they returned to obedience of the Rule. James complied with this request and there ensued an exchange of letters between the two in which Frederick refused to terminate his protection. [78] Meanwhile other disaffected groups were also finding refuge in Sicily.

Matters rested thus during the long vacancy in the papacy, but this period of tranquillity for Frederick and his protégés ended with the accession of John XXII. In 1317 pressure was brought to bear on Frederick by the Pope, by a group of cardinals working through the bishops of Sicily, and by other Sicilians. [79] Frederick was finally forced to make a public pronouncement against the Spirituals. He ordered them to leave the island, but sought asylum for them in Tunis. Some scattered, to Calabria and Naples as well as Tunis, but some remained under the protection of local patrons. In spite of another papal bull against the Spirituals, especially those of Sicily, Frederick seems

[74] *Obres Catalanes*, pp. 241-242.

[75] See *Relaciones*, pp. 47-48; *Obres Catalanes*, p. 45. A portion of the *Constituciones* has been edited by Finke in *Acta Aragonensia* (Berlin, 1908), 2: 695-699.

[76] José Mariá Pou y Martí, "Visionarios, Beguinos y Fraticellos Catalanes, Siglos XIII-XV," *Archivo Iberoamericano*, 11 (1919): 221; idem, *Visionarios, Beguinos y Fraticellos Catalanes, Siglos XIII-XV* (Vich, 1930), p. 102. For the full reference to AIA series, see Bibliography.

[77] Idem, AIA, 11 (1919): 222-223; *Visionarios*, pp. 102-103.

[78] Idem, AIA, 11 (1919): 223-226; *Visionarios*, pp. 103-106.

[79] Idem, AIA, 11 (1919): 228; *Visionarios*, pp. 107-108.

quietly to have protected the remaining ones: he was accused in a letter from his brother James in 1321 of maintaining Beguins (*alios qui sub beguinatus colorato nomine*) who remained disobedient to the Holy See.[80]

His writings link Arnold closely with the movement of Beguins and Franciscan Tertiaries whose influence in Catalonia we shall shortly be tracing. The combination of apocalyptic expectation and lay religious initiative alarmed the authorities by its revolutionary implications, and Arnold's involvement in these developments must have been plain to them. Of the posthumous condemnation of his works at Tarragona in 1316, Pou y Martí comments that "the great solemnity exercised in this matter suggests a grave danger: a popular diffusion of Arnoldian writings and doctrines."[81] In the following year, at the Council of Tarragona, the Beguins and Tertiaries of that province were attacked. More recent research has substantiated Pou y Martí's belief that these groups were disciples of Arnold and that the prohibition made against possessing theological books in the vernacular was especially directed against his writings. We shall see later that Arnold's influence in these circles was important both during and after his death in 1311.

[80] Idem, AIA, 11 (1919): 231; *Visionarios*, p. 110.
[81] Idem, AIA, 11 (1919): 219; *Visionarios*, p. 100. The condemnation is reprinted in Menéndez y Pelayo, *Heterodoxos Espanoles*, 7: 316-322. For discussion of the context of the condemnation, see Perarnau, *Alia Informatio*, pp. 138-141, and infra, p. 59.

4

Beguins and Tertiaries in Catalonia

1. FROM THE EARLY YEARS UNTIL 1316

In spite of a number of studies,[1] the connections and distinctions between the various Joachimist groups who fell under the suspicion of heresy in the late thirteenth and the fourteenth century have never been fully worked out. In particular, the part played by Franciscan Tertiaries in this movement remains obscure.[2] Here an attempt is made to examine these problems in relation to the dissemination of Joachimism in Catalonia and Aragon.

In the fifteenth *quaestio* of Part II in the *Directorium Inquisitorum* Nicholas Eymerich summarizes under a single category the

> heresies and errors of the Beghards, Beguins, Fraticelli, or Brothers of Peni-
> tence [*Fratrum de poenitentia*] of the Third Order of the blessed Francis —
> which is the same thing — who rose up in Provence, and in the provinces of

---

[1] See Felice di Tocco, *Studii Francescani*, 2 (Naples, 1909); Franz Ehrle, "Die Spiritua-len, ihr Verhältnis zum Franzischanerorden und zu den Fraticellen," ALKG, 1 (1885): 509-569; 2 (1886): 106-164, 249-336; 3 (1887): 553-623; 4 (1888): 1-190; Decima Douie, *The Nature and Effect of the Heresy of the Fraticelli* (Manchester, 1932); Malcolm Lambert, *Franciscan Poverty* (London, 1961); Gordon Leff, *Heresy in the Later Middle Ages* (Manches-ter, 1967), 1: 168-255; Raoul Manselli, *Spirituali e Beghini in Provenza* (Rome, 1958); idem, "La Terza Età 'Babylon' e l'Anticristo Mistico," BISI, 82 (1970): 47-79; Livarius Oliger, "Documenta inedita ad historiam Fraticellorum spectantia," AFH, 3 (1910): 253-279, 505-529, 680-699; 4 (1911): 688-712; 5 (1912): 74-84; 6 (1913): 267-290, 515-530, 710-747; idem, "Fr. Bertrandi de Turre processus contra spirituales Aquitaniae (1315) et cardinalis Iacobi de Columna litterae defensoriae spiritualium Provinciae (1316)," AFH, 16 (1923): 323-355; idem, "Acta Inquisitoris Umbriae Fr. Angeli de Assisio contra Fraticellos aliosque anno 1361," AFH, 24 (1931): 63-90; idem, "Beiträge zur Geschichte der Spiritualen, Fratizellen und Clarener im Mittelitalien," *Zeitschrift für Kirchengeschichte*, 45 (1926): 215-242; idem, "Spirituels," *Dictionnaire de Théologie Catholique*, 14.2 (Paris, 1939), pp. 2522-2549; Josep Perarnau, *Alia Informatio*, pp. 108-138.

[2] However, Moorman's *Franciscan Order* (pp. 40-45, 216-225, and 417-428) has cleared the way considerably.

Narbonne, Toulouse, Carcassonne, the island of Sicily, and in Calabria, Tuscany, Germany and various other parts of the world.[3]

Here a number of groups sharing a common intellectual tradition and a connection with the Franciscan Order are lumped together, but in general it was customary to divide them into two broad categories: Fraticelli and Beguins (or Beghards). Thus Pope John XXII, condemning groups of dissidents in Sicily named them as *fraticelli, seu fratres de paupere vita, aut bizocchi sive beghini.*[4]

The term Fraticelli, and the alternative *fratres de paupere vita* which goes with it, usually refers to First Order Franciscans who formed cells within the Order until, in their fight for evangelical poverty, they either detached themselves from formal allegiance to the Minister General or were forced out by persecution. The origin of these groups must be sought in the so-called "Spirituals" within the Order, deriving its inspiration from such men as John of Parma and Hugh de Digne in the first phase and Petrus Johannis Olivi and Angelo Clareno in the second.[5] These leaders communicated an enthusiasm in which passion for evangelical poverty was fused with the apocalyptic expectation of Joachimism. Ultimately those who were forced outside the obedience of the Order splintered into various groups: Poor Hermits of Celestine V, Clarenists, and Fraticelli under various leaders.[6] In passing we should note that the followers of Michael of Cesena were also called Fraticelli, but since the Joachimist aspect seems to have been absent in this case, we shall not be concerned with them. The Joachimist Fraticelli were located mainly in Italy and the islands of the western Mediterranean. They probably contained many Tertiaries, but First Order membership seems more characteristic. Thus Eymerich creates some confusion when he equates Fraticelli with *Fratres de Poenitentia,* the alternative name for the Tertiaries.

The term Beguin was used widely and loosely to cover many groups which appeared in the Netherlands, Germany, France and elsewhere. A number of

[3] Nicholas Eymerich, *Directorium Inquisitorum* (Rome, 1585), p. 299.

[4] Johannes Sbaralea, *Bullarium Franciscanum,* ed. Conrad Eubel (Rome, 1898), 5: 135; Pou y Martí, AIA, 11 (1919): 126; idem, *Visionarios,* p. 19.

[5] The presence of anything as clear-cut as a "Spiritual Party" within the Order is now questioned. Raymond of Fronsac, in "Des Ordensprocurators Raymund von Fronsac (de Fronciacho) Actensammlung zur Geschichte der Spiritualen," ed. Franz Ehrle, ALKG, 3 (1887): 13, and Eymerich, *Direct. Inquis.,* p. 254, both attribute the origin of the Fraticelli to Olivi, but the relationship is more complex than this; see Douie, *Nature and Effect,* pp. 209-216; Lambert, *Franciscan Poverty,* pp. 160, 168-169; Pou y Martí, AIA, 11 (1919): 122-127; *Visionarios,* pp. 16-19.

[6] According to Ehrle, the name Fraticelli was first applied to the Clarenists, ALKG, 4 (1888): 141.

important and significant religious phenomena can be gathered under the term Beguinism but here we confine our attention to the type which contained the Joachimist element. In many ways it can be said that these Beguin groups were the Fraticelli of south France, for their gospel had much the same content. A distinctive characteristic, however, is that they drew their inspiration mainly from Olivi and venerated his writings to a special degree. From his *Postilla in Apocalypsim* they derived their interpretation of their own role in redemptive history.[7] Olivi himself used the term *imbeguiniri* to signify indoctrination with his own views.[8] A second respect in which it seems that we should distinguish them from the Fraticelli is the large part played by Franciscan Tertiaries in these groups of Beguins. This is an obscure matter. It seems strange that the scholar Olivi should have exercised such a popular appeal, but a striking point in the evidence of the Inquisition of Toulouse is the reliance of Beguins on Olivi's works in the vernacular.[9] Moreover, as we shall see, the Beguins are persistently equated with the *Fratres de Poenitentia.*

Further information about the Beguins comes from Bernard Gui in his *Practica Inquisitionis* of 1323.[10] Gui notes the origin of the Beguins in the provinces of Narbonne and Toulouse, and their subsequent spread to Catalonia. According to Gui, the errors of the Beguins began to be detected about 1315, and in 1317 and 1318 large numbers in all three provinces were burned. Gui connects the Beguins with the Tertiaries, notes that there were both male and female adherents, and describes their distinctive habit as brown, worn with or without a cloak.[11]

The works of Olivi, especially the *Postilla*, were highly valued by the Beguins, Gui continues, and were available both in Latin and in the vernacular.[12] The groups co-habited in *domos paupertatis*, and on feast-days and Sundays gathered together at a single house to hear books read in the

---

[7] Supra, pp. 20ff on Olivi's *Postilla.*

[8] Pou y Martí, AIA, 11 (1919): 127-130, 136; *Visionarios*, pp. 20-22, 27; see infra, p. 56. The term "Beguin" was probably used in the same general sense of holding similar views to Olivi by Arnold of Vilanova in his *Informatio Beguinorum.* See *Obres Catalanes*, pp. 29, 63-68.

[9] Infra, p. 61.

[10] Bernard Gui, *Practica Inquisitionis*, Vatican City, Biblioteca Apostolica Vaticana, Vat. Lat. MS 606, fols. 26r-27v, which are reproduced in Perarnau, *Alia Informatio*, pp. 15-16. See also Guillaume Mollat, *Bernard Gui, Manuel de l'inquisiteur* (Paris, 1926), 1: 115-116.

[11] Beguini, igitur, utriusque sexus moderni temporis sic vulgariter appellati, qui se dicunt fratres pauperes de penitencia de tercio ordine sancti francisci, portantes brunum seu de brunello habitum cum mantello vel sine mantello. (*Practica Inquis.*, fol. 26r; *Alia Informatio*, p. 15).

[12] *Practica Inquis.*, fol. 26r; *Alia Informatio*, p. 15.

vernacular.[13] From these books they sucked venom, Gui writes disapproving-
ly. They are a "school of the devil," he says, disguised as a school of Christ,
"simple laymen" preaching privately of matters which should be preached
only in church and only by the proper authorities.[14] Beguins had formulas of
salutation for each other and ritual observances of their own even in public
worship.[15] They obtained money to live by producing goods in their own
houses and by begging from door to door.

Dr. Moorman has elucidated the origin and early history of the Third
Order.[16] Their double title is established by the Rule which Wadding
preserved: *Regula Tertiarorum sive fratrum de Poenitentia.*[17] It is disputed as
to whether St. Francis initially intended to form a fellowship of Penitents
rather than a regular Order under a Rule, or whether when, as at Cannaro
in 1212, everyone in the town wanted to leave all and follow him, he was
nonplussed, not knowing what to do with them. In any event, since the same
phenomenon occurred in many places, he was faced with a problem which
had to be solved: there were so many — both men and women — who wished
to put themselves under a new disciplined way of life but who, for a whole
variety of reasons, could not abandon their social responsibilities. Thus the
idea of the Order of Penitents or Third Order was conceived. In 1214, in his
Letter to the Faithful, St. Francis sketched out the principles of the religious
practice which they should follow. In 1221, encouraged by Honorius III, a
Rule was composed but the earliest surviving Rule of the Third Order appears
to be a little later. The definitive Rule, binding on all congregations, was only
finally laid down by Nicholas IV in 1289; consequently, in the early stages
there was much room for variation and deviation. The movement embraced
many types of people, from urban craftsmen and merchants to princes, nobles
and ladies of royal or noble blood. Patterns of devotion ranged from guilds

[13] *Practica Inquis.,* fol. 27v; *Alia Informatio,* p. 16. For an earlier corroborative description
of the Beguin communities, see the deliberations of the Council of Tarragona of 1317,
summarized in Pou y Martí, AIA, 14 (1920): 7-8, and *Visionarios,* p. 156. See also, Moorman,
Franciscan Order, pp. 218-220. In some cases the Beguins existed alongside but separate from
the Third Order; in others, they were assimilated into the Order. There must have been widely
varying degrees of association and assimilation, since members probably moved rather freely
from one group to another.

[14] *Practica Inquis.,* fol. 27v; *Alia Informatio,* p. 16.

[15] *Practica Inquis.,* fol. 27v; *Alia Informatio,* p. 16.

[16] Supra, n. 2.

[17] Luke Wadding, *Annales Minorum* (Rome, 1732), 2: 9-14; *Seraphicae Legislationis
Textus Originale* (Quaracchi, 1897), pp. 77-94. This text dates from 1289. The oldest extant
Tertiary Rule is that published by Paul Sabatier, *Antiqua Regula Fratrum et Sororum de
Poenitentia seu Tertii Ordinis Sancti Francisci,* in *Opuscules de critique historique,* Fasc. I
(Paris, 1901). See also *Bullarium,* 1 (1759): 99, 108, 532, for references to the Third Order
as *continentes.*

of workers and groups who founded hospitals or hospices to those who pursued the mystical or contemplative life. St. Bonaventura praised the wide appeal of the Third Order, noting that Brothers of Penitence, "living as Christ did [*vivendi modum idem Christi*]," consisted of both clerics and lay people, virgins and married people of both sexes, all pledged to live a communal and penitential life.[18]

In general, and over much of western Europe, the Third Order supplied a tremendous need, but from the beginning its very heterogeneous character created problems for the Church as a whole and for Franciscans in particular. The Friars of the First Order did not want to be involved, and authorities, both ecclesiastical and secular, came up against the Penitents in a number of practical situations. Many congregations, of course, settled down to a life of unexceptionable good works and piety. Indeed, a number of groups, particularly in Germany and the Netherlands, became rapidly more conventional in an almost literal sense by forming settled religious houses. But fervour could take many forms and some of those entering the Third Order were of the type to be carried away by apocalyptic preaching and prophecy. Thus it was that they were often peculiarly open to Joachimist influences and it is with this section of the Tertiary movement alone that we are concerned here.

At an early stage Tertiaries became involved in the struggle between the Spiritual and Conventual concepts of poverty, and Mandonnet has noted how Franciscan control over them fluctuated with changes in the policy of the First Order. When the First Order was conservative in its governance, the Penitents were brought within the orbit of its influence; when progressive elements triumphed, the Penitents found themselves on their own once again. The ebb and flow of the battle between Conventuals and Spirituals within the Order meant that no consistent policy towards the Third Order was developed or maintained during these formative years.[19]

A tendency in the Third Order to harbour dissident and rebellious groups is indicated by successive excommunications by Gregory IX in 1229 and 1239 and Innocent IV in 1245.[20] At this time the rebellious elements seem to have been politically involved in support for Frederick II,[21] but by the early fourteenth century it was their role in the *renovatio ecclesie* that drew extremists among the Tertiaries into the ranks of the Beguins. The twin concepts of evangelical poverty and Joachimist apocalyptic made a powerful

---

[18] St. Bonaventura, *Legenda Maior, Opera Omnia* (Quaracchi, 1898), *Opusculum*, 22, *Legenda Sancti Francisci*, 4, 6, p. 514.

[19] Pierre Mandonnet, *Les Origines de l'ordre de Poenitentia* (Freiburg, 1898), p. 196.

[20] *Bullarium*, 1 (1759): 492. See editor's note 'k'.

[21] See the offer of clemency by Innocent IV, *Bullarium*, 1: 492.

appeal, and possibly it was the popular preaching of men like Bernard Délicieux in the south of France which brought in members of the Third Order.[22] It is worth noting that, whereas the Italian leaders, such as Clareno, Liberato and Ubertino da Casale, inclined to withdraw into the eremitical life in remote places, Beguinism had its home in the cities of southern France.

In the depositions before the Inquisition of Toulouse[23] the Third Order of St. Francis appears clearly as the chosen instrument in the spiritual revolution which the Beguins expect. Thus Bernard de na Jacma is reported as saying that

> he believed that the lord Pope could not bring to nothing the order of Friars Minor, nor the state or order of the Brothers of Penitence or the Beguins, because these states and orders were ordained by the Holy Spirit, and the Pope could not overthrow ordinations of the Holy Spirit.[24]

Again, concerning the Tertiaries condemned for their beliefs, Petrus Gaustadi de Bello Podio said that he believed that those Beguins or "Paupers" of Penitence of the Third Order condemned in Narbonne by the Inquisition were "glorious martyrs."[25]

We shall find the apocalyptic role of the *Fratres de penitencia* developed still further later in the fourteenth century, for it was primarily through the channels of the Tertiaries that Joachimist doctrines, as revised by Arnold of Vilanova and Olivi, continued to be disseminated in the south of France and spread to Spain.[26]

In Catalonia and Aragon the ground for a movement to follow evangelical poverty had first been prepared by the Poor Catholics of Durand de Huesca.[27] These fell under suspicion and in 1237 Gregory IX attempted to reform this group in Spain along the lines of one of the established orders.[28] Pou y Martí suggests that they probably adopted the Tertiary Rule of St. Francis, since

---

[22] On Bernard Délicieux, see Jean Hauréau, *Bernard Délicieux et l'Inquisition Albigeoise* (Paris, 1877); Michel de Dmitrewski, "Fr. Bernard Délicieux, O.F.M., sa lutte contre l'Inquisition de Carcassonne et d'Albi, son procès, 1297-1319," AFH, 17 (1924): 183-218, 313-337, 457-488; 18 (1925): 3-22; Douie, *Nature and Effect*, pp. 18-20.

[23] Limborch, *Lib. Sentent.*, pp. 298-333.

[24] Ibid., p. 307.

[25] Ibid., p. 323.

[26] Infra, pp. 60ff.

[27] On the Poor Catholics see Herbert T. Grundmann, *Religiöse Bewegungen im Mittelalter* (Darmstadt, 1970), pp. 100-118; Pou y Martí, AIA, 11 (1919): 130-132; *Visionarios*, pp. 22-23; Johann Pierron, *Die Katholischen Armen* (Friburg, 1911), pp. 37, 128, 135-140; Christine Thouzellier, "La Profession trinitaire du vaudois Durand de Huesca," *Recherches de Théologie Ancienne et Médiévale*, 22 (1960): 267-289; idem, *Une Somme anti-Cathare: le "Liber contra Manicheos" de Durand de Huesca* (Louvain, 1964).

[28] Pou y Martí, AIA, 11 (1919): 131; *Visionarios*, p. 23.

they had many points of contact.[29] If this surmise is correct, we see already the power of the Tertiaries to absorb dissident groups of laity wishing to follow the life of evangelical poverty. Thus, according to Pou y Marti, the inspiration of the Poor Catholics survived to form a disturbing current in Church life. "It cannot be denied," he writes,

> that ideas concerning poverty and the renovation of the Church reached great proportions in Catalonia, and that the disappearance in the thirteenth century of the Congregation of Poor Catholics could not quickly extinguish the principles which they had formed and directed.[30]

By the end of the thirteenth century a similar current had begun to flow in through Roussillon from the south of France. Contacts were easy. Puigcerdá, Perpignan and Villefranche de Conflent[31] maintained Franciscan convents which fell under the jurisdiction of the Provincial of Provence, as did Castellón de Ampurias, which had formerly belonged to Barcelona and the Province of Aragon. Catalonia maintained good relations with Provence; the region itself had not long been emancipated from the Crown of Aragon. Thus there was easy intercourse with the Franciscan convents of Narbonne, Béziers and Carcasonne, all of which were focal points for the adherents of evangelical poverty and apocalypticism. Narbonne was of special importance, for it was here that Olivi lived during the last years of his life, and died.

In one particular case we have direct evidence of Olivi's reputation and personal influence in Catalonia.[32] In the war between Peter II of Aragon and the Angevin kings of Sicily which followed the Sicilian Vespers, the three sons of Charles II, Louis, Robert and Raymond Berengar, were held as hostages by Aragon from 1288 to 1295. The prisoners were educated by the Franciscans in Barcelona and became interested in evangelical poverty. They engaged in correspondence with Olivi and asked that he should visit them. Olivi attempted to do so, but after various delays, and in spite of being granted permission by the sympathetic General of the Order, Raymond Gaufridi, his request was denied. In a letter written in May 1295, however, Olivi revealed that he had already communicated to the princes his views on poverty and his growing interest in apocalypticism. He may already have been at work on his *Postilla*, which was not completed until 1299.

---

[29] Idem, AIA, 11 (1919): 131; *Visionarios*, p. 23.

[30] Idem, AIA, 11 (1919): 132; *Visionarios*, p. 24.

[31] Villefranche de Conflent had a colony of Tertiaries, maintained under the auspices of the Abbot of St. Michael of Cuxá, where there were also, apparently, Tertiaries; see *Bullarium*, 3 (1765): 136, 304, 401-402.

[32] See ALKG, 3 (1887): 534-540; Pou y Marti, AIA, 11 (1919): 135-138; *Visionarios*, pp. 26-28.

In the letter,[33] Olivi presents the outline of his renovatory scheme for the Church in the sixth age: the upheavals following the opening of the sixth seal; the three unclean spirits (*tres immundi spiritus*) who will gather together the forces of Antichrist; the challenge of the Whore of Babylon against the true evangelical Church in the sixth age; the typology of Noah's Ark and the return of the dove of evangelical peace; the ultimate victory of the preachers of evangelical poverty; the sealing of the twelve tribes in the final age — an idea proscribed by Eymerich — and the ultimate triumph of the Lamb. The interpretation of these symbolic events and their fulfilment is developed in the *Postilla*, and quoted and expounded at length in the *Breviloquium* more than half a century later.

In spite of the efforts of Charles II, Olivi and the Franciscans in Barcelona seem to have succeeded in their efforts to *imbeguiniri* the young princes. St. Louis renounced the throne and world to become a Franciscan friar and eventually Bishop of Toulouse, while Robert harboured and vigorously defended the adherents of evangelical poverty who sought refuge in Naples, among them Philip of Majorca.

At the conclusion of his letter Olivi instructed his charges that they should salute a certain Friar Pere, their companion and teacher. This friar remains unidentified thus far, although he may have been Fr. Pere de Falgar or Fr. Pere Scarez, both of whom are mentioned in Louis' biography.[34] Another friar, named by Wadding and by Marcus of Lisbon as the teacher of St. Louis, has been identified by Pou y Martí as the Fr. Poncio Portugati[35] included by Angelo da Clareno among a group of Olivi's disciples who suffered harsh imprisonment after the visit in 1300 of the Provincial of Aragon, Fr. Arnaldo Olibé.[36] Olibé himself later wrote an account of his visit which included an

---

[33] Oportet, enim, ut in plena apertione sexti sigilli sol et luna graviter obscurentur stellisque de coelo cadentibus, fiat terremotus sic magnus, quod omnes montes et insulae de suis sedibus moveantur ... A sexto enim angelo effundenda est sexta phiala in flumen magnum Eufratem, ut, ejus aquis siccatis, via regibus ab ortu solis venientibus praeparetur, exeantque tres immundi spiritus et ad reges totius terrae procedant, congregare illos in praelium in die magno judicii summi Dei ... oportet fornicariam Babilonem in maris profunda demergi, quando sub sexto capite bestiae hanc meretricem portantis decem cornua tanquam reges una hora accipient potestatem ... Insuper et cum Agno pugnabunt, sed Agnus vincet illos tamquam Rex regum et Dominus dominorum; sicut et archa, superato diluvio, super montes altissimos requievit. Tuncque columba emissa ramum olivae defert suo rostro, id est pacem evangelicam universis praedicabit, juxta quod sexto angelo tuba canente, sub angelo faciem solarem habente. (ALKG, 3 [1887]: 537-538; Pou y Martí, AIA, 11 [1919]: 137; *Visionarios*, pp. 27-28).

[34] Pou y Martí, AIA, 11 (1919): 138; *Visionarios*, p. 29.

[35] Ibid.

[36] Ehrle, "Die Spiritualen," ALKG, 2 (1886): 384, 386; see also R. de Fronsac, ALKG, 3 (1887): 16-17; Pou y Martí, AIA, 11 (1919): 139; *Visionarios*, p. 29.

attack on Olivianist doctrines which he had encountered.[37] Olibé's successor, Fr. Romeo Ortiz, also wrote a polemic against the Spiritual position.

Thus by 1295 the zeal for *renovatio ecclesie* with its concomitant apocalypticism was becoming well established in Catalonia, largely owing to the dissemination of ideas from beyond the Pyrenees. Franciscans of the First and Third Orders were demonstrating their discontent with the existing order of things; the local ecclesiastical authorities were becoming aware of the latent threat to obedience within the Order, among Spirituals of the First Order and Tertiaries, as well as the open threat among the Beguins. Olivi had already acquired a great reputation, and a large number of his adherents were to be found in Catalonia. Both he and his followers enjoyed the sympathy of the House of Aragon and — in the person of Robert of Naples — of Anjou. Thus, although these groups constituted a small and persecuted minority, they had already established a breach within the ecclesiastical structure of Catalonia.

Perarnau has recently discovered and analysed a collection of notarial documents which reveals the presence of at least one community of Beguins in Barcelona at the beginning of the fourteenth century, and which confirms the existence of groups in Vilafranca del Penedès and Valencia.[38] Perarnau's discovery further links the Beguins with Arnold of Vilanova, for, in his defence of the Barcelona Tertiaries, their minister inserts as an explication of his group's beliefs the *Alia Informatio Beguinorum*, which Perarnau has shown to be Arnold's work. The dispersal of Arnold's library to the *Fratres de Penitentia* is further evidence for this link, and justifies the phrase "Arnoldian Beguinism" as a description of the style and substance of Beguin thought in Catalonia.

The first phase of Arnoldian Beguinism, from c. 1302 until the condemnation of the vernacular works of Arnold by the Provincial Council of Tarragona in November of 1316, was one of uneasy tolerance for the Beguins and for Arnold. From the seventeen documents he has analysed, Perarnau has identified two major strands of Arnoldian influence.[39] The first consists of the personal relations between Arnold and various people until his death in 1311, the second of at least one group of Beguins who continued to exist as a cohesive and independent group after Arnold's death. Perarnau notes the

---

[37] Ehrle, "Des Ordensprocurators Raymund von Fronsac," ALKG, 3 (1887): 17; Pou y Martí, AIA, 11 (1919): 140; *Visionarios*, pp. 30-31.

[38] Perarnau, *Alia Informatio*, see esp. pp. 5, 107-144.

[39] Ibid., pp. 108-109, for a reference list of the documents; pp. 87-106 for six documents reproduced.

co-existence and probable contacts between these two parties from May of 1309 to December of 1311.[40]

Five of Arnold's friends in Barcelona can be identified positively; all of them occupied positions of trust within the hierarchies of city and crown. Pere Jutge, an apothecary by profession, conducted business affairs occasionally for James II and for the city of Barcelona;[41] Pere de Montmeló, an official of the crown, founded a hospital with probable Beguin links;[42] Jaume des Pla, a *scriptor* in the royal house, took the last testament of Queen Blanca of Anjou;[43] Miquel Antiga, a notary, served Alphonso the Liberal and James II;[44] Bernat de Llimona, "an advocate of lost causes" according to Perarnau, was a physician who also maintained an interest in Montmeló's hospital.[45] Of the five, Pere de Montmeló was probably the most committed disciple of Arnold's religious views, followed by Miguel Antiga, then Bernat de Llimona. Pere Jutge seems to have been more a friend than a follower, as does Jaume des Pla. Outside Barcelona, in Vilafranca del Penedès, Gerald Pere is probably the Beguin identified as "Fr. Gerald," who was also noted as a friend of Arnold.[46]

The most significant contribution to the perpetuation of Arnold's work made by his circle of friends took place in the home of Pere Jutge.[47] In December of 1311, when news of Arnold's death reached Barcelona, Arnold's executors made an inventory of Arnold's goods which had been left in Jutge's house.[48] The inventory reveals the existence of a *scriptorium* devoted to Arnold's religious tracts, a number of which were found in various stages of completion, some even illuminated. There were three anthologies or *summae* in progress, one which was to contain fifteen works, five in Latin and ten in Catalan; a second of fourteen, mostly in Catalan; and a third of undetermined number, entirely in Catalan. We do not know how long the *scriptorium* had been in operation, but it seems likely to have been the principal source of dissemination for the vernacular works of Arnold, and probably responsible for the flood of works which eventually alarmed the ecclesiastical authorities.

[40] Ibid., pp. 111-112.
[41] Ibid., pp. 113-114.
[42] Ibid., pp. 114-115.
[43] Ibid., p. 116.
[44] Ibid., pp. 116-118.
[45] Ibid., pp. 118-120.
[46] Ibid., p. 17.
[47] Ibid., pp. 122-126.
[48] See R. Chabás, "Inventario de los libros, ropas y demas efectos de Arnaldo de Vilanova," *Revista de Archivos, Bibliotecas y Museos*, 2a época, 9 (Madrid, 1903), pp. 189-203.

Because the *scriptorium* was closed down after Arnold's death, it appears that Arnold himself had instituted and was financing the project, in keeping with his own announced intention to teach and to warn the faithful. Arnold himself visited Barcelona three times between 1300 and 1310, and surely made a significant personal contribution to the growth of Beguinism in Catalonia. His position of favour with the house of Aragon and with the papacy would have made his task easier, as would the positions of his friends, all of whom could have directly and indirectly helped to protect the community of Tertiaries and their sympathizers among other orders.

The manuscripts in Jutge's house found homes among Beguins: the inventory notes that the books found were distributed "to various groups of Penitents [*diversis gentibus de penitentia*]" by Arnold's executors,[49] chief among whom was Pere de Montmeló. Although, as Perarnau has noted, the phrase could refer either to various individuals or to various groups, in either case it clearly indicates that the manuscripts went to those who are consistently identified in the contemporary documents as *fratres de penitencia de tercio ordine beati Francisci*, also referred to as Beguins.[50]

In addition to the indigenous Catalonian followers of Arnold, Perarnau notes evidence for the settlement of a foreign group in Barcelona, probably Provençal in origin (and perhaps recipients of Arnold's books, also), a group referred to by the Archbishop of Tarragona as "certain foreigners who have recently come to this region in that [Beguin] habit."[51] Perarnau also cites as evidence for the infiltration of Beguin influence the movement into Catalonia of the Joan family of Montpellier, who may have transmitted such ideas in the manner of the Cathar families in the Pyrenees.[52]

The documents of 1312 reveal a controversy between the Tertiaries of Barcelona and the ecclesiastical authorities — both Franciscan and secular — over the orthodoxy of the Beguin group. The controversy seems to have been initiated publicly by the vicar of the Franciscans of Barcelona, Fra Arnau de Bonastre, who, in a letter to the bishop of Barcelona, accused the Beguins of having created a new order. In his reply, Guillem Martí, minister of the Beguins, defended his house on the grounds that it followed the rule of the Third Order, and in its practice of poverty followed Christ Himself as closely as possible.[53] Speaking on behalf of "all of the above-mentioned friars of the Third Order," Martí argues that

---

[49] Perarnau, *Alia Informatio*, p. 125.

[50] Ibid., p. 126.

[51] Ibid., p. 127.

[52] Ibid., pp. 128-130. See Emmanuel Le Roy Ladurie, *Montaillou*, (London: Penguin Books, 1980).

[53] Perarnau, *Alia Informatio*, Doc. 13, reproduced on pp. 90-101.

saving the honour of friar Arnau de Bonastre, we neither hold nor serve a new order, but affirm in truth that we hold and serve and live in the Order and Rule of the Brothers of Penitence of the Third Order of St. Francis, an Order which is ancient, and which is approved by the holy mother Church of Rome.[54]

Marti notes that Clement v has recently approved the Order at the Council of Vienne (1311-1313), then goes on to argue that the Order follows the teachings of Christ "in all matters," especially those on poverty.[55] At this point in his document, Marti inserts the text of the *Alia Informatio Beguinorum*, addressed in its Catalan version to the "cultivadors de la evangelica pobrea."[56]

From this exchange of documents we can also confirm that the Beguins of Barcelona lived in the manner described by Bernard Gui.[57] They lived communally, had an internal structure headed by a "minister," practised the Rule of the Third Order, and enrolled both men and women. They wore distinctive habits and lived by the sale of articles manufactured in their house as well as by begging from door to door. It was to virtually all of these practices that the Franciscan establishment objected, objections rooted in a general distrust of the Third Order as an insufficiently disciplined organization whose rule allowed for dangerous new innovations in the interpretation of the lives of both Christ and St. Francis.

Although their suspicions were certainly aroused, the secular authorities of 1312 were cautious in their attempts to restrain the Beguins.[58] In that year, the provincial council of bishops sought information by means of visits on two points: how the Beguins interpreted the articles of faith, and their procedure for electing the minister of their house. They also expressly prohibited two things: the forming of cells within a Tertiary house (*congregaciones vel conventicula inter se*), and any attempt to interpret Holy Scripture.[59] The bishops seemed less concerned than the Franciscan authorities about the daily living arrangements of the Beguins, but saw in the two activities mentioned the danger of a new and unorthodox development of doctrine.

No charges appear to have resulted from this rather moderate inquisition of 1312. The Beguins continued to live in their accustomed manner, under

---

[54] Ibid., Doc. 13, p. 96.
[55] Ibid., Doc. 13, p. 98.
[56] Ibid. See pp. 19-85 for the text of *Alia Informatio*.
[57] Ibid., p. 136.
[58] Ibid., pp. 138-141.
[59] Ibid., p. 139.

suspicion but within the boundaries of orthodoxy, at least for the moment. However, by 1315, further unease over the Tertiaries is revealed in a letter from the bishop of Barcelona to the rector of Vilafranca del Penedès, and by 1316 Arnold's works were considered subversive to the faith. In 1317, John XXII's attack on the Beguins in Provence and Catalonia signalled the end of tolerance for the doctrines of evangelical poverty within the western Church.

The Beguinism of the western Mediterranean was in large part an urban phenomenon, as we have noted, and in Catalonia was closely bound up with the economic advancement of the house of Aragon and the consequent increase in wealth of the Church in the early years of the fourteenth century.[60] In this context, Arnoldian Beguinism may be seen as an attack on the integration of Christian and mercantile values taking place in Barcelona and other cities of the Aragonese empire. "The life of Barcelona society," Perarnau writes,

> from the beginning of that century, without denying other aspects of its life truly worthy of admiration, ... seems to concentrate itself on the gain arising from commerce. The sea voyages to the East ... or to closer countries, the contracts, and every kind of loan for conducting business, without distinction between Christians and Jews, are the matters which most occupy the pages of the manuals of notaries. Consequently, Barcelona society is characterised by a strong demand for instruction, in order to prepare itself for economic competition.[61]

Arnold himself noted an increasing affinity between the desire for knowledge and the desire for social ascent by means of riches, and the crux of his attack on the false religious lay in the desire for worldly things on the part of the clergy. In Perarnau's view, the condemnation of Arnold's work in 1316 demonstrated that it had become impossible for urban-bourgeois Christianity ("cristianism ciu tadà-burgès") to co-exist with a Christianity determined to separate the spiritual from the mercantile,[62] and, it may be added, to do so in a most rigorous fashion. The increasingly vitriolic condemnation of the Christian establishment by Arnold and his successors, combined with their apocalyptic obsession, destroyed beyond repair the delicate fabric of tolerance. After 1317, the Beguins entered into a self-fulfilling future of persecution.

---

[60] Ibid., pp. 142-147.
[61] *Alia Informatio*, pp. 142-143.
[62] Ibid., pp. 143-144.

2. THE PERSECUTION
OF THE CATALONIAN BEGUINS, 1316-1350

The pontificate of John XXII (1316-1334) constituted a watershed for
Fraticelli and Beguins alike, since for the first time the full weight of the
Papacy was brought to bear unequivocally against the upholders of extreme
poverty and the doctrine which underpinned their position. In 1317 the Pope
ordered inquisitors in Languedoc to take action and issued the Bull *Quorundam exigit* against the Spirituals.[63] This aimed at reducing the role of poverty
in Christian discipleship and contained his pronouncement that "poverty is
good but chastity is better and obedience best." Twenty-five Spirituals
attacked this bull on the ground that the Pope had no authority to make
judgements on such matters and four of these were burned in Marseilles on
7 May 1318.[64] The apocalyptic context in which this struggle had now been
placed made the application of prophecy to the new situation immediate and
sharp. Many of Olivi's Joachimist disciples at once recognised John XXII as
the mystic Antichrist of the *Postilla*. In condemning the ideal of poverty
defended by the zealots, John had, in their eyes, completed the transformation of the Church into the Whore of Babylon. Indeed, the appearance of
John must have done for Olivi's *Postilla* what the appearance of the two
mendicant orders had done for Joachim of Fiore's famous prophecy: here
was evidence that Olivi had prophesied correctly. It remained simply to work
out a new time scheme and await the events of the Last Times. This period
in Joachimism saw a concentration upon the ecclesiastical events of the sixth
age; the next era was to focus attention in more detail on events after the
mystic Antichrist.

The Beguins immediately proclaimed the four who had suffered at
Marseilles as martyrs of the Church. The Inquisition responded to the
challenge and throughout the south of France the burning continued. In
Narbonne in 1319, three Beguins were burned, in Cuaresma seventeen in
1321, and large numbers in Béziers, Carcassonne and Pezenas. According
to one computation, 113 persons were executed in Carcassonne between
1318 and 1350.[65] For one of these processes, that against Beguins of the
Third Order at Toulouse in 1321-1322, we possess a full record which casts
a vivid light on their beliefs. The interrogation of Bernard de na Jacma, whom

---

[63] *Bullarium*, 5 (1898): 128; Pou y Martí, AIA, 14 (1920): 11-12; *Visionarios*, p. 159.
[64] Ehrle, "Die Spiritualen," ALKG, 2 (1886): 147; idem, "Des Ordensprocurators Raymund
von Fronsac," 3 (1887): 30; Pou y Martí, AIA, 14 (1920): 12; *Visionarios*, p. 160.
[65] Pou y Martí, AIA, 14 (1920): 13; *Visionarios*, pp. 160-161.

we have already quoted,[66] is representative. He was identified as *Beguinus seu de tercia regula S. Francisci* and charged, among other things, with receiving two classes of dissidents, Spirituals and Beguins.[67] We have already seen that Bernard held the Rule of St. Francis sacrosanct: to act against it was to violate the Gospel, for the *Fratres de Penitentia* were the evangelical men of the third *status*, which is that of the Holy Spirit.[68]

Bernard believed that the Minorites burned at Marseilles were martyrs and saints, as well as other Beguins who had subsequently been burned. He and his friends carried the bones of two martyred Beguins home, and made relics of them. Conversely, Bernard believed that all the persecutors of the Beguins were heretics, since in their persecution of evangelical poverty they erred in the faith. Above all, he revered the memory of Olivi, and believed that all the writing of this "holy father" and "uncanonized saint" was true doctrine (*fidelis et catholica*), except certain chapters condemned by Clement v.[69]

The apocalyptic scheme to which Bernard subscribed was almost entirely that of Olivi, with some occasional fantastic additions which circulated among the Beguins. He believed in the three *status* of the Church, each assigned to a Person of the Trinity, and repeated Olivi's typology of the synagogue, affixing to it an interesting elaboration:

> [Bernard] believed that as the synagogue of the Jews had been reprobate and rejected at the advent of the primitive Church because it had crucified Christ, so in the third *status* at the coming of the new Church our present Church shall be reprobate and rejected because it has persecuted and will continue to persecute the life of the Lord Jesus Christ in the evangelical men. And a third church shall succeed.[70]

The belief in a "third church" seems to perpetuate the view of the *Eternal Evangel* that there will be a new Dispensation to supersede that of the Apostles. Olivi himself did not apparently take this extreme position, but we shall see it appearing again in the work of his followers.

Bernard saw the Roman Church as the Whore of Babylon, and subscribed to the theory of two Antichrists, a mystic and a "true" Antichrist. He equivocated on the question whether John XXII was the mystic Antichrist. He was also not sure whether or not the Pope was a heretic. Certainly his hesitancy in condemning John would suggest a certain prudence on his part, considering the dangerous situation in which he found himself. However,

---

[66] Supra, p. 52.
[67] Limborch, *Lib. Sentent.*, p. 307.
[68] Ibid., supra, p. 52.
[69] Ibid., p. 308.
[70] Ibid., p. 308.

there may also have been real doubt about the nature of John's role in the Joachimist system. He was obviously somewhat confused over Olivi's remarks on the two Antichrists, and at one point had suggested that the mystic and true Antichrists were the same person.[71] In 1330 the great Antichrist would appear, and shortly thereafter, die. Before the advent of this Antichrist, Christ would elect twelve evangelical men to resist him, and after his defeat the third *status* would begin.

The calculations made by Beguins concerning the false pope and great Antichrist of the *Postilla* reveal the growing tendency to assign specific roles in the patterns established by Joachim and Olivi, but they are more confused and crude than, for example, the calculations in the *Breviloquium*. Bernard tells us that the general opinion of Beguins and others was that the false pope described by Olivi would appear in Sicily, elected and established through the power of Frederick of Sicily, as Olivi had written. They believed that the false pope would be either Fr. Henry of Ceva, or Fr. Angelo da Clareno. Frederick, along with the king of Aragon and eight other kings, would defeat in battle the king of France and Robert of Naples. This period would cause such great slaughter of men that women would be forced to embrace trees. During this time the great Antichrist would appear, and he turns out to be Philip of Majorca.[72]

The roles assigned for the Antichrists look forward to Roquetaillade, who sometimes saw Antichrist as a force for good.[73] Since the effect of the work of the Antichrists would be to renovate the church, the Beguins saw in them a pattern resembling the *felix culpa* of the temptation and downfall of Adam, which ultimately was to result in glory for the human race, or at least those chosen ones. Since the church was reprobate, the scourge of God — even though he is called Antichrist — could in theory be a godly man. One can see the germ for this in a passage from Olivi's commentary on Matthew, in which he gives reasons why Christ did not make specific mention of the events to take place before the coming of Antichrist. His third reason is that it is the role of Antichrist to punish the reprobates, paving the way for the final illumination of all the converted after his death, and for the coronation of all the martyrs which he has created.[74]

In general, the Beguins showed more concern for the immediate ecclesiastical situation than for the final historical events. The mystic Antichrist, associated primarily with the religious events of the sixth age, was apparently

---

[71] Ibid., p. 309.

[72] Ibid., p. 309.

[73] Infra, p. 80.

[74] Petrus Johannis Olivi, *Super evangelium Mathei*, Oxford, New College, MS 49, fol. 135v; also quoted infra in *Brev.*, pp. 228-229.

upon them, and they followed Olivi's lead in concentrating upon these events. Olivi also apparently saw the two Antichrists existing contemporaneously,[75] so that the events of the Last Times tended to be telescoped into a brief period. It was not until after John's death that primary attention would perforce be focused upon events after the death of Antichrist. Thus the combination of Olivi's prophecies and the apparently corroborative historical events served to determine the shape of prophecy until the mid-fourteenth century.

The persecutions which had struck at Beguin groups in the south of France were soon extended across the Pyrenees. In 1322 John XXII directed the archbishops and bishops of the Midi in France and of Tarragona in Aragon to begin proceedings against Tertiaries whose orthodoxy was suspect.[76] In this bull John states that unfortunately members of both sexes of the Tertiaries, or Continents, have chosen to condemn themselves by disputing the articles of faith, the sacraments of the Church, the plenitude of apostolic authority and the limits to which this power may be extended. Pou y Martí has noted that within the bull there is evidence that John had been considering a general condemnation of the entire Third Order, but had decided to confine himself to a campaign against the Tertiaries in the areas where the danger of heresy was greatest.[77]

We can gather a little detail concerning the beliefs of persecuted groups of Beguins and Tertiaries in Catalonia in the time of John XXII and the following years. One such group arose at Gerona, led by a certain Durando de Baldach, whose errors, according to Eymerich, included a condemnation of the sacrament of marriage,[78] a view typical of the contemptuous attitude held by many Beguin groups towards marriage. Pou y Martí attributes this view to an attack on the marital estate as non-sacramental.[79] Pou y Martí has uncovered another account of these proceedings in the annals of P. Diago,[80] who reports that in 1321 Durando was brought before the inquisitor as a teacher of Beguin (Beghard) errors, especially the doctrines of Olivi's *Postilla*. Diago also notes that Durando had been arraigned previously before the tribunal in 1317, and had then abjured his beliefs. It was probably for his views on marriage and Beguin doctrines other than poverty that he was tried as a heretic, since it was not until 1321 that the extreme view of poverty was

---

[75] Supra, pp. 24-25.
[76] *Bullarium*, 5 (1898): 222; Pou y Martí, AIA, 14 (1920): 15; *Visionarios*, p. 162.
[77] Pou y Martí, AIA, 14 (1920): 16; *Visionarios*, p. 163.
[78] Eymerich, *Direct. Inquis.*, p. 283.
[79] Ehrle, "Die Spiritualen," ALKG, 2 (1886): 369; Pou y Martí, AIA, 14 (1920): 8; *Visionarios*, p. 156.
[80] Pou y Martí, AIA, 15 (1921): 5-7; *Visionarios*, pp. 194-95.

declared anathema. It is worthy of note that on 12 July 1321, when Durando's sentence was read on the steps of the cathedral, the Infant Peter, along with James II, were in attendance. Durando and one of his companions were burned.

Eymerich provides us with the bulk of our present available information concerning Beguins in Barcelona during this period.[81] He notes first that during the time of John XXII, a certain Peter Oller, from Majorca, was accused of Beguin heresies, along with a certain Fr. Bonanat. Bonanat is of particular interest for two reasons. First, he is listed as leader of the Beguins in Catalonia during the time of Benedict XII (*Begardorum dux in Catalonia*), and secondly, he was probably a Tertiary. Bonanat had a change of heart as he was being burned at the stake; he was taken down immediately and subsequently freed. Pou y Martí believes that this unusual clemency was owing to the priestly office held by Bonanat.[82] Eymerich states further that during the papacy of Benedict XII (1334-1342), Bonanat disseminated Beguin ideas in Vilafranca del Penedés. He acquired many followers, and, according to Pou y Martí, maintained convents, and used as his headquarters one of these establishments.[83] He was eventually seized, however, and his convent was burned.

Bartolomé Janovés also appeared in Barcelona from Majorca at this time, and we learn from Eymerich that he had written a tract on the coming of Antichrist.[84] He preached in Barcelona during the time of Urban V, and announced that Antichrist would appear in 1360. We do not know whether he was a Beguin or Tertiary, but there is no doubt that he belonged to the Arnoldian school of apocalyptic, as Pou y Martí has noted,[85] and professed other ideas which would have found sympathy among Beguin groups, among them that at the time of the appearance of Antichrist the Sacraments of the Church would cease, and that many Christians, marked by the sign of Antichrist, would suffer damnation.[86]

Hitherto unpublished documents[87] reveal the continuing existence of a group of *beguini et aliqui fratres et sorores tertii ordinis Sancti Francisci* in

[81] Eymerich, *Direct. Inquis.*, p. 283; Pou y Martí, AIA, 15 (1921): 7-10; *Visionarios*, pp. 196-198.

[82] Pou y Martí, AIA, 15 (1921): 9; *Visionarios*, p. 197.

[83] Pou y Martí, AIA, 15 (1921): 9; *Visionarios*, p. 197.

[84] Eymerich, *Direct. Inquis.*, p. 284; Pou y Martí, AIA, 15 (1921): 10; *Visionarios*, p. 198.

[85] Pou y Martí, AIA, 15 (1921): 10; *Visionarios*, p. 198.

[86] Eymerich, *Direct. Inquis.*, p. 284.

[87] J.N. Hillgarth and G. Silano, *The Register 'Notule Communium 14' of the Diocese of Barcelona (1345-1348)* (PIMS Subsidia Mediaevalia 13; Toronto, 1983). We are indebted to Professor Hillgarth for this paragraph. See also the work of Josep Perarnau, *Procés inquisitorial contra els beguins de Vilafranca del Penedès (1345-1346)*, Colleció 'Studia, Textus, Subsidia,' Barcelona, Facultat de Teologia.

Vilafranca del Penedés in 1345-1346. The phrase above is cited from a general circular of Bishop Bernat Oliver o.s.a. dated *4 Nonis aprilis*, which commands laymen, even if they are Tertiaries, to desist from living together, gathering alms in public, or proposing their own interpretations of the faith.[88] Ramon Punier, a priest who belonged to this group, died in January 1346 after an interrogation by the bishop and the Dominican inquisitor. Other members of the circle were imprisoned in the episcopal palace in Barcelona.

For Tarragona we possess one very interesting document dated 1345 concerning the fate of a married Tertiary cleric who protested to Clement VI about his treatment by the inquisitor.[89] A certain Bernardo de Camprodón was tried before the Inquisition, presumably for the usual Beguin beliefs. In his subsequent letter to Clement, he complained that his confession had been obtained under false pretences, and without the right of defence having been immediately granted. Clement, in his letter to the Archbishop of Tarragona, summarizes these charges, and asks that an investigation be made. Bernard's confession was obtained by promises of an easy penance in return for his cooperation.[90] However, although he did cooperate, he was kept in prison, tortured, and publicly denounced. The flagrant disregard for his rights described in this document was probably typical of the situation which faced many Beguins in Catalonia during this period. The *Breviloquium*, in its Prologue, speaks of severe conditions.[91]

In Valencia there is evidence for a continuing tradition of Beguin activity from the time of John XXII onwards. After John XXII's time, the leader in Valencia was Fr. Jaime Just, and concerning him and his hospital we have a considerable amount of information, again owing to the diligent researches of Pou y Martí.[92]

In the city of Turía, near Valencia, there was a hospital called Santa Maria, or "dels Beguins."[93] It was founded by D. Ramón Guillén Catalá. In his will, dated 1 May 1334, Catalá discusses the government and administration of this hospital, and declares that he wishes to have the *Fratres de Penitentia* reside there "always." He desires further that the hospital be immune from outside ecclesiastical authority, and be governed rather by the city of

---

[88] Hillgarth-Silano, *The Register*, no. 258.

[89] Pou y Martí, AIA, 15 (1921): 16-17; *Visionarios*, pp. 198-200.

[90] Pou y Martí, AIA, 15 (1921): 17; *Visionarios*, p. 199. See also J. Vidal, *Annales de Saint-Louis des Français à Rome*, a. 10 (1905): 9.

[91] Infra, p. 91.

[92] Pou y Martí, AIA, 15 (1921): 18-25; *Visionarios*, pp. 200-206. Pou y Martí remarks: *Parece que los beguinos, capitaneados por Fr. Jaime Just, eran los mismos del tiempo de Juan XXII, o discipulos, propriamente dichos, de aquellos* (AIA, 18; *Visionarios*, p. 200).

[93] Idem, AIA, 15 (1921): 18; *Visionarios*, p. 200.

Valencia.[94] Fr. Just is mentioned in the document as residing there already, and it was he who eventually took over the administration of the hospital.[95]

Catalá presumably wishes to found a charitable hospital and at the same time offer protection for the Tertiaries. It is likely that he was affiliated with the Order. There is little doubt of their identity as Tertiaries: in 1409 there is a reference in the Municipal Acts of Valencia to "La Casa e Hospital dels de la Terca Regla de Sent Francesch." Pou y Martí is convinced of this identification.[96]

In 1339 Fr. Just was performing his administrative duties for the hospital, for an Act of the City Council tells us that he was engaged in construction at the hospital.[97] But he and his companions were also engaged in the propagation of their beliefs. According to the inquisitor Bertrand de Deux, and to Eymerich, Fr. Just disseminated Beguin beliefs with considerable success, teaching, among other things, that the victims of the inquisition under Clement VI were true martyrs of Christ.[98]

Sometime between 1342 and 1348, Bertrand de Deux began to concern himself with Fr. Just.[99] In 1353, he wrote to the bishop of Valencia and the Inquisitor Ripoll that by mandate of Innocent VI, they should proceed against him. He named also Fr. Guillermo Gilabert and Martin Pere, identifying them along with Just as Tertiaries, and noted that they had already been interrogated at least once by Bernard of Puigcertós. All three were imprisoned for a time, then released. Gilabert and Pere died shortly after their release, but Just returned to the hospital. He was set free on condition that he preach his doctrines no more, and remain in the city. Innocent VI, however, began proceedings against him when Just violated these strictures. In 1353 Just and his exhumed companions were tried again. The two dead bodies were burned; Just, who renounced his heresies, was sentenced to life imprisonment and died shortly thereafter.[100] Although Just cannot be connected directly with the *Breviloquium*, his preaching and his persecution evoke the milieu of our manuscript, which was probably written during the early 1350s, and which also reflects the continual threat of punishment hanging over Beguin groups during these years.

---

[94] Idem, AIA, 15 (1921): 19; *Visionarios*, p. 201.
[95] Idem, AIA, 15 (1921): 19; *Visionarios*, p. 201.
[96] Idem, AIA, 15 (1921): 19; *Visionarios*, p. 201. In 1369 Pedro Brunet had left his possessions to the hospital 'dicto dels Beguins' (AIA, 20 and *Visionarios*, pp. 201-202).
[97] Idem, AIA, 15 (1921): 20; *Visionarios*, p. 202.
[98] Idem, AIA, 15 (1921): 21; *Visionarios*, p. 202.
[99] Idem, AIA, 15 (1921): 21-24; *Visionarios*, pp. 203-205.
[100] Idem, AIA, 15 (1921): 24-25; *Visionarios*, p. 206.

5

Joachimism in Beguin and Tertiary Circles

Two fourteenth-century documents provide us with certain proof that Joachimism was alive in the circles of Beguins and Tertiaries which we have been discussing. The first is a tract, written originally in Catalan, but known to us by the Latin title *De statibus ecclesiae secundum expositionem Apocalypsim.*[1] It was found with various other writings in the possession of a certain Bernard Fuster, a Franciscan of Majorca.[2] Proceedings were instituted against him, not because of any expression of heretical views, but simply because he possessed these writings. It is significant that he had received some of them from a citizen of Gerona where, as we have seen, Durando de Baldach, the leader of a Beguin group, was condemned in 1321.[3] It is possible, as Pou y Marti suggests, that Fuster was connected with this Beguin circle and received his copy of the *De statibus* from Durando.[4]

The form in which the *De statibus* is preserved is that of a Latin document in thirty-two chapters in which offending passages are cited and refuted by the judges of the Inquisition. Unfortunately the Catalan original was presumably destroyed and we can only attempt to reconstruct its contents from the passages which the inquisitors chose to refute and condemn. Fortunately they found much to condemn. They also used the proceedings against the *Eternal Evangel* as the major precedent for their judgement. It does not seem, however, that they knew the Protocol of the Commission of Anagni, for the passages which they quote as from the *Eternal Evangel* are all taken from the Articles drawn up by the Masters of Paris University.[5]

[1] *De statibus ecclesiae secundum expositionem Apocalypsim,* ed. Pou y Marti, AIA, 18 (1922): 29-47; 19 (1923): 25-40; *Visionarios,* pp. 483-512.

[2] Pou y Marti, AIA, 18 (1922): 27; *Visionarios,* p. 255. See also Perarnau, *Alia Informatio,* p. 134.

[3] Supra, p. 63. See Pou y Marti, AIA, 18 (1922): 26; *Visionarios,* p. 255.

[4] Ibid.

[5] The earliest text of the Paris Masters' Articles is given by M. Paris, *Chronica Majora* (ed. Rolls Series), 6, *Additamenta,* pp. 335-339. All the citations from the *Eternal Evangel* made by the inquisitors are close, but not exact, quotations from this text. In one significant detail,

There is little doubt that the work was written by a Franciscan, but his particular affiliation is unknown.[6] Pou y Martí has determined its date as sometime between 7 October 1317 (the date of the bull *Quorundam exigit*)[7] and its condemnation in the spring of 1321.[8] The title of the work is the same as that of chapter three in Joachim's *Liber Introductorius* to the *Expositio*, and its Joachimist foundation is apparent throughout. It begins with a clear statement of the three *status* "on the first page": the first (that of the Father) from the beginning of the world until Christ; the second (that of the Son) from the coming of Christ until Antichrist; the third (that of the Holy Spirit) from the death of Antichrist until the end of the world.[9] The author further follows Joachim in associating the three *status* with the consecutive orders of laity, clergy and religious.[10]

The inquisitors also note that the author elaborated on the theme of the three *status* by borrowing a passage from Olivi. As in the first age, the author writes, God showed Himself as terrible and fearful, bringing down justice on all those who transgressed His laws, so in the second age the Son of God showed Himself full of piety and a teacher of the truth, as the express Word of the Father's wisdom. In the third age God will show Himself as the Holy Spirit, as the "flame and furnace of divine love, as the *cellarium* of spiritual wine, and as the apothecary of spiritual balm."[11]

---

however, the inquisitors' version agrees with that given by the Spanish Inquisitor Eymerich (fl. 1350), rather than with Paris. Thus what they had in hand was clearly a text of the Paris articles, of which there were several versions. In no case do they quote directly from the Protocol of the Commission of Anagni and, indeed, it is unlikely that they would have had the full text of this, since it has survived in very few MSS. Pou y Martí's footnote citations from the Protocol, as edited by Denifle, ALKG, 1 (1885): 99-142, are therefore misleading (*Visionarios*, pp. 490 n. 5, 491 n. 2, 492 nn. 3, 4, 506 n. 5). Moreover he does not give all the references to the Paris articles. In the following list v. = the text of *De Statibus* as published by Pou y Martí, MP. = Mathew Paris's version of the Articles, E. = Eymerich, *Direct. Inquis.*, Pt. 2: v. 484, MP. 339, E. 255; v. 485, MP. 339, E. 255; v. 490, MP. 336, E. 254; v. 490, MP. 338, E. 255; v. 490, MP. 335, E. 254; v. 492, MP. 338, E. 254 (not a quotation, but a summary of articles 4, 5, 9); v. 504, MP. 339, E. 255; v. 506, MP. 336, E. 254; v. 508, MP. 338, E. 255; v. 509, MP. 337, E. 255.

[6] Pou y Martí, AIA, 18 (1922): 27; *Visionarios*, p. 256.

[7] Idem, AIA, 18 (1922): 27-28; *Visionarios*, p. 257.

[8] Idem, AIA, 18 (1922): 27-28; *Visionarios*, p. 257.

[9] Idem, AIA, 18 (1922): 29; *Visionarios*, p. 483.

[10] Idem, AIA, 18 (1922): 29; *Visionarios*, p. 484.

[11] Et sicut in primo tempore Deus ostendit se tanquam terribilem et magni timoris, eo quod faciebat magna judicia et manifesta de eis qui transgrediebantur precepta eius, sic in isto secundo tempore Dei Filius ostendit se plenum pietate et magistrum, doctoremque seu manifestatorem ueritatis, sicut uerbum expressiuum de sapientia Patris. Sed in tertio statu ostendet se Spiritus Sanctus et dabit se sicut flammam et fornacem diuini amoris et sicut cellarium uini spiritalis et sicut apotheca unguentorum spiritualium. Idem, AIA, 18 (1922): 29; *Visionarios*, p. 483. See supra, pp. 20-21, and infra, pp. 104-105.

Although the author of the *De statibus* did not go as far in his claims for the new order as the Commissioners of Anagni felt that Gerard of Borgo San Donnino had done in the *Eternal Evangel*,[12] the inquisitors apparently detected this presumptuous error and, indeed, used the condemnation of the *Eternal Evangel* to dispose of the whole notion of three successive orders in history. The identification of lay people, clerics and religious is held to be an error "condemned in the condemnation of the *Eternal Evangel*," and a similar passage from the second part of the fifth book of Gerard's work is quoted.[13] The author of the *De statibus* follows Olivi in his general view of the events of the end of the second *status* and the beginning of the third. In the end of the second *status* there will be a general judgement of Babylon and of the carnal Church, which will have persecuted the truth of Christ and his "paupers" by condemning the poverty of Christ. The traditional Olivianist typology is used: the Church "will crucify the blessed life and blessed poverty of Christ."[14] The Church will be destroyed by the ten horns of the beast of *Apocalypse* 17, except for the elect who will then found the "spiritual church," and will preach the truth of Christ throughout the world. Olivi's figure of the synagogue's damnation of Christ as the type for the new persecution of the evangelicals by the carnal Church is used, and the carnal Church is named as the Whore of Babylon.[15]

The *De statibus* also sees the sixth age as that of "the renovation of the evangelical life,"[16] a renovation which is to be achieved, of course, through the Rule of St. Francis, which in its renunciation of both personal and common possessions (*in abdicatione habendi in proprio et in communi*), constitutes the true evangelical life.[17] St. Francis himself is the sixth angel of the Apocalypse and will be resurrected before the general resurrection and the end of the world. Those who hold fast to the Rule will be persecuted by the Church in the person of the Pope, and by members of their own order. They will be condemned as schismatics, excommunicates and heretics.[18]

The inquisitors cite the *Eternal Evangel* twice in their condemnation of this passage of the *De statibus*, first in the identification of the established Church as "carnal,"[19] and secondly in the mission of renovation ascribed to

---

[12] Denifle, "Evangelium aeternum," ALKG, 1 (1885): 106-112, 115-118.
[13] Pou y Martí, AIA, 18 (1922): 31-32; *Visionarios*, p. 485.
[14] Idem, AIA, 18 (1922): 32; *Visionarios*, p. 486.
[15] Idem, AIA, 18 (1922): 34-35; *Visionarios*, pp. 487-488.
[16] See supra, pp. 21-22.
[17] Pou y Martí, AIA, 18 (1922): 34-35; *Visionarios*, pp. 487-488.
[18] Idem, AIA, 18 (1922): 36; *Visionarios*, p. 489.
[19] Idem, AIA, 18 (1922): 37; *Visionarios*, p. 490.

the Minorites.[20] The language of *ecclesia carnalis* and of *renovatio* which occurred in the *Eternal Evangel* suggests that Olivi himself may have been influenced by this early Joachite tract.

The author employs the Herod typology which Olivi also derived from the thirteenth-century Joachimist literature[21] and which was to become part of the standard apparatus of Catalonian Joachimism: "A new Herod condemned evangelical poverty." [22] Herod is also linked with Caiaphas and the "boar from the woods" (*aper de Silva*), all of which were identified by Olivi with the mystic Antichrist. Finally, this work displays some post-Olivianist extravagances which were current among his Beguin followers, especially the veneration of Olivi himself, who is seen here as the angel of *Apocalypse* 10 (*illum angelum fortem*) descending from heaven, and to whom above all other doctors the "truth of Scripture and understanding of the Apocalypse has been revealed." [23]

Thus by 1320 the *Postilla* of Olivi had not only been disseminated in Catalonia and Majorca, but had been extensively incorporated into an important vernacular work. It seems likely that the author had some knowledge of a Joachimist work, as the title suggests. In any case, the tract is thoroughly Joachimist in tradition. It is particularly significant that the inquisitors saw it — and Olivi's work — in the tradition of the *Eternal Evangel.*

During this period Roussillon belonged to the crown of Majorca and in ecclesiastical affairs both came under the jurisdiction of a single inquisitor. In the second and third decades of the fourteenth century both regions were centres of continued opposition to John XXII and in both such beliefs as those found in the *De statibus* were being propagated. The chief circle was that of the Infant Philip of Majorca, the uncle of, and regent for the young king, James III, who gathered around him members of both the First and Third Orders. We know the names of the following: Fr. Marcelo, a Tertiary; Guillermo Morull, a Beguin and probably also a Tertiary; Berenguer Guillerm, squire of the Infant; Juan Ginés of Narbonne; a Catalan named Ledo; a Benedictine named Astorgio; most important of all, Fr. Guillermo Hospitaler, a Tertiary. Some of these are described as *familiares* of Philip, *Fratres de Tertia Regula,* who were "of the family" of Philip, and were "incapayronati." [24] This must refer to the distinctive cape of the Tertiaries and

---

[20] Idem, AIA, 18 (1922): 39; *Visionarios,* p. 492.
[21] See supra, pp. 6, 24.
[22] Pou y Martí, AIA, 18 (1922): 46; *Visionarios,* p. 498.
[23] Idem, AIA, 19 (1923): 27; *Visionarios,* p. 501.
[24] Idem, AIA, 12 (1919): 24; *Visionarios,* p. 124.

Beguins. This affiliation of his followers leads Pou y Martí — as it did Zurita — to conclude that Philip himself was a Tertiary.[25]

We also have some slight evidence that Philip of Majorca had a group of female disciples in Catalonia. In a letter which speaks of a certain Fr. Vitale, we are told that approximately a year after the death of Philip, the friar in question was converted to "the truth" by "gentlewomen of Catalonia," all of whom were "disciples of friar Philip and his company."[26] This reference to a circle of female adherents to Philip's tenets is especially interesting as evidence of a highly organized and militant female group, actively disseminating their beliefs. The description of Philip as "friar" constitutes further evidence that he was probably a Tertiary. Fr. Vitale, having been instructed in the true doctrine, was then sent to Fr. Bernard of Azona and his circle, who also held the same observance, and was admitted to his congregation. Fr. Bernard and the majority of his group died in the plague of 1348.[27]

Our knowledge of the beliefs of these groups is mainly derived from the second of the two documents under consideration: the process against Aimar de Mosset of Roussillon. During the regency of Philip (1324-1329) and afterwards there was considerable activity among evangelical groups in Roussillon, activities encouraged by Aimar himself under the patronage of Philip. In 1326, for example, the Franciscan Guillermo Negre was preaching against John XXII and his decretals on evangelical poverty in Villefranche de Conflent.[28] This and other incidents caused the Pope to write in 1330 to the bishop of Elne and the Inquisitor for the kingdom of Majorca directing them to start proceedings immediately against the heretics in their dominions.[29] In the same year the Pope wrote to the new king of Majorca, James, asking him to use his influence to assist the above-mentioned ecclesiastics.[30] The young monarch, who apparently had little love for his uncle Philip, willingly cooperated with John in these matters.

John XXII's campaign culminated in the proceedings against Aimar de Mosset.[31] Aimar took his name from the town near Prades which was under his seigneurie, but he also possessed other domains in Roussillon which Philip had given him in 1330. He enjoyed great prestige at the Majorcan court and had become a close personal friend and admirer of Philip. His confessor was Fr. Guillermo Hospitaler, a companion and spiritual adviser

---

[25] Idem, AIA, 12 (1919): 24; *Visionarios*, p. 124.
[26] Idem, AIA, 12 (1919): 52-53; *Visionarios*, p. 148.
[27] Idem, AIA, 12 (1919): 53; *Visionarios*, p. 149.
[28] Idem, AIA, 14 (1920): 18-19; *Visionarios*, p. 165.
[29] Idem, AIA, 14 (1920): 19; *Visionarios*, pp. 165-166.
[30] Idem, AIA, 14 (1920): 19-20; *Visionarios*, p. 166.
[31] Idem, AIA, 14 (1920): 26-51; *Visionarios*, pp. 166-193.

to Philip. It is, therefore, not surprising that Aimar became involved with Beguins in Roussillon.

After Philip's abdication in 1329 Aimar was unable to maintain his former influence and began to be suspect among inquisitors. In December 1332 he was ordered to account for his activities, and his interrogation began in the spring of 1333. He had already appeared voluntarily before the inquisitor of Perpignan, Fr. Juan Cerda, to denounce Fr. Hospitaler, but this manoeuvre had not been sufficient to satisfy the authorities and John XXII ordered proceedings to commence.

The interrogation[32] consisted of twenty-nine questions put to Aimar which provide us with evidence for the continued dissemination of Joachimist ideas in their revised, Olivianist form. The first question mentioned Fr. Hospitaler by name and asked if he "or any other Beguin of the Third Order" had said to Aimar that in the third *status* the precepts of the apostolic age and the sacraments would be superseded by the New Dispensation of the Holy Ghost.[33]

The inquisitor repeated most of the theories of Olivi on the role of the carnal Church in the time of Antichrist and its destruction before the advent of the great Antichrist. His questions on the decadence of the clergy suggest an Arnoldian tradition. In the inquisitor's summary of suspected views, those who professed the Rule of St. Francis in its entirety — possessing nothing in particular nor in common — were seen as the spiritual leaders of the third age. They were renamed "professors of the Rule of St. Francis and Brothers of Penitence or of the Third Rule"[34] and were expected to endure to the end of the world. The communal Franciscans and even those Fraticelli who held different views would perish along with all other orders. Some of these latter were named: Friars Preacher, because they had impugned the Brothers of Penitence and denied Christ's absolute poverty; Augustinians and Carmelites; Black and White Monks and Canons Regular. All these must perish, as well as all kings, princes and any who had consented to the persecution of the Beguins.[35] Such detailed condemnations are found both in the works of Roquetaillade, to whom we shall turn shortly, and in the *Breviloquium*.

Both the ecclesiastical and secular hierarchies were to be destroyed by the Saracen kings in a climactic battle on the plain of Salses near Elne. There

---

[32] The 29 questions are translated into Spanish by Pou y Marti, AIA, 14 (1920): 31-39; *Visionarios*, pp. 175-183. Subsequent references are to this version.

[33] Pou y Marti, AIA, 14 (1920): 31; *Visionarios*, pp. 175-176. The *Eternal Evangel* is not mentioned, but there is contained here the suggestion of a new dispensation to supersede that of the present.

[34] Pou y Marti, AIA, 14 (1920): 32-33; *Visionarios*, p. 177 (no. 8).

[35] Idem, AIA, 14 (1920): 32-33; *Visionarios*, p. 177.

would be so much blood that horses would be covered to the saddle girth. Afterwards, owing to lack of men, women would share husbands and even in their concupiscence embrace trees. But once the renovation had taken place, a time of great purity would ensue. A young woman would be able to travel from Rome to Santiago without being molested. This epoch would last for one hundred years, after which, little by little, corruption would return and the earth would eventually be once more transformed into Babylon. As in the *Breviloquium*, God would finally be constrained to come in judgement and destroy the sinful world.

The material of question thirteen,[36] based on Olivi and embodying the key Beguin concept of the exalted role of St. Francis in the third age, is also contained in the *Breviloquium*. Before St. Francis began to live by his Rule — i.e. in Olivi's fifth age — the life of Christ and the Apostles had been virtually extinguished in the Church, since all its members had possessions in particular or in common. In pressing upon his followers the vow of absolute poverty Francis had become the renovator of the life of Christ and the most perfect of all the saints after the Apostles. The Spirituals who had died in Marseilles were still venerated as true martyrs, as were all those who died for the cause of evangelical poverty. Olivi was venerated as a saint and was believed to be the angel of *Apocalypse* 10. Among all the doctors of the Church he saw most accurately the corruption of the Church.[37] Furthermore, Olivi's books, and especially the *Postilla*, were held as true to the Catholic faith, containing no errors.[38] Finally, Olivi's sepulchre at Narbonne was considered holy, the object of pilgrimage and the focus of a festival on the anniversary of his death.[39]

John xxii was held to be the mystic Antichrist, precursor of the great Antichrist and his principal champion, especially since he had begun to persecute the Beguins. John xxii was to be to the great Antichrist as John the Baptist had been to Christ.[40] Many Beguins took Olivi's commentary to indicate that the great Antichrist would appear during the lifetime of the mystic Antichrist. Among candidates for the former were Philip of Majorca, because he was an apostate from the Friars Preacher, and Angelo da Clareno, because he had left the Franciscan Order. They believed that Olivi had meant the great Antichrist to be an apostate from his Order. Some thought that the lesser Antichrist was Frederick of Sicily, but the historical calculation remained sketchy.

[36] Idem, AIA, 14 (1920): 34; *Visionarios*, p. 178.
[37] Idem, AIA, 14 (1920): 37; *Visionarios*, p. 181 (no. 25).
[38] Idem, AIA, 14 (1920): 37-38 (no. 26); *Visionarios*, pp. 181-182.
[39] Idem, AIA, 14 (1920): 38; *Visionarios*, p. 182 (no. 27).
[40] Idem, AIA, 14 (1920): 38; *Visionarios*, p. 182 (no. 28).

This account of the beliefs with which Aimar was taxed is gleaned entirely from the 29 questions put by the inquisitor. Aimar himself made no doctrinal statements but simply answered "no" to questions which were put to him in this form: had he heard, believed or said any of the following. Aimar continued to play an important role in the court of James III until he transferred his allegiance to Peter IV of Aragon in 1343 and entered the latter's Royal Council. He is an important figure in Peter's Catalan *Crònica.*[41]

Thus these two documents — the *De statibus* and the *Process* — testify to the continuing veneration of Olivi, the increasing isolation and persecution of the Beguins, their own view of the total corruption of the Church, and the Joachimist role in which they cast themselves as the only survivors at the imminent end of redemptive history.

[41] See the English translation with notes by Mary and Jocelyn Hillgarth, PIMS (Toronto, 1980).

6

Jean de Roquetaillade and His Influence
in Aragon and Catalonia

The death of John XXII necessitated another revision of the apocalyptic scheme of Last Things. The more extreme beliefs about his role as mystic Antichrist, co-existent with the great Antichrist, had not been realised; no obvious candidate for the latter had yet appeared. Although John's persecutions had left an indelible mark, so that in many different groups of Fraticelli and Beguins he continued to be cast for a sinister role in the final drama,[1] clearly this part no longer belonged to the last act. John still remained the mystic Antichrist for many, but the re-evaluation of contemporary history took the form of a renewed emphasis on secular events. This chimed with the growing political strife in western Europe. Since apocalypse thrives upon the topical, it was necessary to read the signs of the times anew in the mid-fourteenth century.

The person most influential in this shift of emphasis was Jean de Roquetaillade (or Rupescissa), who was born at Marcolès near Aurillac and entered the Minorite Order in 1322.[2] Although he was the heir to the Spiritual Franciscan tradition, his prophetic utterances were sufficiently secular to give him great popularity in the later fourteenth century with the general public. Amongst these was Froissart, who fastened on Roquetaillade's apparent prediction of the Hundred Years' War. Froissart says that Roquetaillade was imprisoned by Innocent VI in the castle of Bagnols

---

[1] See Reeves, *Influence*, pp. 212-215.

[2] The most important studies are those of Jeanne Bignami-Odier in her book *Études sur Jean de Roquetaillade* (Paris, 1952), which she has now revised in "Jean de Roquetaillade (de Rupescissa), Théologien, Polémiste, Alchimiste," *Histoire Littéraire de la France*, Tom. 41 (Paris, 1981), pp. 75-284. Footnote references to these two versions are given below as R and HL. See also Pou y Marti, *Visionarios*, pp. 289-307.

because of the great marvels which he described, which would fall principally upon the prelates and presidents of the holy Church, on account of their excesses and the overweening pride which they exhibited; and also upon the kingdom of France and upon the great Christian lords, on account of their oppression of the common people.[3]

This two-fold emphasis is indeed characteristic of Roquetaillade's work and is representative of the new balance between ecclesiastical and secular prophecy in this age.

Roquetaillade's contribution to the history of Joachimism may be divided into four themes: first, the identification of Antichrist by the analysis of contemporary political events, especially the growing power of Aragon; secondly, the prediction of a schism within the Church; thirdly, the triumph of the Franciscan remnant and the Angelic Pope, in partnership with the French crown; fourthly, the ordering and the timing of the Last Things.

Frederick II had been the most promising candidate for Antichrist among the early Joachites and his death in 1250, with expectations unfulfilled, had been a rude shock to them. As we have seen,[4] in a group of pseudo-Joachimist prophecies between 1250 and c. 1268 the earlier programme had been revised and attention had been focused anew on a prince from the seed of Frederick, and finally on the vague and portentous Third Frederick, as the coming Antichrist. Because of its Hohenstaufen connections Sicily held, in all these earlier writings, a special prophetic place. When the Hohenstaufen line was extinguished there, the focus of prophetic significance passed to the House of Aragon, since Peter II had married Constance, daughter of Manfred. With the establishment of Peter's son Frederick in Sicily, the seed of the Hohenstaufen was held to have returned. Thus Sicily again occupied a key prophetic position. Olivi had looked for crucial events there and some of his Beguin followers had singled out Frederick of Sicily as their candidate for Antichrist.[5]

Roquetaillade inherited this political tradition from the pseudo-Joachimist writings. Among them he seized particularly on the *Oraculum Cyrilli*, to which he wrote a commentary. As we have seen,[6] the emphasis had been shifted somewhat in this work from secular to religious prophecy, but there were still sufficient enigmatic political pronouncements for Roquetaillade's purpose and he exploited these as well as the religious prophecies to the full. The historical events of the period between the Emperor Frederick II and the

---

[3] Ed. Jean Buchon, *Les Chroniques de Sire Jean Froissart* (Paris, 1835), 1: 428.
[4] Supra, pp. 8-11.
[5] Supra, p. 73.
[6] Supra, pp. 13-14.

time of Antichrist are dealt with in some detail in the commentary on Cyril.[7] After summarizing the fortunes of the Empire up to Frederick II, Roquetaillade expounds the struggle between Frederick and Innocent IV and the ensuing battles against Manfred and Conradin as earlier acts in the cosmic conflict. The prophetic significance of Sicily is part of the tradition he has inherited, and he incorporates it into his programme for the future. Thus his first candidate for Antichrist was Louis of Sicily, son of Frederick, who inherited the Hohenstaufen role through the House of Aragon.[8] Roquetaillade maintains in both the *Commentum Beati Cyrilli* (c. 1348) and in the *Liber Secretorum Eventorum* (1349) that Louis was to be the Antichrist, but in the *Liber Ostensor* — Louis having died at the age of fifteen — he nominates his successor, Frederick IV (or II) (1355-1377).[9]

We have seen that Joachim expected many manifestations of Antichrist and, in particular, had envisaged Antichrist both in the form of one great political tyrant, the seventh head of the Dragon, and as a diabolical partnership between the Beast from the Land and the Beast from the Sea.[10] Under the latter figure he expected a false religious leader and a political power, usually seen as the infidel. The thirteenth-century Joachites had naturally turned Frederick II into the seventh, later the sixth, head of the Dragon. Olivi had fastened on the second figure, developing the concept of the two Antichrists, the mystic and great, of which the first would be the pseudo-pope and the second the political scourge. Roquetaillade brings the two figures together by making the mystic Antichrist the seventh head of the Dragon (following Frederick II as the sixth), and the Great Antichrist the eighth head.[11] In so doing he changes the mystic Antichrist from a religious into a political figure. He casts the Emperor Louis of Bavaria for this part rather than adopting the previous candidate, John XXII.[12] This revision reflects both previous hesitations as to whether John did fulfill this role and the need to bring the programme up-to-date. As Roquetaillade interpreted the *Postilla* of Olivi, the reign of the mystic Antichrist, the precursor of the great Antichrist, would extend through that of three popes, beginning with John XXII.[13] In this capacity Louis of Bavaria would persecute the Church and be followed by

---

[7] *Commentum super prophetiam Cyrilli*, Paris, Bibliothèque Nationale, MS Lat. 2599, fols. 12v-16r. See also Bignami-Odier, R, pp. 53-109; HL, pp. 106-117.

[8] *Liber Secretorum Eventorum*, Paris, Bibliothèque Nationale, MS Lat. 3598, fol. 2v. See also Bignami-Odier, R, pp. 113-129; HL, pp. 121-133.

[9] See Bignami-Odier, R, pp. 140-156; HL, pp. 142-147.

[10] Supra, p. 4.

[11] *Com. Cyrilli*, fols. 54v-56r.

[12] Ibid., fol. 54v.

[13] Ibid., fol. 56r.

many false prelates and religious as well as by Peter IV of Aragon. He is identified not only with the Beast from the land but also with the *altera aquila* of the Erythrean Sibyl.[14] The great Antichrist, the last head of the Dragon, must come from Sicily and is, therefore, Frederick IV. He is also the Beast from the sea and the *leo fortissimus ab occidente* of the Erythrean Sibyl.[15]

Although the race of Frederick of Hohenstaufen is clearly the embodiment of evil for Roquetaillade as the diabolical root from which the great Antichrist must spring, his attitude towards Aragon and its king, Peter IV, is ambivalent. Aragon is inextricably bound up with the Hohenstaufen through the marriage of Manfred's daughter, Constance, to Peter II. Yet Roquetaillade obviously has a special interest in and regard for the Spanish kingdom. Mme. Bignami-Odier summarizes his attitude towards the House of Aragon as "more well-disposed than ill-disposed."[16] No doubt the importance he attributed to Catalonia and Sicily was the main reason for Roquetaillade's popularity in these parts. There were Catalan translations of his writings[17] and we shall trace his influence, not only in the *Breviloquium*, but also in the work of the Infant Peter and Fr. Eiximenis.[18]

The expectation of a false pope went back through Olivi to Joachim himself. But it was from the *Oraculum Cyrilli* that Roquetaillade took the prophecy of a great schism, prefigured in the story of Rehoboam and Jeroboam and caused by the election of two popes, one canonical, the other schismatical.[19] This would be greater than any previous schism because the false pope would be supported by Antichrist (*partem antipape sustinebit*), who, as the Beast ascending from land, would force the entire Empire to obey the antipope.[20] Most churchmen would follow the antipope, who would seduce the cardinals and persecute the followers of the true pope. The faithful would be misled and the Church attacked by Jews, Saracens, Turks, Tartars, schismatics and heretics. Referring to Joachim, Roquetaillade expected the Beast from the land (the antipope) to adore the Beast from the sea (Antichrist). The antipope was to bear the mark of Antichrist on his brow, as in *Apocalypse* 13.[21] In the meantime the true pope will suffer persecution and

---

[14] Ibid., fol. 58r.

[15] *Lib. Sec. Event.*, fol. 15r.

[16] Bignami-Odier, R, p. 206; HL, p. 201.

[17] R, pp. 241, 248; HL, pp. 228, 234. Bignami-Odier lists a Catalan translation of the *Lib. Sec. Event.*, MS Carpentras, Bibliothèque Inguimbertine, 336, fols. 1-54v, and of *Vade Mecum*, ibid., fols. 55r-75r. See also her discussion of Roquetaillade's influence in Spain, R, pp. 209-213; HL, pp. 202-206.

[18] Infra, pp. 83, 86-87.

[19] *Com. Cyrilli*, fol. 110v.

[20] Ibid.

[21] Ibid., fol. 111v.

go into hiding in France. His integrity will be tried as gold in the furnace, as the cardinals turn against him and elect a false pope.[22]

Following the Cyril tradition, Roquetaillade castigates all the orders of the Church as hypocritical (*totus status putridus ypocritarum*).[23] The prelates are described as "fornicators," and simony is repeatedly attacked.[24] All will be destroyed: "No hypocrite shall remain." [25] The religious orders fall especially under his condemnation; in particular, the Friars Preacher, Augustinians, Carmelites, Templars and Hospitallers are marked for extermination: "Not one shall remain." [26] His attitude towards his own order is typical of the Beguin view. He castigates the hypocrites among the Franciscans and sees Michael of Cesena as the type of a false minister-general, who will champion the Antichrist when he appears.[27] All this congregation, whose head is the pseudo-pope, is that foul Whore of Babylon, of which John speaks in *Apocalypse* 17.[28] But their destruction by the Saracens is at hand.

At this point the doctrine of the saving remnant — so dear to extreme Joachites — appears in dramatic form. The whole Franciscan Order is due for destruction with the rest except for a small portion of it — the *Fratres de Penitentia.* Roquetaillade finds the destruction of all but a remnant typified in the flight of the Israelites from Egypt. Just as Joshua and Caleb alone saw the Promised Land — the rest having all been destroyed for their sins — so only a few will survive the destruction to come.[29] This Old Testament symbolism is matched by the New Testament typology of the flight of the Holy Family — a typology already used in an interesting way in the *Super Esaiam*[30] and to be used again in the *Breviloquium.*[31] Those who hold to the true faith will be forced to flee from the carnal Church and hide in grottos. The remnants of these true Franciscans will eventually return, when the wordly edifices of the false Franciscans have become ruins, the habitation of serpents.[32]

---

[22] Verus papa effundetur ut in fornace aurum ut fiat ymago Christi vicarii per electionem veram qui ut aurum erit plenus caritate et fide probatus in fornace consistorii per cardinales, et argentum, scilicet antipapa, per malos cardinales electus heretice *ut tibi fundat* electum. (*Com. Cyrilli*, fol. 110v).

[23] Ibid., fol. 126.

[24] Ibid., fol. 36v. The phrase is "fornicantes cum sponse [? sponte] virginibus."

[25] Ibid., fol. 126r.

[26] Ibid., fol. 132v.

[27] Ibid., fol. 124r.

[28] Ibid., fol. 143v.

[29] Ibid., fol. 138r.

[30] *Super Esaiam*, fol. 14r.

[31] Infra, p. 121.

[32] Reliqui ... veri filii sancti patris Francisci ... multiplicentur et impleantur totum mundum ... Erunt fratres et superba edificia que fratres contra intentionem sancti Francisci usque ad

The agents of the *renovatio ecclesie* now appear in full force. From the *Oraculum Cyrilli* Roquetaillade derived the expectation of an angelic pope, symbolised in the miraculous bear (*ursus mirabilis*).[33] Ecclesiastically, his allies are the Franciscan remnant who return in triumph when the false religious are destroyed. They are the true seed with which the world will now be sown and which will spring up and multiply.[34] Politically, his staunch champion is the King of France. He alone supports the true pope during the schism and the rule of the great Antichrist. He will restore the Angelic Pope at the end of the tribulation.[35] Here Roquetaillade seizes upon and develops a partnership of Angelic Pope and French monarchy which had already been hinted at in the *Liber de Flore*[36] and which was to become the distinctive mark of a later "French" Joachimism.[37] Together they will carry out a programme of political and religious transformation which will bring the whole world into one flock under one shepherd.

Although his system varies in some of its particulars from work to work and is sometimes self-contradictory in detail, Roquetaillade's scheme for the Last Times follows a consistent general pattern based on an extended version of the *renovatio ecclesie*. The mystic Antichrist was Louis of Bavaria, the precursor of the great Antichrist due to appear in 1365 or 1366.[38] The coming of the great Antichrist would coincide with the great schism in the Church between the anti-pope and the Angelic Pope.[39] The schism would last for only a short period, perhaps only for one and one-half years, during which time Antichrist would play a useful role in his persecution of the corrupt clergy.[40] These times would be marked by famine, pestilence and war.[41] Antichrist would die near Rome in 1370, after a series of battles in which he would ultimately be defeated by the Angelic Pope with the aid of the French king.[42] There would follow a period of wars from 1370 to 1415. Then all Jews and heretics would be converted and the two prophets of the

---

nubes hodie construxerunt in perpetuam memoriam abhominationes malorum dabuntur in drachones deserti. Et loca ipsa aut destruentur ut ad grandem humilitatem reducantur aut remanebunt perpetuo desolata, et ibi ... serpentes excrescent. (*Com. Cyrilli*, fols. 133v-134r). See also the *Brev.*, infra, p. 241.

[33] Supra, p. 13.
[34] *Com. Cyrilli*, fols. 133v-134r.
[35] Bignami-Odier, R, pp. 102-103; HL, p. 117.
[36] Supra, p. 14.
[37] Reeves, *Influence*, pp. 326, 355, 375.
[38] *Com. Cyrilli*, fols. 54v-55v; Bignami-Odier, R, p. 71; HL, p. 114.
[39] *Lib. Sec. Event.*, fol. 7r-v; Bignami-Odier, R, p. 119; HL, p. 125.
[40] Bignami-Odier, R, pp. 119-121; HL, pp. 125-128.
[41] Idem, R, p. 118; HL, p. 125.
[42] Idem, R, pp. 103, 123-125.

Apocalypse would announce a millennium of peace. The power of the empire would be transferred to Jerusalem and the Franciscan remnant would convert the whole world to Christ.[43] But one thousand years after the death of Antichrist the Church would degenerate again and heretics appear. These signs would herald the onslaught of Gog and Magog, the loosing of Satan for his last rule and the final appearance of Christ in Judgement.[44]

Roquetaillade is not quoted directly by the author of the *Breviloquium*, but in the general shape of its predictions for the approaching crisis, as well as in some of its details, the *Breviloquium* shows probable direct influence. It may have been that our author derived ideas from those works of Roquetaillade which were circulating in Catalan.[45] Whatever the manner of derivation, the author of the *Breviloquium* shares Roquetaillade's ideas on the coming struggle between pope and antipope and the consequent schism; the appearance of the great Antichrist yoked with the world-emperor as the sixth and seventh heads of the dragon; the survival of the evangelical remnant; the importance of the house of Aragon and the kingdom of Sicily, and the war between England and France; the dates for the immediate crisis; and the events which are to culminate in the appearance of Gog and Magog at the end of history.[46] However, our author incorporated all the above events into his own original reading of events, and in his political attitude was anti-French.

Further evidence of Roquetaillade's influence in Aragon and Catalonia is found in the writings of two important people, the Infant Peter of Aragon, writing approximately twenty years after the author of the *Breviloquium*, and Fr. Francesc Eiximenis, who was writing at the turn of the fifteenth century. Both were Franciscans and both were indebted to Roquetaillade, but their contrasting styles of prophetic utterance represent two extremes: on the one hand, the new political topicality, and on the other, a relatively cautious approach to prophecy through a total view of history. As we shall see later, the author of the *Breviloquium* struck the most successful balance between topicality and world history in fourteenth-century prophecy.

The Infant[47] gained prominence as a seer in 1365 with the sensational announcement that God had instructed him to go to Avignon to inform Urban v that he should move his residence to Rome in order to remedy the

---

[43] Idem, R, p. 125; HL, p. 130.
[44] Idem, R, p. 126; HL, p. 131.
[45] Supra, note 17.
[46] See the *Brev.*, Dists. 4, 9, 13.
[47] On the Infant Peter, see Pou y Marti, AIA, 22 (1924): 281-326; 23 (1925): 10-58; *Visionarios*, pp. 308-396.

grave ills of the Church. If Urban did not obey, the Infant was to announce the Pope's death.[48] The Infant's reputation as a respected churchman and member of the powerful House of Aragon probably explains the sympathetic response of the Curia. He was cordially received in Avignon, and his prophecy studied and endorsed. In 1367 Urban went to Rome.

This astonishing success gave great weight to the Infant's later prophecies, among them a proposal for war against the Mohammedans, presented to him by God, according to the Infant, as a fulfilment of the *De Exitu Israel* figure.[49] But even the Infant's reputation could not survive unscathed when in 1379 he plunged into the controversy of the Schism by declaring for Urban VI against Clement VII. The King of Aragon, Peter IV, had maintained a strict neutrality in the matter, no doubt as a matter of political expedience, and his uncle's support of Urban VI probably embarrassed him. He also wanted to find out whether the Infant was correct, and so appointed a group of divines from various orders to study his uncle's prophecies and report to him on their integrity. The group spoke to the Infant in his cell at San Francisco in Barcelona, and received from him all his prophecies. Their opinions of his work differed, and they submitted, as groups and as individuals, conflicting appraisals to Peter IV, who apparently took no further action on the matter.

It is clear, however — and it must also have been clear to Peter IV — that the members of the examining board voted according to their allegiances to Rome or Avignon, and wished to use the king's uncle as a pawn in the Urban-Clement struggle. The arguments on both sides rested on the legitimacy of the claims made by each pope. Pedro de Ribés and Tomás Alsina argued that the Infant's visions were false because they attacked Clement VII, who, they said, "truly presides over the entire Church of God.";[50] Bernard Broll concluded that because Urban VI had been elected in concord (*concorditer*) and canonically through the agency of the Holy Spirit (*per viam Sancti Spiritus*), the Infant's revelations were true.[51]

Since ecclesiastical politics were uppermost in the mind of the Infant in 1365 and 1379, and certainly in the minds of his examiners, it is little wonder that there is almost no mention of other aspects of the Infant's prophecy. There is only one reference to his interest in the *renovatio ecclesie*, and that takes the form of a rhetorical question in Broll's *apologia*: "Who in his right mind can say that the reformation of prelates of the sacred Roman Church, if they fall away, is not a saintly event, influenced by the Holy Spirit

---

[48] Idem, AIA, 23 (1925): 30; *Visionarios*, p. 373.
[49] Idem, AIA, 23 (1925): 37; *Visionarios*, pp. 373-374.
[50] Idem, AIA, 23 (1925): 46; *Visionarios*, p. 383.
[51] Idem, AIA, 23 (1925): 50; *Visionarios*, p. 387.

and occurring specifically by such means?"[52] For a view of the Infant's interpretation of this renovation and of the Last Times, we must turn to one of his prophecies written in Catalan in 1377, the *Exposició de la visió damunt dita*.[53] This consists of a commentary on a vision written in 1297 by a Cistercian, and reveals again the Infant's interest in contemporary politics, as well as the nature of his debt to Joachimism.

The Infant's sketchy and somewhat confused account in the *Exposició* of the crucial years about to commence is patterned in general after Roquetaillade, although the central historical personage seems to be the Infant's own choice. That person is Henry of Castile, identified as Saturn in an astrological passage, and later more conventionally as the *bestia occidental*, who will conquer the whole of Spain and then turn his might against the Mohammedans. Within fifteen years there will be "one God and one faith"; Henry will have taken ship to the Holy Land to rededicate Jerusalem to God, and to make the city safe for Christians. Then will follow fifteen years of *gran tranquilitat*, during which time, however, Antichrist, the *leon oriental*, will begin to subvert men. There is implied here Roquetaillade's pattern of a decline from the golden age into a final period of degeneration, but the Infant is not explicit about this. He differs from Roquetaillade on the role of the French, and predicts misfortune for them.

The Infant speaks of the *renovatio ecclesie* only briefly, first to deliver a specific indictment of Gascons and Germans.[54] Then, following the manuscript he has at hand, he states that there will be one God and one faith, but the "mendicant orders and many other sects ... will deteriorate and come to nothing."[55] The Infant is not specific in noting a time sequence for this decline: "When it is to occur," he concludes, "only God knows."[56]

The Infant cites several sources during the course of the tract, usually to support a specific point. His authorities for the role of Henry in defeating the Mohammedans are the prophecies of Merlin, the Abbot Joachim, Johannes de Rupescissa, the tract *Ve mundo in centum annis*, and the Hermit of Lemposa.[57] Roquetaillade and works ascribed to Joachim are the Infant's main sources. He specifically mentions Roquetaillade's *Liber conspectorum*

---

[52] Idem, AIA, 23 (1925): 47-48; *Visionarios*, p. 384. Broll is the only writer to offer any detailed subsidiary evidence which is not politically oriented. The *reformatio prelatorum* cannot be said to be entirely non-political, but Broll is also concerned with such abstract theological issues as the nature of free will.

[53] Idem, AIA, 23 (1925): 33-36; *Visionarios*, pp. 370-373.

[54] Idem, AIA, 23 (1925): 34-35; *Visionarios*, p. 371.

[55] Idem, AIA, 23 (1925): 35; *Visionarios*, p. 371.

[56] Idem, AIA, 23 (1925): 35; *Visionarios*, p. 371.

[57] Idem, AIA, 23 (1925): 34; *Visionarios*, pp. 370-371.

secretorum archanorum in visu Dei, and concludes his work with a quotation from the pseudo-Joachimist *Super Hieremiam*. The formal apparatus of Joachim is absent from the work, and suggests that, like Roquetaillade, the Infant was not familiar with the Abbot's authentic canon.[58] He cites a work which he ascribes to Joachim in corroboration of his prediction in the *Exposició* that Henry's work will culminate within fifteen years in "one God and one faith." According to the Infant, Joachim speaks of the conquest of the infidels in 1390 by the "Spanish lion," a discrepancy in dating of only three years, he says, between Joachim and the *Exposició*.[59] He notes further that such a conquest was preached in the *Eternal Evangel*.[60] The infant also uses Joachim as a parallel source in the identification of the *bestia occidental* with Henry and the *leon oriental* with Antichrist.[61] Finally, he uses the *Super Hieremiam* to support his prediction of misfortune for France.

It can readily be seen from the foregoing examples that the Infant's brand of apocalypticism does not find its fundamental roots in the Joachimist redemptive history. Aspects of that tradition — the general scheme of Last Things, the *renovatio ecclesie* — were certainly important in shaping his view of the course of human events, and in this respect the Infant can be called a Joachimist, but his Joachimism is an accoutrement to what was primarily a process of direct revelation. The Infant believed that God spoke to him directly, not simply through the Scriptures, as his most important pronouncements demonstrate. Further, he saw himself as a messenger of God empowered to deliver spectacular yet very simple prescriptions for setting aright the political and ecclesiastical problems of his time. He was concerned almost exclusively with events of the present and near future; even in his Joachimist *Exposició* he demonstrated no interest in the broader context of history, and little interest in the events which were to bring the downfall of the *gran tranquilitat* he predicted. His mind seems very much like that of Roquetaillade: a visionary zealot passionately interested in the issues of his

[58] There is a three-fold pattern in the *Exposició*, but it is a subordinate figural pattern, not in the classical Joachimist manner. See Pou y Martí, AIA, 23 (1925): 35-36; *Visionarios*, p. 372.

[59] Idem, AIA, 23 (1925): 34; *Visionarios*, p. 371. The Infant introduces another subsidiary or complementary pattern of three sevens which ties into the pattern given in note 58: *Spanya, nodrica de la malyada secta de Mafomet, per batalles d uns ab altres será destruida, car los regnes de aquella se levarán uns contra altres e quan lo pollí jumental dia del Rey Pere de Castella, que fo, aurá tres VII anys, que fan XXI anys* (Idem, AIA, 23 (1925): 35; *Visionarios*, pp. 371-372). This calculation is taken directly from Roquetaillade, who had prophesied that in 1366 a great flagellation would begin; in the tenth year, according to the Infant, a *humiliació* would begin.

[60] Pou y Martí, AIA, 23 (1925): 34; *Visionarios*, p. 371.

[61] Idem, AIA, 23 (1925): 35; *Visionarios*, p. 371.

day, who amasses in eclectic and disorganized fashion whatever material supports the revelation which he believes has been vouchsafed to him.

In contrast to the florid strokes of the Infant are the more formal and subdued compositions of Fr. Francesc Eiximenis.[62] Eiximenis was the leading Catalonian churchman of his time, whose predilection for the Joachimist view of history is evidence in itself for the strong appeal such ideas continued to have in Catalonia. In every other respect, Eiximenis was an orthodox and highly esteemed Franciscan. His Joachimism is relatively cautious, as one might expect. He is more interested in issues than personalities, he makes no sensational revelations or charges, and he works always within the classical Joachimist patterns of three *status* and seven *etates*.

Eiximenis was familiar with a number of apocalyptic works, among them the pseudo-Joachimist *Oraculum Cyrilli* and probably the prophecies of Merlin and the Sibyls. His most important sources, however, were Arnold of Vilanova and Jean de Roquetaillade. He was especially impressed by Arnold as an exemplar of austerity and absolute poverty: "He travelled always on a donkey, did not possess a house, and belonged to the Third Order of St. Francis."[63] Eiximenis's denunciation of the evils of the Church is strongly Arnoldian in tone. His apocalypticism is expressed mainly in two works, the Latin *Apparatus de triplici statu mundi*, of unknown date, and the *Vida de Jesuchrist*, written in Catalan shortly before 1404. In the *Apparatus* he works from a framework of the three *status*; in the *Vida* from a version of the seven ages of the Church.

The *Apparatus* divides the history of the world into three ages in the traditional Joachimist manner: the first from Adam to Christ, the second to the reign of Antichrist and the renovation of the Church, the third from the death of Antichrist to the end of the world. These are, of course, assigned to the Father, Son and Holy Spirit. There is a link with the *Breviloquium* in the sequence of three *operationes*: in the first God demonstrated His power, in the second His wisdom, in the third His love.[64] We only possess one

---

[62] On Eiximenis, see Pou y Martí, AIA, 23 (1925): 349-369; *Visionarios*, pp. 397-415; P. Andrés Ivars, "El Escritor Fr. Francisco Eiximénéz en Valencia," AIA, 15 (1921): 76-104; 19 (1923): 359-398; 20 (1923): 210-248; 24 (1925): 325-382; 25 (1925): 5-48, 289-333; Atanasio López, "Apparatus de triplici statu mundi," *Revista de Estudios Franciscanos*, 3 (1901): 21-24; AIA, 2 (1901): 229-240; Pere Bohigas (Balaguer), "Prediccions i profecies en les obres de Fra Francesc Eiximenis," *Franciscalia* (Barcelona, 1928): 23-38; idem, "Profecies catalanes dels segles XIV i XV, Assaig bibliografic," *Butlletí de la Biblioteca de Catalunya*, 6 (1920-1922): 24-47; Jocelyn Hillgarth, *The Spanish Kingdoms, 1250-1516* (Oxford, 1978), 2: 641, 654; Josep Perarnau, "Bibliografia Teológica Catalana," AST, 45 (1972): 121-235.

[63] Pou y Martí, AIA, 23 (1925): 363; *Visionarios*, p. 409, quoting from *Lo Crestià*, 1.68.

[64] Pou y Martí, AIA, 23 (1925): 363; *Visionarios*, p. 409. Since this sequence occurs otherwise, so far as we know, only in the *Breviloquium*, its use by Eiximenis suggests that he knew this work, cf. infra, pp. 104-105.

manuscript of the *Apparatus*, but this, significantly, was copied in 1473 in Catalonia.[65] Taken in conjunction with the fact that the two dated manuscripts of the *Breviloquium* belong to 1455 and 1488,[66] this demonstrates the continuing interest in prophecy in the fifteenth century.

The scheme of the *Vida* is that of the seven ages of the Church, which are distinguished as those of the primitive Church, of the martyrs, of the doctors, of the time of laity, of the evangelical life, of the opening of the sixth seal, and of the final kingdom. Here Eiximenis follows Olivianist tradition and hence sees the fifth age as one of decay.[67] The clergy during this age was given to avarice, ambition and pride, while princes became negligent of the people's welfare. At the end of the fifth age, c. 800 or 900 AD, Christ intervened for men, sending leaders who began to reform the Church.[68]

The first of these leaders was St. Benedict, who founded the Black Monks; the second, St. Bernard, founder of the White Monks; the third, St. Dominic, founder of the *Praedicatores*. The fourth and greatest was St. Francis, "standard-bearer of Christ," and hailed by St. John in *Apocalypse* 19.7.[69] He instituted the evangelical life and founded his three orders against the three great sins of the world. In the sixth age, however, spiritual decay had again set in and the present state was, if anything, worse than that of the fifth age. Now, all honesty among religious men, all virtue and justice in Christian princes, and all good among the Christian populace, has been destroyed, so that Christians, in their innumerable crimes, seem rather to turn to madness and vanity, at the instigation of the devil, than to the wisdom of Christ.[70] Eiximenis concludes that within a short time, perhaps in the present centenary, there will occur a tribulation for all Christendom second only to that of the flames of the Last Judgement.[71]

In both the *Apparatus* and the *Vida* Eiximenis follows Roquetaillade on the crucial events of the sixth age.[72] The Franciscan Order will be split into three parts, two of which will fall into cupidity while the third, the spiritual branch, will flee to the mountains. Monasteries, cities and religions will be destroyed and God will show forth many signs in the sky. During this time

---

[65] López, REF, 3 (1901): 23.
[66] See infra, p. 151.
[67] Pou y Martí, AIA, 23 (1925): 364; *Visionarios*, p. 410.
[68] Idem, AIA, 23 (1925): 364; *Visionarios*, p. 410.
[69] Idem, AIA, 23 (1925): 364-365; *Visionarios*, p. 411.
[70] López, REF, 3 (1901): 22.
[71] Idem, REF, 3 (1901): 22; Pou y Martí, AIA, 23 (1925): 365; *Visionarios*, p. 412.
[72] López, REF, 3 (1901): 22-23; Pou y Martí, AIA, 23 (1925): 366-367; *Visionarios*, pp. 412-413. Bignami-Odiers point out that Eiximenis appears to be the first to translate Rupescissa as Rochatallada, and that he, like other Catalan authors, may have thought he was of Catalan origin (R, p. 26; HL, p. 84).

there will arise a *princeps mundi*, a fraudulent and fierce ruler, pretending piety and humility, but inwardly rapacious. He will be mighty on the sea and will win naval battles, conquer islands, subjugate many nations and humiliate many kings. He will force his subjects to worship him as God and instigate persecution against the Church. After he has conquered the Christian kingdoms he will subjugate the Holy Land. He will be thought to be Antichrist because of the persecution he will bring upon the carnal Church, but Eiximenis does not believe he will be the true Antichrist, who must come at the end of the world. He may, however, be the mystic Antichrist.

The *Vida* gives a description of the Schism, which by the time of Eiximenis had become a reality. It also follows Roquetaillade and cites sources similar to those of the Infant in describing the two figures of the final age, the World Emperor and the Angelic Pope. These two will fulfill the work of St. Francis and St. Dominic. The opening of the sixth seal, Eiximenis writes,

> occurred when St. Francis and St. Dominic came to preach to the world, and will last until the above-mentioned renovation of the Holy Church has been completed. Joachim, Cyril, and many others have spoken at length on this matter, as well as the Hermit of La Lemposa, and Johannes of Rupescissa of the order of Friars Minor.[73]

Eiximenis is far more cautious and non-committal than the Infant — and, indeed, more so than Roquetaillade — in the matter of dates and personalities, because, he says in *Apparatus de triplici statu mundi*, he has seen so many predictions proved wrong (*nam propter hoc vidi multos defecisse que determinate loquebantur de temporibus futuris ponentes annorum Kalendarium determinatum*).[74] He is concerned rather to elucidate the Holy Scriptures and books written about crucial passages, as Arnold had instructed his followers to do.[75] He is diffident about identifying the universal monarch, claiming that he has no wish to follow his predecessors in determining the lineage and name of this ruler.[76] He seems, however, to have been interested in the house of Aragon, for elsewhere he had stated that from that house "it is prophesied that there shall come a world monarch."[77] In another work, *Lo Crestià*, he reflects Roquetaillade's interest in France; at the conclusion of the fourteenth century only France will remain untouched in the general destruction of

[73] Pou y Martí, AIA, 23 (1925): 366; *Visionarios*, p. 413.

[74] Idem, AIA, 23 (1925): 367; *Visionarios*, p. 413.

[75] See supra p. 33.

[76] Pou y Martí is suspicious of this professed indifference, see AIA, 23 (1925): 367; *Visionarios*, p. 413.

[77] Idem, AIA, 23 (1925): 367; *Visionarios*, p. 413.

kingdoms, owing to its defence of the Church and its harbouring of the true pope during the Schism.

This particular prophecy, made in 1391, had an interesting sequel. John I, a friend of Eiximenis, found it offensive, apparently because it did not give sufficient importance to the house of Aragon. Eiximenis wrote to John in defence of his work,[78] pointing out that he had deliberately refrained from predicting the disappearance of the house of Aragon, and that Roquetaillade had given it a very important place in the scheme of Last Things. John replied that he had indeed been aware of other "astrologers" who had predicted great things for Aragon; he himself left such matters to God's providence.[79] Nevertheless, he invited Eiximenis to discuss the matter further with him, but there the correspondence ends. The discussion may have taken place, but it seems reasonable to assume from the tone of the exchange that Eiximenis was not terribly interested in, and certainly not fanatical about, the subject of specific roles in the Last Times. As in his writings, he defers in such matters almost entirely to Roquetaillade. Tact seems to have governed his conduct in the matter of the house of Aragon, and one can speculate that he must have been amused at the irony of John's attack on his prophecy. One wonders what the Infant might have said or done in a similar situation.

So Eiximenis only dabbled in the assigning of roles in his prophecies; the bulk of his work demonstrates that his real apocalyptic interests lay in the entire sweep of ecclesiastical history and in the continuing problem of the frailty of the temporal church. He hoped for a renovation aided by a world emperor and an Angelic Pope, but was not very interested in identifying these figures. Thus his Joachimism contrasts with that of the Infant, who saw himself as an active participant in the political resolution of the Last Times.

---

[78] Idem, AIA, 23 (1925): 367-368; *Visionarios*, p. 414.
[79] Idem, AIA, 23 (1925): 368; *Visionarios*, p. 413.

7

The Author of the *Breviloquium*
and the Beguins

Eiximenis and the Infant Peter represent two contrasting threads of Joachimist influence in Catalonia which survived late into the fourteenth century.
However, the focal point of this study lies a generation earlier, in the
mid-century, when the last major synthesis of Joachimist prophecy was
prepared for those Penitent and Spiritual groups who were most active in the
struggle to maintain the tenets of evangelical poverty. This central surviving
document of the early 1350s is the *Breviloquium*.[1]

The *Breviloquium* is closely identified with the Beguin houses of the Third
Order. The author's insistence that adherents of evangelical poverty must
maintain the discipline of a rule (*ibi est religio ubi est regularis obseruatio*)[2]
even if they leave their present order is very much in the spirit of Guillem
Martí's defence of the discipline of the Barcelona Beguins.[3] The reliance of
the author on the work of Olivi is a hallmark of the Beguin tradition, and the
rules set forth for the preservation of the circle to which the *Breviloquium* was
addressed confirm in several instances our present knowledge of Beguinism.[4]
Finally, the influence of Arnold of Vilanova permeates the work.

However, the author had connections with other orders which suggest
more complex relationships among disaffected regulars. First, several of the
rules the author lists are concerned wholly or in part with the practical
problems of existence for the dissenter within an order rather than with the
harmonious collaboration of a house of Beguins.[5] The author, in his capacity
as spiritual adviser to his flock, counsels movement from one house or rule

---

[1] For the dating of the *Brev.*, see pp. 160-161.
[2] *Brev.*, p. 174.
[3] Supra, pp. 52-58; Perarnau, *Alia Informatio*, Doc. 13, pp. 96-98.
[4] For these rules, see *Brev.*, pp. 174-176.
[5] For these rules (Nos. 2, 4, 6, 7), see infra, pp. 91-92.

to another in certain extreme instances, but never apostasy from ecclesiastical discipline. Secondly, he is a committed Franciscan, is familiar with at least one of the standard accounts of the life of St. Francis,[6] and devotes long sections to Francis and the nature of his ministry. He follows Olivi in seeing Francis as the renovator of the Church, and salutes the three orders of his rule as the leaders of the *renovatio ecclesie* in the second opening of the sixth age:

> Therefore under this opening occurred the first great transformation and miraculous renovation throughout the entire Church: St. Francis, in whom the image of Christ or the Crucifixion was renewed, renewed in turn the evangelical state, the state of the Ladies of Poverty,[7] and the state of the Brothers of Penitence.[8]

In a later passage we are also told that the order of St. Francis will be singled out from among the other orders and persecuted, just as the eleven brothers acted against Joseph, a time in which the evangelical order and the rule of St. Francis will be "condemned, excommunicated and crucified, along with all its followers and believers," and expelled from the synagogue.[9]

A further refining process from the First to the Third Order is then described, based upon the correspondences drawn in *Distinctio* 2 which link the Tribe of Joseph with the First Order, and the Tribe of Benjamin with the Third Order.[10] In *Distinctio* 6, the author bases his elevation of "these holy

---

[6] A reference to the removal of one of the twelve associates of Francis points to the use of the *Actus Beati Francisci et Sociorum Ejus*, ed. Charles Paul Sabatier (Paris, 1902), p. 2. Other references to the life of St. Francis could also have come from St. Bonaventura, and possibly Thomas of Celano.

[7] *Ordo Pauperum Dominarum* is the name used in the *Legenda Maior* (4.6, p. 514) by St. Bonaventura for the Order of St. Clare, who is herself described as the *mater Pauperum Dominarum*. They are also referred to in the *Bullarium* as *Ordinis Sororum Pauperum, quam Beatus Franciscus instituit*, in *Bullarium*, 1 (1759): 671.

[8] For the Tertiaries, supra, pp. 50-51. This view of the role of the three orders is consistent with Bonaventura's in the *Legenda Maior*, quoted by Wadding, *Annales Minorum*, 2 (1732): 17. Bonaventura writes: *Nam instar reparatae triplicis fabricae ipsius sancti Viri ducatur, secundum datum ab eo formam, regulam, et doctrinam, Christi triformiter renovanda erat Ecclesia, trinaque triumphatura militia salvandorum: sicut et nunc cernimus esse completum.* However, the author of the *Breviloquium* goes beyond this orthodox Franciscan opinion by implying that it is only the adherents of evangelical poverty within the three orders who, after a further renovation, will truly fulfill the mission of St. Francis as the Joachimist tradition saw it.

[9] *Brev.*, p. 224.

[10] Tertiaries were commonly called *continentes* as well, as they are in *Dist.* 2. A sixteenth-century Tertiary document lists three names for the Order: *Et habet tria nomina: O vero diremo ch'questo modo de vivere se chiama: Tertia Regula, Ordine de Continenti, Ordine de fratri et sorore de Penitentia.* From the *Regula Tertii Ordinis Sancti Francisci cum Ceremoniis ad induendum fratres et sorores*, fol. 22 (British Library, 1512 [?]).

men, who follow His path, and by whom the Christian nation shall attain perfect life," on a passage from *Zachariah* 13.7-9: *And I will turn my hand upon the little ones* [*paruulos*], *and it shall come to pass that in all the land, says the Lord, two parts shall be cut off and die, but the third shall be left therein. And I will bring the third part through the fire, and will refine them as silver is refined, and I will try them as gold is tried.*[11] There follows a specific identification of the Tertiaries with Benjamin:

> When the Order of those Friars Minor appeared, the final *status* was de-monstrated, not without great mystery, in Benjamin and his Tribe, in whose sack or religion, in the time of that severe threshing [*trituratione*] of all the tribes, the cup of silver placed by Joseph [in Benjamin's sack], which is the cup of the evangelical truth of Christ the King, should be revealed. At that time the fall of the new Babylon will draw near, when great joy shall be found again.[12]

Thus does the author place the Tertiaries or Tribe of Benjamin foremost among the new spiritual men, purified to a greater degree than their forbears in evangelical truth, the First Order or Tribe of Joseph. There is a suggestion here that only the Third Order is to emerge from the great "refining," but the general context of the discussion of the Order and its dissidents calls for caution in assigning salvation only to Tertiaries. The author does not explicitly make that claim. However, there is no doubt in his mind that the Tertiaries are to play the paramount role in the *renovatio*.

On the other hand, several of the rules "for the present necessity" listed in the Prologue suggest that the *Breviloquium* was intended for circulation to evangelicals in all the Franciscan orders, with a view to the salvation of these groups as well as of the Tertiaries. Rule No. 2 counsels believers not to reveal the "secrets" concerning the present condition to those who are "enemies of God" or "of brutish understanding," because such an action will "bring about great danger."[13] Rule No. 4 allows three justifications for movement from one Order of the Rule to another: "for greater perfection in observance, for the impossibility of observance of a rule, or for the reason of intolerable persecution."[14] Apostasy from the Rule of St. Francis is to be avoided at all costs. Rule No. 6 calls for dissimulation when necessary to avoid persecution, and Rule No. 7 cautions against any familiarity beyond a superficial level with

[11] *Brev.*, p. 225.

[12] *Brev.*, p. 225. The author may have been influenced in his choice of Benjamin as the type for the Tertiaries by an identification made by Gregory the Great in a work from which the author of the *Breviloquium* quotes. In *In Primum Regum Expositiones* (PL 79.262), Gregory says that the *terra Benjamin sancta Ecclesia est.* For the reference to Joseph's cup placed in Benjamin's sack, see *Genesis* 44.2.

[13] *Brev.*, p. 174.

[14] Ibid., p. 174.

"false religious." [15] These rules suggest that the Spiritual must attempt to live as best as he can in one of the Franciscan orders; he is not enjoined to move specifically to the Third Order in order to ensure his fidelity to evangelical poverty and, as a consequence, to salvation.

There is considerable evidence for communications between various types of evangelicals, among them personalities we have already discussed. Bernard de na Jacma, it may be recalled, received both Beguins and Fraticelli in his home, [16] and the Franciscan Bernard Fuster, possessor of the *De statibus ecclesiae*, had received documents from a citizen of Gerona, possibly Durando·da Baldach, the Beguin leader. [17] Philip of Majorca also had a mixed group of Tertiaries and Spirituals in his retinue. [18] Finally, in his work on the dispute over evangelical poverty, the Portuguese Franciscan Alvaro Peláez places both Spirituals and Penitents in the same camp in the struggle against their less zealous brothers:

> At present and for some time there have been in the Order adherents of the purity of the Rule, opponents of the betrayal of it, who often suffer persecution wherever they reside by prelates of the Order and by their carnal brothers ... for the Spirituals and Penitents can only remain silent, and avoid the prevarications of other brothers by not permitting themselves to join their company. [19]

Thus were Spirituals and Penitents grouped together by their contemporaries, and thus no doubt did they feel allied in their common cause and common persecution. Also, Peláez's picture of the contempt shown by Spirituals and Penitents alike for those whom they believed to err in the rule of St. Francis is certainly consistent with Rule No. 7 of the *Breviloquium*, and with the letter and spirit of Rule No. 2, both cited above. [20]

The evidence presented thus far identifies the author as a Franciscan regular, most likely of the Third Order, but whose *summula* was intended for circulation among both Beguin and Spiritual groups within the Franciscan orders. The circumstances of the author's own learning and the appeal to groups outside Beguin circles suggest that he himself may have left another order to join the Tertiaries, but also leave open the possibility that he might still be a First Order Franciscan.

The evidence for a Catalonian provenance for the *Breviloquium* is most immediately discernible in the extant MSS: all four are Iberian in style, one

---

[15] Ibid.

[16] Supra, p. 61.

[17] Supra, p. 67.

[18] Supra, pp. 70-71.

[19] *De Planctu Ecclesiae*, Lyon, Bibliothèque Municipale, MS II, 67, fol. 219r; cited in P. Alejandro Amaro, O.F.M., "Fr. Alvaro Pelagio," AIA, 5 (1916): 19-20.

[20] For these rules, see Note 11.

remains in Tarragona, and two were copied in Barcelona; Catalonia and the house of Aragon are given special prominence in the text; there is one piece of philological evidence which points to a Catalonian origin.[21] In the matter of its content, and in spite of any reservations we may have concerning the precise status of its author, the *Breviloquium* is rooted in Beguin rather than Spiritual tradition, and, more specifically, in doctrine, style and emphasis is redolent of Arnold of Vilanova. It echoes the passionate language of Arnold, denounces the failings of Church and State in similar imagery and with similar urgency, and may be viewed as an example of the mid-century evolution of Arnold's teaching. The almost total absence of direct quotation from Arnold may be ascribed to two reasons: first, that the author belonged to a group immersed in the vernacular tradition of the transmission of Arnoldian ideas;[22] secondly, that he has gone back to Joachim — and, of course, to Olivi — for the formal structure of his concords. We shall postpone discussion of the formal aspects of his apocalypticism to the following chapter, and concentrate here on the exposition of Beguinism as it relates to Arnold's teachings.

As we noted earlier, Perarnau has called attention to the importance of Arnoldian ideas concerning the dangers of temporal business,[23] a theme which is central to both the doctrine and structure of the *Breviloquium*. In the *Raonament d'Avinyó*, Arnold had instructed Frederick and James to avoid business if they wished to pursue justice: "Reject, in your heart, all thoughts of business, if you wish to nourish justice with unalloyed zeal." [24] Love of money ("amor de florins"), Arnold continued, would bring upon them the wrath of God and the desolation of their people.[25] In the *Breviloquium*, the fifth rule admonished the circle of followers "not to enmesh oneself too much in temporal affairs, because they seize the entire heart, and dissipate, and completely withdraw it from the service of God. This is inimical to all your effort." [26] In the sixth age especially, the author writes, it will come about that

---

[21] See the Introduction to the Text, infra, p. 152.

[22] The phrase "vernacular tradition" does not exclude Latin MSS, but is intended to suggest a preponderance of texts circulated in Catalan, as well as reading and discussion in the manner described by Bernard Gui (supra, pp. 49-50). The basic tenets of Arnold's teaching on evangelical poverty were undoubtedly transmitted orally as well as in vernacular texts, and would have been part of the author's own vocabulary. Consequently, he would have little need to find expressions of the themes themselves from other Latin works, except to illustrate and amplify them with Biblical quotations, to make the obligatory citations from Olivi, and to cite patristic sources when appropriate.

[23] See *Alia Informatio*, pp. 166-169, and supra, p. 59.

[24] *Obres Catalanes*, p. 185. See also supra, pp. 39, 43, for further remarks by Arnold on business.

[25] *Obres Catalanes*, p. 188.

[26] *Brev.*, p. 175.

"business shall beget business, occupation shall beget occupation, and labour shall beget labour," with the result that these things will carry all other things along with them, and "the name and number of the Beast shall be given a place."[27]

This conception of temporal business is also central to the author's exposition of the Donation of Constantine, which we shall discuss later. Here we need only note that he regards the division of roles between Silvester and Constantine as essential "lest those who like apostles serve under God should implicate themselves in temporal business."[28]

The Arnoldian themes of the study of Scripture and the importance of "consolation" are established by the author of the *Breviloquium* in his opening sentences, the first of which reads as follows:

> Although it is not for us except by divine revelation or inspiration to know the *times or the moment that the Father has established in His own power*, we can nevertheless with His help have recourse to that one method alone by which through the ladder of generations or times in the Old Testament, figuratively we can perceive similar grades of concord in the New.[29]

In this sentence, which alludes to Christ's injunction in *Acts* 1.7 against predicting the Last Times, the author evokes in a highly condensed form the entire train of argument Arnold brought to bear against the Paris doctors, the nature of which we discussed in an earlier chapter.[30] For the author of the *Breviloquium*, Arnold's answer to the criticism of apocalypticism is the established model, and requires no more than this brief evocation.

In his second sentence, the author of the *Breviloquium* moves from a defence of his undertaking to the reason for its efficacy, which he finds rooted in the words of *Romans* 15.4: *"whatsoever things were written aforetime, were written for our learning, that we through patience and comfort [consolationem] of the Scriptures might have hope."* "Consolation" is the key word here for the author of the *Breviloquium*: "Therefore," he continues,

> as a consolation and solace for the humble heart, this work or *summula* of concords has been gathered together from the *Concordia* of Joachim and other works of his, and collected from other works of notable persons which deal in this fashion with the concordance of the Old and New Testaments, and with the order of the "ladders," or generations, and times, all of which are brought together in a compendium.[31]

---

[27] Ibid., p. 175.
[28] Ibid., p. 280.
[29] Ibid., p. 168.
[30] Supra, pp. 33-34.
[31] *Brev.*, p. 168.

The special significance attached to the term *consolatio* by Arnold and the Beguins has been noted by Perarnau;[32] its importance can be further exemplified by its use in the *Breviloquium*. In the passage quoted above, *consolatio* is granted to those who have humble hearts (defined throughout the *Breviloquium* as a special attribute of Beguins), and who are open to and worthy of knowledge of the imminent coming of the Last Times. The absence of this gift of God is ascribed to the company of the false religious, who cling to worldly values and who refuse to heed apocalyptic warnings. In descriptions of the time of abomination and desolation, the temple of the Christian religion is "destitute of divine consolation,"[33] and in another passage which describes the fallen Church, "the entire Church shall be deprived and destitute of all grace, spiritual society, and the consolation of God."[34] From these passages, we may deduce that *consolatio* is virtually a docrinal passkey to Beguinism, an attribute of those who have the grace of God, humility in their practice of evangelical poverty, knowledge of the coming tribulation, and assurance that they are of the evangelical elect.

This concept of *consolatio* derives from Arnold, who also connects "consolació" with the favour shown by God to adherents of evangelical poverty. In the *Llicó de Narbona*, Arnold writes that "he who gives consolation to the poor rather than the rich pleases our Lord the more";[35] and in the *Alia Informatio* that "to those who in the present life through Jesus Christ renounce riches and temporal abundance is given in this present life spiritual consolation."[36] Arnold also describes the consolatory function of study and writing in which Beguins themselves should engage: "The law of Jesus Christ which we follow obliges us in our works to help one another, and to console and comfort by service, by good works, and by holy colloquies."[37] It was for such consolation that the Beguins described by Bernard Gui gathered to hear readings from holy works, a practice certainly encouraged here by Arnold. Arnold's view of prophecy as "consolatory" is probably derived in turn from Joachim's injunction to study the Scriptures in search of the future, a view to which Arnold subscribed in his earlier work.[38]

The *uigilate* motif is another important Arnoldian theme which, as we have noted, appears in the prefatory poem and in the introductory *distinctio*.[39] The

---

[32] *Alia Informatio*, p. 39.
[33] *Brev.*, p. 230.
[34] *Brev.*, p. 231.
[35] *Obres Catalanes*, p. 156.
[36] *Alia Informatio*, p. 36.
[37] Ibid., p. 52. See also p. 51.
[38] Supra, pp. 49-50.
[39] *Brev.*, p. 164 and p. 174. See supra, p. 33.

author quotes Christ's warning: *"Be vigilant and pray, in order that you do not enter into temptation,"* and comments that "vigilance refers to truth, temptation to error, prayer to true devotion."[40] Thus "vigilance" also seems to have a special resonance for Beguins, implying as it does here another attribute of those who have special knowledge of what is to come, and embodying a warning that they are about to be severely tested.[41] In the *Confessió de Barcelona*, Arnold links the advent of Antichrist to the testing and suffering of the followers of poverty. It is necessary that evangelicals have knowledge of that time of Antichrist, Arnold writes, for two reasons:

> First, in order to know completely and clearly the truth of our lord Jesus Christ and to fix it in their hearts, so that the enemy shall be forced from his hold over all Christians; secondly, to guard passionately within their hearts all the virtues, and especially that of charity and love of our Lord, and also that virtue of contempt for the fleshly life and temporal goods, in order that they may withstand the persecution which will fall upon all those who love Jesus Christ.[42]

The author concludes his introduction to this work of "consolatory" prophecy with a description of the fourteen chapters into which his work is divided. This division probably owes its origin to Arnold, whose work *Dialogus de elementis catholicae fidei* (1297) occupied itself with numerology, and as we saw earlier, was deliberately constructed in fourteen parts.[43] The author of the *Breviloquium* appears at times hard-pressed to achieve such an order; *Dist.* 11 and *Dist.* 12 are probably the result of his effort to follow Arnold's advice.

Arnold's broadest and most florid strokes are found in his descriptions of the sufferings of the true evangelical men, the excesses of a reprobate clergy, and his conviction that a great renovation would herald the end of time. These same themes are familiar to the *Breviloquium*.

Both Arnold and the author of the *Breviloquium* use the imagery of the Slaughter of the Innocents as a metaphor for the sufferings of the true followers of Christ and as an identification of the evangelicals and of their suffering. In the *Llicó de Narbona*, Arnold speaks of the false clergy who destroy the true faith: they are all Herods, he writes, "for all of them kill their

---

[40] Ibid., p. 174. See *Matthew* 26.41.

[41] In the *Raonament d'Avinyó*, Arnold refers specifically to male and female Beguins as persons to emulate, and laments their persecution. He recommends that seculars live in poverty, "axí com són beguins e beguines. Los quals, si no són lurs devots o per qualque obligació sotsmeses a ells, tots los perseguexen cruelment ab diffamacions e ab calúmpnies de vicis e de heretgia, no tan solament en sermó, mas encara en cort de prelats e de príceps.", p. 206.

[42] *Obres Catalanes*, pp. 107-108.

[43] See Ch. 3, n. 32.

children spiritually, just as Herod killed them in the flesh."[44] The Herod imagery occurs in the *Breviloquium* in *Distinctio* 11, in which the persecution of the innocents by Herod is compared to that of the "evangelical children or evangelical life" under the second Herod or mystic Antichrist.[45] The author of the *Breviloquium* also develops the imagery of infants into the children (*paruuli*) of the Introduction, those who attain the true wisdom or *consolatio* and who are contrasted with those who attain merely to worldly wisdom.[46] He pursues further concords between the suffering of Christ and the suffering of the Beguins, and notes that just as Christ was denied in the garden of Gethsemane by his own followers so would many of His faithful leave Him during the tribulations to come,[47] a concord which ties in with the *uigilate* motif. These concords have an Olivianist origin, but this emphasis on the events of Christ's mission as a lesson for Beguins in time of tribulation is very much a part of the Arnoldian tradition as well.[48]

Arnold's denunciation of clergy (and laity) often takes the form of a catalogue of their dress, which shows them to be consumed by temporal vanity. In the *Llicó de Narbona*, they "wear gold, silver, pearls, precious stones and other adornments on their vestments ... and wear exquisite fabrics of various colours, all of which produces only vainglory ...."[49] The author of the *Breviloquium* dwells on this same theme, choosing for his premier example of the worldly vanity of the clergy a passage from *Isaiah* 3.17-26:

> *The Lord will smite the crown of the daughters of Sion and shall strike off their hair. In that day the Lord will take away all their ornaments,* that is, from ecclesiastics who walk in secular vanity, *and chains, bracelets, mufflers, bonnets, ornaments of the legs, earrings, rings, nose, jewels, suits of apparel, mantles, wimples, crisping pins, glasses, fine linen, and hoods and veils.*[50]

The danger from false prophets, another variation on the false religious, is very much on Arnold's mind, and in the *Confessió de Barcelona* he paraphrases *Matthew* 7.15 on the subject: "Be mindful of false prophets, and flee from them, for they will come among you in the false dress of sheep."[51] He also alludes to the commentary in the *Glossa Ordinaria*: "That is, according to the *Glossa*, in the appearance of religious men ... full of covetousness, and desirous of accumulating worldly goods."[52]

---

[44] *Obres Catalanes*, p. 159.
[45] *Brev.*, p. 267.
[46] Ibid., pp. 172-174.
[47] Ibid., pp. 174-175.
[48] See *De statibus*, supra, p. 69.
[49] *Obres Catalanes*, p. 158.
[50] *Brev.*, p. 193.
[51] *Obres Catalanes*, pp. 118-119.
[52] Ibid., pp. 118-119.

The author of the *Breviloquium* also chooses *Matthew* 7.15, and attaches a commentary ascribed to St. Bernard. In his rules for the conduct of his circle, he cautions against having much to do with people of contrary intention, "especially with the false religious," and quotes the "false prophets" passage. According to St. Bernard, he continues,

> there are certain perverse men in the dress of sheep and walking in the garb of honesty, who wish to be humble without practising humility, paupers without lacking anything, well dressed without care of others ... Within they are rapacious wolves, receivers of the goods of the present, givers-up of the reward of the future.[53]

In the *Raonament d'Avinyó*, Arnold says that the false religious will fall into two abominations: false preaching, and the persecution of the evangelical Church,[54] roles for which they are similarly cast in the *Breviloquium*.

Arnold also interested himself in the condition of secular monarchs during the last times. While he saw James and Frederick fulfilling a positive role in the last times, he was in general as critical of secular rulers as he was of those with spiritual authority. In the *Raonament d'Avinyó* he damns the two in tandem ("caps de compaya són prelats ecclesiàstics et prínceps seglars"),[55] and later puts them in the same company as the false religious:

> Just as prelates and princes fall into great difficulty through the love of riches, honours, and temporal delights, so also do all those fall who also profess love for the same things, and whom the Scriptures call the false religious.[56]

The author of the *Breviloquium* believed that this dual breakdown of authority had commenced during the reign of John XXII and Louis of Bavaria in the 1320s, and would be consummated at the climax of the 45 days of silence described in Daniel. He finds concords for this in the 45th generation of the Old Testament, when "all the leaders of the priests and the people transgressed."[57] He is also interested in the House of Aragon, but uses different sources for his prediction of its ultimate fate.

Finally, Arnold looked for a great renovation at the end of the sixth age, a triumph of the evangelical men crowned by the enthronement of an Angelic Pope, as we have noted in a previous chapter: *"There shall be one sheep-fold and one shepherd."*[58] Evangelical men will appear, marked with the sign of God just as St. Francis bore the stigmata of Christ. The author of the

---

[53] *Brev.*, pp. 175-176.
[54] *Obres Catalanes*, p. 195.
[55] Ibid., p. 173.
[56] Ibid., p. 195.
[57] *Brev.*, p. 216.
[58] Supra, pp. 31, 45.

Breviloquium also shares Arnold's expectation of reformation, and sees the type for the Angelic Pope in Zorobabel, who will rebuild the "temple and walls of the city of the universal Church, so that *there shall be one sheep-fold and one shepherd.*"[59]

Are there any direct allusions to specific works of Arnold in the *Breviloquium*? We have noted only one, and that to the Latin *Expositio super Apocalypsim*, in which Arnold identifies Pope Silvester as the angel of *Apocalypse* 20.1.[60]

The papacy of Silvester is a key event in the *Breviloquium*, as we shall see, largely because of this identification. One of several such allusions occurs as follows:

> From the time of pope Silvester until the time of this second opening of the sixth age there were a thousand years. According to certain others, this Silvester is the angel of Apocalypse 20, who has *the key to the abyss, and a great chain in his hand. And he apprehended the dragon, the ancient serpent who is the devil and Sathan, and bound him for a thousand years. And he sent him into the abyss, and closed it, and made a sign over him* after Constantine and the Empire had been converted, *so that he should not seduce more people until a thousand years had passed.* In the interval, dominion and peace were given to the Christian nation.[61]

The most likely source of the allusion "according to certain others" is the *Expositio super Apocalypsim*, in which Arnold makes this identification and comments in some detail on the interval of a thousand years.[62] In Arnold's view, *he saw an angel* (*Apocalypse* 20.1) refers to both Christ and Silvester; *signed upon him* refers to "the mark of evangelical truth,"; *that he should not seduce more people* refers to Silvester's binding of the dragon of Rome so that worldly idolatry should cease. The binding was intended to have two results: "the decline of the general seduction of the peoples, and the spiritual progress of the faithful."[63] This positive view of the Donation contrasts sharply with the opprobrium cast upon Constantine's action by other evangelicals, and constitutes the best evidence that Arnold's *Expositio* is the source of a similar attitude in the *Breviloquium*.[64]

In Arnold, the *mille annorum* signifies that period in which spiritual authority holds sway over the temporal, a period which is coming to an end as secular vanity overtakes the true spiritual life, when "the fleshly life is

[59] *Brev.*, p. 297.
[60] ESA, p. 253.
[61] *Brev.*, p. 215.
[62] ESA, pp. 253-256.
[63] Ibid., p. 254.
[64] For the traditional evangelical view of the Donation, see Ch. 8, n. 21.

institutionalised and the spiritual life is everywhere extinguished."[65] The subsequent loosing of Satan for a brief time occurs, Arnold adds, so that those who have been proven in the trial of faith will manifest themselves.

The identification of Silvester as the Angel of the Abyss and the consequent time-span of one thousand years opened up new possibilities for the author of the *Breviloquium*. The period of one thousand years after the papacy of Silvester coincided almost precisely with the reign of John XXII and the time of tribulation predicted by Arnold. By joining the 45 days of silence in *Daniel* to his first figure,[66] the author found an appropriate means to bring Arnold's chronology up-to-date, to flesh out the theory of empire and papacy adumbrated in this passage, and to fit it into his structure of concords.[67]

Why are there no further borrowings from Arnold's *Expositio*? Perhaps because at this point in his commentary Arnold diverges from the entire Joachimist tradition to argue that the sixth age will contain the final tribulation, and that Gog and Magog do not symbolize a later cataclysm in the seventh age:

> No further persecution of the Church of Christ is described, beyond that which is to be inflicted by Antichrist. Those commentators who believed that after the persecution of Antichrist the Church would endure a severe persecution by Gog and Magog were deceived by the multiple enigmas of this book.[68]

In his commentary on *Apocalypse* 8.1, Arnold made the same point, and squeezed Naman and Antiochus into the sixth age as well.[69] For the author of the *Breviloquium*, drinking as he was from the very fount of the Joachimist tradition, such a denunciation of this portion of the abbot's writing simply would not do.

In sum, the author of the *Breviloquium* reveals himself as a true Joachite with a pastoral mission to his brethren in this time of trial and persecution which heralds the climax of history. Although possibly belonging to the First Order of St. Francis himself, he has a special affinity with the Tertiaries or Beguins. Arnold of Vilanova, and to a lesser extent Olivi and Roquetaillade, have helped to shape his immediate world view, but the fundamental structure of his vision of history is derived directly from the works of the Abbot Joachim.

[65] ESA, pp. 254-255.
[66] The author of the *Brev.* enumerates 44 days of silence and sees the 45th as ushering in the Third *status*.
[67] See Ch. 9 for this material.
[68] ESA, p. 257.
[69] Ibid., p. 120.

8

The Structure of Concord
in the *Breviloquium*

In the history of Joachimist writings the *Breviloquium* occupies a unique position. As we have seen,[1] the authors of the thirteenth-century pseudo-Joachimist tracts aimed at pressing home certain specific interpretations, both ecclesiastical and political. They assumed Joachim's system and wrote what purported to be the Abbot's own further applications of his principles in contemporary prophecy. Olivi and Arnold of Vilanova had revised the Joachimist scheme of history to bring it up to date.[2] Olivi in particular had built his interpretation on a pattern of concords which he derived from Joachim, but he did not treat these systematically. Both were mainly preoccupied with the spiritual crisis and revolution which they expected in the Church, as were also the authors of the prophecies on the Popes. Roquetaillade redressed the balance between ecclesiastical and secular signs of the coming age. We have noted[3] that he turned more and more to the political currents of his day to plot out a detailed scheme of the Last Times. His method, however, was often haphazard and capricious. His visions and projections were narrowly topical at times, and he was hampered by a lack of Joachim's canon. The result in his work is a wealth of detail within an essentially topical framework rather than within a general framework of the redemptive history of the world.

The author of the *Breviloquium* sets out to restore this total view of history to the later Joachites and he accomplishes this by a return to the formal structure of Joachim himself. He is naturally influenced by the revisions of Joachimism which we have traced, and, along with Roquetaillade, involves himself in the topical assignment of political roles. However, the fundamental influence upon him remains Joachim's concept of concords and his deep

[1] Supra, pp. 6-11.
[2] Supra, pp. 21-22, 40-42.
[3] Supra, pp. 75-78.

desire to determine the overall pattern and purpose of history.[4] He proceeds at once to a lengthy discussion of the kinds of concord he believes to be important and the method he intends to use in his analysis of these patterns.[5] Because he regarded his work as a handbook or compendium, our author set out to assimilate and reconcile previous writings, often comparing conflicting interpretations and striving consistently for synthesis. Like Joachim, and Arnold after him, he believed that it was the only method by which one dared presume to read the signs of the times.

The author of the *Breviloquium* established three categories of concord: of time alone; of events alone; of time and events together. It was with the latter two that he was most concerned. As an example of the first type he cited the correspondence of two generations or ages, such as the first generation of the New Testament with that of the Old. In this method events and persons would not be considered.[6]

Events or personalities alone constituted the second method.[7] An example would be the correspondence of Adam and Ozias (Hezekiah), the king of Judah who reigned in the days of Isaiah. Both were righteous in the beginning, then sinned through pride and were punished, and both were expelled from a holy place as "lepers." Thus they corresponded in deeds but not in similarity of generation or age. Using this method, our author jumped among generations: Christ had points of concord with Abel, Isaac, Joseph and Moses. These examples, notably that of Adam and Ozias, were taken from Joachim who actually based these concords on time as well as circumstance, so that none were fortuitous, all exemplified different types of pattern. But Joachim used a bewildering variety of number patterns and it would seem that our author did not always understand these but rationalised them in his own way.[8]

The third, and most important, method of concord occurs when the generations correspond with the ages, and when age and event in turn correspond.[9] Here Christ and Adam correspond by concord, for Adam was the first parent according to the flesh, and Christ was the first parent

---

[4] All references to the *Breviloquium*, unless otherwise stated, are to the edited text in this volume.

[5] *Brev.*, pp. 168-172.

[6] *Brev.*, pp. 168-169.

[7] *Brev.*, p. 169.

[8] Joachim's theory of concords arises directly from his Trinitarian doctrine of history. The events and persons of the first two Testaments embody the work of Father and Son respectively. They must be matched, facing each other, as it were, in order that the work of the Spirit, the *Spiritualis Intelligentia*, may be discerned proceeding from both. This doctrine is clearly stated at the beginning of the *Lib. Conc.*, fol. 7r-v.

[9] *Brev.*, p. 169.

according to the spirit. Adam was created on the sixth day of creation, and in the sixth age of the world Christ was incarnate; from Adam came Eve, and from Christ the Woman who is the Church, and so on. There follows an astonishingly detailed list of concords. By this type of concord, Abraham corresponds with Zachariah, Isaac with John the Baptist: Abraham and Zachariah were both old and righteous, had barren wives, and procreated sons through the intervention of an angel; Abraham begat Isaac and Zachariah begat John the Baptist; Isaac in turn begat Jacob, and John the Baptist begat Christ spiritually by means of baptism. Thus Christ and Jacob correspond both by time or generation, and by similarities in the events of their lives: both were supplantors, one of his brother and the other of the devil; both fought, one against an angel and the other against the devil; Jacob was the fleshly father of the twelve patriarchs, Christ was the spiritual father of the twelve Apostles.[10]

The concords of regions and nations fall in part under this third category, but also have a special figural and sometimes etymological significance of their own. Thus concord exists through the interpretation of names, in which Old Testament places are linked with New Testament places and institutions. The link thus exists partly under event, or time and event, and partly through the interpretation of the name. For example, the kingdom of Judah corresponds to the universal Church militant, and the kings of Judah signify by concord the Roman Pontiffs; Jerusalem, also interpreted as the vision of peace, signifies the universal Church, and the place or city in which the pope and his curia reside. Both Rome and Babylon signify the Church, the latter name applying when it has received Antichrist.[11]

The three categories of concord distinguished in the *Breviloquium* would, one suspects, be too academic for Joachim. His concords usually have a time and event element in them (*ex concordia numerorum et operum*),[12] but because he uses such a variety of time-patterns, his concords need not always follow the same time-sequence. Thus Adam and Ozias correspond because they initiate the first and second *status* respectively, and because they are forty-two generations apart.[13] Joachim makes a special point of their concords as "lepers" when, at the end of the *Liber Concordie*, he develops

[10] The concords of the three Patriarchs with Zacharias, John Baptist and Christ, and of the twelve Patriarchs with the Apostles, are favourites with Joachim and essential parts of the architecture of some figures in the *Lib. Fig.* See *Lib. Conc.*, fols. 7v-8v, 10r, 22v-23r, 38v, 57r; *Expos.*, fols. 9v, 147v; *Lib. Fig.*, Pls. 3, 4, 5, 6, 9, 10.

[11] *Brev.*, p. 171.

[12] *Lib. Conc.*, fol. 23r.

[13] Ibid., fols. 8r-9v, 10v, 18v.

a new time-pattern of seven concords each forty-two generations apart.[14] At one point, again thinking of the two testaments and the *spiritualis intellectus* proceeding from them, he conceives of Adam and Ozias as the two "supports" (*parietibus*) from which one web is woven.[15] Again, the concords can change with the time-patterns. Joachim gives examples of people who can be seen in different concords according to different patterns, but there must be a "cause of concords [*causa concordie*]."[16] Thus, for instance, Isaac is in concord with Christ in a Trinitarian relationship, but Jacob is in concord with Christ in the sequence of great men later to be used in the *Breviloquium*.[17] In the invention of concords, Joachim remains the master.

In the *Breviloquium*, the author shows himself further as a pupil of the Calabrian master by building each *Distinctio* on concord, emphasizing his debt to Joachim by stating the concords of the three general *status* in the first chapter.[18] This is all the more significant because Joachim's *Liber Concordie* does not put the pattern of three *status* in the forefront.[19] The author clearly feels the need — like so many other students of Joachim's writings — to bring into one system the various patterns of concords upon which Joachim's mind plays with such kaleidoscopic speed. So our author begins by gathering as many concords as possible into the pattern of threes. The first *status* lasted from Adam to Christ; it belonged to God the Father and was characterised by the matrimonial order; it had five *etates*, seven seals, sixty-three generations, or, according to "another concord," it terminated in Ozias and had forty-two generations;[20] it was marked by three "noble persons," Abraham, Isaac and Jacob, twelve patriarchs, two "nephews" (*nepotes*), Manasseh and Ephraim. In this *status* God revealed Himself as "exceedingly powerful and terrible": this is proved by three examples and three reasons. The *status* had

---

[14] Ibid., fol. 134v.

[15] Ibid., fol. 23v. For Adam and Ozias, see also the *Psalt.*, fol. 276r.

[16] *Lib. Conc.*, fols. 18r-19r.

[17] See infra, p. 107. On Abel and Christ, see *Lib. Conc.*, fol. 31r; on Isaac and Christ, fols. 9v, 80r; on Joseph and Christ, fol. 31v; on Moses and Christ, fols. 30v, 31v.

[18] *Brev.*, pp. 178-186.

[19] Joachim's first statement on the three *status* comes in Bk. 2, Tract 1, ch. 5 of the *Lib. Conc.*, fols. 8r-v. Up to this point Joachim has been occupied with the concords of the two Testaments. He has postulated the *intellectus spiritualis* proceeding from these concords, but he is slow in formulating the concept of the three *status* of history which flows from this. See Reeves, Hirsch-Reich, *The Figurae of Joachim of Fiore*, pp. 121-122, for an examination of the stages by which he reaches this understanding.

[20] This is a characteristic point for Joachim, connected with his desire to press the Trinitarian symbolism to its limit. As the Son proceeds from the Father and the Spirit from both, so the second *status* and its *ordo clericorum* must have its *initiatio* within the first *status*, and the third *status*, with its *ordo monachorum*, must have a double *initiatio* in the first and second *status* (see *Lib. Conc.*, fols. 8v-11v, 13v, 56v-57v). The author of the *Brev.* gets these *initiationes*, but not the Trinitarian significance behind them.

its dawn, midday and evening, ending in the "great night" of the Jewish rejection of Christ.

The second *status* is worked out on exactly the same pattern of concords. It is characterised by the "wisdom" of Christ; its dawn was in the time of the first Christians; its midday under Pope Silvester.[21] It will end in the evening of the advent of the great Antichrist and the night of the Church's defection to him. The third *status*, from the death of the great Antichrist to the end of the world, again follows exactly the same pattern: to it belong the seventh *etas*, the sixth and seventh *tempora* or seal-openings of the Church, an uncertain number of generations,[22] three great persons, St. Benedict, St. Bernard and St. Francis, twelve evangelical men, and two who correspond to Manasseh and Ephraim in the Old, and Mathias and Joseph in the New Testament. According to the second system of concord it began in St. Benedict when the second beginning (*initiatio*) of the monastic orders took place (the first having been under Ozias). It will pass through the same dawn, midday, evening and final night or third abomination in which Satan will be loosed before the Last Judgement. In some final concords of threes we have three expulsions: as Dan was expelled from the Order of Patriarchs and Manasseh substituted, and as Mathias was substituted for Judas among the Apostles, so one of the Franciscans will be expelled and another installed in his place. This prompts the idea of a "diabolical tempest" in each *status*, of which the second is that of the synagogue against Christ and the third of carnal Christians against *alius homo*. Finally, there are three Judgements: of the Jewish synagogue, of the carnal church, and of all in the Last Day.

It will be obvious that the concords have been brought up to date by introducing the eschatological role of St. Francis and his followers into the pattern and by incorporating Olivi's juxtaposition of the synagogue and the carnal church. Yet it is noteworthy that the author feels the need to go back

---

[21] The apotheosis of the Church under the Emperor Constantine and Pope Silvester is again a characteristic interpretation of Joachim (see *Lib. Conc.*, fols. 17v, 44r-45r, 52r, 66v; *Expos.*, fols. 62r-v, 163v; *Quat. Evang.*, pp. 106-107; *Lib. Fig.*, Pls. 16, 17). It is striking to find it here, however, since in the intervening period the upholders of evangelical poverty among Fraticelli, Beguins etc. had translated the Donation of Constantine into the source of evil which began the corruption of the Roman Church and its transformation into the Babylonish Whore. On one interpretation of the pageant in the Earthly Paradise, Dante was stressing here the sinister effects of the Donation, as he does elsewhere in the *Divina Commedia* (see *Inferno*, 19, 15-17; *Purgatorio*, 32, 124-129; *Paradiso*, 20, 55-60). For a Fraticelli view, see Luigi Fumi, *Eretici e Ribelli nell'Umbria* (Todi, undated), pp. 158-159. See Ch. 9 for a further explication of our author's view of the Donation.

[22] See *Brev.*, p. 182: ... *haberet generationes decem et nouem, unde haberet initium in generatione quadragesima quinta scilicet persone crucis. Si uero habet initium simpliciter in morte magni antichristi, habebit generationes decem et septem ....*

to the foundation of Joachimism, which is the doctrine of the three general *status*. Does he, however, fully understand the roots of this in Joachim's thought? Joachim derived the historical concords of "threes" from his belief that history itself was structured to reflect the nature of the Triune God.[23] In contrast, the author of the *Breviloquium* sees the threefold sequence of the natural world — dawn, midday, evening — as the key to this pattern and so conceives of each *status* as following the curve of nature. The Trinitarian meaning of history is subordinated to this new concept.[24] It is true that Joachim's thought — based on theological, not natural, considerations — contains an essential element of judgement, even deterioration, at the end of each *status*, including the third, since even the third, as part of the time-process, stands under judgement, *sub specie eternitatis*. But his main emphasis is upon the work of each Person in successive *status*, leading onwards in a spiritual progression and culminating in the apotheosis of history which is the work of the Holy Spirit. It is true also that Joachim uses biological metaphors from nature and the author of the *Breviloquium* is following him closely when he sees the second *status* as having a secret germination (or *initiatio*) in Ozias and the third in St. Benedict. But Joachim's symbolism here springs from the mystery of Son and Spirit proceeding from the Father, a concept never referred to in the *Breviloquium*. Moreover, Joachim uses his biological metaphors gloriously: his trees stand erect and crowned with triumph;[25] there is no hint of their decline into senectitude and death. In the *Breviloquium* the tremendous forward drive contained in Joachim's Trinitarian doctrine of history has become somewhat muted. The author works out the Trinitarian sequences conscientiously — even adding one of the attributes to the Persons not found in Joachim's writings[26] — but the *status* sometimes seem to be equal rather than progressive. The changed attitude of this fourteenth-century Joachite is also to be seen in the statement that in the third *status* Christ the Sun "shall shine seven-fold brighter than in the previous *status*." This gives a greater Christological emphasis to the third *status*, a shift of emphasis already found in the thought of Olivi and other Franciscan Joachites.[27] It is reinforced by the Gloss which — no doubt with heretical

---

[23] See Reeves, *Influence*, pp. 16-21.

[24] We may also note that twice — in the opening words of *Distinctiones* 1 and 11 — our author introduces the proverb "nothing new under the sun" in connection with the idea of concord: whatever is in the Old Testament must be repeated in the New (*Brev.*, pp. 178 and 265). This seems to reduce concord to repetition and is far from Joachim's concept of progressive revelation through meditation on concords.

[25] See *Lib. Fig.*, Pls. 1, 2, 5, 6, 22, 23.

[26] *Brev.*, p. 180.

[27] See Reeves, *Influence*, pp. 198, 209-210. But see also Reeves, "The Originality and Influence of Joachim of Fiore," *Traditio*, 36 (1980): 289-291, for a revised view of Joachim's Christology.

charges in mind — stresses the point that this does not refer to greater understanding of truth than now, "but rather to fuller knowledge of the many miracles which shall occur throughout the world and to the greater plenitude of conversion to Christ and His faith."[28] In spite of this hope the thought of the *Breviloquium* is tinged with the symbolism of the natural order, in which decay and death must follow birth and maturity. The author's other original concords — three expulsions, three tempests, three dark nights — all underline decline and fall in a way which Joachim's admission of three Judgements does not.

The second *Distinctio* deals with concords of Noble Persons at the beginning of each *status*.[29] These can be arranged in three sequences of threes: Abraham, Zacharias, St. Benedict; Isaac, John the Baptist, St. Bernard; Jacob, Christ, St. Francis. Except for St. Francis, these concords are derived from the *Liber Concordie*. Joachim never actually makes the third series of St. Benedict, St. Bernard and Another, but he links the first two with the Patriarchs and the extension of the pattern is easy to make.[30] The author then develops an intricate pattern of concords in twelves and twos from which he passes to an exposition of twelve tribes, churches and monasteries which is based on Joachim's number pattern of $5 + 7 = 12$.[31] The fives belong to Peter and therefore to the church of the second *status*; the sevens to John and the third *status*. The "sacrament of the entire third *status*, as it is set forth in Joachim's *concordia*"[32] is contained in the transitions which these number-patterns express: there will be twelve "evangelical men" to match patriarchs and apostles; twelve monasteries to match tribes and churches; two "most illustrious and holy men," like Moses and Aaron, to lead the elect people into the Promised Land. Here the author shows his grasp of some of the number sequences most important to Joachim.[33] He adds an original sequence of judgements: as ten tribes were led away captive by Assyria, so before the fall of New Babylon ten religious orders will suffer a threefold fall. These are listed in concord with the tribes of Israel.[34] They include, besides monastic orders and clergy, the crusading orders, the Dominicans and

---

[28] *Brev.*, p. 182.

[29] *Brev.*, p. 187.

[30] See references supra under n. 10; also *Lib. Conc.*, fols. 57r-60r, and the tree-figure, fol. 14r; *Vita St. Benedicti*, pp. 11-13.

[31] See *Lib. Conc.*, fols. 31v, 44r, 57v-58v; *Expos.*, fol. 17; *De Vita Sancti Benedicti et de Officio Divino secundum eius doctrinam*, ed. Cypriano Baraut, AST, 24 (1951): 21-22. For an explanation of this number-symbolism, see Reeves, "Liber Figurarum," MARS, 2 (1950): 77-79.

[32] *Brev.*, p. 194.

[33] See the full table of references to the work of Joachim.

[34] *Brev.*, p. 192.

Franciscans and the "Order of Continents" (*ordo continentium*), thus high-lighting vividly the smallness of the remnant to be saved.

The third *Distinctio* deals with concords of Cruel Persons who mark the evening of each *status*,[35] as the three *sollempnes personae* had marked its dawn. First came the "dragon" Pilate, the "beast" Herod, and the "false prophet" Caiaphas, with their followers; at the end of the second will come the "dragon or emperor," the "beast or pagan king," and the "false prophet or pontiff ... false and symoniac," together with the prelates, doctors and religious who follow them. These three will condemn the "life and teaching of Christ and His Church" in a persecution which is described in a long quotation from Olivi.[36] As Christ and the Apostles had been opposed by the forces of Judaism and Rome, so again the might of authority would come against the few. At the end of the third *status* the spiritual church will suffer similarly. It is specifically stated that because this is the third *status* the "third abomination" will be blasphemy against the Holy Spirit to whom the *status* is attributed. Thus again we see an extension of the pattern of threes which mutes the full triumph of the third *status*. At the same time it is noteworthy that the early pseudo-Joachimist works — obsessed as they were by the "unjust" condemnation of Joachim[37] — provided the typology of the infamous three whom we shall find appearing a number of times in the *Breviloquium*.

It is not until the fourth *Distinctio* that the author of the *Breviloquium* turns to the patterns of sevens which occupied more of Olivi's attention than the concept of the three general *status*.[38] He begins with the seven ages of the world (*etates*) which, after mentioning alternative interpretations, he expounds by "a more accurate method," that is, the method of Joachim and Olivi.[39] At the end of each *etas* he sees a terrible judgement of God: in the time of Noah, on Sodom, on the Egyptians in the time of Moses, on Eli and Saul, on the carnal synagogue, on the "church of carnal Christians," where he enlarges on the various manifestations of evil — and at the Last Judgement. Under the sixth *etas* he expounds the meaning of the four Beasts of Daniel 7 as the four great kingdoms of his day.[40] In the fifth *Distinctio* the seven "times" or periods (*tempora*) of the Church appear, with the seven wars or persecutions to be endured, the seven heads of the Dragon and the seven Orders of the true Church.[41] These are apostles, martyrs, doctors,

---

[35] *Brev.*, p. 196.

[36] See table of references.

[37] See supra, pp. 6-7.

[38] *Brev.*, p. 201.

[39] The author claims the authority of the Church for this system: ... *et sic tenet ecclesia* (*Brev.*, p. 201).

[40] Infra, p. 118.

[41] *Brev.*, p. 212.

anchorites and hermits, religious in regular orders, having temporal possessions, evangelical men (*viri evangelici*) possessing nothing, and "saintly men"
(*viri sancti*) of the seventh *tempus* from the death of Antichrist to the end
of the world. This sequence represents four stages of development: first, the
four traditional orders of the Church; secondly, Joachim's tentative extension
to seven; thirdly, the eschatological role claimed by the Spiritual Franciscans;
fourthly, our author's relegation of these to sixth place in order to leave the
great seventh place still open.[42] In dealing with the sixth *tempus*, which began
in St. Francis and will endure until the death of Antichrist, the author goes
into more detail, for he is seeking the signs of the times.[43] This is the time
in which there first occurred a "miraculous renewal" throughout the Church.
The forty-fifth generation after Christ will see a spiritual baptism, followed
by a flight of the church of the elect into the wilderness, thus reenacting the
life of Christ. Finally, prefigured in the Resurrection, the Christian people
will obtain victory over Antichrist "through the new spiritual Church." The
seventh, or sabbath, *tempus* is described in Joachim's words from the *Liber
Concordie.*[44]

The sixth *Distinctio* develops the concords between the seven *etates* of the
world and the seven *tempora* of the Church, drawing heavily on Olivi's
works.[45] These quotations include the key-passage quoted above in which
Olivi draws out the parallel roles of Christ and St. Francis.[46] In the elaboration of this pattern our author prophesies the triumph of the evangelical
order, "when the church of carnal Christians has expired." The new order
will subjugate "all the beasts and all the land, both Christian and pagan, and
will raise the fish and the birds, that is, the religious, to governance."[47] He
crowns this with a quotation from the *Liber Concordie* on "that future holy
people and order of the righteous," typified in Solomon, which is to appear
"near the end."[48]

The seventh and eighth *Distinctiones* work out concords between the seven
tempora of the Church and, first, the seven days of Creation, secondly, the
seven sacraments. The seventh[49] is almost wholly quoted from Olivi, includ-

[42] In dealing with the four *apertiones* of the sixth *status*, the author refers to Joachim (*ut
narrat Ioachim*) in connection with the head of the dragon *quasi occasum* which revives again.
This is probably a reference to *Expos.*, fols. 164v-165v.

[43] Infra, p. 117.

[44] *Lib. Conc.*, fol. 96r.

[45] *Brev.*, p. 222.

[46] Supra, p. 22.

[47] *Brev.*, pp. 224-225. Here the author seems to imply the triumph of the whole Franciscan
order (cf. supra, p. 80) and this prophecy is reinforced in a marginal note: *nota de excelantia
ordinis minorum fratrum super ordines aliorum.*

[48] *Lib. Conc.*, fol. 69v.

[49] *Brev.*, pp. 227-232. See table of references. Referring at the end to the persecution

ing his concord between the creation of Man, to whom God subjected all other living creatures, on the sixth Day and the emergence of the "evangelical order ... formed, as rational Man, in the image of God" in the sixth *tempus* of the Church, to whom all other orders would be subordinated. Similarly, the concords in the eighth *Distinctio*[50] are taken from Olivi, with the addition of a passage on Leah and Rachel as types of Synagogue and Church, and then of the active and contemplative churches, which is drawn from Joachim.[51] In the ninth *Distinctio*[52] the author expounds the pattern of double sevens: seven seals in the Old Testament matched with seven openings in the New. Here he incorporates Joachim's little tract *De Septem Sigillis*.[53] When he reaches the opening of the fifth seal, however, he interpolates a passage on Frederick II, the king of France and Louis of Bavaria as persecutors of the Church, especially mentioning the attack on Boniface VIII. The exposition of the sixth seal is also extended and at its opening our author abandons Joachim to give a detailed exposition of events which we shall examine later.[54] He returns again to Joachim's brief text for the seventh seal and its opening and the concluding paragraph on the winding-up of history.[55] In his last exploration of the concords of sevens – the tenth *Distinctio*[56] – the author makes a double-seven sequence of his own by taking the seven heads of the Dragon, commonly identified with tyrants in the Christian era, and matching them with seven tyrants in the Old Testament.[57] In the New Dispensation he follows Joachim for the first four – Herod, Nero, Constantius Arrianus, Mahomet – but for his fifth, while turning, like Joachim, to the German *Imperium*,[58] he names Frederick, "emperor and

---

of the elect, the author puts an interesting accusation into the mouths of the persecutors: *Dicent regulam euangelicam esse mathematicam nec ad salutem esse necessarium ... (Brev.,* p. 231).

[50] *Brev.*, pp. 233-234.

[51] These two form part of a typology of Biblical women (Hagar and Sarah, Rebecca, Leah and Rachel, Elizabeth and Mary) which Joachim examines a number of times and forms into various patterns of concords. The *Brev.* does not quote Joachim directly but gives a simpler, more clear-cut version which presses home more sharply the symbolism of Leah's supercession by Rachel. See *Lib. Conc.*, fols. 56v-57r, 70r, 83r; *Expos.*, fols. 12r-v, 18v-20r.

[52] *Brev.*, pp. 235-256.

[53] For this work, see supra, p. 4.

[54] Infra, pp. 117-120.

[55] *Brev.*, pp. 255-256.

[56] *Brev.*, pp. 257-264.

[57] This double sequence seems to be the author's own, not traceable to Olivi, while the expanded section on the sixth New Testament head (*Brev.*, pp. 259-262) is obviously original in its Spanish and Sicilian bias (see infra, pp. 129-130).

[58] Joachim does not always give exactly the same sequence. *Expos.*, fol. 10r has Herod, Nero, Constantius Arrianus, Cosdroe, king of Persia (for Mahomet), one of the kings of Babylon (i.e. German Emperor), Saladin, Antichrist; fol. 196v gives for the fifth *qui primus in partibus occiduis cepit fatigare ecclesiam pro investitura ecclesiarum* (i.e. Henry IV). The *Lib.*

Bavarian." The sixth head is the Eleventh King of *Daniel* 7.24, who will cause the election of the *papa antichristus*.[59] Here he quotes a sibylline oracle, beginning *De porta Yspanie egredietur infans*, which points to Peter IV as candidate for the sixth head, on whose role he discourses at some length.[60] This passage culminates in a reference to the Angelic Pope.[61] The seventh head is Antichrist and the tail will be "that worst man who is called Gog," representing the unloosing of Satan at the end of the seventh time and followed by the end of history.[62]

The third way in which the *Breviloquium* treats of concords — by generations — occupies the whole of the last part of the book. The eleventh *Distinctio*[63] is concerned with "special concords to reveal the certain time of those things to be accomplished in the new era through comparison with those enacted in the old." This is basically a pattern of twos. Blocks of ten generations are matched and the important concords then sought. This recalls one of Joachim's methods in the *Liber Concordie*.[64] A notable concord is established between the ten generations from Joash to the transmigration of old Babylon and those from Celestine V to the transmigration of new Babylon. The author follows Joachim in his general units of sixty-three generations to each Dispensation, as well as in his search for special concords which are forty-two generations apart.[65] Here some of the concords contain echoes of Joachim's interpretations, for example, Elisha matched with St. Benedict, the Pharisees and Sadducees prefiguring new orders, now identifed as Dominicans and Franciscans, the conversion of Samaria pointing to the return of the Greek Church to its true obedience.[66] Other concords

---

Fig. has Melsemutus for the fifth. The author of the *Brev.* may well have seen the Dragon in the pseudo-Joachimist collection of figures preceding the *Super Esaiam* which usually had Henry I, Saladin, Frederick II for the last three heads, see, for example, Vatican City, Biblioteca Apostolica Vaticana, MSS Vat. Lat. 4959, fol. 2v; Vat. Ross. 552, fol. 3v; London, British Library, MS Add. 11439, fol. 101v; Prague, National Museum, MS XIV.B.17, fol. 3v; also printed editions: *Super Esaiam* (1517); *Expositio* (1527).

[59] See infra, p. 122.

[60] See infra, p. 118.

[61] We have been unable to trace the source of this sibylline oracle, but in style it resembles thirteenth-century Joachimist works such as the *Expositio super Sibillis et Merlino* and the *Oraculum Cyrilli*. The reference to the Angelic Pope suggests a late thirteenth-century date when this concept was just emerging.

[62] *Brev.*, pp. 262 and 264. This is Joachim's standard interpretation, see especially *Lib. Fig.*, Pl. 14. Joachim's concession to the return of tribulation before the end is seen in his use of Antiochus Epiphanes before the First, and Gog before the Second Advent. But the Seventh Head was the crucial climax of evil whose conquest made valid the triumphant Sabbath Age, while the tail was merely the tail.

[63] *Brev.*, pp. 265-271.

[64] See *Lib. Conc.*, fol. 43v.

[65] *Brev.*, pp. 266 and 271. See *Lib. Conc.*, fol. 134v.

[66] *Brev.*, pp. 266-268. For Elisha and St. Benedict, see *Lib. Conc.*, fols. 11v, 23r, 57v.

reflect more immediate experiences, such as the slaughter of the Innocents prefiguring the persecution of the new evangelical children (*pueri euangelici*) and Noah's Flood as typifying the destruction of New Babylon when only the remnant of the spiritual church will be saved. Some concords, based on Joachim's calculations, carry the projections further: 1260 years from the descent of Jacob and the patriarchs into Egypt to the sixth seal of the Old Testament, in which there was a double tribulation, is matched by 1260 years from the descent of Christ and the Apostles into the land of the Gentiles to the double tribulation of the mystic and great Antichrists.[67] Here Herod appears again. Furthermore, in the forty-fifth generation after Abraham came forth "that poisonous serpent Caiphas" and his pseudo-prophets to condemn Christ; equally in the forty-fifth generation from Christ will appear a similar poisonous serpent (*venenosus coluber*) with his train, uttering heresies against the life and doctrine of Christ.[68] As the apostolic order (*ordo apostolicus*) once stood firm on the foundation of Peter, so also will the evangelical order (*ordo euangelicus*). Again, as at the end of the forty-fifth generation after Abraham the sceptre was taken from Judah and given to the new leader (*novus dux*) Jesus Christ, so in the parallel time will be revealed the new leader or pontiff of new Jerusalem.[69] Events in the life of Christ are projected typologically into the future and finally the rule of Pilate is matched with that of the Eleventh King.[70] In the forty-sixth generation from Abraham the *transmigratio ecclesie* prefigured the "translation" which must be made from the Roman imperium or Christendom to the nations, "that is, to the Holy Land and to other infidel nations."[71]

Joachim uses the Pharisees only, as the type of a new religious order, see ibid., fols. 23r, 57r-v, and notes to the list of generations, fol. 11v. In many passages the schism of the Greek and Roman churches is seen typified in the split between Israel and Judah. The return of the Greek Church to Rome is expected in *Lib. Conc.*, fols. 17v, 117r (where Greece = Samaria), 125v-126r. The passage which most fully expresses these ideas is *Expos.*, fols. 142v-145v, a passage in which incidentally there is a reference to Daniel's prophecy of the Eleventh King (fol. 143r).

[67] 1260 was, of course, the key number for Joachim, arrived at by several proofs. But he always maintained that there could be no certainty about the times which were in God's hands and refused to tie his programme to the *date* 1260. After the year 1260 had passed, some of his disciples contrived to push the date on to 1290 by reckoning *a passione* instead of *a nativitate*. A further revised calculation is used here.

[68] Again, the prophecies are projected further forward by carrying the concords beyond the forty-second to the forty-fifth generation. This places the dating of these last events beyond 1350.

[69] See *Lib. Conc.*, fol. 56r, where Joachim uses almost the same words, but with Zorobabel as the type and calculating the generation as the forty-second after Jacob and after Christ.

[70] *Brev.*, pp. 268-269.

[71] This would bring the date to 1380, but, in fact, the author of the *Brev.* makes it 1367 by calculating a shortened forty-sixth generation. See table of dates of the Last Times, infra, p. 161.

In the twelfth *Distinctio*[72] the author tackles a problem which occupied Joachim considerably: the differing lengths of generations between the Old and New Dispensations. Here he quotes Olivi in a passage in which Olivi refers to Joachim.[73] Like Joachim he begins by calculating the New Testament generations in thirty-year spans, so that forty-two generations would bring him to 1260 which had been the great Joachimist date. This now needs revision. By making the starting point either the Passion of Christ — which reconciles the 1260 with the 1290 days of *Daniel* 12 — or the second generation after Christ — which would bring the date up to 1320 — he is able to bring the critical period nearer his own time. After the next generation he postulates a transitional half-generation from 1350 to arrive at the moment of crisis, a calculation consistent with his placement of the 44 days of silence which are to begin in the 1320s.

In the thirteenth *Distinctio*[74] the author surveys the whole sweep of the concords from Adam to Christ and from Christ to Antichrist. The Old Testament generations follow the genealogy of St. Matthew and in the New Dispensation each thirty years is designated in the pope reigning at its beginning. Here his fundamental pattern is Joachimist. This is notable in his concord of David's triumph in Jerusalem with Constantine and Pope Silvester, and in other concords, such as that between Judah and Israel and schism between the Latin and Greek churches, both commonplaces of Joachim's system. The Abbot is directly quoted on Zorobabel as the *novus dux* prefiguring the *novus pontifex* to come. Our author goes solidly through the generations, annotating each with lists of names. He follows Joachim in using the miracle of the sun going ten degrees backwards in the time of Hezekiah to make the necessary adjustments of generations, referring to one of Joachim's trees in this connection.[75] He is original, however, in finding special significance in the terminal generations at either end of the Old Dispensation, that is, the last eleven from Zorobabel to Christ and the first six from Jareth back to Adam. These together make a special concord with the seventeen generations expected in the third *status*: "Those final six generations from the first parent until Enoch and those eleven final genera-

---

[72] *Brev.*, pp. 272-277.

[73] See table of references. Olivi's allusion to Joachim is probably a reference to *De Semine Scripturarum*, a work written quite outside Joachimist circles and probably first ascribed to Joachim by Arnold of Vilanova, see Raoul Manselli, *La Religiosità D'Arnaldo da Villanova* (Rome, 1951), pp. 12-15, cited supra, p. 29.

[74] *Brev.*, pp. 278-297. The opening paragraph on the four *animalia* of the Apocalypse adapts one of Joachim's favourite themes.

[75] The mystical meaning of this famous episode in Hezekiah's reign fascinated Joachim. He refers to it many times, but see especially *Lib. Conc.*, fols. 15r-16v, 44r. See table of references. The reference to the *arbor Ioachimi* is difficult to identify.

tions from Zorobabel to the coming of Christ as Man make a total of seventeen, and signify the span of the Last Times or third *status* of the world."[76] Here we have an ingenious extension of Joachim's number symbolism in order to project the generations of the third *status* – a development from which Joachim himself had drawn back. In the forty-fifth generation, in concord with Jechonias, the *summus pontifex*, John XXII, is taken captive by Babylon. But in three generations Babylon will have been overthrown by the new Persians, i.e. Sicily, and the new Zorobabel will rebuild the new Jerusalem.

The fourteenth and last *Distinctio* of the *Breviloquium* repeats many of these concords in an extensive Table of Concords, modelled on Joachim's but called in the title to the fourteenth *Distinctio* not a *tabula* but a *scala generationum utriusque testamenti*.[77] In the introductory paragraph this is specifically connected with Jacob's ladder, an interesting point, since Joachim had not explicitly used the symbolism of Jacob's ladder to any great extent. In his *Liber Figurarum*, however, there is a pair of tree-ladders in which possibly an allusion to this sacred ladder is intended.[78] It may be that the author of the *Breviloquium* had this in mind, but it was one of the two pairs of tables of concords in the *Liber Figurarum* which he definitely followed.[79] This is made clear in a number of features: the double line of generations in the Old Testament from Joseph to Samuel: the synchronising of the seven seals and openings and the double-seven conflicts with the generations; the assignation of XXX years to each New Testament generation; the incorporation of the twelve Patriarchs/Tribes matched by Apostles/Churches; some of the distinctive notes, for example the double *initiatio* of clergy and monks in the Old Dispensation and the New. One specific detail proves beyond doubt that the author had before him these particular tables: the original – for whatever reason – had made a mistake in assigning the generation beginning in 1200 to Celestine III (d. 1298) instead of Innocent III;[80] in the *Breviloquium* this entry is carefully repeated. On the other hand, the notes throughout demonstrate the special emphases of Joachimism as revised by Franciscans. Thus a note at the generation of Noah draws attention to the contrasts of the raven and dove;[81] the special symbolism

---

[76] *Brev.*, p. 287.

[77] *Brev.*, p. 298.

[78] *Lib. Fig.*, Pls. 20, 21. See Reeves, Hirsch-Reich, *The Figurae of Joachim of Fiore*, p. 169 for a discussion of this point.

[79] *Lib. Fig.*, Pls. 3, 4.

[80] On the possible significance of this error, see Reeves, *Influence*, p. 28.

[81] *Coruus spiritalis ex archa ecclesie egressurus ad archam ultra non reuertetur quia cadaueribus se immisset; columba uero contemplatiua et innocens et per celum uolans, post*

which Joachim found in Manasseh and Ephraim is now applied to Dominic and Francis;[82] the significant place which Joachim allots to the rise of the Order of Pharisees is again picked out in order to establish a concord with the Mendicants.[83] The author uses his initiative in another way by trying to tie every possible pattern of history into one tabulation, including all Joachim's patterns scattered throughout his works and some of his own as well. Thus double Dragon's Heads, the seven visions of the *Apocalypse*, the five and seven Churches, all find a place. Our author is far more systematic than Joachim himself.

From 1200 onwards, of course, the table becomes original, though still using Joachim's general patterns. Frederick II figures as the fifth head of the Dragon, appearing several times in the notes. St. Francis, St. Dominic and their Orders find a natural place in the fortieth generation from Christ. Under the opening of the sixth seal come the "spiritual transmigration" from Jerusalem, the "violent tempest" of the sixth and seventh Dragon's heads and the "persecution of new Babylon." The sixth head is the Eleventh King and the seventh the great Antichrist; between them will supervene the brief period of peace when the Holy City will be recovered and rebuilt. But the seventh king, Antichrist, will usurp the seat of God and Satan unloosed will seduce the peoples. This programme is sketched in the note accompanying the forty-first generation and elaborated under the next generations. The last pope named in the table is Martin IV thus:

Generatio XLIII	Martinus cum Quinque	Anni ab incarnatione
Anni XXX		MCCLXXXX

The next entries give dates but substitute Old Testament kings for popes. Thus at 1320 we have Jechonias. As we have seen, this ill-fated ruler certainly represented John XXII and the readers of the *Breviloquium* would probably understand this. Near the end of his genealogy the author says that only God knows who these pontiffs of the third *status* ought to be,[84] but his audience could quickly draw its own conclusions from his calculations. The forty-sixth generation is designated in Salatiel and is precisely dated 1367. At this point occurs the great upheaval of the Eleventh King and Antichrist.

---

diluuium Babilonis noue, in signum pacis portans ramum oliue uirentibus foliis reuerteretur. (*Brev.*, p. 300).

[82] *Brev.*, p. 303. See *Lib. Conc.*, fols. 27r-28v; *Expos.*, fol. 32v. In the *Lib. Fig.*, Pl. 23 Joachim again uses this typology of Manasseh and Effraim in a tree which was certainly known to Joachites and used to express the aspirations of different orders, see Reeves, Hirsch-Reich, *The Figurae of Joachim of Fiore*, p. 132.

[83] See supra, p. 111, n. 66.

[84] *Quot autem erunt pontifices in isto tercio statu generali soli Deo relinquendum est, qui omnia nouit* (*Brev.*, p. 319).

After this no more dates are given. The forty-seventh generation is designated in the new Zorobabel, while the sealed tribes (which derive from Joachim's table), the fragmentary reference to apostles and the entry of six and six monasteries bring us into the third *status*.[85] This is confirmed in the accompanying note where the Sibyl is cited as promising that "1335 years after the immolation of the Lamb there will commence a paschal age which has not been seen from the beginning of the world until that time."[86] The crucial transition to the third *status* is thus placed in the forty-fifth and forty-sixth generations; the last *status* itself begins in generation forty-seven:

> In the forty-seventh generation from the Advent of Christ, after the earlier general tribulation has been endured, and the wheat has been diligently separated from the universal chaff of sinners, a new Zorobabel or new leader shall arise, a universal pontiff of the new universal church of Jerusalem, who is to be revealed in the forty-sixth generation, just as Christ as new leader and pontiff was revealed in the forty-sixth generation from Abraham, when circumcision was superseded by baptism and the figure of the Paschal Lamb was superseded by the institution of the Sacrament of the Eucharist. This age is distinguished by generations and pontiff-kings, because the Lord Jesus Christ was both king and priest.[87]

Thus the rulers of the third *status* will be priest-kings, who are designated according to the system explained in the previous *distinctio*, that is, by the last eleven and first six of the Old Testament generations.[88] Reckoning Jechonias and Salatiel as representing transitional generations, the forty-seventh to fifty-seventh are designated in Zorobabel to Joseph, "the husband of Mary," and the fifty-eighth to sixty-third go backwards from Jareth to Adam. The note beside Elyachim (forty-ninth) describes the seventh time, the Sabbath age of justice and abundant peace which will last until the opening of the seventh seal, when Satan will be unloosed and the final persecution of Gog take place. The third *status* appears to be lived under the shadow of impending doom, for notes to the generations from the fifty-second to fifty-fourth give the Fifteen Signs of the Last Judgement. When the genealogy turns back to the beginning, the end is near. At "Caynam"

---

[85] See *Lib. Fig.*, Pls. 3, 4. For the twelve monasteries which will match the twelve tribes and churches, see *Lib. Conc.*, fol. 57v.

[86] We have not been able to trace the reference to the Sibyl, but the phrase *tempus paschale quale non fuit ab initio mundi* etc. identifies the source as a Joachimist one. For a similar use of this phrase, see *Lib. Conc.*, fol. 133r; *Expos.*, fols. 15v, 206r-v, 213r-v; *Vita S. Benedicti*, pp. 102-103; *Lib. Fig.*, Pl. 19. See table of dates, infra, p. 161, for further confirmation of the beginning of the third *status*.

[87] *Brev.*, p. 318.

[88] *Supra*, p. 113.

(sixtieth), Christ's fold is split in three parts; at Enos (sixty-first) the "open and last Antichrist, Gog and Magog" appear; at Adam (sixty-third) come the "signs of judgement [*Signa Iudicii*]." The closing words are "the Judgement is set and the Books are opened." (*Daniel*, 7.10).

If we now examine the political programme of the *Breviloquium* in more detail, we find that the author has been considerably influenced by Olivi and Roquetaillade in bringing the prophecies up-to-date but remains independent in some of his interpretations. He sees the sixth *tempus* of the Church as having four *initia* or *apertiones*.[89] The first, initiated by St. Francis, was marked by Frederick II, identified not only as the fifth dragon's head but also as the beast "wounded unto death" of *Apocalypse* 12.3. In it "the evangelical state, the state of the Ladies of Poverty, and the state of the Brothers of Penitence" were renewed.[90] The second was that of the mystic Antichrist, described in Olivi's terms as "the apostate beast from the land of the religious, having two horns of false religious and false prophets," placed on the papal throne by the emperor and instituting a time of "strongest temptation."[91] Our author assigns this time to John XXII and Louis of Bavaria, and since this mystic Antichrist was a pseudo-pope to be, he was probably to be identified with John himself. Here the *Breviloquium* does not follow Roquetaillade, but rather the common Beguin tradition. As with Roquetaillade, however, the mystic Antichrist is ceasing to be a symbol of paramount importance: his time is past. This period saw also the beginning of the war between England and France. The third, marked by the "beginning of the mission of the Holy Spirit which God will give to the evangelical men," is the present, a period given to the true Church to order its defences against the coming great Antichrist, to prepare for the new baptism by the Spirit and to make ready for flight into the desert. The fourth will see a general commotion under the ten kings.

It is to the tribulations of these last two periods that our author devotes most attention. In effect, he abandons the partnership of the mystic and great Antichrists, as used by Olivi,[92] and returns to those other figures of the Dragon's heads and the Beasts of Daniel, making the sixth and seventh heads the Eleventh King and the great Antichrist. He is especially concerned with the structure of contemporary politics and notably with the identity of the

---

[89] *Brev.*, p. 214.
[90] Supra, p. 90.
[91] *Brev.*, p. 215.
[92] Supra, pp. 23-25.

Eleventh King and his connection with the House of Aragon and with Sicily.[93]

Here he relies greatly on expositions of the Book of Daniel, particularly concerning the four great beasts who ascend from the infidel sea to destroy the land of the faithful.[94] The first, the lion, signifies Rome or Italy; the second, the bear, signifies Germany; the third, the panther, Greece; the fourth, Spain. This fourth beast, terrible, marvellous and exceedingly strong, is the main focus of attention. It has ten horns and a greater horn which will arise after them, signifying in the Old Dispensation Antiochus who arose from Alexander's kingdom, entered Jerusalem and placed the Abomination of Desolation upon the altar. This same sequence is to be repeated in the New Dispensation. In the fifth age, in the time of Charlemagne, the Roman empire was divided into ten kingdoms. Now an eleventh kingdom has arisen from these and an eleventh king must come forth from the seed of the eagle, i.e. from Frederick II. Here one sees how crucial to the argument of the *Breviloquium* is Roquetaillade's emphasis on the importance of the marriage of Constantia and Peter III,[95] which our author discusses in *Distinctio* 13. Whether he took it directly from Roquetaillade cannot be determined. He lists the present eleven kingdoms of the Roman Empire as follows: Cyprus, Hungary, Bohemia, Sicily, France, England, Aragon, Majorca, Navarre, Castille and Portugal. In terms of the four beasts, Spain, as the fourth, is the most important and Aragon in particular is marked, since this house was united with the eagle of Frederick II. Thus it is in the gate of Spain, in Catalonia and Aragon, that the Eleventh King will arise.

Throughout *Distinctio* 4 the author avoids explicitly naming Peter IV of Aragon as the Eleventh King, but gradually leads the reader to the unequivocal identification. He is to be known primarily as he fits the description given in *Daniel* 7; he will be greater than those who preceded him, he will bring low three kings, he will preach against God, and will believe that he can change the times and the laws. The empire of Catalonia and Aragon has had eleven rulers, the author continues, five in Aragon,[96] three in Majorca[97] and three in Sicily:[98] one of these is to be the Eleventh King (*qui nunc est. Erit*

---

[93]   *Brev.*, pp. 206-208.

[94]   Joachim expounds this vision of Daniel in *Lib. Conc.*, fols. 40v, 127v-128v; *Expos.*, fols. 24r, 162v-163v, but does not apply it to the kingdoms of his own day.

[95]   Supra, pp. 76-77.

[96]   Peter III (1276-1285); Alfonso III (1286-1291); James II (1291-1327); Alfonso IV (1327-1336); Peter IV (1336-1387).

[97]   James II (ob. 1311); Sancho (ob. 1324); James of Majorca (ob. 1349).

[98]   Frederick II (ob. 1337); Peter II (ob. 1342); Louis (ob. 1355).

ille),[99] but he is not yet named. His works will reveal his identity to those who have eyes for the truth.

In the following paragraphs, more hints are given concerning his present situation and the role he is to play in the Last Times. The etymological identification of Catalonia as "devastation" is given, and he is compared with Alexander the Great, who rose from a "small kingdom" and was a formidable warrior.[100] There then follows a passage which can only apply to Peter IV: he will bring down three kings from his own nation or his own blood, one of whom he has already brought low, deposed and decapitated.[101] This is a clear reference to the death and decapitation of James of Majorca, who died in 1349 in an attempt to regain the island from Peter, who had captured it in 1343. The remainder of *Distinctio* 4 concerns the actions of the Eleventh King which are yet to come, based on Daniel's predictions, cited above: his preaching against God, his attempt to change the times and the laws, and his warfare against kings, princes and *"communitates,"* "both on land and on sea."[102] In *Distinctio* 9, where his story is once again taken up, the Eleventh King is described, along with Alexander, as a person small in stature (*paruus persona*).[103] Finally, in *Distinctio* 14, the date 1367 is given as the year in which the Eleventh King's actions are to fulfill his eschatological promise, and we are told that at that time "Peter began, and Peter shall bring the end."[104]

Peter IV (also known as Pere III) possessed the personal attributes and pursued the kind of career which virtually ensured that he should have a leading role in the drama fashioned by the author of the *Breviloquium*. Born prematurely at the age of seven months, Peter was short in height, a deficiency for which he compensated by wearing splendid robes, carrying himself majestically and engaging in elaborate ceremonial. He crowned himself in Saragossa at the age of 16 in 1336, believed that he had a divine mission as ruler of Aragon and Catalonia, displayed a life-long interest in history, and had chronicles of his reign written. He was a man of passion and violence, filled with hatred and suspicion of his relatives, and, as Hillgarth has said, "took every crisis to its most extreme conclusions."[105]

His political aspirations, especially up to 1356, were also of the kind to excite an apocalyptic mind. Although the Catalan-Aragonese confederation

---

[99] *Brev.*, p. 207.
[100] Ibid., pp. 207-208, 204-205.
[101] Ibid., p. 208.
[102] Ibid., p. 208.
[103] Ibid., p. 245.
[104] Ibid., p. 317.
[105] Jocelyn Hillgarth, *The Spanish Kingdoms* (Oxford, 1978), 1: 349.

had nominal control of the Balearic Islands, Sicily and Sardinia, when Peter took the throne all these possessions had become independent or were in danger of being lost. However, Peter was the first of his line to see the possibility of a Mediterranean empire, so that his long reign, Hillgarth states, "was largely devoted to the integration of his ancestors' conquests under Catalan rule." [106] He abandoned expansion by land against Castile, but recaptured Majorca, allied himself with Venice, and carried on a war with Genoa. The war with Genoa (1351-1353) took his galleys as far as the Bosphorus in 1352, where the allied Catalan-Venetian-Byzantine fleet defeated the Genoese. Taken in the context of his victory in civil war with the nobility of Aragon and Valencia in 1348, and with the death of James of Majorca in 1349, Peter's supremacy in the western Mediterranean and the power he seemed capable of wielding in the eastern seas made him a very convincing candidate for the part of Eleventh King. [107]

Peter's antipathy toward the established church also fit the circumstances necessary for his apocalyptic role. He had a number of papal processes and Bulls publicly burnt, and, when angered by papal officials, threatened them and sometimes caused them physical violence. Peter insisted on control over church appointments, with the result that "after 1350 almost no foreign name appeared among the bishops of Pere's realms." [108]

Because the Eleventh King is to conquer Sicily, it seems likely that Peter IV was seen as the heir to Louis and that the *Breviloquium* was written during Louis' reign (1342-1355). [109] This would account for the absence of Frederick IV from the list of Sicilian kings. If Peter is intended to fulfill his destiny in Sicily — and he is closely associated with that island in *Distinctio* 9 — the author of the *Breviloquium* has made use of the Joachimist tradition on the destiny of Sicily in an original way. We learn in *Distinctio* 4 that he will also attack France, will contend with the pope and temporarily overwhelm the Church. Above all, he will be in league with the great Antichrist who, as we shall see, was to be "ecclesiastical rather than secular." Daniel's time of silence and the power of darkness belong to this forty-sixth generation, and the reign of the Eleventh King will culminate in great destruction.

---

[106] Ibid., p. 347.

[107] In fact, Peter never again conducted military or naval operations in the east, but thereafter concentrated on the western Mediterranean. He did interest himself in the duchy of Athens in the 1380s, and in certain ecclesiastical appointments in the east, but these were peripheral to his major interests.

[108] Hillgarth, *The Spanish Kingdoms*, p. 355. Peter himself was a religious man who took seriously his own duty "to see to the religion of his subjects.", ibid., p. 356.

[109] Peter wished to acquire Sicily, but the task was not accomplished until the reign of Joan I. See the section on chronology and dating in the introduction to the text, infra, pp. 160-161.

In the ninth *Distinctio* our author shifts the perspective to the five great symbolic events at the end of the Old Dispensation as prophecies of those to come in the New.[110] These are the transmigration of Jerusalem, i.e. of the spiritual church; the persecution of new Babylon; the first tribulation under the Eleventh King; the rebuilding of the temple and walls of the city; and finally, the second tribulation under the great Antichrist. The first event is, therefore, the separation of the true church — the spiritual Jerusalem — from Babylon, the carnal church. The author probably follows Olivi here in dating the beginning of this separation from the time of Innocent IV, which saw the beginning of the struggle over evangelical poverty. He evokes a variety of supporting typology. As Moses and Aaron and Paul and Barnabas were called to lead the chosen people out of persecution, so two men have been appointed to lead the faithful out of the *ecclesia carnalis*. The flight of the Holy Family from Herod[111] and subsequent return to Jerusalem gives an important concord with Innocent IV's flight from Frederick II and the flight-to-come of someone from the unnamed seed of Frederick. Again, Christ's withdrawal to the desert after baptism prefigures "the flight or transmigration which certain spiritual men must make from Christianity to the infidel nations." Finally, the flight of the disciples after the arrest of Christ "in that dark night of capture and condemnation of the life and person of Christ," when without a shepherd the flock dispersed to the desert and to caves of the mountain, signifies the "terrible flight" which must be made by the evangelical men during "that dark night of the condemnation of the life and doctrine of the evangelical state," when they shall flee as a flock dispersed without a shepherd.[112] The conclusion of this part of the redemptive drama is figured in one of Joachim's favourite types: the return of Judith which signifies the preaching of the word of God by the new spiritual men at the end of the age.[113]

The second great "event" will be the persecution of new Babylon, formerly Jerusalem, whose populace will be said to be Christian but will be in fact "the synagogue of Satan."[114] Great battles will occur, and the Saracen hordes will invade the Christian nations. The "true Christians," our author states, will be liberated from the tribulations of this event by the fulfillment of the typology of the flood, which brings renovation:

---

[110] *Brev.*, p. 240.
[111] See the use made of this typology in the *Super Hier.*, fols. 43v-44v.
[112] *Brev.*, p. 241.
[113] See *Lib. Conc.*, fols. 117v-119r.
[114] *Brev.*, p. 242.

Just as the first flood of the waters over the sinners of the earth in the Old Testament time of Noah corresponds with the first flood of the infidel nations over Jerusalem in the New Testament of Titus and Vespasian, so does this second inundation of old Babylon foreshadow the second inundation of new Babylon.[115]

Next comes the first tribulation, the persecution by the Eleventh King, "head of the bestial nations." The key passage, interpreting *Daniel* 7, concerns the modern types of the kings of the Medes, Persians, and Greeks. Our author, basing himself probably on Olivi or Roquetaillade,[116] identifies the Medes with France, Greece with Spain, Persia with Sicily, and Macedonia with Catalonia. As Alexander came from Macedonia as a small person and was at first despised, so from Catalonia will come a small person, at first despised, who will persecute Darius, i.e. the king of France. This process was begun by Peter II who conquered Sicily from Charles II and defeated the king of France. It will be completed by Peter's seed, Peter IV, who is the Eleventh King. He will ally with the infidel and persecute the Church, causing a three-fold overthrow of prelates, religious, and laymen. The false Christians will support the Eleventh King in the election of a false pope, but the elect in all three groups will practise the true faith in secret and be saved. His end implies a last-minute conversion to righteousness: after his humiliation of three kings, he will journey to the Holy Land to overcome the pride of the Saracens, and just before expiring there will hand over that "glorious land" to the Angelic Pope.

But in the fourth "event" of the sixth *tempus* — the rebuilding of the temple under the new Zorobabel — the King of Persia, i.e. Sicily, must take part, and this king would also seem to be Peter IV in his role of conqueror of Sicily. It is an original idea to place this symbolic rebuilding between the two tribulations, for Joachim had used the ascent of Zorobabel to Jerusalem to typify the triumphant ushering in of the third *status* and seventh age.[117] In the *Breviloquium*, however, it is only an interlude, followed by the fifth "event," the tribulation of the great Antichrist, which the author finds described in *Daniel* 11, *"Behold three Kings shall govern in Persia,"* identified as Sicily. This passage implies an alliance between the resuscitated Eleventh King and the great Antichrist who will be a religious leader, a pseudo-pope. This is again an original idea, reversing the roles of great and mystic Antichrists

---

[115] Ibid., p. 243.
[116] The source for this passage has not yet been identified. It might be either Olivi or Roquetaillade.
[117] *Lib. Conc.*, fol. 56r-v.

according to Olivianist and other interpretations, though using the same imagery of Nero and Simon Magus.[118]

The role of the House of Aragon and of Peter IV in particular is obviously crucial. As the seed of Frederick II it carries sinister implications and Peter himself as the Eleventh King seems to epitomise the political forces of evil. Yet, seen as the conqueror of Sicily and therefore identified with the king of Persia, he also seems to support the new Zorobabel and side with the forces of righteousness. France occupies an inferior position. It is due to be destroyed by the Eleventh King and, except in the identification with the *Rex Austri* cited above, is not seen among the forces for good. Again, attitudes towards the Papacy are ambivalent. Innocent IV's flight from Frederick II is treated as a persecution of the true Church. Although John XXII seems to be the mystic Antichrist, he is also Jechonias, the victim of Babylon, not its leader. A schism is expected between true and false popes, but this is in the future and there is no echo of the Fraticelli view that from John XXII onwards the Roman pontificate had become the Babylonish Whore.

It is particularly striking that no identification of the final powers of righteousness, either political or religious, are made. There is no clue as to the identity of the *nouus Zorobabel* or the succeeding priest-kings. The Angelic Pope is mentioned, but in contrast to the authors of the *Liber de Flore*, to Roquetaillade and to the later fourteenth-century Telesphorus of Cosenza, no detailed programme coloured by national and religious loyalties is worked out. The holy alliance of World-Emperor and Angelic Pope disappears, for the sword and the crook are joined in unknown hands. The third *status* itself is not altogether convincingly delineated. It is described in common Joachimist terms of peace and abundant justice, with the conversion of Jews and infidels and the gathering of all into *unum ouile sub uno pastore*.[119] But the theme of the *spiritualis intellectus* proceeding from the letter of the Old and New Testaments, so essential to Joachim's concept of the Age of the Holy Ghost, is quite lacking. A new baptism with the Holy Spirit is expected, but its implications are not explored. The spiritual quality which receives most emphasis is the pursuit of absolute evangelical poverty.

---

[118] For the legend of Nero and Simon Magus, see J. Hastings, *Encyclopaedia of Religion and Ethics*, 11 (Edinburgh, 1934), p. 515. For Joachimist references to it, see *Expos.*, fols. 5r, 8r, 24v, 167v-168r; *Lib. Fig.*, Pl. 14; *Super Hier.*, Preface, fol. 18v.

[119] *Brev.*, pp. 296-297.

9

Empire and Papacy in the *Breviloquium*

In Ch. 7 we examined the Arnoldian themes and imagery of the *Brevilo-quium*, and in Ch. 8 the formal structure of concord which the author derived primarily from Joachim's *Liber Concordie* and the *Liber Figurarum*, up-dated by Olivi's *Postilla*. In this chapter we seek to demonstrate how the evangelical theme and the Joachimist structure of concord are blended by the author in his mid-fourteenth-century version of the Last Times.

The *Breviloquium*'s synthesis of Joachimist/Beguin thought centres upon the theme of empire and papacy and is sketched out in its broadest form in *Distinctiones* 13 and 14. Although Joachim's *schema* is fundamental to the conception of the two swords of temporal and spiritual authority in history, the author of the *Breviloquium* modifies and adapts Joachim's structure by building upon an interplay of three concepts: 1. the role of the House of Judah in the Old Testament, 2. Christ as both priest and king in the New Testament, 3. the significance of the Donation of Constantine. The kings of Judah had exercised both royal and priestly power under God; Jesus was anointed by the Holy Spirit and is therefore both king and priest; Constantine, in recognition of this dual nature in Christ, offered his kingdom to Pope Silvester as homage owed to Christ as king.[1] Because the kingdom of Christ is not of this world, however, Silvester only accepted the gift conditionally. It behoved the Roman pontiffs, our author says, to accept power as a debt to Christ, but in practice to allow the temporal order to remain in the hands of those who seek worldly glory, in order that those who fight for God in the manner of the Apostles should never be implicated in temporal business.[2]

Thus the Donation of Constantine involved an implicit recognition that the temporal order required the rule of both empire and papacy. But in the

---

[1] *Brev.*, p. 280.
[2] For this theme, supra, pp. 93-94 and p. 97.

consummation of history Christ would subdue all His enemies and gather all power to Himself, not only for the above reason,

> but also because the very nature of the mystery demands it, for the reason that what the kings of Judah signified in the Old Testament must be consummated in Christ and the Roman pontiffs in the New Testament, and what the Roman emperors from Constantine onward signified shall be consummated near the end of the world, when the Lord Jesus Christ shall subject all His enemies under His feet.[3]

Although the Donation of Constantine was, therefore, not in itself evil,[4] the seeds of corruption were sown when the temptation to assume temporal power assailed the ecclesiastical authority. Involvement in "temporal business" (the Beguin phrase) was to bring about the downfall of the Church in that disintegration of spiritual authority which constitutes a major theme in the *Breviloquium*. The author works out these ideas in a series of concords of rulers and pontiffs which he pursues with the single-mindedness of a fourteenth-century Deuteronomist, determined to demonstrate that God's intervention in the latter stages of history has been and will be to punish the enemies of evangelical poverty and to preserve His elect, that is, all who remain steadfast in their devotion to that ideal.

From the beginning of the New Testament, both rulers and pontiffs are named, beginning with Christ and the emperor Tiberius.[5] After Christ, the next generation of importance is the eleventh, which had its initiation under Diocletian in the preceding 30-year span, but was consummated under Pope Silvester and the emperor Constantine, who, 330 years after the Incarnation, "first brought into existence the Christian empire," that is, established Rome as the spiritual as well as the temporal centre of Christianity.[6] The twelfth generation marks the beginning of Christian temporal rule, in concord with the Old Testament twelfth generation after Jacob in the nation of Israel. It is also noted that Silvester is the angel of *Apocalypse* 20, who apprehends the devil and binds him for a thousand years.

After the end of the Roman empire, the author fixes upon the succession of Frankish, Carolingian and Ottonian rulers and their corresponding popes

---

[3] *Brev.*, p. 280.

[4] For the derivation of this view from Arnold, supra, p. 99. See also p. 105, n. 21 for the traditional evangelical view.

[5] *Brev.*, p. 279. Because Christ began his mission at the age of thirty, the same number of years are allotted to the New Testament generations. The author continues the terminology of the Old Testament "begetting," he writes, because the literal process of the Old Testament means in the New that "there shall be a successor," even though in *Dist.* 14 he names only one principal pontiff for each New Testament generation. *Brev.*, p. 279.

[6] Ibid., p. 280.

for generations twenty-five through thirty-four, or the years 750 to 1020.[7]
Generations thirty-five through forty take us to the year 1200, to the time of
Frederick II and Pope Innocent III.[8]

It is in the forty-first generation from the Incarnation that the period of
crisis begins to take shape, and at this point the author returns to the house
of Judah to demonstrate the course of the Church through generations
forty-one through forty-seven. The major kingdoms and cities within this
historical sequence were identified in the previous chapters, but are here
recalled again:[9] the kingdom of Judah corresponds to the universal Church,
the kings of Judah correspond to the popes; Jerusalem is the universal
Church and the place where the pope and his curia reside; Rome or Roman
also refers to the Church. The Church becomes Babylon in the reception of
the mystic and great Antichrists, and is no longer to be called Rome when
those events occur, because Babylon means "confusion," and during the time
of the Antichrists every order of the Church is to be confounded. The
kingdom of Assyria refers to the empire, and Nebuchadnezzar to the
emperors. The first and second Herods constitute a further concord for the
mystic and great Antichrists, and the Crucifixion prefigures the persecution
which is to occur in the forty-sixth generation. By means of these figures the
author delineates a crescendo of iniquity from generations forty-one through
forty-six, followed by the renovation and transformation of papacy and
empire in generation forty-seven.

The Old Testament concord for the forty-first generation centres upon
Manasseh, who committed evil himself and in turn seduced and corrupted
Judah and Jerusalem.[10] Manasseh was handed over to the king of the
Assyrians, and after having fulfilled his penance was restored to his kingdom.
These events are fulfilled in the forty-first generation of the New Testament
(1200-1230) during the pontificates of Celestine III, Innocent III and
Honorius III, under the emperor Frederick II.[11] In this generation the author
sees the first evidence of God's intention to destroy the world because of the
sins of the children of Judah and of Israel, who represent the prelates of the
Greek and Latin churches. Because these prelates had corrupted both Judah
and Jerusalem, or the active and contemplative churches, God gave the
church into the hands of Frederick II, cast here as the king of the Assyrians.
Innocent III, or Manasseh, had to flee, but afterwards was returned to his

---

[7] Ibid., pp. 287-288.
[8] Ibid., pp. 288-289.
[9] See especially *Prologus*, pp. 170-172.
[10] *Brev.*, p. 289.
[11] Ibid., pp. 289-290.

kingdom. This generation saw the founding of the Franciscans and Dominicans, in concord with the founding of the Sadducees and Pharisees.

In the forty-second generation of the Old Testament, Amon increased the evil wrought by his father, and in the New Testament generation (1230-1260), Frederick II continued the evil ways of his line, in spite of the efforts of the reigning popes.[12] Frederick is named as the first manifestation of the fifth head of the dragon of the New Testament, in concord with Nebuchadnezzar.

In the forty-third generation of the Old Testament, Ozias ruled, and Jeremiah predicted the destruction of Jerusalem and Babylon, both of which took place within a few years.[13] In the New Testament, this generation (1260-1290) encompassed the pontificates of Innocent v through John XXI, as well as the reigns of Manfred and Conradin, both overcome by Charles of France during the struggle for Sicily.[14] Of particular importance in this generation was the marriage of Peter II of Aragon to Constantia, the daughter of Manfred, a union which brought Hohenstaufen blood into the house of Aragon, and prepared the way for the fulfillment of the predictions concerning the seed of Frederick II.[15] Peter also conquered Sicily and expelled Charles, while in the church evils continued to multiply.

In the forty-fourth generation of the Old Testament, Jehoiachin reigned in Jerusalem, was conquered by the king of Babylon but later rebelled.[16] The New Testament generation (1290-1320) encompassed the pontificates of Honorius IV through Clement v, under Henry of Luxembourg, who held the place of the Caesars.[17] In this generation, Boniface VIII was captured by Philip IV of France, poisoned, and his successors made servants of the emperor, according to the author of the *Breviloquium*. It was during this generation that Clement v moved the curia to Avignon, in 1308, and that there was some rebellion against this subjugation of the church, in line with Old Testament concord. It is worth noting that the author does not identify Philip with a head of the dragon of the New Testament, probably because there are only enough heads available to mark the peaks of persecution against evangelical poverty. The author was constrained by tradition to name Frederick II as a head of the dragon.[18]

[12] Ibid., p. 290.
[13] Ibid., p. 290.
[14] Ibid., pp. 290-291.
[15] For discussion of this event, supra, pp. 76, 78.
[16] *Brev.*, p. 291.
[17] Ibid., p. 291. The author confuses Philip IV of France with the emperor Henry VII of Luxembourg, and speaks of "Alamania" rather than "Anagni."
[18] See supra, pp. 8, 11.

The forty-fifth generation, which marks the end of the second *status*, is the first of the two generations of most intense crisis, and, along with the forty-sixth, contains the most lengthy descriptions of concord.[19] In the Old Testament, Jeconiah, the son of Jehoiachin, ruled briefly in Jerusalem, then during the transmigration to Babylon begat Judah and his brother, and after the transmigration begat Salatiel. During this generation, the princes, priests and people were defiled, as was the temple itself in Jerusalem. In this generation, Nebuchadnezzar made his first conquest of Jerusalem, captured Jeconiah and led his people captive from Jerusalem, everyone, that is, except the paupers. In the forty-fifth generation of New Testament (1320-1350), the author introduces a second concord, the Crucifixion or the Vigil of the Passion,[20] then enlarges upon his earlier identification of Jeconiah with John XXII, who begat Peter Corvara the antipope,[21] and in the spiritual transmigration to Babylon will beget Salatiel, who remains unidentified. Louis of Bavaria is not mentioned in *Distinctio* 13, but in *Distinctio* 9 he is identified as a second manifestation of the fifth head of the dragon (after Frederick II),[22] and is elsewhere paired with John XXII in the troubles which commence in the 1320s: the condemnation of evangelical poverty by John XXII in *Cum inter nonnullos*, and the beginning of John's struggle with Louis over the issue of the spiritual authority of the papacy over the Empire.[23]

The major events in this generation are seen by the author as primarily ecclesiastical, with their focus on the emergence of John XXII as the mystic Antichrist. Because of John's decision in *Cum inter nonnullos*, and the persecution which followed it (added to that of 1317), there is in this generation, the author writes, almost no difference between the church and the pagans, nor between regulars and seculars. The church is moving closer to empire; in its lust for power and in its vanity it has blurred the distinction between the two swords: Rome has now become Babylon, and only the paupers remain in Jerusalem, the true church. The empire, personified in Louis, with his contempt for the authority of the pope, has also reached its nadir now that spiritual authority has collapsed. Consequently, another Old

---

[19] *Brev.*, pp. 291-296.

[20] Ibid., p. 292.

[21] It is noteworthy that in this *distinctio* the begetting of the antipope Peter of Corvara is ascribed to John XXII rather than to Louis of Bavaria, who in fact created him, and is given credit for that act elsewhere in the *Brev.* (pp. 292 and 215). Here, the pairing of the antipope with Salatiel, the apostolic successor in the next generation, may be intended to emphasise further the author's disgust with the state of the papacy: the spiritual credentials of the canonically elected pope are as worthless as those of the antipope. We should add that there is no evidence to suggest that Louis of Bavaria is to be identified as Jeconiah.

[22] *Brev.*, p. 239.

[23] See table of dates.

Testament concord has been fulfilled: both princes and prelates and all their followers are grievously defiled.[24]

John xxii is also in concord by means of contrast with Silvester in the manner in which the author works out Arnold's remarks on the angel of *Apocalypse* 20. John's term (1316-1334) occurred one thousand years later than Silvester's (314-335), which, in the author's view, makes John a new manifestation of the exterminating angel, whose role is to distort the Scriptures with false teachings, and in whose time Satan has been released again.[25] Great and terrible sin has begun in the Church, the author warns, and the 44 days of silence have begun during John's pontificate.[26] What Silvester wrought, John has destroyed.

The forty-sixth generation of the Old Testament continues the story of the Babylonian transmigration, and includes the wars waged against Babylon.[27] Salatiel is named as the successor of Jeconiah, but the nation of Israel is also described here as without an effective leader and in thrall to the power of darkness begun under Jeconiah. However, Salatiel begat Zorobabel, who brought back his people to Jerusalem. During the captivity, Babylon was persecuted by the Medes and the Persians, and the children of Israel suffered two tribulations, which are recounted in the story of Judith and in the book of Esther.[28] In the forty-sixth generation of the New Testament (1350-1367), at the beginning of which the author was probably writing, the Old Testament is fulfilled in the coming of the Eleventh King and the great Antichrist, followed by the final renovation under Zorobabel.[29] Much space is given here to political events, which reflect the concord with the Old Testament generation. These events are discussed in more detail in earlier chapters of the *Breviloquium*, but are reviewed here in order to demonstrate the resolution of the empire-papacy theme.

In the forty-sixth generation, with the spiritual transmigration of new Babylon largely completed, the Eleventh King, who is Peter iv of Aragon, will rise from Spain to persecute both the universal church and the empire.[30] He is identified as the sixth head of the dragon of the New Testament, in concord with Nebuchadnezzar both as king of Assyria and as king of Babylon; he is to be the scourge of the empire, yet at the same time its final manifestation. He also fulfills the promise of the temporal empire of Catalonia begun by

---

[24] See supra, pp. 77-78.
[25] *Brev.*, p. 215.
[26] Ibid., p. 293.
[27] Ibid., pp. 294-295.
[28] For these concords, see *Brev.*, p. 295.
[29] *Brev.*, pp. 295-296. For the shortening of this generation, see table of dates, and *Dist.*, p. 296.
[30] *Brev.*, pp. 207-209.

Peter III, who wrested Sicily from Charles of France, and is linked to a secondary concord with Philip of Macedon and Alexander the Great. Peter IV is to bring down the sanctuary of the legitimate pontiff, encourage and abet the corruption of all the orders of the church, bring down the kings of France and Sicily, and in concert with the remaining rulers of the original ten, overwhelm the Holy Roman emperor. His later actions are to be more positive: he will travel to Jerusalem to destroy the infidel nations, and before expiring himself will hand them over to the new leader or new Zorobabel, after having been in effect a world-emperor.

The Eleventh King also initiates the second major event of the forty-sixth generation, the establishment of the great Antichrist, the seventh head of the dragon yoked to the sixth head, an Antichrist who must rise as a consequence of the temporal power of the Eleventh King. As king of the north, the great Antichrist will overcome the king of the south (the true Church) in spiritual battles, while at the same time temporal conflict rages between Catalonia and France. Owing to the corruption of the clergy by temporal vanities, Antichrist will triumph in a false election, and will continue to persecute the free children of evangelical poverty, who are distinguished from the bonded children of the carnal church. Finally, Antichrist will be destroyed in a great earthquake which will cause his palace and those of other false prophets to fall through great chasms in the earth, a fall occasioned "because of too great abundance of the things of this world."[31] The entire episode, based as it is on the yoking of the sixth and seventh heads of secular and false spiritual authority, may have been intended to represent the ultimate perversion of the Donation of Constantine, in which spiritual power becomes the handmaiden of temporal power.

The third great event of the forty-sixth generation, the beginning of the rebuilding of the temple in Jerusalem, or the true Church, is to begin concurrently with the two other events described above, "in troublous times," that is, during the time of the final throes of empire under the Eleventh King and during the depredations of the great Antichrist.[32] The rebuilding is to begin with the help of the king of the Persians, identified as the king of Sicily, who by this time would be Peter IV. Zorobabel is to make his first appearance in this forty-sixth generation, a generation which constitutes the prelude to the third *status*.

In the forty-seventh generation, which initiates the third *status*, the final renovation occurs.[33] The chaff of sinners is to be separated from the wheat

[31] Ibid., p. 255.
[32] Ibid., p. 296.
[33] Ibid., pp. 296-297.

of the elect, and Zorobabel, the new leader and pontiff, will ascend to Jerusalem. With the help of the Eleventh King, he will complete the rebuilding of the temple, a co-operative venture which may signal the brief restoration of the proper relation between empire and papacy as it was conceived in the time of Silvester. Now, however, the traditional division of the two swords is dispensed with in the third *status*, replaced by a reign of pontiff-kings, leaders who encompass both the temporal and spiritual aspects of authority, men such as Peter and Silvester, "with two swords shining," and with one shepherd reigning, "because the Lord Jesus Christ was both king and priest." [34] With God's enemies destroyed and the "elect poor" triumphant, the Donation of Constantine is superseded as temporal Christianity achieves evangelical purity in the true imitation of Christ, and the concord of Christ as priest and king is fulfilled. Hence the Joachimist expectation is achieved, and the consolatory prophecy embodied in this expectation fortifies the beleaguered group for whom the *Breviloquium* was written.

This moment of apotheosis is to be brief. The line of Angelic Popes is to cease in the final persecution of Gog and Magog, or Antiochus and Naman. Then will come the Last Judgement in that unknown but not far distant future when time is subsumed into eternity.

[34] Ibid., p. 297.

10

The Pictures in the *Breviloquium*

The illustrations are a distinctive feature of the *Breviloquium*. There are forty-four, in addition to the Table of Generations which occupies the last twelve folios in the Madrid manuscript,[1] ending in a full-page dramatic representation of the Last Judgement. The British Library copy reproduces them all faithfully, though in a different style. Their purpose is pictorial, not figurative. They are neatly designed and decorative, visual aids to the text which are full of vivid detail.

As a set of Joachimist illustrations they have no clear affinities with any earlier examples and seem to be more closely related to those of the later fourteenth-century Joachite, Telesphorus of Cosenza, than to any other.[2] As we have seen,[3] the author certainly had Joachim's Table of Concords before him and possibly other parts of the *Liber Figurarum*, yet — the Tables apart — he had a quite different conception of the function of his illustrations from Joachim's. The originality of Joachim's *figurae*, both textual and in the *Liber Figurarum*, lies in their ability to express mysteries of theology, history and prophecy in symbolic forms, some derived from geometry, some Biblical, some "given" in moments of illumination.[4] Recognising Joachim's trees as far from natural specimens, it is fair to say that his only representational picture is that of the Dragon with seven heads, taken from the Apocalypse. The first Joachites certainly used Joachim's *figurae* and by the time the *Super Esaiam* was produced they were imitating as well as adapting them.[5] The significant point is that thirteenth-century Joachites stuck closely both to Joachim's conception of a *figura* and to the type of symbol which he used.

---

[1] Fols. 39r-50r.
[2] On the illustrations to Telesphorus' *libellus*, see Reeves, *Influence*, pp. 375-378, 431.
[3] Supra, pp. 114-115.
[4] See Reeves, Hirsch-Reich, *The Figurae of Joachim of Fiore*, pp. 20-74.
[5] Ibid., pp. 286-287, 288-292.

The pictures of the *Breviloquium*, then, were not derived from the thirteenth-century Joachimist tradition. In the early fourteenth century a new
style of Joachimist picture was introduced in the *Vaticinia de summis
pontificibus*.[6] These were an adaptation of a Byzantine source and were
definitely pictorial. Each showed a scene, usually of a pope, with various
symbolic adjuncts, performing some action which symbolised his character
and reign. Thus a symoniacal Orsini pope was represented distributing
money to little bears. Some pictures were much more enigmatic than others
and there was an element of the oracular riddle in those which were
prophetic rather than descriptive. The author of the *Breviloquium* may have
got the idea of his pictorial scenes from this source, for the *Vaticinia*
originated in a Spiritual Franciscan circle and were widely circulated. But we
have not been able to detect any specific features which derive from this
famous series and, in general, the style is different.

We may consider first the pictures in the *Breviloquium* which simply
represent Biblical themes. Thus each of the seven *etates* in the fourth *Distinctio* is illustrated by a key Biblical episode: Noah's Ark, the destruction of
Sodom, the judgement on the Egyptians at the Red Sea, the judgement on
Eli and his sons, the overthrow of Jerusalem, the four Beasts of Daniel.[7]
Again, in the seventh *Distinctio*, where the seven *status* of the Church are
compared with the seven Days of Creation, we have a straightforward set of
seven pictures illustrating the stages of the Creation and culminating in the
creation of Adam and the Sabbath Day.[8] Here, then, we have patterns of
history represented by the Biblical incidents which are their *figurae*.

In a second group may be placed some illustrations with a rather more
figurative purpose. For example, the *status* of the Church in the fifth *Distinctio* are each characterised by a distinctive picture. The first, the age of the
Apostles, is represented by the Woman clothed with the sun (*amicta sole*)
fleeing from the Dragon;[9] then persecutions of martyrs, doctors, anchorites
and regular religious are depicted for the next four *status*.[10] The sixth is
represented more elaborately with a picture for each of its four divisions, or
initia. For the first, the appearance of the evangelical men is illustrated and

---

[6] On the *Vaticinia*, see Reeves, *Influence*, pp. 58, 193-194, 214-215, 402-407, 412-413,
453-462.

[7] Madrid, Biblioteca Nacional, MS 6972, fols. 11v, 12r, 12v, 13r (subsequently referred to
as "Madrid"); London, British Library, MS Egerton 1150, fols. 21v, 22r, 23r, 23v, 24r
(subsequently referred to as "Brit. Lib."). The descriptions of the pictures given here apply to
the Madrid MS; there are variations in the British Library copy.

[8] Madrid, fols. 19v, 20r; Brit. Lib., fols. 36r, 36v, 37r.

[9] Madrid, fol. 15r; Brit. Lib., fol. 27v.

[10] Madrid, fols. 15r, 15v, 16r; Brit. Lib., fols. 28r, 28v, 29r.

St. Francis and the Emperor Frederick II are depicted rather quaintly seated side by side, the former distinguished by halo and stigmata, the latter by crown and sceptre.[11] In the second, John XXII appears in pontificals and Louis of Bavaria with drawn sword.[12] Thirdly, the new outpouring of the Holy Spirit on the evangelical men is represented by fine lines descending from the Dove upon six bishops and six religious, with their leader in their midst.[13] The fourth is represented by dramatic pictures of "general commotion," with earthquake, falling stars etc.[14] A similar type of figurative picture at the end of the next *distinctio* seeks to translate into visual shape the culmination of history as expressed in the words "thus shall arise a new order with a new leader in which the law, life and cross of Christ shall be renewed." It shows in an upper tier a mitred ecclesiastic with a cross, flanked by four bishops on either side, and below a crowd of religious around one central leader.[15] The tenth *Distinctio* on the double-seven Dragon's heads begins with a dragon picture which, in its heads and in the knotted, snake-body terminating in Gog, is actually reminiscent of some Joachimist examples.[16]

The most extraordinary group of pictures — almost comical in their naivety — consists of those which attempt to portray the main concords between the three *status* in literal pictorial fashion. The first set is of three tabernacles.[17] Each has a three-tier turret, in each division of which sits a halo-ed demi-figure. In two storeys below the turret, the upper contains eleven venerable figures grouped around a mitred head, with one more falling dramatically out of the structure, while the lower contains two figures. The figures represent, of course, the three noteworthy persons (*sollempnes personae*), the Eleven, the ejected one who loses his inheritance and the two "nephews" — the pattern which must be repeated in each *status*. The third in the series shows clearly that the Three are St. Benedict, St. Bernard and St. Francis and that the Eleven are religious, while the expulsion is vividly represented. But the identical structure of each picture in the series puts a visual emphasis merely on the repetition of the concords. There are none of the subtle hints of progression from one *status* to another, such as Joachim puts, for instance, into the recurring pattern of his Tree-Ladders.[18] Moreover,

---

[11] Madrid, fol. 16r; Brit. Lib., fol. 29r.

[12] Madrid, fol. 16v; Brit. Lib., fol. 29v.

[13] Madrid, fol. 17r; Brit. Lib., fol. 30r.

[14] Madrid, fol. 18r-v; Brit. Lib., fol. 30v.

[15] Madrid, fol. 19r; Brit. Lib., fol. 34v.

[16] Madrid, fol. 27v; Brit. Lib., fol. 51r. See *Lib. Fig.*, Pl. 14, and references given in chapter 6, n. 52.

[17] Madrid, fols. 5r, 5v, 6v; Brit. Lib., fols. 9v, 10r, 11v.

[18] See *Lib. Fig.*, Pl. 21, where the foliage, flowers and fruits are successively developed in the three "tree-ladders." See also Pls. 22 and 23 for a similar progression in the foliage.

unlike the profound symbolic forms used by Joachim, there seems to be little point in the choice of the tabernacle-form itself: the mystery of the three *status*, covering the whole meaning of history, can hardly be contained in three neat little tabernacles.

The second set gives the forces of evil in a similar sequence.[19] Each picture shows, in an upper tier, the nefarious coalition of three symbolised in the wicked three at the end of the first *status*: Herod, Caiaphas and Pilate. The crown, mitre and pagan emblem worn by each three represents worldly might brought against goodness. Each has an evil genius (like a frog) proceeding from his mouth. Below, Christ stands with His Cross assailed by soldiers and crowds. Thus at the end of every *status* Christ and His true followers must be persecuted by the wicked three and their evil followers. This is a pattern which belongs exclusively to the *Breviloquium* and clearly arises out of the revolutionary mentality of the extreme Franciscan group. St. Francis and his true disciples had repeated the sufferings of Christ and His disciples at the transition from second to third *status*. It was natural, therefore, to project this experience one stage further and expect a third persecution by three similar powers at the close of the third *status*. But, once again, this serves to obscure the triumph of the third *status* and to put the emphasis on repetition of pattern rather than progression in history.

The table of the generations is organised on Joachim's calculations in his Tables of Concords[20] and is very neatly executed in the Madrid manuscript, with ruled lines and decorative embellishments. It has, however, none of the residual tree-attributes which Joachim's tables retain, nor are the concords stressed by placing the two Dispensations on two facing pages as in his.[21] Rather the table goes successively through the generations of both eras in a continuous descending ladder. Its chief pictorial feature is that each person representing a generation is portrayed by a half-figure, whereas Joachim gives names only. In addition, there are side-portraits, as, for instance, of Cain and Abel and various prophets. From David onwards the generations are marked by crowned and sceptred kings down to Eliud, after which there is a break with no portraits for two generations, but a broken sceptre and falling crown. The last two generations before Christ follow, with portraits of prophets, not kings.[22] The New Dispensation begins with an ornamental head-piece under which Christ with the Cross marks the first generation.[23] St. Peter, mitred,

---

[19] Madrid, fols. 10v, 11v; Brit. Lib., fols. 18r, 19r, 20v.
[20] See supra, p. 114, for the features of Joachim's tables adopted here.
[21] See *Lib. Fig.*, Pls. 3, 4, 9, 10.
[22] Madrid, fol. 44r; Brit. Lib., fol. 80v.
[23] Madrid, fol. 45v; Brit. Lib., fol. 81r.

with keys and cross, initiates at the second generation a sequence of popes, all of whom are similarly represented down the "Martin and five more."[24] "Jechonias," i.e. John XXII, who stands next, at generation XLV, is still given the mitre, keys and cross, but the accompanying caption reads "the time of silence and the power of darkness." The next generation, designated in Salatiel, has no portrait but shows instead the mitre, keys and broken cross falling.[25] Here the captions are menacing: "The Eleventh King and blood; Blood on land and in the sea; Peter began and Peter shall bring the end; Eleventh King, blood, seduction, death, destruction." After two spaces marked simply by a cross we come to *Nouus Zorobabel* at Generation XLVII,[26] the first of the priest-kings in the third *status* and therefore mitred, with keys and cross. The generations of the third *status* follow the genealogy in St. Matthew from Zorobabel down to Joseph and then turn backwards from Jareth to the beginning, following the genealogy of St. Luke.[27] At Caynam (generation LX) there is an empty space, with the caption: "Here the flock appears in three parts."[28] At *Enos* mitre, keys and crown once more fall and the captions read "open and last Antichrist; Gog and Magog." But at the end Seth appears as a tonsured religious, with keys and cross restored, although no mitre, while in the final generation (LXIII), Adam appears similarly restored.[29] At the foot of this last column are the words "signs of judgement" and the next page, in the Madrid copy, closes the *Breviloquium* with a dramatic, full-page representation of the Last Judgement.

Throughout the table there are interesting side-notes and portraits. The most important are the three twelves and their attendant twos. At Jacob the twelve patriarchs are ranged impressively in two tiers, six aside, with two additional pairs, Ephraim and Manasseh, Moses and Aaron.[30] At Christ, similarly, we find the twelve apostles, with Joseph and Mathias, Paul and Barnabas.[31] At "new Zorobabel" the names of the twelve and the pairs are taken from the first sequence, but the figures are mitred bishops and below, on either side, is the caption "six monasteries."[32] Another significant series of concords is that of orders: Elijah and Elisha, symbolising the "first initiation of the monastic orders";[33] "order of Pharisees"; and "order of

---

[24] Madrid, fol. 48r; Brit. Lib., fol. 88v.
[25] Madrid, fol. 48r; Brit. Lib., fol. 89r.
[26] Madrid, fol. 48v; Brit. Lib., fol. 89r.
[27] Madrid, fol. 49r-v; Brit. Lib., fols. 89v-92r. See *Matthew* 1.1-16; *Luke* 3.23-38.
[28] Madrid, fol. 49v; Brit. Lib., fol. 91v.
[29] Madrid, fol. 49v; Brit. Lib., fol. 92r.
[30] Madrid, fol. 41r; Brit. Lib., fol. 74r.
[31] Madrid, fol. 44v; Brit. Lib., fol. 81r.
[32] Madrid, fol. 48v; Brit. Lib., fol. 89r-v.
[33] Madrid, fol. 42r; Brit. Lib., fol. 76v.

Sadducees";[34] "second initiation of the monastic orders," with St. Benedict and St. Basil;[35] "second initiation of the clerical orders," with founders of the orders of regular canons and hermits;[36] St. Bernard, with the "initiation of the order of white monks";[37] St. Francis and St. Dominic, with their orders.[38]

This table constitutes an attempt to push Joachim's calculations to a logical completion and to represent the most dramatic moments of history with visual exactitude. Thus, whereas Joachim never attempted to introduce the mystical third *status* into his tables of concords, the author of the *Breviloquium* bravely plots out the generations of the third *status* by the ingenious device already discussed.[39] Even more interesting is his representation of revolutionary transition from one *status* to another. The disruption of the line of rulers, with the breaking and casting down of the symbols of authority, depicts the violence of the change most vividly. The second revolution, expected shortly, is modelled on the first at the end of the first *status*. The third revolution is expected at the end of time. A curious feature of the transition-pattern is that the revolutionary onslaught occurs a little before the end of each *status* and its final years seem to be a preparation for the next stage. Thus, after a violent overthrow of authority, the last two generations before Christ are represented by prophetic figures. At the end of the second *status* this pattern is not so clear, though it may be indicated by the spaces with crosses. The point emerges most strikingly at the end of the third *status*, where the overthrow occurs in the sixtieth and sixty-first generations, while at the sixty-second order is re-established under the religious symbol of Seth and at the sixty-third Adam prepares to meet his God, not in chaos, but in good religious order.

[34] Madrid, fol. 44r; Brit. Lib., fol. 80r.
[35] Madrid, fol. 46r; Brit. Lib., fol. 84r.
[36] Madrid, fol. 46r; Brit. Lib., fol. 84v.
[37] Madrid, fol. 47r; Brit. Lib., fol. 86r.
[38] Madrid, fol. 47v; Brit. Lib., fol. 88r.
[39] Supra, pp. 113-114.

11

The Joachimist Sources of the *Breviloquium*: Chapter-by-Chapter Analysis

Note. The prefatory poem appears to be the original work of the author.

Prologue

pp. 168-169	Opening sentences and analysis of types of concord:
p. 168	The opening sentence contains a highly-condensed form of Arnold's arguments, first presented in *De tempore adventus antichristi* (Finke, CXLII) and later in *La polémica gerundense*, p. 41. The *consolatio* motif of the second sentence is derived also from Arnold; see *Alia Informatio*, p. 52. The section on concords bears some relation to *Lib. Conc.*, fol. 7r-v.
p. 169	*Sic igitur Adam ... obnoxius est effectus*: largely verbatim, *Lib. Conc.*, fol. 43r. Other concords echo *Lib. Conc.*, fols. 30v, 31r-v.
pp. 169-170	Concord of Adam with Christ: see *Lib. Conc.*, fol. 33v, but the extended comparison here derives from Ambrose.
pp. 170-171	Concords derived from *Lib. Conc.*, fols. 7v, 8v, 18r, 22r-23r, 38v.
p. 171	Concord of Judah with the Roman Church echoes *Lib. Conc.*, fols. 38v-39r; possibly related to *Lib. Fig.*, Pls. XVI-XVII, where the words *Jerusalem Visio Pacis* also occur.
p. 172	*onus Babilonis ... alios sarracenos*: verbatim, *Super Esaiam*, fols. 8v, 10r. *Sicut onus Dumea ... uocacionem gencium*: verbatim, ibid., fol. 39v.
p. 172	(with additions). ... *seculi lubricum ... gentilium*: verbatim, ibid., fol. 8v.

pp. 173-177   Original section on the *paruuli* to whom the mysteries will be opened and the rules they must keep).

p. 177   The division into 14 *distinctiones* is probably derived from Arnold of Vilanova's *Dialogus de elementis catholicae fidei* (*Escritos Condenados*, p. 21).

Dist. 1

pp. 178-186   Material derived chiefly from *Lib. Conc.*, fols. 56v-58r, but reorganised to deal with each *status* in turn, instead of in sequences of threes. See also ibid., fols. 8v-13v, 19v-25r.

p. 181   *Et erit hec tribulacio ... dies illos*: echo of *Lib. Conc.*, fol. 106v.

p. 182   *quia tunc ... Ysaye xxx° dicitur*: paraphrase, Olivi, *Postilla*, fol. 42r.

p. 183   Material derived from *Lib. Conc.*, fols. 9v, 13r-14v.

p. 183   Concord between Dan and Judas Iscariot: explicitly made, *Expos.*, fol. 121r; see also *Lib. Conc.*, fol. 43v.

p. 185   Reference to the Sibyl: unidentified. *tempus paschale*: see *Lib. Conc.*, fol. 133r.

Dist. 2

pp. 187-195   Material derived from *Lib. Conc.*, fols. 43v-44v, expanded, not always arranged in the same order, some phrases quoted or closely paraphrased; pp. 189-190 almost verbatim, ibid., fol. 44r-v.

p. 189   Material derived from *Lib. Conc.*, fols. 7v-8r, 43v.

p. 190   *Concordat igitur beatus Benedictus ... monachorum nigro-rum*: paraphrase, *Vita St. Benedicti*, p. 55, but taken from a different pattern. The concords following appear to be original, following the same pattern in Joachim's style, with some affinity to *Lib. Conc.*, fol. 57v.

p. 192   Concord of Dan with Judas, *euulso de medio*: *Expos.*, fol. 121r; *Lib. Conc.*, fol. 43v. Twelve Patriarchs and Apostles: *Lib. Conc.*, fols. 22v-23r, 43v.

pp. 192-193   Patriarchs and types of religion in the Church: echo of *Expos.*, fol. 19r-v.

p. 194   Text from Psalms (*Exterminauit ... eam*): quoted, *Super Esaiam*, fol. 5v; applied to Spain, ibid., fol. 36r.

p. 194   The reference to the *Apocalypse* bears some relation to *Expos.*, fol. 193r.

p. 194	*Vnde sicut xii patriarche ... diligentibus se*: almost verbatim, *Lib. Conc.*, fol. 22r.
pp. 194-195	References to the *concordia* of Joachim: based on *Lib. Conc.*, fols. 21r-23r, 58r-v.
p. 195	*Consumabitur, ut creditur ... terram anathemate*: verbatim, *Lib. Conc.*, fol. 60r. *Sicut ecciam post xii patriarchas ... lac et mel*: almost verbatim, ibid., fol. 44r.

Dist. 3

pp. 196-197	Pilate, Herod and Caiaphas: possibly derived from *Super Hier.*, fol. 23r-v (Herod and Caiaphas), fols. 43r-44v (Herod and Pilate); slight echo, *Expos.*, fol. 164r.
pp. 198-199	*Vnde Iohannes super Apocalipsis ... consurgens temptacio*: verbatim, Olivi, *Postilla*, fol. 101r-v.

Dist. 4

p. 201	*... ut dicit Iohannes ... septimam ... iudicii*: paraphrase, Olivi, *Postilla*, fol. 104v; cf. *Lib. Fig.*, Pl. xvIIIa, b and *Lib. Conc.*, fols. 72v seq.
pp. 202-203	Judgements at the end of each *etas*: hinted at, *Lib. Conc.*, fol. 43v, but in the context of a different pattern.
p. 203	Four Beasts: cf. *Lib. Conc.*, fols. 127v-128v, *Expos.*, fol. 162v, for different interpretations of the Beasts.
p. 204	Fourth Beast identified as Spain: authority cited as Joachim *figurali misterio*: reference might be to *Lib. Fig.*, Pl. xIV, text, but only a hint here; Fourth Beast associated with Spain, *Expos.*, fol. 116r-v.
p. 208	*Vnde Ioachim ...*
	Dicit Ioachim ... ⎫ unidentified
p. 209	*... ut dicit Ioachim ...* ⎭
	que iam tunc ... poterit appellari: paraphrase, Olivi, *Postilla*, fols. 26v-27r.
p. 209	Euphrates as a symbol of the Roman Imperium: see *Expos.*, fol. 190r-v.
pp. 210-211	*soldanus ... transeuntes per Siciliam ... totam Ytaliam*: paraphrase, *Lib. Conc.*, fol. 52r.

Dist. 5

pp. 212-214	*... vii partes ... mortem Antichristi*: paraphrase, Olivi, *Postilla*, fols. 1v-3v, 81r, to form basic structure.

p. 213   Olivi quotes *Lib. Conc.*, fol. 41r (*complebitur autem ... potestate inimici*).

p. 214   *... unum de capitibus quasi ... reuelasse refertur*: close paraphrase, with some rearrangement, Olivi, *Postilla*, fol. 93r.

p. 216   *Tercia apercio ... ecclesia a sinagoga*: derived partly from *Lib. Conc.*, fol. 106v.

p. 217   *Et sicut Christus post babtismum etc.*: perhaps an echo of *Lib. Conc.*, fol. 106v.

p. 221   *... Et erit in diebus ... pacis*: quoted *Lib. Conc.*, fol. 96r. *Et dominabitur ... ad mare*: quoted ibid., fol. 69v.

Dist. 6

p. 222   References to Constantine here and elsewhere are very probably derived from Arnold's ESA. On p. 254, he writes that *quia tunc quando Silvester ligavit Romae draconem sub Constantino generaliter cessavit idolatria corporalis in orbe.*

pp. 222-224   *... vii tempora ecclesie ... confixus et configuratus*: verbatim, Olivi, *Postilla*, fols. 12v-13r.

p. 223   *... conualuit ordo nouus*: echo of *Lib. Conc.*, fol. 69v.

p. 224   *... conualescet unus ordo ... et sua tribu*: based on *Lib. Conc.*, fol. 69v, with an echo of fol. 56r.

pp. 224-225   *... ut xi fratres contra Ioseph*: echo of *Lib. Conc.*, fol. 87r-v. *... et sicut predictus ordo ... quinto formatis*: related to *Lib. Conc.*, fols. 68v-69r.

p. 225   *Hic est populus ille ... exaudiam eum*: almost verbatim, *Lib. Conc.*, fols. 69v-70r.

p. 226   *Sicut enim in vii^a etate ... laboribus suis*: verbatim, Olivi, *Postilla*, fol. 13r.

Dist. 7

pp. 227-228   *... vii diebus ... tribulacio non fuit*: verbatim, Olivi, *Postilla*, fol. 13r, based on *Lib. Conc.*, fols. 65v-70r.

pp. 228-230   *Quare Christus ... in speciali*: verbatim, Olivi, *Super Euangelium Matthei*, fols. 135v.

pp. 230-231   *Tunc, ut dicit Iohannes ... huius seculi adoretur*: verbatim, Olivi, *Postilla*, fols. 92v-93r.

p. 232   *Dies autem ... opere requieuit*: verbatim, Olivi, *Postilla*, fol. 12v.

Dist. 8

p. 233   *... vii tempora ... eius preparauit se*: verbatim, Olivi, *Postilla*, fol. 12r-v.

pp. 233-234   Symbolism of Leah and Rachel: ideas worked out differently but the basic symbolism is used by Joachim several times, see especially *Lib. Conc.*, fols. 83r-84r; *Expos.*, fols. 12r, 18v-20v, 25r.

p. 234   *Uncio extrema ... eum febris*: verbatim, Olivi, *Postilla*, fol. 13v.

Dist. 9

p. 235   *Sub hoc tempore ... obitum Iosue*: verbatim, *De Septem Sigillis*, pp. 239-240.

pp. 235-236   *Sub hoc tempore ... in hac parte*: verbatim, ibid., pp. 239-240.

p. 236   *Sub hoc tempore ... ad Dauid regem*: verbatim, ibid., p. 241.
             Sub hoc tempore ... sunt ostensa: verbatim, ibid., p. 241.

pp. 236-237   *Sub hoc tempore ... in libris Samuelis*: verbatim, ibid., pp. 241-242.

p. 237   *Sub hoc querto tempore ... rerum ymaginibus*: verbatim, ibid., pp. 241-242.
             Sub hoc tempore ... regem Iuda: verbatim, ibid., p. 242.

pp. 237-238   *Sub hoc quarto tempore ... de abisso*: verbatim, ibid., p. 242.

p. 238   *Sub hoc quinto tempore ... regis babilonis*: verbatim, ibid., p. 243.

p. 238   *Sub hoc quinto tempore ... sanem eos*: verbatim, ibid., p. 243.

pp. 238-239   Angels with phials (*Apocalypse* 16.17-21) as preachers, cf. *Expos.*, fol. 185r seq.
             Sub hoc sexto tempore ... tribulaciones excellens: extended version of *De Septem Sigillis* possibly based on *Expos.*, fols. 7v-8r.

p. 239   Paragraph beginning *Sub apercione* can be related to *Expos.*, fol. 197r.

p. 240   The *Lib. Sec. Ev.* of Rupescissa also cites five disasters before the appearance of the great Antichrist. The number may be derived from this source, but the actual list is different from that in the *Brev.*

p. 240   *Vnde sicut circa principium ... lac et mel*: some phrases quoted almost verbatim from *Lib. Conc.*, fol. 44r, but the sequence breaks off and to complete it the author would have turned either to *Lib. Conc.*, fols. 21r-22r or to fols. 57v-58r.

p. 241   The symbolism of the flight into Egypt is developed in *Quat. Evang.*, p. 99 and *Super Hier.*, fol. 43v.

p. 241   *et sicut columba ... super terram*: ideas from *Lib. Conc.*, fols. 23v, 24v; first part almost verbatim from fol. 23v.

p. 242   *percucio nove Babilonis ... liberandi sunt*: almost verbatim, *De Septem Sigillis*, p. 224.

p. 243   *Vnde sicut primum diluuium ... per concordiam respicit*: cf. *Lib. Conc.*, fols. 23v, 43v.

p. 245   Quotation from Olivi? Possible echo of *Lib. Conc.*, fol. 126r.

p. 246   *... v^e principes christianorum, ut dicit Ioachim, inherebunt sibi ... Dicit enim Ioachim quod in Trinaclia exaltabitur cornu eius ... unde Ioachim: Florentem deflorendo ...* unidentified.

p. 249   *dicit enim Iohachim quod tribus de x regibus ... interea multi ...* unidentified.

p. 249   *interea enim multi ... consumacionem accepit*: verbatim, *De Septem Sigillis*, pp. 244-245, with the interpolation of *ascendente nouo duce, seu nouo pontifice noue Ierusalem ecclesie*: close to *Lib. Conc.*, fol. 56r; *uniuerse, fauore regis perssarum seu Sicilie succurrente*: original.

p. 249   *Hoc autem firmiter teneas, ut dicit Ioachim, quod inperium finiet in Sicilia ...*: from *Super Esaiam*, fols. 39v-40r.

p. 250   *nam per eius ... adorari ut Deum*: verbatim, Olivi, *Postilla*, fol. 101r.

p. 250   *... alter Michael*: cf. *Lib. Conc.*, fol. 132v.

p. 254   *nam, ut dicit Ioachim, de Lombardia seu Ytalia ueniet ...* unidentified.

pp. 254-255   *... seduxit eos ... sulphuris expirabunt*: verbatim, Olivi, *Postilla*, fols. 111v-112r; *qui facit ... solucionis sue*: *De Septem Sigillis*, p. 245.

p. 255   *Sub hoc tempore vii° ... conuersaretur*: verbatim, *De Septem Sigillis*, pp. 245-246.

pp. 255-256   *Sub hoc septimo tempore ... gaudium sempiternum*: verbatim, *De Septem Sigillis*, pp. 246-247.

Dist. 10

pp. 257-264	The pattern is original but the New Testament heads 1-4 correspond closely to Joachim's Dragon's Heads, cf. *Expos.*, fols. 10r, 196v, *Lib. Fig.*, Pl. xɪv. No. 5 is Imperial — one of Joachim's alternatives for the fifth head — but pushes the time on to that of Frederick ɪɪ and Louis ɪv.
pp. 259-260	*Dicit de isto Iohannes super Apocalipsim ... cismatice introductus*: verbatim, Olivi, *Postilla*, fol. 93r.
p. 260	*De istomet rege seu sexto drachonis capite Sibilla dicit: De porta Yspanie egredietur infans ...*: unidentified.
p. 260	*Istud ecciam Ioachim uidetur tangere, dicens; Egredietur regulus cuius nomen est fortitudo ...*: unidentified.
pp. 261-262	*Ab angelo pastor reuelabitur qui duobus aquile filiis ...*: unidentified.
p. 262	Comparison between Naaman and Antichrist based on *Lib. Conc.*, fols. 121v-122v.
p. 263	*Vnde sicut Lucifer ...*: possible derivation from Olivi, *Postilla*, fols. 91r, 57r-v. Symbolism of Dan and Judas Iscariot: cf. *Lib. Conc.*, fols. 28v, 43v; *Expos.*, fol. 121r.
p. 263	Sixth and Seventh Heads of Dragon joined: see *Lib. Fig.*, Pl. xɪv.
p. 264	*Cauda drachonis* as Antiochus in the Old Testament and Gog in the New: see *Lib. Conc.*, fol. 56v, *Expos.*, fols. 9r-10r, *Lib. Fig.*, Pl. vɪɪɪ (*Persecutio Grecorum* = Antiochus).
p. 264	*... erit homo ille pessimus qui uocatur Gog*: verbatim, *De Septem Sigillis*, p. 246.

Dist. 11

p. 265	First paragraph: author's own construction based on material from *Lib. Conc.*, fols. 13r, 14r (some verbatim), 25r, with perhaps an idea from fol. 43v.
p. 266	*Tamen sicut ab Adam ...*: calculation as in *Lib. Conc.*, fols. 11v, 14v, 22v.
p. 266	Concords at the 18th generation from Jacob and from the Incarnation: based on *Lib. Conc.*, fols. 47v-48r. 21st generation: related to *Lib. Conc.*, fol. 49r. Concord of Angels sent to Sodom with John the Baptist and Christ: based on *Lib. Conc.*, fol. 23r.

p. 267   Significance of Pharisees and Sadducees: based on *Lib. Conc.*, fol. 23r, where Pharisees only are mentioned as prefiguring the rise of religious orders in the New Testament era.

                Vnde a descensu Iacob et xii patriarcharum ...: some hints of this paragraph occur in *Lib. Conc.*, fols. 38r, 41v, 134r-v.

p. 269   *Completis autem x generacionibus ... in ciuitate Betulie*: almost verbatim, *Lib. Conc.*, fols. 43v, with 23v.

p. 269   *et si inde emissa columba ... super terram*: related to *Lib. Conc.*, fol. 24v, from which some phrases are taken.

pp. 270-271   *Quod autem in diebus Abrae ... expellendum*: mostly verbatim, *Lib. Conc.*, fol. 24v.

p. 271   *Quod in diebus Obeth ... sint filii resurreccionis eius*: verbatim, *Lib. Conc.*, fol. 25r, except for the following interpolations: a. *aut quod latina ecclesia cepit exterminari per Fredericum imperatorem*; b. *sub pressura illius regis xi, ex semine Frederici predicti.*

Dist. 12

p. 272   *Vnde sicut ab Adam usque ad Christum ... lxiii*: derived from *Lib. Conc.*, fol. 10v.

pp. 272-273   *Spacia enim generacionum ... Mcclx*; partly verbatim, *Lib. Conc.*, fol. 12r-v.

pp. 273-274   *Vnde, cum hec generacio ... tercii status*: based on *Lib. Conc.*, fols. 12v-13r.

p. 274   *Dicit Ioachim ... extimacione annorum*: probably reference to *Lib. Conc.*, fol. 56v: *tempus illud quod supererit usque in finem absque humana extimatione annorum.*

                dicit eciam Iohannes ...: possibly derived from Olivi, *Postilla*, fol. 31v.

p. 275   *tamen Iohannes sic exponit ... conceptus et natus*: verbatim, Olivi, *Postilla*, fol. 114r-v (quotation contains two references to Joachim).

p. 276   *... a natiuitate ... satis claret*: paraphrase, Olivi, *Postilla*, fol. 92v.

p. 277   Although derived from Jerome, the 15 signs heralding the Last Judgement are probably from a Joachimist anthology. (See p. 277, n. 19).

Dist. 13

p. 278	List of rulers: see *Lib. Conc.*, fol. 24v.
p. 279	*Regnauit autem Dauid ... mortuus est*: based on *Lib. Conc.*, fol. 92v.
	In nouo autem testamento ... imperatorum: almost verbatim, *Lib. Conc.*, fol. 44v.
p. 279	*Prima generacio peracta est ... ab incarnacione cccxxx*: almost verbatim, *Lib. Conc.*, fols. 44v-45r.
p. 280	*Duodecima incepit ... sub pedibus eius*: almost verbatim, *Lib. Conc.*, fol. 45r, but with omissions, additions and rearrangements.
p. 281	*Vt autem ... generacione*: almost verbatim, *Lib. Conc.*, fol. 45r.
pp. 281-285	*Primus post Dauid ... in Iudam*: passages taken almost verbatim from *Lib. Conc.*, fols. 45r-50r, but with many omissions, some additions, and rearrangements.
pp. 285-286	*... xiiii annis, et a Dauid ... numerus impleatur*: almost verbatim, text of *Lib. Fig.*, Pl. IV.
p. 287	Generations handled in an original way, related to the Tables of Concords, *Lib. Fig.*, Pls. III, IV.
pp. 287-289	*oportet nos ... operi annotare*: verbatim, *Lib. Conc.*, fol. 50v.
	In xxvi generacione ... papam Alexandrum: adaptation of *Lib. Conc.*, fols. 50v-53v, to fit author's scheme, with additions and omissions; continues with sequence where Joachim leaves off.
p. 289	Allusion to Pharisees: see *Lib. Conc.*, fol. 23r.
p. 290	*... predixit Ieremias ... consumacionem accepit*: almost verbatim, *Lib. Conc.*, fol. 53r.
pp. 290-291	*Ioachim, licet xxix^{vs} sit a Iacob ... contra eum*: related to *Lib. Conc.*, fol. 53r.
pp. 293-294	*Iam enim locuste ... cruciare non cessant*: verbatim, Olivi, *Postilla*, fol. 67v.
p. 295	*... non habuit ... inter utrumque*: almost verbatim, *Lib. Conc.*, fol. 56r.
	... transmigracio Ierusalem ... in angustia temporum: almost verbatim, *De Septem Sigillis*, p. 244.
p. 296	*Reuera enim percucietur ... solucionis sue*: almost verbatim, *De Septem Sigillis*, pp. 244-245.
p. 296	*Ortus quidem ... constitutus*: verbatim, *Lib. Conc.*, fol. 56r.
pp. 296-297	*... peracta prius tribulacione ... ad aduentum Helye*: almost verbatim, *Lib. Conc.*, fol. 56r-v, with omissions.

p. 297   *... post tribulacionem ... ignem eternum*: verbatim, *Lib. Conc.*, fol. 56v.

Dist. 14

The whole table is based on *Lib. Fig.*, Pls. III, IV.

p. 299   *Generaciones enim in veteri ... accipiendum est*: almost verbatim, *Lib. Conc.*, fol. 12r.

p. 301   *Maledictus Chanaan ... populum christianum*: cf. *Lib. Fig.*, Pl. XXII, where "Cham" is the abortive stump; *Lib. Conc.*, fol. 121r.

p. 302   *Sicut Abraam tangit ... consilio materno*: based on *Lib. Conc.*, fols. 79v, 82v-88r.

p. 303   *Manasses, frater maior ... iure hereditario accepit*: based on *Lib. Conc.*, fols. 27r-28v.

                    Primum signaculum ueteris testamenti: this passage and subsequent similar ones recapitulating material on the Seals recall the *De Septem Sigillis*.

p. 308   *Hic cessauerunt ystorie ... conuersaretur*: verbatim, *De Septem Sigillis*, pp. 245-246.

p. 311   The identification of Silvester as the angel of *Apoc.* 20.1 occurs in the ESA, p. 254.

pp. 318-319   *Sub hoc septimo tempore ... in septima parte Apocalipsis*: verbatim, *De Septem Sigillis*, pp. 245-246.

p. 322   *Sicut enim, consumatis ystoriis ... que sit beatitudo*: verbatim, *De Septem Sigillis*, pp. 246-247.

p. 322   *sic, consumatis operibus ... superne Ierusalem*: verbatim, *De Septem Sigillis*, p. 246.

*Summula seu breviloquium
super concordia Novi et Veteris Testamenti*

Edited by Harold Lee and Giulio Silano

Siglorum conspectus

add.	= addidit, addiderunt
codd.	= codices
hom.	= homoeoteleuton
lac.	= lacuna
om.	= omisit, omiserunt
par.	= paragraphus
praem.	= praemisit, praemiserunt
rep.	= repetivit, repetiverunt
tr.	= transposuit, transposuerunt
M^{ac}	= lectio codicis M ante correctionem
M^{pc}	= lectio codicis M post correctionem

Introduction to the Text

PROVENANCE

All the available evidence points to an Iberian provenance for the *Brevilo-quium*. It was certainly widely circulated there. The two manuscripts which offer a date and place of composition were written in Barcelona in 1455 and 1488, and the fourteenth-century Tarragona manuscript has *marginalia* written in Spanish (not Catalan, as might be expected). The earliest extant manuscript (Madrid, National Library MS 6972) is undated and unplaced, but it contains several characteristics of the Iberian Gothic Hand noted by Thomson:[1] minuscule *c* and *t* are not easily distinguishable; *ecciam* or *eciam* are used throughout; the abbreviations *eccia* and *oms* occur; the use of an initial *h* is common, as in *Helisabeth* and *hedificare;* the Iberian spellings *nichil, dupplex, ursus,* and *intollerabiles* occur consistently.[2]

There is also evidence for a specifically Catalonian provenance primarily because the *Breviloquium* reflects a special knowledge of and interest in the house of Aragon.[3] Peter IV of Aragon is the dominant historical personage in the work, and the argument for the importance of Catalonia in the scheme of the Last Times is strongly pressed by the author, even to the extent of etymological proof:

> Hec igitur bestia a principali parte, hoc est a principio et porta Yspanie, scilicet Cathalonia, non uocaliter sed realiter nuncupatur, nam Cathalonia a *logos,* quod est *sermo,* et *cathalicio,* quod est *uastacio,* dicitur quia, ut predictum est, *ultra quam credi potest uniuersa uastabit,* ideo describitur.[4]

---

[1] S. Harrison Thomson, *Latin Bookhands of the Later Middle Ages* (Cambridge, 1969), pls. 109-132. As Thomson notes, this type of evidence can indicate the region in which the scribe learned to write, but that does not necessarily have to be the place where the MS was actually written.

[2] One interesting exception is the *Breviloquium*'s *Yspania* rather than the Iberian *Hyspania.*

[3] Morton W. Bloomfield, in 'Joachim of Flora," *Traditio,* 13 (1957): 251, suggests that the author may have been a Sicilian. Sicily, however, has been important in most of the Joachimist literature, so that its role as the center of climactic events is less a significant indication of provenance than is the interest in Catalonia.

[4] A similar type of etymological significance is given the word "Aragon" by the Infant Peter: *Lo Rey d'Aragó es entés o figurat en Mars, qui, segons los stronomans, est planeta bellicós: aytals son estats los Reys d'Aragó; per ço Aragó es dit ara agonis, que vol dir ara de*

The Sybilline prophecy *De porta Ispanie* is also used to verify the events which are believed by the author of the *Breviloquium* to be taking place within the House of Aragon.[5]

There is also one piece of philological evidence which points to a Catalonian provenance. Throughout the *Breviloquium*, the author writes of the *guerras intestinas inter reges et principes et comunitates* (p. 219). The general context of such passages is that of biblical allusions to events held to prefigure the Last Times, but the word *comunitates* is a non-biblical addition. The term "comunitat" was used in Aragon to denote the federation or leagues formed by one or more municipalities, and may have this meaning in the *Breviloquium*. The French excerpts from the Breviloquium omit the word.

THE MANUSCRIPTS

A. The Iberian Manuscripts

M   Madrid, Biblioteca Nacional MS 6972 (*olim* S-247). s. xiv.

The manuscript consists of 51 parchment folios (gatherings of ten folios with one folio added at the end of the last gathering), mm. 259 × 204 (written surface mm. 190 × 151), to which, in the eighteenth century, five guard paper folios were added at the beginning and four at the end. The parchment has occasionally been repaired with paper in modern times. There is an original foliation, in Roman numerals, in the lower margins, beginning on fol. xi and continuing to the end of the volume. A modern foliation, in pencil, has been entered in the upper margins, but fol. 51 is left unnumbered. The binding, from the eighteenth century, is in parchment and bears, on the spine: "Concordia utriusq[ue] Testamenti"; on the front cover: "53"; on the second guard folio: "Concordia Veteris et Novi Testamenti."

The text is written in one fourteenth-century hand on two columns of 37 lines. Paragraph markings are in green and red; some capitals are left blank. Fol. 50r displays a miniature of the Last Judgement. In addition, there are a large number of illustrations of scenes from the Old and New Testaments, and in *Distinctio* 14 lists of the Old Testament rulers and the papal line accompanied by portraits. Although the pictures have a certain charm, they

---

batalla on se sacrificava a Mars per los idolatres, qui es dit deu de batalles. This passage occurs in the Infant's *Exposició de la visio damunt dita,* quoted by Pou y Martí in AIA, 23 (1925): 33; *Visionarios,* p. 370.

[5] Denifle, Bohigas and Russo all cite the *Breviloquium* as a compendium of Joachim's work.

are crude in execution and of little or no artistic importance. Their substantive importance is discussed above, in Chapter 10.

There is no indication of the date or place of composition. The manuscript is complete, but some passages are very difficult to read, especially those in which previous material has been erased and written over. Chapter headings are missing from the first four *distinctiones*. There are marginal glosses which consist of simple identification of sources, interlinear or marginal additions by the scribe or by later readers, the use of NB and variations to call attention to significant passages, and, finally, full-fledged commentary on several passages.

The Iberian orthography of this manuscript has been noted above; it is further characterized by the doubling of initial consonants, as in *Ffrancia*; moreover, *m* is frequently used for *n* and *s* for *x*.

> Heinrich Denifle, *"Evangelium aeternum,"* p. 92; Pere Bohigas, "Profecies Catalanes," pp. 26-27; Marjorie Reeves, *Influence*, pp. 223-224; Marjorie Reeves and Beatrice Hirsch-Reich, *The Figurae of Joachim of Fiore*, p. 292; P. Francesco Russo, *Bibliografia gioachimita*, p. 205.

T   Tarragona, Biblioteca Provincial MS No. 99. s. xiv.

The Tarragona manuscript is singly-bound in 65 fols., mm. 277 × 205 (page), 200 × 140 (text), in two columns, 26 lines per column. It is written in a fourteenth-century hand, and, along with the Madrid manuscript (M), was probably written within the period 1351-1355, when the original was composed.

The final two folios of T have been almost completely destroyed. The remaining folios are in good condition, written in a large but rather careless hand. Spaces have been left for illumination and for the elaboration of capitals, but this work was never undertaken. However, *Distinctio* 14 does contain the ladder of generations. Some *marginalia* in Spanish are interspersed in spaces left for illumination. The use of terminal *ch* for *c*, although an Iberian characteristic as well, distinguishes the orthography slightly from that of M (Madrid), and relates it to B (British Library) and V (Vatican Library).

> Heinrich Denifle, *"Evangelium aeternum,"* p. 92; P. Francesco Russo, *Bibliografia gioachimita*, p. 20; Marjorie Reeves, *Influence*, pp. 223-224.

B   London, British Library MS Egerton 1150 (Catalogue of Additions, 1848-1853). 1455.

This is a singly-bound manuscript of 92 fols., mm. 200 × 290 (page), 140 × 180 (text), in 12 quires of two columns, 32 lines per column. It has capitals in blue, further decorated with red filigree, and paragraph markings in blue and red. This manuscript is illuminated in a manner similar to that of the Madrid manuscript (M), with a similarly constructed table of generations in *Distinctio* 14. Fol. 74r-v, which contained a portion of the table of generations, has been cut out close to the sewing and subsequently replaced by a smaller paper insert which contains a partial summary of the missing scheme. The verso of the paper is blank.

The colophon of the manuscript informs us that it was copied in 1455 by Pedro Fort, a merchant of Barcelona, and presented by him to the cathedral of Barcelona. It found its way to England in the nineteenth century; the original cover, now [i], is inscribed as "purchased of Tho. Robb., 9 Dec., 1848." The final leaf contains the date 1519, and the inscription *Cathalonia que interpretatur a logos quod est sermo et cathalicio quod est uastatio f° xxii°*, a reference to the passage quoted above on the etymology of Catalonia. Except for the missing folio, the manuscript is in good condition, legibly written, and handsomely presented. It differs from M in orthography by the use of terminal *ch* instead of *c*, as in *tunch* and *nunch*. However, this is also a characteristic of Iberian orthography.

A prefatory note in Spanish has been inserted by Dr. Luis Juan Villeta, present at the Council of Trent. It reads as follows:

Censura del presente libro hecha por
Sr. Villeta, dottor theologico y canonico

Este libro intitulado "Summa de la Concordia del Nuevo y Viejo Testamento" está muy guardado en la libraria del Asseo de Barcelona, escrito de pergameno y figurado con muy lindas figuras, no se sabe su proprio autor, solo se dice, quo lo scrivió Pedro Fort, vecino de Barcelona, en el anno MCCCCLV. Dieron le algunos antigos muy grande autoridad, y el cabildo y ciudad de Barcelona lo tienen en grande cuenta, por lo que lo han oydo alabar a muchos, que haviendo le leyido se maravillavan de las grandes concordantias de los dos testamentos que en el vehían por modo de prophetia, la qual les parescia ser complida en gran part delo passado y assi pensavan que podría ser de lo venidero.

El intento del autor es mostrar el discurso de la yglesia hasta al fin del mundo y assenya ladamente en sus partes principales de los Pontificados, Monarchias, Imperios, Reynos, y otros stados, personas y acaescimientos notables, los quales a punta aver sidos o aver de ser en la yglesia conforme y en correspondentia de lo que acontesció a la synagoga por ser esta figura de aquella. Y con presupuesto que el orden y progreso que huvo en el Viejo Testamento hasta la primera venida de Nuestro Senor Jesu Christo para ser jusgado de los hombres es figura y retrato del orden y progreso del Nuevo

Testamento hasta la secunda venida de Jesu Christo para jusgar a los hombres. Y porque hablar sin fundamento sería grande temeridad o atravimiento humano, quiere lo fundar sobre prophetias reveladas por voluntad divina, especialmente de Daniel en el Viejo Testamento, de la Apochalipsi en el Nuevo: con las interpretaciones de algunos sagrados doctores y muchas veces del Abad Joachim, al qual paresce dar maior autoridad de la que el tiene entre hombres dotos y pios. Por donde paresce que los que tanto se maravillan de esta obra si son hombres entendidos tienen mas cuenta del ingenio e invention del autor que de la autoridad del que en el se trata, cuyo argumento rason y orden se declara en el prologo, de donde con lo que esta dicho se pueden sacar algunas reglas para meior entender el proposito, y entento que lleva el autor.

> P. Francesco Russo, *Bibliografia gioachimita,* p. 20; Marjorie Reeves, *Influence,* pp. 223-224; Marjorie Reeves and Beatrice Hirsch-Reich, *The Figurae of Joachim of Fiore,* p. 292.

v Città del Vaticano, Biblioteca Apostolica Vaticana MS Vat. Lat. 11581, fols. 1-65. 1488.

This manuscript occupies the first 65 fols. of an anthology of 23 quires mm. 320 × 236 (page), one column, 39 lines per column. This codex was assembled from the holdings of two other libraries: the *Breviloquium* comes from Catalonia; the other selections come from France, and include Nicholas Eymerich's *Tractatus contra daemonum invocatores* (fols. 77-143), and William of St. Amour's *Tractatus de Antichristo et eius ministris* (fols. 151-226).

In the manuscript of the *Breviloquium,* spaces have been left for ornamented initials at the beginning of each *distinctio* but are unfilled. No miniatures appear to have been intended. The colophon records the copying of this manuscript by a scribe named Michael in 1488 in Barcelona. It is written in a small but extremely clear hand. I am indebted to Professor Morton W. Bloomfield for bringing it to my attention.

> *Bibliotecae Apostolicae Vaticanae: Codices Vaticani Latini* (*Bibl. Vat.,* 1959), pp. 340-341; Marjorie Reeves, *Influence,* pp. 223-224.

Madrid, Real Biblioteca (Biblioteca Nacional) MS ii, II, fols. 37r-38v. s. xiv or xv.

This manuscript contains a fragment of the *Breviloquium* among a collection of prophecies incorrectly attributed to Arnold of Vilanova. The fragment is taken from *Distinctio* 9. Incipit: *in predictis verbis Danielis ut dixit*

Ioh (Iohannes) describitur casus regni Cicilie et regni Francie et regni ecclesie. Explicit: *pastor pacificus post multam peregrinacionem animam Deo rediret et miraculis fulgebit in morte in provincia sua.*
I have not collated this manuscript.

Pere Bohigas, "Proficies catalanes," p. 27.

Barcelona, Biblioteca de Catalunya MS 490, fol. 104v. s. xiv or xv.

Two fragments of the *Breviloquium*'s prefatory poem, ll. 19-22 and 24-25, are interpolated into a poem about the house of Antequera. See the notes to the prefatory poem.

Pere Bohigas, "Profecies catalanes," pp. 26, 46-47.

B. The French Excerpts

I am indebted to Professor Robert Lerner for the information that the following two French manuscripts contain *Distinctio* 5 of the *Breviloquium*:

F   Rouen, Bibliothèque Municipale MS O. 20, T. I (Catalogue No. 1355), fols. 98r-99r. c. 1379-80.

This anthology of 332 fols. contains a selection of pieces relating to the election of Urban VI in 1378, and to the Great Schism.

F¹   Tours, Bibliothèque Municipale, MS 520, fols. 52v-57v. 1422.

The scribe believed the selections from this anthology of prophetic material to be from either Rupescissa or Joachim: *Ignoratur si opus sequens fecerit de Petrascissa uel Ioachim.* (fol. 52v).

C. The Catalan Excerpt

Carpentras, Bibliothèque Inguimbertine MS Nr. 336, fols. 76v-116v. s. xv.

Professor Lerner has also called my attention to this Catalan translation of *Distinctiones* 9 and 10 of the *Breviloquium* in a Catalan prophetic anthology. This excerpt is preceded by a list of eleven kings differing from that of the *Breviloquium*. Incipit: *Esplegada es la viii distincio comensam la novena e del vell Testament.* Explicit: *E es apellat lo llibre de que aco es stat treyt suma seu breviloquium sobre les concordies del novell e del vell Testament.*

Pere Bohigas, "Profecies catalanes," p. 27.

D. Manuscripts Lost or Incorrectly Attributed

Turin, Biblioteca Nazionale MS K, VI, 32. 1459.

This manuscript was recorded by Denifle, but has since been reported by Russo to have been lost in the burning of the library.

Seville, Biblioteca Capitular Colombina MS N. 1272. s. xv.

This manuscript, recorded by Russo and described in the Seville catalogue as illuminated, is missing. Denifle placed this manuscript in Zaragoza (Caesaraugusta).

Valencia, Biblioteca Universidad MS N. 1205. 1489.

This manuscript exists, but is a copy of Joachim's *Liber Concordie*, incorrectly described by Russo as a copy of the *Breviloquium*. Some modern instances from the *Super Esaiam* have been affixed, on fols. 116v-127r.[6]

THE RELATIONSHIP OF THE MANUSCRIPTS

The Madrid manuscript (M) is the earliest of the four copies collated in this edition, but is not necessarily the original manuscript. The Tarragona (T), British Library (B) and Vatican (V) manuscripts all include the major glosses of M within the text, and all three add a short prose section at the conclusion of the prefatory poem. These latter three also share some word order which differs from M, and also use *ch* for terminal *c*. Consequently, we can posit the existence of a successor to M which included some of the marginal glosses of that manuscript in its text, and also included the remarks following the prefatory poem. It is from this intermediate manuscript that the group BTV is directly descended.

Within the group BTV, there is evidence for the divergence of T from BV. In the crucial passage on the identification of the Eleventh King in *Dist.* 4, BTV all diverge from M in similar fashion for several lines. However, T then returns to M for the kings of Sicily, while BV, both later manuscripts, continue their variation by means of a later list of rulers.

---

[6] Dr. Reeves, who made this identification, has collated this section with the *Super Esaiam* (Venice, 1517), fols. 11v-27v. The list of places in this appendix to the Valencia *Liber Concordie* is taken from the marginal notes, which appear in the original edition. The notes are not always reproduced in the same order, and it is probable that there are some original additions. The marginal notes in the MS of the modern instances are later than those reproduced in the 1517 edition.

There are also a number of unique additions, omissions and errors exclusive to T, and similar kinds of variations shared exclusively by BV.

One interesting error shared by BTV concerns the misreading of the abbreviation *Ioh*, intended in M to stand for Iohannis [Olivi]. Most likely beginning with the lost intermediate manuscript, and continuing through BTV, *Ioh* is resolved as Ioachim. Consequently, Olivi's identity as a major source for the *Breviloquium* begins to be lost quite early, an error which helped give rise to the later supposition that the *Breviloquium* was merely a compendium of Joachim's work.

The French excerpts from Rouen (F) and Tours (F^1) are directly related to one another through common errors. However, the later manuscript F^1 is not directly descended from F; rather, both have a common ancestor which probably circulated in France. The small size of the excerpts makes them difficult to compare with the complete manuscripts, but one piece of evidence links them with the Madrid manuscript (M) and with the BTV group: one of M's glosses is contained in the text of the excerpts, but placed several lines further on than in BTV. The readings of the excerpts tend more to follow M than BTV.

The following *schema* illustrates these relationships:

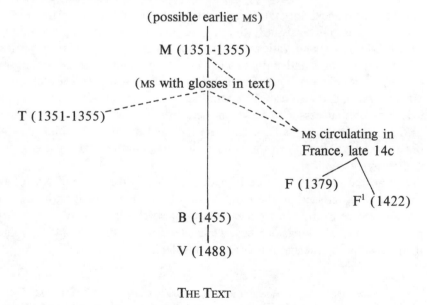

THE TEXT

The text of this edition is, with the exceptions noted below, that of the Madrid manuscript (M). This manuscript has fewer major scribal errors than the Vatican and British Library manuscripts, it is more complete than the

Tarragona manuscript, and is fully illuminated. Because of the nature of historical revision in prophetic manuscripts, it has seemed advisable to use the earliest text, and as far as possible to preserve the differences in each manuscript's treatment of the text. The exceptions to the use of the Madrid manuscript are as follows:

1. The title, and the chapter headings in *Distinctiones* one through three are taken from the later manuscripts, and placed in brackets.

2. Scribal errors in M are corrected by readings from the later manuscripts and cited in the footnotes.

3. Major glosses in M are placed in the text, in conformity with the later manuscripts. Minor glosses and notations in M have been omitted.

4. The orthography of the Madrid manuscript has been modified by eliminating a number of double consonants and by rationalising the spelling of proper names. Other minor changes in orthography have been made when clarity and consistency have been felt to be more important than fidelity to regional spellings.

5. Punctuation, paragraphing and capitalisation have been modernised.

6. Abbreviations have been resolved in conformity with forms established in Adriano Cappelli's *Dizionario di abbreviature latine ed italiane* (Milan, 1961).

The foliation of the Madrid manuscript is as follows:

Prefatory poem	Fols.	1r-v
Prologue		2r-4v
Distinctio 1		4v-7v
2		7v-9v
3		10r-11v
4		11v-15r
5		15r-18r
6		18r-19v
7		19v-21v
8		21v
9		21v-27v
10		27v-29v
11		29v-31v
12		31v-33r
13		33r-38v
14		39r-50r

THE CHRONOLOGY AND DATING OF THE *BREVILOQUIUM*

In the introductory study to this edition, we discussed the content and sources of each chapter of the *Breviloquium* in detail, and placed the manuscript in the context of the development of Joachimism in the Western Mediterranean. In this section, which focuses on the text itself, I should like to concentrate on the chronology of the crucial forty-fifth and forty-sixth generations as they are presented in the *Breviloquium*, and to do so by means of a selected concordance of chapters which mention or allude to particular dates and events during this period. An explication of this chronology is not only valuable in itself, but indispensable to a discussion of the date of the work. In my view, the material in the concordance assembled below demonstrates that 1. with respect to chronology, the crisis of the Last Times is to occur in the mid-1360s, and 2. with respect to the date of the writing of the *Breviloquium*, we can identify the period 1351-1354 as the most probable time of composition, although I would not rule out the possibility of a later date.

The concordance reveals an overall consistency in the chronology of the period in question. However, as with all Joachimist documents, it has inconsistencies and quirks which require some comment, as do certain of my own annotations. In *Dist.* 12, the author notes that although the generations of the Old Testament are uneven, those of the New Testament must be calculated in units of 30 because Christ was 30 when He began his teaching. This scheme is adhered to most rigidly in *Dist.* 14, but in the other chapters, and even at times in *Dist.* 14, it is apparent that the cavalcade of personages and the patterns of dating do not precisely fit such a scheme. For example, in the crucial break between the forty-fourth and forty-fifth generations, both pope and emperor overlap the two generations in their dates, and the crucial events in papacy and empire begin three years after the break. Consequently, throughout the *Breviloquium* there is a tension between a uniform mathematical sequence on the one hand, and the need to fill in a cast of characters and calculate uneven dates on the other. These two ways of approaching the Last Times cause difficulties for both writer and reader. Even though I have reduced the relevant sections to a minimum, the computations do not conform with precision, and there is a risk of imposing a degree of order which the author himself did not intend.

The most difficult date is 1367, which occurs both in *Dist.* 13 and *Dist.* 14, and indirectly in *Dist.* 12, if one accepts the updating of Olivi's calculations concerning a half-generation. It is in the context of the above-mentioned tension that I have suggested one possible way in which this specific date might have been calculated. I wish to emphasize that the figures and comments in brackets are my own interpolations, and are not specifically stated in the *Breviloquium*, a caveat which includes the date 1323. However, the pattern of generational overlaps, as well as the historical personages and events mentioned seem to me to make 1323 a date which must have been much in the mind of the author. Even if this particular date was not calculated in such a manner, the general thrust of the concordance makes it clear that the 1360s were intended to be the time of crisis.

The preponderance of internal evidence suggests that the *Breviloquium* was written in the early 1350s. The last historical event referred to is the death of James of Majorca in 1349, an event characterized as having "recently" taken place. Allowing for writing time, 1351 would seem to be the probable earliest date based on this piece of evidence. It is also significant that, apart from Peter IV, Louis of Sicily, who reigned until October 1355, is the last of the eleven kings mentioned. Frederick of Sicily, Louis' successor, is not mentioned. Based on this evidence, we can assign 1354 (or early 1355) as the terminal date for the composition of the *Breviloquium*.

There is further evidence which points to the period 1351-1354. By placing his own time at the beginning of the forty-sixth generation, the author would be following the usual Joachimist authorial time-scheme, i.e., on the brink of crisis but not actually there. There is also a lack of concrete historical information beyond the early 1350s, and, in the chapters cited in the concordance, a shift in tense which puts events after that time into the future. The period of crisis is consistent with prediction by Roquetaillade of the appearance of the great Antichrist in 1365 or 1366, of schism and other events, and consistent with Arnold of Vilanova's citation of 1368 in the *De mysterio cymbalorum*. Also, the prediction that the Eleventh King is to overthrow the kings of Sicily and France has not yet been fulfilled. Finally, the tone of the *Breviloquium* is characterized by a fidelity to historical sequence which disposes the reader to accept the context as it is presented.

On the other hand, there are also examples of prophecies which are deliberately made to seem earlier than they are. Consequently, there can be no absolute proof that this is not the case with the *Breviloquium*, or that 1367 is not intended to allude to the actual period of composition. The dangers of computation with respect to this manuscript have already been noted. On balance, however, the earlier dating seems more firmly supported.

The Beginning of

Selected Chapters & Events in the *Breviloquium*

Dist. 14 (generations)	*Dist.* 13 (generations)	*Dist.* 12 (2nd & 3rd Status)
Gen. 44 1290-1320 Martin ɪᴠ & 5 others (1281-1314) [Break to next gen. occurs during reign of John xxɪɪ]	*Gen. 44* Martin ɪᴠ (1281-1285) to Clement ᴠ (1305-1314) Philip of France & Henry of Luxembourg Boniface vɪɪɪ (1295-1303) 1308 — Curia to Avignon	Based on calculations in Daniel, and on units of 30 in ɴᴛ: Christ was 30 when He began to give birth to spiritual children.
Gen. 45 1320-1350 [1323-1353] Jeconiah named, but no popes Beginning of 44 days of silence & power of darkness [1323-1367]	*Gen. 45* Jeconiah [John xxɪɪ] begat Peter [Corvara] the antipope Princes & prelates begin to transgress Beg. of 44 days: truth cast down & silence imposed on prophets: [Possible ref. to *Cum inter nonnullos*] Jeconiah begets Salatiel (unidentified)	*Gen. 45* 30 [flight of woman] + 1290 = 1320 Time of Mystic Antichrist & beg. of 44 days of silence Author reconciles 1260 & 1290 as beg. of flight of woman *amicta sole*: 1260 + 30 + 30 1290 + 30
Gen. 46 1350-1367 [1353-1367] Salatiel named, but no popes 1367 — Peter ɪᴠ began, Peter shall end in death & destruction	*Gen. 46* Gen. after John xxɪɪ Salatiel between Jeconiah & Zorobabel Events of previous gen. fulfilled in 1367	*Gen. 46* This gen. to be 14 years in length Transition from 2nd to 3rd status
Eleventh King Antichrist New Zorobabel (first pontiff-king)	Eleventh King to depose kings of Sicily & France Zorobabel appears in 46th gen.	Time of great Antichrist Beg. of the time of plenitude
Gen. 47 No further dates Gens. 48-51 Last Judgement		*Gen. 47* 3rd status: gens. uniform, but length unknown

The Last Times

		Historical Events	
Dist. 5 (6th age)	*Dist.* 4 (Eleventh King)	Papacy	Empire
1st Opening St. Francis & Frederick II Frederick is head of beast almost killed: revived in 4th opening	From 4th beast of Daniel which is Spain Small at first, mighty later To be one of 11 kings of Aragon, Majorca & Sicily	1316: accession of John XXII	
2nd Opening John XXII & Louis of Bavaria 1000 yrs. after Silvester (314-335) War between France & England Tribulations to grow & appear more clearly	To depose 3 kings: 1 deposed already Identification of Peter IV is established here	1323: John XXII condemns poverty in *Cum inter nonnullos* 1324: Louis of Bavaria is excommunicated 1334: death of John 1334: Benedict 1342: Clement VI	1322: Louis defeats Frederick of Austria 1323: Louis claims nothern Italy, denies rights claimed by John 1328: Louis creates antipope Peter of Corvara 1346: Charles IV elected king of Romans
3rd Opening Beg. of gen. 46 Holy Spirit given to evangelical men Antichrist appears End of New Testament Time of plenitude	Ref. to death of James of Majorca [1349] 2 more kings to be brought low	1352: Innocent VI 1362: Urban V 1367: Urban returns to Rome	
4th Opening Attack of 10 kings against church End of 6th age & death of Antichrist No date given			

[INCIPIT PROLOGUS SEU BREVILOQUIUM DE CONCORDIA NOVI ET VETERIS TESTAMENTI.]¹

Exposita sunt tempora per dicta prophetarum,
Plebs det per bona opera moras uigiliarum.
5 Errorum introduccio ne fiat uigilare
Clamat ex euangelio et ueritas orare.
Septimo centenario caterue bestialis
Erit plena destruccio sinagoge carnalis.
Cum alcior uidebitur tunc sedens ut regina,
10 Eius considerabitur propinquior ruina.
Cum uideris silencium ueritati indictum,
Quater x. facto gencium expectabis conflictum,
Quater ix. bis gignicium mulieris a fuga,
Veritatis excidium mutata docet ruga.
15 Mors, fames, pestilencie, bella current et guerre,
Metus, terror, inuidie erunt et motus terre.²
Nam plura edificia in sacro constituta
Ruent, dando presagia per uates instituta,
Casus regnorum plurium, atque comunitatum,
20 Et ciuitatum gencium, et statuum paupertatum.
Castrum, turris et aquilo et uulpis anglicana
Fauebunt cuncti baculo serpente cum griffana
Maioris franci siculi; reges humiliabit
Virtus yspani baculi et patrem captiuabit.
25 Pseudo propheta culmine sedis pontificatus
Regnabit ficto lumine in sancto sublimatus.
Clerus perdet imperium, reptans expoliatus,

Titulum scripsimus cum BTV   concordia] concordancia T   4 Plebe B   7 cate-
rue] externe B   9-10 tunc ... regina *rep. et add.* B *post* considerabitur uidebitur ... ruina
*om.*Tᵈᶜ *et add. in finem col.*   15 gerre M   17 constituta] instituta T   23 siculi]
tituli T   24 baculi] et paciet *add.* Biblioteca de Catalunya MS 490

---

¹ For an edition of ll. 1-20, from M see: Pere Bohigas, "Profecies catalanes dels segles XIV
i XV, assaig bibliografic," *Butlletí de la Biblioteca de Catalunya*, 6 (1920-1922), 25-26.
² Cf. Mat. 24.7.

Cadet in uituperium ut populus fugatus.
Herrorum sagitarius aperte sibilabit,
30   Regnabit mercenarius et pastor emigrabit.
Cuntis tunc mundi gentibus baculus imperabit,
Tribus deiectis regibus ensse cuncta domabit.
Nam surget tunc temptacio toti mundo uentura,
Nec fuit tribulacio talis, nec est futura.
35   Muto tunc inmolabitur in pace a danitis,
Regnum recuperabitur ordinatis leuitis.[3]
Aper de silua uineam Christi exterminabit,
Et ueritatis lineam ferus eradicabit.[4]
Anno climaci consulo tibi fugam parare,
40   Post idest ter facto circulo fugam noli tardare.
In Iudea qui habitant tunc fugiant ad montes,
In agro et qui praticant non redeant ad fontes,
De tecto quis descendere ne curet contemplator,
Rem quam de domo tollere ut sit leuis uiator.[5]
45   Ve autem pregnantibus grossis re temporali,
Pre pondere reptantibus in cursu tam ferali,
Necnon et nutrientibus alimento doctrine,
Salutis indigentibus celestis medicine.
Yems frigens malicie fugat Christi ardorem,
50   Et sabatum accidie carnalem fert merorem.[6]
Ne fiat hec fugacio temporibus pretactis,
Deum uestra oracio pulset in cuntis factis.
Grandis abhominacio in templo desolato
Tunc erit et comocio in mundo perturbato.[7]
55   Iosep peregrinabitur in cruce sublimatus
Christo configurabitur a suis contempnatus.
Anno climacxi populi soluentur infernales
Et ferientur anguli plagis terre uitales.
Nam barbari Hesperiam terrent ab occidente,

---

29 sibibabit V; sibibat B   35 ad annitis T   39 consulo] consilium V   45 autem]
tunc *add.* BTV   grossis] tunc *add.* BV   52 Deum *om.* BV

---

[3] Cf. Iud. 18.
[4] Cf. Ps. 79.14.
[5] Cf. Mat. 24.16-18.
[6] Cf. Mt. 24.19-20.
[7] Cf. Mat. 24.15, 21; Dan. 9.27.

60   Et thursi contra Greciam surgent ab oriente,[8]
      Ethiopes Ytaliam australi ulcione,
      Ferient Alamaniam mauri ab aquilone,
      Vt preparetur regibus uia ab ortu solis
      Cum classe uenientibus obtenebratis polis.
65   Nam decem reges uenient cum bestia uicturi,[9]
      Et Babilonem ferient, ipsam concrematuri,
      Vniuersalis pontifex surget de Babilone
      Micans uirtutum opifex facta confusione.
      Tunc status mundi tercio intrabit a secundo,
70   Et regnabit sublimius Christus in toto mundo.
      Nam sponsa sexti temporis noua Christo parata
      Sede procedit etheris descendens coronata.
      Tunc septimi apercio sigilli gloriosa
      Fiet et reuelacio per orbem radiosa,
75   Nam grandis iubilacio erit et lux serena,
      Et grandis proclamacio cuntorum laude plena.
      Tunc plenitudo gencium sollemniter intrabit
      Ad Christum, qui rex omnium reliquias saluabit,
      Lux solis septempliciter, ut lux septem dierum,
80   Erit lune similiter in contemplando uerum.[10]
      In Beniamin tunc saculo ciffus reperietur
      Argenteus[11] et ferculo regis benedicetur,
      Sed cunta ista gaudea cito sunt finienda,
      Quia tunc sexta feria post palmam est ponenda.
85   Caput drachonis ultimum de carcere soluetur
      Sucitans bellum septimum ut mundus perturbetur.
      Post hec signa iudicii per orbem fulgurabunt
      Et eterni supplicii terrores nunciabunt.
      Ignis e celo ueniens feces mundi purgabit,
90   Post surgens omnis dormiens iudicem contemplabit
      Venientem in nubibus celi. Iam congaudebunt
      Iusti cum sanctis omnibus, sed rei dure flebunt.
      Generalis discucio fiet de toto mundo,
      Et erit retribucio in alto et profundo.

    60-61 contra ... Ethiopes *om.* T^{ac} 70 sublimius] sub lumino T   73 septima T
apercio] aparicio BV   74 orbem] et *add.* T   89 e] de BV   faces T

---

[8] Cf. Dan. 11.2.
[9] Cf. Dan. 7.24.
[10] Cf. Is. 30.26.
[11] Cf. Gen. 44.12.

95 Tunc libri consciencie erunt manifestati,
    Et cuntorum plenarie actus erunt nudati.
    Non proderunt pecunie, nec erunt aduocati,
    Nam cursus tunc iusticie erunt determinati.
    Infernus tunc aperiet os suum ad absorbendum,
100 Prestitutos cuntos feriet, trahens ad comburendum.
    Illa dies miserie, luctus, atque plangendi,
    Dies dure sentencie, sine spe miserendi.
    Sumentur ad conuiuium electi tunc supernum,
    Vbi pax, laus, et gaudium erit in sempiternum.
105 Quam felix illa ciuitas uere deliciarum,
    In qua omnis prosperitas habundat graciarum.
    Illic regina uirginum, cunctorum aduocata,
    Trascendens culmen ordinum, cum Christo collocata,
    Illic ciues angelici semper Deum uidentes,
110 Sub ierarchia triplici misteria implentes,
    Illic sancti dispositi, donis septem dotati,
    Pro dignitate meriti in mundo iam probati,
    Mirantur nec deficiunt, in clara uisione,
    Illius quem prospiciunt mira fruicione.
115 Mater exoret filium pro nobis impetrando,
    Regnum uite et gaudium in fine preparando.
    In hac ualle miserie et plena lacrimarum,
    Mater succurrat filie in uita presurarum.[12]
    Si ergo habes oculum ad uidendum que uides,
120 Considera hoc speculum, ut detur tibi fides.
    Futurorum probacio inceptis comprobatur,
    Dat inceptorum racio ut cursus inpleatur.
    Opusculum qui legerit istud benedicatur,
    Et in mente posuerit gracia repleatur. Amen.

---

99 Infermus M   100 prestitutos] prestitos BTV; precitos M   104 et *om.*
T   112 per dignitatem BV   114 Illius] Illum T   in *add.* BVT   118 succurrat]
occurret T   inuitet BMV; in uite T   124 Amen] Deo gracias, amen. Averte bene quia
rex undecimus, qui erit imperator et malleator seu persecutor ecclesie carnalis, non erit proprie
antichristus, sed ille quem faciet eligere in pseudo papam ille erit antichristus. Dicit Ioachim
quod propter Siciliam capietur summus pontifex et archa federis Domini tradetur in manus
peccatorum. Item Ioachim dicit quod Spiritus sanctus comminabitur multis secundum diuersas
proprietates et condiciones eorum, ut occultet archanum suum. Item dicit Ioachim quod Sicilia
quinque plagis est percucienda, quarum prima fuit a theothonicis, secunda sub hircis regniculis,
tercia sub aquile furiis, quarta a regulo uolanti, quinta quod deducetur in profunda maris et
ultra non apparebit *add.* BTV

---

[12] Cf. *Salve, Regina* (Frederick Raby, *The Oxford Book of Mediaeval Latin Verse* [Oxford,
1959], p. 196).

PROLOGUS. EXPLICIT PROLOGUS SEU BREVILOQUIUM PRESENTIS CONCORDIE. INCIPIT CONCORDIA SEU BREVILOQUIUM NOVI ET VETERIS TESTAMENTI ET PROLOGUS.

Cum non sit nostrum nisi diuina reuelacione seu inspiracione noscere *tempora uel momenta que Pater in sua posuit potestate,*[1] possumus tamen ipsius adiutorio recurrere ad sola illa que per scalam generacionum seu temporum in testamento ueteri per figuram, in nouo autem per misterium concordabi-
5 liter gradu consimili possunt nosci.[2] Quoniam igitur, secundum apostolum, *quecumque scripta sunt, ad nostram doctrinam scripta sunt, ut per consolacionem et passienciam scripturarum spem habeamus,*[3] idcirco ad consolacionem et solamen corde humilium hoc opusculum seu concordie sumula edita est, et de *Concordia* Iohachim et ceteris dictis eius et aliarum aliquarum ecciam
10 notabilium personarum collecta, in qua quidem de huiusmodi testamenti ueteris et noui et noui concordia et de scalarum seu generacionum et temporum ordine sub compendio pertractatur. Vnde ad clariorem noticiam huius operis quatuor per ordinem sunt uidenda: primo, scilicet ipsius concordie diffinicio seu descripcio, et quot sunt modi eius; secundo,
15 concordia aliquarum regionum et nacionum que continentur in testamento ueteri cum aliquibus regionibus et nacionibus que gubernantur sub nouo; tercio, quibus personis hec et alia diuina misteria sunt reuelanda seu aperienda, quia non est tutum nec iustum *sanctum dare canibus;*[4] quarto et ultimo, ordinacio parcium seu distincionum huius operis consimiliter est
20 uidenda.

Concordia igitur est, prout hic sumitur, quidam respectus inter uetus testamentum et nouum secundum quem aut tempore tantum, aut facto

---

Titulum scripsimus cum BV; *om.* M; Incipit prologus seu breuiloquium de concordia noui et ueteris testamenti T   1 Cum] Quoniam V   2 posuit in sua *tr.* BTV   9 corde] cordis BTV   10-11 ueteris testamenti *tr.* T   16 gurbenantur M   17 misteria diuina *tr.* BTV   19 distincionum] uel diffinicionem *add.* BTV   21 et *om.* T

---

[1] Act. 1.17. This opening paragraph is very similar to Arnold of Vilanova's exposition of the same text. See pp. 33-34 of the Introduction.
[2] Cf. *Lib. Conc.*, fol. 7r-v.
[3] Rom. 15.4.
[4] Cf. Mt. 7.6.

tantum, aut tempore et facto simul ad inuicem se concordant. Ex quo
colligitur tres esse concordie modos, scilicet temporis et non facti, facti et
25 non temporis, et temporis et facti simul, quorum duo ultimi huic operi
deseruiunt, primo repulso, sed quia pretactus est per ordinem uideantur.

Primus igitur modus concordie est temporis et non facti, quando scilicet
due generaciones seu duo tempora ad inuicem se concordant, ut prima
generacio noui cum prima generacio ueteris, et secunda cum secunda, et
30 huiusmodi, uel primum tempus ecclesie cum prima etate mundi et primo die
originalium, et secundum cum secunda et secundo, et sic descendendo per
ordinem.

Secundus modus concordie est facti et non temporis, quando scilicet facta
se concordant, sed gradus generacionum et temporum se discordant. Sic
35 igitur Adam primus parens respicit per concordiam Oziam regem Iuda qui
regnauit in diebus Ysaye prophete quia, sicut Adam ob culpa elacionis
fedatus est pudore luxurie, ita Ozias ob reatum superbie pollutus est in-
mundicia lepre, et uterque expulsus est de loco sancto, alius scilicet de
paradiso, et alius de sanctuario Domini, nimirum quia si uterque prius fuit
40 bonus et iustus, usurpando tamen uetitum, uterque preuaricator et culpe
obnoxius est effectus; discordant igitur in gradu generacionis et temporis,
licet concordent in facto. Sic per uiam noui et ueteris Christus concordat cum
Abel quia in Abel occisus est; sic cum Ysaac, quia in Ysaac pedibus colligatus
est; sic cum Ioseph quia in Ioseph uenundatus est; sic cum Moyse, quia in
45 Moyse inuolutus est; sic cum prophetis, quia in prophetis inhonoratus est.
Hic est qui in multis multa passus est, dominus noster Iesus Christus. Hec
Leo papa.[5]

Tercius modus concordie est quando scilicet gradus generacionum et
temporum et tempore et facto ad inuicem se concordant. Sic igitur Adam
50 primus parens, fons et origo cunctarum generacionum secundum carnem,
Christum primum parentem fontem et originem cunctarum generacionum
secundum spiritum per concordiam respicit. Vnde Ambrosius: *Sexta die
originalium factus est Adam et sexta etate mundi incarnatus est Christus; in
prima generacione creacionis mundi Adam, in prima generacione recreacionis
55 mundi Christus; in mense marcii Adam, in mense marcii Christus; sexta feria*

24-25 non ... et[2] *om.* BV *per hom.*   27 Primus igitur] Primo ergo BTV   29 secunda[1]]
secundum BV   31 et secundo *om.* BTV   34 sed] secundum BTV   35 qui] quoniam T   36 Ysaye] Ozie BTV   37 est *om.* BTV   41 igitur *om.* T   42 ueteris]
testamenti *add.* BTV   43 in Ysaac *om.* BTV   a *add.* T   44-45 quia in Moyse
om. BTV   46 est[1] *om.* BTV   multa] sustinuit et *add.* BV; sustinuit et multa
add. T   55-56 Adam ... Christus *om.* T

---

[5] Cf. Leo, *Sermones* 60 (PL 54.344); *Lib. Conc.*, fol. 43r; cf. also fols. 30v-31v.

Adam, sexta feria Christus; in terra promicionis Adam, in terra promicionis
Christus; de terra uirgine Adam, de matre uirgine Christus; ille ad ymaginem
Dei, iste ymago Dei; per mulierem stulticia, per mulierem sapiencia; ex latere
Adam mulier Eua formata est, ex latere Christi mulier ecclesia educta est;
60 *nudus Adam, nudus Christus; mors per arborem, uita per crucem; in deserto*
Adam, in deserto Christus; illa hora in qua Adam fuit formatus, illa hora
Christus fuit captus; illa hora in qua Adam fuit paradisum ingressus, illa hora
Christus in pretorium Pilati est ductus; illa hora qua naufragium perpetratum
est, illa hora Christus de spinis coronatus est; illa hora qua Eua iuit ad lignum,
65 *illa hora Christus ductus est ad suspendium; illa hora qua Adam ad lignum*
manus extendit, illa hora Christus manus et pedes in cruce expansit; illa hora
qua Adam gustauit de ligno, illa Christus fuit potatus felle et aceto; illa hora
qua Adam fuit sentenciatus, illa hora Christus horauit in cruce pro peccatori-
bus; illa hora qua Adam fuit de paradiso expulsus, illa hora expirauit Christus;
70 *illa hora qua Christus sanctis patribus apparuit, illa hora unus miles lancea*
latus eius aperuit; in monte Galuarie Adam intumulatus est, et in monte
Caluarie Christus sepultus est. Hec ille.[6]

Sic ecciam Abraam cum Zacharia concordat, nam uterque senex et iustus
fuit; uterque uxorem sterilem habuit; uterque unicum et unicum procreauit;
75 per angelum iste, per angelum ille; principium ueteris testamenti Abraam,
principium noui testamenti Zacharias; Abraam autem genuit Ysaach, et
Zacharias Iohannem Babtistam. Concordat igitur Ysaach cum Iohanne
Babtista quia uterque de patre sene et iusto, uterque de matre sterili, uterque
per angelus nunciatus et nominatus. Ysaac autem genuit Iacob, Iohannes
80 carnaliter non genuit, sed spiritualiter babtizando Christum, quia ibi confirmata est generacio carnis, hic uero generacio spiritus. Concordat igitur Iacob
cum Christo Domino nostro quia uterque subplantator, ille fratris sui Esau,
iste diaboli in temptacione; uterque luctator, ille cum angelo in scala leticie,
iste cum diabolo in scala paciencie, hoc est, crucis; porta celi illa, porta celi
85 ista. Vetus testamentum fructificauit in Iacob carnaliter, nouum in Christo
spiritualiter; Iacob pater carnalis xii patriarcharum, Christus pater spiritualis
xii apostolorum; Iacob caput xii tribuum, Christus caput xii ecclesiarum;
Iacob autem genuit Iudam et fratres eius carnaliter, et Christus genuit Petrum
et fratres eius, hoc est apostolos, spiritualiter. Concordat igitur Iudas fortis

---

57 matre] Maria T   61 illa[1]] in *praem*. BV   62 illa] in *praem*. BV   63 illa] in
praem. T   66 expandit BTV   illa[2]] hora *add*. BTV   71 eius latus *tr*. BV   est
om. T   72 Caluarie *om*. BV   Hec ille *om*. BV   73 ecciam] enim T; *om*. BV
74 et unicum] filium BV   76 Zacharias] genuit *add*. BV   79 Iohannes] autem *add*.
T   84-85 illa porta celi, ista porta celi *tr*. BTV   85 carnaliter *om*. T

---

[6] Cf. Ambrose, *Expositio Evangelii secundum Lucam* 4.7.8 (PL 15.1614).

90 manus cum Petro robusto quia, sicut Iude et non aliis de suis fratribus dictum
est, *Non auferetur septrum de Iuda et dux de femore eius donec ueniat qui
mittendus est,*[7] et cetera, sic et Petro et non aliis de suis fratribus apostolis
dictum est: *Tu es Petrus et super hanc petram hedificabo ecclesiam meam,*[8]
et cetera. Vtrique septrum regni in predictis uerbis concessum est, illi
95 temporalis regiminis, isti spiritualis gubernacionis. Hec Ioachim.[9]

Circa igitur concordiam aliquarum regionum et nacionum que continentur
in ueteri cum aliquibus que gubernantur sub nouo, uisis modis concordie, est
sciendum quod hec concordia non in uocibus nominum exterioribus, sed in
realibus eorum interpretacionibus consistit. Concordant igitur regiones et
100 naciones et ciuitates earum que in testamento continentur ueteri cum regionibus et nacionibus et earum ciuitatibus que in nouo sub fide catholica
gubernantur, non uoce ut predixi exteriori, sed interpretacione reali. Vnde ea
que in illis ueteris sunt facta concernunt ea que in illis noui modo consimili
sunt fienda.

105 Vnde in primis, sicut regnum Iuda regnum uniuerse militantis ecclesie
tangit, sic et per reges Iuda concordia intelligere pontifices romanos ostendit,[10] et licet Ierusalem, que uisio pacis interpretando dicitur, in generali
uniuersam tangat ecclesiam, tamen in speciali tangit locum seu ciuitatem in
qua sumus sacerdos cum suo collegio trahit moram. Et licet per Romam
110 aliquociens romana intelligatur ecclesia, tamen Petrus ibidem existens, in
prima epistola, sub nomine Babilonis figuraliter Romam significans, ait:
Salutat uos ecclesia que est in Babilone collecta.[11] Babilon enim confusio
interpretatur, nam in recepcione Antichristi non Roma sed Babilon, non
uocaliter sed realiter nuncupabitur, quia tunc in ea omnis ordo christiane
115 religionis turpiter confudetur, *ut tantum nunc qui tenet teneat,* id est romanam
regit ecclesiam et regnat, *donec de medio fiat ille,* scilicet *iniquus,*[12] et cetera.

Hanc igitur materiam seu concordiam Ioachim super Ysaiam in honeribus
generaliter et particulariter satis clare per ordinem tangit, unde causa
breuitatis, dimissis particularibus, superficialiter generalia tantum tangantur.

---

90 de suis fratribus *om.* BTV   92 et²] en B; enim V   fratribus] et *add.* BTV
93 hedificabo ... meam *om.* BTV   97 ueteri] testamento *add.* BV   100 naciones] et
regiones *add.* BV   102 ut predixi *om.* T   106-107 ostendit] intendit BTV
108 speciali] spirituali BV   109 cum] in T   114 realiter] racionabiliter BTV
115 id est] unum BV   116 et *om.* MT   119 tantum generalia *tr.* BTV

---

[7] Gen. 49.10.
[8] Mt. 16.18.
[9] Cf. *Lib. Conc.,* fol. 7v; also fols. 6v, 18r, 22r-23r, 34v.
[10] Cf. *Lib. Conc.,* fols. 38v-39r; *Lib. Fig.,* pls. 16, 17.
[11] 1 Pt. 5.13.
[12] 2 Thess. 2.7-8.

120 Vt inquid Ioachim,[13] onus Babilonis secundum concordiam tangit Romam,
sic Caldea Alamaniam; onus philistini tangit lonbardos et alios ytalicos et
gillemandos; onus Moab et filiorum Amon tangit principes latinos et grecos;
onus deserti maris tangit affricanos et alios sarracenos. Vnde hic nota quod
sicut desertum mare tangit naciones infidelium, ita et nauigancium mare
125 naciones ostendit fidelium; per fluctus uero utriusque maris oceani utriusque
imperii anotantur. Et sicut enim terra firmiter fundata in generali naciones
fidelium tangit, sic et in spirituali ecclesiasticum regnum ostendit. Sicut onus
Dumea uel Ydumea tangit iudeos et omnes negociatores terre et maris
sapientes et legistas et grecos, sic et Grecia hesperios et Macedonia cathali-
130 cios. Onus in Arabia tangit yspanos et marchios; onus uallis uisionis tangit
cuiuscumque ordines regulares. Onus Thiri tangit Siciliam siue siculos,
regniculas et sibi subiacentes, sic et eam Persia tangit, unde addit Ioachim
quod Sicilia quinque plagis est percucienda, quarum prima fuit a theothonicis,
secunda sub yrcis regniculis, tercia sub aquile furiis, quarta a regulo uolanti
135 ab occidente, quinta quod deducetur in profundum maris et ultra non
apparebit. Onus Egypti tangit iudeos, daneos, et francos seu Franciam, sic et
Media tangit eam. Onus iumentorum tangit clericos, prelatos, et rectores
eorum ubique difusos. Onus Damasci tangit tuscos et lugures in gladio uerbi
Domini, et ferro confundendos et conterendos. Onus Niniue tangit mundum
140 pollutum sanguine peccatorum tam in greco populo quam in latino, assirios
aterendum et exterminium paganorum. Onus Abacuc tangit predicatores
seculi, transgressores legis et fidei, iudeos, italicos, aduentum Christi in
carne, crucis patibulum, uocacionem gencium, seculi lubricum et tripudium
saluandorum. Onus uerbi Dei tangit iudeos et populum gentilium, et cetera.
145   Visis concordacionibus regionum et nacionum, seu significacionibus
predictarum in generali, nunc uidendum est que sunt persone quibus hec et
alia diuina sunt misteria reuelanda, seu aperienda, ne sancta canibus mini-
strentur.[14] Horum autem et diffinicio in Mathei euangelio satis claret per
Christum Dominum Deo Patri dulciter alloquentem: *Confiteor tibi, Pater,*
150 *Domine rex celi et terre, quia abscondisti hec a sepientibus et prudentibus, et*

---

123 et alios sarracenos *om.* T   124-125 ita ... fidelium *om.* BTV   125 utriusque[1] ...
oceani *om.* M[ac]   oceani] sic per *add.* BTV   127 spirituali] speciali T   Sicut *om.* M[ac];
Et *praem.* BTV   130 tangit *om.* BTV   132 Ioachim addit *tr.* BTV   138 ibique M
tuscos] rusticos BTV   139 conterendos] contractandos BTV   140 populo] polluto BV
141 predicatores] peccatores BTV   143 lubricum] libitum BTV   144 gencium BTV
145 regionum] regnum BV   seu *om.* T   147 sancta *om.* T   148 et *om.* BTV

---

[13] *Super Esaiam*, fols. 9v-10r; on the plagues to afflict Sicily, cf. *Super Esaiam*, fol. 40v.
[14] Cf. Mt. 7.6.

reuelasti ea paruulis; ita, Pater, quoniam sic iuit placitum ante te.[15] Ex
predictis igitur claret qui et quales sunt isti sapientes et prudentes a quibus
Deus abscondit et abscondere perhibet sua misteria gloriosa, et qui et quales
sunt isti paruuli quibus ea Deus reuelat et reuelare permittit. Isti igitur
155 sapientes et prudentes quibus diuino iudicio alta misteria absconduntur sunt
illi de quibus in euangelio dicitur: *Quia filii huius seculi prudenciores sunt in
generacionibus suis filiis lucis.*[16] Vnde ex hiis colligitur quod sapiencia huius
mundi sit stulticia apud Deum, unde per quendam sapientem dicitur: *Perdam
sapienciam sapiencium et intelligenciam intelligencium reprobabo.*[17] Si uero
160 de talibus amplius querimus, ad romanos i° per apostolum satis claret:
Reuelatur, inquid, *ira Dei de celo super omnem inpietatem et iniusticiam
hominum qui ueritatem Dei in iniusticia detinent, quia quod notum est Dei
manifestum est in illis. Deus enim illis manifestauit, ita ut sint inexscusabiles
quia, cum cognouiscent Deum, non sicut Deum glorificauerunt aut gracias
165 egerunt, sed euanuerunt in cogitacionibus suis et obscuratum est insipiens cor
eorum; dicentes enim se ipsos esse sapientes, stulti facti sunt,*[18] et cetera.

Bene ergo ex predictis claret quibus sunt alta misteria Dei sapiencie
abscondenda. Si uero queris qui et quales sunt isti paruuli quibus illa Deus
reuelat et reuelare permictit, isti sunt illi de quibus legitur in Matheo: *Nisi
170 conuersi fueritis et efficiamini sicut paruuli, non intrabitis in regnum celorum.*[19] Celorum igitur regnum paruulorum est, non mola quantitatis sed
fundamento humilitatis, propter quod sequitur: *Quicumque, ergo,
humiliauerit se sicut paruulus, iste hic maior est in regno celorum.*[20] Quibus
ipse Dominus in Luca loquitur, dicens: *Vobis datum est nosce misterium
175 regni Dei, ceteris autem in parabolis, ut uidentes non uideant et intelligentes
non intelligant.*[21] Igitur ex predictis colligitur quod tales paruuli propter
humilitatem dicantur et maiores regni celorum efficiantur, secundum euangelicum illud, *Qui se humiliat, exaltabitur,*[22] quoniam superbis resistit Deus
et misteria sua abscondit; humilibus uero, quibus mundus crucifixus est,

---

153 perhibet] prohibet M   154 Deus ea *tr.* B   156 euangeliis BV   162 in iniusticia *om.* T   Dei²] Deo M   163 illis¹] illic T   165 incipiens M   167 ergo]
igitur BTV   174 Dominus sap (*lac.*) in Lucha dicens T

---

[15] Mt. 11.25-26; see also: *Lib. Conc.*, fols. 6v-7r, and Arnold of Vilanova's *De tempore*,
p. 132.

[16] Lc. 16.8.

[17] 1 Cor. 1.19.

[18] Rom. 1.18-19, 21-22.

[19] Mt. 18.3.

[20] Mt. 18.4.

[21] Lc. 8.10.

[22] Lc. 18.14.

180 profunda archana reuelat et reuelare permictit.[23] Et quoniam talentum
absconditum non lucratur, uult Deus paruulos predictos reuelantem Spiritum
imitari, ut non sapientibus et prudentibus sed uiris conformibus ea que
reuelata sunt caute et callide propter periculosa tempora intimare. Vnde
uolentibus se prudenter regere, quidam sanctus pater nouem tradit regulas ad
185 hoc necessarie institutas.

Prima est sequi studium sancte oracionis, quia tempore passionis Christus
non monuit discipulos ieiunare, sed pocius orare, dicens: *Vigilate et orate,*
ut non intretis in temptacionem.[24] Vigilancia enim respicit ueritatem, temptacio errorem, oracio uero deuocionem. Nam oracio est magistra sanctorum
190 et porta per quam omnes sancti peruenerunt ad noticiam Dei; qui per istud
ostium non intrauerit, usque ad secreta Dei peruenire non poterit.

Secunda est non reuelare seu aperire secreta istius temporis inimicis Dei,
nec genti brutalem intellectum habenti, quia magnum periculum est. Non est
decens margaritas inter porcos seminare, nec sancta canibus ministrare.[25]
195 Vnde apostolus, huius temporis periculum tangens, dicit: *Veniet enim tempus*
cum homines sanam doctrinam non sustinebunt, sed ad desideria sua coace-
ruabunt sibi magistros, prurientes auribus; et a ueritate quidem auditum
aduertent, ad fabulas autem conuertentur.[26]

Tercia est uoluntario corde loqui de Deo et de maliciis et secretis istius
200 temporis, et hoc cum personis concordibus intellectu, quia loqui de Deo est
uita anime, et est una uiarum per quam anima leuius ascendit in Deum.

Quarta est nullam facere notabilem mutacionem de statu suo ad alium
statum sine magno consilio alicuius spiritualis persone de qua homo bene
possit confidere, que ecciam noticiam habeat de maliciis temporis supradicti.
205 Et dico notabilem mutacionem, uendere scilicet possessiones, uel mutare se
de loco ad locum, uel religionem intrare, uel se ab una in aliam mutare, quod
in tribus casibus licitum est, scilicet causa maioris perfeccionis, uel perfec-
cioris obseruacionis, quia ibi est religio ubi est regularis obseruacio, uel causa
remedii seu impossibilis obseruacionis, uel causa intollerabilis persequucio-
210 nis, et hoc propter periculum desperacionis uel appostasie ab ordine et

---

184 se *post* prudenter *rep.* BTV   tradidit BTV   186 est *om.* BTV   188 ut non]
ne BTV   temptacionem] et cetera *add.* BTV   194 inter porcos *om.* T   195 dicit]
ait BTV   enim *om.* BTV   196 sua desideria *tr.* BTV   201 leuis BTV   in] ad BTV
202 Quarta] regula *add.* BTV   204 possit] posset BV; potest T   205 scilicet
om. BTV   208 est[2] *om.* BTV

---

[23] Cf. 1 Pt. 5.5; Jac. 4.6.
[24] Mt. 26.41.
[25] Cf. Mt. 7.6.
[26] 2 Tim. 4.3-4.

quandoque a fide, quod nimis palam non in modico numero ecclesiasticorum
tempore Antichristi mistici est fiendum. Vnde licet per Petrum intelligatur
ordo clericorum, tamen postquam ter negauit Christus, *egressus foras fleuit
amare.*[27] Et licet per Iohannem euangelistam intelligatur ordo uirorum
215 euangelicorum, tamen in tempestate illius noctis capcionis Christi, relicto
pallio, fugerit, qui post ad consolandum matrem Christi ad pedem crucis
reuersus est.[28] O quanti clerici in pressura illius temporis loco Petri egredien-
tur foras Ierusalem, hoc est ecclesiam uniuersam, negato ordine et fide
Christi, sed utinam flerent amare. O quanti religiosi in illa nocte tenebrarum
220 sub pressura temporum illius regis xi, relicto pallio, id est abitu, fugient, sed
utinam post reuertentur ad consolandum matrem Christi, hoc est ecclesiam,
in pede crucis. Et hic nota quod Christus ante passionem comisit matrem
ecclesiam Petro, et pendens in cruce ipsam matrem comisit propriam
Iohanni quia Petrum oportebat expirare in cruce, Iohannem uero manere, ut
225 ipse Dominus dixit: *Sic eum uolo manere donec ueniam.*[29]

Quinta regula hec est: non implicare se nimis in negociis temporalibus,
quia totum cor rapiunt et difundunt et retrahunt totaliter a seruicio Dei et hoc
inimicus toto conatu suo, ecciam si de abisso sciret ea extrahere maxime
amicos Dei, in isto sexto tempore procurabit ut negocium adducat negocium,
230 et occupacio occupacionem, et labor laborem, et hec ut omnia secum tradat
et ecciam ut caracteri aut nomini aut numero nominis bestie locus detur.

Sexta regula hec est: conformare se aliis christianis; in casu tamen in quo
imperfeccio uel nullum peccatum mortale incurrat, ecciam dissimulare se,
quia nostra infirmitas, que adhuc non est apta ad tollerandum tribulaciones
235 uel persequuciones uel labores, in prefacto tempore hoc requirit.

Septima regula est non habere familiaritates nimias uel profundas cum
gente contrarie intencionis, sed superficialiter transire cum eis, maxime cum
falsis religiosis, dicente Deo: *Attendite a falsis prophetis qui ueniunt ad uos
in uestimentis ouium intrinsecus sunt autem lupi rapaces.*[30] De quibus sanctus

---

211 ad fidem V   ecclesiasticorum] clericorum BTV   213 postquam] priusquam
BV   216 ad] a B   218 hoc est] scilicet BV   et *om.* BV   218-219 Christi
fidei T   219 O *om.* BV   221 reuertantur BTV   consolandum] confortandum BTV
223-224 propriam commisit Iohanne BTV   224 ut] et T   226 nimis secularibus
negociis uel temporalibus BV; secularibus negociis T   228 toto] totus BV   ea *om.*
TV   231 locum BTV   238 Deo] Domino BTV   a *om.* T   239 autem sunt in
tr. et add. B; autem sunt *tr.* TV

---

[27] Cf. Lc. 22.62.
[28] Cf. Mc. 14.51-52.
[29] Jn. 21.22.
[30] Mt. 7.15.

240 Bernardus loquitur, dicens: *Sunt quidam peruersi homines sub ueste ouina et*
honestatis pallio gradientes qui uolunt esse humiles sine despectu, pauperes
sine defectu, bene uestiti sine sollicitudine, delicate pasci sine labore, aliis
adulantes, aliis detrahentes, mordaces ut canes, dolosi ut uulpes, superbi ut
leones, intrinsecus autem sunt lupi rapaces, mercedem presencium capientes,
245 *futurum premium euomentes; uolunt esse sine autoritate iudices, sine uisu*
testes, et postremo sine actu accusatores. Hec ille.[31]
   Octaua regula est ut omnes anxietates et dubitaciones et temptaciones quas
homo habet alicui spirituali persone de qua bene confidere possit sine dubio
reuelet, quia hoc est unum supremum remedium per quod homo multum
250 leuiter temptaciones euadit. Vnde inimicus toto posse suo conatur ad hoc,
ne homo anxietates et dubitaciones et temptaciones quas habet possit alicui
reuelare, et hoc ut de errore incidat in errorem, et desperato animo nullum
possit remedium inuenire.
   Nona regula est quod quilibet ponat studium totum suum ad trahendum
255 alios ad noticiam Dei quia, ut dicit beatus Franciscus, *Nullum sacrificium est*
ita Deo acceptum sicut trahere unam animam ad Deum.[32] Vnde si uis ut
parcat tibi Deus omnia peccata tua et saluet te, trahe alios ad Deum, quia ista
caritas operit, secundum dictum Pauli, *multitudinem peccatorum.*[33] Heu me,
quid dicam, utinam in ciuitate Ierusalem magna, que iam nunc spiritualiter
260 Egyptus et Sodoma appellatur,[34] decem operatores huiusmodi uerbo reperi-
rentur et facto;[35] *nunc autem et flens dico, inimicos crucis Christi.*[36]
   Iam enim in loco sancto, seu in templo christiane religionis, quasi desolato
spiritu et diuino solacio destituto, nimis aperte hec que sequuntur abhomi-
naciones per ordinem reperiuntur, scilicet religiosi sine bona doctrina,
265 predicatores sine bona uita, doctores sine fructus utilitate, regulares sine
castitate, clerici sine sciencia, pastores sine ouium cura, principes absque
iusticia, iudices et aduocati corrupti pecunia, officiales detractores et dolosi,
procuratores fures et maliciosi, notarii corruptores et falsarii, artifices de-

---

241 despectu] et *add.* BTV   244 autem] aut M   rapaces] rapientes BTV
245 uisu] usu BV   247 et temptaciones *om.* BTV   248 possit *om.* M[ac]   249 reuelare BTV   251 et temptaciones *om.* V   254 suum totum *tr.* BTV   255 est *om.* M
258 Pauli] apostoli BTV   259 spiritualiter nunc *tr.* BTV   260 operaciones T
huiusmodi] de *add.* B   261 flens] falsos BTV   263 aperte] apparent T
265-266 regulares ... castitate *om.* BV   268 procuratores ... maliciosi *post* falsari *tr.* BV

---

[31] Cf. Bernard, *Ad pastores in synodos congregatos*, 5 (PL 184.1088-1089). See also the
Introduction, pp. 91-92.
[32] Cf. Thomas of Celano, *Vita I*, c. 131; *Actus Beati Francisci*, c. 16; St. Bonaventure,
Legenda Maior, c. 9.
[33] 1 Pt. 4.8.
[34] Cf. Apoc. 11.8.
[35] Cf. Gen. 18.32.
[36] Phil. 3.18.

ceptores et periurii, diuites absque pietate, mercatores sine ueritate, socii sine
270 fidelitate, peccatores sine humilitate, senes putrefacti in criminibus, filii
rebelles parentibus, consanguinei sine uera amicicia, et mulieres sine uere-
cundia. Quid igitur aliud expectatur, nisi ut alter Nabugodonosor, nouus rex
Babilonis, insurgat et abominandum ydolum pseudo prophetam in loco
sancto instituat, ut quicumque non adorauerit occidatur et ab uniuersa
275 sinagoga tam uiuens quam corporaliter mortuus ut hereticus turpiter confun-
datur, et cetera.[37]

Viso igitur que sunt persone quibus hec et alia diuina misteria sint
reuelanda et aperienda, uidendum est de ordine distincionum seu parcium
principalium huius libri. Iste namque liber in partes seu distinciones quatuor-
280 decim generaliter est diuisus, ut ea que continentur in eo clarius uideantur.[38]
In prima parte seu distincione agitur de tribus statibus generalibus totius
mundi et de eorum concordis; in secunda, de concordia notabilium personarum in principio cuiuslibet status; in tercia, de concordia crudelium personarum in fine cuiuslibet generalis status; in quarta, de vii etatibus mundi et de
285 mirabili punicione facta a Deo in fine cuiuslibet etatis; in quinta, de vii
temporibus ecclesie et de vii bellis contra ecclesiam datis a vii capitibus
drachonis; in sexta, de concordia vii ecclesie temporum cum vii etatibus
huius mundi; in septima, de concordia vii ecclesie temporum et vii dierum
originalium; in octaua, de concordia vii ecclesie temporum cum vii sacramen-
290 tis; in nona, de vii sigillis noui et ueteris testamenti concordatis; in decima,
de vii capitibus drachonis noui et ueteris concordatis; in undecima, de
concordia in speciali ad inueniendum certum tempus eorum que sunt in nouo
fienda per ea que in ueteri consimili modo sunt facta; in duodecima, de
numero et differencia et concordia diferenciarum generacionum noui et
295 ueteris testamenti; in terciadecima, de ordine generacionum ab Adam usque
ad Christum, et a Christo usque in finem mundi, et de concordia eorum; in
quartadecima, de scalis generacionum utriusque testamenti, et de aliquibus
notabilibus, ut in suo ordine et suis marginibus satis claret.

---

270 peccatores] idest oratores *add.* BTV   271 et *om.* BTV   272 nouus Nabuchodonosor *tr.* BTV   275 turpiter *om.* BTV   275-276 confudatur M   278 est *om.* T
280 uideamur M   282 de¹ *om.* BTV   concordis] cordis M^{ac} 284 mundi] huius
praem. BTV   285 a] id est BTV   288 mundi huius *tr.* BTV   288 vii¹ *om.* BTV
290 concordantibus BTV   291 ueteris] testamenti *add.* BTV   concordantibus BTV
293 simili T   296 in¹] ad BTV

---

[37] This might be a reference to the practice of exhuming the bodies of heretics so that they
might be burned, as occurred in the case of the companions of Fr. Just; see the Introduction,
p. 66.
[38] See Arnold of Vilanova's remarks on the number 14 in the *Dialogus de elementis
catholicae fidei*, as noted in the Introduction, p. 36.

[EXPLICIT PROLOGUS. INCIPIT PRIMA DISTINCTIO, IN QUA AGI-
TUR DE TRIBUS STATIBUS GENERALIBUS TOTIUS MUNDI ET DE
EORUM CONCORDIIS.]¹

Cum secundum sapientem, *nichil nouum sub sole, et quid est quod fuit,* nisi
Christum, *ipsum quod futurum est, et quid est quod factum est nisi ipsum quod
fiendum est,*² et tres status mundi generales in scriptura legantur, ex predictis
colligitur quod primus respicit secundum tanquam signum et figuram eius,
5 secundus uero signatus et figuratus per primum tercium per misterium
respicit. Vnde facta primi status sunt signancia tantum, facta secundi signata
et signancia simul, facta tercii signata tantum dicuntur, quia nullum alium per
concordiam respiciunt, quia post tercium statum non subsequitur alius status
cum quo, per principia, media et fines, possit per concordiam respondere.³
10 Nam illa gloria ita nobis incipiet quod nec medium nec finem habebit.

[PRIMUS STATUS]

Primus igitur status generalis istius seculi, siue primum seculum, sumpsit
inicium ab Adam et durauit usque ad Christum, in quo uiguit ordo matrimonii,⁴ et describitur Deo Patri, cui apropriatur potestas, nam in prefacto
15 statu potentissimum ac terribilem se ostendit: primo, in creacione mundi,
quem de nichilo creauit; secundo, in diluuio non solum potentem, ymmo

---

Titulum *om.* M   in qua *om.* T   2 Christum *om.* BTV   5 figuratus] figuram
M; est *add.* BV   primum] et *add.* BTV   11 *Rubricam om.* M

---

¹ The material of this Distinction is derived chiefly from the *Lib. Conc.,* fols. 56v-58r, but
reorganized to deal with each status in turn, rather than in sequences of three. See also *Lib.
Conc.,* fols. 8v-13v, 19v-25r.
² Eccles. 1.9-10.
³ *Lib. Conc.,* fol. 9v.
⁴ For the three orders — matrimonial, clerical, and monastic — and for the assignment of
Father, Son, and Holy Spirit to the three ages, see the *Lib. Conc.,* fols. 8v-9r; for a summary
of initiators and consummators, see *ibid.,* fols. 4, 5, 8, 9; for the combination of *status* and
etates, see *ibid.,* fols. 20v-25r; for disasters at the conclusion of each period, see *ibid.,* fols.
23v-24v, 25r-v, 44r-v.

multum terribilem, quia tunc, exceptis octo personis quas saluauit, totum humanum genus et omnes creaturas in aere et in terra uiuentes destruxit, exceptis aliquibus quas in archa pro semine reseruauit; tercio, ostendit se
20 potentem et dominum et quasi crudelem in corrigendo populum suum quem timore et asperitate alligari oportebat, et ideo in diuersis promissionibus quas fecit mundo iratum ac terribilem se ostendit, et ideo in scripturis sanctis Deum belli et Dominum exercituum se appellat. Quare autem Deus tam grandia atque grauia iudicia fecit in ueteri testamento triplex racio assignatur:
25 prima est ut toti mundo ostenderet suum dominium et potenciam suam magnam; secunda est quia populus ille erat totus carnalis et rudis et dure ceruicis, et quia tales decuit ipsum fortiter corrigere et se ei terribilem ostendere et acriter ecciam castigare; tercia est quia principes huius mundi, quando nouiter intrant possessionem alicuius terre, ostendunt se terribiles et
30 fortes dominatores, et hoc ut ponant populum in timore; modo asimili, in isto primo statu Deus Pater intrauit possessionem et dominium huius mundi, et hac de causa debuit se terribilem ostendere et potentem, et hoc ut poneret populum in timore.

Iste status continet in se v etates, septem sigilla, generaciones lxiii.
35 Secundum enim aliam concordiam, habuit inicium in Adam et terminauit in Oziam, in quo inceperunt tempora prophetarum, in quo eciam fuit iniciacio prima ordinis clericorum, et secundum hoc contineret generaciones xlii, et cetera.

Iste status pro sollempni principio tres sollempnes personas habuit —
40 Abraam, Ysaac, et Jacob — et duodecim patriarchas, scilicet Iudam, Ruben, Gath, Aser, Neptali, Dan, Symeon, Leui, Ysachar, Zabulon, Ioseph, Beniamin, et duos nepotes patriarcharum, scilicet Manassem et Effraym. Et ne patriarcharum numerus per corporalem mortem defficeret, per xii tribus singulas principes in suplendis locis patriarcharum eligebantur.
45 Et hic nota quod quilibet istorum trium statuum est sicut unus dies, habens suum mane, suum meridiem, et suum uesper. Mane autem illius primi status sumpsit inicium in Abraam, cui fuit facta promissio incarnacionis Filii Dei, qui uerus est sol iusticie et salutis. Medium autem et meridiem fuit tempore Dauid et Salomonis, qui hedificauit templum Deo et stabiliuit cantores in
50 magno numero ad laudandum Deum in templo, et ex diuersis mundi partibus uenientes adoratores magnificauit, et fecit sacrificia legis Dei. Vesper uero

---

17 terribilissimum BTV   19 se *om.* T   22 terribilissimum BTV   24 grandia] ira *add.* T   27 ipsum decuit *tr.* T   terribilium B; terribilissimum T   29 intrauit T 34 lxiiii BV   37 continet T; continentur BV   48 est uerus *tr.* BTV   49 hedificauerunt BV

siue finis istius primi status fuit tempore quo Christus Filius Dei humanam
carnem assumpsit de uirgine, et fuit tam grandis nox et tam grauis et tam
tenebrosa quod tota sinagoga iudeorum errauit in Christum, scilicet principes
55 sacerdotum, Annas et Cayfas cum ceteris prelatis sinagoge, et omnes
magistratus et legis doctores, et ecciam omnes religiosi et seniores populi,
necnon et Herodes et Pilatus et omnes herodiani, et in tantum errauerunt
quod condempnauerunt uitam et doctrinam Christi, et tradiderunt eum
morti, et excommunicauerunt omnes confidentes et credentes in eum, ita ut
60 extra sinagogam fierent. Hec est abominacio prima sedens in loco sancto.

[SECUNDUS STATUS]

Secundus status generalis istius seculi, siue secundum seculum, sumpsit
inicium a Christo et durabit usque ad mortem Antichristi, in quo uiguit ordo
clericalis, et describitur Dei Filio benedicto, cui sapiencia apropriatur quia
65 Dei Filius in prefacto statu suam supernam sapienciam toto mundo ostendit,
maxime in duobus: primo, quia misterio sue profundissime humilitatis et
sapiencie, diabolo deuicto in cruce, humanum genus ab inferno eripuit et
aperuit ostium paradisi; secundo, quia ueritas fidei nostre, que detinebatur
sub uelamine littere ueteris testamenti, que sanctis patribus fuit obscura et sub
70 uelamine detenta, fuit nobis reuelata et manifestata per predicacionem
apostolorum, qui prius erant simplices piscatores, ad dandum intelligi quod
Dei Filius benedictus per sapienciam suam operatus est in illis et non
sapiencia mundana.[5] Fuit ecciam nobis manifestata per alios doctores seu
predicatores noui testamenti, ita quod in isto statu lux solis ueritatis fidei
75 septempliciter resplenduit quam in primo,[6] deiecta a se uetustate et uelamine
litere primi status et primi seculi.

Iste status continet in se sextam tantum etatem, quam Christus Dominus
suo consecrauit aduentu, et habet de septem temporibus ecclesie in se
quinque, et de vii sigillis similiter, et generaciones xlii a fuga mulieris, que est
80 ecclesia. Secundum enim aliam concordiam, habuit inicium in Ozia, in quo
fuit iniciacio ordinis clericorum prima, et habet in se generaciones xlii
similiter, circa quorum finem, ut Zacharias ante Christum, sanctus Benedic-

---

52 siue *om.* BTV   istius *om.* BTV   54 tota] in *praem.* BV   55 et[2] *om.* BTV
56 ecciam *om.* BTV   57 et[1] *om.* BV   61 *Rubricam om.* M   64 quia] qui
BTV   71 piscatores] pastores M   73 manifestata nobis *tr.* T   78 habet] hec
BTV   81 se *om.* BTV   82 finem] fuerunt BV   sanctus] factus BV

---

[5] Cf. 2 Cor. 3.12-18.
[6] Cf. Is. 30.26; Olivi opens his *Postilla* with the citation of this text.

tus in mundo claruit, in quo fuit secunda iniciacio ordinis monachorum. Isti
statui pro sollempni sui principio date sunt tres persone sollempnes, scilicet
85 Zacharias, Iohannes Babtista, et Dominus Iesus Christus, necnon et duodecim apostoli, scilicet Petrus, Andreas, Thomas, Symon, Iudas, Mathias,
Iacobus frater Domini, Matheus uel Leui, Philippus, Bartholomeus, Iohannes, Iacobus, et loco duorum patriarcharum nepotuum datis sunt Mathias et
Ioseph, qui cognominatur iustus, et sicut in ueteri testamento, deficiente uno
90 patriarcharum per corporalem mortem, ne numerus deficeret, per tribus xii
eligebatur princeps ad suppledum locum preteriti patriarche, sic in nouo de
tota ecclesia.

Mane autem istius secundi status sumpsit inicium a conuersione iudeorum
in regno Iudee facta per apostolos, de quo scribitur quod nullus illorum
95 habebat proprium, sed omnia erant eis comunia et nullus erat pauper inter
illos.[7] Meridies fuit tempore sancti Siluestri pape, qui conuerterit imperatorem Constantinum, qui quidem imperator subiugauit imperium ecclesie et
dedit libertatem frabicandi ecclesias per totum romanum imperium, et tunc
quasi totum imperium fuit conuersum ad fidem Christi. Vesper uero erit in
100 temporibus Antichristi, et durabit usque ad mortem eius, et erit tam grandis
nox et tam grauis et tam tenebrosa quod tota fere ecclesia errabit in Christum,
et uita et doctrina eius sollempniter condemnabitur per principes sacerdotum
et ceteros prelatos ecclesie, necnon per magistratos et doctores et legis
peritos, et ecciam per religiosos et seniores populi, et per herodianos, seu
105 tirannos romani imperii sub primo et secundo Herode, seu sub mistico et
magno Antichristo, et erit hec tribulacio tam grandis et tam seductoria quod
ab inicio mundi similis non fuit neque postea expectatur, et nisi breuiaret
Deus dies illos, *non fieret salua omnis caro, sed propter electos breuiabuntur
dies illi.*[8] Hec est abominacio secunda stans in loco sancto, seu in templo iam
110 quasi spiritualiter desolato.

[TERCIUS STATUS]

Tercius status generalis istius seculi, siue tercium seculum, sumet inicium a
morte magni Antichristi et durabit usque ad finem mundi, et describitur

---

83 monachorum] clericorum M^{ac}   84 principis BV   85 Christus Iesus *tr.* T
86-87 Matthias *et* Matheus *tr.* BTV   87 Domini] Dei M   87-88 Iohannes] et *add.* BV
93 secundi *om.* BTV   status] seculi BV   94 illorum] eorum T; *om.* BV   106 hec
om. B; hec erit *tr.* TV   109 Hec] autem *add.* BTV   110 quasi] de *add.* T
111 *Rubricam om.* M

---

[7] Cf. Act. 2.44-45.
[8] Mt. 24.22; cf. also Mt. 24.21 and *Lib. Conc.*, fol. 106v.

Spiritui sancto, cui apropriatur bonitas, quia tunc Spiritus sanctus ostendet
115 se tam bonum et largum toti mundo in diuersis donis, ita quod uidebitur esse
sicut fornax ignis prenimio ardore amoris,[9] et sicut ypotecaria pregrandissi-
mis odoribus spiritualium delectacionum, uel sicut sol septem dierum
prenimio splendore spiritualium reuelacionum, unde tunc sol, qui Christus
est, lucebit septempliciter quam in statibus supradictis, quia liber Apoca-
120 lipssis, qui uisus est a Iohanne vii sigillis clausus, tunc erit manifeste apertus.
Vnde Ysaie xxx° dicitur: *Erit lux lune sicut lux solis, et lux solis ut lux septem*
dierum in die qua alligauerit Dominus uulnus populi sui, et percussionem plage
eius sanabit.[10]

[*Glosa.* Cum dicit sol, qui Christus est, lucebit septempliciter quam in
125 statibus supradictis, quoad ueritatem fidei nostre hoc sano modo intelligas;
non enim pleniori modo quoad ueritatem fidei nostre christiane tunc quam
nunc lucebit, *quia tunc cognoscam ut cognitus sum,*[11] ut ait apostolus, set
quoad pleniorem noticiam multorum mirabilium que tunc fient in uniuerso
mundo, et quoad pleniorem conuersionem uniuersalis mundi ad Christum et
130 ad fidem eius, quia liber reuelacionis articulorum fidei Christi, qui primo
christianis fuit clare apertus, tunc omnibus iudeis, paganis, et ceteris infidelibus manifeste aperietur, *et fiat unum ouile et unus pastor,*[12] et cetera.]

Iste status continet in se septimam seu ultimam mundi etatem, et de vii
temporibus ecclesie habet duos, sextum et septimum, et de septem sigillis
135 similiter, ut post uigiliam passionis sequatur gaudium spiritualis et generalis
resurreccionis tocius mundi ad fidem Christi, *ut fiat unum ouile et unus*
pastor.[13] Et secundum hoc haberet generaciones xix, unde haberet inicium in
generacione xlv[a], scilicet prime crucis. Si uero habet inicium simpliciter in
morte magni Antichristi, habebit generaciones xvii, propter quod ille due
140 generaciones, scilicet xlv[a] et xlvi[a], relinquentur, et licet cadant in numero
temporum, non cadunt in numero generacionum, sed sub ueritatis silencium
currunt. Vnde tempus fuge mulieris, que est ecclesia, usque ad xlv[am] generacionem se extendit et non plus. Daniel totum illud tempus predictarum
duarum generacionum sub numero xliiii dierum seu annorum tacet, et

---

119 quia] qui T   121 dicit BV   lux[1] ... et] lux lumen sic lux solis, ut V   ut] sicut
BV; dicitur sic T   122 Dominus *om.* BTV   sui *om.* BTV   125-126 hoc ... nostre
om. V *per hom.*   126 quam] quasi BTV   130 articulorum] in articulo BTV Christi *om.*
T   132 et cetera *om.* BTV   133 vii] v[e] MV   134 de *om.* T   135 similiter *om.*
BTV   139 ille *om.* BTV   141 sed *om.* BTV   142-143 generacionem *om.* M[ac]
144 et *om.* BTV

---

[9] Cf. *Postilla*, fol. 42v.
[10] Is. 30.26.
[11] 1 Cor. 13.12.
[12] Jn. 10.16.
[13] Jn. 10.16.

145 quadragesimum quintum diem seu annum nominat, quia est finis pressure et
principium omnis pacis, et ideo relinquntur racione uigiliarum propter
pressuram, quia specialiter in ultima illarum quasi ab uniuersis cantabitur:
Beati uentres et steriles qui non genuerunt, et ubera que non lactauerunt,[14] et
cetera. Relinquntur ecciam profete preteritorum temporum secundi status.

150   Secundum enim aliam concordiam, a beato Benedicto iste status habuit
inicium, in quo fuit secunda iniciacio ordinis monachorum, qui ab Ozia
completis xl generacionibus, et ab Helizeo, tempore regis Ioram, in quo fuit
prima iniciacio ordinis monachorum, xlii generacionibus, quo tempore
Helias est eleuatus in celum, ipse predictus sanctus apparuit in hoc mundo.[15]

155   Iste autem status pro sollempni principio habuit tres personas sollempnes,
scilicet sanctum Benedictum, qui fuit pater monachorum nigrorum, et
sanctum Bernardum, qui fuit pater monachorum alborum, et sanctum
Franciscum, cum Christo confixum, qui fuit pater fratrum minorum, seu
caput euangelici status. In similitudinem xii patriarcharum et apostolorum,

160 dandi sunt isti statui xii uiri euangelici, forte de santi Francisci gremio
reuelandi, qui sunt in frontibus Christi miliciam in Antichristi temporibus
signaturi. Vnde sicut Iacob xii principes habuit in quibus fuit sinagoga fundata
in primo statu, Dan euulso de medio, Manasse dato pro eo, et sicut Christus
alios xii principes habuit in quibus fuit ecclesia fundata in secundo statu, Iuda

165 Scariothis euulso, Mathia dato pro eo, sic et sanctus Franciscus, plagis
passionis Christi ueraciter insignitus, xii principes euangelicos in isto statu
habebit, in quibus illa noua nupta agni temporis sexti, que est electorum
ecclesia, uno euulso de medio et alio dato pro eo, in isto fundabitur statu.[16]
Similitudo autem Manasses et Effraym, uel Mathie et Ioseph, suo tempore

170 reuelabitur, et sicut in principio primi status, feria sexta, de terra uirgine
formatus est homo ad ymaginem et similitudinem Dei, et fuit tota tempestas
illa dyabolica contra eum per inuidiam, et sicut in principio secundi status,
etate sexta, de matre uirgine formatus est alius homo, non solum ad
ymaginem et similitudinem Dei, sed ecciam pura ymago et similitudo Patris,

175 scilicet Iesus Christus Filius Dei, et fuit tota illa tempestas dyabolica sinagoge

---

145 quintum] sextum BTV   146 ideo *om.* TV   uigilarum M   152-153 et
ab ... generacionibus *om.* T *per hom.*   154 sanctus *om.* M[ac]   155 sollempnes personas *tr.* TV   156 sanctum] beatum BTV   162 signandis BTV   166 passionis *om.*
BTV   169 autem *om.* BV   175 Dei] uiui *add.* BTV

---

[14] Lc. 23.29. The statement which follows suggests that, in the tradition of the *Eternal
Evangel*, the third *status* will bring forth a dispensation to supersede that of the primitive
Church and of the Apostles.
[15] Cf. *Lib. Conc.*, fols. 8v, 13r-v.
[16] Cf. *Lib. Conc.*, fol. 44v. The concord between Dan and Judas is explicitly made in
Expos., fol. 121r. See also *Lib. Conc.*, fol. 43r.

carnalium iudeorum contra eum per inuidiam, sic modo assimili in principio
tercii status, tempore sexto, in ualle uirginis formandus erat alius homo, non
solum ad ymaginem et similitudinem Dei, ymo ecciam ad ymaginem et
similitudinem uite et doctrine et passionis Christi, in quo debeat renouari uita
180 Christi quasi obliuioni tradita, passio et crux, contra quam tota illa tempestas
sinagoge carnalium christianorum per inuidiam, ut xi fratres contra Ioseph,
erit fortissima contra eum. Et sicut a Iacob patriarcha exclusiue, completis
xli generacionibus, in xlii^a Christus intrauit, sic a Christo completis xli
generacionibus, in xlii^a hic uir seraficus religionem euangelicam incoauit, et
185 sicut Christus tercia decima die a natiuitate sua regibus orientis apparuit, sic
circa tercii decimi centenarii annorum principium, hic alter angelus ascendens ab ortu solis, habens signum Dei uiui, tanquam seruus Dei seu Christi
miliciam in frontibus signatus, gentibus et regibus multis ipsum deuote
recipientibus, ut alter Lucifer ante solem, preco auentus iudicii magni regis
190 radiosus apparuit, ut ecciam circa finem predicti centenarii a passione Christi
sub primo Herode, seu mistico Antichristo, exaltaretur in cruce et in
subsequenti generacione, sub secundo Herode seu magno Antichristo, passio
Domini celebretur, et die, seu generacione, tercia a primo Herode generalis
resurreccio ad fidem Christi omnium infidelium inchoetur.
195   Mane autem istius tercii status sumet inicium, ut dictum est, in morte
magni Antichristi, quando totus mundus incipiet conuerti ad fidem. Et de isto
tempore Danielis xii° dicitur: *In tempore illo consurget Michael princeps*
magnus qui stat pro filiis populi tui, et ueniet tempus quale non fuit ab eo ex
quo gentes esse ceperunt usque ad tempus illud. Et in tempore illo saluabitur
200 *populus tuus omnis qui inuentus fuerit scriptus in libro uite, et multi de hiis qui*
dormierunt in puluere terre euigilabunt, hii in uitam eternam et hii in suplicium
sempiternum. Qui autem docti fuerint, fulgebunt quasi splendor firmamenti;
tu, autem, Daniel, claude sermones tuos et signa librum usque ad tempus
statutum. Et dixi ego Daniel uiro qui indutus erat lineis, qui stabat super aquas
205 *fluminis: Vsquequo finis horum mirabilium? Et audiui uirum qui, cum*
leuasset dexteram et sinistram suam in celum et iurasset per uiuentem in
eternum, quia in tempus, et tempora, et dimidium temporis; et cum completa
fuerit dispersio manus populi sancti, complebuntur uniuersa hec. Et ego audiui
et non intellexi, et dixi: Domine mi, quid erit post hec? Et ait: Vade, Daniel,

---

176 carnalium] corporalium BTV   179 et² *om.* BTV   187 Christi] Iesu
praem. BTV   191 Antichristo] passio Domini celebretur *add.* BV   193 et] a BTV
194 fidelium M^ac   196 fidem] Christi *add.* BTV   de *om.* M^ac   197 xii°] vii° *codd.*
cum surget B; cum surge V   199 illud] istud BTV   202 fuerunt M   208 uniuersa]
omnia T; *om.* BV   209 dixi] dixit BV   Et ait *om.* T   209-210 Vade ... quia *om.* BTV

210 *quia clausi sunt signatique sermones, usque ad tempus prefenitum. Eligentur,*
et dealbabuntur, et quasi ignis probabuntur multi, et impie agent impii, neque
intelligent omnes impii, porro docti intelligent, et a tempore cum ablatum fuerit
*iuge sacrificium, et posita fuerit abominacio in desolacionem, dies mcclxxxx*ᵃ.
Beatus qui expectat et peruenit usque ad dies mcccxxxv.[17]

215 Hic enim Daniel describit tempora, seu annos, tocius secundi status, ad
uigilia scilicet passionis Christi, in qua ablatum fuit a Deo iuge sacrificium,
cessante figura agni pascalis per institucionem sacramenti eucharistie. Et tunc
uere in crastino sequenti fuit posita abominacio, quando scilicet in templo
Dei et in consilio sacerdotum sedit Cayphas, una cum eis dans sentenciam
220 mortis in Filium Dei; tunc, ut dictum est, abominacio desolacionis et
destrucionis uniuersalis templi filiorum Iuda stetit in loco sancto.

Describit igitur Daniel, ut predictum est, tempora seu annos predicti status
a uigilia prefata usque ad tempus plenitudinis, seu tercii status, sub numero
dierum, seu annorum, mcccxxxv. Illos uero xliiii dies, seu annos, quos Daniel
225 sub silencio tenet, qui sunt infra numerum predictum, scilicet mcclxxxx et
mcccxxxv, totaliter excluduntur per racionem superius iam prefatam, et
ecciam quia principium horum describitur sub furia mistici Antichristi, finis
uero eorumdem sub furia Antichristi magni, propter quod silentur, quia non
est nisi tempus tenebrarum et silencium euangelice ueritatis.

230 De isto ecciam tempore istius tercii status, Sibilla dicit quod, completis
mcccxxxv annis ab occisione agni, tunc erit tempus paschale quale non fuit
ab inicio mundi usque ad tempus illud.[18] Meridies istius status erit quando
totus mundus erit conuersus ad fidem Christi, et tunc diligetur Deus tantum
in terra quod gentes non curabunt de alio, nisi quomodo possint timere et
235 amare Deum et dare illi gloriam et honorem, ita quod quasi uidebitur illa
celestis Ierusalem de celo in terra descendisse. Vesper uero, siue finis, istius
tercii status erit in fine mundi, quando iterum soluendus est Sathanas in
occulto fine, id est in xvᵃ generacione huius status, ut ab aliquibus dicitur, ad
introducendum terciam abominacionem desolacionis in locum sanctum, ut
240 tercia die, seu generacione, ab ipsa sit resurreccio uiuorum et mortuorum;
quid horum erit uel non erit soli Deo relinquendum est. Cum omnes
resurgemus, erit enim tam grandis nox et tam grauis et tam tenebrosa quod

---

210 signati T   214 expectat] spectat T; spectater B   et *om.* B   217 agni] anni
BV   220-221 et destrucionis *om.* BTV   222 Describitur Mᵃᶜ   223 a] ad V
228 sub ... magni] sub signa mistici Antichristi T   228-229 quia ... ueritatis *rep.* T
239 introducendam BT   240 resurreccio *om.* Mᵃᶜ

---

[17] Dan. 12.1-12.
[18] For the *tempus paschale* see: *Lib. Conc.*, fol. 133r.

fere totus mundus efficietur hereticus et in errore positus et fides Christi ad nichilum quasi deueniet, ut Luce xviii° dicitur: *Cum uenerit Filius hominis,*
245 *putas ut inueniat fidem super terram?*[19] quasi dicat quod quando ueniet dies iudicii tota fides erit perdita, et quasi omnes erunt heretici, et ideo per ignem a Deo punientur, et tunc Deus, quasi coactus, ueniet ad iudicium, tercia abominacione desolacionis et destrucionis tocius mundi in loco sancto impleta.

250 Vnde ex predictis patet quod primus status habuit finem in iudicio facto de sinagoga iudeorum, secundus habebit finem in iudicio fiendo de ecclesia carnalium christianorum; tercius habebit finem et terminum in die generalis iudicii, et hoc iudicium erit aliorum magis terribile, eo quod Deus magis ostenderit bonitatem suam in isto statu quam in secundo et primo. Et hec de
255 tercio statu generali sufficiant.

---

244 quasi *om.* T; quasi ad nichilum *tr.* BV   xviii°] xvii° *codd.*   248 et destrucionis *rep.* T   256 statu] et *add.* BV

---

[19] Lc. 18.8.

[EXPLICIT PRIMA DISTINCITO. INCIPIT SECUNDA DISTINCTIO, IN QUA AGITUR DE CONCORDIA NOBILIUM PERSONARUM IN PRINCIPIO CUIUSLIBET STATUS.][1]

Cum enim, ut iam supra dictum est, tres status generales in toto cursu mundi legantur, pro quorum principio in quolibet date sunt persone sollempnes sese per concordiam respondentes, est sciendum quod persone que fuerunt in principio primi status respiciunt per signum, tanquam signancia, personas
5 que fuerunt in principio secundi status, et econuerso tanquam signata signancia intuentur; hec uero que in principio secundi illas que erunt in principio tercii, unde prime sunt signancia, secunde signata et signancia, tercie signata solum. Igitur Zacharias respicit Abraam, tanquam signatus ab eo, et respicit sanctum Benedictum tanquam signum eius; Iohannes Babtista
10 respicit Ysaac, signatus ab eo, et respicit sanctum Bernardum tanquam signum eius; Dominus Iesus Christus respicit Iacob, signatus ab eo, et respicit sanctum Franciscum ut signum eius, non quoad paritatem persone, sed racione concordie; duodecim apostoli duodecim patriarchas respiciunt tamquam signati ab eis, et respiciunt duodecim uiros euangelicos ut signa eorum
15 in tercii generalis status tempore reuelandos.

Concordat igitur Zacharias cum Abraam quia uterque iustus et senex, uterque uxorem sterilem habuit, uterque unicum et unicum filium de sterili procreauit, per angelum iste, per angelum ille; principium ueteris testamenti Abraam, principium noui testamenti Zacharias. Sic Helisabeth cum Sarra,
20 quia utraque ecclesiam significans, sancta mulier et sterilis fuit, utraque uisitata diuinitus concepit et peperit in senectute sua.[2] Abraam autem genuit Ysaac, et Zacharias Iohannem Babtistam. Concordat igitur Iohannes Babtista

Titulum om. M   1 iam ut *tr.* BTV   3 est] et M   4 signancia] intuentur *add.* M^ac
7 tercii *om.* BV   signata] sunt significate BT   signancia[2]] unde prime sunt signantis
add. V   8 signata] significate BTV   10 signatus] signatur V   Bernardum]
Benedictum BM^acV   15 status generalis *tr.* BV   17 et unicum *om.* BV filium] Dei *add.*
BV   22 Zacharias] genuit *add.* BV

[1] The material in this Distinction is derived chiefly from *Lib. Conc.*, fols. 43v-44v, and expanded.
[2] Cf. *Lib. Conc.*, fols. 7v-8r; for Elizabeth and Sara, see *Lib. Conc.*, fol. 13v.

cum Ysaac quia uterque de patre iusto et sene, uterque de matre sterili,
uterque per angelum nunciatus et nominatus. Sic Maria mater Domini cum
25 Rebecca matre Iacob,[3] quia utraque significat ecclesiam, illa actiuam, ista
contemplatiuam; prima Petro commissa est, secunda Iohanni donata est;
prima Petro ante passionem promissa, secunda Iohanni est in passione
commissa, quia Petrum oportebat expirare in crucem, Iohannem autem
manere, dicente Domino: *Sic eum uolo manere donec ueniam.*[4] Ysaac autem
30 genuit Iacob, Iohannes Babtista non genuit carnaliter sed, cum xxx esset
annorum, babtizauit Christum, quia in illo confirmata est generacio carnis ut
esset pater carnalis, in isto generacio spiritus ut esset pater secundum
spiritum.

Concordat Christus Dominus cum Iacob quia uterque subplantator, ille
35 fratris sui Esau, iste dyaboli in temptacione; uterque luctator, ille cum angelo,
iste cum dyabolo in cruce, ille in scala leticie, iste in scala paciencie, porta
celi illa, porta celi ista; uetus testamentum fructificauit in Iacob carnaliter,
nouum in Christo spiritualiter; Iacob pater carnalis xii patriarcharum,
Christus pater spiritualis xii apostolorum; Iacob caput xii tribuum, Christus
40 caput xii ecclesiarum.

Sic Maria mater Iohannis et Iacobi cum Rayele matre Ioseph et Beniamin,
nam utraque spiritualem significat ecclesiam, unde sicut pro Iuda patriarcha
datus est Petrus, ita et pro Ioseph euangelista Iohannes, pro Beniamin autem
Iocobus frater Domini locum tenet. Iacob autem genuit Iudam et fratres eius
45 carnaliter, et Christus genuit Petrum et fratres eius spiritualiter. Concordat
igitur Petrus robustus cum Iuda fortis manu. Nam sicut iura primogeniture
domus Ruben in domum Iudam mutata sunt, sic et ipsa iura primogeniture
de domo Iuda in domum Petri mutata sunt, unde sicut solo Iude et non aliis
de suis fratribus dictum est: *Non auferetur septrum de Iuda et dux de femore*
50 *eius donec ueniat qui mitendus est,*[5] sic Petro et non aliis apostolis dictum est:
Tu es Petrus, et super hanc petram hedificabo ecclesiam meam,[6] et cetera, et

---

23 et] cum T   24 mater] matre M   25 quia *rep.* M^ac   26 donata] est *praem.* M^ac
32 esset] eciam T   in ... pater *om.* BV   35 uterque] hec *add.* T   36 paciencie]
presiencie M   37 illa ... celi *om.* V *per hom.*   39 caput] pater BTV   41 mater]
matre M   43 et *om.* BTV   pro¹] per BTV   euangelista *om.* M^ac; Iohannes
euangelista *tr.* BV   46-47 iura ... Iudam] sicut Iuda promogeniture domus Ruben BV
47 mutata ... iura] domus Ruben mutate sunt; Ruben mutate sunt, sicut eciam ipsa iura T
48 soli BV   50 sic *om.* T

---

[3] Cf. *ibid.,* fol. 44v.
[4] Jn. 21.22.
[5] Gen. 49.10.
[6] Mt. 16.18.

iterum: *Ego autem orabo pro te ut non deficiat fides tua,*[7] et cetera. Vnde sicut
Iudas de numero duodecim patriarcharum principium generacionis Christi
post Iacob secundum carnem et septrum tenuit, sic et Petrus de numero xii
55 apostolorum principium generacionis secundum spiritum post Christum
tenuit, et militantis ecclesie ab eo septrum accepit, et cetera.

Concordat, ut dictum est, Iohannes euangelista, plus ceteris dilectus a
Christo, cum Ioseph, plus ceteris amatus a patre; ille interpretator sopnio-
rum, iste reuelator uisionum; nam uterque uisionibus plenus, ille per somp-
60 nia, iste per reuelaciones, ille futurus dominator fratrum suorum temporaliter,
iste futurus dominator fratrum suorum spiritualiter, et cetera.

Sic Ruben primogenitus cum Andrea, qui primo uenit ad Christum; sic
Dan cum Iuda Scariothis, quia uterque sublatus est de ordine suo: ille de
numero patriarcharum, iste de numero apostolorum. Sic Mathias et Iosep,
65 qui cognominatus est iustus, cum Manesse et Effraym, et sic de ceteris, ut
infra patebit, et cetera.

Quid enim magis simile queri potest quam quod Abraam et Zacharias alter
et alter senex de sterili et de sterili unicum et unicum procreauit, nec enim
de simile extimatur quod Ysaac patriarcha genuit Iacob, Iohannes autem non
70 genuit sed baptizauit Christum, quia in Iacob confirmata est generacio carnis
ut esset pater carnalis populi, qui ex patris cognomine uocatus est Ysrael; in
isto generacio spiritus ut esset pater secundum spiritum, populi scilicet qui
dicitur christianus; ut enim populus ille per xii patriarchas, ita et iste per xii
apostolos procreatus est, excepto quod ibi, *quod natum ex carne, caro est,*[8]
75 et hic, *quod natum est ex spiritu, spiritus est.*[9] Sicut enim post xii patriarchas,
Moyses et Aaron uiri nominati eduxerunt populum Israel de Egypto ita, post
xii apostolos, electi sunt a Domino Paulus et Barnabas, qui prepararent uiam
populo fideli egresso de sinagoga iudeorum ut, transeuntes per deserta
gentilium, introirent in terram fluentem lac et mel. Sicut ecciam abeunte
80 Moyse successit Iosue qui diuisit vii[em] tribubus hereditatem, sic recedente

---

52 orabo] rogaui BTV   te] Petre *add.* BTV   53 Iudas] fuit *add.* BTV   principium]
sit *add.* BV   generacionis Christi *om.* T   Christi *om.* BV   55 principium] et *add.*
BV   generacionis] Christi *add.* BTV   57 Iohannis M   58 amatus] sit *add.* BTV
ille *om.* BV   58-59 interpretator ... plenus *rep.* B   63 est *om.* BV   65 cognominatus]
iustus *add.* BV   69 de *om.* V   dissimile BT   extimator M; stimatur BV   71 ex]
est BV   72 generacio] genero BV   scilicet *post* dicitur *tr.* T   73 et] ut BV
74 excepto ... ibi] ex quod ibi quo ibi T   natum] est *add.* BV   75 hic *om.* V   ex
om. T   post] per V

---

[7] Lc. 22.32.
[8] Jn. 3.6.
[9] Jn. 3.6.

Paulo a regione Asye successit Iohannes qui scripsit librum Apocalipsis vii^{em} ecclesiis que fuerunt in ea. Sicut uiuente adhuc Iosue possiderunt filii Israel terram promissionis, siue chananeorum, sic uiuente adhuc sancto Iohanne, obtinuerunt ex magna parte fideles largas possessiones gentilium. Sicut
85 obeunte Iosue confluxerunt gentes ille contra filios Israel usque ad tempora Dauid regis, sic obeunte Iohanne pugnauerunt pagani contra christianos usque ad tempora sancti Siluestri pape. Sicut in tempore illo non erat rex unctus in Israel usque ad tempus Saul et Dauid, sic in tempore isto quod decursum est a Christo usque ad sanctum Siluestrum et Constantinum
90 Augustum non fuit rex sollempniter unctus crismate in populo christiano, sed unusquisque uiuebat in arbitrio suo, et sicut fuit longa concertacio inter domum Saul in tribu Beniamin et domum Dauid in tribu Iuda, sic inter grecorum ecclesiam et romanam; obtinuit autem domus Iuda, obtinuit et romana ecclesia.[10] Hec igitur misteria in xii generacionum spacio consumata
95 sunt.

Concordat igitur beatus Benedictus cum Abraam quia sicut Abraam, iussu Dei egressus est de terra sua et de cognacione sua, et de domo patris sui, et uenit in terram quam sibi monstrauit Deus, ibique benediccione accepta creuit in gentem magnam,[11] sic beatus Benedictus inspiracione diuina egres-
100 sus est de terra sua, et de cognacione sua, et de domo patris sui, renuncians scilicet omnibus que habebat, et uenit in terram heremi quam Deus inspirauit sibi, ibique benediccione accepta, uere et nomine Benedictus, creuit in gentem magnam monachorum nigrorum. Sic concordat cum Zacharia quia, sicut Zacharias fuit primus pater et primus patriarcha tocius secundi status
105 et Abraam primi, sic beatus Benedictus fuit primus pater et primus patriarcha tocius tercii status, tenendo uiam secundi modi concordie tercii status. Zacharias principium ecclesie actiue, sanctus Benedictus ecclesie contemplatiue, et cetera.

Concordat sanctus Bernardus cum Ysaac quia, sicut Ysaac fuit filius
110 carnalis primi patris et primi patriarche primi status, sic beatus Bernardus primi patris et primi patriarche secundi status spiritualis, et racione eiusdem ordinis seu eiusdem regule obseruacionis, et racione capitalis imitacionis,

---

82 ea] Asya T   84 possessionis M^{ac} 87 erat *om.* M^{ac} 97 est *om.* T
103 magnam] scilicet *add.* BTV   quia] qui T   104 status] seculi *add.* BTV   105 primi] primus BTV   107 sanctus] secundus M   109 Bernardus] Benedictus
V   110-111 primi^3 ... patriarche *om.* V   111-114 racione ... obediencie] racionem capitalis imitacionis quia caput monachorum alborum sanctus Bernardus extitit filius obediencie V

---

[10] *Lib. Conc.*, fol. 44r-v.
[11] Cf. Gen. 12.1-3; see also: *Vita S. Benedicti*, p. 55; *Lib. Conc.*, fol. 57v.

quia caput monachorum nigrorum sanctus Benedictus fuit, et caput monachorum alborum sanctus Bernardus; extitit filius obediencie Ysaac, filius
115 obediencie sanctus Bernardus. Et quia passio Christi precedit resurreccionem, beatus Benedictus sumpsit habitum nigrum in signum lamenti dominice
passionis, et sanctus Bernardus album in signum gaudii dominice resurreccionis. Sic et cum Iohanne Babtista sanctus Bernardus concordat, nam
utriusque pater patriarcha, ille secundi status, iste tercii status; pater spiri-
120 tualis Iohannes, pater spiritualis sanctus Bernardus; uirgo ille, uirgo iste; ille
in deserto, iste in deserto; sanctus ille, sanctus iste, et cetera huiusmodi.

Concordat sanctus Franciscus cum Iacob patriarcha et Domino Iesu
Christo, non quoad paritatem persone, ut dixi, sed racione concordie quia,
sicut Iacob subplantauit fratrem suum Esau et luctatus est cum angelo, et sicut
125 Christus Sathanam in temptacione et luctatus est cum eo in cruce, ita et
sanctus Franciscus fuit subplantator fratris, seu corporis sui, crucifigendo
ipsum, cum uiciis et concupiscenciis diuersis asperitatibus affligendo, ecciam
cum mundo et dyabolo, utriusque deuictis in cruce humilitatis et passiencie
luctator effectus est, uel forte cum angelo abissi, in pede scale paupertatis
130 euangelice, luctator efficiendus est, ipsum angelum subplantando sua religione in tres partes diuisa, dicens: *Si percusserit Esau,* seu angelus prefatus,
unam turmam, saluabitur altera,[12] et cetera. Et sicut Iacob ordinauit tres
acies, seu tres turmas, roboratas uirtute humilitatis et paciencie contra fratrem
suum, ut sic uinceret eum, dicens: *Si percusserit Esau unam turmam,*
135 *saluabitur altera* et sicut Christus ordinauit tres acies responcionum de sacra
scriptura sumptas, roboratas uirtute humilitatis et paciencie, ut sic suum
temptator uinceret, sic beatus Franciscus tres acies religionum roboratas
uirtute humilitatis et paciencie, contra hostem suum drachonem anticum, qui
tres cateruas demonum contra humanum genus semper roborat, ordinauit. Et
140 sicut Iacob fuit genitus ab Ysaac carnaliter in primo statu, et Christus Iesus
a Iohanne Baptista sacramentaliter in secundo statu, ita et in tercio statu
sanctus Franciscus fuit genitus a beato Bernardo similitudinaliter quoad
forme habitus in modum crucis assumpcionem. Et sicut Abraam tenuit tipum

---

113 quia ... et *om.* B   115 Bernardus] Benedictus M^ac   116 Benedictus] Bernardus BM^acV   119-120 pater ... Iohannes *om.* BV   120 Iohannes *rep.* T   121 huiusmodi *om.* BTV   123 parilitatem M^ac   quia] qui BV   124 Esau *om.* BTV   125 in^1
om. T   et ita *tr.* T   127 ipsum] eum V   128 utrique M^ac   132 et cetera] eius T
133 seu] artes seu *add.* B   136 sumptas] et *add.* BTV   137 roboratas] ordinauit
add. BTV   139 tres] acies seu *add.* BTV   ordinauit *om.* BV   140 sicut] sic V
Iesus Christus *tr.* BV   141 et *om.* M^ac

---

[12] Gen. 32.8.

Patris, et Ysaac typum Filii, et Iacob tipum Spiritus sancti, sic sanctus
145 Benedictus tenuit tipum Patris, sanctus Bernardus tipum Filii, et sanctus
Franciscus tipum Spiritus sancti. Et quia Spiritus sanctus procedit a Patre et
Filio, sic sanctus Franciscus, mixtis coloribus ex habitus colore utriusque
patris in signum lamenti dominice passionis et in signum gaudii dominice
resurreccionis, abiectis egypciis, nudis pedibus, fune cinctus, nudus post
150 nudum in cruce pendentem, habitum sinericum in furma crucis assumpsit. Et
sicut Iacob in numero xii patriarcharum, Dan euulso de medio, et Christus
in numero xii apostolorum, Iuda Scariothis euulso de medio, sic et sanctus
Franciscus fructificauit in numero xii apostolicorum sociorum, uno deuulso
de medio, ut in uita eius legitur.[13]
155   Sic enim, ut iam supra tactum est, xii patriarche sub uno capite Iacob cum
xii apostolis sub uno capite Christo concordant; sic xii tribus Israel cum xii
religionibus ecclesie conformant, et sicut ante exterminium ueteris Babilonis
x predictarum tribuum per regem assiriorum depopulate sunt, sic ante
exterminium noue Babilonis x predictarum religionum per illum regem
160 undecimum exterminande sunt. Hoc autem exterminium tripliciue seu triplici
casu est subtiliter intuendum. Ordo autem sequitur:[14]

	Iuda	Petrus
	Ruben	Andreas
	Gath	Thomas
165	Aser	Symon
	Neptalim	Iudas
	Dan	Iudas Scariothis
	Manasses	Mathias
	Symeon	Iacobus frater Domini
170	Leui	Matheus
	Zabulon	Philippus
	Isachar	Bartholomeus
	Ioseph	Iohannes

---

144 et *om.* BTV   sanctus] beatus BTV   146 Spiritus[2] *post* sanctus *rep.* M
149 resurrecionis] raconis M[ac]   egypciis] uniuersis *add.* BTV   152 et *om.* BTV
153 numero] medio T   apostolicorum *om.* BTV   euulso BTV   155 supra iam *tr.* BTV
156 Christo *om.* T   sic] sicut V   157 exterminum M   158 sunt *om.* BTV
159 exterminum M   160 sunt *om.* BTV   tripliciue] triplici T   161 Ordo ... sequitur
om. V; sequitur *om.* M   167 Scariothis *om.* MT   169 Dei MT   173 Ioseph *om.* BTV

---

[13] See: Paul Sabatier, ed., *Actus Beati Francisci*, p. 2. For the concord of Dan with Judas, see *Expos.*, fol. 121r, *Lib. Conc.*, fol. 43v. For the twelve Patriarchs and the Apostles, see *Lib. Conc.*, fols. 22v-23r, 43v.

[14] Cf. *Expos.*, fol. 19r-v.

	Beniamin	Iacobus
175	Tribus Iuda	Ordo monachorum nigrorum
	Tribus Ruben	Ordo hospitalis
	Tribus Gath	Ordo templi
	Tribus Aser	Ordo clericorum
	Tribus Neptalim	Ordo predicatorum
180	Tribus Manasses	Ordo cartusiensium
	Tribus Symeon	Ordo heremitarum
	Tribus Leui	Ordo canonicorum regularium
	Tribus Ysachar	Ordo monachorum alborum
	Tribus Zabulon	Ordo carmelitarum
185	Tribus Ioseph	Ordo fratrum minorum
	Tribus Beniamin	Ordo continencium.

Primus igitur casus exterminacionis earum est quia extra terminos ueritatis euangelice sunt ponende, quod sub casu stelle clauem putei abissi habentis in Apocalipsi describitur, et in putei apercione, et cum fumi fornacis de
190 predicto puteo ascencione, et solis et aeris ex predicto fumo obscuracione, et locustarum ex prefato puteo egressione habencium super se regem angelum abissi, cui nomen exterminans, et cetera.[15]

Secundus casus exterminacionis predictarum est eo quod extra terminos possecionum rerum temporalium sunt ponende, seu uelint seu nolint sunt
195 expoliande et sicut cursores leues fiende, de quo in Ysaya dicitur: *Decaluabit Dominus uerticem filiarum Syon et crinem earum nudabit. In die illa auferet Dominus omne ornamentum,* scilicet ecclesiasticum, quod uere de seculi uanitate processit, *et lunulas, et torques, et monilia, et armillas, et olfatoria, et inaures, et anulos, et gemmas, et mutatoria, et pallia, et linteamina, et acus,*
200 *et specula, et sindones, et mitras, et theristra, et erit pro suaui odore fetor, et pro zona funiculus, et pro crispanti crine caluicium, et pro fascia pectorali cilicium. Pulcherrimi uiri tui gladio cadent, et fortes tui in prelio, et merebunt atque lugebunt porte eius, et desolata in terra manebit,*[16] unde in tempore illo,

---

174 Iacobus *om.* BTV   176 hospitalis] a. s. M   177 templi] c. n. M 178 clericorum] c. t. M   179 predicatorum] p. d. M   180 cartusiensium] h. p. M 181 heremitarum] t. p. M   182 canonicorum regularium] m. a. M   183 monachorum alborum] c. m. M   184 carmelitarum] m. n. M   185 fratrum minorum] m. n. M 186 continencium] c.° T. M   187 Primus] Primus casus *Rubrica praem.* BV   quia] quod BTV   188 quod] quos T   habentis abissi *tr.* BTV   193 eo *om.* BV 196 crimen M; ex crimine T   198 et⁵ *om.* T   201 fascia] facie *codd.*   202 pulcherrimi] et *praem.* T   mereabunt *codd.*

---

[15] Cf. Apoc. 9.1-3, 11.
[16] Is. 3.17-26.

aperiet Dominus ora mutorum contra illam, et linguas infancium contra illam
205 *faciet disertas,*[17] et cetera. De quo exterminio in psalmo dicitur: *Exterminauit*
eam aper de silua et singularis ferus depastus est eam.[18] Hec enim silua
Yspania est, ut dicit Ioachim.

Tercius casus exterminacionis predictarum religionum est quia extra
terminos uniuersalis Ierusalem sunt dispergende, partim et interficiende et
210 partim in captiuitatem ducende, ut inpleant uisionem, unde Apocalipsis xvi°
dicitur quod in effusione septime fiale ire Dei in aere, seu ecclesiam, *factus*
est terre, seu terrenorum, *motus,* in uniuerso scilicet romano imperio, *qualis*
non fuit ex quo homines esse ceperunt talis terre, seu terrenorum, *motus, et*
ciuitas magna, que est ecclesia, *facta est in tres partes,* quarum due dispergen-
215 tur, seu in captiuitatem ducentur, tercia uero igni orrende tribulacionis
tradetur, *et ciuitates gencium,* scilicet paganorum, *in terre,* seu terrenorum,
motu aduentus illorum x regum cum bestia, *ceciderunt,* quoniam *ipsa Babilon*
magna uenit in memoriam ante Deum dare et calicem ire indignacionis sue.
Tunc enim *omnes insule,* seu abbacie in medio maris romani imperii
220 site, *fugerunt, et montes,* seu regna ecclesiastica, *non sunt inuenti,* nam
tunc uniuersus status ecclesiasticus per totum orbem est funditus subuerten-
dus, et cetera.[19] Vnde sicut xii patriarche ecciam designant omnes patres xii
tribuum quorum ipsi fuerunt primi usque ad finem primi status, et sicut xii
principes qui ceciderunt in deserto cum hiis qui egressi fuerant de Egypto
225 designant xii apostolos cum successoribus eorum, quorum manet temptacio
et ruina corporum usque ad finem secundi status, sic et xii principes qui
ingressi sunt terram promissionis patres tercii status designant, quorum primi
erunt xii, qui omnes uisuri sunt illam pacem quam promisit Deus diligentibus
se.[20]
230 Hoc autem sacramentum tercii status, ut traditur in Concordia Ioachim,
perfectius et clarius reuelabitur circa tempus in quo conculcabunt gentes
ciuitatem sanctam, ut pretactum est, mensibus xlii^bus, regnante illo rege xi° qui
scriptus est in Daniele propheta, qui *et super quam credi potest, uniuersa*

---

204 aperuit T   205 desertas M^ac   exterminio] contra illam *add.* M^ac   206 silua²]
et singularis *add.* M^ac   207 est Yspania *tr.* BTV   208 quia] quare T   209-210 et²
... ducende *om.* V   210 in ... ducende *om.* B   captiuitate T   212-213 in uniuerso ...
motus *om.* V *per hom.*   215 tribulacionis] tribula *praem.* V   216 ciuitas T   219 imperii romani *tr.* BTV   220 cite M   223 quorum] quando T   224 qui¹ *om.* M^ac
233 qui] cui BV

---

[17] Sap. 10.21.
[18] Ps. 79.14; this text is quoted in *Super Esaiam*, fol. 5v, and applied to Spain, fol. 36r.
[19] Cf. Apoc. 16.17-21; *Expos.*, fol. 193r.
[20] Cf. Is. 64.4; 1 Cor. 2.9.

uastabit.[21] Vnde in predicta Concordia dicitur quod in anno illo quo uenturi
235 sunt, sicut tenet ecclesia, Enoch et Elyas, eligendi sunt xii uiri similes
patriarcharum et apostolorum ad predicandum iudeis, et erunt preclarissima
monasteria similia xii tribuum et xii ecclesiarum, quamuis pro eo quibus
quinque tribus acceperunt hereditatem, et quinque principales ecclesie
pertinentes ad Petrum precesserint illas vii^em quas hedificauit Iohannes, et
240 cetera.[22]

Consumabitur, ut creditur, similitudo Zacharie, Iohannis Babtiste et
hominis Christi Iesu, in quorum manifestacione erit quoque, ut credimus,
manifesta similitudo xii apostolorum, maxime Iohannis Euangeliste, et vii^em
ecclesiarum que fuerunt in Asia, siue vii^em tribuum que postreme acceperunt
245 hereditatem. Predicabitur tunc euangelium regni in uniuersum orbem et
perueniet spiritualis intellectus usque ad iudeos, et confringet quasi quidam
tronitus duriciam cordis eorum, ut compleatur illud quod scriptum est in
Malachia propheta: *Ecce, ego mictam uobis Heliam prophetam antequam
ueniat dies Dei magnus et orribilis, et conuertat corda patrum ad filios et corda*
250 *filiorum ad patres eorum, ne forte ueniam et percuciam terram anathemate,*[23]
et cetera.[24]

Sicut ecciam post xii patriarchas Moyses et Aaron, uiri nominatissimi,
eduxerunt populum Israel de Egypto per desertum in terram fluentem lac et
mel, et sicut post xii apostolos electi sunt a Domino Paulus et Barnabas, qui
255 prepararent uiam populo fideli egresso de sinagoga iudeorum, ut transeuntes
per deserta gentilium introyrent in terram fluentem lac et mel,[25] sic et post
xii uiros euangelicos supradictos eligendi sunt a Deo duo uiri nominatissimi
et sancti ad educendum siue preparandum uiam populo electorum egressuro
de sinagoga carnalium christianorum, ut transeuntes per deserta gentilium
260 introeant in terram fluentem lac et mel, et cetera.

---

237 quibus *om.* M^pc   238 acceperit BV   et] pro eo *add.* T   239 processerunt V   239-240 et cetera *om.* BV   242 Iesu Christi *tr.* BTV   243 xii *om.*
BTV   247 durissima BV   249 et²] ut BTV   252 Sicut] Sic T   255 preperarent M
255-256 transeuntes *post* gentilium *tr.* BTV   256 introyrent *rep.* B

---

[21] *Lib. Conc.*, fols. 21r-23r, 55r, 58r-v; Dan. 8.24.
[22] *Lib. Conc.*, fol. 22r.
[23] Mal. 4.5-6.
[24] *Lib. Conc.*, fol. 60r.
[25] *Lib. Conc.*, fol. 44r; cf. Ex. 3.8; Act. 13.

[EXPLICIT SECUNDA DISTINCTIO. INCIPIT TERCIA DISTINCTIO, DE CONCORDIA CRUDELIUM PERSONARUM IN FINE CUIUSLIBET GENERALIS STATUS.]

Cum quilibet generalis status, ut pretactum est, sit sicut unus dies habens suum mane et suum uesper, et pro mane, seu pro principio, date sint persone sollempnes in fide et ueritate et bonitate et cordis simplicitate fundate, sic pro uespere, seu pro fine, dande sunt, licet secundum mundum, notabiles persone
5 sine fide et ueritate et bonitate, et cordis dupplicitate seu dolositate fundate, quod apostolus iii° ad Thimotheum describens, ait: *In nouissimis diebus instabunt tempora periculosa et erunt homines seipsos amantes, cupidi, elati, superbi, blasphemi, parentibus non obedientes, ingrati, scelesti, sine affeccione,* scilicet uere amicicie, *sine pace, criminatores, incontinentes, inmites,*
10 *sine benignitate, proditores, proterui, tumidi, ceci, uoluptatum amatores magis quam Dei, habentes speciem pietatis,* scilicet diuini cultus et zeli animarum et religionis, *uirtutem autem eius abnegantes.*[1]

Vnde sicut primus status pro mane seu pro principio habuit iii sollempnes personas, scilicet Abraam, Ysaac, et Iacob, et xii patriarchas et duos nepotes
15 patriarcharum, scilicet Manassem et Effraym, in fide et ueritate et bonitate, et cordis simplicitate fundatas, sic prefatus status pro uespere seu pro fine habuit tres pessimas et maliciosas personas, quamuis secundum mundum notabiles, supradictis oppositas et contrarias, sine fide et ueritate et bonitate, in tenebris errorum et in uerbo mendacii, et in operum falsitate seu calliditate,
20 corde dupplici et doloso, cum suis secuacibus pari modo fundatas, quarum prima fuit dracho, seu Pilatus, caput et domesticus in regno Iudee; secunda fuit bestia, seu Herodes paganicus a predicto regno alienus, qui illis diebus erat Ierusalem; tercia fuit pseudo propheta, caput pseudo prophetarum,

---

Titulum om. M   generalis] generacionis T   2 pro¹] per V   3 in] et T
fundate *om.* BTV   sic] et BTV   5 cordis] pro uespere persone *praem.* BTV
6 secunda ad Timotheum tercio BV   8 scelerosi BTV   11 speciem] spiritum BTV
12 eius *om.* BV   13 pro² *om.* BTV   15 et³] in BV   18 bonitate] et cordis
simplicitate *add.* BTV   20 fundata T   22 paganus BTV   qui] quod BT

---

[1] 2 Tim. 3.1-5.

scilicet Cayphas pontifex anni illius, hoc est symoniacus. Hii tres uno ore et
25 concordi consilio condempnauerunt Christum et doctrinam eius, nuncii uero
ad hoc concurrentes tanquam rane inflate per superbiam et fetide per
luxuriam, garrientes contra Christum et doctrinam eius. Primi fuerunt milites
a bestia, seu ab Herode, missi, de quibus in euangelio Iohannis dicitur: *Et
milites quidem hec fecerunt.*² Secundi fuerunt doctores, siue legis periti, qui
30 scirent tortuose allegare scripturas, et isti fuerunt missi a pseudo propheta,
seu Caypha, unde dixerunt: *Nos legem habemus, et secundum legem debet
mori, quia filium Dei se fecit.*³ Inter hos enim fuerunt quidam pseudo religiosi,
drachonis fallacia et ypocresis fraudulencia pleni, et missi sunt hii per
quandam anthonomasiam a drachone, hoc est a Pilato, unde postquam
35 Pilatus dixit Christo: *Michi non loqueris? Nescis quia potestatem habeo
crucifigere te, et potestatem habeo dimittere te?*⁴ et postquam populus a
summis pontificibus et a senioribus seductus, clamauit ad Pilatum: *Tolle,
tolle, crucifige eum,*⁵ et facto responso a Pilato, scilicet: *Accipite eum uos et
crucifigite,*⁶ pharisei, scilicet qui Christi mortem tractauerant, dolo et fallacia
40 pleni, responderunt dicentes: *Nobis non licet interficere quemquam.*⁷ Oppositi
uero, seu contrarii xii patriarcharum, fuerunt omnes prelati sinagoge, et
omnes magistratus et doctores, seu legis periti, et seniores populi. Oppositi
uero, seu contrarii, duorum nepotum patriarcharum fuerunt due religiones
sinagoge, scilicet phariseorum et seduceorum. Hii omnes supradicti unanimi-
45 ter condempnauerunt uitam et doctrinam Christi, et tradiderunt eum morti,
et excommunicauerunt omnes confitentes et credentes in eum, ita ut extra
sinagogam fierent. Hec est abominacio prima.

Sicut ecciam secundus status pro mane, seu pro principio, habuit tres
personas sollempnes, scilicet Zachariam, Iohannem Babtistam et Dominum
50 Iesum Christum, et xii apostolos, et pro duobus patriarcharum nepotibus
Mathiam et Ioseph, qui cognominatur iustus, in fide et ueritate et bonitate
et cordis simplicitate fundatas, sic prefatus status pro uespere, seu pro fine,

---

29 Secundi *om.* V   30 sciuerunt BTV   33 fallaciam M   34 a² *om.* BTV
35 Non scis T   36 crucifigere ... et¹ *om.* BT   et¹ ... te *om.* V   37 a *om.* BTV
37-38 Tolle ... eum¹ *om.* T   39 scilicet *om.* BV   mortem Christi *tr.* BTV   tractabant
BTV   46 exconunicauerunt M   48 ecciam] enim BV   50 patriarcharum *om.* V
51 iustus *rep.* T   bonitate et ueritate *tr.* BV

---

² Jn. 19.24.
³ Jn. 19.7; cf. *Super Hier.*, fols. 23r-v, 43r-44r; *Expos.*, fol. 164r.
⁴ Jn. 19.10.
⁵ Jn. 19.15.
⁶ Jn. 19.6.
⁷ Jn. 18.31.

habebit tres pessimas et maliciosas personas, quamuis secundum mundum
notabiles, supradictis oppositas et contrarias. Prima erit dracho, seu impe-
55 rator, in romano imperio caput et domesticus; secunda erit bestia, seu rex
paganicus, caput bestialium nacionum, alienus ab inperio, qui illis diebus erit
Ierusalem magna, qui legit intelligat; tercia erit pseudo propheta, caput
pseudo prophetarum, pontifex anni, seu temporis, illius, uere pseudo et
symoniacus. Hii tres, uno ore et concordi consilio, condempnabunt uitam et
60 doctrinam Christi et ecclesiam eius. Vnde Iohannes super Apocalipsis xvi°,
hanc materiam tangens, textum premitens, dicit: *Vidi de ore drachonis, et de
ore bestie, et de ore pseudo prophete exire tres spiritus inmundos in modum
ranarum. Hii sunt tres spiritus demoniorum missi ad reges terre ad congregandum eos in prelium ad diem magnum ire Dei omnipotentis, in locum qui
65 dicitur Hermagedon,*[8] et cetera. Per hos tres spiritus designantur tam subies-
tiones astute et subtiles et quasi spirituales, quas demones, per se et per ora
hominum malignorum, suggerentes sunt et inducentes, quam quosdam
homines astutos et dolosos, Antichristi nuncios et ambaxiatores et quasi
correptarios, ad congregandum omnes homines mundi et reges ut ueniant in
70 prelium contra Babilonem, seu ecclesiam carnalium christianorum. Dicuntur
autem tres a trino ore exire tum in misterium trinitatis pessime, sancte
trinitati personarum Dei et uirtutum eius opposite, tum quia a duplici gente,
seu a duobus capitibus eius, in quibus dracho seu dyabolus erit principalis et
primus motor, mitentur scilicet a rege gentis paganice uel sarracenice milites
75 seu militares, a pseudo propheta mitentur falsi magistri seu doctores. Inter
hos autem erunt quidam pseudo religiosi, drachonis fallacia et ypocrisis
fraudulencia magna pleni, et hii per quandam anthonomasiam mittentur a
drachone uel, secundum Ioachim,[9] dracho stat hic pro Antichristo, in quo
dracho quasi unus cum eo adorabitur et per quem principalius et familiarius
80 loquetur et operabitur; dicit ecciam, *inmundos in modum ranarum,* ut
monstret uilitatem et feditatem et susurractoriam garriditatem ipsorum
spirituum seu nunciorum et suarum suggestionum; per hoc autem quod dicit,
quod *sunt spiritus demoniorum facientes signa,*[10] ostendit quod demones

---

56 panicus M^ac   59 tres *om.* T   60 eius ecclesiam *tr.* BTV   61 materiam hanc
tr. BV   meteriam M   63 sunt *om.* T   65 et cetera *om.* BV   tam] tres MSS
65-66 subiecciones BV; suggestiones T   astute] statue BV   67 sunt *om.* M   68 et^1
om. BTV   et^2 *om.* BTV   et^3 *om.* BTV   70 Dicunt T   72 et *om.* M^ac
76 ypocrisi *codd.*   80 ecciam] enim BV   81 uilitatem] utilitatem T   82 nunciorum]
iniciorum B

---

[8] Cf. Apoc. 16.13-16; *Postilla,* fol. 101r-v.
[9] Cf. *Postilla,* fol. 101r.
[10] Apoc. 16.14.

erunt sic familiares illis nunciis per quos facient signa, seu illi per ipsos
85 demones, quod quasi sensibiliter poterit scribi ipsis spiritibus demonum.
Cum autem dicit eos ire *ad congregandum,* seu congregandos, *reges,* uidetur
quod antequam congregarent eos non essent illi reges omnino subiecti
Antichristo, nisi forte uadant ad reges ad hoc, ut libencius et animosius ad
ad bellum conueniant et concurrant. Putatur autem quod respectu diuerso-
90 rum temporum utrumque sit uerum, unde et quidam putant quod tam
Antichristus institutus quam proprius et magnus erit pseudo papa, caput
pseudo prophetarum, et quod per eius et suorum pseudo prophetarum
consilia et cohoperaciones acquiretur imperium illi regi per quem statuetur
in suo falso papatu. Sed ille rex qui statuet magnum faciet ipsum ultra hoc
95 adorari ut deum. Nec ecciam ex hoc quod dicit, *in locum qui uocatur*
Hermagedon hebraice. Quidam hanc diccionem habent ab "a", alii ab "h"
cum "e" uocali; utraque autem diccio inuenitur in interpretacionibus, prima
sub littera "a", ubi dicitur quod Armagedon interpretatur mons furius uel
globosus; secunda uero sub lictera "h", ubi dicitur quod Hermagedon
100 interpretatur consurgens temptacio; utrumque autem nomen et utriusque
interpretacio congruit huic loco, nam Antichristus et sui reges et eorum
exercitus erunt sicut mons per temporalem potenciam et superbiam et furium,
per rapacem fraudulenciam, et globosus per uersuciam; ecclesia autem contra
quam et super quam congregabuntur erit tunc mons furium et globosus;
105 utrobique ecciam erit consurgens temptacio. Oppositi seu contrarii xii
apostolorum erunt pro maiori parte omnes prelati predicte ecclesie et omnes
magistratus et doctores seu legis periti et seniores populi. Oppositi seu
contrarii Mathie et Ioseph erunt feces duarum religionum ecclesie predicte
que tunc tempore preualebunt, necnon et aliorum religionum eisdem coher-
110 rencium. Hec est abominacio secunda; hec de secundo statu.

Sicut ecciam tercius status pro mane, seu pro principio, habuit tres
sollempnes personas, scilicet sanctum Benedictum, sanctum Bernardum et
sanctum Franciscum, et in breui habiturus est xii principes seu uiros euangelicos, et pro duobus patriarcharum nepotibus, seu duobus Christi discipulis
115 Mathia et Ioseph, duas sollempnes personas qui suo tempore elucessent in
fide et ueritate et bonitate et cordis simplicitate fundatas, sic prefatus status

---

84 famuliares M   85 quod *om.* T   sencibiliter M   87 essent] erint T
omnino reges *tr.* BTV   88 ad²] et BV   91 papa] ac *add.* T   91-92 caput
pseudo prophetarum *om.* BV   97 diccio ... in] dicem BTV   in *om.* Mᵃᶜ   98 furius
uel *om.* Mᵃᶜ   99 uero] furium uel *add.* Mᵃᶜ   101 huic] habuit M   104 et super quam
om. T *per hom.*   108 feces] fratres T   109 preualebunt] scilicet minorum et predicatorum *add.* Mᵃᶜ   et *om.* BTV   religiosorum BTV   110 hec²] et hec dicta sunt
BTV   111 Sicut] *Rubrica* Tercius status *praem.* BV   113 sanctum] beatum BTV

pro uespere, seu pro fine, habebit tres pessimas et maliciosas personas, quamuis secundum mundum notabiles, supradictis oppositas et contrarias: prima erit dracho, secunda erit bestia, tercia pseudo propheta, caput pseudo
120 prophetarum, ex qua causa concordie seu more prophetico sequitur quod Christi ouile, si unum est ouile et pastor, in tres partes scindetur, quarum prima, que erit spiritualis electorum ecclesia, a duobus sequentibus persequuta, sequestrabitur ab aliis non corpore, sed mente, cuius caput erit uerus papa. Secunda erit secta patterinorum, siue hereticorum tunc insurgencium,
125 tanquam paganica, cuius caput erit bestia cum bestiali caterua suorum nobilium. Tercia uero, in duas partes diuisa, duobus capitibus preualebit: in prima, caput temporalis regiminis erit dracho, seu imperator illius temporis, qui in eisdem hereses incidet cum gente sua seductus; in secunda, caput ecclesiastici regiminis erit pseudo papa, seu pseudo propheta, caput pseudo
130 prophetarum, a quibus, propter nimiam habundanciam rerum temporalium, hic error libertatis spiritus cum multis aliis huic contiguis trahet originem, et quia iste status Spiritui sancto atribuitur, ideo ista blasphemia ipsum tanget. Tantus enim erit in isto tempore inordinate libidinis in toto mundo excessus quod non fuit ab inicio tantus, nec ecciam in Pentapoli est inuentus. Dignum
135 idcirco erit ut, quia contra spiritum ignis caritatis qui in principio istius status regnaturus est, spiritus ignis orrende libidinis in fine huius insurgendus est, igne finaliter ulcionis extremi iudicii extingatur ac ecciam deleatur.

Misterium autem nunciorum, seu excitatorum predictorum errorum, et xii oppositorum, seu contrariorum predictorum sanctorum xii uirorum euangeli-
140 corum, et aliorum duorum predictorum xii sequencium, tempora Gog nouissimi reuelabunt. Hec est abominacio tercia, qua impleta Deus quasi coactus ueniet ad iudicium et destruet totum mundum per ignem. Hec de tercio statu.

---

117 uesper M   habet V   121 si unum om. B   si ... ouile om. V   cindetur M
122 que om. BTV   ecclesia] etiam BV   125 cum bestiali] erit bestialis BTV
126 nobilium V   127 temporalis] temporale BT   129 caput] regiminis erit add. T
130 a om. BT   132 atribuitur Spiritui sancto tr. BTV   136 surgendus BTV   138 et om. T   141 quasi om. BTV   142 Hec] et add. BTV   143 statu] dictum est add. BTV

[EXPLICIT DISTINCTIO III^a. INCIPIT IIII^a, IN QUA AGITUR DE VII. ETATIBUS MUNDI ET DE MIRABILI PUNICIONE FACTA A DEO IN FINE CUIUSLIBET ETATIS.]

Circa quartam distincionem est notandum quod totus decursus huius mundi in vii partes distingitur, que etates communiter ab omnibus dicuntur, quas diuersimodo diuersi distingunt. Quidam enim dicunt septimam esse a Christo usque in finem mundi, et ordinant eas sic: primam, scilicet ab Adam usque
5 ad Noe, secundam a Noe usque ad Abraam, terciam ab Abraam usque ad Moysen, quartam a Moyse usque ad Dauid, quintam a Dauid usque ad transmigracionem Babilonis, sextam a transmigracione Babilonis usque ad Christum, septimam uero a Christo usque in finem mundi. Alii dicunt terciam ab Abraam usque ad Dauid, et sextam a Christo usque ad mortem
10 Antichristi, et ordinant eas sic: primam ab Adam usque ad Noe, secundam a Noe usque ad Abraam, terciam ab Abraam usque ad Dauid, quartam a Dauid usque ad transmigracionem Babilonis, quintam a transmigracione Babilonis usque ad Christum, sextam a Christo usque ad mortem Antichristi, septimam a morte Antichristi usque ad finem mundi.[1] Alii uero ipsas ueriori
15 modo contemplantes, ut dicit Iohannes super Apocalipsi,[2] et sic tenet ecclesia, ponunt terciam ab Abraam usque ad Moysen, quintam uero a Dauid usque ad Christum, et ordinant eas sic: primam ab Adam usque ad Noe, secundam a Noe usque ad Abraam, terciam ab Abraam usque ad Moysem, quartam a Moyse usque ad Dauid, quintam a Dauid usque ad Christum,
20 sextam a Christo usque ad mortem Antichristi, septimam a morte Antichristi usque ad diem iudicii, et in fine cuiuslibet etatis Deus fecit terribile iudicium et uindictam de inimicis suis.[3]

2 distinguntur T   4 in] ad T   scilicet *om.* BTV   ab] sub BTV   5 ad² *om.* T
9 terciam] sic *add.* BTV   15 et sic *om.* T

[1] Cf. *Lib. Fig.*, pl. 18; *Super Hier.*, fol. 35; *Lib. Conc.*, fol. 72v.
[2] *Postilla*, fol. 104v.
[3] The judgements at the end of each *etas* are suggested in the *Lib. Conc.*, fol. 43v, but in the context of a different pattern.

Prima etas. Prima igitur etas fuit ab Adam usque ad Noe, et in fine istius etatis Deus fecit unum terribile iudicium de inimicis suis quia aquis diluuii
25 perdidit omnem carnem, octo personis exceptis, scilicet Noe cum tribus filiis et iiii^{or} feminabus.

Secunda etas. Secunda etas fuit a Noe usque ad Abraam, et in fine istius etatis Deus fecit unum terribile iudicium, quia igne et sulfure destruxit quinque ciuitates in quibus uigebat peccatum contra naturam, et non fuerunt
30 saluate ex eis nisi quatuor persone, scilicet Loth et uxor sua cum duabus filiis suis; tamen uxor sua, contra preceptum angeli aspiciens retro, conuersa est in statuam salis.

Tercia etas. Tercia etas incepit in Abraam et durauit usque ad Moysem, et in fine istius etatis fecit Deus unum terribile iudicium, quia x plagis
35 percussit Egyptum persequentem populum Dei, quarum ultima fuit mortifera persecucio primogenitorum ab homine usque ad animancia omnia in una eadem hora noctis, ita quod uiui non sufficiebant ad sepeliendum mortuos, et paulo post totam miliciam Egypti cum Pharaone submersit in mare rubrum, et vii regna ydolotrancia destruxit, et totus populus iudeorum, qui
40 egressus fuerat de Egypto, propter incredulitatem et rebellionem factam Moysi, mortuus est in deserto ita quod, duobus exceptis, scilicet Caleph et Iosue, nullus illorum uenit in terram promissionis.

Quarta etas. Quarta etas incepit a Moyse et durauit usque ad Dauid, et in fine istius etatis Deus fecit multum terribile iudicium, quia tunc rex Saul
45 propter peccatum inobediencie fuit reprobatus a Deo, et totum genus suum destruxit. Modo asimili Heli summus pontifex cum toto suo genere fuit a Deo reprobatus et fractis ceruicibus mortuus est, eo quod non correxit filios suos fornicantes in templo, grauantes populum in sacrificiis legis Dei.[4]

Quinta etas. Quinta etas incepit a Dauid et durauit usque ad Christum, et
50 in fine istius etatis Deus fecit ualde terribile iudicium, quia tunc Deus reprobauit sinagogam carnalium iudeorum, et per principes infidelium, scilicet Titum et Vespesianum, destruxit eam, et in tantum ascendit reprobacio eorum et destrucio quod xxx iudei pro denario uendebantur, quemadmodum ipsi Christum pro xxx denariis uendiderunt, et per omnes naciones
55 mundi fuerunt dispersi propter peccatum quod comiserunt in Christum.

---

23 etas igitur *tr.* BTV   Adam] Abraam V   27 *Rubricam om.* BTV   31 conuersa]
retrouersa BTV   33 *Rubricam om.* BTV   38 submersa T; submersi V   40 rebellionem] tribulacionem BTV   43 *Rubricam om.* BTV   44 illius T   Deus *om.* BV
45 a Deo] ab eo BTV   46 simili T   pontifex summus *tr.* BV   48 in²] ad M
49 *Rubricam in finem par., post* Christum *tr.* M; *om.* BTV   52 eam *om.* BTV   actendit B   54 ipsi] dederunt *add.* BTV   dinariis M   uendiderunt ... omnes] uel
emerunt ideo per omnes BTV

---

[4] Cf. 1 Sam. 4.

Sexta etas. Sexta etas incepit a Christo et durabit usque ad mortem Antichristi, et in fine istius etatis Deus faciet unum terribile iudicium de ecclesia carnalium christianorum et per x reges infidelium destruet eam. Tunc enim implebitur illud euangelii,[5] *et erit in terris pressura gencium pre confu-*
60 *sione sonitus maris* infidelium nacionum *et fluctuum* tirannorum romani imperii contra ecclesiam insurgencium, quia tunc surget regnum infidelium et regnum imperii contra regnum ecclesie. Cum igitur regnum imperii predicta habeat incipere, ab ipso seu in ipso incohandum est, ut sic per ordinem ad propositum ueniamus. Vnde sicut mare, ut iam in prologo
65 pretactum est, naciones infidelium tangit, sic et terra supra firmam petram fundata per eandem concordiam fidelium naciones ostendit, et quatuor bestie grandes de mari nacionum infidelium ascendentes quatuor regna sonant que de mari nacionum infidelium in terram nacionum fidelium figuraliter, racionabili translata misterio, Daniele testante demonstrant; ait inquid: *Quatuor*
70 *bestie grandes de mari,* scilicet ascendentes, *quatuor regna erunt, que de terra consurgent,*[6] et cetera. Vt ea que in nouissimo malediccionis super totum romanum imperium ac super uniuersum orbem euenienda sunt clarius ostendantur, quia iacula que preuidentur minus feriunt, ut ait Gregorius,[7] et quoniam omne regnum in se ipsum diuisum desolabitur. Oportebat ex
75 predictis ut regnum Iuda in iiii[or] tetrarchias, romanum imperium in quatuor partes, scindi et cuilibet parti suam bestiam per concordiam assignari.[8]

Vnde prima pars ipsius imperii est ipsa Roma, seu Ytalia sub leena, tanquam regina tocius orbis, alas aquile habente descripta, donec sunt ale eius euulse et in uirorum ecclesiasticorum iudicium date; hec est prima bestia.
80 Secunda pars est Alamania, sub urso qui tres ordines dencium in ore habebat et in dentibus tres principes, qui et sic dicebant ei: *Surge et comede carnes plurimas.*[9] Reuera quia primus ordo dencium seu bellatorum et primus princeps tangunt tempora mistici Antichristi, secundus ordo et secundus

---

56 *Rubricam om.* BTV   57 fecit BV   58 et] quia BTV   59 euangelium BV
62 imperii] idest insule *add.* BTV   regnum[3]] persecucio BTV   66 fundata] idest
terram regni Aragonie *add.* BTV   eadem BV   naciones fidelium *tr.* BTV   68 in
om. BTV   69 inquid] Daniel *add.* BTV   71 ea que] quod T   72 uenienda BTV
73 minus feriunt et preuidentur *add. et tr.* V   76 cindi M; secundi BTV   parti] partem
BTV   79 iudiciorum BV   est *post* bestia *tr.* T   80 Alamaniam M   tres *om.* T
81 et[2] *om.* BV   ei] sibi T   83 et] est T

---

[5] Lc. 21.25-26.
[6] Dan. 7.3, 17.
[7] Gregory, *Homiliarum in Evangelia,* 2.35.1 (PL 76.1259).
[8] Cf. *Lib. Conc.,* fols. 127v-128v; *Expos.,* fol. 162v.
[9] Dan. 7.5.

princeps tangunt tempora magni Antichristi, tercius ordo et tercius princeps
85 tangunt tempora Gog nouissimi, quia in ipsis tribus ad comedendum carnes
plurimas Alamania est surgenda.

Tercia pars est Grecia, sub pardo, *et alas habebat auis iiii^{or} super se, et*
quatuor capita erant in bestia, et potestas data est ei.[10] Hic enim pardus
uariatus diuersorum errorum coloribus, Grecia est, in qua quatuor capita seu
90 ciuitates et iiii^{or} ale, seu regna, sunt in quibus ipse pardus principaliter in suis
erroribus dominatur, scilicet Constantinopolis et regnum eius, Philipa et
regnum eius, Tessalonica et regnum eius, Artha et regnum eius, *et potestas*
data est ei, super ista iiii^{or} regna principaliter, in suis scilicet erroribus, usque
ad tempus ut ipsi grecorum errores sint hostium posteriorum errorum qui sub
95 quarta bestia, sexto ecclesie tempore, regnante illo rege xi°, subsequentur.

Quarta pars est Yspania, sub iiii^{a} bestia descripta: *Terribilis atque mirabilis,*
et fortis nimis; dentes ferreos habebat magnos, comedens atque comminuens,
et reliqua pedibus suis conculcans. Dissimilis enim erat ceteris bestiis quas
uideram ante eam, et habebat cornua x. Considerabam cornua, et ecce cornu
100 *aliud paruum ortum est de medio eorum, et tria de cornibus primis euulsa sunt*
a facie eius. Et ecce occuli quasi hominis erant in cornu isto, et os loquens
ingencia, et faciebat bellum aduersus sanctos, et preualebat eis.[11] Sequitur:
Bestia quarta quartum regnum erit in terra, quod maius erit omnibus regnis,
et deuorabit uniuersam terram et cominuet eam. Porro cornua x ipsius regni,
105 *decem reges erunt, et alius consurget post eos, et ipse potencior erit prioribus,*
et tres reges humiliabit, et sermones contra Excelsum loquetur, et sanctos
Altissimi conteret, et putabit quod possit mutare tempora et leges, et tradentur
in manu eius usque ad tempus, et tempora, et dimidium temporis.[12]

Sic enim in quinta etate mundi, sub rege Alexandro, totus mundus pro
110 maiori parte inter multos reges diuisus est; sic et in quinto ecclesie tempore,
sub rege Karulo magno, consimiliter inter decem reges catholicos romanum
inperium pro maiori parte diuisum est. Et sicut de medio predictorum aliud
regnum paruum egressum est, de quo postquam multiplicata fuerunt mala in

---

85 tribus M^{ac}   87 et^{1}] secundum Danielem *add.* BTV   super se et *om.* TV *per hom.*
89 errorum *om.* BV   colorum BTV   qua *om.* BTV   90 et *om.* BTV   92 eius]
Filipa et regnum eius *add.* BTV   Artha ... eius *om.* BV   93 iiii^{or} *om.* T   94 sint]
sicut BTV   98 suis pedibus *tr.* BTV   erit BMV   ceteris *om.* T   102 bellum
om. BTV   aduersos M   103 maior est T   106 sermones] francos V   108 et
tempora *om.* T   et^{2} *om.* M^{ac}   109 Sicut TV   110 est *om.* T   112 pro *om.* BV
est *om.* T   sicut] sic T   113 postquam] priusquam BV

---

[10] Dan. 7.6.
[11] Dan. 7.7-8, 21.
[12] Dan. 7.23-25.

terra, egressus est ille Anthiocus, illustris filius Anthioci regis, qui postquam
115 deposuit Ptolomeum regem Egypti, ascendit Ierusalem et comminuit omnia
uasa domus Dei et omnes thesauros tulit secum, et captiuas duxit mulieres
et natos earum, et abstulit sacrificium, et statuit abominandum ydolum
desolacionis super altare Domini, et deieccit locum sanctificacionis eius, et
ciuitatem succendit, et muros et domos eius destruxit,[13] *et factus est plantus*
120 *magnus in omni Israel, et uniuersa domus Iacob induit confusionem,*[14] et
cetera. Sic consimiliter de medio istorum aliud regnum paruum egressurum
est, de quo postquam multiplicata erunt mala in terra; egrediendus est ille rex
xi[us], de quo supra dictum est quod, *potencior erit prioribus,*[15] et cetera, qui
postquam deposuerit Ptolomeum regem Egypti, seu Francie, ascendet Ierusa-
125 lem et cominuet omnia uasa, scilicet aurea et argentea, domus Dei, seu
summi sacerdotis, et omnes thesauros feret secum et captiuas ducet mulieres,
hoc est prelatos et rectores tunc temporis, molles, delicatos, pictos, comptos
et ornatos, et instabiles sicut mulieres, et natos seu creatos eorum, qui non
ex Deo, sed ex sanguinibus, seu corruptibilibus symonie, tunc tempore pro
130 magna parte nacendi seu procreandi sunt. Et auferet sacrificium, et statuet
abominandum ydolum desolacionis, scilicet pseudo papam seu Antichristum,
super altare seu super sedem Domini, hoc est summi sacerdotis et deiciet
locum sanctificacionis eius, et ciuitatem succendet, et muros et domos eius
destruet, *et erit planctus magnus in omni Israel,* in Christianitate scilicet
135 uniuersa, *et uniuersa domus Iacob,* hoc est uniuersa Christi ecclesia, *induet*
confusionem, et cetera.[16]
   [*Glosa.* Sicut enim, secundum concordiam facti, tempore Iechonie regis
Iude, uniuersi principes sacerdotum et populus preuaricari ceperunt et
preuaricati sunt inique iuxta uniuersas abominaciones gencium, et polluerunt
140 domum Domini, quam sanctificauit sibi in Ierusalem, sic in xlv[a] generacione
a Christo, ut in iii[a] distincione huius libri clarius materia tangitur, uniuersi

---

115 ascendit] in *add.* BTV   117 et[3] *om.* BV   119 succendit] igni *add.* T
120 confusione M   120-121 et cetera *om.* BV   122 postquam *om.* B   multiplicata
om. BTV   123 erit] sit M[ac]   124 ascendit T   125 argentes et aures BTV   126 fert
T   127 compotos T   128 et instabiles *om.* M[ac]   129 symoniis BTV   temporibus
BTV   130 nacendi ... sunt *om.* M[ac]   auferetur BV   133 succedit BV   134 in[2]
om. BV   137 concordiam *om.* T   138 preuaricari ... et *om.* BV   140 sibi] ceperunt T sic] sicut B   141 libri] hec *add.* BTV   clarius *post* tangitur *tr.* V

---

[13] 1 Mac. 1.
[14] 1 Mac. 1.26, 29.
[15] Dan. 7.24.
[16] 1 Mac. 26, 29.

principes sacerdotum, populus scilicet ecclesiasticus, et omnis religio et
omnis mundus, preuaricari incipient et preuaricabuntur inique nouis enormitatibus et seleribus scandalosis, necnon et excessibus irregularibus iuxta
145 uniuersas abominaciones gencium, et domum Domini turpiter polluere tam
temporaliter quam spiritualiter, quod tacendum plusquam dicendum est, et
ideo mulieribus comparantur, molles, delicati, et cetera, et eciam ut passionis
uigilia Domini in membris suis in hoc tempore celebretur, dicendo: *Vado
Romam iterum crucifigi,*[17] et cetera.]
150   Hic igitur primo, sub ista quarta bestia, describitur diuisio tocius romani
pro maiori parte imperii circa principium quinti temporis post Karulum
magnum in x regna, seu inter decem reges, de quorum medio iam aliud, seu
xi[um], regnum ortum cernitur, de quo *cum creuerint iniquitates,* ut dicit
Daniel,[18] egrediendus est ille xi[us] rex predictus ex semine aquile, seu impe-
155 ratoris Frederici secundi, ut multi asserunt, qui tres reges de predictorum
regum numero debet deponere de corona.
    Vnde iam in regna, seu reges xi catholicos, romanum imperium pro maiori
parte diuisum cernitur, qui sunt isti, scilicet rex Cipri, rex Vngarie, rex
Boemie, rex Sicilie, rex Francie, rex Anglie, rex Aragonie, rex Maioricarum,
160 rex Nauarre, rex Castelle, rex Portugalie. Sed quia, ut superius iam predictum
est, ipsa quarta bestia, que totum designabat imperium, in tetrarchiam ipsius
imperii occidentis, que Yspania est, figurali misterio secundum Ioachim per
concordiam est translata,[19] quod idcirco sequitur uideamus. A tempore autem
quo domus Aragonie cepit regnum Valencie et regnum Maioricarum de manu
165 sarrecinorum et regnum Murcie de manu regis Castelle, necnon et regnum
Sicilie de manu regis Karuli, et unica pulla aquile regi domus predicte unita
est, domus ipsa in diuersas propagines domorum regalium se expansit, nec
simile pro hoc misterio preterquam in portis Yspanie, scilicet Cathalonia et
Aragonia, reperitur. Tunc enim illa quarta Danielis bestia de mari infidelium
170 in quartam tetrarchiam occidentis terre fidelium est translata, quando inde

---

142 sacerdotum] et *add.* BTV   147 ideo] loco T   moles M   eciam] enim BV
151 imperii *ante* pro *tr.* BTV   152 seu[2]] scilicet BTV   153 creuerit M
154 regrediendus BTV   est *om.* T   156 numero regum *tr.* V   159-160 rex[5] ...
Portugalie] rex Castelle, rex Portugalie, rex Nauarre, rex Neapolim BTV   161 in] et T
162 est *om.* BTV   164 quod dominus T; rex *add.* BTV   165 et[1] ... Castelle *om.* T
170 terre] tervia V

---

[17] Richard Lipsius and Max Bonnet, eds., *Passio sanctorum apostolorum Petri et Pauli*, in
Acta apostolorum apocrypha (Lipsiae, 1893), p. 171. See also *ibid.*, *Martyrium beati Petri
apostoli a Lino episcopo conscriptum*, pp. 7-8.
[18] Dan. 8.23.
[19] Cf. *Lib. Fig.*, pl. 14. The fourth beast is associated with Spain in the *Expos.*, fol. 116r-v.

extirpatis infidelibus ad manus catholicorum fidelium est deuenta; ex tunc enim domus illa, ut pretactum est, in diuersas propagines domorum regalium expansa est et ex illa radice x reges coronatis ostenduntur egressi, necnon et xi^us de medio eorum, seu de uno eorum, ex semine aquile ortus ostenditur.

175 Quis horum erit qui in subscripto ordine continetur sua tempora reuelabunt. Venturi enim et unde uenientes habenti oculos hoc misterium iam ostendunt. Ex illa namque radice predicta egressi sunt et regnauerunt in ipsa Aragonia et Cathalonia quinque, scilicet rex Petrus, qui cepit Siciliam, cui predicta pulla aquile unita est, rex Alfonsus, rex Iacobus, rex Alfonsus qui cepit

180 Sardiniam, et rex Petrus qui nunc est, qui regnum Maioricarum cepit iterum et ipsum regem de corona deposuit. In regno Maioricarum fuerunt tres, scilicet rex Iacobus, rex Sancius, et rex Iacobus, qui nuper depositus et decapitatus est. In regno Sicilie fuerunt tres, scilicet rex Fridericus, rex Petrus, et rex Lodouicus qui nunc est. Erit ille xi^us rex? Sua tempora

185 reuelabunt, nam xlvi^a generacione ab incarnacione Christi, *ultra quam credi possit uniuersa uastabit,*[20] licet in fine xlv^e incipiat sua principia exercere.

Hec igitur bestia a principali parte, hoc est a principio et porta Yspanie, scilicet Cathalonia, non uocaliter sed realiter nuncupatur, nam Cathaloniam a *logos,* quod est *sermo,* et *cathalicio,* quod est *uastacio* dicitur, quia, ut

190 predictum est, *ultra quam credi potest uniuersa uastabit.* Ideo describitur *terribilis,* terrorem enim inmictet cunctis gentibus, *atque mirabilis,* tacenda

---

173 expensa BV   coronatos M   et² *om.* BTV   174 seu ... eorum *om.* T *per hom.* aquile *om.* BTV   176 hoc misterium *om.* BV   177 Ex] Et T   178 quinque] isti BV; ipsi T; reges *add.* M^pc   179 Iacobus] et *add.* T   180 qui ... est *om.* BTV   181-186 In regno ... exercere] Rex Alfonsus, qui cepit Sardiniam, et rex Petrus, qui deposuit regem Iacobum de regno Maioricarum, ubi fuerunt tres reges, scilicet Iacobus, et rex Sancius, et ille depositus. *Sed isti non procedunt ex recta linea ab aquila,* ideo sunt computandi in regno Sicilie quatuor (tres T), scilicet rex Fredericus, rex Petrus, et rex Ludouicus (qui nunc est *add.* T) BTV; Et aduch sunt tres in regno Aragonie, scilicet rex Iohannes, rex Martinus, et rex Robertus. Martinus bret in regno Sicili, et iste undecimus est, prout sua tempora manifestant, nam undecimus iste ab incarnacione Christi quadragesima sexta uastabit *add.* BV   188 non ... Cathaloniam *om.* BTV *et add.* que interpretatur   189 dicitur *om.* BTV   190 uastabit] ille undecimus a pulla aquile et a petra *add.* BTV

---

[20] Dan. 8.24. The kings of Aragon to whom reference is here made are Peter III (1276-1285), Alfonso III (1286-1291), James II (1291-1327), Alfonso IV (1327-1336), and Peter IV (1336-1387). The kings of Majorca are James II (ob. 1311), Sancho (ob. 1324), and James, who was killed and afterwards decapitated in 1349, following an unsuccessful attempt to recover the island from Peter IV, who had captured it in 1343. The kings of Sicily are Frederic II (ob. 1337), Peter II (ob. 1342), and Louis (ob. 1335). For the dating of M, it is important to note that Louis's successor, Frederick III of Sicily (1355-1377), is not mentioned, consequently M appears to have been written before 1355. It is Peter IV of Aragon who is here cast as the eleventh king of Daniel 7.

enim sunt plusquam dicenda ea que iste rex cum sua gente facturus est, *et fortis nimis,* non enim erit ei resistencia aduersorum, *dentes enim ferreos et magnos habebat,* hoc est bellatores fortes, magnates, et inmisericordes,
195 *comedens et comminuens,* hoc est bellans et interficiens, *et reliqua pedibus suis conculcans,* hoc est uilipedens et ad terram prosternens, *dissimilis enim erat ceterris bestiis quas uideram,*[21] quoniam a seculo tam grandia nec tam terribilia per precedentes bestias uel regna seu reges fuerunt uisa, seu facta, qualia iste rex facturus est, et ideo sequitur quod potencior erit prioribus.[22]
200 Vnde Ioachim: quando omnia regna et omnes communitates, tam in terra quam in mari, erunt in declinacione propter magnas diuisiones et guerras mortales, solum regnum istius magnificabitur, ampliabitur et exaltabitur, cui omnes communitates inclinabuntur et deficient.[23]

Sequitur: *Et tres reges humiliabit*[24] de gente sua, seu de sanguine suo. Dicit
205 Ioachim quod multos reges humiliaturus est uersus orientem et uersus meridiem, tamen de gente sua, seu de sanguine suo, tres humiliabit, seu de corona deponet.[25] Vnus enim iam humiliatus, depositus et decapitatus est; de reliquis uero, scilicet de casu regni Sicilie et regni Francie in sexta parte ix[e] distinccionis huius libri dicetur, in qua quasi de consimili materia agitur.

210 Sequitur: *Et sermones contra Excelsum loquetur;*[26] orientur enim tunc cause et occasiones inter ipsum et summum pontificem, propter que et uerba et scandala et facta non modica inter ipsum et summum pontificem siue ecclesiam insurgent, in quibus ipsa ecclesia temporaliter opprimetur et uituperia et obpropria tam in se quam in suo capite sustinebit, et ideo
215 sequitur: *Et sanctos Altissimi conteret,*[27] non sancti scilicet realiter, sed uocaliter cuncti ecclesie ministri sunt dicti; non enim uocati, sed soli electi Dei realiter sancti dicuntur. Vnde uidetur hic quod tunc tempore ordo clericorum et ceterorum ecclesiasticorum non modicam sustinebit pressuram.

---

192 ea] illa BTV   193 ferreos] fortes T   196 ad ... prosternens *om.* V   198 uel regna *om.* BTV   facta seu uisa *tr.* BTV   205 quod *om.* V   207 est] sed quid de rege Petro Castelle qui captus, depositus, et decapitatus fuit *add.* BV   208 parte] et in *add.* BTV 209 agitur] seu loquitur *add.* BTV   210 Sequitur *om.* BV   212 et[1] *om.* BV   213 et] ut V   214 ideo] in Deo V   216 dicti] sancti *add.* BTV   sed *om.* T 217 temporis BTV   218 sustinebunt BV

---

[21] Dan. 7.7.
[22] Dan. 7.24.
[23] Unidentified source.
[24] Dan. 7.24.
[25] Unidentified source.
[26] Dan. 7.25.
[27] Dan. 7.25.

Sequitur: *Et putabit quod possit mutare tempora et leges;*[28] tempora a Deo
220 scilicet constituta et ordinata non mutabit, nec mutare poterit, nisi forte
permissiue detur sibi a Deo propter peccata, sed tempora ecclesiasticis
legibus et ciuilibus stabilita mutabit, et cunctas leges destruet et cassabit,
propter quod sequitur: *Et tradentur in manu eius post tempus et tempora et
dimidium temporis,*[29] hoc est tribus annis dimidio, quibus finitis, ut alter
225 Nabucodonosor, Babilonis rex reducetur, ut dicit Ioachim,[30] et hoc per
sanctum pastorem qui cum ceteris regibus ad sanctum sepulcrum transsibit
et alias infidelium partes ad conterendum eorum superbiam et diuino cultui
subiugandum.

Cum igitur, ut pretactum est, in fine istius etatis fiendum sit a Deo terribile
230 iudicium de ecclesia carnalium christianorum, que iam tunc non Christi
ecclesia, sed sinagoga demoniorum seu Babilon noua, propter terribilem
casum eius et propter multitudinem reproborum in ea poterit appellari, est
sciendum quod cum quatuor flumina de paradiso deliciarum descendencia
quatuor huius mundi inperia significent,[31] siue regna que per iiii[or] predictas
235 bestias grandes de mari nacionum infidelium ascendentes sunt per Danielem
ostensa,[32] idcirco principale flumen, quod Eufrates dicitur,[33] principale
mundi imperium, quod romanum est, per eum in omnibus sui partibus
ostendetur. In hoc igitur flumen magnum, quod est inperium in quatuor
tetrarchias diuisum, in sue destruccionis signum, sextus angelus sexto eccle-
240 sie tempore, siue sexti sigilli apercione, ad hoc scilicet diuino iudicio cum
suis complicibus malignis spiritibus ad complendum Dei iudicia ordinatus,
effusurus est, ymo iam effundere cepit, phialam ire Dei, de quo Apocalipsis
xvi° dicitur: *Et sextus angelus effudit phialam suam plenam ira Dei in flumen
magnum Eufrates ad cicandum aquas fluminis ut preparetur uia regibus ab
245 ortu solis,*[34] et cetera.

[*Glosa.* Licet enim hic angelus sexte phiale spiritus seu angelus bonus sit,
non propter hoc obstat quin complices malignos spiritus ad hoc habere

---

219 Sequitur *om.* T   223 quod *om.* T   225 ut] et T   226 ad *om.* T
227 partes *om.* T   eorum] corum *add.* T   232 est] et *add.* BTV   235 sunt *om.* T
237 sui *post* partibus *tr.* M[ac]   partibus suis BTV   238 ostendet B; ostenditur T
239 detrarchias M   241 Domini BTV   242 effusus BV

---

[28] Dan. 7.25.
[29] Dan. 7.25.
[30] Unidentified source.
[31] Cf. *Postilla*, fols. 26v-27r.
[32] Dan. 7.3.
[33] Cf. *Expos.*, fol. 190r-v.
[34] Apoc. 16.12.

possit, quia aliud est phialam iracundie Dei effundere, aliud uere ipsam effusionem in execucionem deducere. Angeli enim boni et effusores seu
250 reuelatores iudiciorum Dei super terram suis a Deo preordinatis temporibus sunt; mali uero ipsa iudicia in execucionem deducunt, pro quo in psalmo dicitur: *Misit in eos iram indignacionis sue, indignacionem, et iram, et tribulacionem, inmissiones per angelos malos,*[35] et cetera.]

Et quoniam aque multe populi multi sunt, Apocalipsis xvi°, idcirco hic
255 angelus ad cicandum aquas, hoc est minuendum multos ipsius imperii populos, sextam effundere plenam fialam ire Dei conatur per mortalitates et guerras intestinas inter reges et principes et comunitates tam in terra quam in mari, et hoc ut non sit resistencia hiis qui foris sunt, propter quod sequitur: *ut preparetur uia,* id est ingressus, *regibus ab ortu solis,*[36] contra scilicet
260 inperium et contra ecclesiam uenientibus. Viam enim eis et ingressus preparatus erit quia, quod durum est, tanta erit propter guerras diminucio populorum quod uix erit qui contra infideles exeat ad resistendum, et cum non poterunt se conuerti ad bellum, conuertent se ad luctum. Dicuntur autem isti reges uenire ab ortu solis quia, licet multi reges principaliter ab ortu solis
265 ueniant ad percuciendum fornicariam, tamen ab ortu solis, hoc est ab origine mundi, a Deo preordinatum est ut multi reges infidelium nacionum a quatuor partibus mundi conueniant ad delendum romanum inperium et ecclesiam carnalium christianorum.

Isti igitur reges sunt illi iiii[or] angeli in flumine magno Eufrates alligati
270 propter multitudinem populorum eis resistencium, *qui parati erant in horam et diem et mensem et annum, ut interficerent terciam partem hominum.*[37] Prima enim in mortalitate generali de terra sublata est, secunda in guerris et in tempestate ista gladio ferienda est, tercia ad complendum electorum numerum pro semine reseruanda est. Predicta autem fiala effusa soluentur
275 quia non erit resistencia, nam mauri siue tartari aquilonares cum suis regibus percucient Vngariam et Alamaniam, turci et tartari orientales cum suis regibus percucient Greciam et uenient usque Romam; soldanus cum tota

---

252 dicit T   sue] in *add.* T   254 Et ... aque] Et redeundo ad exposicionem dicendum quod adque BTV   xvii° M   256 phialam plenam *tr.* BTV   257 comunitates] ciuitates BTV   258 non *om.* BTV   259 ingressibus T   261 est] audire *add.* BTV   tanta] enim *add.* BTV   264 principaliter ... solis *om.* BTV   269 Eufrates] magno *add.* M[ac] 270 in] ad BTV   272 est *om.* T   273 ista] ita BTV   274 autem *om.* BV soluetur BTV   275 siue] sunt V   277 usque] ad *add.* BTV

---

[35] Ps. 77.49.
[36] Apoc. 16.12.
[37] Apoc. 9.14-15.

furia, Egyptus, Arabia, et Caldea, et que sunt in plaga meridionali, cum suis
regibus, transeuntes per Siciliam percucient insulas maris et totam Ytaliam.[38]

280 Omnia regna que sunt a plaga meridionali usque ad occasum mundi cum suis
regibus percucient Yspaniam, Angliam, Scociam, Yberniam, Franciam, et
omnem terram usque ad montes Lombardie. Omnes predicti congregabuntur
contra fornicariam et inperium ad diem magnum ire Dei omnipotentis, unde
Ieremie 1° dicitur: *Ecce, ego adducam in Babilonem congregacionem gencium*

285 *magnarum.*[39] Sequitur: *Ecce, populus uenit ab aquilone, et gens magna, et*
reges multi a finibus terre, crudeles et inmisericordes, contra te, filiam
Babilonis. Audiuit rex Babilonis famam illorum, et dissolute sunt manus
eius.[40] Et Ysaie xiii°: *Et erit Babilon illa gloriosa in regnis, sicut subuertit*
Dominus Sobdomam, et replebuntur domus eorum drachonibus, et habitabunt

290 *ibi struciones, et pilosi saltabunt ibi.*[41] Et Apocalipsis xviii°: *Cecidit, cecidit*
Babilon illa magna, et facta est habitacio demoniorum, et custodia omnis
spiritus inmundi, et custodia omnis uolucris inmunde et odibilis, quia de ira
fornicacionis eius biberunt omnes gentes et reges qui cum illa fornicati sunt.[42]
Dicit bis *cecidit* propter dupplicem casum eius, et cetera.

295 *Septima etas.* Septima etas erit a morte Antichristi et durabit usque in
finem mundi, et in fine istius etatis Deus faciet extremum et finale iudicium
de toto mundo, et destruet totum mundum per ignem, et uita hominum non
erit amplius in terra seu in hoc mundo.

---

278 Egypto *codd.*   Caldea] caldura BV   282 ad *om.* T   283 ad diem
magnum *om.* T   285 ueniet BV   289 Sobdomam] et Gomorram *add.* BTV
290 ibi¹ *om.* BT   struciones ... ibi² *om.* T *per hom.*   Et] in *add.* BT   292 in-
munde] mundi T   294 Dicit] et *praem.* BV   et cetera *om.* BTV   295 *Rubricam*
om. M et *om.* T   in] ad BTV   298 mundo] et hec sit finis septime etatis *add.* BTV

---

[38] *Lib. Conc.*, fol. 52r.
[39] Jer. 50.9.
[40] Jer. 50.41-43.
[41] Is. 13.19, 21.
[42] Apoc. 18.2-3.

EXPLICIT IIII^a DISTINCTIO. INCIPIT V^a, IN QUA AGITUR DE VII^{em}
TEMPORIBUS ECCLESIE ET DE VII^{em} BELLIS CONTRA ECCLESIAM
DATIS A VII^{em} CAPITIBUS DRACHONIS.[1]

Circa quintam distinccionem est notandum quod totus status ecclesie a
Christo usque in finem mundi in vii partes seu tempora uel status distinguitur,
et in quolibet statu fuerunt data bella crudelissima contra electos Dei.

Primus status apropriatur apostolis et incepit in Christo et durauit usque
5 ad Neronem imperatorem. In tempore istius status fuerunt sancti apostoli per
iudeos orribiliter persequti quia ipsi interfecerunt Christum et lapidauerunt
sanctum Stephanum et decapitauerunt sanctum Iohannem, et decollauerunt
sanctum Iacobum minorem et sepe discipulos flagellauerunt, ut habetur in
Actibus,[2] et tantum ascendit ista persequucio quod discipuli Christi fuerunt
10 compulsi ut desererent regnum iudeorum et conuerterent se ad gentes. Hic
est fuga mulieris seu ecclesie a facie serpentis in desertum gentilitatis, ubi
pascitur dies, hoc est annos, Mcclx in quarum fine soluendus est Sathanas
seu primus aduersarius ad temptandum Christum in menbris suis.

Secundus status apropriatur martiribus et incepit a Nerone imperatore et
15 durauit usque ad sanctum Siluestrum, et in tempore istius status sancti
martires per xi imperatores romanorum fuerunt grauissime debellati, qui
quidem imperatores dederunt xi bella grauissima contra ecclesiam et effuderunt sanguinem sanctorum, *ultra quam credi potest,*[3] et durauerunt bella ista
et status iste tricentenis annis.

Titulum temporibus ... bellis *om.* T   1 quintam] diffinicionem uel *add.* BV   2 in¹] ad
BFTV   2 distinguntur BTV   3 Dei *om.* FF¹   4 in] a BFF¹V   incipit a T
5 ad *om.* T   In] Et FF¹   6 terribiliter FF¹   7 Iohannem] Babtistam *add.* BTV
8 et *om.* F¹   sepe] septem BF¹TV   habetur] scriptum *add.* F   9 Actibus]
apostolorum *add.* FF¹V   tantum] quantum T; et *add.* FF¹   10 ut desererent] deferre
FF¹   Hic] Hoc F; Hec F¹   11 fuga] figura BT   12 dies] Mcclx *add.* FF¹   13 pri-
mus] principalis BTV   15 istius] illius BTV   16 xi] duodecim BTV   romanorum *om.* T;
Roma manu BV   17 xi] duodecim BV; *om.* FF¹

---

[1] The seven ages of this Distinction are those of the *Postilla*, fols. 1v-3v; for the seven heads,
see: *Postilla*, fol. 81r. Olivi quotes the same passages from the *Lib. Conc.*, fols. 38v-39v, as
below, on the opening of the seven seals. This Distinction is found anthologized in two French
manuscripts; see the Introduction to the Text, above, p. 000.

[2] Act. 5.40, 7.54-60, 8.1-3.

[3] Dan. 8.24. The scribe of M may have been trying to correlate the emperors and their
persecutions with the eleven kings of the earlier passage.

20   Tercius status apropriatur doctoribus et incepit in sancto Siluestro et
durauit usque ad sanctum Anthonium abbatem. In tempore istius status sancti
doctores per hereticos arrianos et per diuersos imperatores sectam arrianorum tenentes fuerunt grauissime debellati, et tantum creuit heresis illa quod
papa Liberius incidit in eadem, et quasi totam ecclesiam pro maiori parte
25 fedauit.

    Quartus status apropriatur anochoritis et heremitis et sanctis monachis
uiuentibus solitarie in desertis, et durauit a sancto Anthonio abbate usque ad
Karolum magnum. In tempore istius status fuit ecclesia per sarracenos et alios
infideles qui tunc surrexerunt terribiliter debellata, et in diuersis partibus
30 mundi, maxime in Iudea et in terra Egypti, ubi predicti sancti patres in maiori
multitudine habitabant, fuerunt in magno numero interfecti. Complebitur
autem sub sexta aparicione quod sub quarta est, ut credimus, inchoatum, cum
sub eadem intelligencia illud quoque consumacionem accipiet quod scriptum
est in Daniele propheta: *Bestia quarta quartum regnum erit in mundo et*
35 *destruet uniuersam terram.*[4] Sicut igitur sub quarto signaculo ueteris, preualentibus assiris, humiliata est superbia Israel, sic sub apercione quarti signaculi noui, preualentibus sarracenis, humiliata est superbia gentis grecorum,
datis magnis illis ecclesiis, que patriarchatus fungebantur officio et honore,
in manus alienorum, et primiceris illorum sedibus in potestate inimici.[5] Iste
40 autem status non durauit per centum annos.

    Quintus status apropriatur regularibus religiosis possessiones temporales
habentibus in comuni, et incepit a Karulo magno, qui diuersas dotauit
ecclesias ac monasteria multa, et durauit usque ad sanctum Franciscum. In
tempore istius status fuit ecclesia per manicheos uariis doctrinis erroris
45 grauissime debellata, unde primo dixerunt quod quilibet poterat habere
quamcumque uellet mulierem sine peccato, et in hoc condempnauerunt
statum matrimonii; secundo, dixerunt quod nullus prelatus potest habere
auctoritatem beati Petri nisi sibi esset sanctitate equalis, et ista insurrexerunt

---

20 in] a FF[1]   23 heresis *om.* T   illa heresis *tr.* FF[1]   24 easdem F   27 et
durauit] durante V   28-29 et ... surrexerunt *om.* FF[1]   29 insurrexerunt B   30 in
Iudea *rep.* F[1]   et in *om.* FF[1]   31 multitudinem M   habitabunt M; habitant BTV;
habitabant FF[1]   fuerunt] fueruntque ibi BTV   32 cum] tamen FF[1]   35 destruet *om.*
FF[1]   quarto] decimo BTV   36 superbia *om.* FF[1]   sub] super BTV   36-37 signa-
culi] sigilli BT   38 dantis illis magnis FF[lac]   40 status] quartus *praem.* FF[1]   non
om. BTV   41 religiosis *om.* FF[1]   temporales *om.* BTV   42 a] de T   43 sanctum
om. F[1]   44 manicheos] monachos T   erroribus BV   46 quacumque M   uellent
F   48 ista *om.* T

---

[4] Dan. 7.23.
[5] *Lib. Conc.*, fol. 40v; *Postilla, loc. cit.*

in principio quinti status propter nimiam laxacionem prelatorum, et hoc ex
50 nimia habundancia rerum temporalium, et ecciam tantum habundauit numerus pessimorum in isto quinto statu et uita corrupta carnalium quod facti
sunt in scandalum et persequucionem bonorum, ut habenti oculos satis claret.
Vnde est sciendum quod sub quinto signaculo facta est primo mencio de
Babillone, et nimirum, quia multitudo christianorum, que a principio ecclesie
55 pro maiori quantitate bonorum dici iure poterat Ierusalem, iam nunc, pro
infinita numerositate malorum, dicenda est pocius Babilon, quamuis nec tunc
defuerint qui pertinerent ad Babilonem, nec modo qui pertineant ad Ierusalem.[6]

Sextus status apropriatur uiris euangelicis qui nec in proprio nec in comuni
60 aliquid possident, incepit in beato Francisco et durabit usque ad mortem
Antichristi; tamen hic nota quod iste status habet quatuor inicia, siue iiii[or]
aperciones. Prima apercio habuit inicium in sancto Francisco et imperatore
Frederico secundo qui, ut opinantur multi,[7] fuit unum de capitibus quasi
occisum illius bestie Apocalipsis xiii° ascendentis de mari,[8] cuius plaga mortis
65 in aliquo de suo semine sub quarta apercione istius status ita curabitur et
reuiuiscet ut non solum romanum imperium, sed ecciam francis ab eo
deuictis, obtineat regnum francorum, quinque regibus christianorum sibi
coherentibus, ut narrat Ioachim, et ecciam ex quibusdam sociis, scilicet fratre
Leoni et quibusdam aliis quibus sanctus Franciscus secrete reuelasse refertur.[9]
70 Sub ista igitur apercione prima fuit facta mutacio non modica et mirabilis
renouacio in tota ecclesia; nam sanctus Franciscus, in quo ymago Christi seu
crucifixi fuit renouata, renouauit statum euangelicum et statum dominarum
pauperum et statum fratrum de penitencia.

---

49 et] ex F[1]   et hoc *om.* T   50 tantum *om.* T   51 carnalium] corporalium FF[1]
quod] quo BTV   52 ut] unde T; et BV   claret] patet F[1]   53 sciendum est *tr.* BTV
54 Babillone] beatitudine F[1]   et] ut *praem.* FF[1]   quia] per F   55 poterit iure BTV
dici *post* poterat *tr.* FF[1]   iam] nam T   56 ducenda FF[1]   nec *om.* BTV   57 defuerunt M[ac]   pertinent BTV; pertineant F   ad[1] *om.* M   59 apropriatur] ad *add.* F[1]
proprio] primo B   60 incepit] et praem FF[1]   beato] sancto BTV   61 iste]
hic BTV   iiii[or] *om.* F   62 et] in *add.* BTV   63 qui] quia FF[1]   multi oppinantur
tr. FF[1]   64 illi BTV   67 obtineant T   68 ex *om.* F[1]   scilicet] beati
Francisci *add.* BTV   69 sanctus Franciscus *om.* F[1]   70 apercione *rep.* F[1]; aparicione
V   prima *om.* FF[1]   71 nam] in qua surrexit FF[1]   seu] figura *add.* F   72 fuit
renouata] renouat F et statum *om.* F   72-73 pauperum dominarum *tr.* F

---

[6] *Lib. Conc.*, fol. 41r; *Postilla, loc. cit.*

[7] *Postilla*, fol. 93r-v.

[8] Apoc. 13.3.

[9] The quotation from the *Postilla* ends here; Olivi adds: "et quod tempore Antichristi idest
reuiuiscat in aliquo de semine eius."

Secunda apercio habuit inicium in Iohanne papa xxii° et Bauaro impera-
75 tore, in cuius tempore primus ordo dencium seu bellatorum Alamagnie per
secundam bestiam Danielis ostensus,[10] et primus princeps, dux scilicet ipse
seu imperator, insurrexerunt contra ecclesiam et Ytaliam totam. Tunc enim
apostatrix bestia de terra religiosorum cum duobus cornibus, pseudo religiosorum et pseudo prophetarum, falso similibus ueris cornibus agni ascendit in
80 altum, ut Apocalipsis xiii° dicitur,[11] et per ipsum ducem seu imperatorem
super sedem beati Petri in urbe Roma fuit sollempniter sublimata, et hoc in
signum ualidissime temptacionis mistici Antichristi et in signum imitacionis
ceptri ut de domo Iuda in domum Petri, quia Petrum oportebat expirare in
cruce, Iohannem autem manere, quia *sic eum uolo manere donec ueniam.*[12]
85 et ecciam in signum solucionis Sathene. Vnde a tempore sancti Siluestri pape
usque ad tempora istius secunde apercionis huius sexti temporis fuerunt M^e
anni, unde secundum aliquos hic papa Siluester est ille angelus Apocalipsis,
xx°, *qui habebat clauem habissi, et cathenam magnam in manu sua, et
apprehendit drachonem, serpentem antiqum, qui est dyabolus et Sathanas, et
90 ligauit eum per annos M^e, et misit eum in abissum, et clausit et signauit super
illum,* Constantino et inperio conuersis, *ut scilicet non seducat amplius gentes
donec consumentur M^e anni,* interim enim regnum et pax fuit data populo
christiano. Sequitur: *Et post hec oportet illum solui modico tempore,*[13] ad
temptandum Christum, seu ecclesiam uniuersam, *et cum consumati fuerunt
95 M^e anni, soluetur Sathanas de carcere suo, et exibit, et seducet gentes,* cum
signis et prodigiis mendacibus, *que super iiii^{or} angulos terre,* seu Christianitatis sunt, *Gog et Magog,* gibellinos et guelfos, *et congregabit eos in prelium.*[14]
Tunc enim inceperunt guerre inter reges francorum et anglorum, et inter alios
reges et principes et comunitates[15] populi christiani, tam in terra quam in

---

74 apparicio V   Bauaro] romano *add.* F^1 75 cuius] casus BV   tempore *om.*
FF^1 seu *om.* FF^1 76 ostensus *om.* BFF^{1}TV   78-79 cum ... religiosorum *om.* BV
79 pseudo *om.* F^1 80 et] ut FF^1 81 romana BTV   hoc *om.* T   83 ut
om. T   84 quia ... manere *om.* BV *per hom.*   85 in signum *om.* BTV   86 istius
secunde] huius tercie BTV   89 comprehendit BTV   92 enim *om.* BV   populo
om. F   93 christiano *om.* FF^1 hec *om.* BTV   94 Christum] christiani F^1 seu
om. F^1 95 exibet F^1; exibebit M   96 et *om.* F^1 97 sunt] scilicet FF^1 et^3
om. BFF^{1}V   98 ceperunt T   et^2 *om.* M^{ac} 99 populi propter BV; hoc T

---

[10] Cf. Dan. 7.5.
[11] Cf. Apoc. 13.11 *et seqq.*
[12] Jn. 21.22.
[13] Apoc. 20.2-3.
[14] Apoc. 20.7.
[15] The term *comunitat* was used in Aragon to denote the leagues formed by municipalities,
consequently its use here constitutes evidence for the Catalonian provenance of the *Breviloquium.*

100 mari, que usque nunc non sine magno aucmento fuerunt, nec erunt usque ad
prefinitum tempus illius regis xi^mi et perdicionis filii Antichristi. Tunc enim,
sicut tempore Iechonie seu Ioachim regis Iuda, uniuersi principes sacerdotum
et populus preuaricati sunt inique iuxta uniuersas abominaciones gencium, et
polluerunt domum Domini, et cetera. Sic ex tunc uniuersi principes sacerdo-
105 tum, seu prelati uniuersi, et populus, seu omnis clerus, et omnis religio et
omnis mundus preuaricari ceperunt inique, hoc est in nouas enormitates et
in enormia selera, et in enormes excessus et abusiones iuxta uniuersas
abominaciones gencium, inceperunt cadere, et domum Domini turpiter
polluere, quod tacendum plusquam dicendum est. Tunc ecciam non modica
110 tumultuacio, nec modicum sisma, nec modica mutacio in tota ymo uniuersali
ecclesia fuit facta. Ex tunc ecciam tribuli cissurarum diuersorum cismatum et
magnarum heresum, ex quibus ille uenenosus coluber Antichristus magnus
egrediendus est, inceperunt cressere, ut in breui clarius apparebit, unde in
tanta excecacionis et iniquitatis habundancia, de malo in peius gradatim
115 descendendo, iam in omni statu est lux tocius caritatis extincta. Tunc ecciam
cometa quasi quatuor mensium in spera ignis apparuit, et hinc inde cir-
cumscribendo articum polum, infinita mala uentura suis pronosticacionibus
indicauit; terre ecciam motus magni per loca et pestilencie et fames et
mortalitas generalis qualis non fuit ab inicio mundi, terroresque ecciam de
120 celo per partes mundi diuersas, hec autem omnia inicia sunt dolorum.

Tercia apercio habebit inicium in missione Spiritus sancti quam Deus dabit
uiris euangelicis ad ordinandum suas acies contra Antichristum sub iiii^a
apercione huius temporis sexti uenturum, ad reprehendendum omnes errores
et malicias huius mundi, et ecciam ad preparandum sibi uiam, seu fugam, a
125 facie serpentis, et predicare euangelium in deserto gentilitatis. Hec autem
dacio Spiritus cognoscetur quando filii libere a filiis ancille se incipient
segregare, ut Israel ab Egypto et ecclesia a sinagoga.[16] Sic isti per Spiritum

---

100 usque nunc] hucusque FF^1   fuerunt om. F^1   usque^2 om. FF^1   101 tempore F
102 sicut] in add. BTV   104 domum] templum V   et cetera om. FF^1   105 uniuersi]
omnes F   uniuersi ... religio om. F^1   clericus F   107 enormia] enarrabilia F^1
108 ceperunt BTV   109 polluerunt BTV   est post tacendum tr. BTV   ecciam] enim
BV; om. T   110 nec^2] non BTV   111 Ex] et praem. BV   ecciam om. F^1V
cissurarum] confisurarum B; consisurarum T; scissure F cismatum om. FF^1   112 coluber
om. FF^1   113 cressere] exercere BV   115 descendo BV; ascendendo FF^1   115-
116 Tunc ... cometa om. FF^1   116 mensium M   118 et^2 om. T   119 ecciam om. BTV
120 omnia om. F^1   121 apparicio FF^1; operacio V   habuit BV   122 uiris] in
praem. F^1   123 aperacione V; apparacione F   omnes om. FF^1   125 predicandum
F   euangelia V   autem om. FF^1   126 Spiritus] sanctus add. F^1

---

[16] Cf. Lib. Conc., fol. 106v.

sanctum incipient sibi ecclesiam componere et ordinare, ut ecclesia que
sanctorum est ab ecclesia que malignancium est, ut granum a paleis, segre-
130 getur.

[*Glosa.* Non intendas hic quod aliam ecclesiam ab illa quam Christus
hedificauit isti sibi componant, sed illuminati Spiritu sancto ipsam quam
Christus hedificauit ecclesiam renouando ad pristinum statum reducent.]

Vnde sicut a natiuitate Abraam, patris circumcisionis, usque ad babtismum
135 Christi, in quo datus est Spiritus sanctus in specie columbe, in quo ecciam
Christus aquas suo tactu sacratissimo consecrauit, fuerunt generaciones xlv,
sic a natiuitate Christi usque ad donacionem huius Spiritus predictis uiris
erunt generaciones totidem, et eorum predicacionis tactu aque fidelium
conuertentur. Et sicut illud babtisma fuit finis ueteris et principium noui, sic
140 in isto spirituali babtismate donacionis huius Spiritus in specie columbe, ut
simplicitatis columbine sine felle predicti uiri efficiantur, erit quodammodo
finis noui et principium temporis plenitudinis. Et sicut magna mirabilia et
nouitas non modica in tota sinagoga fuerunt facta, et multa sanctorum
corpora qui dormierant surrexerunt cum Christo in fine illorum ueterum et
145 in principio nouorum, sic et magna mirabilia et nouitas non modica in fine
noui et in principio plenitudinis in tota ymmo uniuersali Dei ecclesia, seu in
tota Christianitate, absque dubio sunt fienda, et multa sanctorum corpora
secundum Danielem resurgent.[17] Et sicut Christus post babtismum immediate in desertum ascendit, sic et facta ista donacione Spiritus, mulier que est
150 ecclesia a facie serpentis fugam capiet iterum in desertum.[18] Vnde illo eodem
Spiritu quo ductus est Christus Dei Filius in desertum, illo eodem Spiritu
adducetur hec mulier, hoc est electorum ecclesia, iterum in desertum
quousque percuciatur noua Babilon per infidelium naciones. Interea tamen
multi coronabuntur martirio et hedificabitur rursum sancta ciuitas, que est
155 ecclesia electorum, uel Christus, seu populus christianus, transibit in desertum nacionum infidelium, percussa prius noua Babilon, ad eorum superbiam

---

128 sanctum *om.* FF[1]   sibi *om.* BTV   ecclesiam *om.* FF[1]   133 reducent] in fine
illorum et in fine nouorum *add.* F[1]   134 patre *codd.*   135 Christi *om.* BFV   Spiritus sanctus *om.* BTV   136 sanctissimo FF[1]   137 ad] a T   huius] sancti F[1]
predictis] imo in *praem.* F   138 tactu] tactum MFF[1]; tantum BTV   aque *om.* F[1];
a *add.* V   139 sic] et *add.* F[1]   ut] sic *add.* F   140-141 ut ... columbine *om.* BTV
142 plenitudinis temporis *tr.* BTV   sicut] sunt T   143 nouitates non modicas BTV
144-145 in fine ... nouorum *om.* F[1]   145 sic *om.* T   146 ecclesia Dei *tr.* BTV
147 corpora sanctorum *tr.* BTV   148-149 in mediatate M   149 Spiritus] sancti *add.*
BF[1]TV   149-150 que est ecclesia *om.* F   150 eodem illo *tr.* V   153 Interea] Tercia V

---

[17] Dan. 12.2.
[18] Cf. *Lib. Conc.*, fol. 106v.

conterendum et diuino cultui subiugandum, in qua pascetur, seu quam
possidebit, dies Mcclx, qua quadragesima mensium expleta, surget temptator
et seductor, scilicet magnus Antichristus, et eisdem temptacionibus in quibus
160 Adam in paradiso et Christus in deserto experuit, easdem humano generi
obiciat, ut uniuersum mundum in dimidio ebdomadis exerceat et seducat. Et
sicut Christus, habita uictoria de temptatore, predicacionem euangelicam
eligendo sibi xii discipulos incoauit, in cuius principio in nupciarum cele-
bracione aquas in uinum conuertit, et completis predicacionibus et miraculis
165 in trium annorum et trium mensium spacio, ad passionem uenit et die tercia
resurrexit, sic de Antichristo uictoria habita, populus christianus per spiritualem ecclesiam nouam, scilicet nuptam agni, predicabitur euangelium, et
tanquam primum miraculum in nupciis, in illis generalibus nupciis noue
nupte agni sex ydrie aque, seu sex inperia infidelium, ad fidem Christi
170 conuertentur, quibus consumatis, sicut in Mathei euangelio dicitur, *ueniet
consumacio,*[19] et tunc Christus ueniet ad passionem et die seu generacione
tercia illius temporis, ut supra dictum est, fit resurreccio uiuorum et
mortuorum.

    Quarta apercio huius sexti temporis habebit inicium in generali comocione
175 illorum x regum, seu tocius orbis, contra uniuersam ecclesiam carnalium
christianorum, de qua quidem comocione sub apercione vi[ti] sigilli Apocalipsis vi° dicitur: *Et cum aperuisset sigillum sextum, ecce terre motus magnus
factus est* qualis numquam fuit ex quo homines fuerunt super terram talis terre
motus, *et sol factus est niger tamquam sacus silicinus, et luna tota facta est*
180 *sanguis, et stelle ceciderunt super terram, sicut ficus emittit grossos suos cum
a uento magno percutitur, et celum recessit sicut liber inuolutus, et omnis mons
et insule de locis suis mote sunt, et reges terre et principes et tribuni et diuites
et fortes et omnes, seruus et liber, absconderunt se in spelunccis et petris
moncium, et dicent montibus et petris, 'Cadite super nos, et abscondite nos a*
185 *facie sedentis super thronum et ab ira agni quoniam uenit dies magnus ire
ipsorum, et quis poterit stare?',*[20] et cetera.

---

158 completa FF¹T   159 temptatoribus FF¹; temporibus T   160 experuit] ex-
primit F; temptauit F¹   161 ut] et BTV; in FF¹   obdomadis *codd.*   162-
166 uictoria ... habita *om.* FF¹ *per hom.*   166 per *om.* BTV   168 primum *om.* BTV
169 seu *om.* F¹   170 dicitur] habetur BV   171 Christus *om.* BTV   ueniet] idest
ecclesia Christi in persona Christi ad passionem Domini *add.* FF¹   ad *om.* M[ac]   et *om.*
BTV   172 tercia *om.* BTV   est] ut *add.* BTV   fit *om.* FF¹T   175 carnalium *om.*
F¹   177 vi°] quinto T   179 tota *om.* BTV   180 suos *om.* F   182 et¹ *om.* F¹
terre *om.* BTV   183 omnis BFF¹TV   et petris *om.* BTV   184 et³ ... nos² *om.* BV
per hom.   186 et cetera *om.* BF¹V

---

[19] Mt. 24.14.
[20] Apoc. 6.12-17.

Et ecce, scilicet iam in breui, *terre,* seu terrenorum, *motus magnus factus est,* quia in toto orbe, maxime in romano imperio, fiendus est per guerras scilicet intestinas inter reges et principes et comunitates tocius populi
190 christiani, tam in terra quam in mari, et multorum regum infidelium contra romanum inperium et ecclesiam insurgencium, ut dixi, fiendus est, qualis nunquam fuit ex quo homines fuerunt super terram talis terre, seu terrenorum, motus. *Et sol,* seu summus pontifex, qui solus est in dignitate sua, *factus est niger,* seu obscurus quasi cuntis credentibus, radiis utriusque potencie
195 obfuscatis, nam in tantorum errorum et persequucionum caligine erunt omnibus in derisum, *sicut sacus silicinus,* de pillis porcorum propter uilem et corruptam uitam cunctorum ecclesiasticorum in omni statu. *Et ideo luna,* seu uniuersus status inferioris ierarchie tocius ecclesie, *facta est tota sanguis,* et diuersis uiciorum infeccionibus et scandalis mestruata, et in magnum
200 deducta obprobrium et temporalibus perfidiis destituta, sanguis eius, seu suorum ecclesiasticorum, usque ad frenos equorum fundetur. Sequitur: *Et stelle,* seu cardinales et prelati alii cum tota media gerarchia ecclesie, *ceciderunt super terram,* primo de celesti statu diuini cultus, secundo de sedibus seu locis suis uelint nolint, ut cursores leues effecti ab omnibus bonis in
205 quibus confidebant temporalibus destituti, *sicut ficus emittit grossos suos cum a uento magno percutitur,* grossi enim ficus sunt tumefacti exterius, putrefacti interius, et a magno uento percussi, de locis suis inmediate cadunt, sic predicti, tumefacti per superbiam et infecti per luxuriam, ab isto tam magno uento huius temptacionis percussi, deficient et cadent. Sequitur: *Celum*
210 *recessit sicut liber inuolutus,* hoc est electorum ecclesia, ne simul iustus cum impio pereat, recessit, seu in desertum gentilitatis iter arripuit, secundum illud euangelicum: *Tunc qui in Iudea sunt, fugiant ad montes,*[21] et cetera. *Sicut liber,* scilicet secretorum diuine sapiencie, *inuolutus,* seu clausus, ut scilicet, uidentes non uideant, et intelligentes non intelligant.[22] Sequitur: *Et*
215 *omnis mons,* seu omne regnum tam temporale quam ecclesiasticum, *et insule,* seu abbacie tanquam insule in medio maris uite mundane romani imperii constitute, *de locis suis mote sunt,* quia in casu imperii in aduentu illorum

---

188 tota urbe FF[1]   189 comunitates] comociones FF[1]   194 seu *om.* FF[1]
195 nam] uere BV; uera T   196 sicut] et *praem.* BTV   198 tota *om.* FF[1]
199 uiciorum ... et[2] *om.* F[1]   200 deducta *om.* BTV   202 aliis T   204-205 in quibus *om.* M[ac]   206 a *om.* FF[1]   207 in medietate M   sic] sed FF[1]   210 cum *om.* T   211 gentilitatis desertum *tr.* BTV   212 fugient BV   213 scilicet *om.* BFTV   214 et[1] *om.* B; audientes non audiant et *add.* FF[1]   Et[2] *om.* FF[1]   215 seu] siue BTV   temporale *ante* tam *rep.* F   insule *om.* FF[1]   216 maris *om.* BV
217 constitute ... imperii *om.* V *per hom.*

---

[21] Mt. 24.16.
[22] Cf. Mt. 13.13-14.

regum non solum omnia regna pro maiori parte temporalia destruentur, ymmo uniuersus status ecclesiasticus, ut predictum est, funditus subuertetur.

220 Vnde Apocalipsis ix° dicitur quod, *in diebus illis querent homines mortem, et non inuenient eam, et desiderabunt mori, et fugiet mors ab eis.*[23] Et ideo sequitur: *Et reges terre et principes et tribuni et diuites et fortes et omnes, seruus et liber,* manducantes linguas suas pre dolore et timore et terrore magno eorum que super se sencient euenire, incipient blasphemare Deum

225 celi, pre doloribus et uulneribus suis, habentem potestatem super plagas has. Sequitur: *Et abscondent se in speluncciis et in petris moncium, et dicent,* scilicet cum fletu et planctu, *montibus et petris: Cadite super nos et abscondite nos a facie sedentis super thronum,* seu a facie illius dyabolici exercitus illorum regum uenientis ex permissione et uoluntate Christi sedentis super

230 thronum equitatis et iusticie de carnalium christianorum ecclesia tunc fiende, *et ab ira agni,* qui tunc contra illam insurget, dare ei calicem indignacionis sue. Sequitur: *Quoniam uenit dies magnus ire ipsorum,* et magnis seu antiquis temporibus prophetatus uenit, hoc est apropinquauit illa dies magna et amara ualde xlii^bus mensibus duratura. Sequitur: *Et quis poterit stare?* Ve autem illis

235 qui in tempore illo fugam consilii euangelici non arripuerint, ut dicitur in Matheo;[24] unde in tempore illo aperiet Dominus ora mutorum contra illam, et cetera.[25] Vnde in Iohele dicitur: *Canite tuba in Syon, ululate in monte sancto meo, pastores; conturbentur omnes habitatores terre quia prope est dies Domini, dies tenebrarum et caliginis.*[26] Sequitur: *Populus multus et fortis et*

240 *similis ei non fuit a principio, et post eum non erit ante faciem eius ignis uorans, et post eum exurens flama, quasi ortus uoluptatis terra coram eo, et post eum solitudo deserti. Vrbes ingredientur et in muro current, domos ascendent et per fenestras intrabunt; a facie eius contremuit terra et moti sunt celi,*[27] et cetera.

---

218 solum] in *add.* V   219 ecclesiam F; *om.* F¹   221 et² *om.* F¹   mors fugiet *tr.* BTV   223 per T   timore et dolore *tr.* FF¹   224 se *om.* F¹   uenire BTV   225 pre] pro T   suis uulneribus *tr.* BTV   226 se *om.* F¹   229 ueniencium BF¹V; uiencium T   230 equitantis M   232 et] a BFF¹TV   233 prophanatus FF¹   235 qui ... illo *om.* F¹   illo fugam *om.* BTV   euangelium BV   235-236 in Matheo dicitur *tr.* V   237 Iohele] Iohanne T   Syon] et *add.* BTV   240 ei] enim T eum] exurens flama *add.* M^ac   242 similitudo BTV   muro] numero BM   244 et cetera *om.* FF¹

---

[23] Apoc. 9.6.
[24] Cf. Mt. 24.15-19.
[25] Cf. Sap. 10.21.
[26] Joel 2.1-2.
[27] Joel 2.2-3, 9-10.

245   Septimus status apropriatur uiris sanctis illius temporis, sicut in Daniele dicitur, quod post mortem illius xi regis suscitabit Deus celi regnum, quod durabit in eternum, *et potestas et magnitudo regni, que est subter omne celum, tradetur populo sanctorum Altissimi.*[28] Vnde istud tempus habebit inicium in morte magni Antichristi et durabit usque in finem mundi. Hic iterum
250 incarcerandus est Sathanas et cessabunt aperciones sigillorum et labor exponendorum librorum testamenti ueteris, *dabiturque sabbatissimus populo Dei.*[29] *Et erit in diebus illis iusticia et habundancia pacis, et dominabitur Dominus a mari usque ad mare,*[30] et sancti eius regnabunt cum eo usque ad occultum finem illius temporis in quo soluendus est diabolus de carcere suo,
255 et regnaturus est homo ille pessimus qui uocatur Gog, de quo tam multa scripta sunt in libro Ezechielis prophete.[31] *Relinquetur ergo,* ut dicit apostolus, *sabbatissimus populo Dei,*[32] in cuius fine futura est tribulacio ista, postquam premisso Helya uenturus est Dominus ad extremum iudicium. Hoc tamen firmiter habeas, quod bellum istius Gog non erit bellum seductorium
260 sicut primum; tunc enim reprobi non poterunt facere illusiones miraculorum, nec simulabunt in ypocrisi sanctitatem.

---

246 dicitur] legitur BTV   regis undecimi *tr.* BTV   regnum quod] regem qui BTV
248 illud BTV   249 in] ad BF¹TV   250 carcerandus FF¹   est *om.* FF¹
251 dabitur BTV   253 Dominus *om.* F¹V   254 diabolus *om.* T   256 propheta F
257 cuius] casus BV   258 promisso Mᵃᶜ   iudicium extremum *tr.* BV; iudicium christianorum T   259 habeas firmiter *tr.* FF¹

---

[28] Dan. 7.27.
[29] Heb. 4.9.
[30] Ps. 71.7-8.
[31] Cf. Ez. cc. 38, 39.
[32] Heb. 4.9.

Explicit vᵃ Distinctio. Incipit vɪᵃ, in qua agitur de concordia vɪɪᵉᵐ ecclesie temporum cum vɪɪᵉᵐ etatibus huius mundi.[1]

Circa sextam distinccionem huius libri est notandum quod vii tempora ecclesie septem mundi etatibus et vii notabilibus preliis conformantur. Sicut enim in prima etate mundi creatus est orbis et generacio Cayn occiso Abel segregata est a generacione filiorum Dei, hoc est a generacione Seth, sic in
5   primo statu ecclesie formata est ecclesia et generacio iudeorum, pro eo quod Christum interfecerunt, segregata est a filiis Christi; sicut enim tunc prima generacio per diluuium est deleta quia comiscuit se generacioni Chayn, sic prima ecclesia ex circumcisione uocata fuit in fine deleta quia pro legalibus cerimoniis iudaismi nimium zelum contra fidem Christi assumpsit.
10   Sicut in secunda etate Noe per archam iussu Dei fabricatam saluatur a diluuio, leuaturque archa per diluuium super omnes montes altissimos, sic in secundo statu ecclesie per robur catholice fidei saluatur populus christianus a diluuio paganorum, et tam per hoc diluuium quam per diluuium sanguinis martirum tunc effusi eleuaturque fides et ecclesia super uerticem regum et
15   romani imperii conuerso Constantino ad fidem ex diluuio ydolatrie excitato.[2]
Sicut enim in tercia etate, submersis sodomitis in mari mortuo et egyptiis in mari rubro, data est lex populo Dei, et Chore, Dathan et Abiron cismaticos ceterosque de filiis Israel contemptores Dei absorbuit ira eius, sic in tercio statu ecclesie, luxuria et ydolatria gencium per mortem et sanguinem
20   Christi submersa, data est lex ecclesiasticorum decretorum et regularium statutorum populo Christi, et contra cismaticos et hereticos efferbuit ira Dei; sicut ecciam tunc, propter superbiam turris Babel, confuse et diuise sunt

---

Titulum temporum ecclesie *tr.* BV   3 mundi *om.* BTV   4 filiorum ... est] segregata est BTV   5 eo] et BV   9 zelum *om.* T   10 Sic BTV   13 per diluuium *om.* BV   16 Sic BTV   17 Dathan et *om.* T   Dathan et Core *tr.* BV   18 absorbuit] eos in *add.* BTV   20 regalium BV   21 et¹ *om.* BV; sanguinem Christi *add.* T efferbuit] absorbuit T

---

[1] This Distinction is based on the *Postilla*, fols. 12v-13r. The description of the five ages and of the beginning of the sixth and seventh are taken almost verbatim from Olivi; the elaboration of the sixth age seems to be original.
[2] Cf. Arnold of Vilanova, *Expositio super Apocalypsim*, p. 254.

lingue remanente prima et recta lingua in domo hebreorum, ac deinde linguis
ceteris in ydolatriam demonum ruentibus, in sola domo Abraam fides et
25 cultus unius ueri Dei remansit, sic propter superbiam plurium in turrem fidei
Christi introductorum lingua et confessio unius uere fidei Christi est in plures
hereses diuisa et confusa, remanente prima lingua et uera et confessione fidei
in domo Petri. Sicut ecciam tunc Abraam fidelis cum cccxxviii uernaculis
reges gencium superauit et Loth fratrem suum eripuit de manu eorum, sic
30 Christus cum cccxxviii presbiteris in niceno consilio congregatis superauit
arryane heresis principes et eripuit simplicitatem fidelis populi de manu
eorum.

Sicut enim in quarta etate Dauid, deiectis siriis et philisteis ceterisque
hostibus suis, reduxit cum vii choris archam Dei in Ierusalem, et propter
35 pestem populo suo inmissam angelo sibi apparente statuit locum templi in
monte Mora, sic in quarto statu ecclesie, sub Iustiniano imperatore, extirpati
sunt heretici arriani de Grecia et de Affrica et Ytalia, et paulo post, sub
Gregorio magno, extirpati sunt de Yspania, et propter pestem et ruinam
Rome inmissam, ordinati sunt per Gregorium vii cori lateniarum seu roga-
40 cionum, cessauitque plaga apparente angelo gladio tenente in loco qui Rome
adhuc castrum sancti angeli appellatur, restituitque archam diuini cultus in
sede Petri, ordinauitque ecclesiasticum officium sollempnius quam foret ante,
sicut Dauid ordinauit officia canticorum et leuitarum et pontificum sollempnius quam foret ante.

45 Sicut in quinta etate, destructa Iudea et Ierusalem per caldeos et prius x
tribus per assirios, restitutus est populus Iuda in terram suam, nec extunc
pullulauit in eis spina ydolatrie sicut ante, sic destructis orientalibus ecclesiis
per sarracenos et latina ecclesia fere per eos uastata, et ecciam per lombardos
prius paganos et factos postmodum arrianos, restitutus est populus latinus
50 per Karulum imperatorem, nec extunc ydola magnarum heresum inundaue-
runt in eis sicut ante, quamuis sicut tunc circa finem fuit tota heresis
seduceorum, sic circa finem huius quinti temporis serpit secta heresis
manicheorum.

Sicut ecciam in sexta etate mundi, reiecto carnali iudaismo et uetustate
55 prioris seculi, conualuit nouus ordo[3] cum nouo duce, scilicet Christo Iesu,
cum noua lege et uita et cruce, sic in sexto statu ecclesie, reiecta carnalium

---

25 unicus BV   Dei ueri *tr.* BT   27 fidei] uere fidei Christi BTV   28 cum
om. BTV   30 cccxxviii *om.* V   33 ciriis M   37 de[1] *om.* BV   de Affrica *om.*
BTV   38 ruinam] magnam *add.* T   43 officium BTV   45 Sic V   52 sic] tunc
V   quinti] septimi BTV   53 manicheorum heretis *tr.* BTV   54 Sic BT   55 duce
nouo *tr.* BTV

---

[3] Cf. *Lib. Conc.*, fol. 69v.

christianorum ecclesia et uetustate prioris seculi, conualescet nouus ordo cum nouo duce, in quo renouabitur Christi lex et uita et crux, propter quod in eius principio sanctus Franciscus apparuit, plagis Christi passionis ueraciter
60 insignitus, et Christo totus confixus et configuratus. Vnde sicut a natiuitate Abraam, caput et principium circumcisionis cui dedit Deus arietem pro filio inmolandum, completis xlv generacionibus, in sinagoga iudeorum conualuit ordo nouus, scilicet apostolicus, reiecta prius carnali sinagoga iudeorum, conualuit quidem cum nouo duce, scilicet Petro, in Christo et sua euangelica
65 lege fundatus, in Iuda et sua tribu rutilanti misterio figuratus, sic a natiuitate Christi, quem dedit Deus sinagoge pro ariete immolandum, in babtismate terminans circumcisionem et figuram agni thipici, in institucione eucharistie sacramenti, tanquam mediator utriusque legis, signancia terminans et signata conseruans, completis quidem totidem generacionibus, reiecta prius carna-
70 lium christianorum ecclesia, conualescet unus ordo,[4] scilicet euangelicus, cum nouo duce seu pontifice noue Ierusalem in Christi euangelii et beati Francisci regule perfeccione fundatus, in Ioseph et sua tribu ecciam rutilanti misterio demonstratus. Et sicut sinagoga iudeorum contra Christum et predictum apostolicum ordinem, condempnando uitam et doctrinam eius et
75 ipsum crucifigendo, et ipsum predictum ordinem et omnes credentes et confitentes eum excommunicando et extra sinagogam faciendo, et finaliter de suis terminis expellendo, nimium zelum sumpsit propter quod habuerunt ad populum gencium transmigrare, et cetera, sic et ecclesia carnalium christianorum, ut xi fratres contra Ioseph,[5] contra predictum ordinem euangelicum
80 et sancti Francisci regulam condempnando, excommunicando, et crucifigendo cum omnibus confidentibus et credentibus in eum, et extra sinagogam faciendo, eciam finaliter de suis terminis expellendo, nimium zelum assumet, propter quod habebunt ii ad populum gencium transmigrare. Et sicut populus gencium tunc per apostolos conuersus est, sic et per istos euangelicos uiros
85 iterum conuertendus est, unde in Mathei euangelio dicitur: *Predicabitur hoc euangelium regni iterum in toto orbe, in testimonium omnibus gentibus, et tunc ueniet consumacio,*[6] et sicut predictus ordo apostolicus, expirante sinagoga, preualuit in terra et subieccit sibi omnes bestias et

---

60 confixus] infixus *add.* T   et configuratus *om.* V   61 Deus dedit *tr.* BTV
63 nouus ordo *tr.* BTV   apostolico BTV *et rep.* scilicet   64 sua *om.* BTV
67 triplici V   in *om.* BV   69 totidem] totis BTV   71 euangelium BTV
74 predictum *om.* BTV   76 eum] in *add.* T   et[1] *om.* BTV   82 eciam] et BTV
assument BTV   84 per[2] *om.* BTV   85 euangelio Matthei *tr.* BTV   88 subient BV

---

[4] Cf. *Lib. Conc.*, fols. 69v, 56r.
[5] Cf. *Lib. Conc.*, fol. 87r-v.
[6] Mt. 24.14.

omnem terram, hoc est omnes fidelium et infidelium naciones, et prefuit
90 picibus et auibus, hoc est omnibus religionibus in quinta etate in sinagoga
formatis, sic predictus ordo euangelicus, expirante ecclesia carnalium christianorum, preualebit in terra et subiciet sibi omnes bestias et omnem terram,
seu infidelium et fidelium naciones, et preherit picibus et auibus, hoc est
omnibus religionibus in ecclesia christianorum tempore quinto formatis.[7] Et
95 sicut predictus ordo apostolicus, quasi in uirum et uxorem, in prelatorum et
subditorum collegio est distinctus, sic et iste ordo euangelicus consimiliter
distinguetur et dominabitur a mari usque ad mare, et a flumine usque ad
terminos orbis terrarum, de quo dicit angelus Danieli: *Regnum autem et*
potestas et magnitudo regni que est subter omne celum dabitur populo
100 *sanctorum Altissimi.*[8] Hic est populus ille,[9] sanctus ordo iustorum circa finem
futurus, de quo in thipo Salamonis dictum est a Domino per Nathan
prophetam: *Ego ero illi in patrem, et ipse erit mihi in filium.*[10] Neque enim,
secundum quod aperte docet angelus in scriptura Danielis uisione, de solo
Filio Dei intelligenda sunt uerba ista, sed tam de ipso quam de hiis qui sunt
105 eius, de illis scilicet sanctis hominibus circa finem uenturis qui sequentur ad
integrum uestigia eius, et in quibus occursurus est populus christianus in
uirum perfectum et in mensuram etatis plenitudinis Christi, quos Zacharias
tangens dicit: *Extendam manum meam ad paruulos et erunt in omni terra,*
dicit Dominus; partes due in ea dispergentur, et deficient, et tercia pars
110 *relinquetur in ea, et educam terciam partem per ignem, et uram eos sicut uritur*
argentum, et probabo eos sicut probatur aurum. Ipse inuocabit nomen meum,
et ego exaudiam eum,[11] et cetera. Cum autem apparuerit ordo illorum fratrum
minimus, ultimus seculi status in Beniamin et sua tribu non sine magno
misterio demonstratus est, in cuius saculo, seu religione, in illa tam ualida
115 trituracione omnium tribuum cifus argenteus per Ioseph inpositus, scilicet
ueritatis euangelice regis Christi, inclusus reperiendus est, tunc casus noue
Babilonis apropinquabit cum festinancia reuelandus.

---

90 hoc est *om.* T   91-92 christianorum carnalium *tr.* BTV   93 fidelium et infidelium *tr.* BTV   hoc est *om.* T   94 religionibus] regibus BV   97 a[1]] de T   99 et
om. BV   103 aperte] a patre V   104 ipso] isto BTV   106 occursus BV
107 quod T   108 Extendans T   110 ducam BTV   per] in T   sicuti BTV
114 est *om.* M

---

[7] Cf. *Lib. Conc.*, fols. 68v-69r.
[8] Dan. 7.27.
[9] *Lib. Conc.*, fols. 69v-70r.
[10] 2 Sam. 7.14.
[11] Zach. 13.7-9.

Sicut enim in vii^a etate mundi, a sabbato quietis Christi iniciata, continet in pace et quiete sanctas animas defunctorum, sic in vii° statu ecclesie 120 complebitur illud Apocalipsis: *Beati mortui qui in Domino moriuntur; dicit enim Spiritus ut requiescant a laboribus suis*,[12] et cetera.

---

119 sic] sicut B   statu] etate BTV   120 illud *om.* T   Apocalipsis] primo *add.* BTV   121 ut] et BV

---

[12] Apoc. 14.13; *Postilla*, fol. 13v.

EXPLICIT VI^a DISTINCTIO. INCIPIT VII^a, IN QUA AGITUR DE CONCORDIA VII^{em} ECCLESIE TEMPORUM ET VII^{em} DIERUM ORIGINALIUM ET EORUM OPERUM.[1]

Circa vii^{am} distinccionem huius libri est notandum quod vii tempora ecclesie vii diebus originalibus et eorum operibus conformantur; nam in primo statu ecclesie ortus est Christus, lux mundi, eiusque fides illuxit orbi diuisitque fideles ab infidelibus, quasi lucem a tenebris, et factum est uespere et mane,
5 dies primus.[2]

In secundo uero statu ecclesie factum est in celo, id est in celesti ecclesia, firmamentum paciencie et constancie martirum, per quem desideria uite superne diuisa sunt a desideriis uite terrene, quasi aque superiores ab aquis inferioribus, et factum est uespere et mane, dies secundus.[3]

10 In tercio autem statu ecclesie sequestrate sunt aque nacionum ydolatrancium a terra fidelium, et protulit erbam uirentem simplicium et ligna pomifera doctorum fructum spiritualis doctrine emitencium, et factum est uespere et mane, dies tercius.[4]

In quarto uero statu ecclesie fulserunt anachorite in celo et in uita celesti,
15 quasi luminaria celi, quorum patres fuerunt sicut sol, multitudo uero fuit sicut stelle in locis suis fixe et solitarie; quidam actiui et inferiores fuerunt sicut luna, et factum est uespere et mane, dies quartus.[5]

In quinto uero statu ecclesie fuerunt spirituales monachi quasi aues uolantes, clerici uero gentibus comixti fuerunt quasi pisces in aquis. In hac
20 autem die primo dictum est, *Crescite et multiplicamini,*[6] et cetera, quia

---

Titulum vii^{em} ecclesie temporum *om.* BTV   operum] cum septem temporibus ecclesie *add.* BTV   1 libri huius *tr.* BTV   4 fideles] fides T   et²] a T   6 uero *om.* T   8 terrene] eterne T   10 autem *om.* V   11 erbem M   15 fuit] fuerunt BTV   16 solidate T   16 et²] autem ut BV; autem et T   20 et cetera *om.* BV

---

[1] This Distinction is based primarily on the *Postilla*, fol. 12v, a section based in turn on the *Lib. Conc.*, fols. 66r-70r.

[2] Cf. Gen. 1.1-5; *Lib. Conc.*, fol. 66r-v.

[3] Cf. Gen. 1.6-8.

[4] Cf. Gen. 1.9-13.

[5] Cf. Gen. 1.13-19.

[6] Gen. 1.22.

numquam in preteritis temporibus sic monasteria uel ecclesie in tali uita que conueniret pluribus ordinate fuerunt quomodo in tempore quinto, quia non tantum clericorum et monachorum, uerum ecciam ecclesiarum et monasteriorum que sunt propagate in tempore quinto in hac autem occidentali
25 ecclesia colligere numerum non est facile.[7] Vnde quamuis uita monachorum quarti temporis fuerit clarior, non tamen fecundior, nec sic habens sensum uiuum et tenerum pietatis, aues enim et pisces habundant in sensu luminaribus celi. Notandum est quod in quinta die creata sunt munda pariter et immunda;[8] sunt pisces secundum legem mundi et immundi, aues quoque
30 similiter. Qui legit intelligat; quod enim Deus non reprobauit homo non contempnat. Nam factus est uespere et mane, dies quintus.[9]

In sexta autem die primo creata sunt animalia, scilicet iumenta et reptilia et bestie, et post hec creatus est homo ad ymaginem Dei factus cum muliere ex ipso formata.[10] Ordo euangelicus sexto ecclesie tempore formatus, tan-
35 quam homo racionalis ad ymaginem Dei factus, et ipse subiciet bestias et omnem terram, et preherit piscibus et auibus, idest omnibus ordinibus tempore quinto formatis; distinguetur autem in prelatos et collegium subditorum quasi in uirum et uxorem. Iumenta sunt simplices, ad obedienciam prompte et ad honera actiue. Bestie enim et reptilia sunt regna paganorum
40 et secte pseudo prophetarum que in vi° tempore ecclesie contra ipsam atrocius insurgent et seuire permictentur[11] in tantum quod ab inicio talis tribulacio non fuit.

Posset autem queri quare Christus non fecit expressam mencionem de finale temptacione ecclesie precedente temptacionem Antichristi et dispo-
45 nente ad illam. Ad hoc est breuiter respondendum, unde Iohannes Super euangelium Mathei ad hoc quatuor raciones ponit per ordinem.[12] Prima est quia non posset ille facere se adorari ab ecclesia nisi prius multipliciter esset instructa et seducta et excecata. Secunda est quod prima temptacio erit pocius

---

21 uel] seu T; *om.* BV   22 quoquomodo BV   23-24 monasteriorum] occultorum monasterium T   30 non[1] *om.* BTV   32 autem *om.* BTV   creata ... iumenta] sunt creata scilicet iumenta animalia *tr.* BTV   33 factus] est *add.* BTV   34 euangelicus] angelicus TV   35 factus] cum muliere *add.* M[ac]   36 idest] et M[ac]   39 prompte] promicti M; producti BTV   40 et *om.* V   tempore *om.* T   ipsamque V   41 insurgentes atrocius T   permictetur M   45 breuiter est *tr.* BTV   Ioachim BT 48 seduta M

---

[7] *Lib. Conc.*, fol. 69r.
[8] *Lib. Conc.*, fol. 68v.
[9] Cf. Gen. 1.20-23.
[10] Cf. Gen. 1.24-31.
[11] *Lib. Conc.*, fol. 69r.
[12] *Super Evang. Mathei*, fols. 135v-136r.

ad excecandum carnales christianos sub specie ueritatis et uere fidei Christi
50 quam ad illuminandum. Tercia quia illa que erit propria Antichristi erit ad
punicionem excecandorum et ad finalem illuminacionem omnium conuer-
tendorum post eius mortem et ad perfectam coronacionem omnium marti-
rizandorum sub ipso; ista est igitur aperte predicanda, illa uero non, nisi
mistice et oculte; tantus enim erit temptacionis excessus quod electi fere in
55 errorem caderent, nisi singulari Dei gracia custodirentur. Quarta est quia
Antichristus et sui facient multa que uidebuntur miraculosa et supernaturalia,
et ideo ne talibus tanquam ueris crederetur, oportebat de eis expressam facere
mencionem. In prima uero nichil fiet, quin per ea que sunt expressa in fide
possint conuinci et agnosci, nisi temporum malicia subuertat intellectum, et
60 hac eadem racione Christus heresim arrianorum, aut cisma grecorum, aut
alias notabiles hereses et cissuras non expressit in speciali. Et ideo qui non
uult errare in secunda caueat se a prima, ut scilicet intelligat quid est
abominacio sedens in templo Dei ad condempnandum uitam Christi, sicut
Cayphas condempnauit personam Christi, unde ut breuiter auertatur quo-
65 modo omnia possunt ad unumquodque predictorum temporum coaptari.

Primo ergo breuiter aplicemus omnia ad primum tempus, scilicet figure,
ut per eum causa intellectus misterii subsequatur. Constat igitur quod inminente tempore seu excidio Ierusalem sub Thito et Vespesiano non fuit
periculum erroris in electos, quale in euangelio ponitur, nec tunc fuerunt
70 multi pseudo Christi facientes signa ad seducendum electos. Circa autem
mortem Christi fuit proprie periculum, quando apostolis dictum est: *Omnes*
uos scandalum paciemini in me in ista nocte.[13] Tunc autem iudeorum
pontifices et scribe fuerunt quasi pseudo Christi et pseudo prophete, prophetantes scilicet Christum adhuc uenturum nondumque uenisse, et ex scripturis
75 et ex tota auctoritate sua et ex tota specie sui zeli sueque religionis dederunt
signa forcia ad seducendos electos; tunc proprie fuit tribulacio magna in
capite ecclesie, scilicet Christo et matre eius, cui nulla fuit similis neque erit,
et nisi Deus ad solum triduum mortis Christi breuiasset dies illos, electi
desperacione peribant. Quando ecciam in templo Dei et in consilio sacer-
80 dotum sedit Cayphas pontifex una cum eis dans sentenciam mortis in filium
Dei, tunc utique abominacio desolacionis stetit in loco sancto, in qua re fuit

---

49 carneles M prius *praem.* BTV   53 a parte BV   uero *om.* BTV   57 ex-
pressam] specialem BTV   59 possent BTV   61 speciali] spirituali BV   64 per-
sonam] uitam T   ut] et V   65 coabtari M   67 igitur *om.* BTV   71 est] et B
75 specie ... zeli] spe licet T; spe luzeli BV   77 scilicet] a BV   erit *om.* T   78 ad
solum *om.* M^ac   80 cum *om.* T   in *om.* M^ac   81 re fuit] refert BTV

---

[13] Mt. 26.31.

opus maioris intelligencie quam quando per Pilatum fuit posita in templo
ymago Cesaris; per hanc igitur proprie fuit desolatum templum et destitutum,
et tota sinagoga omni gracia et spirituali societate et consolacione Dei priuata
85 et destituta. Statim autem post tribulacionem hanc, sol obscuratus est in
Christi morte, et stelle, idest doctores sinagoge, de celo, seu de celesti statu
diuini cultus, ceciderunt et angelice uirtutes comote sunt contra eos.[14] Post
hec autem apostoli, Spiritu sancto pleni, traditi sunt in uarias tribulaciones
et mortes et dispersi sunt per mundum, et in breui tempore sic predicauerunt
90 euangelium. Et post hec subsequuta sunt *prelia et opiniones preliorum,*[15] et
uenit finis et consumacio sinagoge subito; uenit autem in die iudeis ignota,
a tempore autem resurreccionis. Tunc Christus cepit uenire in romanis
imperatoribus uirtute magna, et sic uenit potenter super iudeos quod omnes
tribus terre fuerunt in planctum; missi sunt autem apostoli quasi angeli ad
95 congregandos electos de gentibus uniuersi orbis.

Coaptatis igitur et aplicatis predictis ad primum tempus, scilicet figure,
coaptanda et applicanda sunt ad secundum tempus, scilicet figurati, ut causa
intellectus misterii clarius agnoscatur. Nam a simili apropinquante uel inminente excidio romani imperii, seu ecclesie carnalium christianorum, sub
100 pressura temporum illius regis xi per x reges infidelium fiendo, non erit
periculum erroris in electos quale in euangelio ponitur, nec tunc erunt multi
pseudo Christi facientes signa ad seducendum electos. Circa autem sollempnem condempnacionem uite et doctrine Christi, seu perfeccionis euangelici
status, ut Cayphas condempnauit personam Christi, tunc erit proprie pericu-
105 lum. Tunc, ut dicit Iohannes,[16] surgent pseudo Christi et pseudo prophete qui
facient ab hominibus adorare cupiditatem et carnalitatem, seu terrenam
gloriam bestie secularis, dabuntque ad hoc signa magna: primo, scilicet, sue
ecclesie auctoritatis, cui contradicere uidebitur inobediencia et rebellio
cismatica; secundo, uniuersalis sentencie omnium magistrorum et doctorum
110 suorum, et ecciam tocius multitudinis seu comunis opinionis omnium, cui
contradicere uidebitur stultum et insanum, et eciam hereticum; tercio, dabunt
signa racionum et scripturarum falso intortarum, et eciam signa alicuius
superficialis ac uetuste et multiforme religionis per longam successionem ab

---

82 quando *om.* BTV   84 gracia] Grecia T   85 in *om.* M   86 seu] siue BTV
87 sunt *om.* T   91 iudeis] iudici BTV   92 autem *om.* BTV   93 quod] ita *praem.*
BTV   99 sub] et *praem.* BTV   104 Christi personam *tr.* BTV   105 Ioachim BTV
108 contradicere] contradicetur primo BTV; quia *add.* BT; quod *add.* V   111 insanum]
consilium *add.* BTV   112 et¹] eciam BTV   113 et *om.* T

---

[14] Cf. Mt. 24.29.
[15] Mt. 24.6.
[16] *Postilla,* fols. 92v-93r.

antiquo firmate et sollempnizate, ita ut cum hiis signis ignem diuine ire super
115 contradictores uideantur facere descendere, et econtra quasi ignem sancti
Spiritus et apostolici zeli uideantur ipsi de celo in suos discipulos facere et
descendere; statuent eciam ut qui non obedierit anathematizatur, et de
sinagoga eiciatur et, si oportuerit, brachio seculari tradatur. Facient eciam
quod ymago bestie, scilicet pseudo papa a rege prime bestie sublimatus,
120 adoretur, hoc est ut sibi plusquam Christo et eius euangelio credatur et ut
adolator quasi Deus huius seculi adoretur. Tunc enim ecclesiasticorum
pontifices et ceteri prelati ecclesie pro maiori parte necnon et magistri et
doctores et legis periti, et eciam religiosi et seniores populi, ut pseudo Christi
et pseudo prophete, dantes predicta signa ex tota auctoritate sua et ex tota
125 specie sui zeli sueque religionis ad seducendum electos prophetantes et
prenunciantes, dicent regulam euangelicam esse mathematicam, nec ad
salutem esse necessariam, et quia Christus sic eam non intellexit, *et erit tunc*
tribulacio in electis qualis non fuit ab inicio mundi, et nisi breuiati fuissent dies
illi, non fieret salua omnis caro, sed propter electos breuiabuntur dies illi,[17] seu
130 tempus illud; non enim dies pro anno dabitur, sed dies pro die intelligetur.
Quando eciam in templo Dei, seu in romano capitulo uel consilio, sedebit
Cayphas, pseudo papa seu Antichristus, una cum toto collegio dans sentenciam et dampnans uitam et doctrinam euangelicam Christi, stabit utique
abominacio desolacionis in loco sancto, qua in re maioris intelligencie erit
135 quam quando per illum regem xi^{um} ymago Cesaris seu Antichristi ponetur in
templo. Per hanc igitur proprie erit templum desolatum et destitutum et tota
ecclesia omni gracia et spirituali societate et solacio Dei erit modo asimili
priuata et destituta. *Statim autem sol,* hoc est Christi euangelium, *obscura-*
bitur, instituto prophetis silencio ueritatis, *et stelle,* idest doctores et prelati
140 ecclesie, *de celo,* seu de celesti statu diuini cultus, *cadent, et angelice uirtutes*
commouebuntur contra eos.[18] Post hec autem uiri euangelici Spiritu sancto
pleni tradentur in uarias tribulaciones et mortes et dispergentur per mundum
in breui tempore; sic predicabunt euangelium. Et post hec subsequentur

---

115-117 et econtra ... descendere *om.* BV *per hom.*   117 obedierint anathe-
matizentur BTV   118 eiciantur BTV   119 papa] propheta T   120 sibi] si BV
sibi ... et^1] plus sibi quam T   121 adolatorem M   enim *om.* BTV   122 et^2 *om.* BTV
123 et^2] ac BTV   et^3 *om.* T   124 ex^2 *om.* BV   127 non sic eam *tr.* T   129 salua
omnis] salvacionis T   sed propter ... illi *om.* BTV   131 uel] in *add.* BTV
137 asimili] erit *add.* BV   139 instituto] et *praem.* BV   stelle] stile BTV
140 celesti] electis V   142 mortes] temptaciones et *praem.* BT   143 in *om.* BTV

---

[17] Mt. 24.21-22.
[18] Mt. 24.29.

prelia et opiniones preliorum,[19] *et ueniet finis et consumacio*[20] ecclesie carna-
145 lium christianorum subito; ueniet enim in die christianis ignota, ueniet enim
tunc temporis Christus in uirtute magna in regibus orientalibus, et sic ueniet
potenter super ecclesiam carnalium christianorum quod omnes tribus terre
erunt in planctu. Mitentur autem uiri euangelici quasi angeli ad congregandos
electos de gentibus uniuersi orbis, et factum est uespere et mane, dies
150 sextus.[21]

Dies autem septimus erit benedictus et sanctificatus, et liber ab omni opere
seruili, et fruens pace que exsuperat omnem sensum,[22] nam Deus *diei septimo*
benedixit, in quo ab omni quod patrarat opere requieuit.[23]

---

145 ueniet[1]] deueniet T　　　enim[1] *om.* BV　　　145-146 enim[2] ... uirtute *om.* BV
148 euangelici] idest *add.* T　　149 factus M　　152 Deus *om.* BV　　153 opera *om.* T

---

[19] Mt. 24.6.
[20] Cf. Mt. 24.14.
[21] Cf. Gen. 1.31.
[22] *Postilla,* fol. 12v; cf. Phil. 4.7.
[23] Gen. 2.2; cf. *Lib. Conc.,* fol. 70r.

Explicit VII^a Distinctio. Incipit VIII^a, in qua agitur de
Concordia VII ecclesie temporum cum septem sacramen-
tis.[1]

Circa viii distinccionem superficialiter sub breuibus est notandum quod vii
tempora ecclesie septem sacramentis per ordinem conformantur. Primus
enim status fundacionis ecclesie babtismali regeneracioni conformatur; sicut
enim prima illa ecclesia, seu iudeorum sinagoga, in sacramento circumci-
5 sionis fuit fundata in primo tempore illius, sic et ista in sacramento babtis-
matis in tempore sui primo, et cetera. Secundus status milicie martirum
conformatur confirmacioni per quam christiani ponuntur in statu pugili et
roborantur ad pugnam, unde in signo crucis insignuntur in fronte, et cetera.
Tercius status doctorum sacerdotalibus ordinibus conformatur, et cetera.
10 Quartus uero sanctorum patrum solitarie in deserto cum puritate uiuentium
congruit pani uite. Sacramentum autem penitencie expedit et congruit
hominibus infirmantibus quinti status, et cetera. Matrimonium uero nupciarum Christi et ecclesie congruit sexto statui, et ideo in sexta uisione
Apocalipsis pro eo dicitur: *Gaudeamus et exultemus et demus gloriam Deo*
15 *quia uenerunt nupcie agni, et uxor eius preparauit se.*[2] Vnde sicut Lya
significat sinagogam, sic et Raxel ecclesiam, et sicut ueniente Rachel et
incipiente parere cessauerunt partus Lye, sic adueniente ecclesia et incipiente
parere seu eligere, cessauerunt partus seu eleciones sinagoge, et sicut nupcie
sinagoge fuerunt celebrate in cenaculo Iacob cum suos filios benediceret
20 futura pretangens, sic et nupcie ecclesie fuerunt celebrate in cenaculo Christi
cum suos filios, seu apostolos, benediceret, quos tunc ordinauit presbiteros
et futura predixit. Et sicut in primis nupciis non defuit Dan, coluber
uenenosus, sic nec in secundis nupciis defuit Iudas, serpens antiqus; et sicut
similiter Lya actiuam significat ecclesiam, sic et Rachel contemplatiuam; et

---

4 sinagoga iudeorum *tr.* TV   6 milicie] miliore B   8 roborat T   pugnandum
BV   signancium BTV   et cetera *om.* BTV   11 panis *codd.*   18 eleciones
om. BV; electi T   24 actiuam] antiquam BV   24-27 et² sicut ... actiue *om.* BTV

---

[1] This Distinction is based on *Postilla*, fol. 12r.
[2] Apoc. 19.7.

25 sicut adueniente Rachel et incipiente parere cessauerunt partus Lye, sic
adueniente contemplatiua ecclesia, et incipiente parere seu eligere, cessabunt
partus seu eleciones ecclesie actiue.[3]

[*Glosa.* Non hic intendas ecclesiam contemplatiuam esse aliam ab illa
quam Christus hedificauit, nec actiuam similiter, set quando segregabuntur
30 filii ancille a filiis libere, scilicet peccatores a turbis iustorum in generali
tribulacione antichristiane persecucionis, electi ecclesie in filiis libere perma-
nebunt quia tunc *omnia cornua peccatorum confringam et exaltabuntur
cornua iusti,*[4] et cetera.]

Et sicut nupcie prime celebrate sunt in cenaculo Christi cum suos filios,
35 seu apostolos, benediceret, sic secunde celebrande sunt in cenaculo illius
noui et uniuersalis pontificis noue Ierusalem reuelandi, in quo suos filios
euangelicos benedicet. Et sicut prime nupcie fuerunt celebrate in uigilia
passionis Christi, sub Pilato et Caypha principe sacerdotum, sic et secunde
celebrabuntur in uigilia passionis ecclesie, sub illo rege xi° et perdicionis filio
40 pseudo papa. Et sicut in primis non defuit Iudas, coluber uenenosus, sic nec
in secundis deherit unus de duodecim, serpens antiquus.

Uncio extrema congruit suauitati et paci, unde et ultimo statui congruit in
quo uerificabitur illud de filio reguli: *Quia heri hora septima reliquit eum
febris,*[5] et cetera.

---

28 hic] ut *add.* BTV   29 set] se V   32 tunc *om.* M   35 celebrate BTV
37 primo BTV   38 sic *om.* T   40 sicut] sic T   sic] sicut T   41 serpen-
tibus T   42 ultimi *codd.*   43 Quia] de quo dicitur quod BTV   eri M

---

[3] Cf. *Lib. Conc.*, fols. 83r-84r; *Expos.*, fols. 12r, 18v-20v, 25r.
[4] Ps. 74.11.
[5] Jn. 4.52; cf. *Postilla*, fol. 13v.

Explicit VIII Distinctio, Incipit IX, in qua agitur de VII sigillis novi et veteris testamenti.[1]

Circa ix distinccionem est notandum quod, sicut totus decursus noui et ueteris testamenti in vii tempora ad se inuicem sese per concordiam respondencia distinguitur, sic et in vii sigilla per concordiam mutuo se cernencia parcietur, ut per ea que facta sunt in ueteri ea que in nouo fienda sunt
5 intellecta conspiciantur, ut per ordinem claret.[2]

Primum ueteris. Primum igitur signaculum ueteris testamenti incepit in Iacob patriarcha, licet inicium habuerit in Abraam; consumacio uero eius fuit in Moyse et Iosue, sub quo fuit conflictus egypciorum contra filios Israel per Pharaonem regem Egypti. Sub hoc tempore continetur de Abraam, Ysaac,
10 et Iacob, de filiis et nepotibus, et de mora eorumdem filiorum Israel in Egypto, et de percucione Pharaonis et transitu maris rubri, et de donacione legis in monte Synay, et de exitu filiorum Israel de Egypto, et de Moyse et Aaron, et de xii principibus populi, necnon et de lxxii senioribus qui fuerunt egressi ex Egypto. Sub hoc quoque tempore duodecim tribus hereditatem
15 acceperunt, primo quinque, nouissime vii. Completa sunt autem ista omnia a diebus Abrae patriarche usque ad obitum Iosue.

Primum noui. Sub apercione primi signaculi noui testamenti continetur persequucio iudeorum contra ecclesiam Christi. Sub hoc tempore continetur specialiter principium euangelii Luce, in quo agitur de Zacharia sacerdote et
20 Iohanne filio eius, a quo babtizatus est Christus, de natiuitate quoque Christi et passione eius, et de duodecim apostolis, et de ceteris discipulis, scilicet

---

Titulum ix] distinccio *add.* BTV   3 distingatur M^ac; distinguntur BTV   4 per ea *rep.* T   fienda] facienda BTV   6 *Rubrica*] Primum igitur signaculum ueteris testamenti *rep.* BTV   incipit T   8 et *rep.* T   8-9 egypciorum ... Egypti] in Egypto et de persecucione Pharaonis regis Egypti BTV   13 de^1 *om.* BV   15 omnia ista *tr.* BTV   17 *Rubrica*] Primum igitur signaculum noui testamenti BTV   Sub] Primum signum *praem.* BTV   18 Christi] christianorum M^ac; Dei seu *praem.* BTV   continetur *om.* BTV   21 scilicet] eius BT

---

[1] This Distinction is based upon, and is in large part drawn verbatim from, *Septem Sigillis.*
[2] For the seven seals and for the conflicts within the ages they mark, see *Lib. Conc.,* fols. 27r, 38v-42r. For the first seal of the Old Testament, see *Septem Sigillis,* pp. 239-240.

lxxii. Similiter et liber Actuum apostolorum editus ab eodem Luca, in quo
et scriptum est de separacione fidelium a sinagoga iudeorum, de aduentu
Spiritus sancti super fideles, de duobus apostolis nouissimis, Paulo et
25 Barnaba, qui in predicacione gencium facti sunt primi, usque ad dormicionem
sancti Iohannis Euangeliste. Continetur quoque spiritualiter sub ipso prima
pars libri Apocalipsis, in quo dicit Iohannes factam sibi reuelacionem
misteriorum *in dominica die*,[3] pro eo scilicet quod tempore resurreccionis
dominice sacra misteria reuelari ceperunt. Sub hoc quoque tempore fundate
30 sunt quinque principales ecclese et alia vii que fuerunt in Asia, de quibus
agitur in hac parte.[4]

Secundum signaculum ueteris. Secundum signaculum ueteris testamenti
incepit a Moyse et Iosue, consumatum uero est in Samuele et Dauid, sub quo
fuit conflictus chananeorum contra filios Israel. Sub hoc tempore continentur
35 pugne filiorum Israel habite cum chananeis et diuersis gentibus, secundum
quod scriptum est in gestis Iosue et libro Iudicum, a diebus scilicet Iosue
usque ad Dauid regem.[5]

Secundum noui. Sub apercione secundi sigilli noui testamenti continetur
persequucio paganorum contra Christi ecclesiam. Sub hoc tempore, ut
40 tactum est, continentur prelia paganorum contra Christi ecclesiam, seu
sanctorum martirum, qui in ara Christi mactati sunt, et ecclesia nimis afflicta
est, secundum quod spiritualiter continetur in secunda parte Apocalipsis, in
qua, apertis vii signaculis, in specie equitum et equorum et aliarum ymaginum
diuersa persequutorum genera sunt ostensa.[6]

45 *Tercium signaculum ueteris testamenti.* Tercium signaculum ueteris testamenti incepit in Samuele et Dauid, consumatum uero est in Helia et Heliseo,
sub quo fuit conflictus siriorum, primo contra decem tribus, secundo contra
utrumque regnum. Sub hoc tempore continentur pugne filiorum Israhel
habite cum siriis, philisteis et aliis gentibus, siue eciam inter Iudam et
50 Ysrahel, propter cisma quod accidit in diebus Roboam filii Salamonis,
quando Ieroboam filius Nabath abstulit sibi x tribus, quas et fornicari faciens
a Deo suo docuit colere deos alienos, hoc est duos uitulos aureos, et recedere

---

22 libri BTV   editi BTV   23 et *om.* BTV   28 scilicet *om.* BTV   32 ueteris[1]]
testamenti *add.* BTV   33 est *om.* T   36 scilicet] Ysrael BV   38 *Rubrica*] Secundum signaculum noui testamenti BTV   sigilli] signaculi BTV   testamenti] incepit in
Samuel *add.* M^ac   39 hoc *om.* T   tractum BV   41 in *om.* T   nimis]
minus BTV   43 aperte BV   49 siue] que T

---

[3] Apoc. 1.10.
[4] *Septem Sigillis*, pp. 239-240.
[5] *Septem Sigillis*, p. 241.
[6] Apoc. 6, 9.17; *Septem Sigillis*, p. 241.

a domo Domini. Neque, interfecto eo, redirent ad Ierusalem et ad Dauid
regem suum; perseuerauit autem concertacio ista inter domum Dauid et
55 domum Ioseph ab exordio regni Roboam usque ad Heliam prophetam,
secundum quod scriptum est in libris Samuelis.[7]

Tercium signaculum noui testamenti. Sub apercione tercii signaculi noui
testamenti continetur persequucio arrianorum contra ecclesiam Christi. Sub
hoc tempore continentur conflictus catholicorum doctorum habiti cum
60 quibusdam gentibus arriane perffidie maculatis, gotis scilicet, uandalis, et
longobardis, siue eciam cum gentibus perssarum; similiter inter ecclesias
latinorum et grecorum, sicut inter Ierusalem et Samariam, discensio facta est,
et perseuerauit error arrianus et alii multi errores in ecclesiis grecorum usque
in finem, sicut quondam in filiis Israel usque ad tempora transmigracionis
65 sue, et non defuerunt in eis reliquie, sicut in tribubus Ysrahel. Continetur
autem conflictus iste quem habuerunt catholici cum hereticis in tercia parte
Apocalipsis in thipo angelorum vii canencium tubis et diuersarum rerum
ymaginibus.[8]

Quartum ueteris. Quartum signaculum ueteris testamenti incepit in ascensu
70 Helie et Helisei, consumatum uero est in Ysaia et Ezechia rege Iuda, sub quo
fuit conflictus assiriorum, et x tribus depopulate sunt. Sub hoc quarto
tempore continentur gesta Helye et Helisei ducencium uitam solitariam et
filiorum prophetarum uitam comunem, quibus eciam ad tempus prefuit
Heliseus, sed et pugne Aczaelis regis assiriorum preualencium contra filios
75 Ysrahel, secundum quod continetur in quarto Regum uolumine, a diebus
Helie et Helisey usque ad Ysayam prophetam et Ezechiam regem Iuda.[9]

Quartum signaculum noui testamenti. Sub apercione quarti signaculi noui
testamenti continetur persequucio arabum siue sarracenorum, seu quarte
bestie ascendentis de mari habentis capita vii et cornua x Apocalipsis xiii°.[10]
80 Sub hoc quarto tempore claruerunt uirgines et heremite. Sed et bella sarrace-

---

53 Dauid] domum *add.* V   54 concertacio] conseruacio V   55 Ioseph] Iosaphat BTV   58 Christi ecclesiam *tr.* BTV   60 scilicet] uidelicet BTV   et *om.*
BTV   62 est *om.* T   69 *Rubrica*] Quartum signaculum ueteris testamenti BTV
incepit *om.* BV   71 conflictus] regis *add.* BTV   x] nouem BTV   72 geste *codd.*
74 preualuerunt BTV   75 a] et V   77 quarti] sigilli *add.* T   79 mari] et *add.* BTV
80 et[2] *om.* BTV

---

[7] *Septem Sigillis*, pp. 241-242.
[8] *Septem Sigillis*, p. 242; Apoc. 8.6.
[9] *Septem Sigillis*, p. 242.
[10] Apoc. 13.1.

norum orta sunt sub hoc tempore quarto, secundum quod in quarta parte
Apocalipsis ostenditur in specie bestie ascendentis de abisso, et cetera.[11]

    Quintum signaculum ueteris testamenti. Quintum signaculum ueteris tes-
tamenti incepit in Ysaya et Ezechia rege Iuda, consumatum uero est in
85 excidio Ierusalem et transmigracione Babilonis, sub quo fuit conflictus
caldeorum. Sub hoc quinto tempore cessauerunt prelia assiriorum datis x
tribubus in manibus eorum, et confirmatum est regnum Iuda in manu
Ezechie, qui fecit mundare domum Domini et restaurauit officia leuitarum,
ut quererent Dominum Deum suum prophetantibus Ysaya, Osee, Michea,
90 Sophonia, et Ieremia, et aliis uiris sanctis qui effuderunt phialam iracundie
Dei super inmundicias populorum a diebus Ysaye prophete usque ad transmigracionem Babilonis, annunciantes mala uentura super Iudam et Egyptum
et Babilonem, et super multos populos qui erant in uicinis regionibus, licet
in spiritu non de illis sed de aliis populis eisdem similibus loqueretur. Fuit
95 autem persequucio quinta contra filios Iuda et Iechonie regis Egypti et
Nabuccodonosor regis Babilonis.[12]

    Quintum signaculum noui. Sub apercione quinti signaculi noui testamenti
continetur persequucio alamagnorum querencium ancillare libertatem ecclesie. Sub hoc quinto tempore cessauerunt bella saracenorum, datis illis x
100 ecclesiis in manibus eorum, et confirmata est latina ecclesia in manu Gregorii
magni, et egressi sunt ex ea uiri spirituales qui zelati sunt zelo Dei, *ad*
faciendam uindictam in nacionibus,[13] et incredibilibus, non gladio ferri sed
gladio uerbi spiritualis, secundum quod continetur in quinta parte Apocalipsis, in thipo templi Dei, et angelorum vii exiliencium ex eo et effunden-
105 cium phialas iracundie Dei in terram ad excecandas mentes peccatorum qui
morantur in ea,[14] iuxta illud Ysaye: *Exceca cor populi huius et aures eius*
agraua, et claude oculos eius ne forte conuertantur et sanem eos.[15] Isti uero
angeli,[16] seu prophete uel religiones, inceperunt effundere phialam predicacionis a diebus Ozie, seu Gregorii magni, et usque ad transmigracionem
110 Babilonis effundent, annunciantes mala uentura super Iudam, seu regnum

---

    88 qui *om.* BTV   90 ueris V   95 Iechonie] Iechao M   rex M   96 rex M
97 *Rubrica*] Quinti signaculi M   noui[1]] testamenti *add.* BTV   100 et *om.* T
104 Dei] Domini BT   107 et[2] *om.* T   109 a *om.* BTV   et *om.* T   110 effun-
derunt BTV

---

[11] *Septem Sigillis*, p. 242.
[12] *Septem Sigillis*, p. 243.
[13] Ps. 149.7.
[14] Apoc. 16.
[15] Is. 6.10.
[16] Cf. *Expos.*, fol. 185r.

romane ecclesie, et Egyptum, seu regnum Francie, et Babilonem, seu
Romam, et super multos populos qui sunt in uicinis regionibus predictarum.
Et licet quinta persequucio contra clericos incepta fuerit per imperatorem
Fredericum et postea per Nachaonem regem Egypti, seu Francie, sub quo
115 papa Bonifacius captus et pocionatus est, seu eciam per ducem Bauarie seu
imperatorem, sub quo diuisa fuit uniuersalis ecclesia, constituto ydolo pseudo
papa in ciuitate romana, tamen circa finem huius temporis et in principio
sexti, sub Naboccodonosor romano cesare, ex semine Frederici predicti,
qualis ab inicio non fuit tribulacio seu persequucio contra ecclesiam expec-
120 tatur, et hoc in transmigracione predicta, sicut in apercione sexti sigilli,
clarius apparebit.

Sextum signaculum ueteris testamenti. Sextum signaculum ueteris testamenti incepit in Ezechiele et Daniele, consumatum uero est in Hesdra et
Neemia. Sub hoc sexto tempore continetur transmigracio Ierusalem et
125 percucio Babilonis, necnon et tribulaciones due quam maxime orte contra
filios Ysrahel, in quibus timore insolito concussa sunt corda eorum: prima
fuit sub Ezechiele et Daniele, que legitur in libro Iudith, sub Nabucodonosor
rege assiriorum; secunda fuit sub Iosue sacerdote magno et Zorobabel filio
Salatiel, sub quibus edificatum est templum Domini et muri ciuitatis in
130 angustia temporum,[17] prophetantibus in Iudea Aggeo et Zacharia, et post
ipsos Malachia. Ista tribulacio legitur in Ester, sub rege Assuero, qui regnauit
super cxxviii prouincias, siue sub Anthioco rege, cunctas aliorum temporum
tribulaciones excellens, et cetera.

Sextum signaculum noui testamenti. Sub apercione sexti signaculi noui
135 testamenti continetur iterata persequucio quarte bestie Apocalipsis xiii° siue
regni quarti et x regum suorum insurgencium contra romanum imperium et
contra ecclesiam, unde pro hoc Apocalipsis xvii° dicitur: *Et x cornua que
uidisti in bestia x reges sunt qui regnum nondum acceperunt, sed potestatem
tamquam reges,* una hora seu uno et eodem sexto concurrente tempore,
140 *accipient,* hii unum consilium habebunt contra Christianitatem, scilicet *et
potestatem suam bestie,* seu soldano, *tradent;*[18] sedes enim bestie Babilonia
est. Sequitur: *Hii hodient fornicariam,* seu carnalem ecclesiam, licet enim

---

112 super *om.* T   116 ecclesia *om.* T   117 et *om.* T   in² *om.* BV   120 hoc
om. BTV   in¹ *om.* T   sexti] tercii BTV; signaculi seu *add.* TV   123 uero *om.* BV
127 et Daniele *om.* T   legis BTV   129 Domini *om.* BTV   131 Assuero rege *tr.*
BTV   132 supra T   134 *Rubrica*] Sub isto continetur iterata persecucio BTV
136 suorum *om.* BTV   136-137 et contra ecclesiam *om.* T   137 dicitur *post* hoc
tr. BTV   138 que nondum regnum T   142-143 licet ... ecclesiam *om.* T *per hom.*

---

[17] Cf. *Septem Sigillis,* p. 244; cf. also *Expos.,* fols. 7v-8r.
[18] Apoc. 17.12.

contra Christum et uniuersam ecclesiam tunc insurgant, Christus tamen non tradet eorum manibus nisi ecclesiam carnalium christianorum. Sequitur: *Et*
145 *desolatam facient illam, et nudam, et carnes,* seu simplices, *eius manduca-bunt,*[19] seu ad manducandum bestie tradent, et fame et gladio deuorabunt, et ossa eius, seu forciores eius, igne ardebunt, unde ibidem vi° dicitur quod, *data est illis potestas interficere gladio, fame, et morte, et bestiis terre.*[20] Sequitur: *Deus enim dedit in corda eorum ut faciant quod illi placitum est, ut dent*
150 *regnum suum,* seu potestatem suam, *bestie, donec consumentur uerba Dei. Et mulier quam uidisti est ciuitas magna,* seu ecclesia per totum orbem diffusa, *que habet regnum super omnes reges terre,*[21] et cetera.

Sub hoc tempore sexto incipiet transmigrare spiritualis Ysrahel quousque percuciatur noua Babilon,[22] unde quinque sunt hic actendenda que in ueteri
155 modo consimili continentur: primo, transmigracio Ierusalem, seu spiritualis ecclesia; secundo, percucio Babilonis noue; tercio, tribulacio prima sub illo rege xi°; quarto, rehedificacio templi et murorum ciuitatis; quinto et ultimo, tribulacio secunda sub magno Antichristo.[23]

Primum igitur quod tangitur hic est transmigracio illa spiritalis Ierusalem,
160 seu ecclesie electorum, ad deserta gentilium a facie serpentis Antichristi. Vnde sicut circa principium primi status ueteris, post xii patriarchas, Moyses et Aaron uiri nominati eduxerunt populum Ysrael de Egypto a facie populi egypciaci persequentis, et sicut circa principium secundi status noui, post xii apostolos, electi sunt a Domino Paulus et Barnabas, qui prepararent uiam
165 populo fideli egresso de sinagoga a facie populi iudaici persequentis, sic circa principium tercii status plenitudinis, post xii uiros euangelicos, eligentur duo uiri notabiles a Spiritu sancto ad preparandum uiam populo fideli egressuro de ecclesia carnalium christianorum a facie populi babilonici persequentis, ut transeuntes per deserta gentilium introheant in terram fluentem lac et mel.[24]

---

144 christianorum carnalium *tr.* BTV   149 eorum] ipsorum BTV   150 seu ... suam *om.* T   consumetur M   152 et cetera *om.* BTV   153 Sub] et *praem.* BTV 154 ueteri] testamento *add.* BTV   163 sicut *om.* BV   165 populo *om.* BV 167 preparandum] predicandum uel *praem.* BV   fidei BV   168 ut] et BTV

---

[19] Apoc. 17.16.
[20] Apoc. 6.8.
[21] Apoc. 17.17-18; cf. *Lib. Conc.*, fol. 41v; *Expos.*, fol. 197r.
[22] Cf. *Septem Sigillis*, pp. 244-245.
[23] The *Liber secretorum eventorum* of Johannes de Rupescissa also cites five disasters that will occur before the appearance of the great Antichrist, but his list differs from this one.
[24] *Lib. Conc.*, fol. 44r, and see also fols. 21r-22r, 57v-58r.

170   Illa enim fuga quam Christus fecit cum matre sua de Ierusalem in Egyptum
      a facie Herodis,[25] et tum sexto anno reuersus est Ierusalem, ubi fuit sub
      secundo Herode passus, significat illam fugam seu transmigracionem quam
      fecit summus pontifex cum matre ecclesia de Roma in dominium regis
      Francie a facie imperatorum, scilicet Frederici et ceterorum qui opprimebant
175   eam, et si de manu imperatoris Frederici et aliorum in quinto tempore uoluit
      euadere, ad manus tamen eiusdem Frederici in aliquo de suo semine et
      romanorum tirannorum sexto anno, seu sexto tempore eius, uelit nolit,
      oportebit eam redire, sub quo in ea Christus iterum passietur, sicut ipse Petro
      dixit: *Vado Romam iterum crucifigi,*[26] et hoc ut transmigracio babilonica
180   misterialiter impleatur.
         Illa autem fuga seu ascensus ille spontaneus quem Christus fecit post
      babtismum de Iordano in desertum significat illam fugam spontaneam seu
      transmigracionem quam aliqui uiri spirituales debent facere de Christianitate
      ad partes infidelium nacionum. Illa similiter fuga quam fecerunt omnes
185   discipuli, cena facta, in illa nocte tenebrarum capcionis et condempnacionis
      uite et persone Christi, fugientes hinc inde sicut grex dispersus sine pastore,
      per deserta et speluncas moncium, nec unus alium expectabat, significat illam
      fugam terribilem quam facturi sunt uiri euangelici et uiri spirituales, cena
      facta, in viiiª distincione huius libri expressa. In illa nocte tenebrarum
190   condempnacionis uite et doctrine euangelici status fugient hinc inde, sicut
      grex dispersus sine pastore, per deserta et speluncas moncium, nec unus
      alium expectabit. Illa uero fuga quam fecerunt omnes Christi discipuli ad
      gentes inminente excidio Ierusalem et sinagoge illam significat fugam que
      tangitur hic, quam omnes electi de ecclesia pro maiori parte facient ad gentes
195   inminente excidio romani imperii, seu ecclesie romane, et sicut columba ex
      archa egressa atulit ramum oliue in signum pacis, et sicut castissima Iudith,
      egressa de Bethulia, filiis Israel truncato capite Olofernis retulit uerbum pacis,
      sic ex artitudine arche spiritualis ecclesie egressura est quasi columba et quasi
      altera Iudith spiritualis quedam turba iustorum per donum Spiritus sancti
200   sicut columba effecta ad predicandum uerbum Dei, que reuersura nunciet
      pacem dandam uelocius super terram.[27]

---

170 enim] tamen T   fecit Christus *tr.* T   de] in T   173 dominium] domum BTV
178 redire] reddere T   183 transmigracionem] transfiguracionem BV   186 dis-
persus] fuit *add.* T   188 facti TV   uiri euangelici et *om.* T *per hom.*   190 con-
dempnacionis] damnacionis BTV   doctrine] Christe et *add.* BTV   192 Christi
discipuli] populi Christi T   192-193 ad gentes *om.* BTV   194 de ecclesia *om.* BTV
198-199 ecclesie ... spiritualis *om.* BV *per hom.*   200 reuersa BTV

---

[25] Cf. *Quat. evang.*, p. 99; *Super Hier.*, fol. 43v.
[26] *Passio sanct. apost.*, p. 171.
[27] *Lib. Conc.*, fol. 24v, and see also fols. 23v-24v.

Secundo tangitur sic percucio noue Babilonis que scripta est in sexta parte
Apocalipsis, reuera enim percucietur Babilon, populus scilicet qui dicitur
christianus et, *non est, sed est sinagoga Sathane;*[28] qui ueri autem sunt
205 christiani a cunctis harum tribulacionibus liberandi sunt.[29] Hec enim percucio
ita subito ueniet et ita in die christianis innota et improuisa ut hii qui
intrinsecus sunt nesciant quid agere debeant contra tam terribiles exercitus
eorum qui foris sunt, uel erunt, ex omni parte et ex omni plaga, orientali
scilicet et septentrionali, occidentali et australi, in furore magno et in inpetu
210 spiritus uenientes. Tunc enim, *peribit a sapiente consilium,*[30] et fugiet a sene
discrecio,[31] et a diuite spes et a leui cursore fuga;[32] non enim erit eis fuga. *In
tempore autem illo querent homines mortem, et fugiet mors ab eis; desiderabunt mori et non inuenient eam.*[33] Vnde Mathei xxiiii° pro ista materia dicitur:
*Sicut autem fuit in diebus Noe, ita erit aduentus Filii hominis; sicut enim erant
215 in diebus ante diluuium comedentes et bibentes, nubentes et nuptui tradentes,
usque ad eum diem quo intrauit in archam Noe, et non cognouerunt donec
uenit diluuium et tulit omnes, ita erit aduentus Filii hominis,*[34] in regalibus
scilicet exercitibus orientis. Sequitur: *Tunc duo erunt in agro,* scilicet culture
ecclesie, *unus assumetur et alius relinquetur;*[35] *duo in lecto,* scilicet contempla-
220 tiue, *unus assumetur et alius relinquetur, et due molentes in mola,*[36] scilicet
actiue; sicut enim differt mulier a uiro, sic actiua et contemplatiua, tamen una
assumetur et alia relinquetur; tunc enim in omni statu fiet segregacio filiorum
Dei a filiis hominum. Tantus enim timor et tremor et pauor tunc irruet in
populum christianum quod ante perderent spem uictorie et confidenciam
225 uirium quam perueniatur ad bellum. Et quoniam et in Apocalipsi dicitur quod
tercia pars maris facta est sanguis, et tercia pars nauigii interiit,[37] oportebit

---

203 scilicet *om.* T   204-205 autem ueri christiani sunt *tr.* BTV   208 uel erunt *om.*
M[ac]   209 et[1] *om.* BTV   in[2] *om.* BTV   210 uenientes] Ezechielis septimo *add.* BTV
210-211 Tunc ... fuga *om.* V   210 consilium *ante* a *tr.* BTV   211 a leui] alieni T
fuga[2]] ruga T   212 mors fugiet *tr.* BTV   213 inueniet M   Vnde *om.* T
214 Sicut[1]] Sic M   erant enim *tr.* BTV   215 nupcii M   218 scilicet] siue BTV
219-220 contemplacionis BTV   220 et[1] *om.* T   221 sic] uita *add.* BTV   et *om.*
M[ac]   223 enim] erit *add.* BTV   225 superueniatur T   et[2] *om.* BTV

---

[28] Apoc. 2.9.
[29] *Septem Sigillis,* p. 244.
[30] Cf. Is. 29.14; Jer. 18.18.
[31] Cf. Ez. 7.26.
[32] Cf. Jer. 2.23, 9.23.
[33] Apoc. 9.6.
[34] Mt. 24.38-39.
[35] Mt. 24.40.
[36] Lc. 17.34; Mt. 24.41.
[37] Apoc. 8.8-9.

tres communitates christianorum in mari per guerras ad bella insurgere, et
tercie partis mare sanguine tingere et terciam partem nauigii interire, ut sic
iam excitato sexto drachonis capite, destructis uniuerse Christianitatis muris
230 seu comunitatibus in mari, hii qui foris sunt, scilicet sarraceni, sine bellatorum resistencia liberum habeant in ipsam Christianitatem ingressum; quid
enim aliud predicant nisi ut, si daretur oportunitas, Christianitatem possent
destruere et legem macumeticam ampliare? Vnde sicut primum diluuium
aquarum inumdancium super peccatores terre tempore ueteri, scilicet Noe,
235 primum dilluuium aquarum infidelium nacionum cum Thito et Vespesiano
inumdancium super Ierusalem, seu super sinagogam iudeorum tempore
nouo, scilicet Christi, per concordiam respicit,[38] sic secundum dilluuium seu
exterminium ueteris Babilonis secundum diluuium seu exterminium noue
Babilonis ostendit. Igitur callidus nauta a primo dilluuio temporis ueteris
240 usque ad secundum, scilicet ueteris Babilonis, computet miliaria seu generaciones, ut inter duo temporis noui sciat quid tenet; a Noe autem usque ad
Zorobabel, sub quo fuit ruina ueteris Babilonis, fuerunt incluse generaciones
xliiii; a resurreccione Domini usque ad excidium Ierusalem fuerunt anni xlii,
ex quibus prefatis materia satis claret.
245   Tercio tangitur hic prima tribulacio sub Nabocodonosor rege assiriorum,
qui sexto ecclesie tempore, tamquam caput bestialium nacionum, cum
omnibus regibus aquilonaribus et orientalibus contra romanum imperium et
contra ecclesiam insurget, ut uerificetur illud Yeremie i°: *Quia ab aquilone*
pandetur omne malum super omnes habitatores terre,[39] et cetera. Tamen
250 Assiria secundum sui interpretacionem, que dirigens aut direccio seu sus-
tollens laborantes interpretatur, aliquod regnum infra romanum imperium
seu christianorum metas designat, in quo iste rex xi^us qui debet laborantes
extollere et terram quasi desertam ponere dirigetur. Vnde respectu sui regni
proprii rex assiriorum dicitur, rex uero Babilonis respectu romani imperii
255 nuncupatur, ut quod in fine quinti temporis per eum incipiendum est, in
tempore sexto per eundem sub utroque nomine impleatur, unde pro presenti
materia Danielis viii° dicitur: *Et ecce aries unus stabat ante paludem, habens*
duo cornua excelsa, et unum excelsius altero atque succrescens, et postea uidi
arietem uentilantem contra occidentem, et contra aquilonem, et contra
260 *meridiem, et omnes bestie non poterant resistere ei neque liberari de manu*

---

228 terciam] tercia *codd.*   interire] in terra V   241 inter duo] in triduo BTV
autem *om.* BTV   242 quo] que BTV   245 regis *codd.*   246 tempore *om.* M^ac
tamquam *om.* BV   249 Tamen] In T   250 interpretacionem sui *tr.* BTV
250-251 sustollens] sensus tollens BTV   251 aliquid BTV   252 designat BTV   255 ut]
unde T   258 altero *om.* BV   succrecetis BV; sucresecutis T   260 ei *rep.* M

---

[38] Cf. *Lib. Conc.*, fols. 23v, 43v.
[39] Jer. 1.14.

eius, fecitque secundum uoluntatem suam et magnificatus est. Ecce yrcus caprarum ueniebat ab occidente super faciem tocius terre et non tangebat terram, porro yrcus habebat cornu insigne inter oculos suos, et uenit usque ad arietem illum cornutum et efferatus est in eum, et comminuit duo cornua eius,
265 *et non poterat aries resistere ei, cumque eum misisset in terram, conculcauit et nemo poterat liberare arietem de manu eius. Yrcus autem caprarum magnus factus est nimis, cumque creuisset fractum est cornu magnum et orta sunt iiii^{or} cornua subter illud; de uno autem ex eis egressum est cornu unum modicum, et factum est grande contra meridiem, et contra orientem et contra fortitudi-*
270 *nem, et magnificatum est usque ad fortitudinem celi, et deiecit de fortitudine et de stellis et conculcauit eas, et usque ad principem fortitudinis magnificatum est, et ab eo tulit iuge sacrificium et deiecit locum sanctificacionis eius. Robur autem datum est ei contra iuge sacrificium propter peccata et prosternetur ueritas in terra et faciet et prosperabitur.*[40]

275 Sequitur: *Aries, quem uidisti habere cornua, rex medorum atque persarum est. Porro yrcus caprarum rex grecorum est, et cornu grande, quod erat inter oculos, ipse est rex primus, quod autem fracto illo surrexerunt iiii^{or} pro eo, quatuor reges de gente eius consurgent, sed non in fortitudine eius, et post regnum ipsorum, cum creuerint iniquitates, consurget rex inpudens facie et*
280 *intelligens proposiciones, et roborabitur fortitudo eius, sed non in uiribus suis, et supra quam credi potest uniuersa uastabit, et prosperabitur, et faciet, et interficiet robustos et populum sanctorum secundum uoluntatem suam, et dirigetur dolus in manu eius, et cor suum magnificabit, et in copia rerum omnium occidet plurimos, et contra principem principum consurget, et sine*
285 *manu conteretur,*[41] et cetera.

[*Glosa.* Licet enim Alexander rex quatuor successores principales habuerit, qui non suis uiribus set iure hereditario regna consecuti sunt adoptiuo modo, de uno quorum egressus est ille Anthiocus, illustris rex inpudens facie, et cetera, tamen finaliter inperium eius inter reges multos pro maiori parte
290 diuisum est, de uno quorum predictorum, et cetera.]

---

261 eius] ecce yrcus caprarum ue *add.* M^{ac}   fecitque ... est *om.* BTV   270 et¹ *om.* T   271 magnificatus M   273 et] ut *add.* BTV   274 prosperabitur] uerbi dicit *add.* BTV   275 Sequitur] textus *add.* BTV   276 est¹ *post* medorum (l. 275) *tr.* BTV 277 eo] quod *add.* BV   281 uniuersa] terra *add.* T   283 in² *om.* BV   286 rex Alexander *tr.* BTV   286-287 habuerit] habundant BV   289-290 tamen ... cetera *om.* T *per hom.*

---

[40] Dan. 8.3-12.
[41] Dan. 8.20-25.

In predictis enim uerbis, ut dicit Iohannes, describitur casus regni Sicilie, regni Francie, et regni ecclesie.[42] Vnde sicut regnum medorum regnum francorum per concordiam tangit, sic regnum grecorum regnum yspanorum per eamdem ostendit, et sicut Persia uel Perssidis tangit Siciliam, ita
295 Macedonia Cathaliciam seu Cathaloniam, et sicut de Grecia seu Macedonia Alexander, rex paruus persona et despectus, ad percuciendum Darium regem medorum et ad cominuendum duo cornua eius egressus est, sic de Yspania, seu Cathalonia, egressurus est unus rex paruus persona et despectus ad percuciendum Darium regem francorum et ad cominuendum radicitus duo
300 cornua eius, ut quod per regem Petrum qui cepit Siciliam inceptum est, scilicet Karulo de Sicilia expulso et rege Francie in Cathalonia mortuo et eius exercitu tam in terra quam in mari deuicto, sub isto rege, seu cornu paruo de suo semine, totaliter impleatur,[43] et sicut per pullam aquile ille, sic et per pullam aquile iste excitandus est, et sicut regnum medorum et regnum
305 perssarum per duo cornua arietis, unum maius altero, ad licteram testante Daniele tanguntur, sic regnum Francie et regnum Sicilie per ipsa duo cornua, unum scilicet maius altero, figurali misterio ostenduntur, et cetera. Primum igitur cornu yrci insigne fuit rex primus, hoc est rex Petrus prefatus, cui unica pulla aquile unica est, qui tanquam horum que sequntur misteriorum princi-
310 pium, *ab occidente,* hoc est ab Yspania, *ueniens, super faciem tocius terre,* seu terrenorum sibi contradicencium, *et non tangebat terram,* per mare enim pro magna parte earum que fecit, et que in aliquo de suo semine facturus est, adimplebit. *Et comminuit,* et eciam radicitus in suo semine comminuet, *duo cornua eius,* et cetera, propter quod yrcus caprarum, seu regnum ipsius primi
315 cornus, seu regis predicti, magnum factum est. *Cumque creuisset,* scilicet in potencia, *fractum est,* per mortem scilicet corporalem, *et orta sunt iiii^{or} cornua,* hoc est iiii^{or} reges seu regales subter illud, de suo scilicet semine, in suis regnis diuisi sibi, quasi in concurrentibus temporibus succedentes,

---

291 Ioachim BTV   292 regni Francie *om.* BTV   293 francorum] et regnum medorum *add.* BV   294-295 ita ... Cathaliciam *om.* BV   295 sicut] sic T   Mace-donia] egressus est *add.* BTV   297 medorum] francorum BTV   297-299 duo ... cominuendum *om.* BTV *per hom.*   300 cepit *om.* T   301 scilicet Karulo] rege Karolo BTV   302 mari quam in terra *tr.* BTV   303 ille *om.* M^{ac}   et² *om.* BV   306 per] propter T   307 ostendunt T   311-312 pro ... semine *om.* M^{ac} 313 et² *om.* BV   315 regis] primi *add.* BTV   scilicet *om.* T   316 scilicet *om.* T   318 diuisum BTV   in *om.* BTV   currentibus M^{ac}

---

[42] This probably refers to some unidentified place in the *Postilla*; see also: *Lib. Conc.,* fol. 126r.

[43] The king described as *rex paruus persona* is Peter IV (Pere III); allusion is here also made to the victory of Peter II over Charles of Anjou, in 1283, by which the Aragonian monarchy gained control of Sicily, and of his defeat of Philip III's attempt to invade Catalonia in 1285.

scilicet rex Alfonsus, rex Iacobus, rex Fredericus, et infans Petrus. Sequitur:
320 *Sed non in fortitudine eius,* non enim iure belli, sed iure hereditario cunse-
quuti sunt regna.

[*Glosa.* Cum dicit casum regni ecclesie temporalem tantum, non spiritualem, intelligas; nauicula enim ecclesie, quamuis diuersis impellatur fluctibus, semper in sua uirtute manebit, quoniam fundata est supra firmam
325 petram, unde dixit Dominus Symoni: *Ecce, Sathanas expetiuit uos ut cribraret
sicut triticum; ego autem orabo pro te ut non defficiat fides tua.*[44]]

Sequitur: *Et post regnum ipsorum,* seu mortem ipsorum, *cum creuerint
iniquitates,* de uno ex eis, seu de semine unius illorum, egressum seu
egressurum est cornu unum modicum, hoc est unus rex paruus persona et
330 despectus, *inpudens facie, et intelligens proposiciones,* scilicet ueri et falsi.
Callidus enim et discernens erit, *et roborabitur fortitudo eius,* tempore enim
tocius discencionis et guerre in omni mundo, ut dicit Ioachim,[45] potencia
istius roborabitur et coronatos reges deponendo ampliabitur et magnificabitur. Sequitur: *Sed non in uiribus suis,* omnia enim euenient sibi facta, tum
335 quia propter intestinas guerras et diuisiones inter principes et tirannos et
communitates multi populi et multe regiones unientur sibi, tum quia v[e]
principes christianorum, ut dicit Ioachim, inherebunt sibi, tum quia propter
ligam quam faciet cum soldano multe infidelium naciones quibus in Apuliam
per Siciliam transitum dabit coadiuuabunt sibi. Dicit enim Ioachim quod in
340 Trinaclia exaltabitur cornu eius propter quod sequitur quod, *factum est
grande contra meridiem et contra orientem;* omnes enim meridionales et
orientales partes suo subiugauit imperio et debellando reges ortus usque ad
siccam arborem pertransibit. Sequitur: *Et contra fortitudinem,* scilicet romani
imperii, domibus duorum regum, scilicet Francie et Sicilie, radicitus commi-
345 nutis, unde Ioachim: *Florentem deflorendo subiciet et uniuersa lilia euellendo
conteret et confringet.* Sequitur: *Et magnificatum est usque ad fortitudinem
celi.* Hic incipit describere persequucionem regni ecclesie, unde Gregorius:
Regnum celorum presentis temporis ecclesia dicitur.[46] Nam sicut in celo sunt

---

320 enim *om.* T   hereditatis BTV   322 Cum dicit] Nota hic glosa super illud
quod superius dicitur BTV   323 impleatur T   324 super T   325 petram] ad partem
add. T   326 orabo] rogaui BTV   tua] et cetera *add.* BTV   327 Sequitur] de predictis *add.* BTV   328 de[2] *om.* BV   egressum seu *om.* BTV; seu egressurum *om.* M[ac]
333 et *om.* BTV   337 quia *om.* BTV   339 et adiuuabunt BT; et adiuuabit V
344 radicitus] penitus et *praem.* T   345 uniuersa lilia] uniuersalia BV   347 ecclesie
regni *tr.* BTV

---

[44] Lc. 22.31-32.
[45] The work to which reference is here repeatedly made has not been identified.
[46] Gregory, *Homiliarum in Evangelia,* 2.38.2 (PL 76.1282).

tres ordines stellarum, scilicet superiorum, que in firmamento, mediocrum
350 seu errancium, que in regione planetica, et inferiorum, que in spera ignis
prenostice nuncupantur; uel eciam superiorum, que circa polum artichum,
mediarum seu mediocrum, que scilicet infra circulum articum et antarticum,
et inferiorum, que circa polum antarticum stabili fixione consistunt, sic et tres
gerarchie seu gradus in ecclesia esse dicuntur, scilicet superiorum, qui est
355 prelacionis, mediorum, qui est religionis, inferiorum, qui est tocius multitudinis. Et sicut omnes stelle uno sole illuminantur, sic omnes supradicti status
uno papa seu summo pontifice gubernantur, unde iste rex dicitur magnificatus usque ad fortitudinem celi, quia usque ad fortitudinem ecclesie
magnificandus est, ut eciam de fortitudine et de stellis deiciat, et ideo
360 sequitur: *Et deiciet de fortitudine et de stellis;* non enim dicit, *deiciet fortitudinem,* sed *de fortitudine,* non enim fortitudinem spiritualis regiminis, que
firmiter supra firmam petram a Deo stabilita est, deiciet seu deicere poterit,
sed regiminis temporalis, quia fortitudo illorum tamquam stellarum errancium in suo motu, non in firmamento diuine sapiencie, sed in spera uolubili
365 mundane confidencie est firmata, propter quod de celo, seu firmamento
predicto, triplici casu, spirituali scilicet et temporali necnon et eternali,
finaliter erunt iudicio diuino deiecti. Illi uero qui in celo seu firmamento
predicto firmati sunt tantum temporalem portabunt. Et ideo *deiciet,* hoc est
ad sui consensum uel minis, uel precibus, uel promissionibus inclinabit, ut
370 scilicet consenciant in illum quem ipse uoluerit instituere principem in loco
sancto, hoc est filium perdicionis in templo. Illi uero qui tanto sceleri
assensum dare noluerint de locis suis seu sedibus deiciet et alios sibi
consencientes in illis scilicet locis instituet, propter quod sequitur: *et
conculcauit eos,* hoc est iuxta uolumtatem et placitum duxit eas, seu fecit de
375 eis, in predictam scilicet elecionem prebendo consensum, et ideo sequitur:
et usque ad principem fortitudinis magnificatus est; princeps enim predicte
fortitudinis summus pontifex est, qui non de spirituali sede, sed temporali,
per istum regem debet deponi, et alius pseudo loco eius institui. Sequitur: *et
ab eo tulit iuge sacrificium;* occasiones enim et cause multe orientur inter
380 ipsum regem et summum pontificem antequam ad eius deposicionem et

---

349 qui in *om.* BV   351 antarticum BTV   352 que] sunt *add.* T   351-
352 artichum ... et² *om.* B *per hom.*   353 circa] polum antarticum mediarum que infra
circulum sunt, scilicet articum et antarticum que circa *add.* V   356 sole] solo lumine BTV
357 summo] supremo BV   rex] dominus *add.* M^ac   358 celi] ecclesie *add.* M^ac
360 et de stellis *om.* BTV   dicit *om.* T   361 enim] licet BTV   spiritualis M
362 est *ante* a *tr.* BTV   364 in² *om.* T   366 eternali] carnali BV   368 portabunt]
penam *add.* BTV   370 illum *om.* T   371 est] in *add.* T   seleri M   372 dare]
dant uel *praem.* BTV   seu] de *add.* BV   373 in *om.* T   restituet BV   374 pla-
citum] suum *add.* BTV   377 summus *om.* BTV   378 istum] illum BV   eius] sui
BTV; debet *add.* BTV   379 enim] licet BV; scilicet T

sacrificii ablacionem perueniatur. Sequitur: *et deiciet locum sanctificacionis eius;* iste inquid locus sanctificacionis aut stricto modo aut largo sumi potest; si autem stricto modo sumatur, pro ecclesia et palacio summi sacerdotis, seu Rome seu Auinione fundatis, potest intelligi; si autem largo modo sumitur,
385 pro omnibus ecclesiis in uniuersa Christianitate fundatis potest exponi, que tunc sub pressura istius regis, tam per sonitum maris nacionum infidelium quam per fluctus tirannorum inperii romani, deicientur et ad terram prosternentur. Sequitur: *Robur autem datum est ei,* hoc est potencia permicione diuina, contra iuge sacrificium; tot enim et tanta erunt abominaciones et
390 scelera et scandala clericorum et religiosorum per uniuersum orbem, ut ab uniuersis in uituperio et contentu eorum sacrificium habeatur, et isti regi detur potencia ut premissum sacrificium faciat cessare ubique, et ideo sequitur, *propter peccata,* et quoniam nondum segregate erunt palee pessimorum a tritico electorum, quia nondum de electis noticia erit plena, quoniam
395 habitus non facit monacum, ab illis qui uere stelle sunt, in cauernis seu in spelunciis moncium sacrificium continuabitur in occulto. Sequitur: *Et prosternetur ueritas,* scilicet euangelica, *in terra,* primo sub mistico Antichristo, secundo sub Antichristo magno per condempnacionem diuinitatis in Christo; dicent enim Christum non esse Deum, sed illum pseudo prophetam cuius
400 aduentus in signis et prodigiis mendacibus secundum operacionem Sathene erit, ut ait apostolus,[47] unde Matheus, xxiv°: *Tunc si quis uobis dixerit: Ecce, Christus hic est, aut illic, nolite credere; surgent enim pseudo Christi et pseudo prophete, et dabunt signa magna et prodigia, ut in errorem inducantur, si fieri potest, eciam electi. Ecce, predixi uobis,*[48] et cetera. Sequitur: *et faciet,* scilicet
405 iste rex, *secundum uoluntatem suam, et prosperabitur,* scilicet de bono in melius, *et in copia rerum occidet plurimos,* quosdam scilicet spiritualiter et quosdam corporaliter, ut prefatum est, *et interficiet robustos,* seu magnates et tirannos, *et populum sanctorum secundum uoluntatem suam,* nam etsi corporaliter iusti pereunt, eternaliter semper uiuunt, *et dirigetur dolus,* huius

---

382 stricto] scripto M^ac   summi M   383 stricto] scripto M   sacerdotis]
pontificis BTV   383-384 seu ... seu] siue ... siue BV   384 summitur M   386 tunc]
currit T   maris *om.* BTV   387 imperio romano BTV   390 orbem] mundum BTV
393 et *om.* T   nondum] sunt *add.* T   394 de *om.* M^ac   395 sunt stelle *tr.*
BTV   400 aduentus] est *add.* BV   402 Christus *post* est *tr.* BTV   illic] et
cetera *add.* BTV   403 magna *post* prodigia *tr.* V; in populo ita *add.* BTV   inducantur] transeant et inducant BTV   404 scilicet] suple BTV   405 scilicet *om.* BTV
406 quosdam ... et *om.* V *per hom.*   407 seu] et T   408 et *om.* BV   etsi *om.* T

---

[47] Cf. 2 Thes. 2.9.
[48] Mt. 24.23-25.

410 perquucionis scilicet, *in manu eius,* quoniam, ut predictum est, *ultra quam credi potest uniuersa uastabit.* Sequitur eius finis: *et sine manu conteretur,* non enim in furore nec in prelio, sed morte sua morietur; dicit enim Ioachim quod, tribus de x regibus per eum humiliatis, transibit cum reliquis ad conterendam superbiam infidelium soldanorum et in terra gloriosa, quam
415 summo pontifici tradet, animam Deo reddet.[49]

Quarto tangitur hic rehedificacio templi et murorum ciuitatis in angustia temporum seu duarum tribulacionum; interea enim multi fidelium coronabuntur martirio et hedificabitur rursum sancta ciuitas, que est ecclesia electorum, ascendente nouo duce, seu nouo pontifice noue Ierusalem ecclesie
420 uniuerse, fauore regis perssarum seu Sicilie succurrente, sicut factum est in diebus Zorobabel et Iosue et Esdre et Nehemie, sub quibus illa uetus Ierusalem consumacionem accepit, et cetera.[50]

Quinto et ultimo tangitur hic secunda tribulacio, sub magno scilicet Antichristo, de quo in Danielis xi° dicitur: *Et ecce, tres reges stabunt in*
425 *Persside,* seu in Sicilia post scilicet regem Petrum Aragonum, qui cepit eam, per rectam lineam descendentes, *et quartus,* scilicet rex a predictis, *ditabitur opibus nimis super omnes, et cum inualuerit diuiciis, concitabit omnes,* scilicet magnates suos et nobiles, *aduersus regnum Grecie,* et obtinebit uniuersum regnum Grecie et omnia regna terre tradentur in manu eius ut alter rex
430 Perssarum, cum Zorobabel pontifice nouo rehedificabit templum Domini et muros ciuitatis sancte, et erit in pace imperium eius. Hoc autem firmiter teneas, ut dicit Ioachim, quod inperium finiet in Sicilia in semine imperatoris Frederici secundi.[51]

[*Glosa.* Cum dicit, *et quartus scilicet rex a predictis,* non per rectam
435 generacionis lineam descendendo, sed per transuersalem ueniendo intelligas; non enim per rectam lineam a predictis tribus regibus descendet, sed per transuersalem ueniet, in cuius temporibus ille iniquus seu aduerssarius perdicionis filius in templo Dei, tanquam sit Deus, sublimandus est.]

---

410 ultra] autem T   413 de *om.* T   transibit ... ad *om.* BTV   414 super-
biam] inimicorum scilicet *add.* BTV   415 animam] et *add.* T; et tunc *add.* BV   419 seu]
siue BTV   421 et[2] *om.* BV   424 in ... dicitur] dicitur in Daniele BTV   Et *om.* BTV
426-427 ditabitur ... omnes *om.* T   427 nimis] multis B   430 pontifice] principe BTV
432 finiet] fiet BTV   434 Cum dicit] Dicit glosa super hoc BV   Cum ... predictis
om. T   436 non] nam T   437 seu *om.* BTV   438 filius prediccionis BTV
est] textus *add.* BV; ceptus *add.* T

---

[49] Dan. 8.24-25; Joachim's work is unidentified.
[50] *Septem Sigillis,* pp. 244-245; cf. *Lib. Conc.,* fol. 56r.
[51] Dan. 11.2; *Super Esaiam,* fols. 39v-40r.

Sequitur: *Surget uero rex fortis*; iste inquid rex fortis non secularis sed
440 ecclesiasticus erit, qui non in suis uiribus, sed in uiribus predicti scilicet regis
quarti seu xi[i] surget, *et faciet quod placuerit illi,* nam per eius et per suorum
pseudo prophetarum consilia et sue sequele potenciam et cooperaciones
aquiretur imperium dicto regi, per quem statuetur in suo falso papatu, ut dicit
Iohannes,[52] et propter signa et mirabilia que dabuntur illi facere, ut deceptus
445 tanquam alter Nero a Simone mago, ipsum faciet adorari ut Deum. Sequitur:
Et cum steterit, scilicet in suo forti dominio mensibus scilicet xlii[bus], ut in
Apocalipsi dicitur,[53] *conteretur regnum eius in iiii[or] uentos celi,* hoc est in
uirtute predicancium euangelium a quatuor partibus mundi, ut post eum non
sit successor in potencia, *qua dominatus est,* et ideo sequitur: *sed non in*
450 *posteros eius, neque in potencia illius qua dominatus est,*[54] in cuius temporibus, *confortabitur rex austri,*[55] seu summus sacerdos. Hic uidetur quod
nondum erit deposita domus Francie, sed tunc erit principium destruccionis
sue quia, seducta pecunia et diuersis ecclesie adiutoriis et eciam comota
propter casum regni Sicilie, sumet occasiones contra illum regem xi[um] et
455 contra Antichristum, et ideo sequitur: *et de principibus eius,* rex scilicet austri,
preualebit super eum,[56] scilicet Antichristum, seu regem fortem prefatum, qui
et hic rex aquilonis figuraliter nuncupatur; oportebit enim regem austri, seu
uerum pontificem, ne lupi rapaces sub manu tam orrendi mercenarii possint
gregem suum inuadere, tanquam alter Michael et angeli eius contra dracho-
460 nem serpentem antiquam, scilicet aquilonis regem, et spiritualiter et temporaliter preliare.[57]
[*Glosa.* Hic tamen notes quod istud bellum inter regem austri et regem
aquilonis, hoc est inter uerum pontificem et pseudo pontificem Antichristum,
totum erit spirituale, sed mediantibus istis regibus, scilicet Francie et illo rege
465 undecimo, erit temporale. Vnde et hic, quo ad bellum spirituale, uerus

---

439 Surgendo BV   uero *om.* BV   440 non *om.* T   sed in uiribus *om.* T   scilicet predicti *tr.* T   441 per[2] *om.* BTV   442 et[1] *om.* T   potencia *codd.*
443 dicto] dicti *codd.*   statuentur BV   444 Ioachim BTV   446 steterit] sederit BTV
scilicet[1] *om.* BTV   scilicet[2] *om.* BTV   447 conteret T   eius *om.* BTV
449-450 et ideo ... est *om.* BV *per hom.*   453 et[2] *om.* BTV   454 sument BV
455 Antichristum] et ideo ... est, *ex ll. 449-450 add. et* in cuius ... Antichristum *ex ll. 450-455*
rep. BV   458 ne] ut T   460-461 temporaliter et spiritualiter *tr.* BTV   462 regem
austri et *om.* BV *per hom.*   464 scilicet *om.* V

---

[52] *Postilla,* fol. 101r.
[53] Apoc. 13.5.
[54] Dan. 11.3-4.
[55] Dan. 11.5.
[56] Dan. 11.5.
[57] Cf. *Lib. Conc.,* fol. 132v.

pontifex rex austri dicitur et pseudo pontifex rex aquilonis, nam Deus ab astro ueniet et ab aquilone pandetur omne malum, et cetera; quo ad bellum uero temporale, rex Francie rex austri dicitur, et ille rex undecimus rex aquilonis, et ideo rex austri, prouocatus multis auxiliis, et cetera.]

470 Sequitur: *Filiaque regis austri,* hoc est ecclesia seu legati ecclesie, timendo scilicet potenciam illius regis xi, *ueniet ad regem aquilonis facere amiciciam,* ut scilicet cum blandiciis et promissionibus possit ipsum a suo errore retrahere et a tanto malo et periculo deuiare. Sequitur: *Et non obtinebit fortitudinem brachii,* illius regis scilicet dominantis, sed *tradetur ipsa,* scilicet

475 ecclesia seu legati ecclesie, *et qui adduxerunt,* seu sociauerunt, *eam adolescentes eius et qui confortabant,* idest manu tenebant, *eam* detinebuntur, seu in capcione ponentur, *in temporibus,*[58] hoc est annis aliquantis, *et prouocatus rex austri egredietur, et pugnabit aduersus regem aquilonis, et preparabit multitudinem nimiam, et dabitur multitudo in manu eius. Et capiet multitu-*

480 *dinem, et exaltabitur cor eius, et deiciet multa milia, sed non preualebit.*[59] Rex uero aquilonis, *stabit in loco eius uilissimus,* scilicet quoad Deum, *et indignus decore regio, et in paucis diebus conteretur, et stabit in loco eius despectus,* quia in prefato bello uictoriam minime hebere potuit, *et non tribuetur ei honor regius, sed ueniet,* seu surget, *clam,* callido scilicet modo et palliato, *et*

485 *obtinebit regnum,* seu apostolicam sedem, *in fraudulencia,* et cum modico populo superabit, *et brachia pugnantis,* scilicet regis austri, *expugnabuntur a facie eius,*[60] *et filiam feminarum dabit illi ut auertat illum, et non stabit, nec illius erit.*[61] Hec enim filia feminarum erit quedam caterua ecclesiasticorum ab omni ecclesiastica gererchia egressa, ut filii ancille a filiis libere, molles,

490 delicati, picti, compti et ornati, tumultuosi, leues, mobiles et instabiles sicut femine, et ideo *filia feminarum* non per generacionem sed per mutacionem caterua predicta dicitur, que *dabit illi,* scilicet regi aquilonis, uocem scilicet et potestatem tocius elecionis, *ut euertat illum,* scilicet pontificem uerum, *et non stabit illa,* scilicet elecio, quoad Deum, *nec illius erit,* quia Deus eam non

495 approbabit, sed pocius reprobabit, *et in fine temporum annorum rex aquilonis,* seu Antichristus, *preparabit multitudinem maiorem quam prius, et ueniet*

---

470 Sequitur] textus *praem.* BTV   470-471 timendo ... potenciam] scilicet timendo suam potenciam scilicet BTV   472 posset BTV   475 associauerunt BTV 477 aliquantis] et transactis *add.* BV   484 seu] siue BTV   scilicet callido *tr.* BTV 487 dabitur BTV   491 mutacionem] imitacionem BV   492 predicitur T   494 nec] neque BV   496 prius] primus BV   ueniens BTV

---

[58] Dan. 11.6.
[59] Dan. 11.11.
[60] Dan. 11.20-22.
[61] Dan. 11.17.

prosperans et inundans cum exercitu magno et opibus nimiis, et capiet urbes
munitissimas, et brachia austri non sustinebunt.[62] *Et in temporibus illis multi*
consurgent aduersus regem austri; filii quoque preuaricatorum, permutacio-
500 nem scilicet, *extollentur,* per superbiam scilicet indignati, aliqua occasione
accepta, contra regem austri, *et corruent,*[63] hoc est ad partem opositam se
conuertent. *Et consurgent electi,* scilicet regis austri, *ad resistendum, et non*
erit fortitudo. Et ueniet super eum rex aquilonis iuxta placitum suum, et non
erit qui stet contra facem eius. Et stabit in terra inclita,[64] in qua Dominus
505 scilicet in corpore mistico tunc est iterum crucifigendus, sicut ipse dixit
Petro: *Vado Romam iterum crucifigi.*[65] Sequitur: *Et contra firmissimas*
cogitaciones inibiit, consilia *usque ad tempus,*[66] nam *propter electos breuiabun-*
tur dies illi.[67] *Et concitabitur fortitudo eius, et cor eius aduersus regem austri*
in exercitu magno, et rex austri prouocabitur ad bellum multis auxiliis et
510 *fortibus nimis, et non stabit quia inibunt aduersus eum consilia, et comedentes*
panem cum eo, conterent illum, exercitusque eius opprimetur, et cadent
interfecti plurimi.[68] *Et reuertetur,* scilicet rex aquilonis, *in terram suam cum*
opibus multis et cor eius aduersus testamentum sanctum, seu Christi euangelium, *statuto tempore reuertetur, et ueniet ad austrum,* hoc est ad partes regis
515 austri, *et non erit priori simile nouissimum, et uenient romani, et percucietur,*
et reuertetur, et indignabitur contra testamentum sanctuarii, hoc est euangelium, *et faciet,* idest euangelium condemnpabit, *reuerteturque et cogitabit*
aduersus eos qui dereliquerunt testamentum sanctuarii, circa scilicet munera
danda, *et brachia ex eo stabunt, et polluent sanctuarium fortitudinis,* tam
520 spititualiter quam corporaliter, *et auferent iuge sacrificium, et dabunt abomi-*
nacionem in desolacionem,[69] doctrina scilicet euangelica et uita seu diuinitate
in Christo sollempniter condempnata, et ymagine et cruce Christi de
predicto sanctuario deiectis, et ibidem ymagine Antichristi constituta et
adorata, ipsam abominacionem predictam sic per ordinem ut forcius poterunt
525 aucmentabunt. Sequitur, quod periculosum est, *et impii in testamentum*

---

499 preuaricacionem T   502 uertent BTV   electi *om.* BV   503 ueniet *om.* T
504-505 scilicet Dominus *tr.* BTV   505 iterum] initium B   crucifigendus] est *add.* BTV
509 et¹ *om.* BTV   517 reuertiturque M; reuertitur quoque BV   520 dabit T
521 in] et BTV

---

[62] Dan. 11.13.
[63] Dan. 11.14.
[64] Dan. 11.15-16.
[65] *Passio sanct. apost.,* p. 171.
[66] Dan. 11.24.
[67] Mt. 24.22.
[68] Dan. 11.25-26.
[69] Dan. 11.28-31.

simulabunt fraudulenter;[70] tantus enim dolus decepcionis et prodicionis tunc incipiet currere quod eciam nec uicinus in uicino poterit confidere. Sequitur: *Et docti in populo docebunt plurimos,*[71] ne tota scilicet fidelium massa pereat. Sequitur: *Et ruent in gladio et in flamma et in captiuitate et in rapina dierum,*
530 *cumque corruerint subleuabuntur auxilio paruulo,* seu paruulorum, propter intensam infirmitatem, *et aplicabuntur eis plurimi fradulenter,*[72] quod maximum erit periculum, et qui stat uideat ne cadat.[73] Sequitur: *Et de eruditis ruent,* in errores et in luxurias et in alias fragilitates multas, *ut* postea, tamquam alter Lazarus, vi^a feria seu sexto tempore suscitandus, *conflentur,*
535 *et eligantur, et dealbentur.*[74] Sequitur: *Et faciet iuxta uoluntatem suam rex, et eleuabitur, et magnificabitur aduersus omnem Deum,* quia nullum reputabit, *et aduersus Deum deorum loquetur magnifica,* dicendo se scilicet esse filium eius et messiam in lege promissum, *et dirigetur, donec impleatur iracundia: perpetrata quippe est difinicio. Et Deum patruum suorum,* Dominum scilicet
540 Iesum Christum, *non reputabit, et erit in concupiscenciis feminarum,*[75] quod non esset nisi esset purus homo, *et multiplicabit gloriam, et diuidet terram gratuito et in tempore prefinito preliabitur aduersus eum rex austri, et quasi tempestas ueniet contra illum rex aquilonis in curribus et in equitibus et in classe magna, et ingredietur terras, et conteret, et pertransiet, et introybit in*
545 *terram gloriosam,* hoc est Romam, in qua gloriosus sanguis sanctorum effusus et effundendus est, *et multe,* terrarum scilicet et prouinciarum naciones, *corruent, et mittet manum suam ad terras,* subiugando scilicet, *et terra Egypti,* seu Francie, *non effugiet, et dominabitur thesaurorum auri et argenti et in omnibus preciosis Egypti. Hee autem sole saluabuntur de manu eius: Edom,*
550 *et Moab, et principes filiorum Amon,* hoc est hebrei, gibellini, et greci, qui tanquam principes seu principales erunt in sui recepcione; *per Libiam quoque et Ethiopiam pertransibit,*[76] Libia enim ueniens uel introiens interpretatur;

---

527 in *om.* BV   528 Et *om.* BTV   docti] dicti BV   529 flamma] fama M^{ac} rapinam M   530 paruulo seu *om.* BTV   532 de *om.* T   534 suscitando BTV; sucitandus M   537 loquetur *om.* M^{ac} scilicet *om.* BTV   538 impleatur *post* iracundia *rep.* M^{ac} 541 diuidetur V   542 et^1 *om.* BTV   543 et^1 *om.* BV   in^3 *om.* BV   544 et^1 *om.* BTV   545 est] in *add.* T   effusus] est *add.* BTV 547 manus suas BTV   terra] scilicet *add.* BTV   548 seu ... effugiet] non effugient seu Francie BTV   in *om.* BTV   549 autem *om.* BTV

---

[70] Dan. 11.32.
[71] Dan. 11.33.
[72] Dan. 11.33-34.
[73] Cf. 1 Cor. 10.12.
[74] Dan. 11.35.
[75] Dan. 11.36-37.
[76] Dan. 11.39-43.

nam, ut dicit Ioachim,[77] de Lombardia seu Ytalia ueniet et, quod non licet, seductorie usurpando in potenciam introybit. Ethiopia uero caligo uel tene-

555 bre interpretando sonat, nam Grecia, que in tota ecclesia fuit fons tocius ueritatis, facta est nunc, et peius fiet tunc, fons tocius cismatis et erroris, ut in recepcionem Antichristi non Grecia sed Ethiopia nuncupetur, unde et in psalmo dicitur: *Dracho iste quem formasti ad illudendum ei; dedisti eum escam populis ethiopum.*[78]

560 Tota enim ecclesia, tam in Grecia quam in Ytalia et Alamagnia, quam in Francia et Yspania et insulis maris pro maiori parte ipsum recipiet uelut Deum circumcisionis, caratire insignita quod in manu dextra per opera et in fronte manifesta prophecione portabunt. Nam sedens in templo tamquam sit Deus, ut sequitur, *fama turbabit eum ab oriente et aquilone,* predicancium

565 scilicet euangelium in partibus orientalibus et aquilonaribus contra eum, *et ueniet in multitudine magna ut conterat et interficiat plurimos,* sibi scilicet rebellantes, *et figet tabernaculum suum,* seu palacium hedificabit *inter* duo *maria,* adriaticum scilicet et romanum, *super montem inclitum et sanctum,*[79] in quo illa inclita sedes Christi, seu eius uicarii, et locus sanctificacionis eius

570 consistunt, necnon et beatorum Petri et Pauli apostolorum et aliorum sine numero sanctorum corpora requiescunt. Sequitur: *Et ueniet usque ad sumitatem eius,*[80] tamquam scilicet in palacium et triumphum glorie regni sui. Sequitur eius finis: *Et nemo auxiliabitur ei,*[81] quia *Dominus Iesus interficiet eum spiritu oris sui, et destruet illustracione aduentus sui,* ut dicit apostolus.[82]

575 Vnde Apocalipsis xix° dicitur quod scilicet, *aprehensa est bestia, et cum ea pseudo propheta qui fecit signa coram eam, quibus seduxit eos qui acceperunt caracterem bestie, et qui adorauerunt ymaginem eius; uiui missi sunt hii duo in stagnum ignis ardentis et sulfuris.*[83] Dicit Iohannes quod in illo tam magno

---

553 ut *om.* T   555-556 ueritatis tocius *tr.* BTV   556 fiet peius *tr.* BTV   557 numcupetur M   unde *om.* BTV   561 Ymspania M   et²] in *add.* Mᵃᶜ   recipient BTV 562 per opera *om.* BTV   563 professionem T   564 et] ab *add.* BTV   564-565 predicancium *post* euangelicum *tr.* BTV   567 et] etiam BTV   seu] papilionem seu *add.* BTV   569 inclita *post* Christi *tr.* TV   571-572 sumitatem] ciuitatem BTV 572 eius *om.* T   573 Sequitur ... ei *om.* Mᵃᶜ   Dominus] noster *add.* T   Iesus] Christus *add.* BV   575 Vnde] in *add.* BT   scilicet] quod *add.* BV   est *om.* T 576 eam] ea BTV   577 uiui *om.* BV   578 Ioachim BTV

---

[77] Unidentified source.
[78] Ps. 103.26; 73.14.
[79] Dan. 11.44-45.
[80] Dan. 11.45.
[81] Dan. 11.45.
[82] 2 Thes. 2.8.
[83] Apoc. 19.20.

terre motu qui fiet in morte Antichristi cadet palacium eius et palacia
580 multorum pseudo prophetarum, et quod terra uoraginose aperietur et tam
soldanus caput bestialium nacionum in loco suo quam Antichristus caput
pseudo prophetarum in loco suo, absorbebit eos uiuos usque ad profunda
inferni et missi uiui in stagnum ignis et sulphuris expirabunt;[84] sed et
Sathanas, seu dracho, qui facit omnia mala hec, incarcerandus est in abisso
585 ut non seducat amplius gentes usque ad statutum terminum solucionis sue.[85]

Septimum signaculum ueteris testamenti. Septimum signaculum ueteris
testamenti incepit in Esdra et Nehemia, consumatum uero est in Iohanne
Babtista et Domino Iesu Christo. Sub hoc tempore vii° cessauerunt ystorie
et prophecie et concessus est *sabbatissimus populo Dei,*[86] et reliquis iudeorum
590 data est pax usque ad Anthiocum regem, qua persecucione peracta, non
longe post, premisso Iohanne, unigenitus Dei filius uenit in mundum, ita ut
in terris uideretur et cum hominibus conuersaretur.[87]

Septimum signaculum noui testamenti. Sub apercione septimi signaculi
noui testamenti continetur persequucio Gog nouissimi. Sub hoc septimo
595 tempore, quod in proximo futurum est, cessabunt aperciones signaculorum
et labor exponendorum librorum testamenti ueteris, dabiturque re uera
sabbatissimus populo Dei,[88] et erit *in diebus eius iusticia et habundancia pacis,*
et dominabitur Dominus a mari usque ad mare,[89] et sancti eius regnabunt cum
eo usque ad ocultum finem istius temporis, in quo soluendus est Sathanas de
600 carcere suo et regnaturus est homo ille pessimus qui uocatur Gog, de quo tam
multa scripta sunt in libro Ezechielis prophete. *Relinquitur ergo,* ut dicit
apostolus, *sabbatissimus populo Dei,* in cuius fine futura est tribulacio ista
postquam, premisso Helya, uenturus est Dominus ad extremum iudicium,
secundum quod continetur in septima parte Apocalipsis.[90]
605 Consumatis ystoriis ueteris testamenti et passo unigenito Filio Dei, qui
factus est *sub lege, ut eos qui sub lege erant redimeret,*[91] aduenit tempus

---

583 missi] sunt *add.* BTV   sulphuris] in quo *add.* BTV   585 gentes amplius
tr. BTV   sue *om.* BTV   587 incepit] fuit BTV   Nehemia *om.* BV   589 et² *om.*
M^{ac}   confessus BTV   593 *Rubrica rep.* BTV   septimi signaculi M   595 in]
tempore *add.* BTV   est *ante* in *tr.* T   596 dabitur BV   600 ille homo *tr.* BTV   601-
602 sabbatissimus *ante* ut dicit *tr.* BTV   603 postquam] plusquam BV   605 Con-
sumatis] *Rubrica*: Consumatis ystoriis *praem.* BTV   et passo *om.* BV   606 eis T

---

[84] *Postilla,* fols. 111v-112r.
[85] *Septem Sigillis,* p. 245.
[86] Heb. 4.9.
[87] Cf. Bar. 3.38.
[88] Heb. 4.9.
[89] Ps. 71.7-8.
[90] *Septem Sigillis,* pp. 245-246.
[91] Gal. 4.5.

resurreccionis, in quo, *et multa corpora sanctorum, qui dormierant,*[92] suscitata
sunt, et collecta in unum in turbam fidelium, effusa est illa habundancia pacis
que eciam repleta est Spiritu sancto, aduenitque sic beatitudo de qua dicit
610　propheta: *Oculus non uidit, Deus, absque te, que preparasti diligentibus te.*[93]

Consumatis eciam operibus testamenti noui, peracta tribulacione illa
maxima que erit in diebus Gog, simili quidem illi que facta est sub Anthioco,
significata uero in passione Domini, aduenit tempus resurreccionis mortuorum et consolacionis superne Ierusalem, qua influxit ex eo tempore fluuius
615　aque uiue, secundum quod continetur in octaua parte libri Apocalipsis,[94] et
erit in ea gaudium sempiternum.[95]

---

609 aduenitque] agnouitque *codd.*　　　beatitudo] Deus *add.* BV　　　610 propheta]
quod *add.* BTV　　　611 Consumatis] *Rubrica:* Consumatis operibus *praem.* B　　　eciam
om. M^ac　　　illa tribulacione *tr.* BTV　　　612 Gog] et Magog *add.* BTV　　　614-615 influxit ... quod *rep.* BV

---

[92] Mt. 27.52.
[93] Is. 64.4; *Septem Sigillis*, pp. 246-247.
[94] Apoc. 22.1.
[95] *Septem Sigillis*, pp. 246-247.

EXPLICIT IX. INCIPIT X, IN QUA AGITUR DE VII CAPITIBUS DRACHONIS NOVI ET VETERIS TESTAMENTI.

Circa x distinccionem est notandum quod, sicut ille antiqus serpens seu dracho usque ad Christi aduentum in ueteri testamento in suis capitibus, hoc est regibus, per vii^{em} tempora contra populum iudaicum debellauit, sic et in nouo testamento usque ad ultimum Christi aduentum in consimilibus suis
5 capitibus seu regibus per similia vii^{em} tempora Christi ecclesiam expugnabit. Vnde dracho iste, prout hic sumitur, est in numerosa multitudo peruersorum atque impiorum hominum cum suis capitibus seu regibus iniquis, per quos uniuersa multitudo electorum ab Abel iusto usque ad ultimum electum tam in ueteri quam in nouo persequucione passa est, et ecciam pacietur. Vnde in
10 Apocalipsi dicitur quod dracho *stetit super arenam maris,*[1] tangendo scilicet condicionem populi supradicti innumerabilis, ficus sine humore alicuius pietatis et sine fructu alicuius bonitatis; talis dominus, talis seruus. Et ideo tam in ueteri quam in nouo cum vii^{em} capitibus et cauda describitur, tangens principium eius et finem, ut per ordinem claret.
15 *Quinque ceciderunt, unus est, alius nondum uenit,* sed cum uenerit, oportet ipsum stare modico tempore; Apocalipsis.[2] Ista duo capita simul iuncta sunt, primum et secundum, quia due tribulaciones ecclesie sub uno sexto tempore germinabuntur, et eciam quia vii^{us} non in suis uiribus, sed in uiribus vi^{ti} debet ascendere.[3]
20 *Primum caput drachonis ueteris testamenti.* Primum caput drachonis ueteris testamenti fuit Pharao, rex egypciorum, persecutor populi Dei seu

---

Titulum ix] distinctio *add.* BTV   x] distinctio *add.* BTV   1 antiqus] hostis *add.* BV; Antichristus hostis *add.* T   9 nouo] testamento *add.* BTV   in^3 *om.* M^{ac}
10 stetit] fiet T   13 nouo quam in ueteri *tr.* BTV   14 claret] *Rubrica*: Primum caput drachonis *add.* BV; Caput drachonis *add.* T   16 Apocalipsis] uicesimo *add.* BTV   16-17 sunt ... secundum *om.* BTV   17 due *om.* M   20 *Rubrica om.* T

---

[1] Apoc. 12.18.
[2] Apoc. 17.10.
[3] The pattern which follows is original, but the first four heads of the New Testament correspond closely to *Expos.*, fols. 10r and 196v, and to *Lib. Fig.*, pl. 14. The fifth head is imperial, which is one of Joachim's alternatives for the fifth head, but advances the time to that of Frederic II and Louis IV.

Israel, finaliter a Deo x plagis percussus, cum tota milicia Egypti in mari
rubro submerssus est.

    Primum caput drachonis noui testamenti. Primum caput drachonis noui
25 testamenti fuit Herodes, persequutor populi innoscencium, necnon et Pilatus
et Cayphas, qui Christum condempnauerunt et discipulos eius persequuti
sunt, finaliter a Deo una cum omnibus suis cateruis per Titum sunt et
Vespisianum percussi et per uniuersum mundum dispersi.

    Secundum caput drachonis ueteris testamenti. Secundum caput drachonis
30 ueteris testamenti fuit Iebin, rex cananeorum, contra filios Israel; *clamauerunt
filii Israel ad Dominum,*[4] et liberati sunt.

    Secundum caput drachonis noui testamenti. Secundum caput drachonis
noui testamenti fuit Nero et Symon magus et persequucio paganorum, a
quibus multitudo martirum in ara Christi mactata est et ecclesia uehementer
35 afflicta; clamauit ad Dominum, et liberata est.

    Tercium caput drachonis ueteris testamenti. Tercium caput drachonis
ueteris testamenti fuit Benedab, rex siriorum, contra filios Israel, primo
contra x tribus, secundo contra utrumque regnum; clamauerunt ad Dominum, et liberati sunt.[5]

40   *Tercium caput drachonis noui testamenti.* Tercium caput drachonis noui
testamenti fuit Constantinus imperator, filius Constantini, et persequucio
arrianorum contra ecclesiam electorum, cui mox uandalica pressura et
longobardica addite sunt; iuxta Danielem, tercia bestia similis erat pardo, et
quatuor capita habebat super se.[6]

45   *Quartum caput drachonis ueteris testamenti.* Quartum caput drachonis
ueteris testamenti fuit Atzahel, rex assiriorum, contra filios Israel, et preualentibus assiriis decem tribus depopulate sunt.[7]

    Quartum caput drachonis noui testamenti. Quartum caput drachonis noui
testamenti fuit Macumetus et persecucio arabum seu sarracenorum, a quibus
50 grecorum ecclesie, uersus orientalem et meridionalem plagam incolentes,
multa discrimina perpessa sunt, nec longe post affricana ecclesia ad nichilum
penitus est redacta.

---

24 Primum²] asimili *praem.* BTV   25 et *om.* BMᵃᶜTV   27 omnibus *post* cateruis
tr. BTV   27-28 sunt² *ante* percussi *tr.* BTV   30 fuit *om.* Mᵃᶜ   34 quibusdam BV
mactata] tracta T   35 clamauerunt BTV   liberati sunt BTV   37 fuit *om.* T
38 clamauerunt *om.* Mᵃᶜ   42 mox] morum T   44 capitura M   50 plaga BTV
52 redacta *om.* BV

---

[4] Cf. Jud. 4.3.
[5] Cf. Jud. 3.9; 4 Reg. cc. 6, 7.
[6] Dan. 7.6.
[7] Cf. 4 Reg. c. 13.

Quintum caput drachonis ueteris testamenti. Quintum caput drachonis
ueteris testamenti fuit Nabuccodonosor, rex Babilonis, et conflictus caldeo-
55 rum contra filios Israel, sub quo sanctus ignis consumptus est et muri ciuitatis
prostrati sunt in terram et templum consumptum est et populus est ductus
in Babilonem captiuus.[8]

Quintum caput drachonis noui testamenti. Quintum caput drachonis noui
testamenti fuit imperator Fredericus, necnon et Bauarus, et persequucio
60 Alamagnorum querencium ancillare libertatem ecclesie; iam enim tipum
Babilonis regni suos uires exercet ut, consumpto igne sancto, per
condempnacionem sollempnem euangelice uite, mater Syon de sua ciuitate
emigrare compellatur. O mater ecclesia, que nouerca crudelis poteris appellari, cur caros filios tuos legitimos, qui tibi obediebant et te uenerabantur
65 subieccione fideli, cogis maria transfretare et ire ad barbaras naciones, et
congregas sub alis tuis filios alienos, habentes supra se regem angelum, seu
pontificem, abissi cui nomen exterminans, tocius scilicet uite euangelice
ueritatem? Propter quod muri tui in terram prosternentur et, consumpto
templo seu loco sanctificacionis tue, populus tuus in Babilonem ducetur
70 captiuus.

Sextum caput drachonis ueteris testamenti. Sextum caput drachonis ueteris
testamenti fuit Nabocodonosor, rex assiriorum, sub cuius pressura percussa
est Babilon, et cetera, ut superius satis claret.

Sextum caput drachonis noui testamenti. Sextum caput drachonis noui
75 testamenti erit ille rex xi[us] seu cornu paruum de quo, ut predictum est, in
Daniele dicitur quod *potencior erit prioribus* et quod *tres reges humiliabit,*[9] et
cetera. Dicit de isto Iohannes super Apocalipsim quod statuet in pseudo
papam quendam falsum religiosum qui contra regulam euangelicam excogita-
bit et faciet dispensacionem dolosam, promouens in episcopos professores
80 regule prefate sibi consencientes, et exinde expellens clericos et priores
episcopos, qui semini Frederici et illi imperatori et sibi et suo statui fuerant
aduersati, ac persequens omnes qui regulam predictam ad purum et plene
uoluerint obseruare et defensare. Addit ecciam quod tunc in parte implebitur
illud apostoli, ii[e] ad Thessalonicenses ii°: *Nisi uenerit discecio primum,*[10] et
85 cetera.

---

56 sunt *om.* BTV   ductus est *tr.* T   61 suo BTV   64 legimos T   66 super
BTV   regem *om.* V   66-67 seu pontificem *om.* BTV   69 tue] tuis BV
babilonetur M   dicetur M; duceturque BTV   73 superius] supra V   satis *om.*
BT   75 ut *om.* B   77 Et de isto dicit BTV   Ioachim BTV   78 papam] propheta BV; prophetam T   82 aduersarii BTV   ac] et BTV   persequens] conse-
quens M[pc]   84 ii°] capitulo *add.* BTV   nisi] si BV

---

[8] Cf. 4 Reg. c. 17.
[9] Dan. 7.24.
[10] 2 Thes. 2.3; *Postilla,* fol. 93r.

[*Glosa.* Auerte bene quod rex xi[us], qui erit imperator et malleator seu persecutor ecclesie carnalis, non erit proprie Antichristus, sed ille quem faciet eligere in pseudo papam erit Antichristus.]

    Dicit enim quod tunc omnes discedent ab obediencia ueri pape et se-
90 quentur illum pseudo papam, qui quidem erit pseudo quia heretico modo errabit contra ueritatem euangelice paupertatis et quia forte ultra hoc non erit canonice electus, sed cismatice introductus.

    De istomet rege seu sexto drachonis capite, Sibilla dicit: *De porta Yspanie
egredietur infans, cuius nomen in petra fundabitur, cui pulla aquile unica*
95 *coniungetur, ex cuius semine in petra fundato egredietur regulus ad inperium
uolans qui, lilia omnia cum baculo in terram deiciens, bestias grossas hinc
inde per totum imperium, concassatis capitibus, castigabit et Petri nauiculam,
falsis prophetis qui in uestibus ouium uenerant extirpatis radicitus, ad portum
ecclesie primitiue conducet et, nobilibus ortus de toto imperio debellando*
100 *expulsis, tribus de sua gente euulsis regibus, cum ceteris ad terram inclitam
pertransibit quam diuino cultui et Christi uicario subiugauit,*[11] et cetera.

    Hec est enim illa petra Danielis ii° abcisa de monte, seu de regno suo egressa, ad percuciendum noue statuam Babilonis et comminuendum aurum et argentum, hes, ferrum et testam eius et, deletis omnibus regnis, crescat in
105 montem seu imperium magnum.[12] Hec est illa petra scandali que debet ponere terram desertam, necnon illa Ezechielis limpidissima petra,[13] in cuius manibus regnum Sicilie debet dari.

    Istud ecciam Ioachim uidetur tangere, dicens: *Egredietur regulus, cuius
nomen est fortitudo, et in manu eius potestas dominantis iusticie, et ueniet*
110 *garriens et confringens hostes, et municionum diripiet ianuas, et uastabit turres
excelsas, et regnabit conculcans terram, et sedebit inperans super aquas, super
uniuersum scilicet mare; agricolas ecclesiasticos capiet et predabit in tantum
ut, debachati dolore, ad locum unde primitus exierunt timidi reuertantur;
florentem deflorendo subiciet et hostes undique dissipabit, et quis sibi resistere*
115 *poterit, cum potestatem habeat ab Excelso?*[14] Ve, ue abitatoribus circa eam

---

90 papam] prophetam T; *om.* BV   qui ... pseudo[2] *om.* BV   91 forte *om.* BTV
92 introductus] intronizatus et *praem.* BV   94 unica *om.* BV   96 hinc] habuit BV
98 ad *om.* BTV   100 terram] sanctam seu *add.* BTV   103 nouem T   104 testam]
testamenta V   deletis] de locis BV   106 Ezechielis] Ysaye *codd.*   111 aquas]
et *add.* BTV   112 agricolas] scilicet *add.* T   113 debecati M   114 et[1] *om.* BTV
115 ue[2]] ue *add.* BTV

---

[11] Unidentified source.
[12] Dan. 2.34-35.
[13] Cf. Is. 8.14; Ez. 26.4.
[14] Unidentified source.

quia, cum garrire incipiet, contremiscere faciet ecciam montes altos. Ipsa est enim filia aquile ferocissime, que hucusque prostrata dormiuit, que, cum excitata fuerit, expandet alas in predam et ungulas acuet in capturam, rostrum aperiet ut deuoret inimicos; ciuitates et castra alarum sonitu perturbabit et
120 destruet subuertendo quia dure ceruicis populo sociabitur, qui centuplum restituet pro receptis, et erit luctus nimius qualis non fuit a diebus preteritis, et uniuersa lilia euellendo conteret et confringet et destruet spolia multitudinis cum furore, nec erit qui sibi resistere possit nec ecciam obuiare. Nam uniuersas destruet acies paganorum et soldanorum acubitus extinget, et terras
125 quas comprimunt infideles, cum iam tempus eorum incipiat breuiari, restituet uicario crucifixi.

Sub pressura temporum istius principis, regna in declinacione erunt, magnates ruent et comunitates tam in terra quam in mari inclinabuntur et cadent, ut illud quod in Apocalipsi dicitur impleatur, scilicet, quod *tercia pars*
130 *maris facta est sanguis, et tercia pars nauigii interiit*,[15] nam interim ceruigosa Sicilia triturabitur et, infatuata consiliis, sedebit eius acies in ruina, subcidiis infirmabitur et tam a suis domesticis quam ab externis populis lacerata manebit, propter quod cuncta in ea erunt corda micancia et, a suis aduersionibus resupina, cumque unge aquile desinent eam restringere, gemina
135 procella deuorabitur. Nauale bellum deponente in Siciliam, ueniet quod non solum opressos in ea liberabit, sed per terram et per mare in regnum ueniens, Neapolim a quatuor angulis igne et gladio deuorabit. Populus uero insularis ut pila rotunda effectus, hinc inde per diuersas partes fugiens, uix locum quietum in aliqua orbis parte poterit inuenire; sic fugabitur Calabria et Ianua
140 porta lugurium, idest Lombardia, in securi, et Acia deicietur in terra, necnon et pisanorum plebs hemula erit protinus in suis aduersionibus impedita; ledetur in suo flore Florencia et furens Fauencia confundetur; calcabitur semel et iterum Gallia et trahetur in terram; gallus cantabit et Anglia subcumbet, cuius uulgus in sagena fortiter oprimetur; Yspania deficiet,
145 Affrica et Arabia repelletur, cadet oriens et aquilo conticescet, flagellabitur Thucia et Licora plaga incredibili discindetur; confundetur Grecia et manus aquile non euadet. Ab angelo pastor reuelabitur qui duobus aquile filiis

---

116 ecciam faciet *tr.* V; ecclesiam faciet T   Ipsa est] Et ipsam BTV   117 enim] scilicet petra est *add.* BTV   118 excitata] exita T   120 associabitur BTV centuplum] templum T   121 pro] quod T   nimis BT   130 maris ... pars *om.* T *per hom.*   133 mirancia BV; minancia T   134 cum BTV   139 quietem BTV 140 Acia *forte perperam pro* Asta   143 et[2] *om.* T   144 comprimetur BTV   deficiet] scilicet *add.* T   146 Liconia BTV

---

[15] Apoc. 8.8-9.

benedicet, quem romanum monarcham in Ytalia constituet, cui Grecia
unietur; Roma quasi ad nichilum in temporalibus deueniet, sed in spirituali-
150 bus crescet. Pastor pacificus, post multam peregrinacionem, animam Deo
reddet et miraculis fulgebit in morte in prouincia sua inter flumen et lacum
in planicie iuxta montem.

    Septimum caput drachonis ueteris testamenti. Septimum caput drachonis
ueteris testamenti fuit Naaman, qui secundus fuit a rege Assuero, qui regnauit
155 supra cxxvii prouincias, ut dicitur in libro Hester,[16] sub quo decretum erat
periclitari modis omnibus populum hebreorum, nisi eis diuina clemencia
mirabiliter affuisset; uerumtamen Zorobabel, percussa prius Babilon, cum
multis qui sequuti sunt eum ascendit Ierusalem, et rehedificauit templum Dei
et muros ciuitatis in angustia temporum.

160   *Septimum caput drachonis noui testamenti.* Septimum caput drachonis
noui testamenti erit Antichristus, alter Naaman, sub quo tum inciperit
periclitari modis omnibus populum realiter christianum, qui nomen eius seu
caracterem eius in fronte uel dextra manu non habuerit, ut predixi, unde eius
seduccionem ii[e] ad Tesalonicenses ii[o] apostolus tangens dicit: *Videte ne quis*
165 *uos seducat ullo modo quoniam, nisi uenerit discescio primum, et reuelatus*
fuerit homo peccati, filius perdicionis, qui aduersatur et extollitur supra omne
quod dicitur Deus, aut quod colitur, ita ut in templo Dei sedeat tamquam sit
Deus. Nunc autem quid detineat scitis, ut reueletur in suo tempore, ut tantum
qui tenet teneat, donec de medio fiat, et tunc reuelabitur ille iniquus quem
170 *Dominus Iesus interficiet spiritu oris sui, et destruet illustracione aduentus sui,*
cuius aduentus est secundum operacionem Sathane, in omni uirtute et signis
mendacibus,[17] et cetera. Discescio enim omnium regnorum a romano imperio et omnium ecclesiarum patriarchalium et illarum que sunt in Asia ab
ecclesia romana facta est, uno lumine iam solo uigente; *nunc autem quid*
175 *detineat scitis,* ipsa scilicet intestina dissecio per cismata diuersorum errorum
et cissuras magnarum heresum, ex quibus iam fumus incipit ascendere et
grossis nebulis solem et aerem obscurare, *ut tantum qui tenet teneat,* hoc est,
qui regit romanam ecclesiam regat, *donec de medio,* ipsius scilicet ecclesie seu
imperii, et cissarum predictarum et cismatum, *fiat ille,* scilicet *iniqus, et tunc*

    148 in] et T   149 unietur] uenietur T   151 inter] in T   153 drachonis[2] caput[2]
tr. BV   156-162 populum ... omnibus *om.* V *per hom.*   161 tum inciperit] decretum
erat BT   162 populo M   164 ii[e] *om.* BTV   apostolus ad Thessalonicenses quinto
BTV   165 uenit T   discencio BTV   167 ut] quod T   169 teneat *om.* BV
tunc *om.* T   172 Discencio BTV   175 scitis ipsa] satis ipso T   discencio BTV
177 obscurare] seu *add.* T

[16] Est. 1.1; cf. *Lib. Conc.*, fols. 121v-122r.
[17] 2 Thes. 2.3-9.

180 *reuelabitur quem Dominus Iesus,* et cetera. Et licet dicant aliqui quod in
Babilonia debet nasci, discordando a lictera non discordant a sensu; tres
enim Babilones seu Babilonie in scriptura leguntur, quarum prima est inabi-
tabilis et deserta, in qua regnauit ille Nabocodonosor rex magnus; secunda
est populata, in qua regnat soldanus; tercia figurata, scilicet Roma, in qua
185 regnat populus christianus.

Vnde sicut Lucifer per apostasiam euulsus est de superiori ierarchia
ecclesie, et forte de ordine tronorum, uolens sibi usurpare honorem diuinum,
sic iste, ut dicit Iohannes, per apostasiam euellendus est de superiori iererchia
militantis ecclesie, et forte de ordine prelatorum, usurpando sibi honorem
190 summorum pontificum, ymo pocius in adorando diuinum.[18] Et sicut de
numero xii patriarcharum Dan euulsus est de medio, sortitus sortem
ministerii sui in illius loco seu ministerio Manasse instituto, et sicut de
numero xii apostolorum Iudas Scariothis euulsus est de medio, sortitus
sortem ministerii sui Mathias in illius loco seu ministerio instituto,[19] sic, ut
195 tenent multi, de numero illorum xii uirorum euangelicorum in proximo
reuelandorum iste perdicionis filius euellendus est et egrediendus ad sorcien-
dum sortem ministerii sui, et in loco eius et ministerio alius instituendus, de
quo ipse preuaricator erit expulsus, *cuius aduentus erit secundum operacio-*
nem Sathane, in omni uirtute et signis et prodigiis mendacibus, et in omni
200 *seduccione iniquitatis,* et cetera, ut dicit apostolus.[20]

Sub uno igitur tempore sexto hec tribulacio, scilicet vi[ti] et vii[mi] drachonis
capitis, gemminata insurget,[21] ut sit temporis breuiacio electorum et ecciam
quia vii[us] non in suis uiribus sed in uiribus vi[ti] debet ascendere, de quibus
Danielis xi° dicitur: *Duorum quoque regum cor erit ut maleficiant, et ad*
205 *mensam unam loquentur mendacium, et non proficient, quia adhuc finis in*
aliud tempus.[22] Hoc autem in secundo bello Antichristi proficietur, unde tunc
ipse et rex xi[us] ad mensam unam conuenient, loquentes circa condempnacio-

---

187 ecclesie] triumphantis *praem.* BTV   188 Ioachim BTV   191 medio] et *add.*
BTV   192 ministerio] misterio BT   193 xii *om.* T   est *om.* T   medio] et *add.*
BTV; sortitus est *add.* BTV   194 ministerii] misterium T   illius] ipsius BTV
ministerio] misterio M   196 est *om.* BTV   197 ministerii] misterii BTV   et²] in
add. T   ministerio] misterio M   instituendus] est *add.* BTV   199 mendacibus]
mediantibus T   202 sit] si T   203 in¹] est T   204 dicitur *ante* Danielis *tr.* BTV
erit] unum *add.* BT   205 in] idest T   206 proficientur T

---

[18] *Postilla,* fols. 91r, 57r-v.
[19] Cf. *Lib. Conc.,* fols. 28v, 43v; *Expos.,* fol. 121r.
[20] 2 Thes. 2.9-10.
[21] Cf. *Lib. Fig.,* pl. 14.
[22] Dan. 11.27.

nem ecclesie mendacium, et ideo non proficient nec in hoc prosperitatem habebunt quoniam finis horum in tempore alio expectatur, in tercio scilicet
210 bello, in quo omnia iuxta suum desiderium implebuntur, ubi dicitur, *et iuxta uoluntatem suam faciet rex,*[23] et cetera.

   Cauda drachonis ueteris testamenti. Cauda drachonis ueteris testamenti fuit rex Anthiocus, radix peccati,[24] cunctas aliorum temporum tribulaciones excellens, quibus finitis, in fine septimi temporis seu septimi apercione sigilli,
215 Christus Iesus Filius Dei secundum carnem uenit in mundum et generaciones carnis, quas Deus Pater a mundi principio confirmauerat, carnem assummendo de uirgine, in sinagoga mirabili ordine adimpleuit, et generaciones Spiritus, tamquam mediator Dei et hominis, in sua ecclesia inchoauit, ut amodo non secundum carnem sed secundum spiritum uiuant.

220 *Cauda drachonis noui testamenti.* Cauda drachonis noui testamenti erit homo ille pessimus qui uocatur Gog.[25] Tunc enim soluendus est Sathanas de carcere suo in oculto fine illorum temporum; hec enim tribulacio non minor vi[ti] capitis drachonis erit, sed equalis, excepto quod non erit seductoria sed aperta, quibus finitis, in fine septimi temporis seu vii[mi] sigilli apercione, Iesus
225 Christus Filius Dei in natura assumpta de uirgine ad generale iudicium est uenturus. Generacionum adimplebit ordines ut amplius non sit uita hominum in hoc mundo sed, execucionis sentencia promulgata, alii ibunt in uitam eternam, alii uero in suplicium sempiternum.

---

209 scilicet in tercio *tr.* T   210 in quo *om.* T   213 cunctis BTV   214 sigilli apercione *tr.* BTV   216 principio mundi *tr.* T   218 hominum BTV
222 temporum] tempestatis V

---

[23] Cf. Dan. 8.24-25.
[24] Cf. *Lib. Conc.*, fol. 56v; *Expos.*, fols. 9r-10r; *Lib. Fig.*, pl. 8.
[25] *Septem Sigillis*, p. 246.

EXPLICIT DECIMA DISTINCCIO. INCIPIT XI[a], IN QUA AGITUR DE
CONCORDIIS IN SPECIALI AD INVENIENDUM CERTUM TEMPUS
EORUM QUE SUNT IN NOVO FIENDA PER EA QUE IN VETERI
CONSIMILI MODO SUNT FACTA.

Cum, ut superius tactum est, *nichil nouum sub sole,* et *quid est quod fuit,* in
ueteri scilicet, nisi *ipsum quod,* scilicet in nouo, *futurum est?*[1] Cum igitur per
figuram ueterum nouorum misteria concordatis gradibus congnoscantur,
idcirco sciendum est quod sicut ab Adam usque ad Noe,[2] sub quo factum est
5 diluuium et archa aquis diluuii tradita est, fuerunt generaciones x, sic a
Christo usque ad sanctum Marcellum papam, sub quo factum est diluuium
paganorum et archa ecclesie in manus eorum tradita est, fuerunt generaciones
x. Et sicut a Noe usque ad Abram, sub quo facta est submersio sodomorum,
fuerunt generaciones x, sic a sancto Marcello papa usque ad sanctum
10 Gregorium papam, in quibus temporibus facta est submersio ecclesiarum
orientalium per sarracenos, fuerunt generaciones x. Et sicut ab Abraam usque
ad Obeth, qui fuit contemporaneus Heli de Silo, in cuius diebus data est archa
Dei in manus alienigenarum et postmodum restituta est archa in terram
suam, fuerunt generaciones x, sic a sancto Gregorio papa usque ad Iohannem
15 papam v[um], in quibus temporibus tradita est archa latine ecclesie in manus
sarracenorum et postmodum per Karulum magnum restituta est in terram
suam, fuerunt generaciones x. Et sicut ab Obeth usque ad Ioas, in cuius
diebus cepit exterminari Ysrael ab Azahel regi Syrie, fuerunt generaciones x,
sic a Iohanne papa predicto usque ad Celestinum papam, in quibus tempori-
20 bus cepit exterminari ecclesia per imperatorem Fredericum regem Sicilie,
fuerunt similiter generaciones x.

Titulum nouo] testamento *add.* BTV   ueteri] testamento *add.* BTV   1 nouum
post sole *tr.* T   2 ueteri] testamento *add.* BTV   scilicet[2]] fuit T   3 ueterum *om.*
BTV   concordans BTV   4 ab *om.* T   8 sicut] sunt V   8-11 Et sicut ... x
om. T *per hom.*   11 ab *om.* T   18 exterminacio T   regis M

---

[1] Eccles. 1.9-10.
[2] The Old Testament generations in the passages which follow are taken verbatim from *Lib. Conc.*, fol. 14r; other material is added from fols. 13r, 25r, 43v.

Si autem sicut a Ioas usque ad transmigracionem ueteris Babilonis fuerunt generaciones x, et a predicta transmigracione usque ad Iohannem Babtistam fuerunt totidem, tribus trium regum tacitis quos Matheus de genelogia
25 Saluatoris excludit, erunt a Celestino papa predicto usque ad transmigracionem seu ruinam noue Babilonis, et exinde usque ad uentum Helie totidem, tribus trium regum, scilicet Neronis et mistici et magni Antichristi, tacitis? Soli Deo relinquendum est; tum, propter aliquas contrarias concordias superius tactas, plus concordiam facti esse credo quam temporis et facti
30 simul. Tamen sicut ab Adam usque ad primum aduentum Christi generaciones lxiii esse cernuntur, sic a Christo usque ad secundum aduentum eius a multis et lxiii consimiliter esse creduntur, non quoad paritatem temporum, sed numerum generacionum, et sicut ille primus status magnos patres et sanctos prophetas et religiones diuersas mundo obtulit, ut Christi aduentum
35 in carnem ad homines nunciarent, sic iste secundus status magnos patres et sanctos predicatores et religiones diuersas mundo obtulit qui in potencia spiritus et uirtute uerborum ultimum Christi aduentum ad iudicium annuncient hominibus et annunciare non cessent.

Vnde sicut xviiiª generacione a Iacob Helias est heleuatus in celum et
40 Heliseus indutus est duplici spiritu, sic xviiiª generacione a Christo sanctus Benedictus euolauit in celum et ordo eius indutus est dupplici spiritu, spiritualium scilicet et temporalium in communi.[3] Sicut enim completis xxi generacionibus a Iacob, tempore Ozie regis Iuda incepit tempus prophetarum currere, sic, completis totidem generacionibus a Christo, inceperunt diuerse
45 predicancium religiones in ecclesia apparere.[4] Sicut ecciam tempore Abraam, in quo fuit principium ueteris testamenti, misit Deus duos angelos in Sodomam et Gomorram ad liberandos electos suos de medio populi excecati, ne simul perirent cum eis, et sicut ecciam tempore Zacharie, in quo fuit principium noui testamenti, misit Deus alios duos angelos, scilicet Iohannem
50 Babtistam et Dominum Iesum Christum, ad liberandum electos suos de medio populi excecati domus Iuda et domus Israel ne simul perirent cum eis,[5] sic, completis xl generacionibus a duobus primis, missi sunt a Deo alii

---

22 a *om.* T   Babilonis ueteris *tr.* T   24 fuerunt] generaciones *add.* BV quos *om.* V   26 uentum] aduentum BTV   28 concordias contrarias *tr.* T   32 consimiliter] similiter BV; simul T   temporum] ipsorum BV   35 patres *om.* T   36 in *om.* T   43 generacione M   a] et BV   45 predicacionum BT   48 ecciam] ecclesia BV   48-51 et sicut ... Israel *rep.* V   49-50 scilicet ... Christum *om.* V   52 xl] quatuor *add.* BTV

---

[3] *Lib. Conc.*, fols. 47v-48r.
[4] Cf. *Lib. Conc.*, fol. 49r.
[5] Cf. *Lib. Conc.*, fol. 23r.

duo angeli, scilicet sanctus Dominicus et sanctus Franciscus, in quibus
tempus plenitudinis sumpsit inicium, et hoc ad liberandum populum suum
55 de medio populi excecati latinorum ecclesie et grecorum, ne iustus cum inpio
puniatur. Et sicut per vi generaciones ante ortum ueritatis euangelice legis in
sinagoga iudeorum due religiones, phariseorum scilicet et seduceorum,
inceperunt apparere,[6] sic per vi generaciones ante ortum temporis plenitudinis in ecclesia christianorum due noue religiones, predicatorum scilicet et
60 minorum, inceperunt similiter apparere. Et sicut, completis xliiii^{or} generacionibus a natiuitate Abraam, fuit persequucio contra pueros innocentes primo
Herode regnante, sic, completis totidem generacionibus, erit persequucio
contra pueros euangelicos seu euangelicam uitam, primo Herode seu mistico
Antichristo regnante. Vnde a descensu Iacob et xii patriarcharum in terra
65 Egypti usque ad apercionem sexti signaculi ueteris testamenti fuerunt anni
Mcclx, in cuius tempore illa dupplex tribulacio vi^{ti} et vii^{mi} drachonis capitis
in sinagoga surrexit; consimiliter a descensu Christi et xii apostolorum in
terram gencium usque ad apercionem sexti signaculi noui testamenti, in cuius
tempore consimiles tribulaciones debent consurgere sub predicto primo et
70 secundo Herode, hoc est mistico et magno Antichristo, erunt anni totidem;
hic est uolatus et pastus mulieris Apocalipsis in solitudinem a facie serpentis,
dies seu annos Mcclx, in cuius fine soluendus est Sathanas ad temptandum
Christum in membris suis, et cetera.[7]

Sicut ecciam, completis xlv generacionibus a natiuitate Abraam, fuerunt
75 orte in sinagoga iudeorum opiniones diuerse de Christo, de quarum cauerna
egressus est ille uenenosus coluber, scilicet Cayphas, cum multis pseudo
prophetis accepta occasione condempnandi Christum ad mortem, sic,
completis totidem generacionibus a natiuitate Christi, orientur in ecclesia
christianorum diuerse secte hereticorum et diuerse opiniones heresum tan-
80 gendo uitam et doctrinam Christi, ut de orribili cauerna predictorum egrediatur ille uenenosus coluber cum caterua multorum pseudo prophetarum ad
condempnandum tocius ueritatis semitam, scilicet Antichristus. Et sicut ordo
apostolicus super firmam petram fundatus tunc conualuit, sic et ordo euangelicus supra firmam petram fundatus finaliter conualescet, et cetera.
85   Sicut ecciam, a natiuitate Habraam completis xlv generacionibus, defuit
dux et regalis uncio de domo Iuda in populo Israel et reuelatus est nouus dux

---

63 euangelicam] tenentes *praem.* BTV   70 et magno *om.* M^{ac} 72 in ... Sathanas
om. V   83 supra BT   84 super BTV   86 Ysrael populo *tr.* TV   nouus] nobis T

---

[6] Cf. *Lib. Conc.*, fol. 23r, where the Pharisees are said to prefigure the rise of religious
Orders in the New Testament era.
[7] Cf. *Lib. Conc.*, fols. 38r, 41v, 134r-v; Apoc. 12.6.

de sinagoga, uniuersalis pontifex noue Ierusalem Iesus Christus Filius Dei, sic, a natiuitate Christi completis totidem generacionibus, deficiente duce in populo christiano et regali uncione de domo Petri, reuelabitur quasi nouus
90 dux, pontifex noue Ierusalem ecclesie uniuerse, et cetera. Et sicut, completis xlv generacionibus a natiuitate Abraam, in babtismate Christi datus est Spiritus sanctus in specie columbe, sic, completis totidem generacionibus a natiuitate Christi, daturus est Spiritus sanctus euangelicis uiris in specie columbe, ut columbine simplicitatis efficiantur, missi agni inter lupos,
95 prudentes sicut serpentes et simplices sicut columbe.[8]

Et sicut, completis xlv generacionibus a natiuitate Abraam, in principio xlvi[e] Christus transfigurauit se et ostendit gloriam suam ad confirmandum corda discipulorum antequam ueniret ad passionem, aparentibus ibi Moysen de inferno seu limbo et Helia de celo seu de paradiso, sic, completis totidem
100 generacionibus a natiuitate Christi, in principio xlvi[e] reuelata facie manifestabitur gloria Domini et ueritas Dei nostri ad confirmandum corda suorum uere discipulorum antequam Christus ueniat Romam iterum crucifigi, nec dubium quin tunc tam de profundo inferni quam de excelso supra signa miranda reuelentur.
105 Sicut ecciam, completis xlv generacionibus a natiuitate Abraam, in xlvi[a] Christus eiecit omnes uendentes et ementes de templo, sic, completis totidem generacionibus a natiuitate Christi, in xlvi[a] eiciendi sunt iterum in forti manu omnes uendentes et ementes de ecclesia, ut templum ab atrio segregetur, et cetera. Et sicut, completis xlv generacionibus a natiuitate Abraam, in xlvi[a],
110 hora quasi vi, conuersa est Samaria ad Christum, sic, completis totidem generacionibus a natiuitate Christi, in xlvi[a], sub apercione quasi sexti sigilli, est Grecia ad obedienciam romane ecclesie reuertenda.

Sicut ecciam, completis xlv generacionibus a natiuitate Abraam, in xlvi[a], sexta feria, Lazarus quatridianus fetens in monumento resuscitatus est, sic,
115 completis totidem generacionibus a natiuitate Christi, in xlvi[a], sub apercione vi[ti] sigilli, multi quatridiani fetentes per infamiam de monumento consueti uicii suscitabuntur ut alter Lazarus, misericordia preuenienti diuina, unde Danielis xi[o] dicitur: *Et de eruditis ruent,* scilicet in luxurias et fragilitates diuersas propter intensam infirmitatem, *ut* postea *conflentur, et eligantur, et*
120 *dealbentur,*[9] et cetera.

---

89 regalis uncio *codd.*   93 datus BV   sanctus *om.* M[ac]   96 sicut] sic T
99 paradiso] terrestri *add.* BTV   100 principio] primo aduentu BTV   facie] a *praem.*
BTV   101 suorum corda *tr.* BTV   112 reuertenda] et est conuertenda *add.* M[ac]
116 vi[ti]] quasi *praem.* B   117 alter *om.* T   118-120 Et ... cetera *om.* B *et rep.:* sexti
sigilli est Grecia ad obedienciam romane ecclesie reuertenda   119-120 et[2] ... cetera *om.* V

---

[8] Cf. Mt. 10.16.
[9] Dan. 11.35.

Sicut ecciam, completis xlv generacionibus a natiuitate Abraam, in xlvi^a Christus uenit ad passionem et sub Pilato a quatuor militibus in pede crucis nudus expoliatus est, sic, completis totidem generacionibus a natiuitate Christi, in xlvi^a ecclesia ueniet ad passionem et sub illo rege xi° a quatuor
125 christianorum regibus in pede crucis ab omnibus temporalibus nuda expolianda est, unde et in Iohannis euangelio dicitur: *Et si me persecuti sunt, et uos persequentur,*[10] et cetera; *non enim est discipulus super magistrum,*[11] ut ait Christus, et cetera.

Sicut ecciam, completis xlv generacionibus a natiuitate Abraam, in xlvi^a
130 facta est transmigracio ecclesie seu discipulorum Christi de regno Iudee ad gentes, sic, completis totidem generacionibus a natiuitate Christi, in xlvi^a fiendum est passagium christianorum de romano imperio seu Christianitate ad gentes, hoc est in terram sanctam, et ad alias infidelium naciones. Sicut a natiuitate Abraam completis xlv generacionibus, in xlvi^a incepit predicacio
135 Iohannis Babtiste, sic, a natiuitate Christi completis xlv generacionibus, in xlvi^a in aduentum Helie incipiet predicacio eius.

Completis autem x generacionibus ab Adam usque ad Noe, in xi^a, facta inundacione diluuii, perdidit Deus peccatores terre, saluato Noe et domo eius in archa. Asimili, completis x generacionibus ab Ozia usque ad Salatiel, in
140 xi^a facta est inundacio gencium contra Babilonem, saluatis reliquiis filiorum Israel in ciuitate Betulie.[12] Primum igitur ueteris temporis, scilicet Noe, primum diluuium noui temporis, scilicet Christi, per concordiam respicit, et si ibi fuit inundacio aquarum, quibus Deus perdidit peccatores terre, et si inundacio gencium sub Thito et Vespesiano, quibus Deus perdidit peccatores
145 sinagoge; et si ibi saluatus est Noe et domus eius in archa, et hic Petrus et domus eius in arcitudine arche spiritualis ecclesie saluatus est, et si inde emissa columba ac tulit ramum oliue in signum pacis, et hic quedam turba iustorum per donum Spiritus sancti, sicut columba effecta ad predicandum uerbum Dei, que reuersura die vii°, seu vii° ecclesie tempore, per misterium
150 nunciet pacem dandam uelocius super terram.[13]

---

126 euangelio Iohannis *tr.* BTV   127-128 non ... cetera *om.* T *per hom.*   133 ad^2 *om.* V   Sic T   134 generacionibus] nacionibus BTV   137 facta] est *add.* M^ac
138 eius] sua BTV   142 scilicet *om.* T   143 si ibi] sibi T   143-145 et ... sinagoge *om.* V *per hom.*   145 sinagoge *om.* B   est *ante* ibi *tr.* V   145-146 in ... eius *om.* TV   146 arcitudine] multitudine B   147 emissa] est *add.* BTV   ac] que BTV quendam M^ac   148 effecta *om.* BV   149 que *om.* BV   reuersura] reuera B; in reuersa V   vii° ^1] ecclesie *add.* BV; ecclesie die *add.* T   seu ... ecclesie *om.* V   ecclesie] et *add.* BV

---

[10] Jn. 15.20.
[11] Mt. 10.24.
[12] *Lib. Conc.*, fols. 43v, 23v.
[13] Cf. *Lib. Conc.*, fol. 24v.

Secundum consimiliter diluuium seu exterminium ueteris Babilonis diluuium seu exterminium secundum noui temporis, noue scilicet Babilonis,
per misterium tangit, et si ibi fuit inundacio gencium, et hic inundacio
infidelium nacionum erit; ut enim tunc reliquie filiorum Israel saluate sunt a
155 Domino in ciuitate Bethulie, sic enim et nunc reliquie spiritualis ecclesie in
eadem ciuitate interpretatiue saluabuntur, que uirgo uel casta a Domino et
dolens a Domino interpretatur, in quibus non solum uirgines, sed casti et
penitentes tacti saluabuntur in sincera ueritate fundati, donec egrediatur ex
ea quasi altera Iudith reuersura filiis Israel et, truncato capite Olofernis seu
160 interueniente morte magni Antichristi, referat uerbum pacis. Vnde callidus
nauta a primo diluuio ueteris temporis usque ad secundum eiusdem temporis
computet miliaria seu generaciones, ut inter duo excidia noui temporis sciat
quid tenet. Hoc autem firmiter teneas, quod quot fuerunt generaciones in
testamento ueteri, ab Abraam scilicet usque ad babtismum Christi, tot erunt
165 in testamento nouo usque ad temporis plenitudinis ortum, et sicut magna
mirabilia in fine illorum ueterum et in principio nouorum et nouitates non
modice in sinagoga fuerunt facte, sic et in principio temporis plenitudinis, ut
narrat Daniel,[14] mirabilia magna et nouitates non modice in ecclesia Dei fient,
et cetera.
170 Quod autem in diebus Abrae, completis a Sem x generacionibus et ab
Adam xx^{ti}, missi sunt duo angeli ad Sodomam et Gomorram ut, saluato Loth
et domo eius, perderent ciuitates impiorum, aut quod in diebus Zacharie,
completis a Zorobabel x generacionibus et ab Ozia xx^{ti}, missi sunt duo magni
angeli seu prophete, licet dissimiliter magni ut, saluatis reliquiis, traderent
175 sinagogas hebreorum Sathane in obscuracione cordis sui, et ut fierent uelud
aqua sulfurea et stagnum malediccionis, significat id quod futurum est in
diebus illorum duorum prophetarum qui uenturi sunt quando, electis de
ecclesia grecorum et latinorum aliquantis reliquiis, ceteri omnes cecabuntur,
ut non uideant ueritatem propter infinita selera quibus repleta est terra, et
180 efficiantur sinagoga Sathane et ecclesia demoniorum, ut quod Adam expulsus
est de paradiso et Ozias de templo pro peccatis suis monstret non solum

---

151 seu *om.* BV   153 hic *om.* M^{ac} 154 erit] est BM^{ac}TV   a] in T
155 enim *om.* T   156 saluabuntur] idest *add.* BTV   que] in BV   a Domino
om. BTV   157 et *om.* T   158 egrediatur *om.* T   159 et *om.* M   160 referre T
161 usque ... temporis *om.* T *per hom.*   162 computent M   ut] et BV; *om.* T
163 teneas] teneat *om.* M^{ac} 166 illarum BV   167 ut *rep.* M   168 fient in ecclesia
V   170 in] a *codd.*   a Sem. *om.* BTV; assem M   172 eius *om.* V   174-175 licet ...
Sathane *om.* T   174 traderetur BV   175 ut *om.* BTV   uelud] uultu BV   176 est
om. T   178 cecabuntur *Lib. Conc.*; calcabuntur *codd.*

---

[14] Dan. 12.

iudeorum populum, ymmo ecciam istum babilonicum esse de loco sancto pro suis reatibus expellendum.[15]

Quod in diebus Obeth contritus est Israel et data est archa Domini in
185 manus philistinorum, aut in diebus Marcelli pape, imperantibus Diocliciano et Maximiano, afflictus est uehementer populus christianus et tradita est ecclesia iustorum in manus paganorum designat futuram ipsam calamitatem in quam ecclesia Dei tradetur in manus scilicet peccatorum donec ueniat tempus consolacionis ipsius.[16]

190 Quod regnum Samarie datum est in manu Atzaelis regis Sirie, aut quod ecclesia orientalis tradita est in manu Cosdroe regis perssarum, aut quod latina ecclesia cepit exterminari per Fredericum imperatorem designat futuram calamitatem quam passurus est populus christianus in fine huius secundi status, quando et calcabunt gentes ciuitatem sanctam mensibus xlii[bus] sub
195 pressura illius regis xi ex semine Frederici predicti. Cessio illa magna capitum israeliticarum designat ruinam illam mencium que denotatur in libro Apocalipsis, ubi dicitur: *Atrium quod est foris templum eice foras, et ne meciaris illud quia datum est gentibus,*[17] et cetera.[18]

Quod populus babilonicus infra quem illo in tempore detinebantur captiui
200 filii Iuda percussus est a medis, aut quod noua Babilon percucietur a x regibus et exercitibus eorum significat uniuersale illud iudicium quod erit in fine, quando exibunt angeli et separabunt malos de medio iustorum, et mittent eos in caminum ignis ardentis simul cum dyabolo et angelis eius. Quod autem post hos labores, seu ibi seu hic, relicturus est sabatissimus populo Dei
205 significat illam requiem futuram quam habituri sumus in regno Dei post consumacionem seculi, quando neque nubent neque nubentur, sed filii erunt Dei cum sint filii resurreccionis eius.[19]

---

182 ecciam] et BTV   sancto loco *tr.* T   184 in¹ *om.* T   185 pape] propter V   185 Diodiciano *codd.*   186 afflictus] astrictus T   187 ipsam futuram *tr.* BTV 192 recipit BV   195 magna illa *tr.* T   196 mensium *codd.*   198 quia *om.* BTV 199 in *om.* V   203 eius] suis BTV   206 neque¹ *om.* V   207 sint] suis T   eius *om.* T

---

[15] *Lib. Conc.*, fols. 24v-25r.
[16] *Lib. Conc.*, fol. 24v.
[17] Apoc. 11.2.
[18] *Lib. Conc.*, fol. 24v, except, of course, for the interpolated references to Frederic II.
[19] *Lib. Conc.*, fol. 24v.

EXPLICIT UNDECIMA DISTINCTIO, INCIPIT XII, IN QUA AGITUR DE
NUMERO ET DIFFERENCIA ET CONCORDIA DIFFERENCIARUM
GENERACIONUM NOVI ET VETERIS TESTAMENTI, ET CETERA.

Circa xii^{am} distinccionem est notandum quod, sicut Dominus Iesus Christus,
mediator Dei et hominis, ut lapis angularis copulans ad se duas parietes,[1]
faciens pacem hiis qui prope et pacem hiis qui longe, in medio duorum
testamentorum, in medio duorum animalium in presepio, in medio doctorum
5 in templo, in medio discipulorum in cena, in medio duorum latronum in
cruce, et bis in medio discipulorum ianuis clausis inuentus est, sic, ut
opinantur multi, tenet medium et corporalis apparuit in medio cunctarum
generacionum ab Adam usque ad ultimum electum, non quoad paritatem
temporum, sed numerum generacionum. Vnde sicut ab Adam usque ad
10 Christum fuerunt generaciones lxiii, sic a Christo usque in finem mundi erunt
generaciones lxiii[2]
    Spacia enim generacionum in ueteri testamento uaria et inequalia fuerunt:
alie sub longiori annorum spacio, alie sub breuiori. A natiuitate autem Noe
usque ad natiuitatem Sem fuerunt anni quingenti; Sem uero c erat annorum
15 quando genuit Arphasat, et Arphasath, cum esset annorum xxxvi, genuit
Sale. Vnde est notandum quod ab Adam usque ad Noe maiora fuerunt spacia
generacionum quam a Noe usque ad Dauid. Porro a Dauid usque ad
transmigracionem Babilonis non a natiuitate unius usque ad natiuitatem
alterius accipiendum est tempus generacionis, sed a regno in regnum, ex qua
20 re accidit ut omnino breuiora sint spacia generacionum, ut aliquis xvi annis,
alius tribus annis, alius tribus mensibus regnante referantur, et tamen
unumquodque spacium regni sub una generacione accipiendum est, et
cetera.[3]

Titulum generacionum] generalium T   et cetera *om.* T   2 hominum BTV   3 pacem[2] *om.* BV   9 temporum] corporum BV   numeracionem Y   10 lx T   in]
ad BTV   12 enim *om.* T; erunt *add.* BTV   15 et Arphasath *om.* T   17 a[1] *om.* BV
20 aliquis] aliis BV   21 regnante] generante V

---

[1] Cf. Eph. 2.20.
[2] Cf. *Lib. Conc.*, fol. 110v.
[3] *Lib. Conc.*, fol. 12r.

Differt enim uetus testamentum a nouo ex predictis, et luna a sole;
25 oportebat enim generaciones prioris testamenti, ad modum lune crescentis
et decrescentis, uarios et dissimiles accipere cursus, in nouo autem manere
stabiles sicut sol, qui semper manet in iubare claritatis sue, et reuera sicut sol,
quia sol iusticie Christus est, qui regnat in populo christiano sicut hebreorum
in populo Moyses, cuius splendor faciei lune similitudinem expressit. Igitur
30 in testamento nouo non secundum carnem accipienda est generacio, sed
secundum spiritum, secundum illud euangelii: *Quod natum est ex carne, caro
est, et quod natum est ex spiritu, spiritus est.*[4] Et quoniam xxx annorum erat
Dominus quando cepit habere filios spirituales, recte spacium generacionis
in nouo testamento xxx annorum numero terminatur, et nimirum, quia
35 perfeccio ipsius numeri ad fidem pertinet Trinitatis. Igitur generaciones
ecclesie sub spacio xxx annorum singule sub singulis tricenariis accipiende
sunt, ita ut, sicut Matheus comprehendit tempus primi status ab Abraam
usque ad Christum sub spacio generacionum xlii[rum], ita tempus secundi status
a fuga mulieris sub eodem generacionum numero non sit dubium terminari,
40 cum hoc ostendatur figuratum in numero dierum quo mansit absconditus
Helias a facie Acab, et quo mulier amicta sole, que designat ecclesiam, mansit
abscondita in solitudine a facie serpentis diebus seu annis Mcclx, que fuga
in suo toto fuit in fine secunde generacionis a Christo.[5] Erit igitur duracio
tocius secundi status usque ad clarum tempus plenitudinis secundum Da-
45 nielem a uigilia passionis Christi, quando cessauit figura agni tipici, dies seu
anni Mcccxxxv,[6] ex quo sequitur quod ultima istarum generacionum erit xiiii
annorum a tempore prefacto, et erit finis generacionum xxx annorum, nec
mirum, quia tam in ipsa quam in sequenti generacione ab ea omnia sunt
mutanda, ut in Apocalipsi noua nupta agni et noua Ierusalem, ciuitas sancta,
50 et agni nupcie sub ingenti gaudio ostenduntur, ecciam et celum nouum et
terram nouam uise sunt, *et dixit qui sedebat in trono: Ecce, noua facio omnia.*[7]
Vnde, cum hec generacio xiiii annorum sit medium inter generaciones xxx
annorum tocius secundi status et generaciones tocius tercii status, datur

---

26 decrescentis] recrescentis BV   28 quia] qui BV   sicut] sunt BV   34 numero]
spacio *add.* T   35 ipsius] illius T   38 generacionum] numerum *add.* BTV   secundi]
sancti T   41 et] ex BTV   44 tocius] seculi *add.* BTV   secundi *om.* M[ac]   ad]
status *add.* T   claram T   tempus *om.* M[ac]   45 quando] quam T   46 anni] agni
M   47 a] in T   et *om.* T   53 et ... status *om.* V *per hom.*

---

[4] Jn. 3.6.
[5] *Lib. Conc.*, fol. 12r-v.
[6] Dan. 12.12.
[7] Apoc. 21.5.

intelligi quod generaciones secundi status longe maiores fuerunt et sunt
55 sequentibus generacionibus tocius tercii status.[8]

Et ne uideatur discordia inter numerum Danielis et numerum fuge
mulieris, actendat lector in diuersis radicibus unum finem. Dicitur Danielis
xi°: *A tempore quo iuge ablatum fuerit sacrificium et posita fuerit abominacio
dies Mcclxxxx,*[9] et cetera. Daniel incipit computare a principio secunde
60 generacionis a Christo, hoc est a uigilia passionis; fuga uero mulieris fuit in
fine eiusdem generacionis, unde numerus Danielis a radice sua ponit
Mcclxxxx usque ad misticum Antichristum, seu primum Herodem doctorum,
fuga uero mulieris ponit Mcclx, quod totum est unum, licet sit radix diuersa.
Illos autem xliiii°ʳ dies quos usque ad tempus plenitudinis Daniel tacet non
65 est nisi labor et dolor, tempus tenebrarum et silencium ueritatis, in quorum
principio misticus, in fine uero magnus Antichristus regnabit, ut primus
Herodes in natiuitate Christi, secundus uero in passione. Generaciones uero
que ab Adam usque ad Dauid de natiuitate unius in natiuitatem alterius
fuerunt; generaciones tocius secundi status de natiuitate in natiuitatem seu
70 successionem, in successionem non carnalem sed spiritalem respiciunt, ut
quod in ueteri testamento designabant reges Iuda, in nouo testamento usque
ad tempus plenitudinis in Christo et in romanis pontificibus consumatum.
Generaciones uero que a Dauid usque ad Zorobabel de regno in regnum
fuerunt generaciones tocius tercii status consimili modo respiciunt, ut quod
75 romani imperatores a Constantino et deinceps significauerunt in tercio
generali statu misterialiter impleatur, quia Dominus Iesus Christus rex fuit
pariter et sacerdos.

Spacia uero generacionum huius temporis per racionem superius dictam,
ut creditur, equalia erunt; quantorum annorum uero erit generacionis spa-
80 cium soli Deo relinquendum est, suo enim tempore experimenta docebunt.
Dicit Ioachim quod illud tempus tocius tercii status erit absque humana
extimacione annorum;[10] dicit eciam Iohannes quod tam magna mirabilia et
tam magne mutaciones et nouitates que in tempore illo sunt fiende non
modico annorum spacio indigebunt, ut per totum mundum Dei mirabilia
85 clarius et spaciosius elucescant;[11] tamen contrarium in euangelio legitur, ubi

---

57 actendatur BTV   60 generaciones M^ac   61 sua *om.* BTV   63 radix sit *tr.* T
64 Daniel tacet *ante* usque *tr.* BTV   65 est *om.* M^ac   et[2] *om.* T   68 in *om.* BV
70 sed] seu B   71 designabant ... testamento[2] *om.* V *per hom.*   82 annorum] domorum
T   eciam *om.* V   Ioachim BTV   83 que *om.* BTV

---

[8] Cf. *Lib. Conc.*, fols. 12v-13r.
[9] Dan. 12.11.
[10] *Lib. Conc.*, fol. 56v.
[11] Cf. *Postilla*, fol. 31v.

dicitur quod, *statim post tribulacionem dierum illorum sol obscurabitur, et luna non dabit lumen suum.*[12] Sequitur: *Et tunc apparebit signum Filii hominis in celo, et uidebunt Filium hominis uenientem,*[13] et cetera. Vnde, licet lictera uideatur contrarium dicere, tamen Iohannes sic exponit: *statim,* idest

90 in eodem statu tercio, scilicet generali, et non in alio, quia post ipsum non sequitur alius generalis seu temporalis status, sed illa gloria que neque medium neque finem habebit. Vnde, ad clariorem euidenciam duracionis horum temporum secundum scripturarum diuersum datum numerum, est sciendum quod a construccione turris Babel, ut dicit Ioachim, in qua diuisis

95 linguis remansit lingua ebrea, usque ad Christum secundum xxii^{as} licteras ebreorum fuerunt xxii centenaria annorum, sic, secundum xxiii licteras latinorum, erunt xxiii centenaria annorum a construccione urbis Rome, in qua est principalis sedes latinorum et ecclesie Christi, usque ad extremam mutacionem sanctuarii, et inter cetera Ioachim sumit hec mistice ex Danielis

100 viii°, ubi dicit angelus: *Vsque ad uesperam et mane, dies duo milia tricenti, et mundabitur sanctuarium,*[14] diem sumendo pro anno. Tempore autem Danielis fluxerant c anni a construccione urbis predicte, unde Daniel erat tunc in secundo centenario per "b" designato. Primus autem centenarius cepit circa tempus captiuitatis x tribuum, in quo cepit Dei sanctuarium

105 conculcari, unde ex predictis Christus uenit in octauo centenario designato per "h", quod non est lictera sed aspiracio, sic et Christus non per humanum opus, sed per aspiracionem Spiritus sancti est de uirgine conceptus et natus.[15]

Creditur autem quod iste octauus centenarius fuit completus in excidio Ierusalem, completis xlii^{bus} annis a resurreccione Christi, unde a tempore

110 raptus Christi, seu ascensionis in celum, usque ad centenarium designatum per "x" in mistico Antichristo sunt, secundum latinas licteras, anni Mcclxxxx, et a fuga mulieris Mcclx, ut in x lictera, que crucem significat, in suo centenario sub Nabocodonosor et Naaman turpiter conculcetur et in ipso eodem centenario super uertices omnium regum tocius orbis ut Deus

---

87-88 Filii hominis *om.* BTV   89 Ioachim BTV   93-94 diuersum ... sciendum] datum est diuersarum numerum et sciendum T   95 lingua] est *add.* TV   98 sede M 102 fluxerunt BV; fluxiit T   104 tempus *om.* M^{ac}   105 conculcari] occultari T designato *om.* BTV   106 quod *om.* V   108 completus fuit *tr.* BTV   110 designacio T   111 x] Christum BTV   112 ut in x lictera *om.* BTV   113 in *om.* V 114 super] sunt BTV

---

[12] Mt. 24.29.
[13] Mt. 24.30.
[14] Dan. 8.14.
[15] *Postilla*, fol. 114r-v. Olivi takes this material from *De semine scripturarum*, which he ascribes to Joachim; for Arnold of Vilanova's use of the tract, see the Introduction, pp. 34-35.

115 honorabiliter exaltetur. Ecciam super ista materia Iohannes, partem Apocalipsis tangens, scilicet, *numerus hominis et numerus bestie est dclxvi*,[16] dicit
quod a natiuitate hominis Christi usque ad primam exaltacionem bestie
sarracenice uinctis persis et captis Damasco, Phenice, Egypto et Ierusalem,
fuerunt anni dclxvi, et ab ista prima exaltacione istius bestie usque ad
120 misticum Antichristum sunt similiter anni dclxvi, et a tempore uigilie
passionis, quando cessauit figura agni tipici, usque ad secundam exaltacionem bestie predicte per Affricam et Asyam sollempniter diuulgate fuerunt
anni dclxvi, et ab ista secunda exaltacione bestie predicte usque ad magnum
Antichristum erunt anni dclxvi. Si autem terminus utriusque tribulacionis sub
125 utroque Antichristo in numeris supradictis includitur aut excluditur, cautus
lector materiam haberet pre manibus satis claret.

Tamen, ut presentem materiam concludamus, concordatis passibus Danielis, isto scilicet, *usque ad uesperam et mane dies duo milia tricenti et
mundabitur sanctuarium*,[17] cum predicto, scilicet, *a tempore quo iuge ablatum*
130 *fuerit sacrificium et posita fuerit abominacio dies,* seu anni, *Mcclxxxx; beatus
qui peruenerit ad dies,* seu annos, *Mccccxxxv*,[18] istis igitur passibus concordatis
a prima mundacione sanctuarii post mortem magni Antichristi usque ad
secundam mundacionem eiusdem, quando exibunt angeli et separabunt
malos de medio iustorum post mortem illius Gog, essent cc^{ti} et vii anni sub
135 "z" lictera terminandi; tum quid horum erit uel non erit soli Deo relinquendum est. Generaciones uero illorum temporum, si trium mensium uel
trium annorum, ad perfeccionem tocius trinitatis; uel quatuor mensium uel
iiii^{or} annorum, ad perfeccionem iiii^{or} uoluminum euangeliorum; uel quinque
mensium uel quinque annorum, ad perfeccionem quinque librorum Moysi;
140 uel mensium vi uel vi annorum, ad perfeccionem vi ydriarum aque que tunc
conuertentur in uinum, idest vi imperia infidelium ad fidem Christi; uel vii
mensium uel vii annorum, ad perfeccionem vii beatitudinum que in fine illius
temporis in generali resurreccione dabuntur, et huiusmodi ascendendo, ut
tamen predixi, soli Deo relinquendum est.

---

115 honorabilis BTV   Ioachim BTV   partem] personalitatem BTV   116 est *om.*
BTV   118 uinctis *om.* M^{ac} 119 ista] illa BTV   124 tribulaciones M   126-127 haberet ... materiam *om.* V *per hom.*   126 satis] ut *praem.* BTV   claruet M   129 a *om.*
BTV   131 Mccccxxxvi BTV   134 essent] centum B   et *om.* BTV   135 terminanda tunc T   tum] tamen BV   136 si] scilicet BTV   138-139 uel quinque mensium *om.* BV   140 ydrianum M   142 perfeccionum M

---

[16] Cf. Apoc. 13.18; *Postilla*, fol. 92v.

[17] Dan. 8.14.

[18] Dan. 12.11.

145 Et sicut signa magna precesserunt resurreccionem Christi in sole et luna
et stellis et elementis in fine illorum ueterum, ita et signa non minus magna
in fine nouorum precedent generalem resurreccionem, unde Ieronimus dicit
se uidisse in libris iudeorum quindecim signa ante diem iudicii.[19] In prima
die eriget se mare xl cubitis super altitudinem moncium, stans in loco suo
150 quasi murus; in secunda die tantum descendet quod uix uideri poterit; in
tercia die marine belue apparentes super mare dabunt rugitos usque ad celum;
in quarta die ardebunt mare et aque; in quinta die erbe et arbores dabunt
rorem sanguineum; in sexta die ruent hedificia; in septima die petre collidentur ad inuicem; in octaua die generalis fiet terremotus; in nona die adequa-
155 bitur terra; in x die exibunt homines de cauernis terre et ibunt uelut amentes,
nec poterunt sibi mutuo loqui; in undecima die stabunt ossa mortuorum
super sepulcra; in duodecima die cadent stelle de celo, et sol conuertetur in
tenebras, et luna in sanguinem; in terciadecima die morientur omnes uiuentes
ut cum mortuis resurgant; in quartadecima die ardebunt celi et terra ut
160 ascensus et descensus usque ad locum ignis; in quintadecima die fiet celum
nouum et terra noua et resurgent omnes ad iudicium, unde Aggey secundo:
Adhuc unum modicum, et ego mouebo celum et terram. Sequitur: *Et ueniet*
desideratus cunctis gentibus, dicit Dominus exercituum.[20] Tunc enim uidebit
omnis caro salutare Dei,[21] ad extremum scilicet iudicium uenientis, et cetera.

---

145 sicut *om.* BTV   et[2] *om.* BTV   148 sedecim BTV   150 poterit
uideri *tr.* T   151 marine] maxime V   152 aque] omnes *add.* BTV   erbe] orbe T
153-154 collidetur M   155 homines] de cauernis terre uel *add.* T   162 Et sequitur
tr. BTV   164 uenientem BTV

---

[19] This list of the fifteen signs of the Last Judgement, attributed to Jerome, occurs in two
manuscript anthologies circulating in Joachite circles. The first, in Catalan, is listed in M. Beti,
"Noticies de dos manuscrits," p. 58; the second, in Latin, is in Paris, Bibliothèque Nationale
MS Lat. 3319, fols. 87v-88r.

[20] Ag. 2.7-8.

[21] Lc. 3.6.

EXPLICIT XII DISTINCTIO. INCIPIT XIII, IN QUA AGITUR DE ORDINE GENERACIONUM AB ADAM USQUE AD CHRISTUM ET A CHRISTO USQUE AD FINEM MUNDI, ET DE CONCORDIA EARUM.

Circa xiii distinccionem est notandum quod, sicut quatuor Apocalipsis animalia senas alas habencia primas quatuor sigillorum aperciones senas generaciones habentes in apercione cuiuslibet tangunt, sic et sedes in celo posita ad restringendum penas et ampliandum gracias, et xx^{ti} iiii^{or} seniores
5   circa eam sedentes quinti signaculi et sexti apercionem ostendunt ut, dicte sedi seu paci xx generacionibus datis, in apercione sexti a quatuor mundi partibus pressure guerrarum et signa magna insurgant, et faciant euigilare dilectam.[1] Vnde in primis a Iacob inchoandum est et usque ad Dauid tempora percurrendum ut, sub duabus primis sigillorum apercionibus peractis illis in
10   figura et misterio que de natiuitate in natiuitatem sunt generacionibus, ad illas que de regno in regnum sunt per ordinem ueniamus, ut in subsequentibus claret.

	Iacob
	Iudas
15	Phares
	Esron
	Aram
	Aminadab
	Naason
20	Salmon
	Booz
	Obeth
	Iesse
	Dauid.[2]

Titulum xiii] distinccio *add.* BTV   eorum *codd.*   1-2 animalia Apocalipsis *tr.* BTV
3 in¹ *om.* M^ac   aperciones M^ac   et *om.* T   3-4 posita in celo *tr.* V
6 sedi *om.* T   apercione] cuiuslibet *add.* M^ac   8 a] ad T   9 ut] et T   signaculorum T   11 ordinem] sunt *add.* T   sequentibus BV

[1] Cf. Apoc. 4.
[2] *Lib. Conc.*, fol. 24v.

25   Regnauit autem Dauid in Ebron annis vii^em, in Ierusalem uero xxxiii; totum
autem tempus quo ipse regnauit fuit xxxx annorum, et mortuus est.[3] In nouo
autem testamento xii generaciones decurse sunt ab incarnacione Domini
usque ad extrema tempora sancti Siluestri pape, generaciones seu succes-
siones dico spirituales, non carnales. Computandi enim sunt in nouo testa-
30 mento xxx anni per singulas generaciones, consideratis annis romanorum
pontificum et imperatorum,[4] unde hic nota quod quot pontifices sub una
generacione continentur, tot ab uno illorum principaliter nominantur, ut
omnes non plures sed unus solus dicantur. Qui uero succidentes in sequenti
generacione ponuntur, non successores sed successor illius precedentis
35 generacionis sic per ordinem habeantur, et quod in ueteri dicitur, "genuit,"
in nouo intelligatur, "successorem habuit uel habebit."

        Prima generacio peracta est sub Domino nostro Iesu Christo, ab anno
incarnacionis eius usque ad annum quintum decimum imperii Tiberii Cesaris,
quo anno, sicut creditur, babtizatus est Christus, anni xxx.[5]

40   Secunda generacio fuit sub beato Petro, principe apostolorum, et imperatoribus romanorum Caio, Claudio et Nerone, anni ab incarnacione lx^a.

        Tercia, incipiens sub beato Petro et Nerone, consumata est in diebus Cleti
pape et Domiciani augusti, anni ab incarnacione lxxxx.

        Quarta incepit sub Domiciano predicto, consumata uero est sub papa
45 Auaristo et Adriano imperatore, anni ab incarnacione cxx.

        Quinta incepit sub Adriano predicto, consumata uero est sub papa
Thelesphoro et Antonino augusto, anni ab incarnacione cl.

        Sexta incepit sub Antonino prefato, consumata uero est in diebus Soteris
pape et Marcii imperatoris, anni ab incarnacione clxxx.

50   Septima incepit sub Marcio predicto, consumata uero est in diebus
Victoris pape et Helii augusti, anni ab incarnacione ccx.

        Octaua incepit sub Helyo prefato, consumata uero sub Ponciano papa et
Maximo augusto, anni ab incarnacione ccxxxx.

        Nona incepit sub Maximo predicto, consumata uero est in diebus Sixti
55 pape et Valeriani augusti, anni ab incarnacione cclxx.

        Decima incepit sub Valeriano predicto, consumata uero est sub Marcello
papa et Diocliciano augusto, anni ab incarnacione ccc.

---

29 enim *om.* T   33 dicatur BTV   34 successor] successoribus T   37 ab anno
om. BV   44 consumato M   49 pape *om.* BTV   50 supradicto BV   52 prefato]
predicto BTV   uero] est *add.* BTV   57 et *om.* BV   anni ... ccc *om.* BV

---

[3] *Lib. Conc.*, fol. 92v.
[4] *Lib. Conc.*, fol. 44v.
[5] See *Lib. Conc.*, fols. 44r-45v, for the list of twelve generations; specific debates are added
by the author of the *Brev.*, perhaps from the *Lib. Fig.*

Vndecima incepit sub Diocliciano prefato, consumata uero est sub beato
Siluestro papa et Constantino imperatore, qui primus christianum ampliauit
60 imperium, anni ab incarnacione cccxxx.
   [*Glosa.* Hic scilicet papa Siluester, secundum aliquos, fuit ille angelus
Apocalipsis qui habebat clauem putei abissi et catenam magnam in manu sua,
et aprehendit draconem serpentem anticum, qui est diabolus et Sathanas, et
ligauit eum per annos M^e, hoc est usque ad tempora casus illius pontificalis
65 stelle que habebat clauem putei abissi. Sequitur: *Et miserit eum in abissum
ne amplius seducat gentes donec consumentur M^e anni,*[6] *et cetera.*]
   Duodecima incepit sub eodem papa et eodem imperatore, consumata uero
est sub Liberio papa et Constantino arriano, filio Constantini predicti, qui
post annos quatuor Iulianum apostatam successorem accepit, et cetera, anni
70 ab incarnacione ccclx.
   Igitur duodecima generacione a Iacob cepit habere regem unctum oleo
populus Israel, et duodecima generacione a Christo cepit habere regem
christianum populus gentilis, calcatis et superatis in utroque populo unice
fidei inimicis. Ibi quoque electa est Ierusalem et sublimata super omnia
75 tabernacula Iacob, hic romana ecclesia sublimata est super omnes orientales
ecclesias; utrique, ut iam dixi, Ierusalem in consimili generacione concessa
est sublimitas regni. Sciendum uero est quod homo Christus Iesus, qui unctus
Spiritu sancto regnat in populo christiano, rex est pariter et sacerdos, quod
intelligens Constantinus imperator beato pape Siluestro imperialem, quam
80 ipse tenere uidebatur, tanquam debitam Christo regi sponte obtulit dignitatem. Verum quia regnum Christi non est de hoc mundo, sic uisum fuit
romanis pontificibus debitam semper Christo accipere potestatem, ut tantum
usus temporalis regiminis illis remaneat qui mundi gloriam querunt, ne hii qui
iusta apostolum militant Deo negociis temporalibus implicentur.[7] Non solum
85 autem propter hoc, sed quia causa misterii exigebat, quia quod in ueteri
testamento designabant reges Iuda, consumatum est sub nouo in Christo et
in pontificibus romanis, et quod significauerunt romani imperatores a
Constantino et deinceps, consumabitur circa finem mundi cum subiecerit
Dominus Iesus omnes inimicos suos sub pedibus eius.[8]

---

58 Vndecima] uero *add.* T   59 papa *om.* BV   60 anni ... cccxxx *om.* BV
66 secudat *om.* T; homines seu *add.* BTV   anni] ab incarnacione *praem.* BTV
M^e] ccxxx *add.* BV; ccc *add.* T   68 est *om.* T   69 et cetera *om.* BM^{ac}TV   70 Mccclx
T   73 et *om.* T   in utroque *rep.* T   unice] ueridice BV; uertice T   75 est
om. BM^{ac}TV   super *om.* M^{ac} 78 regnauit BTV   80 debitum in T   82 Christo
om. BTV   83 gloriam mundi *tr.* T   84 Deo] Christo *praem.* BTV; nunciant *add.* T
implicent T   86 in *om.* BTV   88 et *om.* T

---

[6] Apoc. 20.3.
[7] 2 Tim. 2.4.
[8] *Lib. Conc.*, fol. 45r.

90 Vt autem inter xii et xii statuta meta seruentur, incipiendum est a tercia
decima generacione, hoc est a rege Salomone usque ad Achaz, in quibus sunt
duorum secundorum sigillorum misteria consumata;[9] sub nouo quoque
similiter scribende sunt per ordinem generaciones, uidelicet a tercia decima
usque ad xxiiii^{am} sub duabus consimilibus sigillorum apercionibus ut, notatis
95 temporibus romanorum pontificum et imperatorum, sciatur per singula unde
agendum sit.[10]

Primus post Dauid, qui fuit xii^{us} a Iacob, regnauit Salmon super omnem
Israel annis xl, per quem donauit Deus sapienciam et pacem populo Israel,
et cetera. Tercia decima generacio fuit ab incarnacione Domini sub papa
100 Damaso et Liberio, Constantino augusto filio Constantini, consumata uero
est in diebus pape Zozimi, Ciriaci et Graciani augusti; sub ista generacione,
mortuo Iuliano, qui usurpauerat imperium, in Christi sapiencia, qui semper
regnat in populo christiano, data est pax et requies populo fideli, cessante
persequucione paganorum, et cetera, anni ab incarnacione ccclxxxx[11]
105 Secundus post Dauid fuit Roboam, qui regnauit post Salomonem annis
xvii, sub quo diuisum fuit regnum Dauid in duo regna, hoc est in Iudam et
Effraym, sola tribu Iuda filio Salomonis relicta, et cetera. Quarta decima
generacio ab incarnacione fuit sub romanis pontificibus Ciricio, Anastasio et
Innocencio, et imperatoribus romanis Theodosio, Archadio et Honorio; hic
110 scinduntur ecclesie grecorum ab ecclesia romana, ut regnum Dauid sub
Roboam in duas partes obtinuit domus Iuda, obtinuit romana ecclesia. Nam
grecorum ecclesiis suis arrianis episcopis innitentibus, alii in Christum, alii
in Spiritum sanctum blasphemauerunt, et cetera, anni ab eadem incarnacione
ccccxx.[12]
115 Tercius post Dauid fuit Abia, qui regnauit post Roboam tribus annis, qui
pugnauit contra Ieroboam, et tunc preualuerunt filii Iuda contra filios Israel
eo quod sperarent in Domino Deo suo, et cetera. Quinta decima generacio
ab incarnacione fuit sub papa Innocencio et Honorio augusto, consumata
uero est sub Leone papa, Theodosio iuniore. Hic fuit conuicta grecorum

---

90 et xii *om.* BTV   91 est *om.* M^{ac} 94 ut] et T   notas M^{ac} 99 et cetera
om. BV   generaciones M^{ac} 100 Constantini *om.* BTV   102 usurpauit BTV
107 Decima quarta *tr.* T   109 huic BV   110 regimen BV   113 et cetera
om. M^{ac} 114 cccxx BTV   117 eo quod ... cetera *om.* T   speraret BV   Deo *om.* B
119 conuicta] disiuncta BTV

---

[9] *Lib. Conc.*, fol. 45r.
[10] For the twelve generations after David, see *Lib. Conc.*, fols. 45r-50r; the dates are added
by the author of the *Brev.*
[11] *Lib. Conc.*, fols. 45v-46r.
[12] Cf. *Lib. Conc.*, fol. 46r.

120 ecclesia a romana, sicut regnum Israel a regno Iuda, et cetera, anni a predicta
incarnacione ccccl.[13]

Quartus post Dauid fuit Asa, filius Abie regis Iuda, qui regnauit annis xl.
Contra istum ascendit Zara ethiobs cum decies centenis militis; orauit Asa
toto corde ad Deum et exauditus est, et inimicos eius in fugam conuertit, et
125 cetera.[14] Sexta decima generacio ab incarnacione fuit sub Leone papa et
Theodosio predicto, consumata uero est sub Felice et Simplicio pontificibus
et Zenone augusto. Hic uenit innumerabilis multitudo diuersarum gencium
cum rege Athilia in suis regulis ad perdendum occidentalem imperium, sed
orante rege Asa, hoc est sanctissimo Leone papa, regem Christum uictoriam
130 de eis habita est, et cetera, anni a prefata incarnacione cccclxxx.[15]

Quintus post Dauid fuit Iosaphat, filius Asa regis Iuda, qui regnauit annis
xxv. Hic habuit amiciciam cum impiissimo Acab, rege Israel, et cetera.
Decima septima generacio ab incarnacione inchoata est sub papa Simplicio
et Zenone imperatore, consumata uero est sub papa Sisimacho et Anastasio
135 augusto. Hic impiissima gens gotorum amiciciam habuit cum impiissimo
imperatore Zenone et permissione imperatoris predicti, egressa ab oriente
fedatura latinam ecclesiam, intrauit Ytaliam ut quod operata in Constantinopolim fuerat operaretur et Rome, et cetera, anni a predicta incarnacione dx.[16]

Sextus post Dauid fuit Ioram, filius Iosaphat regis Iuda, qui regnauit annis
140 viii et diebus viii Ochozias filius Achab, rex Israel impiissimus et Dei
inimicus, cum pre solito unitum esset regnum Iuda regno Israel, eo quod
Ioram esset gener Achab, fecit peccare Israel et adorare Baal, et cetera. Hic
Helias est eleuatus in celum et Eliseus indutus est duplici spiritu. Decima
octaua generacio ab incarnacione inchoata est sub Sisimaco papa et Anas-
145 tasio imperatore, consumata uero est sub romanis pontificibus Siluerio et
Virgilio, et Iustino augusto. Hic Theodoricus, rex gothorum impiissimus et
fidei inimicus, cum Iustinus imperator arrianos in oriente positos uellet ad

120 Roma BV   et cetera *om.* M[ac]   121 cccl BTV   123 militis] militum *codd.*
124 Deum] Dominum *praem.* BTV   127 gencium] generacionum BV   129 Asa *om.*
T   130 est *om.* BTV   et cetera *om.* M[ac]   a] ab BV; *om.* M[ac]   ccclxxx T
131 Iuda] Achab *add.* M[ac]   132 xxvi BV   135 gentes M   grecorum *codd.*   im-
piisiimo *om.* BTV   137 operata ac *add.* M[ac]   138 et cetera *om.* M[ac]   140 et diebus
viii *om.* TV dies *codd.*   141 regnum] regem T   regno] regus T   142 gener]
gentiles T   Achab] rex Ysrael *add.* BV   143 inductus M[ac]   145 est *om.* BTV
146 augusto] imperatore BTV   147 imperatore M

[13] *Lib. Conc.*, fol. 46v.
[14] Cf. 2 Par. 14.11.
[15] *Lib. Conc.*, fol. 46v.
[16] *Lib. Conc.*, fol. 47r-v.

fidem catholicam reformare, Theodoricus misit papam Iohannem ad augustum dicens se in Ytaliam claudere ecclesias catholicorum nisi ipse in orientis
150 partibus arrianos dimitteret in quiete. Hic sanctus Benedictus euolauit ad celum et ordo eius indutus est dupplici spiritu, et cetera, anni ab incarnacione predicta dxl.[17]

Septimus post Dauid fuit Ochozias, filius Ioam regis Iuda, qui regnauit anno uno diebus octo. Post ipsum regnauit Athalia, uxor Ioram, annis vii dies
155 xi; hunc occidit Iheu. Hic fecit malum coram Domino; sicut pater eius, ambulauit in uiis Achab, et cetera. Decima nona generacio ab incarnacione inchoata est sub papa Vigilio et Iustiniano augusto, consumata uero est sub Iustino minore. Hic suscitauit Deus spiritum Iustiniani, quasi alterius Iheu, et congregata sinodo episcoporum, tradidit illis condempnandam posterita-
160 tem Anastasii imperatoris heretici et aliorum hereticorum, quasi sacerdotes Baal; et quasi altera Athalia in regno Iuda, secundum concordiam facti tantum, quedam femina in pontificio romano uterque a Deo punita fuit inuenta, anni ab incarnacione predicta dlxx.[18]

Octauus post Dauid fuit Iohas, filius Ochozie regis Iuda, qui regnauit annis
165 xl et diebus xii Hic restitutus est rex in domo Iuda, peractis vii annis ab obitu Ochozie, in quibus Athalia regnauit. Hic licet iustus et pacificus in principio, tamen post ad paternam prauitatem reuersus est, et cetera. Vicesima generacio ab incarnacione inchoata est sub papa Iohanne et Iustino augusto, consumata uero est sub beato Gregorio et Mauricio imperatore. Hic resti-
170 tutus est in Ytalia et amicus romanorum contra arrianos fuit, sed postea, oblitus percepti beneficii sui, ipse cum populo suo, ingressus per uiam patrum suorum, factus est arrianus persecutor ministrorum Domini, et cetera, anni ab incarnacione dc.[19]

Nonus post Dauid fuit Amasias filius Iohas regis Iuda, qui regnauit annis
175 xxix diebus xiiii, qui et ipse, sicut pater et auus, occisus est in selere suo. Istos tres reges supradictos, scilicet Ochozias, Iohas et Amasias, qui occisi sunt gladio, excludit euangelista de geneologia Saluatoris, tamen in numero generacionum cadunt, et cetera. Vicesima prima generacio ab incarnacione inchoata est sub papa Gregorio et Mauricio augusto, consumata uero est in

---

149 in² *om.* M^{ac}   154 diebus] dies *codd.*   157 Iustiniano] Iustino *codd.*
158 Deus] Dominus BV   160 imperatoris] et *praem. codd.*   161 in *om.* BTV
162 quedam ... uterque *om.* BTV   164 filius ... regis] mortuo Ochozia rege BTV
165 dies *codd.*   167 et cetera *om.* M^{ac}   168 et *om.* BTV   171 percepti] et cepti T
172 ministros *codd.*   178 et cetera *om.* BTV

---

[17] Cf. *Lib. Conc.*, fols. 47v-48r.
[18] *Lib. Conc.*, fol. 48r.
[19] *Lib. Conc.*, fol. 48v.

180 papa Honorio et Constantino augusto. Hic predictus Constantinus precursus
est ab Eradio imperatore. Ipse Eradilius, pater predicti Constantini, pugnauit
contra regem perssarum, qui multas prouincias romani imperii et ipsam
Ierosolimam adauxerat regno suo, recuperauit prouincias ante perditas et
restituit christianis, et cetera, anni ab incarnacione predicta dcxxx.[20]

185 Decimus post Dauid fuit Ozias seu Azarias, qui regnauit annis lii diebus
xv, in quibus diebus missi sunt prophete annunciare aduentum Christi in
carne, incipientibus primis omnium Ysaias et Osee; sub isto rege pars
quedam de populo Israel tradita est in manus regis assiriorum, et cetera.
Vicesima secunda generacio ab incarnacione inchoata est sub Honorio papa
190 et Constantino augusto, consumata uero est sub romanis pontificibus
Deodato et Bono et Iustiniano augusto. Hic diuerse religiones inceperunt in
ecclesia apparere annunciantes aduentum Christi ad iudicium; hic suscitauit
Deus spiritum regis arabum, qui per successionem tam regni quam perfidie
descenderat a Machumeto pseudo propheta sarracenorum, et primo quidem
195 deuastauerunt ierusolimanam, anthiocenam et alexandrinam ecclesiam,
deinde alias atque alias, iusto Dei iudicio permictente, ita ut possit dicere
alienus: *Vbi est Deus eorum,*[21] et cetera, anni ab incarnacione dclx. Hic
floruerunt Hylarius et Hambrosius in Ytalia, Ieronimus in Bethleem, Iohannes Grisostomus in Archadia, et Augustinus in Affrica, anni ut supra.[22]

200 Vndecimus post Dauid fuit Ioathan, qui Ozie successit in regnum, qui
regnauit annis xvi diebus xv, in cuius temporibus facta est secunda depopu-
lacio a rege assiriorum, et cetera. Vicesima tercia generacio ab incarnacione
inchoata est sub romanis pontificibus Deodato, Bono, Agatone, Leone,
Benedicto, Iohanne, et cetera, regnantibus in Ytalia longobardis; consumata
205 uero est sub predicto Iohanne papa et sub regno longobardorum. Hic
Iustinianus et Thiberius imperauerunt in partibus orientis, in quorum diebus
plurime ecclesie et prouincie per sarracenos deuastate sunt et depopulate, et
cetera, anni a predicta incarnacione dclxxxx.[23]

---

180 percussus *om.* BTV   181 Eradilius] Heraclius BV   pater] preter T   183 adau-
reat M; adduxerat BTV   suo] et *add.* V   184 et cetera *om.* M[ac]   185 dies *codd.*
187 primis] in *praem.* BTV   191 et[1] *om.* BTV   192 apparare M   Christi *om.*
BTV   194 descenderunt BTV   sarraceno BTV   195 Alexandriam M   196 alias[2]
om. BV posset T   dicere M   197 alienos M   et cetera *om.* M[ac]   199 et *om.* BTV
201 dies MT; diebus xv *om.* BV   xv] xvi T   202 et cetera *om.* M[ac]   203 est
om. BV   206 Thiberius] imperatorem *add.* BV   207 depopulate] fuit *praem.* M[ac]
207-208 et cetera *om.* M[ac]

---

[20] *Lib. Conc.*, fol. 48v.
[21] Ps. 78.10.
[22] *Lib. Conc.*, fol. 49r-v.
[23] *Lib. Conc.*, fol. 49v.

Duodecimus post Dauid fuit Acham, qui successit in regnum Ioathan, qui
210 regnauit annis xvi et diebus xvi, in cuius orologio reuersus est sol x gradibus.
Hic ascendit rex assiriorum in Damascum et, interfecto Rasim rege Syrie,
siros transtulit Cirenem; hucusque perseuerauit regnum Israel in loco suo,
deletum est autem sub sequenti generacione, vi° uidelicet anno Ezechie regis
Iude, et cetera. Vicesima quarta generacio ab incarnacione, regnantibus
215 longobardis in Ytalia, contaminantibus eam Philippus et Constantinus
persequutores seu retrogradi in orologio ueritatis, sub romanis pontificibus
Iohanne et alio Iohanne, Sisinnio et Constantino et Gregorio, qui infinita
grauamina propter multas adinuenciones errorum orientalium augustorum
perpessi sunt, sed Deus, iustus iudex, abenas sarracenorum contra eos
220 dissoluit, qui captis et deuastatis ecclesiis prouinciisque desolatis, totum
pondus impetus sui contra Constantinopolim direxerunt. Sed et sicut in
diebus Acham ascendit rex assiriorum in Damascum et, interfecto Rasim rege
Syrie, siros transtulit Cirenem, sic gens sarracenorum, dimicans contra regem
persarum, superatos et deuictos perssas transtulit in sectam suam, ita ut ex
225 eo tempore sarraceni pariter dicerentur.[24] Et sicut in tempore Ezechie regis
Iuda deletum est regnum Israhel, sic et augusti orientales, qui usque ad
consimilem generacionem participes fuerunt romani, ymmo ecclesiastici,
principatus, ita ut romani imperatores dicerentur, ex hinc, sicut regnum super
quod aliquando regnauerat rex Dauid, sicut et super Iudam desiit esse
230 regnum quia filii Israel, qui elegerant sibi regem Ieroboam, filium Nabath,
amoti sunt de loco suo, sic et imperium grecorum, quoad urbem Romam,
desiit esse imperium quia, *atrium,* inquid Iohannes, *quod est foris templum
eice foras, et ne meciaris illud quoniam datum est gentibus,*[25] et cetera.
Duodecim itaque generacionibus perseuerauit primus temporis cursus in
235 populo Israel, et totidem secundus; sic in ecclesia similis imutacio facta est,
et cetera, anni ab incarnacione prefata dccxx.[26]

Ezechias, uicesimus quintus a Iacob, post Acham regnauit in Iudam xiiii
annis, et a Dauid[27] usque ad ipsum generaciones xiiii; designabant uero
generaciones ecclesie xiiii, que a tempore sancti pape Siluestri usque ad
240 Zacharie pape tempora denotate cernuntur, idest anni ccccxx, ex quibus

---

210 et diebus] dies uero T; dies BMV   212 suo] sancto BV   213 dilectum BV
sequenti] se *add.* BV   214 et cetera *om.* M^ac   quarta] autem T   219 abenas] habentis
B; habeat V   222 interfecit BTV   rege] regenti BV; regem T   223 sarracena BTV
228 imperatoris M^ac   dicerent BTV   230 eligerunt BTV   234 generaciones
codd.   perseuerari BTV   237 a] et T   240 denotatiue BTV

---

[24] *Lib. Conc.,* fol. 49v.
[25] Apoc. 11.2.
[26] *Lib. Conc.,* fol. 50r.
[27] *Lib. Fig.,* pl. 4.

septuagenarii sex perficiuntur, qui uidelicet numerus, pro eo quod perfeccionem designat,[28] turbatis mundi rebus et confusis, finem uniuerse carnis aduenisse Deus omnipotens numerabatur, adeo ut romana ecclesia infirmaretur fide, doctoribus acclamantibus et dicentibus: *Morieris tu et non uiues.*[29]

245 Beatus papa Gregorius, qui similis eloquencie flore iure Ysaye prophete assimilabatur: *Vere exaudiuit Dominus Ezechie fletum, audiuit et romane ecclesie, additis illi xv annis, isti tricenario xv, quorum decem in magna peperit pace, quos sol significauit ad alciora reuersus, quinque uero pro uespertina declinacione accipiendi sunt;*[30] tempora uero siue generaciones que

250 post ista secuntur sunt pro uespere reputande. Protexit quoque Dominus sub illo annorum numero urbem Ierusalem ab assiriorum rege, protegit et romanam ecclesiam a sarracenorum regno donec iste numerus impleatur.[31]

Ne autem uideatur discordia in concordi numero generacionum noui et ueteris testamenti propter retrogradacionem istarum quindecim generacio-

255 num, datis scilicet ueteri ab Adam usque ad Christum lxxviii generacionibus, et a Christo usque ad finem mundi lxiii, uel ab Abraam usque ad babtismum Christi lx generacionibus et a Christo usque ad tempus plenitudinis xlvi, unde est aduertendum quod loco istarum xv generacionum retrogradarum, inter scilicet Ezechiam et Manassem, supplende sunt ille quindecim que sunt in

260 canna arboris Ioachim, scilicet ab Enoch usque ad Iacob patriarcham.[32] Vnde sicut ab Enoch qui fuit eleuatus in paradisum terrestrem, completis quindecim generacionibus, missi sunt duo fratres carnales, scilicet Iacob et Hesau, in quibus figura mirabili incepta est quedam distinccio inter templum et atrium, inter filios libere et filios ancille, sic, concordatis illis xv generacioni-

265 bus retrogradis ueteris, scilicet inter Ezechiam et Manassen, cum illis xv noui testamenti, scilicet a xxv[a], tempore Zacharie pape, in quo, sicut Enoch, eleuata est ecclesia, tanquam in paradisum terrestrem, super uertices regum sub Karolo magno, et datus est locus sedi et paci, ab ista xxv[a] dico usque ad quadragesimam primam, tempore Celestini, Innocencii et Honorii summo-

270 rum pontificum, in diebus Frederici imperatoris, missi sunt alii duo fratres

---

247 addito *codd.*   annos *codd.*   xv[2] *om.* T   248 peperit] reperit BTV; parte *add.* T   253 uideat T   254 quindecim] uiginti BV   258 quod] ex BV 261 sicut] Ioachim scilicet *add.* T   263 mirabiliter BTV   263-264 inter ... atrium *om.* BV   268 locus *post* paci *tr.* BTV   xxvi[a] BTV   dico] dies BV

---

[28] *Lib. Conc.*, fol. 50r.
[29] Cf. 2 Reg. 20.1; Is. 38.1.
[30] *Moralia in Job*, 12.2, 16.10.14 (PL 75.987, 1127).
[31] *Lib. Conc.*, fol. 50r.
[32] *Lib. Conc.*, fol. 50r; Joachim also discusses the revised generations in the *Lib. Conc.*, fols. 44r, 15r-16v; see also the diagram on fol. 14r.

spirituales, scilicet sanctus Franciscus et sanctus Dominicus, tanquam precursores Christi aduentus ad iudicium et signaturi Christi miliciam electorum contra aduersarium Antichristum, sub quorum tempore incepta est quedam mentalis et misterialis distinccio inter templum et atrium, inter filios libere
275 et filios ancille, seu inter filios Ierusalem et filios Babilonis. Vnde generaciones intermedie, inter scilicet Enoch et Zorobabel, quia intermedie sunt, totum intermedium statum mundi inter primum et tercium in generacionum numero et aliis factis mirabilibus non sine magno misterio prefigurant. Ille uero sex generaciones extreme superius, a primo scilicet parente usque ad
280 Enoch, et ille xi extreme inferius, scilicet a Zorobabel usque ad Christi aduentum in carne, illas xvii significant que extreme sunt tocius extremi temporis seu tercii mundi status, que, lege ueterum grauida tanquam testa nuclei in duas extremas partes diuisa, numerum nobis generacionum tocius tercii status et ordinem mirabilium fiendorum per ipsius figuras et noui
285 misteria in ipso ostendunt, ut inmediate post generaciones predictas ad extremum iudicium sequatur Christi aduentus. Ex predictis igitur numeralis concordia generacionum noui et ueteris satis claret ut ab Adam usque ad Christum sint generaciones lxiii, et a Christo usque ad ultimum aduentum eius sint consimiliter generaciones lxiii, et sic de ceteris.
290 Ne autem iste xv generaciones retrograde, eo quod inimici Dei, iusto Dei iudicio, retrogressi sunt, ut darent scilicet locum sedi et paci, transactis temporibus iiii^{or} animalium habencium alas senas, uideantur sub silencio preterire, ut ad inceptum iter redeamus, oportet nos memoratas generaciones sub pontificum romanorum et francorum principum cronica presenti operi
295 annotare, anni ab incarnacione prefata dccl.
In xxvi generacione ab incarnacione prefuerunt ecclesie romane Stephanus, Paulus, Constantinus, Stephanus, in diebus Papini et Karoli regum franchorum, anni ab incarnacione predicta dcclxxx.[33]
In xxvii^a generacione ab incarnacione prefuerunt in ecclesia Adrianus et
300 Leo, in diebus Karoli supradicti, qui postea factus est imperator, anni a predicta incarnacione dcccx.
In xxviii generacione ab incarnacione prefuerunt in ecclesia idem Leo, Stephanus, Pascalis, Eugenius, Valentinus et Gregorius, in diebus Karoli imperatoris primi et Lodouici filii eius, anni a prefata incarnacione dcccxl.

---

271 scilicet *om.* T   tanquam *om.* BV   272 aduentum *codd.*   ad] ac BV
275 filios^1 *om.* T   280 a *om.* T   281 aduentum] uentum M^{ac} que] quia *codd.*
sunt *om.* T   282 lex *codd.*   288-289 et ... lxiii *om.* BTV *per hom.*   290 Dei^2
om. T   295 notare M^{ac} incarnacione] que *add.* BTV   297 regnum M   304 primi
imperatoris *tr.* TV

---

[33] *Lib. Conc.*, fols. 50v-51r, for the generations from the twenty-sixth to the thirty-fifth.

305 In xxix generacione ab incarnacione prefuerunt in ecclesia Sergius, Benedictus, Nicholaus et Adrianus, in diebus Ludouici et Lotharii, anni a dicta incarnacione dccclxx.

In xxxª generacione ab incarnacione prefuerunt in ecclesia Iohannes, Martinus, Adrianus, Stephanus, Romanus et Theodorus, in diebus Karoli 310 secundi et Karoli tercii, anni ab incarnacione dcccc.

In xxxiª generacione ab incarnacione prefuerunt in ecclesia Iohannes, Benedictus, Leo, Christoforus, Sersius, Anastasius, Landus, Iohannes, Leo et Stephanus, in diebus Lodouici tercii et Berengarii primi et Berengarii secundi et Ugonis, anni ab inarnacione predicta dccccxxx.

315 In xxxiiª generacione ab incarnacione prefuerunt in ecclesia Iohannes, Leo, Stephanus, Marinus, Agapitus et Iohannes, in diebus Berengarii tercii et Berengarii quarti et Alberti, anni ab incarnacione predicta dccclx.

In xxxiiiª generacione ab incarnacione prefuerunt in ecclesia Benedictus, Leo, Iohannes, Bonus, Bonifacius, Benedictus, Iohannes et Iohannes, in 320 diebus Othonis primi, Othonis secundi, et Othonis tercii, anni ab incarnacione predicta dcccclxxxx.

In xxxiiiiª generacione ab incarnacione prefuerunt in ecclesia Gregorius, Iohannes, Siluester, Iohannes, Iohannes, Sergius et Benedictus, in diebus Othonis tercii et Henrici primi, anni ab incarnacione mille uiginti.

325 In xxxv generacione ab incarnacione prefuerunt in ecclesia Iohannes, Benedictus, Siluester, Gregorius, Clemens et Damasus, in diebus Henrici predicti et Corradi et Henrici secundi. Hic meridiei seu plenitudini pacis datur finis, sequitur declinacio uespertina, anni ab incarnacione predicta Ml.

In xxxvi generacione ab incarnacione prefuerunt in ecclesia Leo, Victor, 330 Stephanus, Benedictus, Nicolaus et Alexander, in diebus Henrici tercii et Henrici quarti.[34] Hic sub tercio Henrico christianorum gens ad sepulchrum Domini de toto mundo processit, qui Ierusalem a sarracenis uiriliter abstulit, anni ab incarnacione predicta Mlxxx.

In xxxvii generacione ab incarnacione prefuerunt in ecclesia Gregorius, 335 Victor et Vrbanus, qui Gregorius ductus Salernum a duce normanorum, usurpauit cathedram Gilabertus archiepiscopus Rauenne, nominans se ipsum

---

306 Benedictus] Bernardus BTV   308-310 In ... dcccc *om.* T   312 Benedictus] Bernardus BV   317 anni *rep.* Mᵃᶜ   318 in ecclesia *om.* T   320 Othonis primi *om.* V 321 predicte M   323 Sergius] Gregorius BTV   324 incarnacione] prefuerunt *add.* Mᵃᶜ   328 anni *om.* BTV   330 et¹ *om.* BTV   334 incarnacione] predicta *add.* BTV   335 et *om.* BTV   ductus] dictus BV   Salernum *om.* T   normannorum] romanorum BTV

---

[34] *Lib. Conc.*, fol. 53r.

Clementem, in diebus Henrici quarti, Lotharii et Corradi, anni ab incarnacione prefata Mcx.[35]

In xxxviii generacione ab incarnacione uenit rex Henrigus in urbem
340 Romam et cepit papam Pascalem in ecclesia sancti Petri, et tamdiu ipsum
cum multis in custodia tenuit pro inuestitura ecclesiarum donec extorqueret
ab eo priuilegium per quod posset euacuare libertatem ecclesie; tamen hoc
nec papa nec ecclesia sustinuit, quia quod fecerat coactus uigorem constancie
non habebat, anni a prefata incarnacione Mcxl.[36]

345 In xxxix generacione ab incarnacione factum est magnum cisma in ecclesia
occasione Octouiani et pape Alexandri, aliis translatis ad partem imperatoris,
aliis seruantibus libertatem ecclesie; tamen generacione xl[a] facta est pax inter
imperatorem et papam Alexandrum, anni ab incarnacione predicta Mclxx.[37]

In xxxx[a] generacione ab incarnacione prefuerunt in ecclesia Alexander,
350 Lucius, Vrbanus, Gregorius et Clemens, in diebus Octouiani et Frederici
primi; quicquid autem decetero sequitur pro uespere reputatur, a predicta
incarnacione anni Mcc.

In xli[a] generacione oportet reddire ad lineam patrum ueteris testamenti,
unde licet Manasses sit xxvi[us] a Iacob, propter retrogradacionem tamen
355 ponitur hic in xli[a]. Hic *fecit malum in conspectu Domini,*[38] et seduxit Iudam
et Ierusalem ut facerent malum, idcirco tradit eum Dominus in manu regis
assiriorum sed, penitencia inductus, restitutus est in regnum suum. Regnauit
autem annos lv dies xxi, et cetera.

In xxxxi[a] generacione a natiuitate Abraam apparuerunt due religiones in
360 sinagoga, scilicet phariseorum et seduceorum, et cetera.[39] In xli[a] generacione
ab incarnacione prefuerunt in ecclesia Celestinus, Innocencius et Honorius,
in diebus Frederici secundi. Hic Deus iterum uoluit destruere mundum
propter peccata, quia principes filiorum Iuda et filiorum Israel, hoc est prelati
tam latinorum ecclesie quam grecorum, fecerunt malum in conspectu
365 Domini, et suis abominacionibus seduxerunt seu corruperunt Iudam et

---

339 In[1] *om.* BV   342 euacuare] extorquere BTV   344 prefata *om.* V   incarnacione *om.* T   348-349 predicta ... incarnacione *om.* BV *per hom.*   350 in diebus *om.*
BTV   351 reputantur M   a] anni *praem.* BV   351-352 a predicta incarnacione *om.*
M[ac]   354 sit *om.* M[ac]   357 ductus BTV   358 diebus BT   et cetera *om.* BM[ac]V
359 xxxxi prima M   362 iterum Deus *tr.* BTV   363 propter] pro T   Israel *om.* BTV

---

[35] *Lib. Conc.*, fol. 53r.
[36] *Lib. Conc.*, fol. 53r.
[37] *Lib. Conc.*, fol. 53v.
[38] 2 Reg. 21.2.
[39] Cf. *Lib. Conc.*, fol. 23r.

Ierusalem, actiuam scilicet et contemplatiuam, ut facerent malum, idcirco tradidit eos Dominus in manu imperatoris Frederici, qui quidem imperator contra papam Innocencium et eius clerum in tantum surrexit quod dictus papa habuit fugere et clerici plantabantur uiui; et exaudiuit Dominus Manassen in capcione, et exaudiuit papam Innocencium in fuga, utrique restitutum est regnum, et cetera. In ista generacione due religiones in ecclesia inceperunt apparire, scilicet minorum et predicatorum, anni a predicta incarnacione Mccxxx.

Amon, licet xxvii^{us} sit a Iacob, tamen, racione qua supra, ponitur in generacione xlii. Hic *fecit malum in conspectu Domini, sicut et pater eius,*[40] et amplius, et regnauit annos duos et dies xxi, et cetera. In xlii^a generacione ab incarnacione prefuerunt in ecclesia Gregorius, Innocencius et Alexander, secundo Frederico regnante, nec propter hoc tribulaciones ecclesie diminute sunt, quia peccata similiter quam prius aucmentata sunt, et quod per Federicum imperatorem in precedenti generacione inceptum est, in ista fuit pro maiori parte impletum. Implebitur autem perfeccius hoc misterium in aliquo de suo semine, xlvi generacione a Christo, et cetera, anni a predicta incarnacione Mcclx.

Iozias, licet xxviii^{us} sit a Iacob, tamen, racione qua supra, ponitur hic in generacione xliii. In tercio decimo anno regni sui predixit Ieremias propheta ruinam Ierusalem nec minus et excidium Babilonis; utrumque in paucis annis consumacionem accepit; regnauit autem annis xxxi et diebus xxii, et cetera.[41]

In xliii generacione ab incarnacione prefuerunt in ecclesia Innocencius, Vrbanus, Clemens et Iohannes, tempore Frederici predicti et Manfredi filii eius Sicilie regis. Hic enim cepit compleri per concordiam in ecclesia quod super Ierusalem et templum Ieremias predixit, nec desinit compleri usque ad presens, quousque rehedificentur muri Ierusalem, precedente tamen iudicio fornicarie Babilonis. Hic igitur mortuo et deuicto rege Manfredo per regem Karolum in campo beneuentano, Corradinus, predicti Frederici filius, per eumdem Karolum captus, decapitatus est, in quibus temporibus Petrus rex

---

367 in manu *om.* M^{ac} 368 dictus] decus BT   369 clerici] clerius BV   371 destitutum T   et cetera *om.* M^{ac} 374 uicesimus et septimus BTV   376 duos annos *tr.* T   xxi dies *tr.* T   et cetera *om.* M^{ac} 377 ab incarnacione *om.* BTV   380 inceptum] impletum BTV   381 perfeccius *post* misterium *tr.* BTV   382 et cetera *om.* M^{ac} 385 Ieremias] Ysaias BTV   386 nec] non *add.* BTV   paucis] pacis M^{ac} 387 autem *om.* BTV   dies *codd.*   et cetera *om.* M^{ac} 388 generaciones M   prefuerunt] proposuerunt T   389 tempore *om.* M^{ac} 390 reges BT   394 filius] filii *add.* BTV

---

[40] 2 Reg. 21.20.
[41] *Lib. Conc.*, fol. 53r.

Aragonum, qui Constanciam, regis Manfredi filiam, duxit in uxorem, uenit in Siciliam et cepit eam, inde supradicto Karulo rege expulso. Tunc enim inceperunt mala non modica inundare, ut in xlvi generacione a Christo plenius apparebit, et cetera, anni ab incarnacione predicta Mcclxxxx.

400　Ioachim, licet xxix^{us} sit a Iacob, tamen, racione qua supra, ponitur hic in generacione xliiii^a; ipso regnante in Ierusalem, ascendit rex Babilonis contra eum, et factus est Ioachim seruus eius, qui tamen postea rebellauit et noluit illi esse subiectus, et cetera. Regnauit autem annis xi diebus xxiii.

In xliiii generacione ab incarnacione prefuerunt in ecclesia Honorius,
405　Nicolaus, Martinus, Celestinus, Bonifacius, Benedictus et Clemens, in diebus regis Francie, qui locum cesaris tenebat, et Henrici imperatoris. In quibus temporibus papa Bonifacius per regem Francie, seu exercitum eius, captus est et, extractus de Anagnia, ductus Romam pocionatus et mortuus est, et in suis successoribus, scilicet Clemente et ceteris, factus est seruus eius, nam,
410　tractante eodem rege, romana curia sub Clemente descendit de Roma in dominium regni Francie. Tunc enim Roma, que erat domina gencium et princeps prouinciarum, facta est quasi uidua sola a suo pastore relicta; que tamen curia supradicta dicto regi rebellauit et noluit illi esse subiecta quando de dominio regis Francie in Prouinciam se mutauit, et cetera. Hucusque
415　tempus fuge mulieris et Danielis, scilicet Mcclx et Mcclxxxx, diuersis consideratis radicibus, se extendit, anni a prefata incarnacione Mcccxx.

[*Glosa.* Hic tamen notes quod, quamdiu romanum imperium Cesare Augusto, seu imperatore, caruit, semper loco eius domus Francie, usque ad apercionem sexti signaculi, preualebit.]
420　Iechonias seu Ioachim, licet tricesimus sit a Iacob, tamen, racione qua supra, ponitur hic in generacione xlv^a. Regnauit post patrem suum Ioachim in Ierusalem mensibus tribus, diebus xxiiii. Hic in transmigracionem Babilonis genuit Iudam et fratrem eius, et post transmigracionem Babilonis genuit Salatiel, et cetera. In huius generacionis tempore, *uniuersi principes sacer-*
425　*dotum et populus preuaricati sunt inique iusta uniuersas abominaciones gencium, et polluerunt domum Domini, quam sanctificauit sibi in Ierusalem,*[42]

---

398 generaciones M　　　399 et cetera *om.* M^{ac}　　　401 generaciones T　　　402 et²
om. BV　　　402-403 noluit illi esse] non fuit T　　　403 et cetera *om.* M^{ac}　　　xi] xii BV
annos *codd.*　　　405 Benedictus *om.* T　　　406 quibus] omnibus BTV　　　408 Alaniam
codd. Romam *om.* BTV　　　in *om.* T　　　410 tractantem M　　　romana] Roma M^{ac}
412 principes *codd.*　　　413 dicti *codd.*　　　414 et cetera *om.* M^{ac}　　　416 radicibus]
racionibus T Mccxx BV　　　417 Cesare] a *praem.* T　　　420 Iechonias] Sequitur *praem.* BTV
tricesimus] xxvi^{us} T　　　qua *om.* M^{ac}　　　422 dies *codd.*　　　Hic *om.* T　　　423 fratres
BTV

---

[42] 2 Par. 36.14.

et consumpto sancto igne, Naboccodonosor, rex Babilonis, cum magno
exercitu caldeorum uenit Ierusalem et, capto Ioachim seu Iechonia rege Iuda
cum magna parte populi, duxit eum in Babilonem captiuum, ita quod,
430 omnem Ierusalem, exceptis pauperibus, et omnes thesauros domus Domini
transtulit de Ierusalem in Babilonem, et facta diuisione populi, Sedechias per
predictum Babilonis regem fuit in regem Iude constitutus, per quem finaliter
rex Babilonis, occasione accepta, iterum obscedit Ierusalem et, muris ciuitatis
et templo et palacio regis in terra deiectis, Sedechias in fuga captus est et filii
435 eius coram eo in mortem traditi sunt, et uinctus cathenis ductus est in
Babilonem captiuus.[43] In quibus temporibus rex Babilonis, conuocatis cunctis
principibus et iudicibus sapientibus et tirannis ad erigendam statuam auream
et dedicandam, statuit ut quicumque dictam statuam non adoraret occideretur, propter quod Sidrach, Misach et Abdenago missi sunt in fornace ignis
440 et, uisitacione Dei presencie, uidente rege speciem quarti similem Filio Dei,
euaserunt illesi, quam ob rem conuersus rex benedixit Deo Sidrach, Misach
et Abdenago, qui saluos facit sperantes in se, et posuit decretum ut quicumque blasphemauerit Deum Sidrach, Misach et Abdenago dispereat et
domus eius uastetur.[44]
445   In xlv[a] generacione ab incarnacione passionis uigilia celebratur, iam enim
romanum imperium, ut regnum Iuda in quatuor tetharchias diuisum, uigiliam
scilicet tocius desolacionis ostendit. Hic Iechonias genuit Iudam, seu Petrum
antipapam, et fratres eius in spirituali transmigracione Babilonis predicta;
Iechonias genuit, hoc est successorem habebit, Salatiel, et cetera. Hic enim,
450 sicut in tempore Iechonie, *uniuersi principes sacerdotum,* seu prelati omnes,
et populus, idest omnis clerus, et omnis religio et omnis mundus, *preuaricari
ceperunt inique,* nouis enormitatibus et enormis seleribus et abusionibus et
scandalosis excessibus, *iusta uniuersas abominaciones gencium, et domum
Domini* turpiter et spiritualiter et corporaliter *polluere,* quod tacendum
455 plusquam dicendum est. Iam enim inter nos et paganos quasi nulla est
differencia, nec inter religiosos et seculares, ut a planta pedis usque ad
uerticem capitis nulla sit sanitas in statibus supradictis. Necesse est ergo ut

---

428 uenit] fuit BV   429 captum BV   ita quod] itaque V   430 domum]
domos M[ac]   432 fuit] ea uero T   Iudam *codd.*   433 obscedit] ascendit BTV
435 uictus M   437 et[1]] hec B   440 similiter T   444 uastetur] domus eius
add. T   445 ab incarnacione *om.* B   446 tetharchias] ierarchias BV   448 an-
tipapam] in papam BV   449 Salatiel] per *praem.* T   451 et[1] ... omnis[1] *om.* T
452 abusionibus] scandalis *add.* BTV   453 scandalosis *om.* V   454 quod] quid T
455 paganos et nos *tr.* BTV

---

[43] Cf. 2 Reg. 24.13-15.
[44] Cf. Dan. 3.

iudicium incipiat de domo Domini, quod Ieremias defleuit, dicens: *Quomodo
sedet sola ciuitas plena populo,*[45] non suo sed alieno, non filiis Ierusalem sed
460 filiis Babilonis, et cetera.

Consumpta luce ignis templi, scilicet euangelice ueritatis, tenebre condensantur; in tempore igitur confusionis omnia sunt confusa, quia ubi lux
absconditur pro peccatis tenebre ignorancie condensantur, ita ut nesciat
homo peccator ubi sit, et qua die uel hora accidit illud quod dicit Ysayas:
465 *Ecce, dies Domini uenit, crudelis et indignacionis plenus, ire furorisque, ad
ponendum terram in solitudinem et peccatores eius conterendos de ea,*[46] et
apostolus: *Cum dixerint: Pax et securitas,* subauditur, filii Babilonis, *tunc
repentinus irruet interitus, tanquam in utero habenti, et non effugient.*[47]

Hic est enim principium illorum xxxxiiii[or] dierum seu annorum quos
470 Daniel tacet, in quibus erat in terra ueritas prosternenda et prophetis ueritatis
silencium imponendum. Hic est casus illius stelle Apocalipsis que cecidit de
celo, seu de celesti statu suo, que habebat clauem, seu potestatem, aperiendi
puteum abissi, seu soluendi profunditatem scripturarum, cum falsa et callida
in tortura contra euangelicam ueritatem, ut iam fumus erroris, sicut fumus
475 fornacis magne, preualeat et ascendat, et solem et aerem, hoc est Christi
euangelium et ecclesiam, obscuret; non enim modica ex fumo tanti erroris
huius putei, sed magna excecacio et terribilis fere in tota ecclesia est incepta,
ita ut iam non Christi ecclesia, sed sinagoga demoniorum et noua Babilon
spiritualiter nuncupetur. Iam enim locuste, seu religiosi, de fumo casus illius
480 pontificalis stelle et apercionis putei processerunt locuste, seu religiosi illius
erroris secaces, leues, uolatiles, cupidi et carnales, ypocritales et detractores,
qui contra omnes non eis fauentes, ut dicit Iohannes, animosissime conci-
tabuntur, quasi equi currentes ad bellum.[48] *Vox autem alarum,* seu sentencia-
rum suarum, quas altissimas et uolantes esse presumunt, *sicut uox* rotarum
485 et tumultuosi exercitus *currentis in bellum* contra omnem sentenciam
contrariam, quantumcumque ueram.[49] Hec autem iam nimis notoria sunt,

---

458 defluit BV; *om.* T   459-460 filii ... filii BTV   463 non sciat BTV   465 in-
dignacione *codd.*   467 et *om.* BV   subauditur] saluabitur T   468 habentes M[ac];
habentis *codd.*   469 seu annorum *om.* BTV   470 ueritas in terra *tr.* BTV   471 est
om. T   stelle] noni *add.* BTV   474 fumus[2] *om.* BTV   475 et[2] *om.* T   476 fumo]
summo T   tante *codd.*   478 ut ... ecclesia *om.* BV   non iam *tr.* T   480 et *om.*
M[ac]   482 Iohannes] Iob uel Iacob BV; Iob T   483 alarum *om.* T[ac]   485 tumultuosa
M[ac]

---

[45] Lam. 1.1.
[46] Is. 13.9.
[47] 1 Thes. 5.3.
[48] *Postilla,* fol. 67v (commenting on Apoc. 9.1-11).
[49] Apoc. 9.9.

cum continuo tamen aucmento; consumabuntur autem in fine, quando
publice Christi uitam et spiritum in uiris spiritualibus acerbissime inpugna-
bunt et sollempniter condempnabunt, quamuis non permictantur ledere
490 spiritum perfectorum, nec ecciam simplicium, et uxorem spiritus uite Christi
firmiter in se seruancium, et illorum malicias et errores aberrancium et
fugiencium, sicut agricole et agniculi exorent lupos; ceteros hinc inde
uacillantes suis uenenatis aculeis cruciant et cruciare non cessant, habentes
supra se regem angelum abissi, cui nomen exterminans.[50] Dignum enim et
495 rectum Dei iudicium est, ut populus ille babilonicus, qui tamquam locuste de
puteo errorum abissi ascensus est, ducem super se, seu pontificem, regem
abissi angelum habeat cuius nomen exterminans, una cum ipso, tocius scilicet
perfeccionis euangelice ueritatem, et cetera.

Futurum quippe est per concordiam in temporali transmigracione Babi-
500 lonis ut in modernis temporibus nouus rex Babilonis insurgat, et cum magno
exercitu caldeorum ueniat Ierusalem, et capto Ioachim, seu Iechonia, rege
Iuda, seu summo sacerdote, cum magna parte populi, scilicet ecclesiastici,
cum omnibus thesauris domus Domini ducatur in Babilonem captiuus, ut
transmigracio babilonica misterialiter impleatur, et quod est in ista genera-
505 cione inceptum in sequenti ab ista habeat per omnia complementum. Et facta
diuisione populi supradicti per predictum Babilonis regem, instituatur in
regem Iuda, seu romanum pontificem, Sedechias, in cuius temporis fine rex
Babilonis, per ipsum occasione accepta, iterum obsidat Ierusalem, et muris
ciuitatis et templo et palacio summi sacerdotis in terram deiectis, Sedechias,
510 seu summus sacerdos, in fuga capiatur, et filii eius coram eo in mortem
tradantur, et uinctus cathenis in Babilonem ducatur captiuus. In quibus
temporibus rex Babilonis, conuocatis cunctis principibus, magistratibus et
iudicibus sapientibus et tirannis, ad erigendam, seu eligendam, et dedicandam, seu consecrandam, statuam auream, pseudo papam scilicet Antichri-
515 stum, statuet ut quicumque non adorauerit occidatur. Tunc autem electorum
ecclesia, ut tres pueri, in fornace magne tribulacionis probanda est, in cuius
medio, ut species quarti, ad confortandum suos, Filius Dei presencialiter
apparebit, quod agnoscens rex Babilonis, penitencia ductus, reducetur per
sanctum pastorem ad Dominum Iesum Christum.

---

488 acerbissime] et *add.* V   490 perfecciorum V   uxorem] uocem B
493 uacillantes] mollantes T   494 regem *om.* BTV   enim] est BV   495 est *om.*
BTV   497 tocius *om.* BTV   498 et cetera *om.* BTV   500 ut *om.* BV   rex *om.*
BTV   502 sacerdote] pontifice seu *praem.* BTV   508 excepta BV   509 sacerdotis]
pontificis seu *praem.* BTV   511 tradatur TV   captus M   516 magne *om.* T
tribulacione M^{ac}   517 Dei *om.* M^{ac}   518 penitenciam M^{ac}

---

[50] Cf. Apoc. 9.10-11.

520   Salatiel, licet xxxi[us] sit a Iacob, tamen, racione qua supra, ponitur hic in
generacione xlvi[a]. Hic enim non habuit regem proprium nec ducem populus
Israel, quia iam uenerat tempus impiorum et potestas tenebrarum; quod
autem in xlv[a] generacione inchoatum est sub Ieconia et Sedechia, in ista
generacione xlvi[a] fuit pro maiori parte impletum. Siquidem Iechonias des-
525   cendit de Ierusalem in Babilonem et Zerobabel de Babilone ascendit in
Ierusalem, in qua regnauit auus eius, Salatiel autem fuit medius inter utrumque; tamen, uolente Deo, Zorobabel princeps est in populo constitutus. In
ista generacione fuit facta transmigracio Ierusalem et fuit percussa Babilon a
medis et persis, necnon et tribulaciones due fuerunt orte filiis Israel, quarum
530   una continetur in istoria Iudith, altera in libro Hester; uerumtamen templum
Dei et muri ciuitatis rehedificati sunt in angustia temporum.[51]

Quadragesima sexta generacio ab incarnacione similis est diei in qua
passus est Christus, non enim habuit regem proprium aut ducem populus
Israel, unde iudei ducem seu regem proprium abnegantes, scilicet Iesum
535   Christum, dixerunt Pilato: *Non habemus regem nisi cesarem.*[52] Iam enim
aduenerat tempus impiorum et potestas tenebrarum, ut quod in xlv[a] generacione inceptum est, in ista xlvi[a] per omnia impleatur.[53] Sicut enim in tercia
generacione a Iechonia, percussa prius Babilon, Zorobabel de Babilone
ascendit in Ierusalem, sic in consimili generacione a Iechonia, Iohanne papa,
540   populus christianus, percussa prius Babilon, secundum faciet passagium sub
nouo Zorobabel in Ierusalem et alias infidelium naciones, ut tunc tempus
plenitudinis inchoetur. In ista generacione fienda est transmigracio spiritualis
Israel quousque percuciatur noua Babilon a medis et persis. Vnde nota hic
quod, postquam rex xi[us] deposuerit regem Sicilie et regem Francie, gentes
545   regnorum Sicilie et regnorum Francie, tamquam patricide et matricide, ut
canes rabidi et ingrati lacerantes et dilaniantes carnes, seu temporalia, ipsius
matris ecclesie, sic atrocius in ipsam primo insurgent, ut quod in trenorum
per Ieremiam dictum est totaliter impleatur: *Omnes amici eius spreuerunt
eam, et facti sunt ei inimici.*[54] Sequitur: *Qui glorificabant eam spreuerunt eam,*

---

523 et *om.* T   524 generacione] in *add.* T   526 inter] in T   528 fuit[2] *om.* BTV
533 proprium regem *tr.* BTV   534 scilicet] sanctum V   537 est] ut quod *add.* T
539 ascendit *om.* T   540 Babilon] idest ecclesia carnalium *add.* BTV   541 Zoro-
babel] idest sub nouo pastore seu pontifice *add.* BTV   542 est *om.* T   543 percuciatur
om. T   Babilon *om.* T   et] a T   544 regem ... et *om.* V   546 dilaniantes]
delinquentes T   549 eam[1] *om.* M[ac]   eam[2] *om.* T   eam[3] *om.* M[ac]

[51] *Septem Sigillis*, p. 244; see also *Lib. Conc.*, fol. 41v.
[52] Jn. 19.15.
[53] *Lib. Conc.*, fol. 55v.
[54] Lam. 1.2.

550 *quia uiderunt ignominiam eius,*[55] et cetera. Reuera enim percucietur Babilon,
populus scilicet qui dicitur christianus et non est, sed est sinagoga demoniorum.[56] Qui ueri autem sunt christiani in duabus tribulacionibus liberandi
sunt, quarum una similis est ei quam fecit Holofernes, princeps Nabocodonosor regis assiriorum, altera ei quam fecit Naaman; interea tamen multi
555 fidelium coronabuntur martirio et hedificabitur rursum sancta ciuitas, que est
ecclesia, in angustia temporum, sicut factum est in diebus Zorobabel et Iosue
et Hesdre et Nehemie, sub quibus illa uetus Ierusalem consumacionem
accepit. Set et Sathanas, qui facit omnia mala hec, incarcerandus est in abisso,
ut non seducat amplius gentes usque ad statutum terminum solucionis sue.[57]
560 Omnia enim que in ista generacione implenda sunt, iam in precedentibus
distinccionibus dicta sunt, et cetera, anni ab incarnacione predicta Mccclxvii.

Zorobabel, licet xxxii[us] sit a Iacob, tamen, racione qua supra, ponitur hic
in xlvi[a]. Ortus quidem fuit in Babilone, sed tamen, uolente Deo, princeps est
in populo constitutus.[58] Hic suscitauit Deus spiritum regis persarum, in cuius
565 manu Deus celi dedit omnia regna terre, ut edificaret domum Domini in
Ierusalem, que est Iuda. Tunc Zorobabel, percussa prius Babilon, in angustia
temporum de Babilone assendit in Ierusalem, et cum magno sucursu regis
perssarum rehedificauit templum et muros ciuitatis, et cetera.

In xlvii[a] generacione ab incarnacione, peracta prius tribulacione generali
570 et purgato diligenter tritico ab uniuersis zizanis peccatorum, ascendet nouus
dux, seu nouus pontifex noue Ierusalem, ecclesie scilicet uniuerse. Ascendet
autem non gressu pedum, aut mutacione locorum, sed quia dabitur ei plenaria
libertas ad innouandum christianam religionem et ad predicandum uerbum
Dei, incipiente iam regnare Domino exercituum super omnem terram. Non
575 enim regnabunt ultra super populum Domini reges superbi et ydolorum
abominacione polluti, est enim auaricia ydolorum seruitus, sed is qui redemit
nos in sanguine suo, contritis pariter auro, argento, here et ferro et testa,
deletisque omnibus regnis a quibus passa est persequcione omnis ecclesia

---

551 scilicet populus *tr.* T   554 ei] enim BTV   tamen] enim T   557 Neuenie M
Ierusalem uetus *tr.* BTV   559 non *om.* T   561 et cetera *om.* M[ac]   563 in[1] *om.*
BV   564 in[1] *om.* BV   566 est *om.* T   primus BV   567 temporum] descendit
add. T   569 xlvi[a] T   571 pontifices M   576 is] hiis M; hic BTV   577 auro]
et *add.* BTV

---

[55] Lam. 1.8.
[56] Cf. Apoc. 2.9.
[57] *Septem Sigillis*, pp. 244-245.
[58] *Lib. Conc.*, fol. 56r.

iustorum a Iohanne Babtista precursore Domini usque ad aduentum Helye.[59]
580 In ista generacione suscitabit Deus spiritum regis perssarum, seu Sicilie, in
cuius manu Deus celi dabit omnia regna terre, qui hedificabit domum Domini
in Ierusalem, que uisio pacis interpretatur, quia erit in pace imperium eius,
que est in Iuda, in magna scilicet fortitudine et potencia roboratum. Tunc
nouus Zorobabel, seu nouus pontifex, percussa prius noua Babilon, ascendet
585 seu passagiuum faciet in Ierusalem, hoc est in terram sanctam, cum magno
sucursu regis persarum, seu Sicilie, et rehedificabit templum et muros ciuitatis
ecclesie uniuerse, ut scilicet, *fiat unum ouile et unus pastor.*[60] Erit enim
tempus istud quod supererit usque in finem absque humana extimacione
annorum, uelut in sabbatum reputatum absque bello, absque scandalo, absque
590 sollicitudine et terrore, quia Deus benedicet ei et sanctificabit illud, eo quod
in ipso cessabit *ab omni opere suo quod patrauit.*[61]

Hoc autem tempus distinguetur per generaciones et pontifices reges,
tanquam Petrus et Siluester, gladiis duobus fulgentes, in uno uniuersali ouile,
temporaliter et spiritualiter, uno solo pastore regnante, quia Dominus Iesus
595 Christus rex fuit pariter et sacerdos. Ascendet autem predictus pontifex in
ista xlvii[a] generacione, quamuis in xlvi[a] reuelandus sit, ut Christus, nouus dux
et nouus pontifex, in xlvi[a] generacione a natituitate Abraam reuelatus est in
babtismate, terminans circumcisionem et figuram agni thipici in institucione
eucharistie sacramenti. In tempore autem illo quod decursum est a Zorobabel
600 usque ad Christum, circa finem istius temporis, post tribulacionem que facta
est sub Anthioco in populo iudeorum, Christus Iesus Filius Dei uenit in
mundum, qui postquam consumauit opus quod acceperat a Patre, soluens
plaustorum debitum in carne mortali, tandem resurrexit a mortuis cum
testibus resurreccionis, et inter alia magnalia que fecit ascendens in celum et
605 sedens a dextris Dei, promissum Spiritum sanctum in filios adobcionis
effudit. Similiter in fine mundi, post persecucionem quam facturus est Gog,
cum iam uniuersa erunt completa, peracta prius resurreccione mortuorum,
sedebit Dominus Iesus in sede magestatis sue ad segregandos electos suos a
multitudine reproborum, quatinus repleti Spiritu sancto uadant ipsi pariter in
610 uitam eternam, impii uero in ignem eternum.[62]

---

584 prius] pocius V   585 facit M   586 hedificabit BTV   587 enim *om.* T
588 in] ad BV   589 reputata T   bello] et *add.* BTV   590 sollicitudine] solitudine
BV   601 Dei] nouus *add.* BTV   603 protoplaustorum *Lib. Conc.*   604 et[2] *om.* BTV
606 factus T

---

[59] Cf. *Lib. Conc.*, fol. 56r-v.
[60] Jn. 10.16.
[61] Cf. Gen. 2.2.
[62] *Lib. Conc.*, fol. 56v.

Explicit XIII distinccio. Incipit XIIII, qua agitur de scala generacionum utriusque testamenti.[1]

Circa xiiii distinccionem et ultimam huius operis est notandum quod, sicut scala quam uidit Iacob de terra procedens, et eius sumitas angelis ascendentibus et descendentibus celum tangens,[2] scalam generacionum ab Adam procedentem et se usque ad Christi aduentum secundum carnem, angelis, seu
5 patriarchis et prophetis, in Deum per caritatem ascendentibus et ad proximum descendentibus, procedentem, figuraliter tangit, sic et scalam generacionum ab incarnacione Christi similiter procedentem et se usque ad eius aduentum ad finale iudicium, angelis, seu apostolis et ceteris uiris euangelicis, per caritatem modo consimili in Deum ascendentibus et ad proximum
10 descendentibus, extendentem ostendit. Gradus enim generaciones significant et signaculi staciones designant, ut per ea que sequuntur per ordinem clarent.

Generacio		Generacio
Prima	Adam	Prima
Abel		Caym
15 Domus minorum		Domus maiorum

Sunt autem anni mundi ab Adam usque ad aduentum Christi quinque milia cccclxxix.

Cum cxxx annorum esset, Adam genuit Seth, et *facti sunt omnes dies Adam dccccxxx anni, et mortuus est.*[3]
20 Caym, frater maior, propter peccatum inuidie quod commisit in fratrem suum minorem, scilicet Abel, in diluuio Babilonis noue cum tota sua generacione peribit; tunc Abel, frater minor, propter peccatum inuidie in effusione sui sanguinis, ut mater sterilis usque in finem seculi plures filios spirituales generabit.

Titulum qua] distinccio in *praem.* BV   1 ultimam] partem *add.* BTV   7 ab incarnacione *om.* V   10 excedentem BV   11 per[2] *om.* T   claret BV   15 Domus minorum *om.* BT   Domus maiorum *om.* BT; Domus generacio II V   16 autem] sicut B   17 cccccxxix V   18 facti sunt *om.* T   20 Caym] domus minorum generacio II *praem.* BTV   21-22 generacione sua *tr.* BTV   22 periit BTV   23 sui *om.* TV

[1] The table of this Distinction is based on the *Lib. Fig.*, pls. 3, 4.
[2] Cf. Gen. 28.12.
[3] Cf. Gen. 5.5.

25   Generaciones enim in ueteri testamento uarie et inequales fuerunt, alie sub longiori annorum spacio, alie sub breuiori; a natiuitate autem Noe usque ad natiuitatem Sem fuerunt quingenti anni, Sem uero centum erat annorum quando genuit Arphaxath, et Arphaxath, cum esset annorum xxxvi, genuit Sale. Vnde est notandum quod ab Adam usque ad Noe maiora fuerunt spacia
30 generacionum quam a Noe usque ad Dauid; porro a Dauid usque ad transmigracionem Babilonis non a natiuitate unius usque ad natiuitatem alterius accipiendum est tempus generacionis, sed a regno in regnum, ex qua re accidit ut omnino breuiora sint spacia generacionum, ut aliquis xvi annis, alius tribus annis, alius tribus mensibus regnasse referantur, et tamen unum-
35 quoque spacium regni sub una generacione accipiendum est.[4]

Generacio		Generacio
II	Seth	II

Cum cv annorum esset, *Seth genuit Enos, et facti sunt omnes dies Seth dccccxii anni, et mortuus est.*[5]

Generacio		Generacio
III	Enos	III

40

Cum lxxxx annorum esset, *Enos genuit Caynan, et facti sunt omnes dies Enos dccccv anni, et mortuus est.*[6]

Generacio		Generacio
IIII	Caynan	IIII

45

Cum lxx annorum esset, Caynan genuit Malalehel, *et facti sunt omnes dies Caynan dccccx anni, et mortuus est.*[7]

Generacio		Generacio
V	Malalael	V

50 Cum clxii esset annorum, Malalael genuit Iareth, *et facti sunt omnes dies Malalahel dccclxxxxv anni, et mortuus est.*[8]

---

25 Generacio T   26 longiori] tempore *add.* BTV   autem *om.* TV   27 fuerunt ... anni *om.* V   33 xvi] xv BTV   36-39 Generacio ... est *om.* T   38 Cum] Domus generacio secunda *praem.* BV   42 esset annorum *tr.* BTV   43 dccccvi BTV 45 Caynan] Seth et Enos generacio II, Cayn III V   47 Caynan ... est] Malalahel dccclxxxxv anni et mortuus est *per hom. rep.* M   50 annorum esset *tr.* TV

---

[4] *Lib. Conc.*, fol. 12r.
[5] Gen. 5.8.
[6] Gen. 5.10-11.
[7] Gen. 5.12, 14.
[8] Gen. 5.15, 17.

	Generacio			Generacio
	VI	Jareth		VI

Cum clxii annorum esset, Iareth genuit Enoch, *et facti sunt omnes dies Iareth*
55 *dcccclxii anni, et mortuus est.*[9]

	Generacio			Generacio
	VII	Enoch		VII

Cum lxv annorum esset, Enoch genuit Matussalem, *et facti sunt omnes dies*
Enoch ccclxv anni; hambulauitque cum Deo et non apparuit, quia tulit eum
60 *Dominus.*[10]

	Generacio			Generacio
	VIII	Matussalem		VIII

Cum clxxxvii esset annorum, Matussalem genuit Lamech, *et facti sunt omnes*
dies Matussalem dcccclxix anni, et mortuus est.[11]

65	Generacio			Generacio
	VIIII	Lamech		VIIII

Cum clxxxii annorum esset, Lamech genuit Noe, *et facti sunt omnes dies*
Lamech dcclxxvii anni, et mortuus est.[12]

		Generacio			Generacio		
70	Iaphet		X	Noe		X	Cham

Cum quingentorum annorum esset, *Noe genuit Sem, Cham et Japhet,*[13] *et*
facti sunt omnes dies Noe post dilluuium cccl anni, et impleti sunt omnes dies
eius dccccl, et mortuus est.[14]

Coruus spiritalis ex archa ecclesie egressurus ad archam ultra non reuerte-
75 tur quia cadaueribus se immisset; columba uero contemplatiua et innocens
et per celum uolans, post diluuium Babilonis noue, in signum pacis portans
ramum oliue uirentibus foliis reuerteretur.[15]

---

54 Iareth[2]] Enoch M[ac]　　55 dccccxii BMV　　58 esset] est BV　　64 anni *om.* M
67 esset annorum *tr.* BTV　　68 dcclxxii M　　73 dccccl] anni *add.* TV　　74 egressus
BV; regressurus T　　75 quia] eo quod BTV　　innocens *om.* T

---

[9] Gen. 5.18-20.
[10] Gen. 5.21, 23-24.
[11] Gen. 5.25-27.
[12] Gen. 5.28-29, 31.
[13] Gen. 5.32.
[14] Gen. 9.28-29.
[15] Cf. Gen. 8.8-9.

Generacio		Generacio
XI	Sem	XI

80 Cum c annorum esset, Sem genuit Arphasath,[16] et facti sunt omnes dies Sem
dc anni, et mortuus est.

Maledictus Chanaan, seruus seruorum erit fratribus suis. Benedictus
Dominus Deus Sem; sit Chananan seruus eius; dilatet Deus Iapheth et habitet
in tabernaculis Sem, sit Chanaan seruus eius.[17] Sicut Sem tangit populum
85 iudaycum, et Cham, seu Chanaan, populum sarracenicum, sic Japhet tangit
populum christianum.

Generacio		Generacio
XII	Arphaxath	XII

Cum xxxv esset annorum, Arphasath genuit Salem, et facti sunt omnes dies
90 Arphasath cccxxxviii anni, et mortuus est.[18]

Generacio		Generacio
XIII	Sale	XIII

Cum triginta esset annorum, Sale genuit Eber, et facti sunt omnes dies Sale
ccccxxxiii anni, et mortuus est.[19]

95

Generacio		Generacio
XIIII	Heber	XIIII

Cum xxxiiii annorum esset, Heber genuit Faleth, et facti sunt omnes dies
Heber ccccclxiiii anni, et mortuus est.[20]

Generacio		Generacio
XV	Faleth	XV

100

Cum xxx annorum esset, Phaleth genuit Ragau, et facti sunt omnes dies
Phaleth ccxxxviiii anni, et mortuus est.[21]

Generacio		Generacio
XVI	Ragau	XVI

---

89 annorum esset *tr.* BTV   102 anni *om. codd.*

---

[16] Gen. 11.10-11.
[17] Gen. 9.25, 27.
[18] Gen. 11.12-13.
[19] Gen. 11.14-15.
[20] Gen. 11.16-17.
[21] Gen. 11.18-19.

105 Cum xxxii annorum esset, Ragau genuit Seruth, et facti sunt omnes dies Ragau ccxxxviiii anni, et mortuus est.[22]

Generacio		Generacio
XVII	Seruth	XVII

Cum xxx esset annorum, Seruth genuit Nachor, et facti sunt omnes dies
110 Seruth ccxx anni, et mortuus est.[23]

Generacio		Generacio
XVIII	Nachor	XVIII

Cum xxix annorum esset, Nachor genuit Thare, et facti sunt omnes dies Nachor cxxxxix anni, et mortuus est.[24]

115
Generacio		Generacio
XVIIII	Thare	XVIIII

Cum lxx annorum esset, Thare genuit Abraam, et Nachor, et Aran,[25] et facti sunt omnes dies Thare ccv anni, et mortuus est.[26]

	Generacio		Generacio		
120	Aram	XX	Abraam	I	Nachor
Christiani					Pagani

Cum c esset annorum,[27] Abraam genuit Ysaac,[28] et facti sunt omnes dies Abraam clxxv anni, et mortuus est.[29]

Sicut Abraam tangit populum hebreorum, sic Aram tangit populum
125 christianorum, qui genuit Loth, ordinem iustorum a diluuio spiritualis Sodome in futuro tempore liberandum. Nachor, populus paganorum, non habitet cum eis. Frater minor Iacob, subplantator fratris sui maioris Hesau, sua primogenita ante tulit, et secundo benediccionem subripuit consilio materno.[30]

---

233 xxxii *om.* T   106 cxxxviiii T   anni *om. codd.*   110 ccxxx T
113 xxix] xxx M; cxx BTV   117 esset annorum *tr.* BTV   et[1] ... Aran *om.* T
120 Aram ... Nachor *om.* V   120-152 Aram ... accepit *deest* B *causa caesurae fol. 74;*
alia manus addidit summarium generationum omissarum   121 Christiani ... Pagani *om.*
TV   122 annorum esset *tr.* V   123 anni *om.* T   124 sic] sicut TV   125 Loth
om. TV

---

[22] Gen. 11.20-21.
[23] Gen. 11.22-23.
[24] Gen. 11.24-25.
[25] Gen. 11.26.
[26] Gen. 11.32.
[27] Gen. 21.5.
[28] Cf. Gen. 21.1-3.
[29] Gen. 25.7.
[30] Gen. 27.1-29.

130 Generacio   Generacio
         XXI   Ysaac   II

Cum clx annorum esset, Ysaac genuit Iacob, et facti sunt omnes dies Ysaac
clxxx anni, et mortuus est.[31] Ysaac, filius libere, sanctorum ecclesiam respicit,
set Ysmahel, filius ancille, malignancium ecclesiam tangit.[32]

135 Generacio   Generacio
         XXII   Iacob   III
    Iudas Ruben Gath Effraym Aser   Manasses Symeon Levi Ysachar
         Neptali Manasses   Zabulon Ioseph Beniamin

Manasses, frater maior, *erit in populos et multiplicabitur,* set Effraym, *frater*
140 *minor, maior illo illo erit, et semen illius cresset in gentes.*[33] Hec enim fuit
benediccio Iacob super Manassem a dextris et super Effraym a sinistris,[34] sed,
cancellatis manibus, posuit dextram super fratrem minorem, benedicens ut
supra. Nota figuram ordinis predicatorum fratrum et ordinis fratrum minorum.
145 Manasses et Effraym inter patriarchas benediccionem acceperunt, nam pro
Dan patriarcha datus est Manasses. Ioseph, frater minor, postquam peregri-
natus fuerit, a patre apostolico et matre ecclesia et a cunctis suis fratribus, seu
ecclesie religionibus, adorabitur, atque apparuerit Beniamin, ordo illorum
fratrum minimus, ultimus secundi status; tribus Iuda in aduentu noui
150 Zorobabel septrum dimictet. Tunc Ioseph in septrum uniuersalis regni
ascendit et in populos multos cresset; sicut enim Caleph tenuit locum Iude,
ita et Iosue locum Ioseph iure hereditario accepit.

Primum signaculum ueteris testamenti incepit a Iacob patriarcha, licet
inicium habuerit in Abraam; consumacio uero eius fuit in Moyse et Iosue, sub
155 quo fuit conflictus populus egypciorum contra filios Israhel per primum caput
drachonis, scilicet Pharaonem regem Egypti, et cetera.

Secundum signaculum ueteris testamenti incepit a Moyse et Iosue, consumatum uero est in Samuele et Dauid, sub quo fuit conflictus chananeorum
contra filios Israel per secundum caput drachonis, scilicet Iabim regem
160 chananeorum, et cetera.

---

132 Cum *om.* M   lx *om.* TV   135-138 Generacio[1] ... Beniamin *rep.* M *sed in*
primam add.: Vacat propter deffectum.   138 Beniamin] Aaron *add.* T   143 predicatorum fratrum et *om.* V   147 fuerat TV   148 atque] cumque V   149 nouo TV
151 locum *om.* TV   156 et cetera *om.* BTV   158 est uero *tr.* T   159 per *om.* T

---

[31] Gen. 25.26, 35.28-29.
[32] Cf. Gen. 16, 21.10-13.
[33] Gen. 48.19.
[34] Gen. 48.8-17.

	Generacio		Generacio
	XXIII	Iudas	IIII
	Religiones sex		Religiones sex
	Generacio		Generacio
165	XXIIII	Ffares	V
	Generacio		Generacio
	XXV	Esron	VI
	Generacio		Generacio
	XXVI	Aram	VII
170	Generacio		Generacio
	XXVII	Aminadab	VIII
	Generacio		Generacio
	XXVIII	Naason	VIIII
	Generacio		Generacio
175	XXIX	Psalmon	X
	Generacio		Generacio
	XXX	Booz	XI
	Generacio		Generacio
	XXXI	Obeth	XII

180 In diebus Obeth, tempore Hely, expulsum est tabernaculum et data est archa
Domini in manus philistinorum.

	Generacio		Generacio
	XXXII	Iesse	XIII

		Linea iudicum:
185		Ioseph
		Moyses
		Iosue
		Ochoniel
		Ehuth
190		Debbora
		Gedeon
		Abimalech
		Thola
		Iaar
195		Jephte
		Abrissa
		Aylon

163 Religiones sex[1] om. V   195-199 Jephte ... Sanson om. BTV

Abdon
Sanson
200   Heli
Samuel
Saul.

Generacio		Generacio
XXXIII	Dauid	XIIII

205 Tercium signaculum ueteris testamenti incepit in Samuele et Dauid, consumatum uero est in Helia et Heliseo, sub quo fuit conflictus syriorum, primo
contra decem tribus, secundo contra utrumque regnum per tercium caput
drachonis, scilicet Benadab, regem siriorum.

Generacio		Generacio
XXXIIII	Salomon	XV

210

Hic regnum et pax data est populo Israel.

Generacio		Generacio
XXXV	Roboam	XVI

Hic decem tribus scinduntur a domo Dauid.

215

Generacio		Generacio
XXXVI	Abia	XVII

	Generacio		Generacio	
Helyas	XXXVII	Asa	XVIII	Helyseus

Prima iniciacio ordinis monachorum.

220

	Generacio		Generacio	
Sanctus	XXXVIII	Iosaphat	XIX	Ordo
Benedictus				monachorum

Generacio		Generacio
XXXIX	Ioram	XX

225 Hic Helyas eleuatus est in celum. Hic Helyseus indutus est dupplici spiritu.
Quartum signaculum ueteris testamenti incepit in ascensu Helye et Helysei,
consumatum uero est in Ysaya et Ezechia rege Iuda, sub quo fuit conflictus
assiriorum per quartum caput drachonis, scilicet Atzahel, regem syriorum, et
x tribus depopulate sunt.

200-201 Heli, Samuel *om.* BV   202 Saul *om.* T   204 Dauid *om.* BV   XIIII] xv V
206 est uero *tr.* T   208 scilicet *om.* BTV   225 Hic² *om.* BT   indutus] ductus T

230	Generacio		Generacio	
	XXXX	Ochozias	XXI	
	Generacio		Generacio	
	XLI	Ioas	XXII	
	Generacio		Generacio	
235	XLII	Amasias	XXIII	

Istos tres reges impios qui occisi sunt gladio, scilicet Ochozias, Ioas, et Amazias, excludit euangelista a genologia saluatoris.[35]

	Generacio		Generacio	
	Ysaias	XLIII	Ozias	XXIIII	Osee
240	propheta				propheta

Prima iniciacio ordinis clericorum.

	Generacio		Generacio
	XLIIII	Ioathan	XXV

Prima destruccio decem tribuum.

245	Generacio		Generacio
	XLV	Achaz	XXVI
	Generacio		Generacio
	XLVI	Ezechias	XXVII

Quintum signaculum ueteris testamenti incepit in Ysaya et Ezechia rege Iuda,
250 consumatum uero est in excidio Ierusalem et transmigracione Babilonis, sub quo fuit conflictus caldeorum per quintum caput drachonis, scilicet Nabuchodonosor regem Babilonis.

	Generacio		Generacio
	XLVII	Manasses	XXVIII

255 Hucusque filii Israel pacem regni dauitici possederunt; ex hinc translati sunt in assirios, et sola tribus Iuda, de qua Christus erat nasciturus, remansit, cum qua illa Beniamin et Leui ita sunt numerate ut tres una tribus dicantur.

---

236 impios] imperios V   occisi] cessi BTV   246 XLV] XLIIII T   249 cepit T   reges T   255 pacem] patrem BV   257 dicatur BV

---

[35] *Lib. Conc.*, fol. 45v.

	Generacio			Generacio
	XLVIII	Amon		XXIX

260
	Generacio		Generacio	
Ieremias	XXXXIX	Iozias	XXX	
propheta				

Hic prophetauit Ieremias urbis et templi destruccionem ; predixit et uidit, et tocius ruinam populi multiplici alphabeto defleuit.

265
Generacio		Generacio	
L	Ioachim	XXXI	
Generacio		Generacio	
LI	Iechonias	XXXII	Transmigracio
			Babilonis

270 Hic Nabuchodonosor, rex Babilonis, cum magno exercitu caldeorum uenit Ierusalem et, capto Ioachim seu Iechonia rege Iuda cum magna parte populi, duxit eum in Babilonem captiuum, ita quod omnem Ierusalem, exceptis pauperibus, et omnes thesauros domus Domini transtulit de Ierusalem in Babilonem et, facta diuisione populi, Sedechias per predictum Babilonis
275 regem fuit in regem Iuda constitutus, per quem finaliter rex Babilonis, accepta occasione, iterum obsedit Ierusalem, et muris ciuitatis et templo et palacio regis in terram deiectis, Sedechias in fuga captus est, et filii eius coram eo in mortem traditi sunt, et uinctus cathenis ductus est in Babilonem captiuus. In quibus temporibus rex Babilonis, conuocatis cunctis principibus et iudicibus
280 sapientibus et tirannis ad erigendam statuam auream et dedicandam, statuit ut quicumque dictam statuam non adoraret occideretur, et cetera, ut supra.[36]

        Daniel propheta   Ezechiel propheta

Sextum signaculum ueteris testamenti incepit in Ezechiele et Daniele, consumatum uero est in Esdra et Neemia, in quo fuit transmigracio Ierusalem
285 et percucio ueteris Babilonis, necnon et tribulaciones due filiorum Israel sub duobus ultimis capitibus drachonis, scilicet Nabochodonosor, rege assirio-rum, et Naman, secundo a rege Assuero, quarum una continetur in ystoria Iudith, altera in libro Hester. Verumtamen templum Dei et muri ciuitatis rehedificati sunt in angustia temporum.

---

259 XLVIII] XL TV   261-262 Ieremia propheta *sub* Ioachim *tr.* B   261 XXXXIX]
XL T   Iozias *om.* V   263-264 et uidit Ieremias ruinam tocius BTV   268 XXXII]
XXIII V   272 captiuus M   273 sustulit T   274-275 regem Babilonis *tr.* T
278 est *om.* T   captus T   281 et ... supra *om.* BTV   283 accepit T   285 nec-non et tribulaciones *om.* BV   286 rege] regis *codd.* et *praem.* BTV   287 secundus M
288 altera] aliam B; et *praem.* BTV

---

[36] Cf. Dan. 3.1-7.

290   Generacio   Generacio
                LII   Salatiel   XXXIII
             Generacio   Generacio
                LIII   Zorobabel   XXXIIII
                   Aggei, Zacharias, Malachias, Esdras, Neemias

295 Ruina ueteris Babilonis et rehedificacio, et cetera.

             Generacio   Generacio
                LIIII   Abuid   XXXV

Ab Abuid usque ad Ioseph sunt x generaciones, de quibus nulla fit mencio
in auctentico canone ueteris testamenti, qui quidem non carent misterio
300 grandi, sicut iam superius tactum est. Tamen a Zorobabel usque ad tempora
Anthiochi regis non defuit regalis unccio de domo Iuda; tunc enim fuit casus
perpetuus corone et tocius unccionis domus Iude, ut impleretur quod a Iacob
patriarcha Iude filio suo dictum est: *Non auferetur septrum de Iuda, et dux
de femore eius, donec ueniat qui mictendus est,*[37] et cetera. Tunc enim, in fine
305 illorum temporum, Iesus Christus Filius Dei fuit missus a Deo Patre in
mundum, et cetera.[38]

Septimum signaculum ueteris testamenti incepit in Esdra et Neemia,
consumatum uero est in Iohanne Babtista et Domino Iesu Christo; hic
cessauerunt ystorie et prophecie et concessus est sabbatissimus populo Dei,[39]
310 et reliquiis iudeorum data est pax usque ad caudam drachonis, scilicet
Anthiocum regem, qua persequucione peracta, non longe post, premisso
Iohanne, unigenitus Dei Filius uenit in mundum, ita ut *in terris uideatur et
cum hominibus conuersaretur,*[40] et cetera.[41]

             Generacio   Generacio
315   LV   Elyachim   XXXVI
             Generacio   Generacio
                LVI   Azor   XXXVII
             Generacio   Generacio
                LVII   Sadoch   XXXVIII
320   Generacio   Generacio
                LVIII   Achim   XXXIX

---

294 Neemias *om.* BTV   298 Ab *om.* BV   generaciones decem *tr.* BTV   300 a
om. BV   302 a] de TV   305 istorum BTV   315 xxxvi] xxxv B   321 Achim]
Sadoch T   xxxix] xl T

[37] Gen. 49.10.
[38] Cf. Jn. 3.17.
[39] Heb. 4.9.
[40] Cf. Bar. 3.38.
[41] *Septem Sigillis*, pp. 245-246.

	Generacio			Generacio	
Ordo pharise-	LIX	Eliud	XXXX	Ordo seduce-	
orum				orum	

325   Quadragesima generacione ab Abraam, per sex generaciones ante babtismum Christi, surrexerunt in sinagoga iudeorum due religiones, scilicet
phariseorum et seduceorum.

	Generacio			Generacio
	LX	Eleazar	XXXXI	
330	Generacio		Generacio	
	LXI	Natan	XXXXII	

Persequucio Antiochi regis et casus perpetuus corone et unccionis tocius
domus Iuda.

	Generacio			Generacio
335	LXII	Iacob	XXXXIII	
	Generacio		Generacio	
	LXIII	Ioseph	XXXXIIII	
	Zacharias sacerdos		Iohannes Babtista	

Totum tempus quod decursum est a circumcisione uel a natiuitate
340 Habraam usque ad babtismum Christi sub testamento ueteri computatur, quia
non uenit soluere legem sed adimplere.[42]

INCARNACIO DOMINI NOSTRI IESU CHRISTI

Generaciones enim in nouo testamento non secundum carnem, sed
secundum spiritum, accipiende sunt, secundum illud euangelii: *Quod natum*
345 *est ex carne, caro est, et quod natum est ex spiritu, spiritus est.*[43] Et quoniam
xxx annorum erat Dominus quando cepit habere filios spirituales, recte
spacium generacionis in nouo testamento xxx annorum numero terminatur,
et nimirum, quia perfeccio ipsius numeri ad fidem pertinet Trinitatis, igitur
generaciones ecclesie sub spacio xxx annorum singule sub singulis tricenariis
350 accipiende sunt, et cetera.

---

322 Generacio² *om.* BV   325 per *om.* V   330-331 Generacio¹ ... xxxII] Natan B
336-337 Generacio¹ ... xxxxIIII] Ioseph B   338 sacerdos *om.* B   339 de cursu M
est decursum *tr.* BTV   345 caro] spiritus est Mᵃᶜ   350 et cetera *om.* BTV

---

[42] Cf. Mt. 5.17.
[43] Jn. 3.6.

A Christi descensu cum xii^{cim} apostolis in terram gencium usque ad solucionem Sathane sunt anni Mcclx.

Generacio prima anni xxx	Iesus Christus Filius Dei, rex et sacerdos	Anni ab incarnacione xxx
Petrus, Andreas, Thomas Symon, Iudas, Mathias	Iacobus frater Domini, Mathias Philippus, Bartholomeus, Iohannes Iacobus	
Ioseph Paulus Sex ecclesie	Mathias Barnabas Sex ecclesie	

Sub apercione primi sigilli continetur persequucio iudeorum contra Christi ecclesiam, sub qua Christi populus afflictus nimis, relicta sinagoga, uenerunt ad gentes, preeuntibus se Paulo et Barnaba. Continet generaciones sex.

Primus ordo uisionum Apocalipsis respicit primum tempus ecclesie sub primo candelabro, prima stella, prima ecclesia, scilicet Ephesum, primo sigillo, prima tuba, prima fiala plena ira Dei, cum primo capite drachonis, scilicet Herode primo et secundo, uel Pilato et Caypha.

Paulus et Barnabas inter apostolos benediccionem acceperunt, nam pro Iuda proditore datus est Mathias.

Generacio II anni xxx	Petrus	Anni ab incarnacione lx

Secundus ordo uisionum Apocalipsis respicit secundum tempus ecclesie sub secundo candelabro, secunda stella, secunda ecclesia, scilicet e Smirna, secundo sigillo, secunda tuba, secunda phiala plena ira Dei, et secundo capite drachonis, scilicet Nerone et Symone mago.

Exterminium Ierusalem per Titum et Vespesianum factum fuit xlii° anno a resurreccione Christi.

Generacio III anni xxx	Linus et Cletus	Anni ab incarnacione lxxxx
Generacio IIII anni xxx	Clemens cum tribus	Anni ab incarnacione cxx

351 A] Cum BTV   357-360 Matheus, Iohannes, Mathias, Barnabas, Iacobus, Philippus, Bartholomeus *tr.* BTV   361 Sex ecclesie² *sub.* Petrus *tr.* BV   363 Christi *om.* BTV   366 scilicet] ecclesia *add.* BTV   370 traditore BTV   371 II] LII BV   Anni ab incarnacione *om.* T   372 anni xxx *om.* T   374 secunda¹] et BTV   380 lxxxx] cxx BV   381 IIII] III T

	Generacio v		Anni ab incarnacione
	anni xxx	Sixtus cum duobus	cl
385	Generacio vi		Anni ab incarnacione
	anni xxx	Annicius cum duobus	clxxx

Sub apercione secundi signaculi continetur persequucio paganorum a quibus multitudo martirum in ara Christi mactata est, et ecclesia, uehementer afflicta, clamauit ad Dominum et liberata est.[44] Et continet in se generaciones
390 sex.

	Generacio vii		Anni ab incarnacione
	anni xxx	Eleuterius cum duobus	ccx
	Generacio viii		Anni ab incarnacione
	anni xxx	Calixtus cum iiii^{or}	ccxl
395	Generacio ix		Anni ab incarnacione
	anni xxx	Cornelius cum sex	cclxx
	Generacio x		Anni ab incarnacione
	anni xxx	Gayus cum uno	ccc
	Generacio xi		Anni ab incarnacione
400	anni xxx	Marcello cum duobus	cccxxx
	Generacio xii		Anni ab incarnacione
	anni xxx	Siluester cum iiii^{or}	ccclx

Hic tradita est archa ecclesie in manus peccatorum.

Hic, sub Siluestro papa, factum est imperium huius mundi Dei Patris et
405 Christi eius, et populus christianus in ipsa xii generacione a Christo regem habuit christianum, scilicet Constantinum, imperatorem, sicut populus iudaycus in xii similiter generacione a Iacob regem habuit iudeum, scilicet Dauid, et cetera.

Hic scilicet papa Siluester, secundum aliquos,[45] est ille angelus Apocalipsis
410 xx° qui habebat *clauem abissi et cathenam magnam in manu sua, et apprehendit draconem, serpentem antiqum, qui est diabolus et Sathanas, et ligauit eum per annos mille, et misit eum in abyssum.*[46] Interim regnum et pax data est populo christiano. Sequitur: *Et cum consumati fuerunt M anni, soluetur Sathanas de carcere suo,*[47] et cetera.

---

391 vii] vi T   392 ccx] ccxx BV   393 Anni ab incarnacione *om.* T
402 ccclx *om.* T   404 mundi *om.* M^{ac} 409 scilicet *om.* BT   413 fuerint BT

---

[44] Cf. Jud. 3.9, 4.3, 6.7.
[45] Cf. esa of Arnold of Vilanova, p. 254.
[46] Apoc. 20.1-3.
[47] Apoc. 20.7.

415   Sub apercione tercii sigilli continetur persequucio arrianorum contra
Christi ecclesiam, cui mox uandalica, persica, et longobardica addite sunt.
Iuxta Danielem, tercia bestia similis erat pardo et iiii^{or} capita habebat supra
se.[48] Continet autem generaciones sex.
      Tercius ordo uisionum Apocalipsis respicit tercium tempus ecclesie sub
420   tercio candelabro, tercia stella, tercia ecclesia, scilicet Pergami, tercio sigillo,
tercia tuba, tercia phiala plena ira Dei, tercio capite drachonis, scilicet
Constantino arriano, filio Constantini.

	Generacio XIII		Anni ab incarnacione
	anni xxx	Damasus cum duobus	ccclxxxx
425	Generacio XIIII		Anni ab incarnacione
	anni xxx	Zozimus cum tribus	ccccxx
	Generacio xv		Anni ab incarnacione
	anni xxx	Leo cum duobus	ccccl
	Generacio XVI		Anni ab incarnacione
430	anni xxx	Felix cum duobus	cccclxxx
	Sanctus Antonius abbas		Sanctus Paulus primus heremita
	Generacio XVII		Anni ab incarnacione
	anni xxx	Siscimacus cum vii	dx
435	Generacio XVIII		Anni ab incarnacione
	anni xxx	Virgilius cum septem	dxl
	Sanctus Benedictus		Sanctus Basilius
	Secunda iniciacio ordinis monachorum		Ordo calogerorum

440   Sub apercione quarti sigilli continetur persequucio arabum, seu sarracenorum, designata per quartam bestiam ascendentem de mari, et cetera, a quibus
grecorum ecclesie, uersus orientalem et meridionalem plagam incolentes,
multa descrimina passe sunt, nec longe post affricana ecclesia ad nichilum
penitus redacta est. Et continet generaciones sex.
445   Quartus ordo uisionum Apocalipsis respicit quartum tempus ecclesie sub
quarto candelabro, quarta stella, quarta ecclesia, scilicet Tyatira, quarto

---

416 persica] persecucio BTV   419 uisionum *om.* T   420 tercia^2 *om.* BV
421 tercio] et *praem.* T   422 Constantini] arriani T   424 ccclxxxx] cccx BT; *om.* V
426 ccccxx] ccclxxxx BV   429 xvi] xv T   430 cccclxxx] ccccl T   438 Se-
cunda] Sancta T   441 designatam M   ascendentis M   443 post] potest T

---

[48] Dan. 7.6.

sigillo, quarta tuba, quarta fyala plena ira Dei, et quarto capite drachonis, scilicet Macumeto.

	Generacio XIX		Anni ab incarnacione
450	anni xxx	Iohannes cum duobus	dlxx
	Generacio xx		Anni ab incarnacione
	anni xxx	Gregorius cum v	dc
	Generacio XXI		Anni ab incarnacione
	anni xxx	Honorius cum v	dcxxx
455	Generacio XXII		Anni ab incarnacione
	anni xxx	Vellignanus cum vii	dclx
	Sanctus Ambrosius		Sanctus Augustinus
	Sanctus Gregorius		Sanctus Ylarius
			Sanctus Iohannes Crisostomus
460	Ordo regularium		Ordo heremitarum

Secunda iniciacio ordinis clericorum.
Hic Macumetus surrexit.

	Generacio XXIII		Anni ab incarnacione
	anni xxx	Sergius cum iiii^{or}	dclxxxx
465	Generacio XXIIII		Anni ab incarnacione
	anni xxx	Sanctus Gregorius cum iiii^{or}	dccxx

Bestia sarracenica ascendens de mari, habens capita vii et cornua x Apocalipsis xi.

470 Sub apercione quinti sigilli continetur persequucio alamannorum contra Christi ecclesiam querencium ancillare libertatem ecclesie; iam enim typum Babilonis regni suos uires exercet, iam enim mater Syon ex sua ciuitate transmigrare compellitur. Et continet in se generaciones xx.

Quintus ordo uisionum Apocalipsis respicit quintum tempus ecclesie sub
475 quinto candelabro, quinta stella, quinta ecclesia, scilicet Sardis, quinto sigillo, quinta tuba, quinta phyala plena ira Dei, et quinto capite drachonis, scilicet Frederico secundo, qui, quasi mortuus, in aliquo de suo semine in modernis temporibus ita reuiuiscet, ut non solum romanum imperium, ymmo eciam francis ab eo deuictis, obtineat regnum francorum, ut dicit Ioachim.[49]

---

448 Macumeto *om.* T   450 dlxx *om.* T   456 dclx] cxxx T   460 Ordo heremitarum *om.* V   468 de mari ascendens *tr.* T   475 Sardis] et *praem.* BTV

---

[49] Unidentified source.

480	Generacio xxv anni xxx	Zacharias cum iiii[or]	Anni ab incarnacione dccl
	Generacio xxvi anni xxx	Adrianus cum uno	Anni ab incarnacione dcclxxx
485	Generacio xxvii anni xxx	Stephanus cum iiii[or]	Anni ab incarnacione dccc et x
	Generacio xxviii anni xxx	Sergius cum iiii[or]	Anni ab incarnacione dcccxl
	Generacio xxix anni xxx	Iohannes cum octo	Anni ab incarnacione dccclxx
490	Generacio xxx anni xxx	Iohannes cum nouem	Anni ab incarnacione dcccc
	Beatus Bernardus Ordo alborum		Iniciacio ordinis monachorum alborum

[*Glosa.* Ponitur hic sanctus Bernardus racione concordie facti cum Ieremia.]

495	Generacio xxxi anni xxx	Iohannes cum quinque	Anni ab incarnacione dccccxxx
	Generacio xxxii anni xxx	Benedictus cum vii	Anni ab incarnacione dcccclx
500	Generacio xxxiii anni xxx	Iohannes cum vii	Anni ab incarnacione dcccclxxxx
	Generacio xxxiiii anni xxx	Iohannes cum quinque	Anni ab incarnacione M et xx
	Generacio xxxv anni xxx	Leo cum quinque	Anni ab incarnacione Ml
505	Generacio xxxvi anni xxx	Gregorius cum duobus	Anni ab incarnacione Mlxxx
	Generacio xxxvii anni xxx	Pascalis cum tribus	Anni ab incarnacione Mcx
510	Generacio xxxviii anni xxx	Innocencius cum v	Anni ab incarnacione Mcxl
	Generacio xxxix anni xxx	Alexander cum iiii[or]	Anni ab incarnacione Mclxx
	Generacio xxxx anni xxx	Celestinus cum duobus[50]	Anni ab incarnacione Mcc

---

480-481 Generacio ... dccl *om.* V   480 xxv] xxiiii BT   483 anni xxx *om.* M dcclxx T   485 dccc B   491 dccccxxx V   492 Beatus Bernardus *om.* B   ordinis *om.* BTV   493 Ordo alborum *om.* BTV

---

[50] This is the last of the generations in the *Lib. Fig.*

515   Sub papa Innocencio et imperatore Frederico secundo incepit compleri in ecclesia illud quod Ieremia super Ierusalem et templum predixit, nec desinit impleri usque ad presens, quousque percuciatur noua Babilon, et cetera.

    Quadragesima generacione ab incarnacione Christi, per sex generaciones ante tempus plenitudinis, surrexerunt in ecclesia christianorum due religio-
520 nes, scilicet minorum et predicatorum.

Generacio xxxxi		Anni ab incarnacione
anni xxx	Honorius	Mccxxx
Sanctus Franciscus		Sanctus Dominicus
Ordo fratrum minorum		Ordo predicatorum
Generacio xxxxii		Anni ab incarnacione
anni xxx	Gregorius cum iiii^{or}	Mcclx
Generacio xxxxiii		Anni ab incarnacione
anni xxx	Innocencius cum tribus	Mcclxxxx
Generacio xxxxiiii		Anni ab incarnacione
anni xxx	Martinus cum quinque	Mcccxx

    Sub apercione vi^{ti} sigilli continetur transmigracio spiritualis Ierusalem et percusio noue Babilonis sub iterato conflictu quarte bestie, scilicet sarrace-nice, ascendentis de mari, et x regum eorum insurgencium contra romanum imperium, et ualidissima tempestas vi^{ti} et vii^{mi} capitis drachonis, quarum
535 prima erit sub illo rege xi^{o}, seu cornu paruo, secunda sub Antichristo; in intermedio, aliqua pace data, fiet passagium et rehedificabitur rursum sancta ciuitas et templum in angustia illorum temporum, sicut factum est in diebus Zorobabel, et cetera.

    Sextus ordo uisionum Apocalipsis respicit vi^{us} tempus ecclesie sub sexto
540 candelabro, sexta stella, sexta ecclesia, scilicet Philadelfia, sexto sigillo, sexta tuba, sexta phyala plena ira Dei, et sexto et septimo capite drachonis, illo scilicet rege xi^{o} et Antichristo.

    Futurum quippe est per concordiam in modernis temporibus ut nouus rex Babilonis insurgat, et cum magno exercitu caldeorum ueniat Ierusalem et,
545 capto Iechonia rege, seu summo sacerdote, cum magna parte populi, scilicet ecclesiastici, exceptis pauperibus, et cum omnibus thesauris domus Domini, ducatur in Babilonem captiuus, ut transmigracio babilonica misterialiter impleatur. Et facta diuisione populi supradicti per predictum Babilonis

---

516 Ieremia] Ysaia BTV   519 christianorum *om.* BTV   524 ordo *post* minorum *tr.* BV   predicatorum] fratrum *praem.* BTV   532 noue *om.* BV   535 secunda] tercia BTV   in *om.* BTV   537 est *om.* BV   538 et cetera *om.* T   539-540 ecclesia ... stella *tr.* BTV   541 capitibus BTV   543 quippe] quidem BTV   in *om.* BTV   544 cum *om.* M^{ac} 545 sacerdote] pontifice BTV

regem, instituatur in regem Iuda, seu romanum pontificem, Sedechias, in
550 cuius temporis fine rex Babilonis per ipsum occasione accepta, iterum obsidat
Ierusalem, et muris ciuitatis et templo et palacio summi sacerdotis in terram
deiectis, Sedechias in fuga capiatur et filii eius coram eo in mortem tradantur,
et uinctus cathenis in Babilonem ducatur captiuus. In quibus temporibus rex
Babilonis, conuocatis cunctis principibus, magistratibus et iudicibus sapienti-
555 bus et tirannis ad erigendam, seu eligendam, et dedicandam, seu consecrandam, statuam auream, pseuso papam scilicet Antichristum, statuet ut
quicumque non adorauerit occidatur, et cetera.[51]

Iste septimus rex, scilicet Antichristus, prius ueniet quam deficiat sextus,
quia in uiribus vi[ti] debet ascendere, et in templo Dei sedere tanquam sit Deus,
560 *et dabit signa magna et prodigia, ut in errorem inducantur, si fieri potest,*
ecciam electi.[52] *Tunc scandalizabuntur multi,*[53] dicentes: si Christum esset
Deus, non permitteret populum suum christianum in tam diuersas et orribiles
procellas tribulacionum, quasi sine interuallo temporis, incidere. Vt autem
ostendatur istos duos reges in eodem tempore concurrere, Danielis xi°
565 dicitur: *Duorum quoque regum cor erit ut malefaciant, et ad mensam unam*
loquentur mendacium et non proficient, quia adhuc finis in aliud tempus.[54] Hii
duo unum consilium habebunt, et erit eis uotum unum ad complendum opera
patris sui.

Et cum consumati fuerint M anni, soluetur Sathanas de carcere suo, et
570 *seducet gentes que sunt super iiii[or] angulos terre,* et cetera, *et congregabit eas*
in prelium,[55] et cetera.

In dimidio ebdomadis deficiet hostia et sacrificium, et in templo erit
abominacio desolacionis, et usque ad consumacionem et finem perseuerabit
desolacio.[56] Danielis ix°.

550-551 Ierusalem obsidat *tr.* T   551 sacerdotis] pontificis BTV   552 capitur T
in[2] *om.* BV   556 auream] seu *add.* BV; in *add.* T   557 et cetera *om.* BTV   558 primus BTV   559 vi[ti] *om.* BTV   Dei *om.* T   561 ecciam *ante* si (l. 560) *tr.* BTV
562 suum populum *tr.* BTV   563 tribulancium BV   sine] signa M[ac]   564 tempore
om. T   occurrere BV   565 erit cor *tr.* BTV   570 super *om.* M   570-571 angulos
... cetera *om.* M[ac]   571 in prelium *om.* T   et cetera *om.* V *et add.*: Hic imperator
Fredericus secundus a papa Honorio in urbe coronatus.   574 desolacio *om.* M   xi°
codd.   Danielis xi° *post l. 573* desolacionis *tr.* BTV

[51] Cf. Dan. 3.1-7.
[52] Mt. 24.24.
[53] Mt. 24.10.
[54] Dan. 11.27.
[55] Apoc. 20.7.
[56] Dan. 9.27.

575 Generacio xlv   Anni ab incarnacione
      anni xxx   Iechonias   Mcccl

Tempus silencii et potestas tenebrarum, dies xliiii.

Generacio xlvi   Anni ab incarnacione
      anni xxx   Salatiel   Mccclxvii
580 Petrus, Iacobus, Iohannes   Rex undecimus, Antichristus
Helias, Moyses
      Rex undecimus. Sanguis, sanguis in terra et in mari.
      Petrus incepit, Petrus dabit finem. Rex undecimus, sanguis, sedutio,
      mors, interitus.
585   Generacio xlvii
                        Nouus Zorobabel

Iudas, Ruben, Gath   Symeon, Leui, Ysachar
Aser, Neptali, Manasses   Zabulon, Ioseph, Beniamin
     Effraym   Manasses
590   Moyses   Aaron
    Sex monasteria   Sex monasteria

Ex tribu Iuda, xii milia   *Ex tribu Symeon, xii milia*
signati.   *signati.*
Ex tribu Ruben, xii milia   *Ex tribu Leui, xii milia*
595 *signati.*   *signati.*
Ex tribu Gath, xii milia   *Ex tribu Ysachar, xii milia*
signati.   *signati.*
Ex tribu Asser, xii milia   *Ex tribu Zabulon, xii milia*
signati.   *signati.*
600 *Ex tribu Neptali, xii milia*   *Ex tribu Ioseph, xii milia*
signati.   *signati.*
Ex tribu Manasses, xii milia   *Ex tribu Beniamin, xii milia*
signati.   *signati.*[57]

     Manasses et Beniamin inter patriarchas euangelicos benediccionem acci-
605 pient et plenam mercedem portabunt.

---

578 Generacio xlvi *om.* BTV   Anni ab incarnacione *om.* BV   580 Rex ...
Antichristus] Iudas BTV   583 Petrus[2] *om.* TV   604 Beniamin] magnus *add.* BV
605 mercedem] in cedem V

---

[57] Apoc. 7.5-8.

In tempore illo, consurget Michael, princeps magnus, qui stat pro filiis
populi tui, et ueniet tempus quale non fuit ex eo ex quo gentes esse ceperunt
usque ad tempus illud, et in tempore illo saluabitur populus tuus, omnis qui
inuentus fuerit in libro uite, et multi de hiis qui dormierunt in puluere terre
610 *uigilabunt, hii in uitam eternam, et hii in supplicium eternum.*[58] Sequitur: *Et*
a tempore cum ablatum fuerit sacrificium iuge et posita fuerit abominacio, dies
Mcclxxxx; beatus qui expectat et peruenit usque ad dies Mcccxxxv,[59] et cetera.

De isto ecciam tempore Sibilla dicit quod, completis Mcccxxxv annis ab
immolacione agni, erit tempus pascale quale non fuit ab inicio mundi usque
615 ad tempus illud, et cetera.

Iudicium sedit, ut auferatur potencia, et conteratur, et dispereat usque in
finem; regnum autem, et potestas, et magnitudo regni, que est subter omne
celum, detur populo sanctorum Altissimi, cuius regnum sempiternum est, et
omnes reges seruient ei et obedient.[60] Hucusque finis uerbi Danielis septimo.
620 In xlvii[a] generacione ab ortu Christi, peracta prius tribulacione generali et
purgato diligenter tritico ab uniuersis zizaniis peccatorum, ascendit nouus
Zorobabel, seu nouus dux, uniuersalis pontifex noue Ierusalem, ecclesie
scilicet uniuerse, licet in xlvi[a] reuelandus sit, ut Christus, nouus dux et nouus
pontifex, in xlvi[a] generacione a natiuitate Habraam reuelatus est, in baptis-
625 mate terminans circumcisionem et figuram agni pascalis in institucione
eucharistie sacramenti. Hoc autem tempus distinguetur per generaciones et
pontifices reges, quia Dominus Iesus Christus rex fuit pariter et sacerdos.

Sub apercione septimi sigilli continetur persequucio Gog nouissimi. Sub
hoc septimo tempore cessabunt aperciones signaculorum et labor exponen-
630 dorum librorum testamenti ueteris, dabiturque reuera *sabbatissimus populo*
Dei,[61] et erit *in diebus eius iusticia et habundancia pacis, et dominabitur*
Dominus a mari usque ad mare,[62] et sancti eius regnabunt cum eo usque ad
occultum finem istius temporis, quo soluendus est Sathanas de carcere suo,

---

607 ex eo *om.* BTV   611 iuge sacrificium *tr.* BTV   612 et[1] ... ad *om.*
BTV   et cetera *om.* BV   613 Mcccxxxv *om.* BTV   616 sedit *om.* T   in] ad T
617 regni *om.* T   619 eis BTV   620 In *om.* BV   621 nouus] rex *add.* BTV
623-624 sit ... xlvi[a] *om.* BT   624 reuelatus] eleuatus T   in[2] *om.* BV   626-
627 pontifices et *tr.* BTV   627 rex] qui Dominus *add.* M[ac]   632 eo] regnabunt *add.*
BTV   633 finem *om.* T

---

[58] Dan. 12.1-2.
[59] Dan. 12.11.
[60] Dan. 12.26-27.
[61] Heb. 4.9.
[62] Ps. 71.7-8.

et regnaturus est homo ille pessimus qui uocatur Gog. *Relinquitur ergo,* ut
635 dicit apostolus, *sabbatissimus populo Dei,*[63] in cuius fine futura est ista
tribulacio, postquam, premisso Helya, uenturus est Dominus ad extremum
iudicium, secundum quod continetur in septima parte Apocalipsis.[64]

Et ego, Daniel, audiui unum de sanctis loquentem, et dixit unus sanctus
alteri: Vsquequo uisio, et iuge sacrificium, et peccatum desolacionis que facta
640 *est, et sanctuarium, et fortitudo conculcabitur? Et dixit ei: Vsque ad uesperam*
et mane, dies duo milia cccᵗⁱ, et mundabitur sanctuarium. Et cum ego, Daniel,
uiderem uisionem, et quererem intelligenciam, stetit in conspectu meo quasi
species uiri, et clamauit, et ait: Gabriel, fac me intelligere istam uisionem; et
ait ad me: Intellige, fili hominis, quoniam in tempore finis complebitur uisio.[65]
645 *Et uisio mane et uespere que dicta est, uera est; tu uero signa uisionem, quia*
post dies multos erit. Et ego, Daniel, langui et egrotaui per dies, cumque
surrexissem, stupebam ad uisionem, et non erat qui interpretaretur,[66] et cetera.
Danielis octauo.

Septimus ordo uisionum Apocalipsis respicit septimum tempus ecclesie
650 sub septimo candelabro, septima stella, septima ecclesia, scilicet Lahodicie,
septimo sigillo, septima tuba, septima phiala plena ira Dei, sub cauda
drachonis que octaua est, scilicet Gog nouissimi.

Quot autem erunt pontifices in isto tercio statu generali soli Deo relinquendum est, qui omnia nouit; tamen isti qui ponuntur hic post nouum
655 Zorobabel ad hoc solummodo ponuntur, ut per eos generaciones huius
temporis distinguantur. Nauicula enim ecclesie, quamuis diuersis impellatur
fluctibus, tamen usque ad diem iudicii non erit absque pastore; tamen nomina
summorum pontificum et collateralium interscripta, de fine et principio
ueteris temporis sumpta, ut sint *primi nouissimi et nouissimi primi,*[67] non
660 carent misterio grande.

Signa enim ante diem iudicii, ut ait Ieronimus, sunt xv. In prima die eriget
se mare xl cubitis super altitudinem moncium, stans in loco suo quasi murus.

---

634 ille homo *tr.* BTV   635 sabbatissimus *ante* ut *tr.* BV   636 postquam]
post T   637 septima] alia BTV   638 Et *om.* T   641 sanctuarium] sacrificium T
644 me] eum BTV   fine temporis BTV   645 uera est *om.* BV   646 Et *om.* T
647 et cetera *om.* BV   651 septima² *om.* BTV   Dei] et *add.* BT   654 ponitur V   656 appellatur T   658 et collateralium *om.* Mᵃᶜ   659 temporis
ueteris *tr.* BTV   661 prima *om.* T   662 altitudinem] multitudinem T

[63] Heb. 4.9.
[64] Apoc. cc. 19-21; *Septem Sigillis,* pp. 245-246.
[65] Dan. 8.13-17.
[66] Dan. 8.26-27.
[67] Mt. 19.30.

In secunda die tantum descendit quod uix uideri poterit. In tercia die marine
belue apparentes super mare dabunt rugitus usque ad celum. In iiii^a die
665 ardebunt mare et aque. In v die erbe et arbores dabunt rorem sanguineum.
In vi die ruent hedificia. In vii die petre collidentur ad inuicem. In viii^a die
generalis fiet terremotus. In viiii^a die equabitur terra. In x die exibunt homines
de cauernis terre et non poterunt sibi mutuo loqui. In xi die stabunt ossa
mortuorum super sepulcra. In xii die cadent stelle de celo. In xiii die
670 morientur omnes uiuentes ut cum mortuis resurgant. In xiiii die ardebunt celi
et terra. In xv^a die fiet celum nouum et terra noua et resurgent omnes ad
iudicium, et cetera.^68

Et qui non habuerunt partem in resurreccione prima ledentur a morte
secunda, et prohicientur homines in lacum magnum ire Dei ignis et sulphuris,
675 ubi *estuabuntur homines estu magno, et commanducabunt linguas suas pre*
doloribus, et blasphemabunt Deum celi, pre doloribus et uulneribus suis,
habentem potestatem super plagas has.^69 *Et in diebus illis querent homines*
mortem, et non inuenient eam; desiderabunt mori, et mors fugiet ab eis.^70 Et
cruciabuntur igne et sulfure in conspectu angelorum sanctorum et ante
680 conspectum Agni, nec habebunt requiem die ac nocte, et fumus tormentorum
illorum ascendet in secula seculorum. Apocalipsis.^71

Vidi thronum candidum, et sedentem super eum, a cuius conspectu fugit
terra et celum, et locus non est inuentus ab eis. Et uidi mortuos magnos et
pusillos stantes in conspectu throni, et libri aperti sunt, et alius liber apertus
685 *est qui est liber uite, et iudicati sunt mortui ex his que scripta erant in libris,*
secundum opera ipsorum. Et dedit mare mortuos suos qui in eo erant, et mors
et infernus dederunt mortuos suos qui in ipsis erant, et iudicatum est de singulis
secundum opera ipsorum. Et infernus et mors missi sunt in stagnum ignis. Hec
est mors secunda. Et qui non est inuentus in libro uite scriptus, missus est in
690 *stagnum ignis.* Apocalipsis.^72

Generacio XLVIII
Abuid

---

664 celum] mare M^ac   665 aque] omnes *add.* TV   666 petre] paretre B; pareti et
V   667 die^1 *om.* V   670 morientur *post* uiuentes *tr.* BTV   678 et non ... mori *om.*
BTV   679 sulfure] fulgure M   683 celum et terram *tr.* BTV   685 libris] ex hiis
add. T   686 ipsorum] eorum BTV   eo] ipsis T   686-687 eo ... dederunt *om.* V
690 Apocalipsis] Daniele septimo: *Fluuius igneus rapidusque egrediebatur a facie eius*
add. BTV

---

^68 See the Joachite anthologies listed at p. 277, n. 19.
^69 Cf. Apoc. 16.9-11.
^70 Apoc. 9.6.
^71 Cf. Apoc. 20.7-10, 15.
^72 Apoc. 20.11-15.

Generacio XLVIIII
Elyachim
695   Generacio L
Azor
Generacio LI
Sadoch
Generacio LII
700   Achim
Generacio LIII
Eliud
Generacio LIIII
Eliazar
705   Generacio LV
Nathan
Generacio LVI
Iacob
Generacio LVII
710   Ioseph
Generacio LVIII
Iareth
Generacio LIX
Malalahel
715   Generacio LX
Caynan

Hic cindetur ouile in tres partes.
Principium totius erroris spiritus libertatis.

Generacio LXI
720   Enos

Antichristus apertus et ultimus. Gog et Magog.

Generacio LXII
Seth
Generacio LXIII
725   Adam
Signa iudicii.

---

699 LII] LI T   713 Generacio LIX *om.* V   713-715, 719-720 Generacio LIX ...
Enos *om.* T   718 Principium ... libertatis *om.* BV   721 ultimus] Generacio LXIIII
add. B   Gog et Magog *om.* BTV   722 LXIII B   723-725 Seth ... Adam *om.* T
724 LXIIII B   726 Signa iudicii *om.* BV

Sicut enim, consumatis ystoriis ueteris testamenti, ut pretactum est, et
passo unigenito Filio Dei, qui factus est *sub lege, ut eos qui erant sub lege
redimeret*,[73] aduenit tempus resurreccionis, in quo *multa corpora sanctorum*
730 *qui dormierant*[74] suscitata sunt et collecta in unum, et in unam turmam
fidelium effusa est illa *habundancia pacis*,[75] que ecciam, repleta Spiritu
sancto, agnouit que sit beatitudo,[76] et cetera, sic, consumatis operibus
testamenti noui, peracta tribulacione que erit in diebus Gog, simile quidem
illi que facta est sub Antiocho, significata in passione Domini, aduenit tempus
735 resurreccionis mortuorum et consolacionis superne Ierusalem. Tunc enim
sedebit Dominus Iesus in sede magestatis sue ad segregandos electos suos a
multitudine reproborum quatinus, repleti Spiritu sancto, uadant ipsi pariter
in uitam eternam. Amen.

Iudicium sedit et libri aperti sunt.

740 Explicit sumula, seu breuiloquium, super Concordia noui et ueteris testamenti.

---

730 et[1] *om.* T   739 sunt *om.* BTV   740 Concordancia T   740-741 testamenti]
Deo gracias et uirgini Marie, toti curie supernorum *add.* BV Scriptus fuit liber iste per Petrum
Fort, mercatorem in ciuitate Berchenona, anno a natiuitate Domini millesimo quadringentesimo quinquagesimo quinto, ad laudem et honorem omnipotentis Dei, Patris, Filii, et Spiritus
sancti, qui regnat per infinita secula seculorum, amen. Et eum dedit in presenti libreria
constitutum in etate sexaginte quinque annorum, cum eum scripsit *add.* B; Scriptus fuit liber
iste per Michaelem Mirauet, uidellum sedis Barchinone, anno a natiuitate Domini millesimo
quadringentesimo octagesimo, octaua die carnispriuium, xviiii. mensis februarii, ad laudem et
honorem omnipotentis Dei, Patris, Filii, et Spiritus sancti, qui uiuit et regnat per infinita secula
seculorum, amen. Benedicamus Domino. Deo gracias.

---

[73] Gal. 4.5.
[74] Mt. 27.52.
[75] Ps. 71.7.
[76] *Septem Sigillis*, pp. 246-247.

Bibliography

PRIMARY SOURCES

Acta Aragonensia. See Finke, Heinrich.

Arnold of Vilanova. *Alia Informatio Beguinorum.* Ed. by Josep Perarnau. In *L'"Alia Informatio Beguinorum" d'Arnau de Vilanova,* pp. 19-85. Barcelona, Facultat de Teologia de Barcelona, 1978.

——. *Allocutio Christiani de iis quae conveniunt homini secundum propriam dignitatem creaturae rationalis.* Ed. in part by Heinrich Finke. In *Aus den Tagen Bonifaz VIII,* pp. CXCVII-CCI. Munster: Druck und Verlag der Aschendorff-schen Buchhandlung, 1902. See also Città del Vaticano, Biblioteca Apostolica Vaticana MS Vat. Lat. 3824, fols. 217-226r-v.

——. *Allocutio super significatione nominis tetragrammaton.* Ed. by Joaquin Carreras y Artau. In "Arnaldo de Vilanova, Apologista Antijudaico." *Sefarad,* 7 (1947): 49-61; 9 (1949): 75-105.

——. *Confessió de Barcelona.* Ed. by Miguel Batllori with a prologue by Joaquin Carreras y Artau. In *Arnau de Vilanova: Obres Catalanes,* 1: 101-139. Barcelona: Editorial Barcino, 1947.

——. *De tempore adventu Antichristi.* Ed. in part by Heinrich Finke. In *Aus den Tagen,* pp. CXXIX-CLIX. See also Città del Vaticano, Biblioteca Apostolica Vaticana MS Vat. Lat. 3824, fols. 50v-78r.

——. *Dialogus de elementis catholicae fidei.* Ed. in part by W. Burger. In "Römische Beitrage zur Geschichte der Katechese im Mittelalter." *Römische Quartalschrift,* fasc. 4 (1907). See also Città Vaticana, Biblioteca Apostolica Vaticana MS Vat. Lat. 3824, fols. 29-42r-v. See also a Castilian translation ed. by Josep Perarnau. In *Dos Tratados espirituales de Arnau de Vilanova en traducción castellana medieval.* Roma: Instituto Español de Historia Ecclesiástica, 1975-1976.

——. *Eulogium.* Ed. by Joaquin Carreras y Artau. In "La Polémica Gerundense sobre el Antichristo entre Arnau de Vilanova y los Dominicos." *Annales del Instituto de Estudios Gerundenses,* 5 (1950): 33-58.

——. *Expositio super Apocalypsi.* Ed. by Joaquin Carreras y Artau. Barcelona: Institut d'Estudis Catalans, 1971.

——. *Informació espiritual al Rei Frederic de Sicilia.* Ed. by Miguel Batllori. In *Obres Catalanes,* 1: 223-243.

——. *Introductio in librum Ioachim de semine scripturarum.* Ed. by Raoul Manselli. In *La religiosità d'Arnaldo di Villanova,* pp. 43-59. Rome: Istituto Storico Italiano per il Medio Evo e Archivio Muratoriano, 1951.

——. *Llicó de Narbona*. Ed. by Miguel Batllori. In *Obres Catalanes*, 1: 141-166.

——. *Raonament d'Avinyó*. Ed. by Miguel Batllori. In *Obres Catalanes*, 1: 167-221.

——. *Responsio ad cavillationes adversarii veritatis* (old title). *Tractatus quidem in quo respondetur obiectionibus que fiebant contra tractatum Arnaldi de adventu Antichristi* (new title). Ed. by Miguel Batllori. In "Dos nous escrits espirituals d'Arnau de Vilanova." *Analecta Sacra Tarraconensia*, 28 (1955): 45-70. See also Rome, Biblioteca Carmelitana, MS III, Var. I, fols. 49v-90r.

Batllori, Miguel. *Arnau de Vilanova: Obres Catalanes*. See Arnold of Vilanova, *Confessió de Barcelona*.

——. "Dos nous escrits espirituals d'Arnau de Vilanova." See Arnold of Vilanova, *Responsio ad cavillationes adversarii veritatis*.

Betí, Manuel. "Noticies de dos manuscrits de l'Arxiprestal de Morella." *Butlletí de la Biblioteca de Catalunya*, 4 (1917): 47-67.

Buchon, Jean Alexandre. See Froissart, Jean.

Bullarium Franciscanum. Ed. by Joannes Sbaralea and Conrad Eubel. 6 vols. Città del Vaticano, 1759-1902.

Burdach, Karl. See Pseudo-Joachim, *Oraculum Cyrilli*.

Burger, W. "Römische Beiträge zur Geschichte der Katechese im Mittelalter." See Arnold of Vilanova, *Dialogus de elementis catholicae fidei*.

Carreras y Artau, Joaquin. "Arnaldo de Vilanova, Apologista Antijudaico." See Arnold of Vilanova, *Allocutio super significatione nominis tetragrammaton*.

——. "La polémica gerundense sobre el Antichristo entre Arnau de Vilanova y los Dominicos." See Arnold of Vilanova, *Eulogium*.

Denifle, Heinrich. "Das Evangelium aeternum und die Commission zu Anagni." ALKG, 1 (1885): 49-142.

De semine scripturarum. Città del Vaticano, Biblioteca Apostolica Vaticana MS Vat. Lat. 3819. Fols. 1-18r-v. This is the original, non-Joachimist work used by Petrus Iohannis Olivi and Arnold of Vilanova.

De statibus ecclesiae secundum expositionem apocalypsim. Ed. by José María Pou y Martí. AIA, 18 (1922): 29-47; 19 (1923): 25-40; *Visionarios*, pp. 483-512. See also Pou y Martí, José María.

Ehrle, Franz. "Des Ordensprocurators Raymund von Fronsac (de Fronciacho) Actensammlung zur Geschichte der Spiritualen." ALKG, 3 (1887): 1-32.

Eiximenis, Francesch. *Apparatus de triplici statu mundi*. Partially ed. by P. Atanasio López, REF, 3 (1901): 21-24.

——. *Vida de Jesuchrist*. References to this text are from the summary and quotations in Pou y Martí, AIA, 23 (1925): 349-369; *Visionarios*, pp. 397-415. See also Pou y Martí, José María.

Eternal Evangel. See Denifle, Heinrich; Paris, Matthew; Toepfer, Berhard.

Eymerich, Nicholas. *Directorium Inquisitorum*. Rome, 1585.

Finke, Heinrich, *Acta Aragonensia (1291-1327)*. 3 vols. Berlin and Leipsig: Walther Rothschild, 1908.

——. *Aus den Tagen Bonifaz VIII*. See Arnold of Vilanova, *Allocutio Christiani*.

Froissart, Jean. *Chroniques*. Ed. by Jean Alexandre Buchon. *Les Chroniques de Sire Jean Froissart*. 3 vols. Paris, 1835.

Gui, Bernard. *Practica Inquisitionis.* Città del Vaticano, Biblioteca Apostolica Vaticana MS Vat. Lat. 606, fols. 26r-27v. These folios are edited in part by Josep Perarnau in *L'"Alia Informatio Beguinorum" d'Arnau de Vilanova*, pp. 15-16. See Arnold of Vilanova, *Alia Informatio Beguinorum*, and Guillaume Mollat, *Bernard Gui.*

Hillgarth, Jocelyn and Giulio Silano. *The Register "Notule Communium 14" of the Diocese of Barcelona (1345-1348).* PIMS Subsidia Mediaevalia 13. Toronto, 1983.

Hillgarth, Mary and Jocelyn. *Pere III of Catalonia, Chronicle.* PIMS Mediaeval Sources in Translation, 23-24. Toronto, 1980.

Infant Peter. *Exposició de la visió damunt dita.* Summarized and quoted in part by Pou y Marti, AIA, 23 (1925): 33-36; *Visionarios*, pp. 370-373. See Pou y Marti, José Maria.

Joachim of Fiore. *De Septem Sigillis.* Ed. by Marjorie Reeves and Beatrice Hirsch-Reich. RTAM, 21 (1954): 239-247. See Reeves, Marjorie and Hirsch-Reich, Beatrice.

——. *De Vita Sancti Benedicti et de Officio Divino secundum eius Doctrinam.* Ed. by Cypriano Baraut. *Analecta Sacra Tarraconensia*, 24 (1951): 42-118.

——. *Expositio in Apocalypsim.* Venice, 1527.

——. *Liber Concordie Novi ac Veteris Testamenti.* Venice, 1519.

——. *Liber Figurarum.* Ed. by Leone Tondelli, Marjorie Reeves, Beatrice Hirsch-Reich. *Il Libro delle Figure dell'Abate Gioacchino da Fiore.* 2nd ed. 2 vols. Turin: Società Editrice Internazionale, 1953.

——. *Psalterium Decem Chordarum.* Venice, 1527.

——. *Tractatus super Quatuor Evangelia.* Edited by Ernesto Buonaiuti. Rome: Istituto Storico Italiano, 1930.

Limborch, Philippus van. *Historia Inquisitionis, cui subjungitur Liber Sententiarum Inquisitionis Tholosanae, 1307-1313.* Amsterdam, 1692.

Lipsius, Richard. See Ss. Peter and Paul.

López, P. Athanasio. "Apparatus de Triplici Statu Mundi." See Eiximenis, Francesc.

Manselli, Raoul. *La religiosità d'Arnaldo di Villanova.* See Arnold of Vilanova, *Introductio in librum Ioachim de semine scriptuarum.*

Mollat, Guillaume, ed. *Bernard Gui: Manuel de l'inquisiteur.* 2 vols. Paris: Librairie Ancienne Honoré Champion, 1926.

Olivi, Petrus Johannis. *Postilla super Apocalypsim.* Rome, Biblioteca Angelica, MS 382.

——. *Postilla super Evangelium Matthei.* Oxford, New College, MS 49.

——. *Quaestiones Quatuor de Domina.* Ed. by P. Dionysius Pacetti. In "Petrus Ioannis Olivi. O.F.M., Quaestiones Quatuor de Domina." *Bibliotheca Francescana Ascetica Medii Aevi*, 8 (1954): 15-29.

Pacetti, P. Dionysius. "Petrus Ioannis Olivi, O.F.M., Quaestiones Quatuor de Domina." See Petrus Iohannis Olivi, *Quaestiones Quatuor de Domina.*

Paris, Matthew. *Chronica Majora.* Rolls Series, 6, Additamenta, pp. 335-339.

Pelster, Franz. "Die Quaestio Heinrichs von Harclay über die Zweite Ankunft

Christi und die Erwartung des Baldigen Weltendes zu Anfang des XIV Jahrhunderts." *Archivio Italiano per la Storia della Pietà,* 1 (1951): 25-82.

Perarnau, Josep. *L'"Alia Informatio Beguinorum" d'Arnau de Vilanova.* See Arnold
of Vilanova, *Alia Informatio Beguinorum.*

——. *Proces inquisitorial contra els beguins de Vilafranca del Penedes (1345-1346).*
Barcelona: Facultat de Teologia de Barcelona. Forthcoming.

Piur, Paul. See Pseudo-Joachim, *Oraculum Cyrilli.*

Pseudo-Joachim. *De Oneribus Prophetarum.* Ed. by Oswald Holder-Egger. In *Neues
Archiv,* 33 (1907): 139-187.

——. *Joachimi Abbatis Liber contra Lombardum.* Ed. by Carmelo Ottaviano.
Roma: Reale Accademia, 1934.

——. *Oraculum Cyrilli.* Ed. by Paul Piur. In Karl Burdach, *Vom Mittelalter zur
Reformation,* pp. 220-327. Berlin: Weidmannsche Buchhandlung, 1912.

——. *Super Esaiam Prophetam.* Venice, 1517.

——. *Super Hieremiam Prophetam.* Venice, 1516.

——. *Vaticinium Sibillae Erithreae.* Ed. by Oswald Holder-Egger. In *Neues Archiv
der Gesellschaft für altere deutsche Geschichtskunde,* 15 (1889): 155-173
(longer version); 30 (1904-1905): 328-335 (shorter version).

Raymond of Fronsac. See Ehrle, Franz.

*Regula Antiqua Fratrum et Sororum de Poenitentia seu Tertii Ordinis Sancti
Francisci.* Ed. by Charles Paul Sabatier. In *Opuscules de critique historique.*
Fasc. 1. Paris, 1901.

*Regula Tertii Ordinis Sancti Francisci cum ceremoniis ad induendum fratres et
sorores.* 1512 (?). Publisher and date missing. Copy in London, British
Library.

Roquetaillade, Jean de (Rupescissa, Joannes de). *Commentum super prophetiam
Cyrilli.* Paris, Bibliothèque Nationale, MS Lat. 2599.

——. *Liber Ostensor.* Città del Vaticano, Biblioteca Apostolica Vaticana MS Ross.
Lat. 753.

——. *Liber Secretorum eventorum.* Paris, Bibliothèque Nationale, MS Lat. 3598.

Sabatier, Charles Paul. See *Regula Antiqua Fratrum et Sororum de Poenitentia seu
Tertii Ordinis Sancti Francisci.*

St. Ambrose. *Expositio Evangelii secundum Lucam* 4.7-8 (PL 15: 1614).

St. Augustine. *De Civitate Dei* 18.53 (PL 41: 616-617).

St. Bernard. *Ad Pastores in Synodos Congregatos* 5 (PL 184: 1088-1089).

St. Bonaventura. *Legenda Sancti Francisci.* Opusculum 23. In *Opera Omnia.*
Quaracchi, 1898.

St. Gregory the Great. *Homiliarium in Evangelia* 2.35 (PL 76: 1259); 2.38.2 (PL 76:
1282).

——. *Moralium Libri* 12.2 (PL 75: 987); 16.10.4 (PL 75: 1127).

St. Peter. *Martyrium Beati Petri Apostoli a Lino episcopo conscriptum.* Ed. by Richard
Lipsius and Max Bonnet. In *Acta Apostolorum Apocrypha.* Lipsiae, 1893.

Ss. Peter and Paul. *Passio Sanctorum Apostolorum Petri et Pauli.* Ed. by Richard
Lipsius and Max Bonnet. In *Acta Apostolorum Apocrypha.* Lipsiae, 1893.

Sbaralea, Joannes. See *Bullarium Franciscanum.*

Seraphicae Legislationis Textus Originale. Rome: Quaracchi, 1897. Contains the Rule of the Third Order.

Thouzellier, Christine. *Une Somme anti-cathare: Le Liber contra Manicheos de Durand de Huesca.* Louvain: Spiciliegium Sacrum Lovaniense, 1964.

Toepfer, Bernhard (also Töpfer). "Eine Handschrift des Evangelium aeternum des Gerardino von Borgo San Donino." ZG, 7 (1960): 156-163.

Tondelli, Leone; Reeves, Marjorie; Hirsch-Reich, Beatrice. *Il Libro delle Figure.* See Joachim of Fiore, *Liber Figurarum.*

Ubertino da Casale. *Arbor Vitae Crucifixae.* Venice, 1485.

Wadding, Luke. *Annales Minorum.* Vol. 2. Rome, 1732.

SECONDARY SOURCES

Alexander, Paul. "The Diffusion of Byzantine Apocalypses in the Medieval West and the Beginning of Joachimism." In *Prophecy and Millenarianism: Essays in Honour of Marjorie Reeves,* ed. by Ann Williams, pp. 53-106. London: Longman, 1980.

Amaro, Alejandro P. "Fr. Alvaro Pelagio, su vida, sus obras." AIA, 5 (1916): 5-32, 192-213; 6 (1916): 5-28.

Batllori, Miguel. "Orientaciones bibliográficas para el estudio de Arnau de Vilanova." *Pensamiento,* 10 (1954): 311-323.

Bibliotecae Apostolicae Vaticanae: Codices Vaticani Latini. Città del Vaticano: in Biblioteca, 1959.

Bignami-Odier, Jeanne. *Études sur Jean de Roquetaillade.* Paris: Librairie Philosophique J. Vrin, 1952.

——. "Jean de Roquetaillade (de Rupescissa), Théologien, Polémiste, Alchimiste." In *Histoire Littéraire de la France.* 41: 75-284. Paris, 1981.

Bloomfield, Morton W. "Joachim of Fiore." *Traditio,* 13 (1957): 249-311.

Bloomfield, Morton W. and Reeves, Marjorie. "The Penetration of Joachimism into Northern Europe." *Speculum,* 29 (1954): 772-793.

Bohigas, Pere. "Prediccions i profecies en les obres de Fra Francesc Eiximenis." In *Franciscalia,* pp. 23-28. Barcelona, 1928.

——. "Profecies catalanes dels segles XIV i XV. Assaig bibliografic." *Butlletí de la Biblioteca de Catalunya,* 6 (1920-1932): 24-49.

Burr, David. "The Persecution of Peter Olivi." *Transactions of the American Philosophical Society,* ns., vol. 66, Pt. 5. Philadelphia: American Philosophical Society, 1976.

Canovas, Elena and Piñero, Felix. *Arnaldo de Vilanova: Escritos Condenados por la Inquisición.* Madrid: Editora Nacional, 1976.

Carreras y Artau, Joaquin. *Arnau de Vilanova y las culturas orientales.* Barcelona: Consejo Superior de Investigaciones Cientificas, 1954.

——. *Relaciones de Arnau de Vilanova con los Reyes de la Casa de Aragon.* Barcelona: Graficas Marina, S.A., 1955.

Chabás, Roque. "Inventario de los libros, ropas y demas efectos de Arnaldo de Vilanova." *Revista de Archivos, Bibliotecas y Museos*, 2a epoca, pp. 189-203. Madrid, 1903.

Daniel, E. Randolph. "A Re-examination of the Origins of Franciscan Joachitism." *Speculum*, 43 (1968): 671-676.

de Dmitrewski, Michel. "Fr. Bernard Délicieux, O.F.M., sa lutte contre l'inquisition de Carcassonne et d'Albi, son procès, 1297-1319." AFH, 17 (1924): 183-218, 313-337, 457-488; 18 (1925): 3-22.

Donckel, Emil. "Studien über die Prophezeiung des Telesforus." AFH, 26 (1933): 29-104.

Douie, Decima. *The Nature and Effect of the Heresy of the Fraticelli.* Manchester: University of Manchester, 1932.

Egerton MSS. *Catalogue of Additions to the Manuscripts in the British Museum in the Years 1848-1853.* London: British Museum, 1868.

Ehrle, Franz. "P. J. Olivi, sein Leben und seine Schriften." ALKG, 3 (1887): 409-552.

———. "Die Spiritualen, ihr Verhältnis zum Franziscanerorden und zu den Fraticellen." ALKG, 1 (1885): 509-569; 2 (1886): 106-164, 249-336; 3 (1887): 553-623; 4 (1888): 1-190.

Flood, David. *Peter Olivi's Rule Commentary.* Wiesbaden: Franz Steiner Verlag Gmbh, 1972.

Friderich, Karl. "Kritische Untersuchung der dem Abt Joachim v. Floris zuge-schichte: denen Commentate zu Esays u. Jeremias." *Zeitschrift für Wissenschaftliche Theologie*, pp. 349-363, 449-514. Jena, 1859.

Fumi, Luigi. *Eretici e ribelli nell'Umbria: Studio storico di un decennio, 1320-1330.* Todi: Biblioteca Umbra, 1916.

Gieben, Servus. "Bibliographica Oliviana (1885-1967)." *Collectanea Francescana*, 38 (1968): 167-195.

Grundmann, Herbert. "Die Liber de Flore." *Historisches Jahrbuch*, 49 (1929): 33-91.

———. "Die Papstprophetien des Mittelalters." *Archiv für Kulturgeschichte*, 19 (1929): 77-159.

———. *Religiöse Bewegungen im Mittelalter.* Darmstadt: Wissenschaftliche Buchgesellschaft, 1970.

Hastings, James. *Encyclopedia of Religion and Ethics.* Vol. 2. Edinburgh: T. and T. Clark, 1909.

Hauréau, Jean Barthélémy. *Bernard Délicieux et l'inquisition albigeoise, 1300-1320.* Paris, 1877.

Hillgarth, Jocelyn. *The Spanish Kingdoms.* 2 vols. Oxford: The Clarendon Press, 1976, 1978.

Hirsch-Reich, Beatrice. "Alexanders von Roes Stellung zu den Prophetien." *Mitteilungen des Instituts für Österreichische Geschichtforschung*, 47 (1959): 306-316.

Ivars, P. Andres. "El Escritor Fr. Francisco Eximenes en Valencia." AIA, 15 (1921):

76-104; 19 (1923): 359-398; 20 (1923): 210-248; 24 (1925): 323-352; 25 (1926): 289-333.

Ladurie, Emmanuel Le Roy. *Montaillou: Cathars and Catholics in a French Village, 1294-1324.* Trans. by Barbara Bray. London: Penguin Books, 1980.

Lambert, Malcolm David. *Franciscan Poverty.* London: SPCK, 1961.

Lee, Harold. "Scrutamini Scripturas: Joachimist Themes and *Figurae* in the Early Religious Writing of Arnold of Vilanova." JWCI, 37 (1974): 33-56.

Leff, Gordon. *Heresy in the Later Middle Ages.* Manchester: Manchester University Press, 1967.

Mandonnet, Pierre. *Les Origines de l'ordre de Poenitentia.* Freiburg, 1898.

Manselli, Raoul. *La "Lectura super Apocalipsim" di Pietro di Giovanni Olivi.* Rome: Istituto Storico Italiano per il Medio Evo, 1955.

——. *Spirituali e Beghini in Provenza.* Rome: Istituto Storico Italiano per il Medio Evo, 1959.

——. "La Terza Età, 'Babylon' e l'Antichristo Mistico (a proposito di Pietro di Giovanni Olivi)." BISI, 82 (1970): 47-79.

McGinn, Bernard. "Angel Pope and Papal Antichrist." *Church History,* 47 (1978): 155-173.

——. *Visions of the End.* New York: Columbia University Press, 1979.

Menendez y Pelayo, Marcelino. *Historia de los heterodoxos españoles.* Ed. by D. Enrique Sanchez Reyes. 2nd ed. 8 vols. Madrid: Consejo Superior de Investigaciones Científicas, 1963.

Moorman, John. *A History of the Franciscan Order from its Origins to the Year 1517.* Oxford: The Clarendon Press, 1968.

Oliger, P. Livarius. "Acta Inquisitoris Umbriae Fr. Angeli de Assisio contra Fraticellos aliosque anno 1361." AFH, 24 (1931): 63-90.

——. "Beiträge zur Geschichte des Spiritualen, Fratizellen und Clarener im Mittelalter." *Zeitschrift für Kirchengeschichte,* 45 (1926): 215-242.

——. "Documenta inedita ad historiam Fraticellorum spectantia." AFH, 3 (1910): 253-279, 505-529, 680-699; 4 (1911): 688-712; 5 (1912): 74-84; 6 (1913): 267-290, 515-530, 710-747.

——. "Fr. Bertrandi de Turre processus contra spirituales Aquitaniae (1315) et cardinalis Iacobi de Columna litterae defensoriae spiritualium Provinciae (1310)." AFH, 16 (1923): 323-355.

——. "Spirituels." DTC, 14.2, pp. 2522-2549.

Paniagua, Juan Antonio. *Estudios y Notas sobre Arnaldo de Vilanova.* Madrid: Consejo Superior de Investigaciones Científicas, 1963.

——. "Vida de Arnoldo de Vilanova." *Archivo Ibero-americano de Historia de la Medicina y de Antropologia medica,* 3 (1951): 3-83.

Pásztor, Edith. "Le polemiche sulla 'Lectura super Apocalipsim' di Pietro di Giovanni Olivi fino alla sua condanna." BISI, 70 (1958): 365-424.

——. "Giovanni XXII e il Gioachimismo di Pietro di Giovanni Olivi." BISI, 82 (1970): 81-111.

Perarnau, Josep. "Bibliografia teológica catalana." *Analecta Sacra Tarraconensia,* 45 (1972): 121-235.

——. "Troballa de tractats espirituals perduts d'Arnau de Vilanova." *Revista Catalana de Teológia*, 1 (1976): 489-512.

Pierron, Johann Baptist. *Die Katholischen Armen*. Freiburg im Breisgau: Herdersche Verlagshandlung, 1911.

Pou y Marti, José Maria. "Visionarios, Beguinos y Fraticelos Catalanes, Siglos XIII-XV." AIA, 11 (1919): 113-231; 12 (1919): 8-53; 14 (1920): 5-51; 15 (1921): 5-25; 18 (1922): 5-47; 19 (1923): 25-40; 20 (1923): 7-37, 289-320; 21 (1924): 348-368; 22 (1924): 281-326; 23 (1925): 10-58, 349-369; 24 (1925): 198-232; 26 (1926): 5-47.

——. *Visionarios, Beguinos y Fraticelos Catalanes, Siglos XIII-XV*. Vich: Editorial Seráphica, 1930. This book reproduces the above articles in a single volume.

Raby, Frederic. *The Oxford Book of Mediaeval Latin Verse*. Oxford: The Clarendon Press, 1959.

Reeves, Marjorie. "The Abbot Joachim's Disciples and the Cistercian Order." *Sophia*, 19 (1951): 355-371.

——. *The Influence of Prophecy in the Later Middle Ages*. Oxford: The Clarendon Press, 1969.

——. "The *Liber Figurarum* of Joachim of Fiore." MARS, 2 (1950): 57-81.

——. "The Originality and Influence of Joachim of Fiore." *Traditio*, 36 (1980): 269-316.

——. "Some Popular Prophecies from the Fourteenth to the Seventeenth Centuries." In *Popular Belief and Practice*, ed. by G. J. Cuming and Derek Baker, pp. 107-134. Cambridge: Cambridge University Press, 1972.

Reeves, Marjorie and Hirsch-Reich, Beatrice. "The *Figurae* of Joachim of Fiore: Genuine and Spurious Collections." MARS, 3 (1954): 170-199.

——. *The Figurae of Joachim of Fiore*. Oxford: The Clarendon Press, 1972.

——. "The Seven Seals in the Writings of Joachim of Fiore." RTAM, 21 (1954): 211-247. See also Joachim of Fiore, *De Septem Sigillis*.

Russo, P. Francesco. *Bibliografia gioachimita*. Florence: Leo S. Olschki-Editore, 1954.

Simoni, Fiorella. "Il 'Super Hieremiam' e il Gioachimismo francescano." BISI, 82 (1970): 13-46.

Thomson, S. Harrison. *Latin Bookhands of the Later Middle Ages*. Cambridge: Cambridge University Press, 1969.

Thouzellier, Christine. "La profession trinitaire du Vaudois Durand de Huesca." RTAM, 22 (1960): 267-289.

Tierney, Brian. *Origins of Papal Infallibility, 1150-1350*. Leiden: E. J. Brill, 1972.

Tocco, Felice di. *Studii Francescani*. Naples: Nuova Biblioteca di Litteratura, Storia ed Arte, 1909.

Toepfer, Bernard (also Töpfer). *Das kommende Reich des Friedens*. Berlin: Akademie-Verlag, 1964.

Vidal, J. *Annales de Saint-Louis des Français à Rome*. anno 10 (1905): 9.

Index to the Introduction

See also the Index to the Text for persons and place names appearing there.

Index to the Text

This Index includes only names of persons and places which occur in the text proper of the *Breuiloquium*. The orthography of the name at its first occurrence has usually been adopted. Divine names have not been indexed. For subjects see the Index to the Introduction.

Index of Biblical References

DATE DUE

DEC 27 1992			